Accounting

Canadian Sixth Edition

- **Charles T. Horngren**
  Stanford University

- **Walter T. Harrison, Jr.**
  Baylor University

- **Linda Smith Bamber**
  University of Georgia

- **W. Morley Lemon**
  University of Waterloo

- **Peter R. Norwood**
  Langara College

PEARSON

Prentice
Hall

Toronto

National Library of Canada Cataloguing in Publication

Accounting/Charles T. Horngren . . . [et al].—Canadian 6th ed.

Canadian ed. published under title: Accounting/Charles T. Horngren,
Walter T. Harrison, W. Morley Lemon; with Carol E. Dilworth.
Includes index.
Contents: v. 1. Chapters 1–11—v. 2. Chapters 12–18—v. 3. Chapters 19–26.
ISBN 0-13-123362-9 (v. 1) ISBN 0-13-123364-5 (v. 2) ISBN 0-13-123367-X (v. 3)

1. Accounting—Textbooks. 2. Managerial accounting—Textbooks. I. Horngren,
Charles T., 1926-   .

HF5635.A366 2005   657'.044   C2004-900054-3

0-13-123362-9

Vice President, Editorial Director: Michael Young
Executive Editor: Samantha Scully
Director of Marketing, Business and Economics: Bill Todd
Developmental Editor: Anita Smale, CA
Production Editor: Mary Ann McCutcheon
Copy Editor: Carol Fordyce, Anita Smale
Production Coordinator: Deborah Starks
Page Layout: Bill Renaud
Permissions/Photo Research: Sandy Cooke
Art Director: Julia Hall
Interior Design: David Cheung
Cover Design: David Cheung
Cover Image: Getty Images

2 3 4 5   09 08 07 06 05

Printed and bound in U.S.A.

Photo Credits
2 © Michael Mahovlich/Masterfile www.masterfile.com;
52 © Dick Hemingway Photography; 108 Photo Courtesy of WestJet;
163 CP Photo/Richard Lam; 217 Courtesy of Danier Leather; 293 The Forzani
Group Limited; 333 Pearson Education Canada; 387 Getty Images Inc.-Photo
Disc; 437 Courtesy of Research In Motion (RIM); 484 Courtesy of CanJet
Airlines; 535 Bombardier Recreational Products Inc.

BRIEF
Contents

Contents

---

*In each chapter, Assignment Material includes Questions, Exercises, Beyond the Numbers, an Ethical Issue, and
    Problems (Group A and B, and Challenge Problems).
**Extending Your Knowledge includes Decision Problems and a Financial Statement Problem.

About the Authors

Charles T. Horngren is the Edmund W. Littlefield Professor of Accounting, Emeritus, at Stanford University. A graduate of Marquette University, he received his MBA from Harvard University and his Ph.D. from the University of Chicago. He is also the recipient of honourary doctorates from Marquette University and DePaul University.

A Certified Public Accountant, Horngren served on the Accounting Principles Board for six years, the Financial Accounting Standards Board Advisory Council for five years, and the Council of the American Institute of Certified Public Accountants for three years. For six years, he served as a trustee of the Financial Accounting Foundation, which oversees the Financial Accounting Standards Board and the Government Accounting Standards Board.

Horngren is a member of the Accounting Hall of Fame.

A member of the American Accounting Association, Horngren has been its President and its Director of Research. He received its first annual Outstanding Accounting Educator Award.

The California Certified Public Accountants Foundation gave Horngren its Faculty Excellence Award and its Distinguished Professor Award. He is the first person to have received both awards.

The American Institute of Certified Public Accountants presented its first Outstanding Educator Award to Horngren.

Horngren was named Accountant of the Year, Education, by the national professional accounting fraternity, Beta Alpha Psi.

Professor Horngren is also a member of the Institute of Management Accountants, where he has received its Distinguished Service Award. He was a member of the Institute's Board of Regents, which administers the Certified Management Accountant examinations.

Horngren is the author of other accounting books published by Pearson Education Canada: *Cost Accounting: A Managerial Emphasis,* Third Canadian Edition, 2004 (with George Foster, Srikant Datar and Howard D. Teall); *Introduction to Financial Accounting,* Third Canadian Edition, 2001 (with Gary L. Sundem, John A. Elliot and Howard D. Teall); *Management Accounting,* Fourth Canadian Edition, 2002 (with Gary L. Sundem, William O. Stratton, and Howard D. Teall); and *Financial Accounting,* Canadian Edition, 2004 (with Walter T. Harrison, Jr., W. Morley Lemon, and Sandra Robertson Lemon).

Horngren is the Consulting Editor for the Charles T. Horngren Series in Accounting.

Walter T. Harrison, Jr. is Professor of Accounting at the Hankamer School of Business, Baylor University. He received his B.B.A. degree from Baylor University, his M.S. from Oklahoma State University, and his Ph.D. from Michigan State University.

Professor Harrison, recipient of numerous teaching awards from student groups as well as from university administrators, has also taught at Cleveland State Community College, Michigan State University, the University of Texas, and Stanford University.

A member of the American Accounting Association and the American Institute of Certified Public Accountants, Professor Harrison has served as Chairman of the Financial Accounting Standards Committee of the American Accounting Association, on the Teaching/Curriculum Development Award Committee, on the Program Advisory Committee for Accounting Education and Teaching, and on the Notable Contributions to Accounting Literature Committee.

Professor Harrison has lectured in several foreign countries and published articles in numerous journals, including *The Accounting Review, Journal of Accounting Research, Journal of Accountancy, Journal of Accounting and Public Policy, Economic Consequences of Financial Accounting Standards, Accounting Horizons, Issues in Accounting Education,* and *Journal of Law and Commerce.* He is also co-author of *Financial Accounting,* Canadian Edition, 2001 (with Charles T. Horngren, W. Morley Lemon and Sandra Robertson Lemon). Professor Harrison has received scholarships, fellowships, research grants, or awards from Price Waterhouse & Co., Deloitte & Touche, the Ernst & Young Foundation, and the KPMG Peat Marwick Foundation.

Linda Smith Bamber is Professor of Accounting at the J.M. Tull School of Accounting at the University of Georgia. She graduated summa cum laude from Wake Forest University, where she was a member of Phi Beta Kappa. She is a certified public accountant. For her performance on the CPA examination, Professor Bamber received the Elijah Watt Sells Award in addition to the North Carolina Bronze Medal. Before returning to graduate school, she worked in cost accounting at RJR Foods. She then earned an MBA from Arizona State University, and a Ph.D. from The Ohio State University.

Professor Bamber has received numerous teaching awards from The Ohio State University, the University of Florida, and the University of Georgia, including selection as Teacher of the Year at the University of Florida's Fisher School of Accounting.

She has lectured in Canada and Australia in addition to the U.S., and her research has appeared in numerous journals, including *The Accounting Review, Journal of Accounting Research, Journal of Accounting and Economics, Journal of Finance, Contemporary Accounting Research, Auditing: A Journal of Practice and Theory, Accounting Horizons, Issues in Accounting Education,* and *CPA Journal.* She provided the annotations for the *Annotated Instructor's Edition* of Horngren, Foster, and Datar's *Cost Accounting: A Managerial Emphasis,* Seventh, Eighth, and Ninth Editions.

A member of the Institute of Management Accounting, the American Accounting Association (AAA), and the AAA's Management Accounting Section and Financial Accounting and Reporting Section, Professor Bamber has chaired the AAA New Faculty Consortium Committee, served on the AAA Council, the AAA Research Advisory Committee, the AAA Corporate Accounting Policy Seminar Committee, the AAA Wildman Medal Award Committee, the AAA Nominations Committee, and has chaired the Management Accounting Section's Membership Outreach Committee. She served as Associate Editor of *Accounting Horizons,* and served as editor of *The Accounting Review* from 1999 to 2002.

W. Morley Lemon is the PricewaterhouseCoopers Professor of Auditing and the Director of the School of Accountancy at the University of Waterloo. He obtained his BA from the University of Western Ontario, his MBA from the University of Toronto, and his PhD from the University of Texas at Austin. Professor Lemon obtained his CA in Ontario. In 1985 he was honoured by that Institute, which elected him a Fellow; in 2003, he received the Institute's ICAO Award of Outstanding Merit. He received his CPA in Texas.

Professor Lemon was awarded the University of Waterloo Distinguished Teacher Award at the 1998 convocation at the University.

Professor Lemon is co-author, with Arens, Loebbecke, and Splettstoesser, of *Auditing and Other Assurance Services,* Canadian Ninth Edition, published by Pearson Education Canada, and co-authored five previous Canadian editions of that text. He is also co-author, with Harrison, Horngren, and Robertson Lemon, of *Financial Accounting,* Canadian Edition, published by Pearson Education Canada.

He was a member of the Canadian Institute of Chartered Accountants' Assurance Standards Board. He has also served on the Institute of Chartered Accountants of

Ontario Council, as well as a number of committees for both bodies. He has chaired and served on a number of committees of the Canadian Academic Accounting Association. Professor Lemon has served on Council and chaired and served on a number of committees of the American Accounting Association.

Professor Lemon has presented lectures and papers at a number of universities and academic and professional conferences and symposia in Canada, the United States, and China. He has chaired and organized six audit symposia held at the University of Waterloo. He has served on the editorial board of and reviewed papers for a number of academic journals including *The Accounting Review*, *Contemporary Accounting Research*, *Issues in Accounting Education*, *Auditing: A Journal of Practice and Theory*, *Advances in Accounting*, *Journal of Accounting and Public Policy*, and *CA Magazine*. Professor Lemon has co-authored two monographs and has had papers published in *Contemporary Accounting Research*, *Research on Accounting Ethics*, *Journal of Accounting, Auditing and Finance*, *The Chartered Accountant in Australia*, *The Journal of Business Ethics*, and *CA Magazine*. He has had a chapter published in *Research Opportunities in Internal Auditing* and papers published in the following collections: *Educating the Profession of Accountancy in the Twenty-First Century*, *Comparative International Accounting Education Standards*, *Comparative International Auditing Standards*, and *The Impact of Inflation on Accounting: A Global View*. Professor Lemon served as a judge for *CA Magazine's* Walter J. Macdonald Award.

Professor Lemon has received a number of research grants and has served as the Director of the Centre for Accounting Ethics, School of Accountancy, University of Waterloo. He has written a number of ethics cases published by the Centre.

Peter R. Norwood is an instructor in accounting and the Chair of the Financial Management Program at Langara College. A graduate of the University of Alberta, he received his MBA from the University of Western Ontario. He is a Chartered Accountant and a Certified Management Accountant.

Before entering the academic community, Mr. Norwood worked in public practice and industry for over fifteen years. He is a past member of the Board of Evaluators of the Canadian Institute of Chartered Accountants and has served on a variety of committees for the British Columbia Institute of Chartered Accountants. In addition to his duties at Langara College, Mr. Norwood is involved in program development with the Certified Management Accountants of British Columbia and the Certified General Accountants Association of British Columbia. He lectures in the Diploma Accounting Program at the University of British Columbia and is the Chair of the Langara College Foundation.

Norwood is co-author with Jones, Werner, Terrell, and Terrell, of *Introduction to Management Accounting: A User Perspective*, Canadian Edition, published by Pearson Education Canada.

A Letter to Students

Welcome to your introductory accounting course! Accounting is the language of business. Whether you intend to be an accountant or not, you owe it to yourself to develop your skills with this language so that you can give yourself a winning edge in your career.

You will discover in this course that accounting is more than bookkeeping. Accounting requires that you understand issues conceptually in addition to developing the technical ability to record, summarize, report, and interpret financial data.

As instructors, we know that the volume of material covered in introductory accounting can be overwhelming. To help you develop your skills and understanding of accounting principles, we have created a number of tools and resources to support you. These are described in detail in the tour "Developing Your Winning Edge" that is presented over the next few pages.

While you work through your course, we'd like to hear from you. Let us know what you like about this book and your ideas for improving it by visiting our web site at **www.pearsoned.ca/horngren** and clicking on the Feedback link within any chapter.

Best of luck with your course!

Morley Lemon
Peter Norwood

Developing Your Winning Edge

GUIDING Each chapter of *Accounting* includes a number of tools designed to guide you through the process of developing your skills and understanding of key accounting concepts. Please read through the next few pages to learn more about these tools and the many ways in which they will help you learn, understand, and apply accounting concepts.

Chapter Objectives are listed on the first page of each chapter. This "roadmap" shows you what will be covered and what is especially important. Each objective is repeated in the margin where the material is first covered. The objectives are summarized at the end of the chapter.

Chapter openers present a story about a real company or a real business situation, and show why the topics in the chapter are important to real companies. Some of the companies you'll read about include WestJet Airlines, Danier Leather, and The Forzani Group. Students tell us that using real companies makes it easier for them to learn and remember accounting concepts.

The Forzani Group Ltd. (www.forzanigroup.com) is the largest sporting goods retailer in Canada. The company, headquartered in Calgary, started with one location in 1974. Since then, the corporation has expanded aggressively throughout Canada by acquiring various regional and national chains of stores. Forzani now operates a number of chains of stores, including SportChek, Sports Experts, and Coast Mountain Sports.

As a retailer, The Forzani Group Ltd. purchases products from various suppliers and resells them to its customers. The purchased products are included in the inventory account until they are sold, at which time they are transferred to cost of goods sold. As you can imagine, inventory is the largest single current asset for most retailers. A retailer must closely monitor its inventory. Too much inventory is costly; too little inventory may result in loss of...

'It's competitive as hell out there... about that,' Chief Executive Officer B... lysts.

Forzani said its strategy going f... keeping inventories low and negotiati... for exclusive products."

Source : The Canadian Press via COMTEX "S... Forzani Backs Away from Competitive Clothin... 2003, as reported on the website Stock... September 6, 2003).

Weblinks within the body of the text give you the internet address for the companies mentioned in the text. If you want to learn more about a company, use these handy references.

Objectives in the margin signal the beginning of the section that covers the objective topic. Look for this feature when you are studying and want to review a particular objective.

OBJECTIVE 3
Compare the effects of the FIFO, LIFO, and moving-weighted-average cost methods

Comparing FIFO, LIFO, and Moving-Weighted-Cost

What leads SportChek to select the moving-weighted-average cost... Celestica Inc. (www.celestica.com) to use FIFO? The different met... ferent benefits.

Exhibit 6-7 summarizes the results for the three inventory methods... It shows sales revenue, cost of goods sold, and gross margin for FI... moving-weighted-average cost. All data come from Exhibits 6-4, 6-5...

Exhibit 6-7 also shows that FIFO produces the lowest cost of goo... highest gross margin. Net income is also the highest under FIFO w... costs are rising. Many companies wish to report high income to at... and borrow money on favourable terms. FIFO offers this benefit.

LIFO results in the highest cost of goods sold and the lowest gros... leads to the lowest net income when inventory costs are rising. I... LIFO costing method is not allowed for income tax purposes, so ve... nies use this method.

The moving-weighted-average cost method generates gross m... income amounts that fall between the extremes of FIFO and LIFO. C... seek a "middle-ground" solution, therefore, use the average c...

Learning Tips in the margin are suggestions for learning or remembering concepts that you might find difficult.

..., first-out (LIFO) method, cost of goods sold comes from the lat-...cent—purchases. Ending inventory's cost comes from the oldest ...d. LIFO costing does not follow the physical movement of goods ...nies. Canada Customs and Revenue Agency does not allow the ...termine taxable income because it often results in the highest cost ...d the lowest net income. Although LIFO is acceptable for account-...Canada, most Canadian companies do not want to incur the cost ...wo sets of inventory records. Exhibit 6-5 gives a perpetual inven-...he LIFO method.

...hek had 1 ski parka at the beginning of November. After the pur-...

LEARNING TIP
A sand company illustrates the LIFO concept. When a sand company dumps new sand on a pile, the new sand lies on the top. When the company needs sand, it takes the new sand off the top. Thus the last sand (the newest sand) on the pile is the first off the pile.

Exhibits are provided in full colour to make the concepts easier to understand and easier to remember.

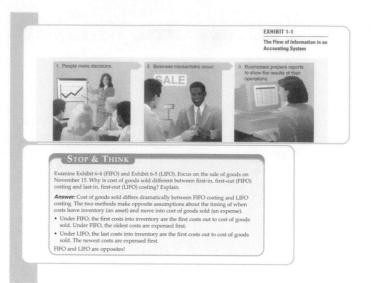

EXHIBIT 1-1

The Flow of Information in an Accounting System

1. People make decisions. 2. Business transactions occur. 3. Businesses prepare reports to show the results of their operations.

Stop and Think boxes are "speed bumps" that allow you to slow down for a moment, review and apply to a decision situation material just covered in the text. These serve as an excellent way to check your progress because the answers are provided in the same box.

> **STOP & THINK**
>
> Examine Exhibit 6-4 (FIFO) and Exhibit 6-5 (LIFO). Focus on the sale of goods on November 15. Why is cost of goods sold different between first-in, first-out (FIFO) costing and last-in, first-out (LIFO) costing? Explain.
>
> **Answer:** Cost of goods sold differs dramatically between FIFO costing and LIFO costing. The two methods make opposite assumptions about the timing of when costs leave inventory (an asset) and move into cost of goods sold (an expense).
>
> - Under FIFO, the first costs into inventory are the first costs out to cost of goods sold. Under FIFO, the oldest costs are expensed first.
> - Under LIFO, the last costs into inventory are the first costs out to cost of goods sold. The newest costs are expensed first.
>
> FIFO and LIFO are opposites!

Working It Out are short calculation questions that appear throughout the chapter. Answers are provided to give you immediate feedback. You can use these questions to check your progress and to prepare for exams.

> **WORKING IT OUT**
>
> Company X receives $3,000 for magazine subscriptions in advance and records it as a liability.
> (1) If $1,600 is unearned at the end of the year, what is the adjusting entry?
> (2) If the subscriptions were originally recorded as revenue, what is the adjusting entry?
>
> **A:**
> (1) Unearned Rev. 1,400
>   Revenue   1,400
> (2) Revenue 1,600
>   Unearned Rev. 1,600
> Only $1,400 of the $3,000 has been earned. The revenue account needs a $1,400 balance. That account must be reduced (debited) by $1,600.

Appendix Exercises

Exercise 3A-1 *Recording supplies tran*

At the beginning of the year, supplies business paid $10,800 cash for supp plies indicates the ending balance is

Required

1. Assume that the business records Therefore, place the beginning ba the above entries directly in the a
2. Assume that the business record account. Therefore, place the beg account, and record the above ent journal.
3. Compare the ending account bal same? Explain.

Exercise 3A-2 *Recording unearned re*

At the beginning of the year, the comp ice revenue collected in advance. Duri receipts of $20,000. At year end, the u

Required

1. Assume that the company record *liability* account. Open T-accounts Revenue, and place the beginni Journalize the cash collection an amounts. As references in the T receipt by *CR*, and an adjustment
2. Assume that the company record *revenue* account. Open T-accounts Revenue, and place the beginning cash collection and adjusting entr ences in the T-accounts, denote a adjustment by *Adj*.
3. Compare the ending balances in same or different.

Appendix Problems

Problem 3A-1 *Recording prepaid rent*
            (Obj. A1, A2)

Johal Sales and Service completed th

Aug. 31   Paid $6,000 store rent coverin
Dec. 1   Collected $6,400 cash in adv
            earned $1,600 each month ov

Thinking It Over are short questions about concepts just covered in the text. Answers are provided to give you immediate feedback. Like the Working It Out questions, you can use Thinking It Over questions to check your progress and to prepare for exams.

> asset account as long as the business
> may refer to the Furniture account to
> mation is useful in a decision about
> nount to pay.
>
> is an *estimate*. Accountants use the
> w the cumulative sum of all amortiza-
> e asset. Therefore, the balance in this
>
> *asset* account, which means an asset
> call from Chapter 2, page 65, that the
> ide of the account where increases are
> guishing characteristics:
>
> .count.
>
> bit or credit) is the opposite of that of
>
> is the contra account that accompanies
> after Furniture. Furniture has a debit
> ization, a contra asset, has a credit bal-
> .nces.
>
> rtization or depreciation account for

> **THINKING IT OVER**
>
> Describe one similarity and one difference between
> (1) prepaid expenses and
> (2) capital assets and the related amortization.
>
> **A:** Similarity: For both prepaid expenses and capital assets, the business first records the purchase as an asset. The business then records the expense later.
> Difference: Prepaid expenses cover a shorter time period than capital assets and the related amortization.

Key Points in the margin highlight important details from the text. These are good review tools for when you prepare for tests or exams.

> **KEY POINT**
>
> Recognize that a dollar change in ending inventory means a dollar change in income. This is one reason auditors examine the ending inventory so carefully. An income statement may be manipulated by altering the amount of ending inventory.

Because ending inventory is *subtracted* in computing cost of goods sold in one period and the same amount is *added* as beginning inventory the next period, the error cancels out after two periods. The overstatement of cost of goods sold in Period 2 counterbalances the understatement for Period 1. Thus, the total gross margin for the two periods combined is correct. These effects are summarized in Exhibit 6-9.

Ethical Issues

No area of accounting has a deeper ethical dimension than inventory. Owners and managers of companies whose profits do not meet expectations are sometimes tempted to "cook the books" to increase reported income. The increase in reported

Mid-Chapter Summary Problem for Your Review gives you another chance to review your understanding of the material covered in the first half of the chapter. A full solution is provided so you can judge whether you should look at the material again or proceed to the last half of the chapter.

Mid-Chapter Summary Problem
for Your Review

The Watch Shop carries only watches. Assume The Watch Shop began June with an inventory of 10 wristwatches that cost $50 each. The Watch Shop sells those watches for $90 each. During June, The Watch Shop bought and sold inventory as follows:

June	3	Sold 8 units for $90 each.
	16	Purchased 10 units at $55 each.
	23	Sold 8 units for $90 each.

Required

1. Prepare a perpetual inventory record for The Watch Shop under each method.
   - FIFO
   - LIFO
   - Moving-weighted-average cost
2. Journalize all of The Watch Shop's inventory transactions for June for each of these cost methods.
3. Show the computation of gross margin for each method.
4. Which method maximizes net income? Which method allowed in Canada (FIFO or moving-weighted-average) minimizes income taxes?

Solution

Requirement 1

Perpetual inventory records:

FIFO

Wristwatches

Date	Purchases Qty.	Unit Cost	Total Cost	Cost of Goods Sold Qty.	Unit Cost	Total Cost	Inventory on Hand Qty.	Unit Cost	Total Cost
June 1							10	$50	$500
3				8	$50	$400	2	50	100
16	10	$55	$550				2	50	100
							10	55	550
23				2	50	100			
				6	55	330	4	55	220
30	10		$550	16		$830	4		$220

Accounting and the E-World or **Accounting Around the Globe** appears in each chapter. These boxes illustrate either how the world of e-commerce influences accounting or how accounting differs around the world. These boxes offer interesting views of accounting that might make you think about accounting in different ways.

Accounting and the *e*-World

How Do E-tailers Manage Inventory?

Bricks-and-mortar retailers like Canadian Tire have large stores with thousands of items on hand so that shoppers can find whatever product they are looking for, from tires to plumbing and electrical fixtures to sporting goods. Each of the 450 Canadian Tire Associate Stores carries a large-dollar inventory to provide this selection. Shoppers at a Canadian Tire store select the item they want from the store's shelves, pay for the item on their way out of the store, take it home, and can use it instantly.

E-tailers, or online merchandisers, are very different from the bricks-and-mortar merchandisers. E-tailers have a large inventory of items for sale over the web but the company itself may not stock all the items it offers for sale. When a customer purchases an item over the web, the e-tailer must locate the item (it may be in a warehouse under the e-tailer's control, in a manufacturer's warehouse, or somewhere else) and arrange to have the item shipped to the customer.

E-tailers typically promise accurate orders and fast delivery, but many customers have had the opposite experience. Stories of late deliveries, receipt of incorrect orders, and billing problems are still common. Bricks-and-mortar retailers advertise that if the product the customer selected is not what was needed, the customer can bring it back for a different product or a refund. Billing problems can be resolved quickly in person.

To combat order and delivery problems, e-tailers have developed relationships with trucking/warehouse companies to be responsible for warehousing and deliveries. The e-tailer takes the order and arranges for the trucking/warehouse company to deliver the product to the customer. The arrangement seems to be a win-win-win situation for the e-tailer, the trucking/warehouse company, and the e-tailer's customer. The e-tailer manages the product delivery arrangements and billing, the trucking/warehouse company expands its business using existing facilities, and the customer gets quicker, and probably more reliable, delivery of the product desired.

Decision Guidelines show how the accounting concepts covered in the chapter are used by business people to make business decisions. This feature shows why accounting principles and concepts are important in a broader business context, not just to accountants. The Decision Guidelines also serve as an excellent summary of the chapter topics.

DECISION GUIDELINES   Guidelines for Inventory Management

Decision	Guidelines	System or Method
Which inventory system to use?	• Expensive merchandise • Cannot control inventory by visual inspection	→ Perpetual system
	• Can control inventory by visual inspection	→ Periodic system
Which costing method to use?	• Unique inventory items	→ Specific-unit cost
	• The most current cost of ending inventory • Maximizes reported income when costs are rising	→ FIFO
	• The most current measure of cost of goods sold and net income	→ LIFO
	• Middle-of-the-road approach for income tax and net income	→ Weighted-average
How to estimate the cost of ending inventory?	• The cost-of-goods-sold model provides the framework	Gross margin (gross profit) method
	• Standard mark-ups from cost price to selling price are used for all inventory items	→ Retail method

Summary Problem for Your Review pulls together the chapter concepts with an extensive and challenging review problem. Full solutions are given so that you can check your progress.

Cyber Coach appears after both the Mid-Chapter Summary Problem for Your Review and the Summary Problem for Your Review. It is a reminder to visit the *Accounting* Companion Website's Online Study Guide and other student resources for extra practice with the new material introduced in the chapter.

Summary appears at the end of each chapter. It gives a concise description of the material covered in the chapter and is organized by objective. Use this summary as a starting point for organizing your review when studying for a test or exam.

Summary

1. **Compute perpetual inventory amounts under the FIFO, LIFO, and moving-weighted-average cost methods.** In a perpetual inventory system, the business keeps a continuous record for each inventory item to show the inventory on hand at all times. Businesses multiply the quantity of inventory items by their unit cost to determine inventory cost. To compute ending inventory and cost of goods sold, a cost is assigned to each inventory item. Three methods of assigning costs to similar items are: *first-in, first-out (FIFO)*, *last-in, first-out (LIFO)*, and *moving-weighted-average*. FIFO reports ending inventory at the most current cost. LIFO reports cost of goods sold at the most current cost. Moving-weighted-average falls in the middle.

2. **Record perpetual inventory transactions.** Since the perpetual inventory system keeps a continuous record for each inventory item, inventory is debited immediately at cost when an item is purchased and inventory is credited immediately at cost when an item is sold. A physical count of inventory at the end of the year or the accounting period is needed to ensure the accounting records are accurate.

3. **Compare the effects of the FIFO, LIFO, and moving-weighted-average cost methods.** FIFO reports ending inventory at the most current cost. LIFO reports cost of goods sold at the most current cost. Moving-weighted-average reports ending inventory and cost of goods sold at amounts between those of FIFO and LIFO. When prices are rising, LIFO produces the high-

4. **Compute the periodic inventory amounts under the FIFO, LIFO, and weighted-average cost methods.** In a periodic inventory system, the business does not keep an up-to-date balance for ending inventory. Instead, at the end of the period, the business counts the inventory on hand and updates its records. To compute ending inventory and cost of goods sold, a cost is assigned to each inventory item. Three methods of assigning costs to similar items are: *first-in, first-out (FIFO)*, *last-in, first-out (LIFO)*, and *weighted-average*. FIFO produces identical balances for ending inventory and cost of goods sold under the periodic and perpetual inventory systems, but LIFO and weighted-average produce different results under the periodic and perpetual systems.

5. **Apply the lower-of-cost-or-market rule to inventory.** The *lower-of-cost-or-market (LCM) rule*—an example of accounting *conservatism*—requires that businesses report inventory on the balance sheet at the lower of its cost or current replacement or net realizable value. Companies disclose their definition of "market" for purposes of applying LCM in notes to their financial statements.

6. **Determine the effects of inventory errors.** Although inventory overstatements in one period are counterbalanced by inventory understatements in the next period, effective decision making depends on accurate inventory information.

7. **Estimate ending inventory by the gross margin method and the retail method.** The *gross margin*

Self-Study Questions allow you to test your understanding of the chapter on your own. Page references are given for each of these multiple-choice questions so that you can review a section quickly if you miss an answer. The answers are provided after the Similar Accounting Terms (see the next page) so you can check your progress.

Self-Study Questions

Test your understanding of the chapter by marking the correct answer to each of the following questions:

1. Suppose a Canadian chain store made sales of $9,363 million and ended the year with inventories totalling $966 million. Cost of goods sold was $6,110 million. Total operating expenses were $2,734 million. How much net income did the chain store earn for the year? (p. 294)
   a. $519 million   c. $5,663 million
   b. $3,253 million   d. $6,629 million

2. Which inventory costing method assigns to ending inventory the latest—the most recent—costs incurred during the period? (p. 296)
   a. Specific unit cost
   b. First-in, first-out (FIFO)
   c. Last-in, first-out (LIFO)
   d. Average cost

3. Assume Amazon.ca began June with 10 units of inventory that cost a total of $190. During June, Amazon purchased and sold goods as follows:

Accounting Vocabulary

Conservatism (p. 303)
Consistency principle (p. 303)
Disclosure principle (p. 303)
First-in, first-out (FIFO) inventory cost method (p. 295)
Gross margin method (p. 306)
Gross profit method (p. 306)
Last-in, first-out (LIFO) inventory cost method (p. 297)

Lower-of-cost-or-market (LCM) rule (p. 304)
Materiality concept (p. 303)
Moving-weighted-average-cost method (p. 298)
Retail method (p. 307)
Specific identification method (p. 295)
Specific-unit-cost method (p. 295)
Weighted-average cost method (p. 302)

Accounting Vocabulary lists all the terms that were defined and appeared in bold type in the chapter. The page references are given so you can review the meanings of the terms. These terms are also collected and defined in the Glossary at the end of the text.

Similar Accounting Terms links
the accounting terms used in the chapter
to similar terms you might have heard
outside your accounting class, in the
media, in other courses, or in day-to-day
business dealings. Knowing similar
terms should make it easier to remember the accounting terms.

These are the Answers to the Self-Study
Questions, mentioned on the previous
page.

Similar Accounting Terms

Cost of goods sold	Cost of sales
Gross margin method	Gross profit method
Weighted-average cost method	Average-cost method

Answers to Self-Study Questions

1. c	5. b		7. b
2. a	6. c [785 × 3 (one debit, one credit, and one		8. b
3. d	to the accounts receivable subsidiaryledger)		9. d
4. b	= 2,355]		10. a

PRACTISING

While practice may not make you perfect, it is still
the best way to make sure you grasp new accounting concepts and procedures.
Working through the end of chapter exercises and problems will help you confirm
your understanding of accounting concepts and develop your accounting skills.
These review and practice materials are described in the following pages.

Questions require short, written answers or short calculations, often on a
single topic.

Questions

1. Why is merchandise inventory so important to a
   retailer or wholesaler?
2. Suppose your business deals in expensive jewellery. Which inventory system should you use to
   achieve good internal control over the inventory?
   If your business is a hardware store that sells
   low-cost goods, which inventory system would
   you be likely to use? Why would you choose this
   system?

inventory costing method should produce the
most accurate data on the income statement?
11. Which inventory costing method produces the
    most accurate data on the balance sheet? Why?
12. How does the consistency principle affect
    accounting for inventory?
13. Briefly describe the influence that the concept of
    conservatism has on accounting for inventory.

Exercises on a single or a small number of topics require you to "do the accounting" and, often, to consider the
implications of the result in the same way
that real companies would. The objectives covered by each exercise are listed
after the brief description of the concepts
covered.

Exercises

Exercise 6-1 *Measuring ending inventory and cost of goods sold in a perpetual system—
FIFO (Obj. 1)*

Picker Paradise carries a large inventory of guitars and other musical instruments.
Picker uses the FIFO method and a perpetual inventory system. Company records
indicate the following for a particular line of Honeydew guitars:

Date	Item	Quantity	Unit Cost
May 1	Balance	5	$70

Serial Exercise in Chapters 2 to 5
follows one company and builds in complexity with each chapter, providing an
excellent review of the accounting cycle.

Serial Exercise

*Exercise 3-17 continues the Melanie Clark Engineers situation begun in Exercise 2-15 of
Chapter 2.*

Exercise 3-17 *Adjusting the accounts, preparing an adjusted trial balance, and preparing
the financial statements (Obj. 3, 4, 5)*

Refer to Exercise 2-15 of Chapter 2. Start from the trial balance and the posted
T-accounts that Melanie Clark Engineers prepared for this engineering practice at
December 18. Make sure the account balances in your trial balance and
T-accounts match those in the trial balance at December 18, 2005, shown on the

Challenge Exercises provide a
challenge for those students who have
mastered the Exercises.

Challenge Exercises

Exercise 6-17 *Inventory policy decisions (Obj. 3)*

For each of the following situations, identify the inventory method that you are
using or would prefer to use, or, given the use of a particular method, state the
strategy that you would follow to accomplish your goal.

a. Inventory costs are increasing. Your business uses LIFO and is having an unexpectedly good year. It is near year end, and you need to keep net income from
   increasing too much.
b. Inventory costs have been stable for several years, and you expect costs to

Beyond the Numbers exercises require analytical thinking and written responses about the topics presented in the chapter.

Ethical Issues are thought-provoking situations that help you recognize when ethics should affect an accounting decision.

Problems are presented in two groups that mirror each other, "A" and "B." Many instructors work through problems from Group A in class to demonstrate accounting concepts, then assign problems from Group B for homework or extra practice. The objectives covered by each problem are listed after the brief description of the concepts covered.

Challenge Problems encourage you to consider the effect of accounting information and apply it to decision situations.

Decision Problems allow you to prepare and interpret accounting information and then make recommendations to a business based on this information.

Beyond the Numbers

Assessing the impact of the inventory costing method on the financial statements (Obj. 3, 5)

The inventory costing method chosen by a company can affect the financial statements and thus the decisions of the users of those statements.

Required

1. A leading accounting researcher stated that one inventory costing method reports the most recent costs in the income statement, while another method reports the most recent costs in the balance sheet. In this person's opinion, this results in one or the other of the statements being "inaccurate" when prices are rising. What did the researcher mean?

Ethical Issue

During 2005, Rooy Electronics changed to the LIFO method of accounting for inventory. Suppose that during 2006, Rooy Electronics changes back to the FIFO method, and in the following year switches back to LIFO again.

Required

1. What would you think of a company's ethics if it changed accounting methods every year?
2. What accounting principle would changing methods every year violate?
3. Who can be harmed when a company changes its accounting methods too often? How?

Problems (Group A)

Problem 6-1A *Accounting for inventory in a perpetual system—FIFO* **(Obj. 1, 2)**

Pier 1 Imports (www.pier1.com) operates almost 1,000 stores around the world. Assume you are dealing with a Pier 1 store in Vancouver. Assume the store began with an inventory of 50 chairs that cost a total of $1,500. The store purchased and sold merchandise on account as follows:

Purchase 1	60 chairs at $35
Sale 1	100 chairs at $60
Purchase 2	80 chairs at $40
Sale 2	70 chairs at $70

Problems (Group B)

Problem 6-1B *Accounting for inventory using the perpetual system—LIFO* **(Obj. 1, 2)**

Assume Toys "R" Us Canada (www.toysrus.ca) purchases inventory in crates of merchandise, so each unit of inventory is a crate of toys. Assume you are dealing with a single department in the Toys "R" Us store in Whitby, Ontario.

Assume the department began January with an inventory of 20 units that cost a total of $1,200. During the month, the department purchased and sold merchandise on account as follows:

Purchase 1	30 units at $65	Purchase 2	70 units at $70
Sale 1	40 units at $100	Sale 2	75 units at $110

Toys "R" Us uses the LIFO cost method.

Challenge Problems

Problem 6-1C *Inventory measurement and income* **(Obj. 3)**

An anonymous source advised Canada Customs and Revenue Agency that Jim Hick, owner of Hick's Grocery Store, has been filing fraudulent tax returns for the past several years. You, a tax auditor with Canada Customs and Revenue Agency, are in the process of auditing Hick's Grocery Store for the year ended December 31, 2004. Hick's tax returns for the past five years show a decreasing value for ending inventory from 1999, when Hick bought the business, to 2003; the return for 2004 shows the same sort of decrease. You have performed a quick survey of the large store and the attached warehouse and observed that both seemed very well stocked.

Decision Problem

1. Assessing the impact of a year-end purchase of inventory—periodic system (Obj. 4)

BackCountry Camping Supplies is nearing the end of its first year of operations. The company uses the periodic inventory method and made inventory purchases of $111,750 during the year as follows:

January	150 units at	$100.00	=	$ 15,000
July	600 units at	121.25	=	72,750
November	150 units at	160.00	=	24,000
Totals	900			$111,750

Financial Statement Problem

allows you to use real financial information from Intrawest Corporation, the successful Canadian ski and resort company, to answer the problem. Selected information from Intrawest's 2003 Annual Report appears in Appendix A of Volume I and Volume II of *Accounting*.

 Media Companion CD-ROM A CD-ROM icon appears beside selected Exercises and Problems to remind you that Excel spreadsheets have been created to answer these questions. You can find these spreadsheets on the Media Companion CD-ROM packaged with your text. You don't have to use the spreadsheets to answer the questions, but you may find they save you time.

In addition to the features above that appear in each chapter, two additional features appear at the end of each part of Volume I and Volume II.

Comprehensive Problem

covers the content addressed in the book so far. This is a relatively long problem that provides an excellent review of all of the topics covered in the chapters in that part. See your instructor for the solution to this problem.

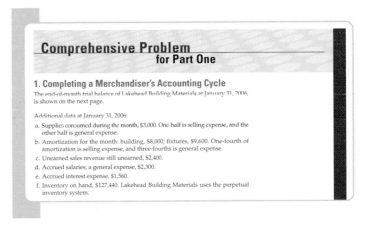

Comprehensive Problem
for Part One

1. Completing a Merchandiser's Accounting Cycle

The end-of-month trial balance of Lakehead Building Materials at January 31, 2006, is shown on the next page.

Additional data at January 31, 2006:

a. Supplies consumed during the month, $3,000. One half is selling expense, and the other half is general expense.

b. Amortization for the month: building, $8,000; fixtures, $9,600. One-fourth of amortization is selling expense, and three-fourths is general expense.

c. Unearned sales revenue still unearned, $2,400.

d. Accrued salaries, a general expense, $2,300.

e. Accrued interest expense, $1,560.

f. Inventory on hand, $127,440. Lakehead Building Materials uses the perpetual inventory system.

 **CBC Video Cases** appear at the end of each of the Parts in Volumes I and II. The CBC videos that accompany these cases are included on the Media Companion CD-ROM packaged with your text.

The videos demonstrate the importance of accounting concepts to real businesses and real entrepreneurs in a truly interesting way.

REINFORCING
Interactive media and supplements can reinforce the material you learn within the text. We have developed series of resources to enhance your experience as you build your accounting skills:

The **Media Companion CD-ROM** that accompanies this book contains an array of tools to help you learn accounting concepts and test your understanding:

- An animated accounting cycle tutorial
- A complete Study Guide with chapter reviews, exercises, problems, and solutions
- The PowerPoint presentations often used in class
- The CBC videos that accompany the CBC Video Cases in the text
- An Excel tutorial that you can use as a refresher
- Excel spreadsheet templates to accompany selected text Exercises and Problems

The **Companion Website (www.pearsoned.ca/horngren)** provides a wealth of resources for you, including:

- An Online Study Guide with quizzes and immediate feedback
- Links to the CBC videos that accompany the CBC Video Cases in the text
- Links to the websites of companies mentioned in each chapter
- A link to our Accounting Online Tutor, an accounting instructor who will help you work through chapter or problem material that you find particularly challenging

Prentice Hall GradeAssist is an online self-assessment and quiz system that, if adopted by your instructor, provides review and problem materials linked directly to *Accounting, Canadian Sixth Edition*. Quizzes and problem assignments are marked automatically for instant feedback on your work. Many of the problems are based on those found in the book, but the content of the problems refreshes itself each time you visit, to allow you to build accounting rather than memorization skills.

The **Working Papers** are a set of tear-out forms that you can use to solve all the exercises and problems in Volume I. Because the forms you need have already been created, you avoid time-consuming set-up and can focus on the accounting right away.

The *Appliance City Practice Set*, Canadian Edition provides you with the opportunity to perform the accounting cycle for a sole proprietorship merchandising business.

The *A-1 Photography Practice Set*, Fifth Canadian Edition gives you the opportunity to complete the accounting cycle for a sole proprietorship service business.

To the Instructor

Welcome to *Accounting*! Instructors have told us that their greatest challenges are effectively teaching students with very different business and accounting backgrounds and motivating students to give accounting the study time and attention it deserves. *Accounting*'s approach and features were designed to help you address and overcome these challenges:

- Instructors have told us that if students miss an accounting class, they must be able to keep up by reading the text. We continue to use an **easy-to-understand writing style** to help students prepare for class or, should they miss a session, catch up without being overwhelmed.

- Wherever possible, accounting principles and procedures are illustrated using **examples from real Canadian companies**. This real-world context enlivens the material, makes difficult concepts easier to grasp, and illustrates the role of accounting in business. In those situations where "live" data drawn from real companies would complicate the material for introductory students, we illustrate the accounting with realistic examples from generic companies to give students the clearest examples possible.

- As instructors, we know that **accuracy in problems and solutions** is every bit as important as clear writing and effective pedagogy. Tremendous effort has been made to ensure that the solutions to problem materials in *Accounting,* Canadian Sixth Edition, are correct. The authors have developed their own problem and solutions materials. Our Developmental Editor, Anita Smale, CA, has reviewed all problems and solutions. And as a final stage in our efforts to bring you the most accurate text possible, technical checkers have reviewed all problems and solutions.

The Canadian Fifth Edition of *Accounting* included a number of changes that were made after considerable discussion with instructors from across the country. We brought on a new co-author, Peter Norwood, to address more directly the needs of instructors and students in the college setting. We introduced a new, full-colour presentation of the material that made concepts easier for students to understand. We moved from a corporate to a sole proprietorship focus in Volume I, because a majority of instructors told us that students grasp owners' equity concepts more easily by learning about proprietorships before learning about corporations. And we added new features like Accounting and the E-World, Accounting Around the Globe, and Management Accounting for a Small Business to illustrate the dynamic and diverse nature of accounting.

As always, market feedback has been crucial in the development of this new edition. With the Canadian Sixth Edition of *Accounting*, we have continued to build on the improvements to the previous edition with the following changes based directly on reviewer and user feedback:

- Reviewers told us that inventory concepts should be covered in consecutive chapters to facilitate instruction, so you will now find **inventory covered in Chapters 5 and 6**.

- Faculty asked for **more single-objective end-of-chapter exercises and problems** to enhance classroom and student review, so we added them.

- Faculty told us that fresh end of chapter exercise and problem materials are an important learning tool. We've listened, **updating or replacing 90% of the end of chapter materials**.

- In response to user feedback, we have **streamlined the amount of marginal material** to simplify ease of text use for students.

- Reviewers indicated that, while well intended, the **"Student to Student" boxes** that appeared in the Canadian Fifth Edition did not particularly aid student learning. We have **removed** them from this edition.

- Many students prefer to learn in an interactive environment. They also appreciate value! To help faculty address these needs, we've added a new **Media Companion CD-ROM** that includes an interactive Accounting Cycle Tutorial, a Study Guide, Excel Spreadsheet Templates, PowerPoints, and CBC Videos.

We also recognize the benefits of an extensive and varied supplement package, so we are pleased to offer the following instructor supplements to support your use of *Accounting*, Canadian Sixth Edition:

Instructor Integrator CD-ROM The next generation of the Instructor's Resource CD-ROM, this CD-ROM provides a fully searchable and integrated collection of resources to help you with lecture preparation, presentation, and assessment. The Instructor Integrator contains the following supplements:

- **Instructor's Solutions Manual** Now provided in both Adobe PDF and MS Word format for ease of use.
- **Instructor's Resource Manual** Also provided in both Adobe PDF and MS Word format, the Instructor's Resource Manual includes Chapter Overviews and Outlines, Assignment Grids, Ten-Minute Quizzes, and other valuable teaching resources.
- **TestGen** This powerful and user-friendly computerized test bank includes well over 100 questions per chapter, ranging from True/False, Multiple-Choice, and Matching to Problems and Critical Thinking Exercises.
- **PowerPoint Teaching Transparencies** For flexibility of use, we provide two sets of transparencies: a brief set with six to eight slides per chapter, and a comprehensive set with 40 to 50 slides per chapter.
- **Exhibits** We are pleased to provide the exhibits from the text in GIF format for use in the classroom and easy conversion to acetate format.
- **CBC/Pearson Canada Video Library** We now offer this excellent teaching and learning resource in digitized format for use in technology-enhanced classrooms.

Adapting Your Lecture Notes These detailed transition notes, including comparison of tables of content, chapter objectives, and chapter content, will facilitate your course preparation if making the switch to *Accounting* from another introductory accounting text.

Printed Solutions Acetates In response to instructor feedback, we continue to provide all text solutions printed on acetates for easy classroom use.

CBC/Pearson Canada Video Library We also continue to provide these videos in VHS format for those instructors who prefer this delivery method.

Corporate Chapters Back by popular demand, the "corporate" version of Chapters 1-5 is available through our Companion Website or for packaging with the text. Solutions are also available on demand.

WebCT, BlackBoard, and CourseCompass These fully prepared courses, including review, self-assessment, and testing tied directly to the text, allow you to incorporate online course management with as little or as much modification as you desire.

Finally, we want to draw your attention to two great services offered by Pearson to further enhance the use of *Accounting* in your course:

Pearson Custom Publishing We know that not every instructor follows the exact order of a course text. Some may not even cover all the material in a given volume. Pearson Custom Publishing provides the flexibility to select the chapters you need, presented in the order you want, to tailor fit your text to your course and your students' needs. Contact your Pearson Education Canada Sales and Editorial Representative to learn more.

Instructor's Asset With every qualifying new adoption, we provide Instructor's Asset – Academic Support and Service for Educational Technologies. This customized training and after-the-sale support program lets you select the level of service and degree of support that you need to make your course successful. Contact your Pearson Education Canada Sales and Editorial Representative to learn more.

Developing high-quality textbooks is an ongoing effort. As you deliver your course, we'd like to hear from you. Let us know what you like about this book and your ideas for improving it by visiting our web site at **www.pearsoned.ca/horngren** and clicking on the Feedback link.

We hope you enjoy *Accounting*!

Morley Lemon
Peter Norwood

Acknowledgements for the Canadian Sixth Edition

We would like to thank Chuck Horngren, Tom Harrison, and Linda Bamber for their encouragement and support.

Particular thanks are due to the following people for either reviewing the previous edition of this text during the planning stages of this edition or reviewing the manuscript for this new edition or both:

Cécile Ashman, Algonquin College
Robert Dearden, Red River Community College
Johan de Rooy, University of British Columbia
Elizabeth Evans, Nova Scotia Community College
Donna Grace, Sheridan College
Sharon Hatten, British Columbia Institute of Technology
Connie Johl, Douglas College
Jane Kaake-Nemeth, Durham College
Ann MacGillivary, Mount Saint Vincent University
Marie Madill-Payne, George Brown College
John Mitchell, Sault College
Jan Nyholt, Southern Alberta Institute of Technology
Penny Parker, Fanshawe College
Traven Reed, Canadore College
Frank Ridley, Seneca College
David Sale, Kwantlen University College
Bob Sproule, University of Waterloo
Rod Tilley, Mount Saint Vincent University
John Vermeer, Humber College

Thanks are due again to our previous edition reviewers, who helped to shape many of the changes we have carried forward into this new edition:

Cécile Ashman, Algonquin College
Dave Bopara, Toronto School of Business
Nada Borden, College of the North Atlantic
Wayne Bridgeman, formerly with CGA-Canada

Chris Burnley, Malaspina University College
Maisie Caines, College of the North Atlantic
James E. Chambers, St. Clair College
K. Suzanne Coombs, Kwantlen University College
Robert Dearden, Red River Community College
Vincent Durant, St. Lawrence College
Richard Farrar, Conestoga College
Albert M. Ferris, University of Prince Edward Island
Dave Fleming, George Brown College
Augusta Ford, College of the North Atlantic
Reiner Frisch, Georgian College
Donna Grace, Sheridan College
Elizabeth Hicks, Douglas College
Larry Howe, University College of the Fraser Valley
Stephanie Ibach, Northern Alberta Institute of Technology
Wayne Irvine, Mount Royal College
Connie Johl, Douglas College
Ann MacGillivary, Mount Saint Vincent University
Rick Martin, College of the North Atlantic
Allen McQueen, Grant MacEwan Community College
Tariq Nizami, Champlain Regional College CEGEP
Penny Parker, Fanshawe College
Carson Rappell, Dawson College
David Sale, Kwantlen University College
Gabriela Schneider, Grant MacEwan Community College
Scott Sinclair, British Columbia Institute of Technology
Bob Sproule, University of Waterloo
Gregg Tranter, Southern Alberta Institute of Technology
Elizabeth Zaleschuk, Douglas College

Thanks are extended to Intrawest Corporation for permission to use its annual report in Volumes I and II of the text once again. Thanks are extended to JVC Canada Inc. for permission to use its invoice in Chapter 5. We acknowledge the support provided by *The Globe and Mail's Report on Business*, the *Financial Post*, and by the annual reports of a large number of public companies.

The Canadian Institute of Chartered Accountants, as the official promulgator of generally accepted accounting principles in Canada, and the *CICA Handbook*, are vital to the conduct of business and accounting in Canada. We have made every effort to incorporate the most current *Handbook* recommendations in this new edition of *Accounting*.

We would like to acknowledge the people of Pearson Education Canada, in particular Vice-President, Editorial Director Michael Young, Executive Editor Samantha Scully, and Director of Marketing Bill Todd. Special thanks to Production Editor Mary Ann McCutcheon, Production Coordinator Deborah Starks, and their teams for their superior efforts in guiding this edition through the various phases of preparation and production. We would also like to acknowledge the editorial and technical support of Anita Smale, CA.

I would like to thank my wife Sandra for her assistance.

W. Morley Lemon

I would like to thank my wife, Helen, and my family very much for their support, assistance, and encouragement.

Peter R. Norwood

The Accounting Profession: Career Opportunities

The accounting profession offers exciting career opportunities because every organization uses accounting. The corner grocery store keeps accounting records to measure its success in selling groceries. The largest corporations need accounting to monitor their locations and transactions. And the dot.coms must account for their transactions. Why is accounting so important? Because it helps an organization understand its business in the same way a model helps an architect construct a building. Accounting helps a manager understand the organization as a whole without drowning in its details.

The Work of Accountants

Positions in the field of accounting may be divided into several areas. Two general classifications are *public accounting* and *private accounting*.

In Canada, most accountants, both public and private, belong to one of three accounting bodies, which set the standards for admission of members and deal with matters like the rules of professional conduct followed by their members: The Canadian Institute of Chartered Accountants (CICA) (www.cica.ca), whose members are called *Chartered Accountants (CA)*; the Certified General Accountants Association of Canada (CGAAC) (www.cga-canada.org), whose members are called *Certified General Accountants (CGA)*; and the Society of Management Accountants of Canada (SMAC) (www.cma-canada.org), whose members are called *Certified Management Accountants (CMA)*. The role and activities of each of these bodies are discussed below.

Private accountants work for a single business, such as a local department store, the St-Hubert restaurant chain, or McCain Foods Ltd. Charitable organizations, educational institutions, and government agencies also employ private accountants. The chief accounting officer usually has the title of controller, treasurer, or chief financial officer. Whatever the title, this person often carries the status of vice-president.

Public accountants are those who serve the general public and collect professional fees for their work, much as doctors and lawyers do. Their work includes auditing, income tax planning and preparation of returns, management consulting, and various accounting services. These specialized accounting services are discussed in the next section. Public accountants represent about a quarter of all professional accountants.

Some public accountants pool their talents and work together within a single firm. Public accounting firms are called CA firms, CGA firms, or CMA firms, depending on the accounting body from which the partners of the firm come. Public accounting firms vary greatly in size. Some are small businesses, and others are medium-sized partnerships. The largest firms are worldwide partnerships with over 2,000 partners. There are four large, international accounting firms:

Deloitte & Touche LLP	KPMG LLP
Ernst & Young LLP	PricewaterhouseCoopers LLP

Although these firms employ less than 25 percent of the more than 60,000 CAs in Canada, they audit most of the 1,000 largest corporations in Canada. The top partners in large accounting firms earn about the same amount as the top managers of other large businesses.

Exhibit 1 shows the accounting positions within public accounting firms and other organizations. Of special interest in the exhibit is the upward movement of accounting personnel, as the arrows show. In particular, note how accountants may move from positions in public accounting firms to similar or higher positions in industry and government. This is a frequently travelled career path. Because accounting deals with all facets of an organization—such as purchasing, manufacturing, marketing, and distribution—it provides an excellent basis for gaining broad business experience.

Accounting Organizations and Designations

The position of accounting in today's business world has created the need for control over the professional, educational, and ethical standards of accountants. Through statutes passed by provincial legislatures, the three accounting organizations in Canada have received the authority to set educational requirements and professional standards for their members and to discipline members who fail to adhere to their codes of conduct. The acts make them self-regulating bodies, just as provincial associations of doctors and lawyers are.

The *Canadian Institute of Chartered Accountants (CICA)*, whose members are chartered accountants or CAs, is the oldest accounting organization in Canada. Experience and education requirements for becoming a CA vary among the provinces. Generally, the educational requirement includes a university degree. All the provincial institutes require is that an individual, to qualify as a CA, pass a national three-day uniform examination administered by the CICA and meet articling requirements. The provincial institutes grant the right to use the professional designation CA.

CAs in Canada generally must earn their practical experience by working for a public accounting firm; subsequently, about half the CAs in Canada leave public practice for jobs in industry, government, or education. A small number of CAs meet their experience requirements working for the federal or provincial governments. CAs in public accounting have the right to perform audits and issue opinions on the audited financial statements in all provinces in Canada.

CAs belong to a provincial institute (*Ordre* in Quebec) and through that body to the CICA. The provincial institutes have the responsibility for developing and enforcing the code of professional conduct that guides the actions of the CAs in that province.

The CICA, through the Accounting Standards Board and the Assurance Standards Board respectively, issues accounting standards or GAAP (discussed in Chapter 1)

EXHIBIT 1

Accounting Positions within Organizations

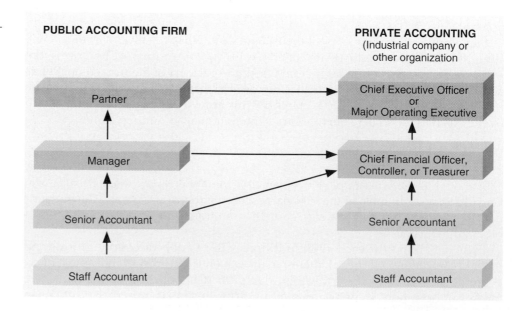

and auditing standards (Generally Accepted Auditing Standards or GAAS). These standards are collected in the *CICA Handbook*. Specific standards are italicized and called *Recommendations*. Accounting Recommendations are the standards or regulations that govern the preparation of financial statements in Canada. The Accounting Standards Board and the Assurance Standards Board publish Accounting Guidelines and Assurance and Related Services Guidelines respectively; these do not have the force of Recommendations, but simply provide guidance on specific issues.

The Emerging Issues Committee (EIC), another committee of the CICA, publishes Abstracts of Issues Discussed, which rank below Accounting Guidelines in terms of authority. A fourth body, the Public Sector Accounting Board (PSAB), issues standards pertaining to public sector accounting.

The CICA supports and publishes research relating primarily to financial reporting and auditing. The CICA publishes a monthly professional journal entitled *CA Magazine*.

The *Certified General Accountants Association of Canada (CGAAC)* is also regulated by provincial law. The experience and education requirements for becoming a CGA vary from province to province, but in all provinces the individual must either pass national examinations administered by the CGAAC in the various subject areas or gain exemption by taking specified university, college, and association courses. Certain subjects may only be passed by taking a national examination. CGA students require a university degree in order to obtain their designation; they do not need to have the degree to enroll as a student.

CGAs may gain their practical experience through work in public accounting, industry, or government. They are employed in public practice, industry, and government. Some provinces license CGAs in public practice, which gives them the right to conduct audits and issue opinions on financial statements, while some other provinces do not require a licence for them to perform audits.

The association supports research in various areas pertaining to accounting through the Canadian CGA Research Foundation. CGAAC publishes a professional journal entitled *CGA Magazine*.

The *Society of Management Accountants of Canada (SMAC)* administers the Certified Management Accountant program that leads to the Certified Management Accountant (CMA) designation. The use of this designation is similarly controlled by provincial law. Students generally must have a university degree. The SMAC administers an admission or entrance examination that students must pass before embarking on a two-year professional program and completing two years of required work experience. After completing the professional program and the work experience, they write a final examination and make a presentation to a SMAC committee, based on the professional program administered by the SMAC, in order to obtain the CMA designation. The SMAC also administers the professional program and the final examination. CMAs earn their practical experience in industry or government, and are generally employed in industry or government, although some CMAs are in public accounting. The Society issues standards relating to management accounting through the SMAC. The SMAC conducts and publishes research relating primarily to management accounting. The SMAC publishes a professional journal entitled *Cost and Management*.

The *Financial Executives Institute (FEI)* is an organization composed of senior financial executives from many of the large corporations in Canada, who meet on a regular basis with a view to sharing information on how they can better manage their organizations. Most of these executives have one of the three designations just discussed. The FEI supports and publishes research relating to management accounting. The FEI also publishes a journal, the *Financial Executive*.

The *Institute of Internal Auditors (IIA)* is a world-wide organization of internal auditors. It administers the examinations leading to and grants the Certified Internal Auditor (CIA) designation. Internal auditors are employees of an organization whose job is to review the operations, including financial operations, of the organization with a view to making it more economical, efficient, and effective. Many

Canadian internal auditors are members of Canadian chapters of the IIA. The IIA supports and publishes research and conducts courses related to internal auditing. The IIA journal is *The Internal Auditor*.

The *Canadian Academic Accounting Association (CAAA)* directs its attention toward the academic and research aspects of accounting. A high percentage of its members are professors. The CAAA publishes a journal devoted to research in accounting and auditing, *Contemporary Accounting Research*.

While it is not an accounting organization or designation, *Canada Customs and Revenue Agency (CCRA)* enforces the tax laws and collects the revenue needed to finance the federal government.

Specialized Accounting Services

As accounting affects so many people in so many different fields, public accounting and private accounting include specialized services.

Public Accounting

Auditing is one of the accounting profession's most significant services to the public. An audit is the independent examination that ensures the reliability of the reports that management prepares and submits to investors, creditors, and others outside the business. In carrying out an audit, public accountants from outside a business examine the business's financial statements. If the public accountants believe that these documents are a fair presentation of the business's operations, they offer a professional opinion stating that the firm's financial statements have been prepared in accordance with generally accepted accounting principles, or, if generally accepted accounting principles are not applicable, with an appropriate disclosed basis of accounting. Why is the audit so important? Creditors considering loans want assurance that the facts and figures the borrower submits are reliable. Shareholders, who have invested in the business, need to know that the financial picture management shows them is complete. Government agencies need information from businesses. All want information that is unbiased.

Tax accounting has two aims: complying with the tax laws and minimizing taxes to be paid. Because combined federal and provincial income tax rates range as high as 53 percent for individuals and 46 percent for corporations, reducing income tax is an important management consideration. Tax work by accountants consists of preparing tax returns and planning business transactions to minimize taxes. In addition, since the imposition of the Goods and Services Tax (GST), public accountants have been involved in advising their clients how to properly collect and account for GST. Public accountants advise individuals on what types of investments to make, and on how to structure their transactions. Accountants in corporations provide tax planning and preparation services as well.

Management consulting is the term that describes the wide scope of advice public accountants provide to help managers run a business. As they conduct audits, public accountants look deep into a business's operations. With the insight they gain, they often make suggestions for improvements in the business's management structure and accounting systems. Management consulting is the fastest-growing service provided by accountants.

Accounting services is also a catchall term used to describe the wide range of services related to accounting provided by public accountants. These services include bookkeeping and preparation of financial statements on a monthly or annual basis. Some small companies have all their accounting done by a public accounting firm.

Private Accounting

Cost accounting analyzes a business's costs to help managers control expenses or set selling prices. Good cost accounting records guide managers in pricing their products to achieve greater profits. Also, cost accounting information shows management when a product is not profitable and should be dropped from a product line.

Budgeting sets sales and profit goals, and develops detailed plans—called budgets—for achieving those goals. Some of the most successful companies in Canada have been pioneers in the field of budgeting.

Information systems design identifies the organization's information needs, both internal and external. Using flow charts and manuals, designers develop and implement the system to meet those needs.

Internal auditing is performed by a business's own audit staff. Many large organizations, Ontario Power Generation Inc., Hudson's Bay Co., and The Bank of Nova Scotia among them, maintain a staff of internal auditors. These accountants evaluate the firm's own accounting and management systems to improve operating efficiency, and to ensure that employees follow management's policies.

Exhibit 2 summarizes these accounting specializations.

As you work through *Accounting* you will learn how to use accounting to make business decisions. With the exciting career opportunities accounting offers, consider a career in accounting.

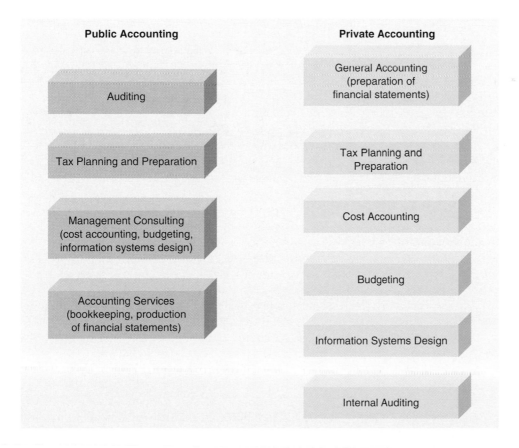

Public Accounting

Auditing

Tax Planning and Preparation

Management Consulting
(cost accounting, budgeting,
information systems design)

Accounting Services
(bookkeeping, production
of financial statements)

Private Accounting

General Accounting
(preparation of
financial statements)

Tax Planning and
Preparation

Cost Accounting

Budgeting

Information Systems Design

Internal Auditing

EXHIBIT 2

Specialization in Public and Private Accounting

1

Accounting and the Business Environment

CHAPTER OBJECTIVES

After studying this chapter, you should be able to

1 Use accounting vocabulary for decision making

2 Apply accounting concepts and principles to business situations

3 Use the accounting equation to describe an organization's financial position

4 Use the accounting equation to analyze business transactions

5 Prepare and use the financial statements

6 Evaluate the performance of a business

 Media Companion CD-ROM

Visit the Media Companion CD-ROM that comes with this book for extra practice with the new material in Chapter 1.

Brad Taylor is a student at Langara College in Vancouver. After successfully completing his first term in December, Brad started looking for a summer job that would pay him enough to cover his expenses for his second year of school. He noticed an advertisement from College Pro Painters. Brad met with the managers of College Pro Painters and was granted a franchise to operate in Richmond, a suburb of Vancouver. Brad's income would be determined by his ability to successfully operate his own business. Overnight, Brad became an entrepreneur. He had to find customers, hire painters, set up an office, and learn some basic bookkeeping. By the time the second term of school had ended in April, Brad had lined up enough work to keep two crews of painters working full time for the entire summer.

"I've never worked so hard in my life," Brad confided. "It's been a lot of fun but a lot of work. I had to learn how to bid for jobs, deal with customers, and find painters. My objective is to make enough income to pay for my tuition, books, and room and board next year. I think I've succeeded, but I won't know for sure until I prepare financial statements at the end of the summer. I never knew keeping track of my expenses would be so important!"

W_{HAT} role does accounting play in this situation? Brad Taylor had to decide how to organize his franchise. He set up his business as a proprietorship—a single-owner company—with Brad Taylor as the owner. As the business grows, he may consider joining forces with a fellow franchisee to form a partnership. If he wants to expand the business after graduation, he could choose to incorporate—that is, to form a corporation. In this chapter, we discuss all three forms of business organization: proprietorships, partnerships, and corporations.

You may already know various accounting terms and relationships, because accounting affects people's behaviour in many ways. This first accounting course will sharpen your focus by explaining how accounting works. As you progress through this course, you will see how accounting helps people like Brad Taylor—and you—achieve business goals.

Accounting: The Language of Business

OBJECTIVE 1
Use accounting vocabulary for decision making

Accounting is the information system that measures business financial activities, processes that information into reports, and communicates the results to decision makers. For this reason it is called "the language of business." The better you understand the language, the better your decisions will be, and the better you can manage the financial aspects of living. A recent survey indicates that business managers believe it is more important for college students to learn accounting than any other business subject. Decisions concerning personal financial planning, education expenses, loans, car payments, income taxes, and investments are based on the *information system* that we call accounting. Financial statements, a key product of an accounting system, provide information that helps people make informed business decisions. **Financial statements** report on a business in monetary amounts, providing information to help people make informed business decisions.

Is my business making a profit? Should I hire assistants? Am I earning enough money to pay my rent? Answers to business questions like these are based on accounting information.

Please don't mistake bookkeeping for accounting. *Bookkeeping* is a procedural element of accounting, just as arithmetic is a procedural element of mathematics.

Increasingly, people are using computers to do detailed bookkeeping—in households, businesses, and organizations of all types. Exhibit 1-1 illustrates the role of accounting in business. The process starts and ends with people making decisions.

Decision Makers:
The Users of Accounting Information

Decision makers need information. The more important the decision, the greater the need for information. Virtually all businesses and most individuals keep accounting records to aid decision making. Here are some decision makers who use accounting information.

Individuals   People use accounting information in day-to-day affairs to manage bank accounts, evaluate job prospects, make investments, and decide whether to rent or buy a house.

Businesses   Managers of businesses use accounting information to set goals for their organizations. They also evaluate their progress toward those goals, and they take corrective action when it is necessary. Decisions based on accounting information may include which building to purchase, how much merchandise inventory to keep on hand, and how much cash to borrow.

Investors   Investors provide the money a business needs to begin operations. To decide whether to invest in a new venture, potential investors evaluate what return they can reasonably expect on their investment. This evaluation means analyzing the financial statements of the business and keeping up with developments in the business press, for example, *The Financial Post* (a part of *The National Post*) (www.financialpost.com) and *Report on Business* published by *The Globe and Mail* (www.globeinvestor.com).

Creditors   Before loaning money, creditors (lenders) such as banks evalauate the borrower's ability to make scheduled payments. This evaluation includes a report of the borrower's financial position and a prediction of future operations, both of which are based on accounting information.

Government Regulatory Agencies   Most organizations face government regulation. For example, the provincial securities commissions, such as the Ontario Securities Commission, dictate that businesses that sell their shares to or borrow money from the public disclose certain financial information to the investing public.

EXHIBIT 1-1

The Flow of Information in an Accounting System

1. People make decisions.
2. Business transactions occur.
3. Businesses prepare reports to show the results of their operations.

Taxing Authorities   Provincial and federal governments levy taxes on individuals and businesses. Income tax is calculated using accounting information. Businesses determine their goods and services tax and sales tax based on their accounting records that show how much they have sold.

Nonprofit Organizations   Nonprofit organizations such as churches, hospitals, government agencies, and colleges, which operate for purposes other than to earn a profit, use accounting information in much the same way that profit-oriented businesses do.

Other Users   Employees and labour unions may make wage demands based on the accounting information that shows their employer's reported income. Consumer groups and the general public are also interested in the amount of income that businesses earn. And newspapers may report "an improved profit picture" of a major company as it emerges from economic difficulties. Such news, based on accounting information, is related to the company's health.

Financial Accounting and Management Accounting

Users of accounting information are a diverse population, but they may be categorized as external users or internal users. This distinction allows us to classify accounting into two fields—financial accounting and management accounting.

   Financial accounting provides information to people outside the company. Creditors and outside investors, for example, are not part of the day-to-day management of the company. Likewise, government agencies and the general public are external users of a company's accounting information. Chapters 2 through 18 in Volumes I and II of this book deal primarily with financial accounting.

   Management accounting generates information for internal decision makers, such as company executives, department heads, college deans, and hospital administrators. Chapters 19 through 26 in Volume III of this book cover management accounting.

The History and Development of Accounting

Accounting has a long history. Some scholars claim that writing arose in order to record accounting information. Account records date back to the ancient civilizations of China, Babylonia, Greece, and Egypt. The rulers of these civilizations used accounting to keep track of the cost of labour and materials used in building structures like the great pyramids. The need for accounting has existed as long as there has been business activity.

   Accounting developed further as a result of the information needs of merchants in the city-states of Italy during the 1400s. In that busy commercial climate, the monk Luca Pacioli, a mathematician and friend of Leonardo da Vinci, published the first known description of double-entry bookkeeping in 1494.

   In the Industrial Revolution of the nineteenth century, the growth of corporations spurred the development of accounting. The corporation owners—the shareholders—were no longer necessarily the managers of their business. Managers had to create accounting systems to report to the owners how well their businesses were doing. Because managers want their performance to look good, society needs a way to ensure that the business information provided is reliable.

   In Canada, the *Accounting Standards Board (AcSB)* of the Canadian Institute of Chartered Accountants (CICA) determines how financial accounting is practised. The AcSB consists of a maximum of nine members from a variety of backgrounds. Members are chosen so that the AcSB has an appropriate balance of competencies and expertise to set accounting standards. As described in the Appendix following

Chapter 1, the federal and provincial legislatures through the various companies' acts and the various provincial securities commissions have given the standards or *generally accepted accounting principles (GAAP)* issued by the AcSB their legal status.

Like other segments of society, accounting must be practised in an ethical manner. We look next at the ethical dimension of accounting.

Ethical Considerations in Accounting and Business

Ethical considerations affect all areas of accounting and business. Investors, creditors, and regulatory bodies need relevant and reliable information about a company. Naturally, companies want to make themselves look as good as possible to attract investors. There is a potential for conflict.

That is why the financial statements that are issued by public companies—those companies that sell their shares to or borrow money from the public—are subject to the greatest scrutiny. The provincial securities commissions dictate that public companies undergo audits. Audits are conducted by independent accountants who verify and certify that the financial statements are materially correct. It is vital that companies and their auditors behave in an ethical manner.

Unfortunately for the accounting profession, accounting scandals involving both public companies and their auditors have made the headlines in recent years. Most of these incidents occurred in the United States. For example, Enron Corporation, which was the seventh-largest company in the United States, allegedly issued misleading financial statements that reported fewer debts than the company really owed. Enron was forced into bankruptcy and its auditors were forced out of business. The impact of the Enron bankruptcy was felt by many different parties, including Enron shareholders who saw their investments become worthless, employees who lost their jobs and their pension funds, and the accounting profession, which lost its integrity and reputation as gatekeepers and stewards for the investing public. Scandals like this shocked the business community and hurt investor confidence.

In this book, we provide several problems that allow you to consider ethical dilemmas. Consider them carefully. The perception that accountants follow the highest standard of professional conduct must also be the reality. In today's business climate, behaving in an ethical manner is crucial.

The Professional Accounting Bodies and Their Standards of Professional Conduct

Chartered Accountants (CAs), Certified General Accountants (CGAs), and Certified Management Accountants (CMAs) are all governed by rules of conduct created by their respective organizations. Many of the rules apply whether the members are public accountants working in public practice or private accountants working in industry or government, while other rules are applicable only to those members in public practice.

The rules of conduct serve both the members of the accounting bodies and the public. The rules serve members by setting standards that they must meet, and providing a benchmark against which they will be measured by their peers. The public is served because the rules of conduct provide it with a list of the standards to which the members of the body adhere. This helps the public determine its expectations of members' behaviour. However, the rules of conduct should be considered a minimum standard of performance; ideally, the members should continually strive to exceed them.

There are certain rules that are fundamental to the practice of accounting and common to the rules of conduct of all three bodies. They concern the confidentiality of information the accountant is privy to, maintenance of the reputation of the profession, the need to perform their work with integrity and due care, competence, refusal to be associated with false and misleading information, and compliance by the accountant with professional standards such as the accounting standards found in the *CICA Handbook*.

There are other rules that are fundamental to the practice of public accounting. They deal with the public accountant's need for independence, and with the rules governing advertising, the seeking of clients, and the conduct of practice.

Codes of Business Conduct of Companies

Many companies have codes of conduct that apply to their employees in their dealings with each other and with the companies' suppliers and customers. Some of these companies mention their code in the annual report or on their website. For example, Vancouver City Savings Credit Union (www.vancity.ca) states on its website:

> **Our Values**
> **Integrity:** We act with courage, consistency and respect to do what is honest, fair and trustworthy.
> **Innovation:** We anticipate and respond to challenges and changing needs with creativity, enthusiasm and determination.
> **Responsibility:** We are accountable to our members, employees, colleagues and communities for the results of our decisions and actions.[1]

The company indicates to its employees and to the general public how management expects employees to behave.

Types of Business Organizations

A business can have one of three forms of organization: proprietorship, partnership, and corporation. In some cases, accounting procedures depend on the organizational form. Therefore, you should understand the differences among the three.

KEY POINT

A proprietorship and a partnership (Ch. 12) are not legal entities separate from their owners, so the income from proprietorships and partnerships is taxable to their owners, not to the business. But in accounting, the owner and the business are considered separate entities, and separate records are kept for each. A corporation (Ch. 13) is a separate legal entity. The corporation is taxed on its income, and the owners are taxed on any income they receive from the corporation.

Proprietorship   A **proprietorship** has a single owner, called the proprietor, who is usually also the manager. Proprietorships tend to be small retail establishments and individual professional businesses, such as those of physicians, lawyers, and accountants, but also can be very large. From the accounting viewpoint, each proprietorship is distinct from its proprietor. Thus the accounting records of the proprietorship do *not* include the proprietor's personal accounting records. However, from a legal perspective, the business *is* the proprietor. In this book, we begin the accounting process with a proprietorship.

Partnership   A **partnership** joins two or more individuals together as co-owners. Each owner is a partner. Many retail establishments and professional organizations of physicians, lawyers, and accountants are partnerships. Most partnerships are small and medium-sized, but some are quite large; there are public accounting firms in Canada with more than 500 partners and law firms with more than 100 partners. Accounting treats the partnership as a separate organization distinct from the personal affairs of each partner. But again, from a legal perspective, a partnership *is* the partners.

Corporation   A **corporation** is a business owned by **shareholders**. These are the people or other corporations who own shares of ownership in the business. The corporation is the dominant form of business organization in Canada. Although proprietorships and partnerships are more numerous, corporations engage in more

---

[1]From Vancouver City Savings Credit Union's website, www.vancity.ca (accessed May 19, 2003).

business and are generally larger in terms of total assets, income, and number of employees. Most well-known companies, such as Bombardier Inc. (www.bombardier.com), McCain Foods Ltd. (www.mccain.com), and the Royal Bank of Canada (www.royalbank.ca), are corporations. In Canada, generally corporations must have *Ltd.* or *Limited, Inc.* or *Incorporated,* or *Corp.* or *Corporation* in their legal name to indicate that they are incorporated. Corporations need not be large; a business with only a few assets and employees could be organized as a corporation.

A business becomes a corporation when the federal or a provincial government approves its articles of incorporation. From a legal perspective, a corporation is a distinct entity. The corporation operates as an "artificial person" that exists apart from its owners and that conducts business in its own name. The corporation has many of the rights that a person has. For example, a corporation may buy, own, and sell property. The corporation may enter into contracts and sue and be sued. Unlike the proprietorship and the partnership, the corporation is not defined by its owners.

Corporations differ significantly from proprietorships and partnerships in another way. If a proprietorship or partnership cannot pay its debts, lenders can take the owners' personal assets—cash and belongings—to satisfy the business's obligations. But if a corporation goes bankrupt, lenders cannot take the personal assets of the shareholders. The *limited personal liability* of shareholders for corporate debts explains why corporations are so popular. People can invest in corporations with limited personal risk.

Another factor in corporate growth is the division of ownership into individual shares. Companies such as BCE Inc. (www.bce.ca), Canadian Imperial Bank of Commerce (www.cibc.com), and Canadian Tire Corporation, Limited (www.canadiantire.ca) have issued millions of shares of stock and have tens of thousands of shareholders. An investor with no personal relationship either to the corporation or to any other shareholder can become an owner by buying 30, 100, 5,000, or any number of shares of its stock. For most corporations, the investor may sell the shares at any time. It is usually harder to sell one's investment in a proprietorship or a partnership than to sell one's investment in a corporation.

Exhibit 1-2 shows how the three types of business organizations compare.

Accounting for corporations includes some unique complexities. For this reason, we initially focus on proprietorships. We cover partnerships in Chapter 12 and begin our discussion of corporations in Chapter 13.

Accounting Concepts and Principles

Accounting practices follow certain guidelines. The rules that govern how accountants measure, process, and communicate financial information fall under the heading GAAP, which stands for **generally accepted accounting principles**.

OBJECTIVE 2
Apply accounting concepts and principles to business situations

EXHIBIT 1-2

Comparison of the Three Forms of Business Organization

	Proprietorship	Partnership	Corporation
1. Owner(s)	Proprietor—one owner	Partners—two or more owners	Shareholders—generally many owners
2. Life of organization	Limited by owner's choice or death	Limited by owners' choices or death	Indefinite
3. Personal liability of owner(s) for business debts	Proprietor is personally liable	Partners are personally liable	Shareholders are not personally liable
4. Legal status	The proprietorship is the proprietor	The partnership is the partners	The corporation is separate from the shareholders

Accounting principles draw their authority from their acceptance in the business community. They are generally accepted by those people and organizations who need guidelines in accounting for their financial undertakings.

GAAP in Canada rests on Section 1000, "Financial Statement Concepts," of the *CICA Handbook. The primary objective of financial reporting is to provide information useful for making investment and lending decisions and for assessing management's stewardship.* Decision makers who require useful accounting information include investors, creditors, members (in the case of not-for-profit organizations such as cooperatives), contributors (in the case of not-for-profit organizations such as charities), and other users, including management. The objective of financial statements appears at the top of the hierarchy shown in Exhibit 1-3.

To be useful, information must be *understandable, relevant,* and *reliable,* as well as *comparable* and *consistent.* The information must be *understandable* to users if they are to be able to use it. *Relevant* information influences decisions and is useful for making predictions and for evaluating past performance. *Reliable* information is free from error and the bias of a particular viewpoint; it is in agreement with the underlying events and transactions. *Comparable* information is information that is

EXHIBIT 1-3

A Hierarchy of Qualities that Increase the Value of Information for Decision Making

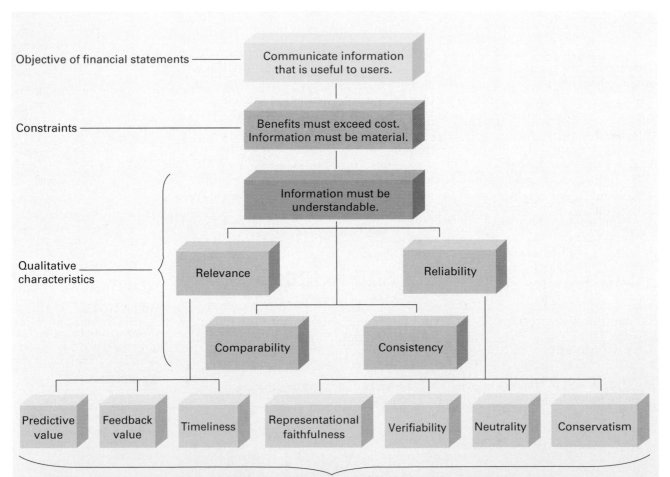

*Section 1000 of the *CICA Handbook* describes these factors as attributes that make accounting information relevant or reliable.
Predictive value: the information can be used to make predictions. *Feedback value:* the information can be used to confirm the accuracy or inaccuracy of earlier predictions. *Timeliness:* the information must be received in time to make decisions. *Representational faithfulness:* the information presented agrees with the underlying transactions. *Verifiability:* the information can be confirmed by reference to other sources. *Neutrality:* the information is free of bias that would influence users' decisions. *Conservatism:* the assets, revenues, and gains are not overstated; the liabilities, expenses, and losses are not understated.

produced by organizations using the same accounting principles and policies, and allows comparison between the organizations. *Consistent* application of these principles over time allows year-to-year comparisons. Exhibit 1-3 summarizes these qualitative characteristics that increase the value of accounting information.

There are two constraints to providing information to users that is understandable, relevant, reliable, comparable, and consistent. The first constraint is that the benefits of the information produced should exceed the costs of producing the information, as stated in Paragraph 1000.16 in the *CICA Handbook*. For example, it may be very costly to produce detailed information beyond that required by GAAP for a forestry company's lumber inventory. If the cost of providing this information exceeds the benefits to decision makers of receiving this information, the detailed information should not be provided.

The second constraint is *materiality*, as stated in Paragraph 1000.17; a piece of information is material if it would affect a decision maker's decision. Materiality is not defined in the standards but is a matter of the information preparer's judgment. For example, information about inventory is important to users of Canadian Tire's financial statements, since a change in inventory could change a decision maker's decision about investing in Canadian Tire or selling products to Canadian Tire. Thus, such information would be provided to decision makers. However, information about the supplies inventory at Coast Capital Savings Credit Union (www.coastcapitalsavings.com) would not likely change the investment decision of a member of the credit union, so details of such information are not provided. Both of these constraints are reflected in Exhibit 1-3.

The characteristics presented in Exhibit 1-3 combine to shape the concepts and principles that make up GAAP. This course will expose you to the generally accepted methods of accounting. We begin the discussion of GAAP in this section and introduce additional concepts and principles as needed throughout the book. Appendix B at the end of Volume I and Volume II summarizes the major elements of generally accepted accounting principles.

The Entity Concept

The most basic concept in accounting is that of the **entity**. An accounting entity is an organization or a section of an organization that stands apart from other organizations and individuals as a separate economic unit. From an accounting perspective, sharp boundaries are drawn around each entity so as not to confuse its affairs with those of other entities.

Suppose you decided to tutor other students, so you started a proprietorship. After the first year, you had $2,000 in your bank account. Suppose only $1,000 of that amount came from your business's operation. The other $1,000 was a gift from your parents. If you follow the entity concept, you will keep separate the money generated by the business—one economic unit—from the money generated by the gift from your family—a second economic unit. This separation makes it possible to view the business's operating result clearly.

Suppose you disregarded the entity concept and treated the full $2,000 amount as income from your business operations. You would be misled into believing that the business produced more cash than it did. Any steps needed to make the business more successful might not be taken.

Consider Petro-Canada (www.petro-canada.ca), a giant company with oil exploration, oil-refining, and retail gasoline sales operations (see Exhibit 1-4). Petro-Canada accounts for each of these divisions separately in order to know which part of the business is earning a profit, which needs to borrow money, and so on. If sales in the retail gasoline division were dropping drastically, Petro-Canada would do well to identify the reason. But if sales figures from all divisions were analyzed as a single amount, then management would not even know that the company was selling less gasoline. Thus the entity concept also applies to the parts of a large organization—in fact, *to any entity that needs to be evaluated separately*. When a company is preparing

> **KEY POINT**
>
> The entity concept requires that the transactions of each entity are accounted for separately from the transactions of all other organizations and persons.

EXHIBIT 1-4

The Entity Petro-Canada

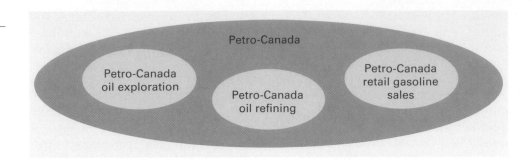

its financial statements for external users, all of these entities are consolidated into a single entity. Thus the divisions of Petro-Canada are combined and reported in the consolidated financial statements of Petro-Canada.

The entity concept also applies to non-profit organizations such as churches, synagogues, and government agencies. A hospital, for example, may have an emergency room, a pediatrics unit, and a surgery unit. The accounting system of the hospital should account for each separately to allow the managers to evaluate the progress of each unit.

In summary, the transactions of different entities making up the whole organization should not be accounted for together. Each entity should be accounted for separately.

The Reliability (Objectivity) Principle

Accounting records and statements are based on the most reliable data available so that they will be as accurate and useful as possible. This guideline is the **reliability principle**, also called the **objectivity principle**. Reliable data are verifiable. They may be confirmed by any independent observer. For example, a purchase of supplies can be supported by paid invoices. A paid invoice is objective evidence of the cost of the supplies. Ideally, accounting records are based on information that flows from activities that are documented using objective evidence. Without the reliability principle, accounting records might be based on whims and opinions and would be subject to dispute.

Suppose you want to open a music store. To have a place for operations, you transfer a small building to the business. You believe the building is worth $200,000. To confirm its value, you hire two real-estate professionals, who appraise the building at $190,000. Is $200,000 or $190,000 the more reliable estimate of the building's value? The real-estate appraisal of $190,000 is, because it is supported by independent, objective observation. The business should record the building cost as $190,000.

The Cost Principle

The **cost principle** states that acquired assets and services should be recorded at their actual cost (also called *historical cost*). Even though the purchaser may believe the price paid is a bargain, the item is recorded at the price actually paid and not at the "expected" cost. Suppose your music store purchased some compact discs from a supplier who was going out of business. Assume you got a good deal on this purchase and paid only $5,000 for merchandise that would have cost you $8,000 elsewhere. The cost principle requires you to record this merchandise at its actual cost of $5,000, not the $8,000 that you believe the compact discs to be worth.

The cost principle also holds that the accounting records should maintain the historical cost of an asset for as long as the business holds the asset. Why? Because cost is a reliable measure. Suppose your store holds the compact discs for three months. During that time, compact disc prices increase, and the compact discs can be sold for $7,000. Should their accounting value—the figure "on the books"—be the actual cost of $5,000 or the current market value of $7,000? According to the cost principle, the accounting value of the compact discs remains at actual cost, $5,000.

The Going-Concern Concept

Another reason for measuring assets at historical cost is the **going-concern concept**. This concept assumes that the entity will remain in operation for the forseeable future. Most assets—that is, the firm's resources, such as supplies, land, buildings, and equipment—are acquired to use rather than to sell. Under the going-concern concept, accountants assume the business will remain in operation long enough to use existing assets for their intended purpose.

To understand the going-concern concept, consider the alternative, which is to go out of business. A store that is holding a Going-Out-of-Business Sale is trying to sell all its assets. In that case, the relevant measure of the assets is their current market value. Going out of business, however, is the exception rather than the rule.

The Stable-Monetary-Unit Concept

We think of the cost of a loaf of bread and a month's apartment rent in terms of their dollar value. In Canada, accountants record transactions in dollars because the dollar is the medium of exchange. French and German transactions are measured in euros. The Japanese record transactions in yen.

Unlike a litre, a kilometre, or a tonne, the value of a dollar or a British pound sterling changes over time. A rise in the general level of prices is called *inflation*. During inflation a dollar will purchase less milk, less toothpaste, and less of other goods. When prices are relatively stable—when there is little inflation—the purchasing power of money is also stable.

Accountants assume that the dollar's purchasing power is relatively stable. The **stable-monetary-unit concept** is the basis for ignoring the effect of inflation in the accounting records. It allows accountants to add and subtract dollar amounts as though each dollar has the same purchasing power as any other dollar at any other time. In certain countries in South America, where inflation rates are often high, accountants make adjustments to report monetary amounts in units of current buying power—a very different concept.

STOP & THINK

Suppose you are considering the purchase of land for future expansion. The seller is asking $100,000 for land that cost her $70,000. An appraisal shows the land has a value of $94,000. You first offer $80,000. The seller counteroffers with $96,000. Finally, you and the seller agree on a price of $92,000. What dollar amount for this land is reported on your financial statements? Which accounting concept or principle guides your answer?

Answer: According to the *cost principle*, goods and services should be recorded at their actual cost. You paid $92,000 for the land. Therefore, $92,000 is the cost to report on your financial statements.

The Accounting Equation

Financial statements tell us how a business is performing and where it stands. They are the final product of the accounting process. But how do we arrive at the items and amounts that make up the financial statements? The most basic tool of the accountant is the **accounting equation**. This equation presents the resources of the business and the claims to those resources.

EXHIBIT 1-5

The Accounting Equation

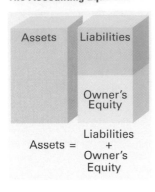

Assets and Liabilities

Assets are economic resources that are expected to be of benefit in the future. Cash, office supplies, merchandise inventory, furniture, land, and buildings are examples of assets.

Claims to those assets come from two sources. **Liabilities** are *outsider* claims, debts that are payable to outsiders. These outside parties are called *creditors*. For example, a creditor who has loaned money to a business has a claim—a legal right—to a part of the assets until the business pays the debt. *Insider* claims to the business assets are called **owner's equity** or **capital**. These are the claims held by the owners of the business. An owner has a claim to some of the entity's assets because he or she has invested in the business. Owner's equity is measured by subtracting liabilities from assets.

The accounting equation in Exhibit 1-5 shows how assets, liabilities, and owner's equity are related. Assets appear on the left side of the equation. The legal and economic claims against the assets—the liabilities and owner's equity—appear on the right side of the equation. As Exhibit 1-5 shows, the two sides must be equal:

Economic
Resources   *Claims to Economic Resources*

ASSETS = LIABILITIES + OWNER'S EQUITY

Let us take a closer look at the elements that make up the accounting equation. Suppose you own Neptune Foods, which supplies seafood to restaurants. Some customers may pay you in cash when you deliver the seafood. Cash is an asset. Other customers may buy on credit and promise to pay you within a certain time after delivery. This promise is also an asset because it is an economic resource that will benefit you in the future when you receive cash from the customer. To Neptune Foods, this promise is called an **account receivable**. A written promise that entitles you to receive cash in the future is called a **note receivable**.

A restaurant's promise to pay Neptune Foods in the future for the seafood it purchases on credit creates a debt for the restaurant. This liability is an **account payable** of the restaurant—the debt is not acknowledged by a formal promissory note. Instead it is supported by the reputation and credit standing of the restaurant. A written promise of future payment is called a **note payable**.

Owner's Equity

Owner's equity is the amount of an entity's assets that remains after the liabilities are subtracted. For this reason, owner's equity is often referred to as *net assets*. We often write the accounting equation to show that the owner's claim to business assets is a residual; something that is left over after subtracting the liabilities.

ASSETS – LIABILITIES = OWNER'S EQUITY

The purpose of business is to increase owner's equity through **revenues**, which are amounts earned by delivering goods or services to customers. Revenues increase owner's equity because they increase the business's assets but not its liabilities. As a result, the owner's share of business assets increases. Exhibit 1-6 shows that owner investments and revenues increase the owner's equity of the business.

Exhibit 1-6 also shows that owner withdrawals and expenses decrease owner's equity. **Owner withdrawals** are those amounts removed from the business by the owner. Withdrawals are the opposite of owner investments. **Expenses** are decreases in owner's equity that occur from using assets or increasing liabilities in the course of delivering goods and services to customers. Expenses are the cost of doing business and are the opposite of revenues. Expenses include the cost of office rent, interest payments, salaries of employees, insurance, advertisements, property taxes, utility payments for water, electricity, gas, and so forth.

◖ KEY POINT ◗

All receivables are assets. All payables are liabilities.

◖ KEY POINT ◗

Increases in cash are not always revenues. Cash also increases when a company borrows money, but borrowing money creates a liability—not a revenue. Revenue results from rendering a service or selling a product, not necessarily from the receipt of cash.

◖ KEY POINT ◗

Decreases in cash are not always expenses. Cash decreases when land is purchased, for example, but the purchase also increases the asset land, which is not an expense. Expenses result from using goods or services in the course of earning revenue, not necessarily from the payment of cash.

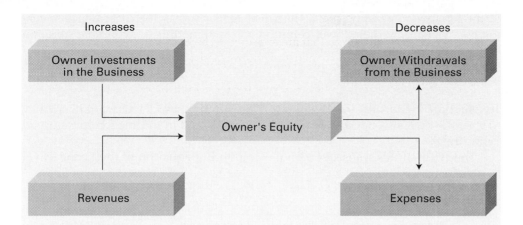

EXHIBIT 1-6

Transactions that Increase or
Decrease Owner's Equity

Accounting and the *e*-World

Using the Internet to Attract Customers

At the beginning of this chapter, you read about Brad Taylor, who spent the summer between his first and second years of college operating a College Pro Painters franchise. Because of the short period of time between being granted the franchise and the beginning of the outdoor painting season, Brad needed to advertise his new business to potential customers quickly. Since he had a limited budget, radio or television advertising was out of the question. As a result, Brad developed a marketing plan with two approaches. First, he had brochures and leaflets printed and distributed in his franchise area. Second, he developed a website for his franchise.

Brad knew that the name College Pro Painters was well known and people using the Internet would likely go to the College Pro Painters website. Brad, in co-operation with the franchisor, linked his franchise's website to College Pro Painters' website.

The results were astounding. Over 20 percent of Brad's franchise's jobs came as a result of the website. For a relatively low cost, Brad was able to increase his sales by attracting customers he would not have been able to meet using more conventional advertising methods.

Accounting for Business Transactions

Accounting records are based on transactions. A **transaction** is any event that affects the financial position of the business entity *and* can be reliably recorded. Many events may affect a company, including elections and economic booms. Accountants do not record the effects of these events because they cannot be measured reliably. An accountant records as transactions only events with dollar amounts that can be measured reliably, such as purchases and sales of merchandise inventory, payment of rent, and collection of cash from customers.

To illustrate accounting for business transactions, let's assume that Don Smith opens a travel agency that he calls EconoTravel. The travel agency offers service in two ways. Some customers phone or email EconoTravel. Other customers do business with the travel agency strictly online. Online customers plan and pay for their trips through the EconoTravel website. The website is linked to airlines, hotels, and cruise lines, so clients can obtain the latest information at any time. The website allows EconoTravel to transact more business and to operate with fewer employees,

OBJECTIVE 4
Use the accounting equation to analyze business transactions

leading to lower operating costs. The travel agency passes the cost savings to customers by charging them lower commissions, making this a favourable situation for the business and the customer. We now consider 11 events and analyze each in terms of its effect on the accounting equation of EconoTravel. Transaction analysis is the essence of accounting.

Transaction 1: Starting the Business   Don Smith invests $100,000 of his money to start the business. Specifically, he deposits $100,000 in a bank account entitled EconoTravel.

The effect of this transaction on the accounting equation of the EconoTravel business entity is

	Assets		Liabilities	+	Owner's Equity	Type of Owner's Equity Transaction
	Cash				Don Smith, Capital	
(1)	+100,000				+100,000	*Owner investment*

For every transaction, the amount on the left side of the equation must equal the amount on the right side. The first transaction increases both the assets (in this case, Cash) and the owner's equity of the business (Don Smith, Capital). The transaction involves no liabilities of the business because it creates no obligation for EconoTravel to pay an outside party. To the right of the transaction we write "Owner investment" to keep track of the reason for the effect on owner's equity.

Transaction 2: Purchase of Land   EconoTravel purchases land for a future office location, paying cash of $80,000. The effect of this transaction on the accounting equation is

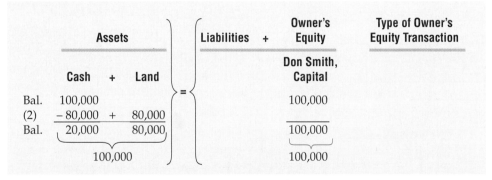

The cash purchase of land increases one asset, Land, and decreases another asset, Cash, by the same amount. After the transaction is completed, EconoTravel has cash of $20,000, land of $80,000, no liabilities, and owner's equity of $100,000.

STOP & THINK

The realtor that arranged EconoTravel's land purchase assures the company that the land is worth $125,000. Could the company ethically record the land at $125,000?

Answer: Regardless of the realtor's belief about the true value of the land, it is recorded at $80,000 because of the *cost principle* and the *reliability principle*. Actual cost is a reliable measure of an asset.

Transaction 3: Purchase of Office Supplies   EconoTravel buys stationery and other office supplies, agreeing to pay $1,000 within 30 days. This transaction increases both the assets and the liabilities of the company. Its effect on the accounting equation is

	Assets						Liabilities	+	Owner's Equity
	Cash	+	Office Supplies	+	Land		Accounts Payable	+	Don Smith, Capital
Bal.	20,000				80,000	=			100,000
(3)			+1,000				+1,000		
Bal.	20,000		1,000		80,000		1,000		100,000
			101,000					101,000	

The asset affected is Office Supplies, and the liability is called an account payable. The term *payable* signifies a liability. Because EconoTravel is obligated to pay $1,000 in the future but signs no formal promissory note, we record the liability as an Account Payable, not as a Note Payable.

Transaction 4: Earning of Service Revenue   EconoTravel earns service revenue by providing travel arrangement services for clients. Assume the business earns $11,000 and collects this amount in cash. The effect on the accounting equation is an increase in the asset Cash and an increase in Don Smith, Capital, as follows:

	Assets					Liabilities	+	Owner's Equity	Type of Owner's Equity Transaction
	Cash	+ Office Supplies	+ Land			Accounts Payable	+	Don Smith, Capital	
Bal.	20,000	1,000	80,000	=		1,000		100,000	
(4)	+11,000							+ 11,000	*Service revenue*
Bal.	31,000	1,000	80,000			1,000		111,000	
		112,000					112,000		

A revenue transaction causes the business to grow, as shown by the increase in total assets and in the sum of total liabilities plus owner's equity. A company like Canadian Tire or Zellers that sells goods to customers is a merchandising business. Its revenue is called *sales revenue*. In contrast, EconoTravel performs services for clients. EconoTravel's revenue is called *service revenue*.

STOP & THINK

EconoTravel has now completed four business transactions. Answer these questions about the business:
1. How much in total assets does EconoTravel have to work with?
2. How much of the total assets does EconoTravel actually own? How much does the business owe to outsiders?

Answers:
1. EconoTravel owns three assets totalling $112,000, which is the sum of cash ($31,000) + office supplies ($1,000) + land ($80,000).
2. EconoTravel or Don Smith owns $111,000, the amount of owner's equity. The business owes $1,000 (Accounts Payable) to outsiders.

Transaction 5: Earning of Service Revenue on Account   EconoTravel performs services for clients who do not pay immediately. In return for the services, EconoTravel issues an invoice and the clients' implicit agreement is to pay the $6,000 amount within one month. This debt is an asset to EconoTravel, an account receivable because the business expects to collect the cash in the future. In accounting, we say that EconoTravel performed this service *on account*. When the business performs a service for a client or a customer, the business earns the revenue. The act of performing the service, not collecting the cash, earns the revenue. This $6,000 of service revenue is as real an increase in the wealth of EconoTravel's business as the $11,000 of revenue that was collected immediately in Transaction 4. EconoTravel records an increase in the asset Accounts Receivable and an increase in Service Revenue, which increases Don Smith, Capital, as follows:

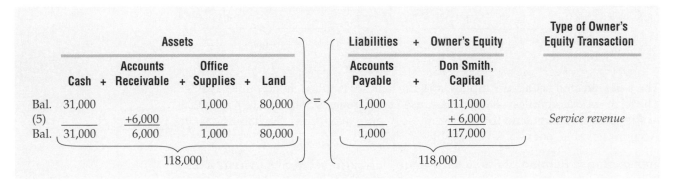

Transaction 6: Payment of Expenses   During the month, EconoTravel pays $5,400 in cash expenses: office rent, $2,200; employee salary $2,400 (for a part-time assistant); and total utilities, $800. The effects on the accounting equation are

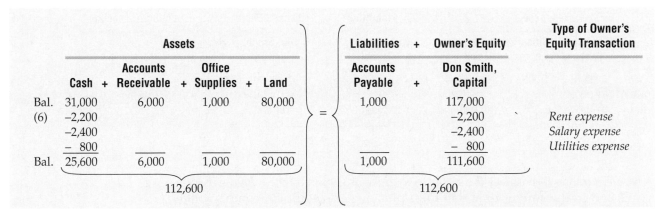

Expenses have the opposite effect of revenues. Expenses cause the business to shrink, as shown by the decreased balances of total assets and owner's equity.

Each expense is recorded in a separate transaction. Here, for simplicity, the expenses are listed together. Alternatively, we could record the cash payment in a single amount for the sum of those three expenses, $5,400 ($2,200 + $2,400 + $800). In either case, the "balance" of the equation holds, as we know it must.

Businesspeople run their businesses with the objective of having more revenues than expenses. An excess of total revenues over total expenses is called **net income**, **net earnings**, or **net profit**. If total expenses exceed total revenues, the result is called a **net loss**.

Transaction 7: Payment on Account   EconoTravel pays $800 to the store from which it purchased $1,000 worth of office supplies in Transaction 3. In accounting, we say that the business pays $800 *on account*. The effect on the accounting equation is a decrease in the asset Cash and a decrease in the liability Accounts Payable as follows:

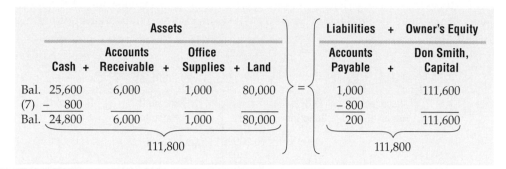

		Assets				Liabilities	+	Owner's Equity
Cash +	Accounts Receivable +	Office Supplies +	Land		=	Accounts Payable	+	Don Smith, Capital
Bal. 25,600	6,000	1,000	80,000			1,000		111,600
(7) – 800						– 800		
Bal. 24,800	6,000	1,000	80,000			200		111,600
		111,800					111,800	

The payment of cash on account has no effect on the asset Office Supplies because the payment does not increase or decrease the supplies available to the business. Likewise, the payment on account does not affect expenses. EconoTravel was paying off a liability, not an expense.

Transaction 8: Personal Transaction   Don Smith remodels his home at a cost of $30,000, paying cash from personal funds. This event is *not* a transaction of EconoTravel. It has no effect on EconoTravel's business affairs and therefore is not recorded by the business. It is a transaction of the Don Smith personal entity, not the EconoTravel business entity. We are focusing now solely on the *business* entity, and this event does not affect it. This transaction illustrates the application of the *entity concept*.

Transaction 9: Collection on Account   In Transaction 5, EconoTravel performed services for clients on account. The business now collects $2,000 from a client. We say that it collects the cash *on account*. It will record an increase in the asset Cash. Should it also record an increase in service revenue? No, because EconoTravel already recorded the revenue when it performed the service in Transaction 5. The phrase "collect cash on account" means to record an increase in Cash and a decrease in the asset Accounts Receivable. The effect on the accounting equation is

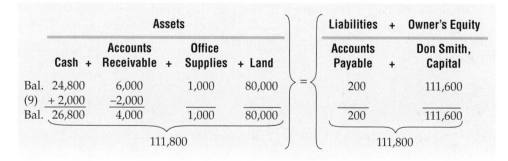

		Assets				Liabilities	+	Owner's Equity
Cash +	Accounts Receivable +	Office Supplies +	Land		=	Accounts Payable	+	Don Smith, Capital
Bal. 24,800	6,000	1,000	80,000			200		111,600
(9) + 2,000	–2,000							
Bal. 26,800	4,000	1,000	80,000			200		111,600
		111,800					111,800	

Total assets are unchanged from the preceding transaction's total. Why? Because EconoTravel merely exchanged one asset for another. Also, the total of liabilities and owner's equity is unchanged.

Transaction 10: Sale of Land   Don Smith sells a parcel of land owned by EconoTravel. The sale price of $44,000 is equal to EconoTravel's cost of the land. EconoTravel sells the land and receives $44,000 cash, and the effect on the accounting equation is

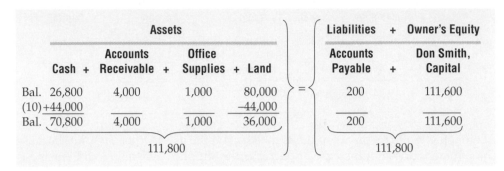

Transaction 11: Withdrawing of Cash   Don Smith withdraws $4,200 cash for his personal use. The effect on the accounting equation is

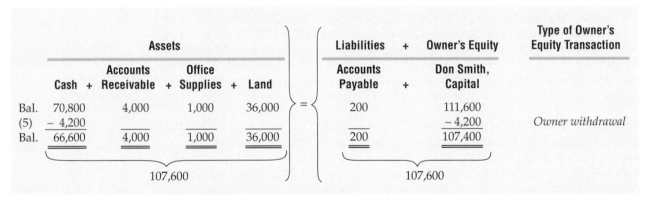

Don Smith's withdrawal of $4,200 cash decreases the asset Cash and also the owner's equity of the business.

The withdrawal does not represent a business expense because the cash is used for the owner's personal affairs unrelated to the business. We record this decrease in owner's equity as Withdrawals or Drawings. The double underlines below each column indicate a final total.

STOP & THINK

Why does Don Smith, or anyone else, go into business? If you could identify only one reason, what would it be? How will accounting serve to meet this need?

Answer: Don Smith went into business to earn a profit—and thereby to make a living. He hopes EconoTravel's accounting revenues exceed its expenses to provide an excess—a net income. Accounting tells Don Smith how much income the business has earned, how much cash and other assets the business has, and how much in liabilities the business owes.

Evaluating Business Transactions

Exhibit 1-7 summarizes the 11 preceding transactions. Panel A of the exhibit lists the details of the transactions, and Panel B presents the analysis. As you study the exhibit, note that every transaction maintains the equality

ASSETS = LIABILITIES + OWNER'S EQUITY

EXHIBIT 1-7

Analysis of Transactions of EconoTravel

Panel A: Details of Transactions

(1) The business recorded the $100,000 cash investment made by Don Smith.
(2) Paid $80,000 cash for land.
(3) Bought $1,000 of office supplies on account.
(4) Received $11,000 cash from clients for service revenue earned.
(5) Performed services for clients on account, $6,000.
(6) Paid cash expenses: rent, $2,200; employee salary, $2,400; utilities, $800.
(7) Paid $800 on the account payable created in Transaction 3.
(8) Remodelled Don Smith's personal residence. This is *not* a transaction of the business.
(9) Collected $2,000 on the account receivable created in Transaction 5.
(10) Sold land for cash equal to its cost of $44,000.
(11) The business paid $4,200 cash to Don Smith as a withdrawal.

Panel B: Analysis of Transactions

	Cash +	Accounts Receivable +	Office Supplies +	Land	=	Accounts Payable +	Don Smith, Capital	Type of Owner's Equity Transaction
(1)	+100,000						+100,000	*Owner investment*
Bal.	100,000						100,000	
(2)	−80,000			+80,000				
Bal.	20,000			80,000			100,000	
(3)			+1,000			+ 1,000		
Bal.	20,000		1,000	80,000		1,000	100,000	
(4)	+ 11,000						+ 11,000	*Service revenue*
Bal.	31,000		1,000	80,000		1,000	111,000	
(5)		+6,000					+ 6,000	*Service revenue*
Bal.	31,000	6,000	1,000	80,000	=	1,000	117,000	
(6)	− 2,200						− 2,200	*Rent expense*
	− 2,400						− 2,400	*Salary expense*
	− 800						− 800	*Utilities expense*
Bal.	25,600	6,000	1,000	80,000		1,000	111,600	
(7)	− 800					− 800		
Bal.	24,800	6,000	1,000	80,000		200	111,600	
(8)	Not a transaction of the business							
(9)	+ 2,000	−2,000						
Bal.	26,800	4,000	1,000	80,000		200	111,600	
(10)	+44,000			−44,000				
Bal.	70,800	4,000	1,000	36,000		200	111,600	
(11)	− 4,200						− 4,200	*Owner withdrawal*
Bal.	66,600	4,000	1,000	36,000		200	107,400	

107,600   107,600

The Financial Statements

Once the analysis of the transactions is complete, what is the next step in the accounting process? How does a business present the results of the analysis? We now look at the *financial statements*, which are the formal reports of an entity's financial information. The primary financial statements are the (1) income statement, (2) statement of owner's equity, (3) balance sheet, and (4) cash flow statement.

Income Statement   The **income statement** presents a summary of the *revenues* and *expenses* of an entity for a specific period of time, such as a month or a year. The income statement, also called the **statement of earnings** or **statement of operations**, is like a video of the entity's operations—it presents a moving financial picture of business operations during the period. The income statement holds perhaps the most important single piece of information about a business—its *net income*, revenues minus expenses. If expenses exceed revenues, a net loss results for the period.

Statement of Owner's Equity   The **statement of owner's equity** presents a summary of the changes that occurred in the entity's *owner's equity* during a specific period of time, such as a month or a year. Increases in owner's equity arise from investments by the owner and from net income earned during the period. Decreases result from a net loss for the period or from owner withdrawals. Net income or net loss comes directly from the income statement. Owner investments and withdrawals are capital transactions between the business and its owner, so they do not affect the income statement.

Balance Sheet The **balance sheet** lists all the assets, liabilities, and owner's equity of an entity as of a specific date, usually the end of a month or a year. The balance sheet is like a snapshot of the entity. For this reason, it is also called the **statement of financial position**.

Cash Flow Statement   The **cash flow statement** reports the amount of cash coming in (*cash receipts*) and the amount of cash going out (*cash payments* or *disbursements*) during a period. Business activities result in a net cash inflow (receipts greater than payments) or a net cash outflow (payments greater than receipts). The cash flow statement shows the net increase or decrease in cash during the period and the cash balance at the end of the period. We focus on the cash flow statement in Chapter 17.

Computers and software programs have had a significant impact on the preparation of the financial statements. Financial statements can be produced instantaneously after the data from the financial records are entered into the computer. Of course, any errors that occur in the financial records will be passed on to the financial statements. For this reason, the person responsible for analyzing the accounting data is critical to the accuracy of the financial statements.

Financial Statement Headings

Each financial statement has a heading, which gives three pieces of data: the name of the business (in our discussion EconoTravel); the name of the particular statement; and the date or time period covered by the statement. A balance sheet taken at the end of year 2004 would be dated December 31, 2004. A balance sheet prepared at the end of March 2005 is dated March 31, 2005.

An income statement or a statement of owner's equity covering a year ending on December 31, 2004 is dated "For the Year Ended December 31, 2004." A monthly income statement or statement of owner's equity for September 2005 has in its heading "For the Month Ended September 30, 2005" or simply "For the Month of September 2005." Income must be identified with a particular time period.

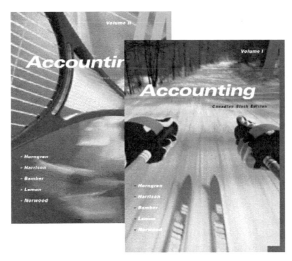

Want to
FIND YOUR WINNING EDGE
in accounting?

This is your Access Code for the *Accounting*, Canadian Sixth Edition, Online Tutor.

Welcome to the *Accounting* Online Tutor, Pearson Education Canada's online resource for accounting students! Here you'll find an online tutor to help you with those tough accounting questions.

What do you do with this access code?

1. **Go to the Online Tutor website:**
   Launch your Web browser and type **www.pearsoned.ca/accountingtutor** into the location area.

2. **Use your Pearson Education Canada access code:**
   The first time you log into the Online Tutor, you will be required to register using the access code provided below. Type in the access code on this page (one word per box) and follow the steps indicated. During registration, you will choose a personal ID and password for logging into the tutor. Your access code can be used only once to establish your subscription, which is non-transferable. Once your registration has been confirmed, you will need to enter only your personal ID and password each time you enter your course.

   This code is valid for 8 months of access to the *Accounting* Online Tutor (from activation date).

   Warning: Once you enter your access code, registration processing may take up to 3 minutes to complete. If you do not wait for confirmation before proceeding, the access code will become invalid.

3. **Log onto the site:**
   Once your registration is confirmed, follow the link to the website to log on with your newly established User ID and password.

CSACO-PLUNK-BOULE-AYERS-HIGHS-HEARD

This pincode is only valid with the purchase of a new book.
For help using this access code, please e-mail us at

online.support@pearsoned.com

Relationships among the Financial Statements

Exhibit 1-8 on page 22 illustrates all four financial statements. Their data come from the transaction analysis in Exhibit 1-7. We are assuming the transactions occurred during the month of April 2005. Study the exhibit carefully, because it shows the relationships among the four financial statements.

Observe the following in Exhibit 1-8:

1. The *income statement* for the month ended April 30, 2005
   a. Reports all *revenues* and all *expenses* during the period. Expenses are often listed alphabetically.
   b. Reports *net income* of the period if total revenues exceed total expenses, as in the case of EconoTravel's operations for April. If total expenses exceed total revenues, a *net loss* is reported instead.

2. The *statement of owner's equity* for the month ended April 30, 2005
   a. Opens with the owner's capital balance at the beginning of the period.
   b. Adds *investment by the owner* and adds *net income* (or subtracts *net loss*, as the case may be). Net income (or net loss) comes directly from the income statement (see arrow ① in Exhibit 1-8).
   c. Subtracts *withdrawals by the owner*. The parentheses around an amount indicate a subtraction.
   d. Ends with the owner's equity balance at the end of the period.

3. The *balance sheet* at April 30, 2005, the end of the period
   a. Reports all *assets*, all *liabilities*, and *owner's equity* of the business at the end of the period.
   b. Reports that total assets equal the sum of total liabilities plus total owner's equity.
   c. Reports the owner's ending capital balance, taken directly from the statement of owner's equity (see arrow ②).

4. The *cash flow statement* for the month ended April 30, 2005
   a. Reports cash flows from three types of business activities (*operating*, *investing*, and *financing* activities) during the month.
      * *Operating activities* bring in revenues and the related cash collections from customers. They also include the payment of expenses.
      * *Investing activities* are the purchase and sale of assets that the business uses for its operations.
      * *Financing activities* are the receipts of cash from people or companies that finance the business and also payments back to those people or companies.
        Each category of cash-flow activities includes both cash receipts, which are positive amounts, and cash payments, which are negative amounts (denoted by parentheses). Each category results in a net cash inflow or a net cash outflow for the period. We discuss these categories in detail in Chapter 17.
   b. Reports a net increase in cash during the month and ends with the cash balance at April 30, 2005. This is the amount of cash to report on the balance sheet (see arrow ③).

EXHIBIT 1-8

Financial Statements of
EconoTravel

ECONOTRAVEL
Income Statement
For the Month Ended April 30, 2005

Revenue:		
Service revenue		$17,000
Expenses:		
Rent expense	$2,200	
Salary expense	2,400	
Utilities expense	800	
Total expenses		5,400
Net income		$11,600

        (1)

ECONOTRAVEL
Statement of Owner's Equity
For the Month Ended April 30, 2005

Don Smith, Capital, April 1, 2005	$ 0
Add: Investment by owner	100,000
Net income for the month	11,600
	111,600
Less: Withdrawals by owner	(4,200)
Don Smith, Capital, April 30, 2005	$107,400

        (2)

ECONOTRAVEL
Balance Sheet
April 30, 2005

Assets		**Liabilities**	
Cash	$66,600	Accounts payable	$ 200
Accounts receivable	4,000	**Owner's Equity**	
Office supplies	1,000	Don Smith, Capital	107,400
Land	36,000		
		Total liabilities and	
Total assets	$107,600	owner's equity	$107,600

ECONOTRAVEL
Cash Flow Statement*
For the Month Ended April 30, 2005

Cash flows from operating activities		
Cash collections from customers**		$13,000
Cash payments to suppliers***	$(3,800)	
Cash payments to employees	(2,400)	(6,200)
Net cash inflow from operating activities		6,800
Cash flows from investing activities		
Acquisition of land	$(80,000)	
Proceeds from sale of land	44,000	
Net cash outflow from investing activities		(36,000)
Cash flows from financing activities		
Investment by owner	$100,000	
Withdrawal by owner	(4,200)	
Net cash inflow from financing activities		95,800
Net increase in cash		$66,600
Cash balance, April 1, 2005		0
Cash balance, April 30, 2005		$66,600

   (3)

*   Chapter 17 explains how to prepare this statement.
** $11,000 + $2,000 = $13,000
*** $2,200 + $800 + $800 = $3,800

Study Exhibit 1-8, which gives the financial statements for EconoTravel at April 30, 2005, the end of the first month of operations. Answer these questions for EconoTravel to evaluate the business's results.

1. What was the business's result of operations for the month of April—a net income (profit) or a net loss, and how much? Which financial statement provides this information?

2. How much revenue did the business earn during April? What was the business's largest expense? How much were total expenses?

3. Is the income statement dated at the last day of the period or for the entire period? Why?

4. How much owner capital did the company have at the beginning of April? At the end of April? Identify all the items that changed owner capital during the month, along with their amounts. Which financial statement provides this information?

5. How much cash does the company have as it moves into the next month—that is, May 2005? Which financial statement provides this information?

6. How much do clients owe EconoTravel at April 30? Is this an asset or a liability for the business? What does the business call this item?

7. How much does the business owe outsiders at April 30? Is this an asset or a liability for the business? What does the business call this item?

8. How is the balance sheet dated? Why is it dated this way? Why does the balance sheet's date differ from the date on the income statement?

Answers:

1. Net income = $11,600. The income statement provides this information.

2. From the income statement: Total revenue = $17,000. Salary was the largest expense, at $2,400. Total expenses = $5,400.

3. The income statement is dated "For the Month Ended April 30, 2005." The income statement is dated for the entire period because the revenues and the expenses occurred *during* the month, not at the end of the month. The income statement reports on the business's operations during the whole span of the period.

4. From the statement of owner's equity:

   Beginning owner capital = $0   Ending owner capital = $107,400

   Increases: Investment by owner = $100,000; Net income for the month = $11,600

   Decrease: Withdrawal by owner = $4,200

5. Cash = $66,600. The balance sheet or cash flow statement provides this information.

6. Clients owe the business $4,000, which is an *asset* called Accounts Receivable.

7. The business owes outsiders $200, which is a *liability* called Accounts Payable.

8. The balance sheet is dated April 30, 2005, which means at midnight on April 30, 2005. The balance sheet is dated at a single moment in time (in this case, April 30, 2005) to show the amount of assets, liabilities, and owner's equity the business had on that date. The balance sheet is like a snapshot, while the income statement provides a moving picture of the business through time.

The Decision Guidelines feature below summarizes the chapter by examining some decisions that businesspeople must make. A Decision Guidelines feature appears in each chapter of this book. The Decision Guidelines serve as useful summaries of the decision-making process and its foundation in accounting information.

DECISION GUIDELINES *Major Business Decisions*

Decision	Guidelines
How to organize the business?	If a single owner, but not incorporated—a *proprietorship*. If two or more owners, but not incorporated—a *partnership*. If the business issues shares of stock to shareholders—a *corporation*.
What to account for?	Account for the business, which is a separate entity apart from its owner (*Entity concept*). Account for transactions and events that affect the business and can be measured objectively. (*Reliability principle*).
How much to record for assets and liabilities?	Actual historical amount (*Cost principle*).
How to analyze a transaction?	The accounting equation: ASSETS = LIABILITIES + OWNER'S EQUITY Note: Owner's equity is called shareholders' equity if the entity is a corporation.
How to measure profits and losses?	Income statement: REVENUES − EXPENSES = NET INCOME (or NET LOSS)
Did owner's equity increase or decrease?	Statement of owner's equity Beginning capital + Owner investments + Net income (or − Net loss) − Owner withdrawals ──────────────── = Ending capital
Where does the business stand financially?	Balance sheet (accounting equation): ASSETS = LIABILITIES + OWNER'S EQUITY
Where did the business's cash come from? Where did the cash go?	Cash flow statement: *Operating activities:* Net cash inflow (or outflow) + *Investing activities:* Net cash inflow (or outflow) + *Financing activities:* Net cash inflow (or outflow) ──────────────── = Net increase (decrease) in cash

Lynn Raffan opens an apartment-locator business in Toronto. She is the sole owner of the proprietorship, which she names Fast Apartment Locators. During the first month of operations, July 2005, the following transactions occurred:

a. Raffan invests $50,000 of personal funds to start the business.

b. The business purchases, on account, office supplies costing $600.

c. Fast Apartment Locators pays cash of $40,000 to acquire a parcel of land. The business intends to use the land as a future building site for its business office.

d. The business locates apartments for clients and receives cash of $3,500.

e. The business pays $200 on the account payable created in Transaction (b).

f. Lynn Raffan pays $3,000 of personal funds for a vacation for her family.

g. The business pays cash expenses for office rent, $1,000, and utilities, $200.

h. The business returns to the supplier office supplies that cost $300. The wrong supplies were shipped.

i. Lynn Raffan withdraws $1,500 cash for personal use.

Required

1. Analyze the preceding transactions in terms of their effects on the accounting equation of Fast Apartment Locators. Use Exhibit 1-7 as a guide but show balances only after the last transaction.

2. Prepare the income statement, statement of owner's equity, and balance sheet of Fast Apartment Locators after recording the transactions. Use Exhibit 1-8 as a guide.

Solution

1. Panel A: Details of Transactions

a. Raffan invested $50,000 cash to start the business.

b. Purchased $600 in office supplies on account.

c. Paid $40,000 to acquire land as a future building site.

d. Earned service revenue and received cash of $3,500.

e. Paid $200 on account.

f. Paid for a personal vacation, which is not a transaction of the business.

g. Paid cash expenses for rent, $1,000, and utilities, $200.

h. Returned office supplies that cost $300.

i. Withdrew $1,500 for personal use.

Cyber Coach

Visit the Study Guide on the Media Companion CD-ROM and the Student Resources area of the *Accounting* Companion Website for extra practice with the new material in Chapter 1.

www.pearsoned.ca/horngren

	Assets				Liabilities	+	Owner's Equity	Type of Owner's Equity Transaction
		Office			Accounts		Lynn Raffan,	
	Cash +	Supplies +	Land		Payable	+	Capital	
(a)	+50,000						+50,000	*Owner investment*
(b)		+ 600			+ 600			
(c)	−40,000		+40,000					
(d)	+ 3,500						+ 3,500	*Service revenue*
(e)	− 200				− 200			
(f)	Not a business transaction							
(g)	− 1,000						− 1,000	*Rent expense*
	− 200						− 200	*Utilities expense*
(h)		− 300			− 300			
(i)	− 1,500						− 1,500	*Owner withdrawal*
Bal.	10,600	300	40,000		100		50,800	

50,900 = 50,900

2. Financial Statements of Fast Apartment Locators

FAST APARTMENT LOCATORS
Income Statement
For the Month Ended July 31, 2005

Revenue:		
Service revenue		$3,500
Expenses:		
Rent expense...	$1,000	
Utilities expense	200	
Total expenses..		1,200
Net Income..		$2,300

FAST APARTMENT LOCATORS
Statement of Owner's Equity
For the Month Ended July 31, 2005

Lynn Raffan, Capital, July 1, 2005	$ 0
Add: Investment by owner...	50,000
Net income for July	2,300
	52,300
Less: Withdrawal by owner..	1,500
Lynn Raffan, Capital, July 31, 2005	$50,800

FAST APARTMENT LOCATORS
Balance Sheet
July 31, 2005

Assets		Liabilities	
Cash..............................	$10,600	Accounts payable	$ 100
Office supplies	300		
Land...	40,000	**Owner's Equity**	
		Lynn Raffan, Capital	50,800
		Total liabilities and	
Total assets	$50,900	owner's equity	$50,900

Summary

1. **Use accounting vocabulary for decision making.** Accounting is an information system for measuring, processing, and communicating financial information. As the "language of business," accounting helps a wide range of decision makers.

2. **Apply accounting concepts and principles to business situations.** *Generally accepted accounting principles (GAAP)* guide accountants in their work. The three basic forms of business organization are the proprietorship, the partnership, and the corporation. Whatever the form, accountants use the *entity concept* to keep the business's records separate from other economic units. Other important guidelines are the *reliability principle*, the *cost principle*, the *going-concern concept*, and the *stable-monetary-unit concept*.

3. **Use the accounting equation to describe an organization's financial position.** In its most common form, the accounting equation is

   Assets = Liabilities + Owner's Equity

4. **Use the accounting equation to analyze business transactions.** A transaction is an event that affects the financial position of an entity *and* can be reliably recorded. Transactions affect a business's assets, liabilities, and owner's equity. Therefore, transactions are often analyzed in terms of their effect on the accounting equation.

5. **Prepare and use the financial statements.** The *financial statements* communicate information for decision making by an entity's managers, owners, creditors, by government agencies, and by other users. The *income statement* summarizes the entity's operations in terms of revenues earned and expenses incurred during a specific period. Total revenues minus total expenses equal net income. The *statement of owner's equity* reports the changes in owner's equity during the period. The *balance sheet* lists the entity's assets, liabilities, and owner's equity at a specific time. The *cash flow statement* reports the cash receipts and the cash payments during the period.

6. **Evaluate the performance of a business.** High net income indicates success in business; net loss indicates a lack of success in business.

Self-Study Questions

Test your understanding of the chapter by marking the correct answer for each of the following questions:

1. The organization that formulates generally accepted accounting principles is (*pp. 4–5*)
   a. Ontario Securities Commission
   b. Public Accountants Council of Canada
   c. Canadian Institute of Chartered Accountants (CICA)
   d. Canada Customs and Revenue Agency (CCRA)

2. Which of the following forms of business organization is an "artificial person" and must obtain legal approval from the federal government or a province to conduct business? (*p. 7*)
   a. Law firm   c. Partnership
   b. Proprietorship   d. Corporation

3. You have purchased some T-shirts for $1,000 and can sell them immediately for $1,500. What accounting concept or principle governs the amount at which to record the goods you purchased? (*p. 10*)
   a. Entity concept
   b. Reliability principle
   c. Cost principle
   d. Going-concern concept

4. The economic resources of a business are called (*p. 12*)
   a. Assets   c. Owner's equity
   b. Liabilities   d. Accounts payable

5. A business has assets of $140,000 and liabilities of $60,000. How much is its owner's equity? (*p. 12*)

   a. $0   c. $140,000
   b. $80,000   d. $200,000

6. If the assets of a business are $174,300 and the liabilities are $82,000, how much is the owner's equity? (*p. 12*)
   a. $256,300   c. $174,300
   b. $92,300   d. $82,000

7. If the owner's equity in a business is $22,000 and the liabilities are $36,000, how much are the assets? (*p. 12*)
   a. $22,000   c. $58,000
   b. $14,000   d. $36,000

8. The purchase of office supplies on account will (*p. 15*)
   a. Increase an asset and increase a liability
   b. Increase an asset and increase owner's equity
   c. Increase one asset and decrease another asset
   d. Increase an asset and decrease a liability

9. The performance of service for a customer or client and immediate receipt of cash will (*p. 15*)
   a. Increase one asset and decrease another asset
   b. Increase an asset and increase owner's equity
   c. Decrease an asset and decrease a liability
   d. Increase an asset and increase a liability

10. The payment of an account payable will (*p. 17*)
    a. Increase one asset and decrease another asset
    b. Decrease an asset and decrease owner's equity
    c. Decrease an asset and decrease a liability
    d. Increase an asset and increase a liability

11. The report of assets, liabilities, and owner's equity is called the (p. 20)
    a. Cash flow statement
    b. Balance sheet
    c. Income statement
    d. Statement of owner's equity

12. The financial statements that are dated for a time period (rather than for a specific point in time) are the (pp. 20–22)

a. Balance sheet and income statement
b. Balance sheet and statement of owner's equity
c. Income statement, statement of owner's equity, and cash flow statement
d. All financial statements are dated for a time period.

Answers to the Self-Study Questions follow the Similar Accounting Terms.

Accounting Vocabulary

Like many other subjects, accounting has a special vocabulary. It is important that you understand the following terms. They are explained in the chapter and also in the glossary at the end of the book.

account payable (p. 12)
account receivable (p. 12)
accounting (p. 2)
accounting equation (p. 11)
asset (p. 12)
balance sheet (p. 20)
capital (p. 12)
cash flow statement (p. 20)
corporation (p. 6)
cost principle (p. 10)
entity (p. 9)
expense (p. 12)
financial accounting (p. 4)
financial statements (p. 2)

generally accepted accounting principles (GAAP) (pp. 7, 47)
going-concern concept (p. 11)
income statement (p. 20)
liability (p. 12)
management accounting (p. 4)
net earnings (p. 16)
net income (p. 16)
net loss (p. 16)
net profit (p. 16)
note payable (p. 12)
note receivable (p. 12)
objectivity principle (p. 10)
owner's equity (p. 12)

owner withdrawals (p. 12)
partnership (p. 6)
proprietorship (p. 6)
reliability principle (p. 10)
revenue (p. 12)
shareholder (p. 6)
stable-monetary-unit concept (p. 11)
statement of earnings (p. 20)
statement of financial position (p. 20)
statement of operations (p. 20)
statement of owner's equity (p. 20)
transaction (p. 13)

Similar Accounting Terms

Accounting equation	Assets = Liabilities + Owner's Equity
Balance Sheet	Statement of Financial Position
Income Statement	Statement of Operations; Statement of Earnings
Net Income	Net Earnings; Net Profit

Answers to Self-Study Questions

1. c	3. c	5. b	7. c	9. b	11. b
2. d	4. a	6. b	8. a	10. c	12. c

Assignment Material

Questions

1. Distinguish between accounting and bookkeeping.
2. Identify five users of accounting information and explain how they use it.
3. Name two important reasons for the development of accounting.
4. Name three professional designations of accountants. Also give their abbreviations.
5. What organization formulates generally accepted accounting principles? Is this organization a government agency?
6. Identify the owner(s) of a proprietorship, a partnership, and a corporation.
7. Why do ethical standards exist in accounting? Which professional organizations direct their standards more toward independent auditors? Which organizations direct their standards more toward management accountants?

8. Why is the entity concept so important to accounting?

9. Give four examples of accounting entities.

10. Briefly describe the reliability principle.

11. What role does the cost principle play in accounting?

12. If assets = liabilities + owner's equity, then how can liabilities be expressed?

13. Explain the difference between an account receivable and an account payable.

14. What role do transactions play in accounting?

15. A company reported monthly revenues of $77,600 and expenses of $81,300. What is the result of operations for the month?

16. Give a more descriptive title for the balance sheet.

17. What feature of the balance sheet gives this financial statement its name?

18. Give another title for the income statement.

19. Which financial statement is like a snapshot of the entity at a specific time? Which financial statement is like a video of the entity's operation during a period of time?

20. What information does the statement of owner's equity report?

21. Give another term for the owner's equity of a proprietorship.

22. What piece of information flows from the income statement to the statement of owner's equity? What information flows from the statement of owner's equity to the balance sheet? What balance sheet item is explained by the cash flow statement?

Exercises

Exercise 1-1   *Explaining assets, liabilities, owner's equity*   *(Obj. 1)*

Shortly after starting Red River Express Company you realize the company needs a bank loan to purchase office equipment. In evaluating the loan request, the banker asks about the assets and liabilities of the business. In particular, she wants to know the amount of the owner's equity. In your own words define *assets*, *liabilities*, and *owner's equity*. What is the *relationship* among assets, liabilities, and owner's equity?

Exercise 1-2   *Explaining the income statement and the balance sheet*   *(Obj. 1)*

Raymond and Lupita Rodriguez want to open a Mexican restaurant in Winnipeg. In need of cash, they ask TD Canada Trust (www.tdcanadatrust.com) for a loan. The bank's procedures require borrowers to submit financial statements to show likely results of operations for the first year and likely financial position at the end of the first year. With little knowledge of accounting, Raymond and Lupita don't know how to proceed. Explain to them the information provided by the income statement (the statement of operations) and the balance sheet (the statement of financial position). Indicate why a lender would require this information.

Exercise 1-3   *Business situations*   *(Obj. 2)*

For each of the following items, give an example of a business transaction that has the described effect on the accounting equation:

a. Increase an asset and increase a liability.

b. Increase one asset and decrease another asset.

c. Decrease an asset and decrease owner's equity.

d. Decrease an asset and decrease a liability.

e. Increase an asset and increase owner's equity.

Exercise 1-4   *Transaction analysis*   *(Obj. 2)*

Cheung Enterprises, a business owned by Sophie Cheung, experienced the following events. State whether each event (1) increased, (2) decreased, or (3) had no effect on the total assets of the business. Identify any specific asset affected.

a. Sophie Cheung increased her cash investment in the business.

b. Paid cash on accounts payable.

c. Purchased office equipment; signed a promissory note in payment.

d. Performed service for a customer on account.

e. Sophie Cheung withdrew cash for personal expenses.

f. Received cash from a customer on account receivable.

g. Sophie Cheung used personal funds to purchase a swimming pool for her home.

h. Sold undesirable land for a price equal to the cost of the land; received cash.

i. Borrowed money from the bank.

j. Cash purchase of desirable land for a future building site.

Exercise 1-5   *Accounting equation*   *(Obj. 3)*

Compute the missing amount in the accounting equation of each of the following three entities:

	Assets	Liabilities	Owner's Equity
Business A	$?	$123,600	$168,800
Business B	91,800	?	68,000
Business C	163,400	119,600	?

Exercise 1-6   *Using the accounting equation*   *(Obj. 3)*

Theresa Hanson owns Common Grounds Coffee House, near the campus of Western College. The company has cash of $4,000 and furniture that cost $24,000. Debts include accounts payable of $2,000 and a $14,000 note payable. What is the owner's equity of the company? Write the accounting equation of Common Grounds Coffee House.

Exercise 1-7   *Accounting equation*   *(Obj. 3)*

Diamond Works, a mineral exploration and development company in Vancouver, had total assets of $440 million and total liabilities of $370 million at January 31, 2004. At the company's year end on January 31, 2005, Diamond Works's total assets were $437 million and total liabilities were $309 million.

Required

1. Did the owner's equity of Diamond Works increase during the period February 1, 2004, to January 31, 2005? By how much?

2. Identify two possible reasons for the change in owner's equity of Diamond Works during the period February 1, 2004, to January 31, 2005.

Exercise 1-8   *Transaction analysis*   *(Obj. 4)*

Indicate the effects of the following business transactions on the accounting equation of a proprietorship. Transaction *a* is answered as a guide.

a. Received $50,000 cash from the owners.

   Answer: Increase asset (Cash)
              Increase owner's equity (Owner, Capital)

b. Paid the current month's office rent of $2,000.

c. Paid $2,700 cash to purchase office supplies.

d. Performed engineering service for a client on account, $5,000.

e. Purchased on account office furniture at a cost of $5,000.

f. Received cash on account, $3,000.

g. Paid cash on account, $1,000.

h. Sold land for $15,000, which was the business's cost of the land.

i. Performed engineering services for a client and received cash of $2,000.

Exercise 1-9 *Transaction analysis, accounting equation* *(Obj. 2, 4)*

Media Companion CD-ROM

Angela Roper D.V.M. opens an animal hospital to specialize in small animals. During her first month of operation, January, the hospital, entitled Angela Roper Veterinarian Services, experienced the following events:

Jan.
6	Roper invested $120,000 in the hospital by opening a bank account in the name of Angela Roper Veterinarian Services.	
9	Angela Roper Veterinarian Services paid cash for land costing $112,500. There are plans to build a clinic on the land.	
12	The business purchased medical supplies for $3,000 on account.	
15	On January 15, Angela Roper Veterinarian Services officially opened for business.	
15–31	During the rest of the month the business earned professional fees of $12,000 and received cash immediately.	
15–31	The business paid cash expenses: employee salaries, $2,100; office rent, $1,500; utilities, $450.	
28	The business sold supplies to another animal hospital at cost for $750.	
31	The business paid $2,250 on account.	

Required

Analyze the effects of these events on the accounting equation of the animal hospital, Angela Roper Veterinarian Services. Use a format similar to that of Exhibit 1-7, Panel B in the chapter with headings for: Cash; Medical Supplies; Land; Accounts Payable; and Angela Roper, Capital.

Exercise 1-10 *Business organization, transactions, and net income*
(Obj. 2, 3, 4)

The analysis of the transactions that Sawada Equipment Rental engaged in during its first month of operations follows. The business buys electronic equipment that it rents out to earn rental revenue. The owner of the business, Steve Sawada, made only one investment to start the business and made no withdrawals from Sawada Equipment Rental.

	Cash	+	Accounts Receivable	+	Rental Equipment	=	Accounts Payable	+	S.Sawada, Capital
a.	+25,000								+25,000
b.	+ 375								+ 375
c.					+60,000		+60,000		
d.			+400						+ 400
e.	− 500								− 500
f.	+ 2,800								+ 2,800
g.	+ 75		− 75						
h.	− 6,000						− 6,000		

Required

1. Describe each transaction of Sawada Equipment Rental.

2. If these transactions fully describe the operations of Sawada Equipment Rental during the month, what was the amount of net income or net loss?

Exercise 1-11 *Business organization, balance sheet* *(Obj. 2, 5)*

Presented below are the balances of the assets and liabilities of Whitehead Consulting Services as of September 30, 2005. Also included are the revenue and expense account balances of the business for September. Darlene Whitehead, the owner, invested $30,000 when the business was formed.

Consulting service revenue	$45,500	Computer equipment	$77,500
Accounts receivable	24,500	Supplies	8,000
Accounts payable	8,750	Note payable	40,000
Salary expense	10,000	Rent expense	3,500
D. Whitehead, Capital	?	Cash	3,750

Required

1. What type of business organization is Whitehead Consulting Services? How can you tell?

2. Prepare the balance sheet of Whitehead Consulting Services as of September 30, 2005.

3. What does the balance sheet report—financial position or operating results? Which financial statement reports the other information?

Exercise 1-12   *Preparing the financial statements*   **(Obj. 5)**

Examine Exhibit 1-7 on page 19. The exhibit summarizes the transactions of EconoTravel for the month of April 2005. Suppose the business completed transactions 1 to 7 and needed a bank loan on April 21, 2005. The vice-president of the bank requires financial statements to support all loan requests.

Required

Prepare the income statement, statement of owner's equity, and balance sheet that EconoTravel would present to the banker on April 21, 2005, after completing the first seven transactions. Exhibit 1-8, page 22, shows the format of these financial statements.

Media Companion CD-ROM

Exercise 1-13   *Income statement for a proprietorship*   **(Obj. 2, 5)**

The assets, liabilities, owner's equity, revenue and expenses of Maclean Company, a proprietorship, have the following balances at December 31, 2005, the end of its first year of business. During the year the proprietor, Nancy Maclean, invested $45,000 in the business.

Note payable	$ 63,000	Office furniture	$ 105,000
Utilities expense	20,400	Rent expense	54,000
Accounts payable	9,900	Cash	10,800
N. Maclean, capital	63,000	Office supplies	14,400
Service revenue	543,600	Salary expense	195,000
Accounts receivable	27,000	Salary payable	6,000
Supplies expense	24,000	Business tax expense	4,200
Equipment	30,000	N. Maclean, withdrawals	?

Required

1. Prepare the income statement of Maclean Company for the year ended December 31, 2005. What is Maclean Company's net income or net loss for 2005?

2. What was the total amount of Nancy Maclean's withdrawals during the year?

Exercise 1-14   *Evaluating the performance of a real company*   **(Obj. 6)**

The 2003 annual report of Bombardier Inc. (www.bombardier.com) reported sales revenue of $23,665 million. Total expenses for the year were $24,280 million. Bombardier ended the year with $29,009 million in total assets and $26,263 million in total liabilities.

During 2002, Bombardier earned net income of $36 million. At the end of 2002, Bombardier reported total assets of $27,243 million and total liabilities of $23,916 million.

Required

1. Compute Bombardier's net income for 2003. Did net income increase or decrease from 2002 to 2003? By how much?

2. Did Bombardier's shareholders' equity (which is the owner's equity of a corporation) increase or decrease during 2003? By how much?

3. Bombardier's management strives for a steady increase in net income and shareholders' equity. How would you rate Bombardier's performance for 2003—excellent, fair, or poor? Give your reason.

Challenge Exercise

Exercise 1-15   *Using the financial statements*   *(Obj. 5)*

Compute the missing amounts for each of the following businesses.

	Oak Co.	Cedar Co.	Maple Co.
Beginning:			
Assets	$220,000	$100,000	$180,000
Liabilities	100,000	40,000	120,000
Ending:			
Assets	$320,000	$140,000	$?
Liabilities	140,000	70,000	160,000
Owner's equity:			
Investments by owner	$?	$ 0	$ 20,000
Withdrawals by owner	220,000	80,000	140,000
Income Statement:			
Revenues	$880,000	$420,000	$800,000
Expenses	640,000	?	600,000

Beyond the Numbers

Beyond the Numbers 1-1   *Analyzing a loan request*   *(Obj. 1, 3)*

As an analyst for CIBC (www.cibc.com), it is your job to write recommendations to the bank's loan committee. Berg Engineering Co., a client of the bank, has submitted these summary data to support the company's request for a $200,000 loan:

Income Statement Data	2006	2005	2004
Total revenues	$445,000	$415,000	$410,000
Total expenses	320,000	285,000	270,000
Net income	$125,000	$130,000	$140,000

Statement of Owner's Equity Data	2006	2005	2004
Beginning capital	$190,000	$200,000	$195,000
Add: Net income	125,000	130,000	140,000
	$315,000	$330,000	$335,000
Less: Withdrawals	(145,000)	(140,000)	(135,000)
Ending capital	$170,000	$190,000	$200,000

Balance Sheet Data	2006	2005	2004
Total assets	$365,000	$360,000	$330,000
Total liabilities	$195,000	$170,000	$130,000
Total owner's equity	170,000	190,000	200,000
Total liabilities and owner's equity	$365,000	$360,000	$330,000

Required

Analyze these financial statement data to decide whether the bank should lend $200,000 to Berg Engineering Co. Consider the trends in net income and owner's equity and the change in total liabilities in making your decision. Write a one-paragraph recommendation to the bank's loan committee.

Beyond the Numbers 1-2   *Transaction analysis, effects on financial statements*   *(Obj. 4)*

Camp Pleasant conducts summer camps for children with disabilities. Because of the nature of its business, Camp Pleasant experiences many unusual transactions. Evaluate each of the following transactions in terms of its effect on Camp Pleasant's income statement and balance sheet.

a. A camper suffered a dental injury that was not covered by insurance. Camp Pleasant paid $500 for the child's dental care. How does this transaction affect the income statement and the balance sheet?

b. One camper's mother is a physician. Camp Pleasant allows this child to attend camp in return for the mother's serving part-time in the camp infirmary for the two-week term. The standard fee for a camp term is $1,000. The physician's salary for this part-time work would be $1,000. How should Camp Pleasant account for this arrangement?

c. Lightning during a storm damaged the camp dining hall. The cost to repair the damage will be $5,400 over and above what the insurance company will pay.

Ethical Issues

Ethical Issue 1

In 1989, an oil tanker, the Exxon *Valdez*, ran aground off the coast of Alaska and spilled its load of oil, causing an environmental catastrophe that resulted in a number of lawsuits, including several class-action lawsuits. The 2002 annual report of Exxon Mobil Corporation, the owner of the Exxon *Valdez*, included a note to the financial statements updating users on the ongoing lawsuits. A portion of the note read: "The ultimate cost to Exxon Mobil from the lawsuits arising from the Exxon *Valdez* grounding is not possible to predict and may not be resolved for a number of years." Generally accepted accounting principles require companies to report in their financial statements the effects of potential losses that the company might suffer as a result of past events.

Required

1. Why is it important that this type of information be disclosed?

2. Suppose you are the chief financial officer (CFO) responsible for the financial statements of Exxon Mobil Corporation. What ethical issue would you face as you consider what to report in Exxon Mobil Corporation's annual report about the *Valdez* oil spill? What is the ethical course of action to take in this situation?

3. What are some of the negative consequences to Exxon Mobil Corporation of not telling the truth? What are some of the negative consequences to Exxon Mobil Corporation of telling the truth?

Ethical Issue 2

The board of directors of Cloutier Inc. is meeting to discuss the past year's results before releasing financial statements to the public. The discussion includes this exchange:

Sue Cloutier, company president: "Well, this has not been a good year! Revenue is down and expenses are up—way up. If we don't do some fancy stepping, we'll report a loss for the third year in a row. I can temporarily transfer some land that I own into the company's name, and that will beef up our balance sheet. Rob, can you shave $500,000 from expenses? Then we can probably get the bank loan that we need."

Rob Samuels, company chief accountant: "Sue, you are asking too much. Generally accepted accounting principles are designed to keep this sort of thing from happening."

Required

1. What is the fundamental ethical issue in this situation?

2. Discuss how Sue Cloutier's proposals violate generally accepted accounting principles. Identify the specific concept or principle involved.

Problems (Group A)

Problem 1-1A   *Entity concept, transaction analysis, accounting equation*   *(Obj. 2, 4)*

Sarah Vallance is an architect and was a partner with a large firm, a partnership, for ten years after graduating from university. Recently she resigned her position to open her own architecture office, which she operates as a proprietorship. The name of the new entity is Vallance Design.

Vallance recorded the following events during the organizing phase of her new business and its first month of operations. Some of the events were personal and did not affect the practice of architecture. Others were business transactions and should be accounted for by the business.

July   1   Sarah Vallance sold 2,000 shares of Royal Bank stock, which she had owned for several years, receiving $110,000 cash from her stockbroker.

      2   Sarah Vallance deposited the $110,000 cash from sale of the Royal Bank stock in her personal bank account.

      3   Sarah Vallance received $300,000 cash from her former partners in the architecture firm from which she resigned.

      5   Sarah Vallance deposited $200,000 into a bank account in the name of Vallance Design.

      5   The business paid office rent for the month of July, $3,800.

      6   A representative of a large real estate company telephoned Sarah Vallance and told her of the company's intention to transfer its design business to her business, Vallance Design.

      7   The business paid $1,100 cash for letterhead stationery.

      9   The business purchased office furniture for the office, on account, for $19,000, promising to pay in three months.

   23   The business finished design work for a client and submitted the bill for design services, $6,000. It expects to collect from this client within one month.

   31   Sarah Vallance withdrew $2,000 for personal expenses.

Required

1. Classify each of the preceding events as one of the following:

   a. A business transaction to be accounted for by the business, Vallance Design.

   b. A business-related event but not a transaction to be accounted for by Vallance Design.

   c. A personal transaction not to be accounted for by Vallance Design.

2. Analyze the effects of the above events on the accounting equation of Vallance Design. Use a format similar to Exhibit 1-7, Panel B.

Problem 1-2A   *Balance sheet*   *(Obj. 2, 5)*

The bookkeeper of Shamanski Insurance Agency prepared the balance sheet of the company while the accountant was ill. The balance sheet contains errors. In particular, the bookkeeper knew that the balance sheet should balance, so she "plugged in" the owner's equity amount needed to achieve this balance. The owner's equity amount, however, is not correct. All other amounts are accurate.

SHAMANSKI INSURANCE AGENCY
Balance Sheet
For the Month Ended October 31, 2006

Assets		Liabilities	
Cash	$ 1,700	Premium revenue	$36,000
Insurance expense	150	Accounts payable	1,500
Land	10,750	Note payable	10,500
Salary expense	1,650		
Office furniture	2,850		
Accounts receivable	6,300	**Owner's Equity**	
Utilities expense	1,050	C. Shamanski, capital	(21,550)
Notes receivable	2,000	Total liabilities and	
Total assets	$26,450	owner's equity	$26,450

Required

1. Prepare the correct balance sheet, and date it correctly. Compute total assets, total liabilities, and owner's equity.

2. Identify the accounts listed above that should *not* be presented on the balance sheet and state why you excluded them from the correct balance sheet you prepared for Requirement 1.

Problem 1-3A   *Balance sheet, entity concept*   *(Obj. 2, 3, 5)*

Laura Cullen is a realtor. She buys and sells properties on her own, and she also earns commission revenue as a real estate agent. She invested $60,000 on March 10, 2004, in the business, Laura Cullen Realty. Consider the following facts as of March 31, 2004:

a. Cullen had $15,000 in her personal bank account and $24,000 in the business bank account.

b. The real estate office had $1,500 of office supplies on hand on March 31, 2004.

c. Laura Cullen Realty had spent $22,500 for a Realty World Canada franchise, which entitled the company to represent itself as a Realty World Canada member firm. This franchise is a business asset.

d. The company owed $55,500 on a note payable for some undeveloped land that had been acquired by the company for a total price of $96,000.

e. Cullen owed $165,000 on a personal mortgage on her personal residence, which she acquired in 2001 for a total price of $360,000.

f. Cullen owed $1,500 on a personal charge account with The Bay.

g. The company acquired business furniture for $21,000 on March 26. Of this amount, Laura Cullen Realty owed $12,000 on account at March 31, 2004.

Required

1. Prepare the balance sheet of the real estate business of Laura Cullen Realty at March 31, 2004.

2. Identify the personal items given in the preceding facts that would not be reported on the balance sheet of the business.

Problem 1-4A   *Business transactions and analysis*   *(Obj. 4)*

Recently, Carole Gallagher formed a management accounting practice as a proprietorship. The balance of each item in the proprietorship accounting equation follows for November 2 and for each of the nine business days given on page 37.

Required

Assuming that a single transaction took place on each day, describe briefly the transaction that was most likely to have occurred beginning with November 9. Indicate which accounts were affected and by what amount. No revenues or expense transactions occurred on these dates.

	Cash	Accounts Receivable	Office Supplies	Land	Accounts Payable	Owner's Equity
Nov. 2	$ 9,000	$21,000	$ 2,400	$33,000	$11,400	$54,000
9	18,000	12,000	2,400	33,000	11,400	54,000
14	12,000	12,000	2,400	33,000	5,400	54,000
17	12,000	12,000	3,300	33,000	6,300	54,000
19	18,000	12,000	3,300	33,000	6,300	60,000
20	14,700	12,000	3,300	33,000	3,000	60,000
22	32,700	12,000	3,300	15,000	3,000	60,000
25	32,700	12,600	2,700	15,000	3,000	60,000
26	32,100	12,600	3,300	15,000	3,000	60,000
30	19,800	12,600	3,300	15,000	3,000	47,700

Problem 1-5A   *Income statement, statement of owner's equity, balance sheet*   **(Obj. 5)**

Media Companion CD-ROM

The amounts of (a) the assets and liabilities of Dempster Office Cleaning as of December 31 of the current year and (b) the revenues and expenses of the company for the year ended on that date appear below. The items are listed in alphabetical order.

Accounts payable	$ 8,500	Land	$ 14,000
Accounts receivable	1,500	Notes payable	18,000
Building	25,500	Property tax expense	1,000
Cash	500	Rent expense	6,000
Equipment	10,500	Salary expense	21,000
Interest expense	2,500	Service revenue	52,000
Interest payable	500	Supplies	11,000
		Utilities expense	1,500

The beginning amount of owner's equity was $30,500. During the year, the owner, Jill Dempster, withdrew $14,500.

Required

1. Prepare the income statement of Dempster Office Cleaning for the year ended December 31 of the current year.

2. Prepare the statement of owner's equity of the business for the year ended December 31.

3. Prepare the balance sheet of the business at December 31.

4. Answer these questions about Dempster Office Cleaning.

   a. Was the result of operations for the year a profit or a loss? How much was it?

   b. Did the business's owner's equity increase or decrease during the year? How would this affect the business's ability to borrow money from a bank in the future?

   c. How much in total economic resources does the company have at December 31 as it moves into the new year? How much does the company owe? What is the dollar amount of the owner's portion of the business at December 31?

Problem 1-6A   *Transaction analysis, accounting equation, financial statements*   **(Obj. 4, 5)**

Terry Thibert operates an interior design studio called Thibert Design Studio. The following amounts summarize the financial position of the business on April 30, 2005:

	Assets				=	Liabilities	+	Owner's Equity
Cash +	Accounts Receivable +	Supplies +	Land	=		Accounts Payable	+	T. Thibert, Capital
Bal. 3,440	4,480		48,200	=		10,800		45,320

During May 2005 the company did the following:

a. Thibert received $28,000 as a gift and deposited the cash in the business bank account.

b. Paid the beginning balance of accounts payable.

c. Performed services for a client and received cash of $2,200.

d. Collected cash from a customer on account, $1,800.

e. Purchased supplies on account, $1,440.

f. Consulted on the interior design of a major office building and billed the client for services rendered, $12,000.

g. Recorded the following business expenses for the month:

 (1) Paid office rent for May 2005—$2,400.

 (2) Paid advertising—$1,320.

h. Sold supplies to another interior designer for $160 cash, which was the cost of the supplies.

i. Withdrew $2,800 cash for personal use.

Required

1. Analyze the effects of the above transactions on the accounting equation of Thibert Design Studio. Adapt the format of Exhibit 1-7, Panel B.

2. Prepare the income statement of Thibert Design Studio for the month ended May 31, 2005. List expenses in decreasing order by amount.

3. Prepare the statement of owner's equity of Thibert Design Studio for the month ended May 31, 2005.

4. Prepare the balance sheet of Thibert Design Studio at May 31, 2005.

Problem 1-7A *Accounting concepts/principles* *(Obj. 2)*

Keith Allen has been operating a plumbing business as a proprietorship (Keith Allen Plumbing) for four years and had the following business assets and liabilities (at their historical costs) on May 31, 2006:

Cash	$30,000
Accounts receivable	15,000
Shop supplies	6,000
Shop equipment	45,000
Accounts payable	15,000

The following transactions took place during the month of June 2006:

June 1 Keith's brother, John, had been in a similar business in the same city and moved to England. He sold Keith his equipment for $27,000. The equipment had cost $51,000 and had a replacement cost of $33,000.

3 The business did some plumbing repairs for Sheldon Kantor, a customer. The business would normally have charged $600 for the work, but had agreed to do it for $450 cash in order to promote more business from the client.

10 The business signed a lease to rent additional shop space for the business at a cost of $2,400 per month. The business will occupy the premises effective July 1, 2006.

18 Finding he was low on cash, Keith Allen went to the bank and borrowed $4,500 on a personal loan.

22 The company did repairs to the plumbing of Mary's Fine Foods for $21,000. Mary's Fine Foods paid $15,000 cash and agreed to pay $6,000 in 90 days.

June 28 Keith Allen withdrew $6,000 from the business and used $4,500 to repay the bank loan of June 18.

Required
Identify the accounting concept or principle that would be applicable to each of the transactions and discuss the effects it would have on the financial statements of Keith Allen Plumbing.

Problem 1-8A *Accounting concepts/principles, transaction analysis, accounting equation, financial statements, evaluation* **(Obj. 2, 4, 5, 6)**

Sheridan Computer Concepts, a proprietorship owned by Melanie Rindt, was started on January 1, 2002, by Melanie Rindt with an investment of $20,000 cash. It has been operating for three years. Rindt has made additional investments of $44,000 but has not made any withdrawals. The company prepares marketing plans for clients and has seen business grow from a small business using rented equipment and having only a few customers to one with the following balances as of December 31, 2004:

Cash	$ 8,000
Accounts receivable	16,000
Software	12,000
Office furniture	48,000
Computer equipment	72,000
Accounts payable	26,000
Owner's equity	130,000

The following transactions took place during the month of January 2005:

Jan. 2 Rindt invested $10,000 in the business.
2 The business paid $2,000 for the month's rent on the office space.
4 The business signed a lease for the rental of additional office space at a cost of $1,600 per month. The lease is effective February 1. The business will pay the first month's rent in February.
6 The business developed a systems design for Fleming Ltd. and received $1,800 now plus additional $1,000 payments to be received on the 15th of the month for the next three months.
10 The business paid $100 to a courier service.
12 Rindt signed an agreement to provide design work to Smith Inc. for $20,000 to be paid upon completion of the work.
14 The company purchased $3,000 of software that will be required for the Smith assignment. The company paid $2,000 and promised to pay the balance by the end of the month.
15 The company received $1,000 as the monthly payment from Fleming Ltd. of January 6.
18 The company purchased computer equipment for $10,000 by paying $3,000 cash with the balance due in 60 days.
23 The company completed a network design for Wong Ltd., which promised to pay $12,000 by the end of the month.
29 The company paid the balance owing for the software purchased on January 14.

Required
1. What is the total net income earned by the business over the period of January 1, 2002, to December 31, 2004?

2. Analyze the effects of the January 2005 transactions on the accounting equation of Sheridan Computer Concepts. Be sure to include the account balances from December 31, 2004.

3. Prepare the income statement for Sheridan Computer Concepts for the month ended January 31, 2005.

4. Prepare the statement of owner's equity for Sheridan Computer Concepts for the month ended January 31, 2005.

5. Prepare the balance sheet for Sheridan Computer Concepts at January 31, 2005.

6. Rindt has expressed concern that although the business seems to be profitable and growing, she constantly seems to be investing additional money into it and has been unable to make any withdrawals for the work she has put into it. Prepare a reply to her concerns.

Problems (Group B)

Problem 1-1B *Entity concept, transaction analysis, accounting equation* *(Obj. 2, 4)*

Bruce Imrie was a civil engineer and partner in a large firm, a partnership, for five years after graduating from university. Recently he resigned his position to open his own consultancy practice, which he operates as a proprietorship. The name of the new company is Imrie Consultants.

Imrie recorded the following events during the organizing phase of his new business and its first month of operations. Some of the events were personal and did not affect his consultancy practice. Others were business transactions and should be accounted for by the business.

July	4	Imrie received $105,000 cash from his former partners in the firm from which he resigned.
	5	Imrie invested $105,000 cash in his business, Imrie Consultants.
	5	The business paid office rent expense for the month of July, $1,800.
	6	The business paid $450 cash for letterhead stationery for the office.
	7	The business purchased office furniture for the office and will pay the account payable, $12,000, within six months.
	10	Imrie sold 750 shares of Dofasco stock, which he and his wife had owned for several years, receiving $27,000 cash from his stockbroker.
	11	Imrie deposited the $27,000 cash from sale of the Dofasco stock in his personal bank account.
	12	A representative of a large construction company telephoned Imrie and told him of the company's intention to transfer its consulting business to Imrie Consultants.
	29	The business finished an assessment for a client and submitted the bill for services, $7,500. The business expected to collect from this client within two weeks.
	31	Imrie withdrew $1,500 cash from the business.

Required

1. Classify each of the preceding events as one of the following:
   a. A business transaction to be accounted for by the business, Imrie Consultants.
   b. A business-related event but not a transaction to be accounted for by Imrie Consultants.
   c. A personal transaction not to be accounted for by Imrie Consultants.
2. Analyze the effects of the above events on the accounting equation of Imrie Consultants. Use a format similar to Exhibit 1-7, Panel B.

Problem 1-2B *Balance sheet for a proprietorship* *(Obj. 2, 5)*

The bookkeeper of Kirkham Services Co., a proprietorship, prepared the balance sheet of the company while the accountant was ill. The balance sheet on page 41 is not correct. The bookkeeper knew that the balance sheet should balance, so he plugged in the owner's equity amount needed to achieve this balance. The owner's equity amount, however, is not correct. All other amounts are accurate.

Required

1. Prepare the correct balance sheet, and date it correctly. Compute total assets, total liabilities, and owner's equity.
2. Identify the accounts listed on page 41 that should *not* be presented on the balance sheet and state why you excluded them from the correct balance sheet you prepared for Requirement 1.

KIRKHAM SERVICES CO.
Balance Sheet
For the Month Ended July 31, 2005

Assets		Liabilities	
Cash..................................	$24,000	Service revenue	$144,000
Office supplies............................	2,000	Note payable..............................	12,000
Land	88,000	Accounts payable.......................	16,000
Advertising expense	5,000		
Office furniture............................	20,000	**Owner's Equity**	
Accounts receivable	26,000	J. Kirkham, capital	9,000
Rent expense...............................	16,000	Total liabilities and	
Total assets	$181,000	owners' equity.......................	$181,000

Problem 1-3B *Balance sheet for a sole proprietorship, entity concept* *(Obj. 2, 3, 5)*

Paul Keeler is a realtor. He buys and sells properties on his own, and he also earns commission revenue as a real estate agent. He organized his business as a sole proprietorship on November 24, 2004. Consider the following facts as of November 30, 2004:

a. Keeler owed $165,000 on a note payable for some undeveloped land. This land had been acquired by the business for a total price of $300,000.

b. Keeler's business had spent $75,000 for a Re/Max Ltd. real estate franchise, which entitled him to represent himself as a Re/Max agent. Re/Max is a national affiliation of independent real estate agents. This franchise is a business asset.

c. Keeler owed $240,000 on a personal mortgage on his personal residence, which he acquired in 2001 for a total price of $510,000.

d. Keeler had $30,000 in his personal bank account and $51,000 in his business bank account.

e. Keeler owed $1,800 on a personal charge account with The Bay.

f. The business acquired business furniture for $51,000 on November 25. Of this amount, the company owed $18,000 on account at November 30.

g. The real estate office had $3,000 of office supplies on hand on November 30.

Required

1. Prepare the balance sheet of the real estate business of Paul Keeler, Realtor, at November 30, 2004.

2. Identify the personal items given in the preceding facts that would not be reported on the balance sheet of the business.

Problem 1-4B *Business transactions and analysis* *(Obj. 4)*

Alberni Suppliers was recently formed. The balance of each item in the business's accounting equation is shown below for June 21 and for each of the nine following business days.

	Cash	Accounts Receivable	Supplies	Land	Accounts Payable	Owner's Equity
June 21	$12,000	$ 6,000	$1,500	$12,000	$6,000	$25,500
22	19,500	6,000	1,500	12,000	6,000	33,000
23	9,000	6,000	1,500	22,500	6,000	33,000
24	9,000	6,000	6,000	22,500	10,500	33,000
25	7,500	6,000	6,000	22,500	9,000	33,000
26	10,500	3,000	6,000	22,500	9,000	33,000
27	21,000	3,000	6,000	22,500	9,000	43,500
28	16,500	3,000	6,000	22,500	4,500	43,500
29	13,500	3,000	9,000	22,500	4,500	43,500
30	3,000	3,000	9,000	22,500	4,500	33,000

Required

Assuming that a single transaction took place on each day, describe briefly the transaction that was most likely to have occurred, beginning with June 22. Indicate which accounts were affected and by what amount. No revenue or expense transactions occurred on these dates.

Problem 1-5B   *Income statement, statement of owner's equity, balance sheet*   *(Obj. 5)*

Presented below are the amounts of (a) the assets and liabilities of Premium Sounds as of December 31 and (b) the revenues and expenses of the company for the year ended on that date. The items are listed in alphabetical order.

Accounts payable	$ 18,000	Insurance expense	$ 1,000
Accounts receivable	11,000	Interest expense	4,500
Advertising expense	6,500	Note payable	62,500
Building	85,000	Rent expense	11,500
Cash	5,000	Salary expense	60,000
Consulting expense	9,000	Salary payable	4,500
Electronic equipment	55,000	Service revenue	127,500
Furniture	10,000	Supplies	1,500

The opening balance of owner's equity was $75,000. At year end, after the calculation of net income, the owner, Shiraz Charania, withdrew $27,500.

Required

1. Prepare the business's income statement for the year ended December 31 of the current year.

2. Prepare the statement of owner's equity of the business for the year ended December 31.

3. Prepare the balance sheet of the business at December 31.

4. Answer these questions about the business:

    a. Was the result of operations for the year a profit or a loss? How much was it?

    b. Did the business's owner's equity increase or decrease during the year? How would this affect the business's ability to borrow money from a bank in the future?

    c. How much in total economic resources does the business have at December 31 as it moves into the new year? How much does the business owe? What is the dollar amount of the owner's portion of the business at December 31?

Problem 1-6B   *Transaction analysis, accounting equation, financial statements*   *(Obj. 4, 5)*

Phyllis Coburn is proprietor of a career counselling and employee search business, Coburn Personnel Services. The following amounts summarize the financial position of the business on August 31, 2005:

	Assets				=	Liabilities	+	Owner's Equity
Cash	+ Accounts Receivable	+ Supplies	+ Furniture and Computers	=	Accounts Payable	+	P. Coburn, Capital
Bal. 5,000	6,000		48,000		16,000		43,000

During September 2005, the following company transactions occurred:

a. Coburn deposited $80,000 cash in the business bank account.

b. Performed services for a client and received cash of $3,600.

c. Paid off the August 31, 2005, balance of accounts payable.

d. Purchased supplies on account, $4,000.

e. Collected cash from a customer on account, $4,000.

f. Consulted on a large downsizing by a major corporation and billed the client for services rendered, $32,000.

g. Recorded the following business expenses for the month:

   (1) Paid office rent for August 2005—$3,600.

   (2) Paid advertising—$400.

h. Sold supplies to another business for $600 cash, which was the cost of the supplies.

i. Phyllis Coburn withdrew $16,000 cash.

Required

1. Analyze the effects of the above transactions on the accounting equation of Coburn Personnel Services. Adapt the format of Exhibit 1-7, Panel B.

2. Prepare the income statement of Coburn Personnel Services for the month ended September 30, 2005. List expenses in decreasing order by amount.

3. Prepare the business's statement of owner's equity for the month ended September 30, 2005.

4. Prepare the balance sheet of Coburn Personnel Services at September 30, 2005.

Problem 1-7B   *Accounting concepts/principles*   *(Obj. 2)*

Michael Chung had been operating his law practice in Mississauga under the name Michael Chung, Lawyer, for two years and had the following business assets and liabilities (at their historical costs) on April 30, 2004:

Cash	$ 9,000
Accounts receivable	4,500
Supplies	600
Furniture and computers	21,000
Accounts payable	3,000

The following business transactions took place during the month of May 2004:

May   1   Chung deposited $30,000 cash into the business bank account.

         3   Chung completed legal work for a home builder. He charged the builder $1,500, not the $2,700 the work was worth, in order to promote business from the builder.

         5   The business bought furniture from Arthur Frame for $6,000, paying $1,500 cash and promising to pay $750 a month at the beginning of each month starting June 1, 2004 for six months.

     10   The company signed a lease to rent additional space at a cost of $1,350 per month. Michael Chung will occupy the premises effective June 1, 2004.

     18   Determining that the business would need more cash in June, Chung went to the bank and borrowed $1,500 on a personal loan and transferred the money to the company.

     22   The company did legal work for CBB Co. for $9,000. CBB Co. agreed to pay $4,500 in 30 days and $4,500 in 90 days.

     25   Chung purchased a painting for his home from one of his clients. He paid for the $450 purchase with his personal credit card.

     28   Chung withdrew $4,500 from the business. He used $1,500 of the money to repay a portion of the loan arranged on May 18.

     31   The business did legal work with a value of $6,000 for Apex Computers Ltd. Apex paid for the work by giving the company computer equipment with a selling price of $12,000.

Required

Identify the accounting concept or principle that would be applicable to each of the transactions and discuss the effects it would have on the financial statements of Michael Chung, Lawyer.

Problem 1-8B *Accounting concepts/principles, transaction analysis, accounting equation, financial statements, evaluation* **(Obj. 2, 4, 5, 6)**

Board City was started on December 31, 2004, by Jason Elliott with an investment of $30,000 cash. It has been operating for one year. Elliott has made additional investments of $20,000 but he has not withdrawn any funds. The company rents out snowboards and related gear from a small store. The balance sheet accounts at November 30, 2005, are as follows:

Cash	$ 2,000
Accounts receivable	18,000
Rental gear	36,000
Rental snowboards	68,000
Store equipment	26,000
Accounts payable	24,000

The following transactions took place during the month of December 2005:

Dec. 1 Elliott borrowed $30,000 from his family and invested $12,000 in the business. The other $18,000 was intended for Elliott's living expenses.

1 The business paid $6,000 for the month's rent on the store space.

4 The business signed a one-year lease for the rental of additional store space at a cost of $4,000 per month. The lease is effective January 1. The business will pay the first month's rent in January.

6 Rental fees for the week were: Gear, $12,000; Boards, $28,000. Half the fees were paid in cash and half on account.

10 The business paid the accounts payable from November 30, 2005.

12 The business purchased gear for $18,000 and boards for $32,000, all on account.

13 Rental fees for the week were: Gear, $6,000; Boards, $12,000. All the fees were paid in cash.

15 The company received payment for the accounts receivable owing at November 30, 2005.

18 The company purchased computer equipment for $8,000 by paying $2,000 cash with the balance due in 60 days.

20 Rental fees for the week were: Gear, $8,000; Boards, $20,000. Half the fees were paid in cash and half on account.

24 The company paid the balance owing for the purchases made on December 12.

27 Rental fees for the week were: Gear, $4,000; Boards, $16,000. All the fees were paid in cash.

27 The company received payment for rental fees on account from December 6.

Required

1. What is the total net income earned by the business over the period of December 31, 2004 to November 30, 2005?

2. Analyze the effects of the December 2005 transactions on the accounting equation of Board City. Include the account balances from November 30, 2005.

3. Prepare the income statement for Board City for the month ended December 31, 2005.

4. Prepare the statement of owner's equity for Board City for the month ended December 31, 2005.

5. Prepare the balance sheet for Board City at December 31, 2005.

6. Elliott has expressed concern that although the business seems to be profitable and growing, he constantly seems to be investing additional money into it and has been unable to make any withdrawals for the work he has put into it. Prepare a reply to his concerns.

Challenge Problems

Problem 1-1C   *Understanding the going-concern concept*   **(Obj. 2)**

The going-concern concept is becoming an increasing source of concern for users of financial statements. There are instances of companies filing for bankruptcy several months after issuing their annual audited financial statements. The question is: why didn't the financial statements predict the problem?

A friend has just arrived on your doorstep; you realize she is very angry. After calming her down, you ask what the problem is. She tells you that she had inherited $25,000 from an uncle and invested the money in the common shares of Always Good Yogurt Corp. She had carefully examined Always Good Yogurt's financial statements for the year ended six months previously and concluded that the company was financially sound. This morning, she had read in the local paper that the company had gone bankrupt and her investment was worthless. She asks you why the financial statements valued the assets at values that are in excess of those the Trustee in Bankruptcy expects to realize from liquidating the assets. Why have the assets suddenly lost so much of the value they had six months ago?

Required

Explain to your friend why assets are valued on a going-concern basis in the financial statements and why they are usually worth less when the company goes out of business. Use inventory and accounts receivable as examples.

Problem 1-2C   *Accounting for business transactions*   *(Obj. 4)*

You and three friends have decided to go into the lawn care business for the summer to earn money to pay for your schooling in the fall. Your first step was to sign up customers to satisfy yourselves that the business had the potential to be profitable. Next, you planned to go to the bank to borrow money to buy the equipment you would need.

After considerable effort, your group obtained contracts from customers for 200 lawns for the summer. One of your partners wants to prepare a balance sheet showing the value of the contracts as an asset. She is sure that you will have no trouble with borrowing the necessary funds from the bank on the basis of the proposed balance sheet.

Required

Explain to your friend why the commitments (signed contracts) from customers cannot be recognized as assets. What suggestions do you have that might assist your group in borrowing the necessary funds?

Extending Your Knowledge

Decision Problems

1. Using financial statements to evaluate a request for a loan (Obj. 1, 3, 6)

Two businesses, Tyler's Bicycle Centre and Ryan's Catering, have sought business loans from you. To decide whether to make the loans, you have requested their balance sheets.

TYLER'S BICYCLE CENTRE
Balance Sheet
December 31, 2004

Assets		Liabilities	
Cash	$ 13,500	Accounts payable	$ 18,000
Accounts receivable	21,000	Notes payable	177,000
Merchandise inventory	127,500	Total liabilities	195,000
Store supplies	750		
Furniture and fixtures	13,500	**Owner's Equity**	
Building	123,000	T. Jones, Capital	125,250
Land	21,000	Total liabilities and	
Total assets	$320,250	owner's equity	$320,250

RYAN'S CATERING
Balance Sheet
December 31, 2004

Assets		Liabilities	
Cash	$ 15,000	Accounts payable	$ 4,500
Accounts receivable	6,000	Note payable	102,000
Office supplies	3,000	Total liabilities	106,500
Inventory	30,000		
Office furniture	7,500	**Owner's Equity**	
Investments*	300,000	R. Smith, Capital	255,000
		Total liabilities and	
Total assets	$361,500	owner's equity	$361,500

*The investments of $300,000 can be sold today for $380,000.

Required

1. Based solely on these balance sheets, which entity would you be more comfortable loaning money to? Explain fully, citing specific items and amounts from the balance sheets.
2. In addition to the balance sheet data, what other financial statement information would you require? Be specific.

2. Using accounting information (Obj. 1, 2, 3, 4, 5)

A friend learns that you are taking an accounting course. Knowing that you do not plan a career in accounting, the friend asks why you are "wasting your time." Explain to the friend:

1. Why you are taking the course.
2. How accounting information is used or will be used:
   a. In your personal life.
   b. In the business life of your friend, who plans to be a farmer.
   c. In the business life of another friend, who plans a career in sales.

Financial Statement Problem

Identifying items from a company's financial statements (Obj. 4)

This and similar problems in later chapters focus on the financial statements of a real, Canadian company—Intrawest Corporation, a developer and operator of such well-known mountain resorts as Whistler/Blackcomb, Panorama, Tremblant, Mont Ste. Marie and Blue Mountain in Canada, and Mammoth, Copper, Stratten, and Showshoe in the United States, as well as resorts in France and a golf course resort in Florida. As you study each financial statement problem, you will gradually build the confidence that you can understand and use actual financial statements.

Refer to the Intrawest Corporation financial statements in Appendix A. Notice that Intrawest reports financial results in U.S. dollars.

Required

1. How much cash and short-term deposits did Intrawest Corporation have at June 30, 2003?
2. What were total assets at June 30, 2003? At June 30, 2002?
3. Write the company's accounting equation at June 30, 2003, by filling in the dollar amounts:

ASSETS = LIABILITIES + SHAREHOLDERS' EQUITY

4. Identify total revenue for the year ended June 30, 2003. Do the same for the year ended June 30, 2002. Did revenue increase or decrease in 2003?
5. How much net income or net loss did Intrawest Corporation experience for the year ended June 30, 2003? Was 2003 a good year or bad year compared to 2002?

Appendix

The History and Development of Accounting

Every technical area seems to have professional associations and regulatory bodies that govern its practice. Accounting is no exception. In Canada, the Canadian Institute of Chartered Accountants (CICA) (www.cica.ca) has had the responsibility for issuing accounting standards that form the basis of **generally accepted accounting principles** or GAAP. GAAP are like the law of accounting—rules for conducting behaviour in a way acceptable to the majority of people. The rules that govern how accountants measure, process, and communicate financial information fall under the heading GAAP.

Responsibility for Setting the Standards

Initially, from 1946, when the first accounting standard was issued by the CICA's Accounting and Auditing Research Committee, until 1972, the CICA assumed for itself the responsibility for issuing accounting standards.[1]

Then in 1972, the Canadian Securities Administrators, a body composed of officials appointed by the provincial governments with securities exchanges to set securities law, issued National Policy Statement 27 (NP 27) designating the *CICA Handbook* as generally accepted accounting principles (GAAP). In 1975, the *Canada Business Corporations Act* did likewise. The *Ontario Securities Act* in 1978 also designated the *CICA Handbook* as GAAP (Exhibit A1-1). In these ways, the CICA became the official promulgator of generally accepted accounting principles. Exhibit A1-1 illustrates how the authority for setting GAAP is delegated to the CICA by the federal and provincial governments and the Securities Administrators.

From the date of the first accounting standard in 1946 until 1968, some 26 "Bulletins" were issued by the Accounting and Auditing Research Committee. In 1968, the CICA changed the format of pronouncements; from that date they became *Recommendations* and were the italicized portions of a looseleaf binder entitled the *CICA Handbook*. Sections 1000 to 4999 of the *Handbook* are concerned with accounting, while Sections 5000 to 9200 are concerned with assurance. The Recommendations are standards or regulations that must be followed, except in those rare cases where a particular Recommendation or Recommendations would not lead to fair presentation. In those cases, the accountant should, using professional judgment, select the appropriate accounting principle. An accountant who determines that the *Handbook* is not appropriate and selects some other basis of accounting must be prepared to defend that decision. The *Handbook* also includes *Accounting Guidelines* and *Assurance Guidelines*. They do not have the force of Recommendations and are issued simply to suggest methods for dealing with issues that are not covered by Recommendations. Frequently, they become replaced eventually by Recommendations on the issues.

In 1972, the Accounting and Auditing Research Committee was split into two committees—the Accounting Research Committee (ARC), renamed in 1982, the Accounting Standards Committee (AcSC) and the Auditing Standards Committee (AuSC). In 1992, the two committees were renamed the Accounting Standards Board and the Auditing Standards Board respectively. The Auditing Standards Board

[1]This material is from George J. Murphy, "A Chronology of the Development of Corporate Financial Reporting in Canada: 1850 to 1983." *The Accounting Historians Journal,* Spring, 1986.

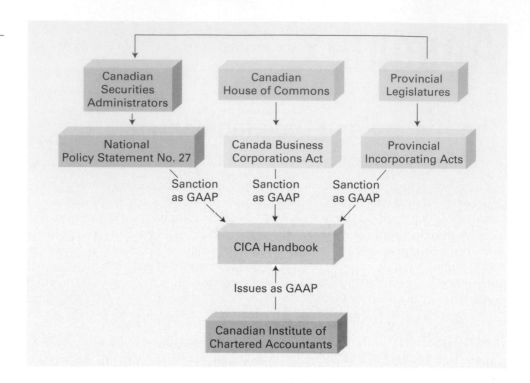

became the Assurance Standards Board in 1998. The former has the responsibility for establishing accounting standards, while the latter has the responsibility for establishing assurance standards.

The CICA established another standards committee in 1981, the Public Sector Accounting and Auditing Standards Committee (PSAAC), and a new handbook to contain the standards issued by that body. The PSAAC, renamed the Public Sector Accounting Standards Board (PSAB) in 1998, issues standards dealing with accounting by public sector entities, such as Transport Canada, provincial liquor commissions, municipalities, hospitals, and school boards. The Recommendations issued by PSAB have the same force as standards issued by the Accounting Standards Board except that they apply only to public sector entities. The CICA formed the Criteria of Control Board in 1992 and the Assurance Services Development Board in 1998.

Each new accounting Recommendation issued by the Accounting Standards Board becomes part of GAAP, the "accounting law of the land." In the same way that our laws draw authority from their acceptance by the people, GAAP depend on the general acceptance by the business community. Throughout this book, we refer to GAAP as the proper way to do accounting.

The Standard-Setting Process

Setting accounting standards is a complex process. The *Accounting Standards Board* determines how accounting is practised. The AcSB is made up of CAs from public accounting, industry, government, and academe, plus individuals nominated by the Canadian Council of Financial Analysts, the Financial Executives Institute of Canada, the Canadian Academic Accounting Association, the Certified General Accountants Association of Canada, and the Society of Management Accountants of Canada. The Accounting Standards Board does research on a particular issue, for example, the proper accounting for a lease. A document called an exposure draft is issued; it is a draft of the proposed new *Handbook* material. The exposure draft is distributed by the Accounting Standards Board to all interested parties, who are asked to make comments by a specified date. The Accounting Standards Board considers the responses to the exposure draft and issues a new Recommendation, which becomes part of the *Handbook*. Occasionally, the proposed *Handbook* section is redrafted and re-exposed as a re-exposure draft to get additional comments before it is incorporated into the *Handbook*.

In 1988, the CICA set up the *Emerging Issues Committee* (EIC) to develop appropriate accounting standards for emerging accounting issues on a timely basis. The abstracts of issues published by the EIC are considered to be an authoritative source of GAAP in the absence of an accounting Recommendation. At the time of this writing, 140 abstracts of issues had been published by the EIC.

Individuals and companies often exert pressure on the Accounting Standards Board in their efforts to shape accounting decisions to their advantage. Occasionally governmental bodies have exerted pressure when they perceived that a proposed standard was not in harmony with government policy. Accountants also try to influence accounting decisions.

We will see that GAAP guide companies in their financial statement preparation. Independent auditing firms of public accountants hold the responsibility for making sure companies do indeed follow GAAP.

Sources of Generally Accepted Accounting Principles

Section 1100 of the *CICA Handbook* is entitled Generally Accepted Accounting Principles. This section establishes the standards for financial reporting in Canada and describes what constitutes generally accepted accounting principles, or GAAP. The primary source of GAAP is the Recommendations in the *CICA Handbook*, sections 1300 to 4460; however, they cannot possibly cover all situations that accountants encounter. Section 1100 lists these five other primary sources of GAAP:

1. Accounting Guidelines. The Accounting Standards Board issues Guidelines, which are that body's interpretations of Recommendations or opinions on issues that are not yet codified as Recommendations.

2. Abstracts of issues discussed by the Emerging Issues Committee.

3. The background documents for the pronouncements in the *Handbook* and the Accounting Guidelines.

4. Examples and illustrations that describe the pronouncements in the *Handbook*, the Accounting Guidelines, and the EIC Abstracts.

5. Implementations Guides authorized by the Accounting Standards Board.

Not all situations encountered in the preparation and presentation of financial information can be dealt with by applying these primary sources. The *Handbook* indicates that in these circumstances, a company should adopt policies and disclosures that are consistent with the primary sources of GAAP and are developed through the exercise of professional judgment and the application of financial statement concepts. Some other sources that may be consulted in order to assist a company in adopting appropriate accounting policies in the event that the primary sources do not provide sufficient guidance include:

1. Pronouncements from other countries

2. Accounting textbooks, journals, studies, and articles

3. Industry practice, provided it is consistent with the primary sources of GAAP listed in Section 1100.

If confronted with an accounting issue that is not dealt with by the *CICA Handbook*, accountants should consider these sources and select the most appropriate treatment, that is, the one that provides the most informative disclosure.

Recording Business Transactions

CHAPTER OBJECTIVES

After studying this chapter, you should be able to

1 Define and use key accounting terms: *account*, *ledger*, *debit*, and *credit*

2 Apply the rules of debit and credit

3 Record transactions in the journal

4 Post from the journal to the ledger

5 Prepare and use a trial balance

6 Set up a chart of accounts for a business

7 Analyze transactions without a journal

 Media Companion CD-ROM

Visit the Media Companion CD-ROM that comes with this book for extra practice with the new material in Chapter 2.

What is your favourite snack food? If you are like most people, it may be Doritos, Earth Chips, or plain potato chips. All of these are Frito-Lay Canada (www.pepsico.com) products. Year in and year out, Frito-Lay Canada leads the prepared snack-food industry. How does this company deliver fresh quantities of chips to thousands of stores every day of the year?

One of Frito-Lay Canada's great advantages is its accounting system. Route managers use hand-held computers to record how many products are sold each day. The data are relayed to company headquarters, and managers can see instantly which products are selling, and where. Suppose Doritos are selling well and potato chips are currentlly out of favour. Frito-Lay Canada managers know they should buy more corn for Doritos and fewer potatoes for chips. The company avoids waste by buying only what it needs to meet consumer demand.

The result? Frito-Lay Canada is very profitable. This chapter shows how Frito-Lay Canada and other companies record their business transactions. The procedures outlined in this chapter are followed by entities ranging from giants like Frito-Lay Canada to a local travel agency such as EconoTravel.

The following diagram summarizes the accounting process covered in this chapter.

Accounting begins and ends with accounts.

CHAPTER 1 introduced transaction analysis and the financial statements. But that chapter did not show how the financial statements are prepared. Chapters 2, 3, and 4 cover the accounting process that results in the financial statements.

Chapter 2 discusses the processing of accounting information as it is actually done in practice. Throughout this chapter and the next two, we continue to illustrate accounting procedure with service businesses, such as EconoTravel, a systems design engineering company, or a sports franchise like the Edmonton Oilers (www.edmontonoilers.com). In Chapter 5 we move into merchandising businesses such as The Bay (www.hbc.com/bay) and Zellers (www.hbc.com/zellers). All these businesses use the basic accounting system that we illustrate in this book.

By learning how accounting information is processed, you will understand where the facts and figures reported in the financial statements come from. This knowledge will increase your confidence as you make decisions. It will also speed your progress in your business career.

The Account

OBJECTIVE 1
Define and use key accounting terms: *account, ledger, debit,* and *credit*

The basic summary device of accounting is the **account**, the detailed record of the changes that have occurred in a particular asset, liability, or item of owner's equity during a period of time. For convenient access to the information, accounts are grouped together in a record called the **ledger**. In the phrase "keeping the books," *books* refers to the ledger. Today the ledger usually takes the form of a computer listing.

Accounts are grouped in three broad categories, according to the accounting equation:

ASSETS = LIABILITIES + OWNER'S EQUITY

Recall that in Chapter 1, page 11, we learned that the accounting equation is the most basic tool of the accountant. It measures the assets of the business and the claims to those assets.

Assets

Assets are economic resources that will benefit the business in the future. Most firms use the following asset accounts.

Cash   The Cash account shows the cash effects of a business's transactions. Cash means money and any medium of exchange that a bank accepts at face value, such as bank account balances, paper currency, coins, certificates of deposit, and cheques. Successful companies such as Frito-Lay Canada usually have plenty of cash. Most business failures result from a shortage of cash.

Accounts Receivable   A business may sell its goods or services in exchange for an oral or implied promise of future cash receipts. Such sales are made on credit ("on account"). The Accounts Receivable account contains these amounts. Most sales in Canada and in other developed countries are made on account.

Notes Receivable   A business may sell its goods or services in exchange for a *promissory note*, which is a written pledge that the customer will pay the business a fixed amount of money by a certain date. The Notes Receivable account is a record of the promissory notes that the business expects to collect in cash. A note receivable offers more security for collection than an account receivable does.

Prepaid Expenses   A business often pays certain expenses in advance. A *prepaid expense* is an asset because it provides future benefits to the business. The business avoids having to pay cash in the future for the specified expense. The ledger holds a separate asset account for each prepaid expense. Prepaid Rent, Prepaid Insurance, and Office Supplies are accounted for as prepaid expenses.

Land   The Land account is a record of the cost of land a business owns and uses in its operations. Land held for sale is accounted for separately—in an investment account.

Building   The cost of a business's buildings—office, warehouse, garage, and the like—appear in the Building account. Intrawest Corporation (www.intrawest.com) owns buildings at Whistler, Tremblant, and its other resorts. Buildings held for sale are separate assets accounted for as investments. Intrawest builds condominiums at its resorts and sells them. These condominiums would, therefore, *not* be included in the Building account; they would be a part of inventory, discussed in Chapter 5.

Equipment, Furniture, and Fixtures   A business has a separate asset account for each type of equipment—Computer Equipment, Office Equipment, and Store Equipment, for example. The Furniture and Fixtures account shows the costs of these assets.

We will discuss other asset categories and accounts as needed. For example, many businesses have an Investments account for their investments in the shares and bonds of other companies.

Liabilities

Recall that a *liability* is a debt. A business generally has fewer liability accounts than asset accounts because a business's liabilities can be summarized under relatively few categories.

Accounts Payable   This account is the opposite of the Accounts Receivable account. The oral or implied promise to pay off debts arising from credit purchases appears in the Accounts Payable account. Such purchases are said to be made on account. All companies, including Frito-Lay Canada, have accounts payable.

Notes Payable   The Notes Payable account is the opposite of the Notes Receivable account. Notes Payable represents the amounts that the business must pay because it signed a promissory note to borrow money to purchase goods or services.

Accrued Liabilities   Liability categories and accounts are added as needed. Utilities Payable, Interest Payable, and Salaries Payable are liability accounts used by most companies.

Owner's Equity

········ **THINKING IT OVER**

Name two things that (1) increase owner's equity;
(2) decrease owner's equity.

A: (1) Investments by owner and net income (revenue greater than expenses)
(2) Withdrawals and net loss (expenses greater than revenue)

The owner's claims to the assets of a business are called *owner's equity*. In a proprietorship, like that of Brad Taylor or Don Smith, described in Chapter 1, or a partnership, owner's equity is often split into separate accounts for the owner's capital balance and for the owner's withdrawals. In a partnership, each partner would have a capital balance and a withdrawal account.

Capital   The Capital account shows the owner's claim to the assets of the business, whether it is Brad Taylor or Don Smith of EconoTravel. After total liabilities are subtracted from total assets, the remainder is the owner's capital. Amounts received from the owner's investment in the business are recorded directly in the Capital account. The Capital balance equals the owner's investments in the business plus net income minus net losses and owner withdrawals over the life of the business. (See the statement of owner's equity in Chapter 1.)

········ **THINKING IT OVER**

Suppose you bought a Honda Civic for $28,000 and had to borrow $18,000 to pay for the car. Write your personal accounting equation for this transaction.

A:
Assets = Liabilities + Owner's Equity
$28,000 = $18,000 + $10,000

Withdrawals   When Don Smith withdraws cash or other assets from EconoTravel for personal use, the business's assets and owner's equity decrease. The amounts taken out of the business appear in a separate account entitled Don Smith, Withdrawals, or Don Smith, Drawings. If withdrawals were recorded directly in the Capital account, the amount of owner withdrawals would not be highlighted and decision making would be more difficult. The Withdrawals account shows a *decrease* in owner's equity.

Revenues   The increase in owner's equity created by delivering goods or services to customers or clients is called *revenue*. The ledger contains as many revenue accounts as needed. EconoTravel would have a Service Revenue account for amounts earned by providing services for clients. If a business lends money to an outsider, it will need an Interest Revenue account for the interest earned on the loan. If the business rents a building to a tenant, it will need a Rent Revenue account.

Expenses   Expenses use up assets or create liabilities in the course of operating a business. Expenses have the opposite effect of revenues; they decrease owner's equity. A business needs a separate account for each type of expense, such as Salary Expense, Rent Expense, Advertising Expense, and Utilities Expense. Businesses strive to minimize their expenses in order to maximize net income whether they are Brad Taylor, EconoTravel, or Frito-Lay Canada.

Exhibit 2-1 shows how asset, liability, and owner's equity accounts can be grouped into the ledger.

Double-Entry Accounting

Accounting is based on a *double-entry system*, which means that we record the *dual effects* of a business transaction. *Each transaction affects at least two accounts*. For example, in Chapter 1, Don Smith's $100,000 cash investment in his travel agency increased both the Cash account and the Capital account of the business. It would be incomplete to record only the increase in the entity's cash without recording the increase in its owner's equity.

Consider a cash purchase of supplies. What are the dual effects of this transaction? The purchase (1) decreases cash and (2) increases supplies. A purchase of supplies

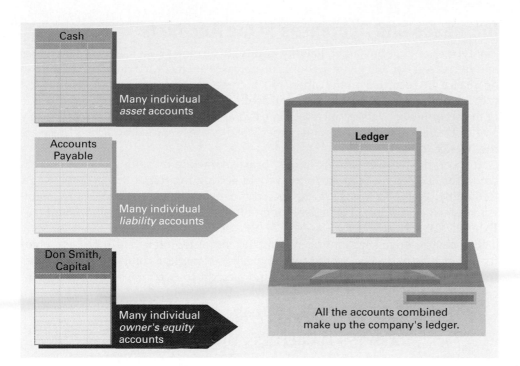

EXHIBIT 2-1

The Ledger (Asset, Liability, and Owner's Equity Accounts)

on credit (1) increases supplies and (2) increases accounts payable. A cash payment on account (1) decreases cash and (2) decreases accounts payable. All transactions have at least two effects on the accounts of the entity.

The T-Account

How do we record transactions? The account format used for most illustrations in this book is called the *T-account* because it takes the form of the capital letter "T." The vertical line in the letter divides the account into its left and right sides, with the account title at the top. For example, the Cash account of a business appears in the following T-account format:

Cash

(Left side)	**(Right side)**
Debit	*Credit*

The left side of the account is called the **debit** side, and the right side is called the **credit** side. The words *debit* and *credit* can be confusing because they are new. To become comfortable using them, simply remember this:

$$\text{debit} = \text{left side}$$
$$\text{credit} = \text{right side}$$

Even though *left side* and *right side* may be more convenient, *debit* and *credit* are deeply entrenched in business.[1] Debit and credit are abbreviated as follows:

- Dr = Debit
- Cr = Credit

> **KEY POINT**
>
> A T-account is a quick way to show the effect of transactions on a particular account—a useful shortcut in accounting.

> **KEY POINT**
>
> The accounting equation must balance after every transaction. But verifying that total assets = total liabilities + owner's equity is no longer necessary after every transaction. The equation will balance as long as the debits in each transaction equal the credits in the transaction.

---

[1] The words *debit* and *credit* abbreviate the Latin terms *debitum* and *creditum*. Luca Pacioli, the Italian monk who wrote about accounting in the fifteenth century, used these terms.

Increases and Decreases in the Accounts

The type of an account (asset, liability, equity) determines how we record increases and decreases. For any given account, all increases are recorded on one side, and all decreases are recorded on the other side. Increases in *assets* are recorded in the left (debit) side of the account. Decreases in assets are recorded in the right (credit) side of the account. Conversely, increases in *liabilities* and *owner's equity* are recorded by *credits*. Decreases in liabilities and owner's equity are recorded by *debits*. These are the *rules of debit and credit*.

In everyday conversation, we may praise someone by saying, "She deserves credit for her good work." In your study of accounting forget this general usage. Remember that *debit means left side* and *credit means right side*. Whether an account is increased or decreased by a debit or credit depends on the type of account (see Exhibit 2-2).

In a computerized accounting system, the computer interprets debits and credits as increases or decreases by account type. For example, a computer reads a debit to Cash as an increase to that account and a credit to Accounts Payable as an increase to that account.

This pattern of recording debits and credits is based on the accounting equation:

ASSETS = LIABILITIES + OWNER'S EQUITY

Assets are on the opposite side from liabilities and owner's equity. Therefore, increases and decreases in assets are recorded in the opposite manner from increases and decreases in liabilities and owner's equity. Liabilities and owner's equity are on the same side of the equal sign, so they are treated in the same way. Exhibit 2-2 shows the relationship between the accounting equation and the rules of debit and credit.

To illustrate the ideas diagrammed in Exhibit 2-2, reconsider the first transaction from Chapter 1. Don Smith invested $100,000 in cash to begin the travel agency. The company received $100,000 cash from Don Smith and gave him the owner's equity. We are accounting for the business entity, EconoTravel. What accounts of EconoTravel are affected? By what amounts? On what side (debit or credit)? The answer is that Assets and Capital would increase by $100,000, as the following T-accounts show:

ASSETS	**=**	**LIABILITIES**	**+**	**OWNER'S EQUITY**
Cash				**Don Smith, Capital**
Debit for Increase, 100,000				Credit for Increase, 100,000

Notice that Assets = Liabilities + Owner's Equity *and* that total debit amounts = total credit amounts. Exhibit 2-3 on page 58 illustrates the accounting equation and EconoTravel's first three transactions.

EXHIBIT 2-2

The Accounting Equation and the Rules of Debit and Credit (The Effects of Debits and Credits on Assets, Liabilities, and Owner's Equity)

The amount remaining in an account is called its *balance*. This initial transaction gives Cash a $100,000 debit balance, and Don Smith, Capital a $100,000 credit balance.

Transaction 2 is an $80,000 cash purchase of land. This transaction affects two assets: Cash and Land. It decreases (credits) Cash and increases (debits) Land, as shown in the T-accounts:

ASSETS		=	LIABILITIES	+	OWNER'S EQUITY

Cash					Don Smith, Capital
Balance 100,000	Credit for Decrease, 80,000				Balance 100,000
Balance 20,000					

Land	
Debit for Increase, 80,000	
Balance 80,000	

After this transaction, Cash has a $20,000 debit balance ($100,000 debit balance reduced by the $80,000 credit amount), Land has a debit balance of $80,000, and Don Smith, Capital has a $100,000 credit balance as shown in the middle section of Exhibit 2-3 (labelled Transaction 2).

Transaction 3 is a $1,000 purchase of office supplies on account. This transaction increases the asset Office Supplies and the liability Accounts Payable, as shown in the following accounts and in the right side of Exhibit 2-3 (labelled Transaction 3):

ASSETS		=	LIABILITIES	+	OWNER'S EQUITY
Cash			Accounts Payable		Don Smith, Capital
Balance 20,000			Credit for Increase, 1,000		Balance 100,000
			Balance 1,000		

Office Supplies	
Debit for Increase, 1,000	
Balance 1,000	

Land	
Balance 80,000	

We create accounts as they are needed. The process of creating a new T-account in preparation for recording a transaction is called *opening the account*. For Transaction 1, we opened the Cash account and the Don Smith, Capital account. For Transaction 2, we opened the Land account, and for Transaction 3, Office Supplies and Accounts Payable.

We could record all transactions directly in the accounts as we have shown for the first three transactions. However, that way of accounting does not leave a clear record of each transaction. You may have to search through all the accounts to find both sides of a particular transaction. To save time, accountants keep a record of each transaction in a *journal* and then transfer this information from the journal into the accounts.

EXHIBIT 2-3

The Accounting Equation and the First Three Transactions of EconoTravel

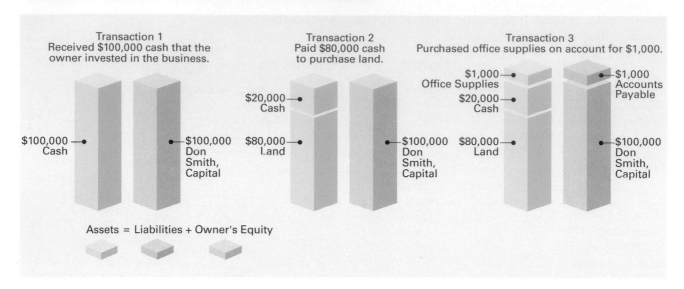

Transaction 1
Received $100,000 cash that the
owner invested in the business.

$100,000
Cash

$100,000
Don
Smith,
Capital

Transaction 2
Paid $80,000 cash
to purchase land.

$20,000
Cash
$80,000
Land

$100,000
Don
Smith,
Capital

Transaction 3
Purchased office supplies on account for $1,000.

$1,000
Office Supplies
$20,000
Cash
$80,000
Land

$1,000
Accounts
Payable

$100,000
Don
Smith,
Capital

Assets = Liabilities + Owner's Equity

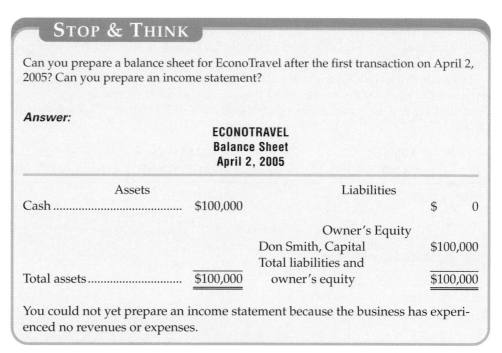

STOP & THINK

Can you prepare a balance sheet for EconoTravel after the first transaction on April 2, 2005? Can you prepare an income statement?

Answer:

ECONOTRAVEL
Balance Sheet
April 2, 2005

Assets		Liabilities	
Cash	$100,000		$ 0
		Owner's Equity	
		Don Smith, Capital	$100,000
		Total liabilities and	
Total assets	$100,000	owner's equity	$100,000

You could not yet prepare an income statement because the business has experienced no revenues or expenses.

OBJECTIVE 3
Record transactions in the journal

Recording Transactions in Journals

In practice, accountants record transactions first in a **journal**, which is a chronological record of the entity's transactions. The journalizing process follows four steps:

1. Identify the transactions from source documents, such as bank deposit slips, sales invoices, or cheque stubs.
2. Specify each account affected by the transaction and classify it by type (asset, liability, or owner's equity).
3. Determine whether each account is increased or decreased by the transaction.

Using the rules of debit and credit, determine whether to debit or credit the account to record its increase or decrease.

4. Enter the transaction in the journal, including a brief explanation for the journal entry. The debit side of the entry is entered first and the credit side last. Total debits should always equal total credits.

Step 4, "Enter the transaction in the journal," means to record the transaction in the journal. This step is also called "making the journal entry" or "journalizing the transaction."

These four steps are completed in a computerized accounting system as well as in a manual system. In step 4, however, the journal entry is generally entered into the computer by account number, and the account name then appears automatically. Most computer programs replace the explanation in the journal entry with some other means of tracing the entry back to its source documents.

Let's apply the four steps to journalize the first transaction of EconoTravel—the business's receipt of Don Smith's $100,000 cash investment in the business.

Step 1. The source documents are EconoTravel's bank deposit slip and the $100,000 cheque, which is deposited in the business bank account.

Step 2. The accounts affected by the transaction are *Cash* and *Don Smith, Capital*. Cash is an asset account, and Don Smith, Capital is an owner's equity account.

Step 3. Both accounts increase by $100,000. Therefore, Cash, the asset account, is increased (debited), and Don Smith, Capital, the owner's equity account, is increased (credited).

Step 4. The journal entry is

Date	Accounts and Explanation	Debit	Credit
Apr. 2[a]	Cash[b]	100,000[d]	
	Don Smith, Capital[c]		100,000[e]
	Received initial investment from owner.[f]		

The journal entry includes (a) the date of the transaction, (b) the title of the account debited (placed flush left), (c) the title of the account credited (indented slightly), the dollar amounts of (d), the debit (left), and (e), the credit (right)—dollar signs are omitted in the money columns—and (f) a short explanation of the transaction.

The journal offers information that the ledger accounts do not provide. Each journal entry shows the complete effect of a business transaction. Consider Don Smith's initial investment. The Cash account shows a single figure, the $100,000 debit. We know that every transaction has a credit, so in what account will we find the corresponding $100,000 credit? In this illustration, we know that the Capital account holds this figure. But imagine the difficulties you would face trying to link debits and credits for hundreds of daily transactions—without a separate record of each transaction. The journal solves this problem and presents the full story for each transaction. Exhibit 2-4 shows how Journal page 1 looks after the first transaction is recorded.

	Journal			Page 1
Date	Accounts and Explanation	Ref.	Debit	Credit
2005 Apr. 2	Cash		100,000	
	Don Smith, Capital			100,000
	Received initial investment from owner.			

EXHIBIT 2-4

The Journal

Regardless of the accounting system in use, an accountant must analyze every business transaction in the manner we are presenting in these opening chapters. Once the transaction has been analyzed, a computerized accounting package performs the same actions as accountants do in a manual system. For example, when a sales clerk runs your VISA card through the credit card reader, the underlying accounting system records the store's sales revenue and receivable from VISA (www.visa.com). The computer automatically records the transaction as a journal entry, but an accountant had to program the computer to do so. A computer's ability to perform routine tasks and mathematical operations quickly and without error frees accountants for decision making.

OBJECTIVE 4
Post from the journal to the ledger

Transferring Information (Posting) from the Journal to the Ledger

Posting in accounting means transferring the amounts from the journal to the accounts in the ledger. Debits in the journal are posted as debits in the ledger, and credits in the journal as credits in the ledger. Debits never become credits, and credits never become debits. The initial investment transaction of EconoTravel is posted to the ledger as shown in Exhibit 2-5. Computers perform this tedious task quickly and without error. In these introductory discussions we temporarily ignore the date of each transaction in order to focus on the accounts and their dollar amounts.

The Flow of Accounting Data

Exhibit 2-6 summarizes the flow of accounting data from the business transaction all the way through the accounting system to the ledger. In the pages that follow, we continue the example of EconoTravel and account for six of the business's early transactions. Keep in mind that we are accounting for the business entity, EconoTravel. We are *not* accounting for Don Smith's *personal* transactions.

Transaction Analysis, Journalizing, and Posting to the Accounts

1. ***Transaction:*** **Don Smith invested $100,000 cash to begin his travel business, EconoTravel.**

   Analysis: Don Smith's investment in EconoTravel increased its asset cash; to record this increase, debit Cash. The investment also increased its owner's equity; to record this increase, credit Don Smith, Capital.

   Journal Entry:
   Cash 100,000
        Don Smith, Capital..............   100,000
   Received initial investment from owner.

   Accounting Equation:

ASSETS	=	LIABILITIES	+	OWNER'S EQUITY
Cash				Don Smith, Capital
+100,000	=	0	+	100,000

   The journal entry records the same information that you learned by using the accounting equation in Chapter 1. Both accounts—Cash and Don Smith, Capital—increased because the business received $100,000 cash and gave Don Smith $100,000 of capital (owner's equity) in the business.

Panel A — Journal Entry

Date	Accounts and Explanation	Debit	Credit
April 2	Cash...	100,000	
	Don Smith, Capital.......................................		100,000
	Received initial investment from owner.		

Panel B — Posting to Ledger

Cash

100,000

Don Smith, Capital

100,000

EXHIBIT 2-5

Journal Entry and Posting to the Ledger

Ledger Accounts:

Cash		Don Smith, Capital	
(1) 100,000			(1) 100,000

2. *Transaction:* **EconoTravel paid $80,000 cash for land as a future office location.**

Analysis: The purchase decreased cash; therefore, credit Cash. The purchase increased the entity's asset land; to record this increase, debit Land.

EXHIBIT 2-6

Flow of Accounting Data

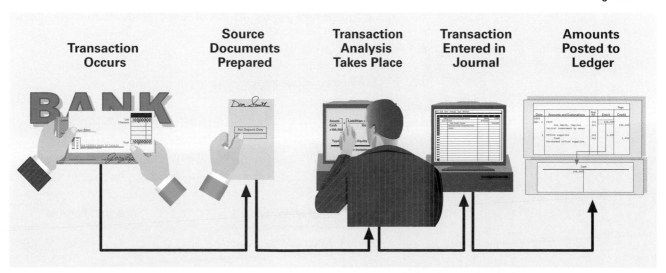

| Transaction Occurs | Source Documents Prepared | Transaction Analysis Takes Place | Transaction Entered in Journal | Amounts Posted to Ledger |

Journal Entry:

```
Land ................................................. 80,000
     Cash ....................................               80,000
Paid cash for land.
```

Accounting Equation:

	ASSETS		=	LIABILITIES	+	OWNER'S EQUITY
	Cash	Land				
	−80,000	+80,000	=	0	+	0

This transaction increased one asset, land, and decreased another asset, cash. The net effect on the business's total assets was zero, and there was no effect on liabilities or owner's equity. We use the term *net* in business to mean an amount after a subtraction.

Ledger Accounts:

Cash		**Land**	
(1) 100,000	(2) 80,000	(2) 80,000	

---

3. Transaction: The business purchased office supplies for $1,000 on account.

Analysis: The credit purchase of office supplies increased this asset, so we debit Office Supplies. The purchase also increased the liability accounts payable; to record this increase, credit Accounts Payable.

Journal Entry:

```
Office Supplies ............................  1,000
     Accounts Payable ...............                1,000
Purchased office supplies on account.
```

Accounting Equation:

	ASSETS	=	LIABILITIES	+	OWNER'S EQUITY
	Office Supplies		Accounts Payable		
	+1,000	=	+1,000	+	0

Ledger Accounts:

Office Supplies		**Accounts Payable**	
(3) 1,000			(3) 1,000

<table>
<tr><td>4.</td><td>*Transaction:*</td><td>**The business paid $800 on the account payable created in Transaction 3.**</td></tr>
</table>

Analysis: The payment decreased the asset cash; therefore, credit Cash. The payment also decreased the liability accounts payable, so we debit Accounts Payable.

Journal Entry:

Accounts Payable 800
    Cash 800
Paid cash on account.

Accounting Equation:

	ASSETS	=	LIABILITIES	+	OWNER'S EQUITY
	Cash		Accounts Payable		
	−800	=	−800	+	0

Ledger Accounts:

Cash				Accounts Payable			
(1)	100,000	(2)	80,000	(4)	800	(3)	1,000
		(4)	800				

<table>
<tr><td>5.</td><td>*Transaction:*</td><td>**Don Smith remodelled his personal residence with personal funds and a loan from his bank. This is not a business transaction of the travel business, so no journal entry is made.**</td></tr>
</table>

<table>
<tr><td>6.</td><td>*Transaction:*</td><td>**Don Smith withdrew $4,200 cash for personal living expenses.**</td></tr>
</table>

Analysis: The withdrawal decreased the entity's cash; therefore, credit Cash. The transaction also decreased the owner's equity of the entity. Decreases in the owner's equity of a proprietorship that result from owner withdrawals are debited to a separate owner's equity account entitled Withdrawals. Therefore, debit Don Smith, Withdrawals.

Journal Entry:

Don Smith, Withdrawals.............. 4,200
    Cash 4,200
Withdrawal of cash by owner.

Accounting Equation:

	ASSETS	=	LIABILITIES	+	OWNER'S EQUITY
	Cash				Don Smith, Withdrawals
	−4,200	=	0		−4,200

Ledger Accounts:

Cash				Don Smith, Withdrawals		
(1)	100,000	(2)	80,000	(6)	4,200	
		(4)	800			
		(6)	4,200			

Each journal entry posted to the ledger is keyed by date or by transaction number. In this way any transaction can be traced from the journal to the ledger, and, if need be, back to the journal. This linking allows you to locate efficiently any information needed.

Accounts after Posting

We next illustrate how the accounts look when the amounts of the preceding transactions have been posted. The accounts are grouped under the accounting equation's headings.

Each account has a balance, denoted as *Bal.* This amount is the difference between the account's total debits and its total credits. For example, the balance in the Cash account is the difference between the debits, $100,000 and the credits, $85,000 (i.e., $80,000 + $800 + $4,200). Thus the cash balance is $15,000. The balances are residual amounts left over after the journal entries have been posted to the accounts. We set an account balance apart by a horizontal line. The final figure in an account below the horizontal line is the balance of the account after the transactions have been posted.

If the sum of an account's debits is greater than the sum of its credits, that account has a debit balance, as the Cash account does here. If the sum of its credits is greater, that account has a credit balance, as Accounts Payable does.

ASSETS		=	LIABILITIES		+	OWNER'S EQUITY	
Cash			**Accounts Payable**			**Don Smith, Capital**	
(1) 100,000	(2) 80,000		(4) 800	(3) 1,000			(1) 100,000
	(4) 800			Bal. 200			Bal. 100,000
	(6) 4,200						
Bal. 15,000							
Office Supplies						**Don Smith, Withdrawals**	
(3) 1,000						(6) 4,200	
Bal. 1,000						Bal. 4,200	
Land							
(2) 80,000							
Bal. 80,000							

The Trial Balance

A **trial balance** is a list of all accounts with their balances—assets first, followed by liabilities and then owner's equity—taken from the ledger. Before computers, the trial balance provided a check on accuracy by showing whether the total debits equalled the total credits. The trial balance is still useful as a summary of all the accounts and their balances. A trial balance may be taken at any time the postings are up to date. The most common time is at the end of the accounting period. Exhibit 2-7 is the trial balance of the ledger of EconoTravel after the six transactions have been journalized and posted.

EXHIBIT 2-7

Trial Balance

ECONOTRAVEL
Trial Balance
April 30, 2005

Account Titles	Balance Debit	Balance Credit
Cash	$ 15,000	
Office supplies	1,000	
Land	80,000	
Accounts payable		$ 200
Don Smith, Capital		100,000
Don Smith, Withdrawals	4,200	
Total	$100,200	$100,200

Normal Balance of an Account

An account's *normal balance* appears on the side of the account—debit or credit—where *increases* are recorded. That is, the normal balance is on the side that is positive. For example, Cash and other assets usually have a debit balance (the debit side is positive and the credit side negative), so the normal balance of assets is on the debit side, and assets are called *debit-balance accounts*. Conversely, liabilities and owner's equity usually have a credit balance, so their normal balances are on the credit side, and they are called *credit-balance accounts*. Exhibit 2-8 illustrates the normal balances of assets, liabilities, and owner's equity.

An account that normally has a debit balance may occasionally have a credit balance, which indicates a negative amount of the item. For example, Cash will have a temporary credit balance if the entity overdraws its bank account. Similarly, the liability Accounts Payable—normally a credit balance account—will have a debit balance if the entity overpays its accounts payable. In other instances, the shift of a balance amount away from its normal column may indicate an accounting error. For example, a credit balance in Office Furniture or Buildings indicates an error because negative amounts of these assets cannot exist.

As we saw earlier in the chapter, owner's equity usually contains several accounts. In total, these accounts show a normal credit balance. An individual owner's equity account with a normal credit balance represents an *increase* in owner's equity. An owner's equity account that has a normal debit balance represents a *decrease* in owner's equity.

KEY POINT

The normal balance of an account is the side on which increases are recorded.

EXHIBIT 2-8

Normal Balances of Balance Sheet Accounts

Assets	=	Liabilities	+	Owner's Equity
Normal Bal. Debit		Normal Bal. Credit		Normal Bal. Credit

Mid-Chapter Summary Problem
for Your Review

On August 1, 2005, Anna Wu opens Wu Computer Consulting. During the business's first ten days of operations, it completes the following transactions:

a. To begin operations, Anna Wu deposits $60,000 of personal funds in a bank account entitled Wu Computer Consulting. The business receives the cash and gives Wu capital (owner's equity).

b. Wu Computer Consulting pays $30,000 cash for a small house to be used as an office and $15,000 for the land on which the house is located.

c. The business purchases office supplies for $750 on account.

d. The business pays $9,000 cash for office furniture.

e. The business pays $300 on the account payable created in Transaction (c).

f. Wu withdraws $2,000 cash for personal use.

Required

1. Prepare the journal entries to record these transactions. Key the journal entries by letter.

2. Post the entries to T-accounts and calculate the ending balance.
3. Prepare the trial balance of Wu Computer Consulting at August 10, 2005.

Solution

Requirement 1

Accounts and Explanation	Ref.	Debit	Credit
a. Cash		60,000	
Anna Wu, Capital			60,000
Record initial investment from owner.			
b. Building		30,000	
Land		15,000	
Cash			45,000
Purchased building for an office and land.			
c. Office Supplies		750	
Accounts Payable			750
Purchased office supplies on account.			
d. Office Furniture		9,000	
Cash			9,000
Purchased office furniture.			
e. Accounts Payable		300	
Cash			300
Paid cash on account.			
f. Anna Wu, Withdrawals		2,000	
Cash			2,000
Withdrew cash for personal use.			

Requirement 2

ASSETS

Cash

(a)	60,000	(b)	45,000
		(d)	9,000
		(e)	300
		(f)	2,000
Bal.	3,700		

Office Supplies

(c)	750	
Bal.	750	

Land

(b)	15,000	
Bal.	15,000	

Office Furniture

(d)	9,000	
Bal.	9,000	

Building

(b)	30,000	
Bal.	30,000	

LIABILITIES

Accounts Payable

(e)	300	(c)	750
		Bal.	450

OWNER'S EQUITY

Anna Wu, Capital

	(a)	60,000
	Bal.	60,000

Anna Wu, Withdrawals

(f)	2,000	
Bal.	2,000	

WU COMPUTER CONSULTING
Trial Balance
August 10, 2005

Account Titles	Balance	
	Debit	Credit
Cash	$ 3,700	
Office supplies	750	
Office furniture	9,000	
Building	30,000	
Land..	15,000	
Accounts payable		$ 450
Anna Wu, Capital		60,000
Anna Wu, Withdrawals	2,000	
Total	$60,450	$60,450

Cyber Coach

Visit the Study Guide on the Media Companion CD-ROM and the Student Resources area of the *Accounting* Companion Website for extra practice with the new material in Chapter 2.

www.pearsoned.ca/horngren

Details of Journals and Ledgers

To focus on the main points of journalizing and posting, we purposely omitted certain essential data. In practice, the journal and the ledger provide additional details that create a "trail" through the accounting records for future reference. For example, a supplier may bill us twice for the same item we purchased on account. To prove we paid the first bill, we would search the accounts payable records and work backward to the journal entry that recorded our payment. To see how this works, let's take a closer look at the journal and the ledger.

Details in the Journal   Exhibit 2-9, Panel A describes two transactions and Panel B presents a widely used journal format. The journal page number appears in the upper-right corner. As the column headings indicate, the *journal* displays the following information:

1. The *date*, which indicates when the transaction occurred. The year appears only when the journal is started or when the year has changed. The date of the transaction is recorded for every transaction

2. The *account title* and *explanation* of the transaction, as in Exhibit 2-4

3. The *posting reference*, abbreviated Post. Ref. How this column helps the accountant becomes clear when we discuss the details of posting

4. The *debit* column, which shows the amount debited

5. The *credit* column, which shows the amount credited

Details in the Ledger   Exhibit 2-9, Panel C presents the *ledger* in three-column format. The first two amount columns are for the debit and credit amounts posted

EXHIBIT 2-9

Details of Journalizing and
Posting

Panel A: Two of EconoTravel's Transactions

Date	Transaction
Apr. 2, 2005	Don Smith invested $100,000 in travel agency. The business received cash and gave Smith owner's equity in the business.
Apr. 3, 2005	Paid $1,000 cash for office supplies.

Panel B: The Journal

Page 1

Date	Accounts and Explanation	Post. Ref.	Debit	Credit
2005				
Apr. 2	Cash	1100	100,000	
	Don Smith, Capital	3000		100,000
	Received initial investment from owner.			
3	Office Supplies	1400	1,000	
	Cash	1100		1,000
	Purchased office supplies.			

Panel C: The Ledger

Account: Cash   **Account No.** 1100

Date	Item	Jrnl. Ref.	Debit	Credit	Balance
2005					
Apr. 2		J.1	100,000		100,000 Dr
Apr. 3		J.1		1,000	99,000 Dr

1 Transfer the date of the transaction from the journal to the ledger.

2 Transfer the page number from the journal to the journal reference column of the ledger.

3 Post the debit figure from the journal as a debit figure in the ledger account.

4 Enter the account number in the posting reference column of the journal once the figure has been posted to the ledger.

Account: Office Supplies   **Account No.** 1400

Date	Item	Jrnl. Ref.	Debit	Credit	Balance
2005					
Apr. 3		J.1	1,000		1,000 Dr

Account: Don Smith, Capital   **Account No.** 3000

Date	Item	Jrnl. Ref.	Debit	Credit	Balance
2005					
Apr. 2		J.1		100,000	100,000 Cr

from the journal. The third amount column is for the account's balance. This three-column format keeps a running balance in the account. The balance is usually indicated by the letters Dr or Cr (indicating a debit or credit respectively) appearing in the third amount column. Each account has its own record in the illustrative ledger. Our example shows EconoTravel's Cash account, Office Supplies account, and Don Smith, Capital account. Each account in the ledger has its own identification number.

The column headings identify the ledger account's features:

1. The date
2. The item column. This space is used for any special notation
3. The journal reference column, abbreviated Jrnl. Ref. The importance of this column becomes clear when we discuss the mechanics of posting
4. The debit column, with the amount debited
5. The credit column, with the amount credited
6. The balance column, with the debit or credit running balance

Posting from the Journal to the Ledger

We know that posting means transferring information from the journal to the ledger accounts. But how do we handle the additional details that appear in the journal and the ledger formats that we have just seen? Exhibit 2-9 illustrates the steps in full detail. Panel A lists the first two transactions of the business entity EconoTravel; Panel B presents the journal; and Panel C shows the ledger. The posting process includes four steps:

After recording the transaction in the journal:

Arrow ①—Copy (post) the transaction date from the journal to the ledger.

Arrow ②—Copy (post) the journal page number from the journal to the ledger. We use several abbreviations:
Jrnl. Ref. means Journal Reference. J. 1 refers to Journal page 1.
This step indicates where the information in the ledger came from: Journal page 1.

Arrow ③—Copy (post) the dollar amount of the debit ($100,000) from the journal as a debit to the same account (Cash) in the ledger. Likewise, post the dollar amount of the credit (also $100,000) from the journal to the appropriate account in the ledger. Now the ledger accounts have their correct amounts.

Arrow ④—Copy (post) the account number (1100) from the ledger back to the journal. This step indicates that the $100,000 debit to Cash has been posted to the Cash account in the ledger. Also, copy the account number (3000) for Don Smith, Capital back to the journal to show that the $100,000 amount of the credit has been posted to the ledger.
Post. Ref. is the abbreviation for Posting Reference.

After posting, you can prepare the trial balance, as we discussed earlier.

Chart of Accounts in the Ledger

OBJECTIVE 6
Set up a chart of accounts for a business

As you know, the ledger contains the business's accounts grouped under these headings:

1. Balance Sheet Accounts: Assets, Liabilities, and Owner's Equity
2. Income Statement Accounts: Revenues and Expenses.

To keep track of their accounts, organizations have a **chart of accounts**, which lists all the accounts in the ledger and their account numbers. These account numbers are used as posting references, as illustrated by Arrow 4 in Exhibit 2-9. This numbering system makes it easy to locate individual accounts in the ledger.

Accounts are identified by account numbers with two or more digits. Assets are often numbered beginning with 1, liabilities with 2, owner's equity with 3, revenues with 4, and expenses with 5. The second, third, and higher digits in an account number indicate the position of the individual account within the category. For example, Cash might be account number 1001, which is the first asset account. Accounts receivable may be account number 1101, the second asset account. Accounts payable may be number 2001, the first liability account. All accounts are numbered by this system. Many numbers remain between 1001 and 1101 in case new accounts with new account numbers are added later.

Organizations with many accounts use lengthy account numbers; some may have more than 25 digits. The account number can provide much useful information. For example, the account number might indicate the type of account (for example, Petty Cash) and the location of the account within the organization (for example, the Moose Jaw branch). The chart of accounts of Brown and Hansell, a law partnership, in Exhibit 2-10, uses a four-digit account number. The assignment material reflects the variety found in practice.

The chart of accounts for EconoTravel appears in Exhibit 2-11. Notice the gap in account numbers between 1200 and 1400. Don Smith realizes that at some later date the business may need to add another category of receivables—for example, Notes Receivable— to be numbered 1210.

Appendix C at the end of Volume I and Volume II gives three expanded charts of accounts that you will find helpful as you work through this course. The first chart lists the typical accounts of a large *service* proprietorship. The second chart is for a *merchandising* corporation, one that sells a product rather than a service. The third chart lists some accounts a *manufacturing* company uses. These accounts will be used in connection with Chapters 19–26. Study the service proprietorship chart of accounts now, and refer to the other charts of accounts as needed later.

The expense accounts are listed in alphabetical order throughout this chapter. Many businesses follow such a scheme for their records and financial statements since computer programs often list accounts alphabetically. The other system of ordering is by balance or size, with the accounts with the largest balances listed first. The service, merchandising, and manufacturing accounts shown in Appendix C are taken from the financial statements of real companies and are listed in the order used by those companies.

EXHIBIT 2-10

Partial Chart of Accounts—Law Practice of Brown and Hansell

Account Number	Account Name
1101	Petty Cash
1110	Cash in Bank
1201	Accounts Receivable
1300	Office Supplies
1601	Office Furniture
1701	Computers
2201	Accounts Payable
2250	Notes Payable
2300	Employee Withholdings Payable
3000	H. Brown, Capital
3001	B. Hansell, Capital
3100	H. Brown, Withdrawals
3101	B. Hansell, Withdrawals
4000	Fee Revenue
5001	Rent Expense
5101	Supplies Expense
5401	Wages Expense

EXHIBIT 2-11

Chart of Accounts—
EconoTravel

Balance Sheet Accounts:

Assets		Liabilities		Owner's Equity	
1100	Cash	2100	Accounts Payable	3000	Don Smith, Capital
1200	Accounts Receivable	2300	Notes Payable	3100	Don Smith, Withdrawals
1400	Office Supplies				
1500	Office Furniture				
1900	Land				

**Income Statement Accounts
(part of Owner's Equity)**

Revenues		Expenses	
4000	Service Revenue	5100	Rent Exp.
		5200	Salary Exp.
		5300	Utilities Exp.

Accounting and the *e*-World

Using Computers and the Internet to Be Successful

Many companies have embraced the opportunities provided by the Internet. They can use the technology to their advantage in a number of ways. As a marketing tool, many companies use their websites to showcase their products and, in many cases, allow customers to purchase products online. Canadian Tire Corporation, Limited (www.canadiantire.ca), for example, lists products on its website and allows customers to "fill a shopping cart" with online purchases.

Many manufacturing companies, such as Bombardier Inc. (www.bombardier.com), also use the Internet to communicate with their suppliers. Orders are placed and invoices are paid electronically. This gives companies like Bombardier greater flexibility in managing their inventory.

The Internet also allows companies to communicate with their offices all over the world. Accounting information can be transferred from subsidiary companies to head office quickly and accurately, for accounting purposes and management purposes.

The Internet is useful for service organizations as well. Your college or university probably allows you to register for courses over the Internet. It wasn't very long ago that students had to line up to register for courses. Now you can register from anywhere in the world—but don't miss your registration time!

Companies are successful because they produce excellent products or services. The Internet allows them to enhance their performance, and successful companies take full advantage of the opportunity.

Expanding the Accounting Equation to Account for Owner's Equity Accounts: Revenues and Expenses

> **KEY POINT**
>
> Because withdrawals reduce owner's equity, the Withdrawals account is sometimes referred to as a *contra equity* account, meaning that it has a normal balance opposite to that of owner's equity.

Owner's equity includes Revenues and Expenses because revenues and expenses make up net income or net loss, which flows into owner's equity. As we have discussed, *revenues* are increases in owner's equity that result from delivering goods and services to customers in the course of operating the business. *Expenses* are decreases in owner's equity that occur from using assets or increasing liabilities in the course of operating the business. Therefore, the accounting equation may be expanded as shown in Exhibit 2-12. Revenues and expenses appear in parentheses to highlight

EXHIBIT 2-12

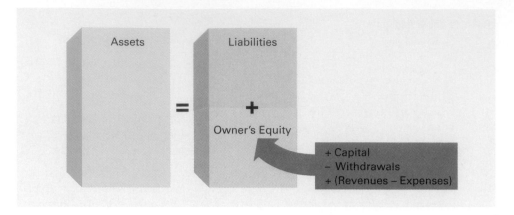

the fact that their net effect—revenues minus expenses—equals net income, which increases owner's equity. If expenses are greater than revenues, the net effect of operations is a net loss, which decreases owner's equity.

Revenues increase owner's equity, so the normal balance of a revenue is a credit. Expenses decrease equity, so the normal balance of an expense is a debit.

We can now express the rules of debit and credit in final form as shown in Panel A of Exhibit 2-13. Panel B shows the *normal* balances of the five types of accounts: *Assets*; *Liabilities*; and *Owner's Equity* and its subparts, *Revenue* and *Expenses*. All of accounting is based on these five types of accounts. **Before proceeding, make sure you know the rules of debit and credit. Also make sure you know the normal balances of the five types of accounts.**

EXHIBIT 2-13

Rules of Debit and Credit, and the Normal Balances of Accounts

Panel A: Rules of Debit and Credit

Assets		=	Liabilities		+	Capital	
Debit for Increase	Credit for Decrease		Debit for Decrease	Credit for Increase		Debit for Decrease	Credit for Increase

		Withdrawals	
		Debit for Increase	Credit for Decrease

		Revenues	
		Debit for Decrease	Credit for Increase

		Expenses	
		Debit for Increase	Credit for Decrease

Panel B: Normal Balances

	Debit	Credit
Assets	Debit	
Liabilities		Credit
Owner's equity—overall		Credit
Capital		Credit
Withdrawals	Debit	
Revenue		Credit
Expenses	Debit	

Compute the missing amount in each account:

(1) Cash		(2) Accounts Payable		(3) S. Scully, Capital	
Bal. 10,000		X	Bal. 12,800	22,000	Bal. X
20,000	13,000		45,600		56,000
Bal. X			Bal. 23,500		15,000
					Bal. 73,000

Answers: (1) The ending balance (X) for Cash is

$$X = \$10,000 + 20,000 - \$13,000$$
$$X = \$17,000$$

(2) We are given the beginning and ending balances. We can compute the debit entry as follows:

$$\$12,800 + \$45,600 - X = \$23,500$$
$$\$12,800 + \$45,600 - \$23,500 = X$$
$$X = \$34,900$$

(3) The Capital account has an ending credit balance of $73,000. We can calculate the beginning credit balance as follows:

$$X + \$56,000 + \$15,000 - \$22,000 = \$73,000$$
$$X = \$73,000 - \$56,000 - \$15,000 + \$22,000$$
$$X = \$24,000$$

Expanded Problem Including Revenues and Expenses

Let's account for the revenues and expenses of the law practice of Jacob Letourneau, Lawyer, for the month of July 2005. We follow the same steps illustrated earlier in this chapter: Analyze the transaction, journalize, post to the ledger, and prepare the trial balance.

Transaction Analysis, Journalizing, and Posting

1. **Transaction:** Jacob Letourneau invested $30,000 cash in a business bank account to open his law practice. The business received the cash and gave Letourneau owner's equity.

Analysis: The business asset cash is increased; therefore, debit Cash. The owner's equity of the business is increased, so credit Jacob Letourneau, Capital.

Journal Entry:
```
Cash .............................................  30,000
      Jacob Letourneau, Capital                          30,000
Received investment from owner.
```

Accounting Equation:

ASSETS	=	LIABILITIES	+	OWNER'S EQUITY
Cash				Jacob Letourneau, Capital
+30,000	=	0	+	30,000

Ledger Accounts:

Cash		Jacob Letourneau, Capital	
(1) 30,000			(1) 30,000

2. Transaction: Letourneau provided legal services for a client and received $9,000 cash.

Analysis: The asset cash is increased; therefore, debit Cash. The revenue account service revenue is increased; credit Service Revenue.

Journal Entry:

Cash 9,000
    Service Revenue 9,000
Performed service and received cash.

Accounting Equation:

ASSETS	=	LIABILITIES	+	OWNER'S EQUITY	+	REVENUES
Cash						Service Revenue
+9,000	=	0			+	9,000

Ledger Accounts:

Cash			Service Revenue		
(1)	30,000			(2)	9,000
(2)	9,000				

---

3. Transaction: Letourneau provided legal services to HK Co. and billed the client for $1,500 on account. This means HK Co. owes the business $1,500 and Letourneau expects to collect the $1,500 later.

Analysis: The asset accounts receivable is increased; therefore, debit Accounts Receivable. Service revenue is increased; credit Service Revenue.

Journal Entry:

Accounts Receivable 1,500
    Service Revenue 1,500
Performed service on account.

Accounting Equation:

ASSETS	=	LIABILITIES	+	OWNER'S EQUITY	+	REVENUES
Accounts Receivable						Service Revenue
+1,500	=	0			+	1,500

Ledger Accounts:

Accounts Receivable			Service Revenue		
(3)	1,500			(2)	9,000
				(3)	1,500

---

4. Transaction: Letourneau provided and billed legal services of $2,100 to a doctor, who paid $900 cash immediately. Letourneau billed the remaining $1,200 to the doctor on account.

Analysis: The assets cash and accounts receivable are increased; therefore, debit both of these asset accounts. Service revenue is increased; credit Service Revenue for the sum of the two debit amounts.

Journal Entry:

Cash 900
Accounts Receivable 1,200
    Service Revenue 2,100
Performed service for cash and on account.

Accounting Equation:

	OWNER'S			
ASSETS	= LIABILITIES +	EQUITY +	REVENUES	

					Service
ASSETS					Revenue
Cash	Accounts Receivable				
+900	+1,200	=	0	+	2,100

Note: Because this transaction affects more than two accounts at the same time, the entry is called a *compound entry*. **No matter how many accounts a compound entry affects—there may be any number—total debits must equal total credits.**

Ledger Accounts:

Cash			**Accounts Receivable**	
(1)	30,000		(3)	1,500
(2)	9,000		(4)	1,200
(4)	900			

Service Revenue	
(2)	9,000
(3)	1,500
(4)	2,100

---

5. *Transaction:* **Letourneau paid the following cash expenses: office rent, $2,700; employee salary, $4,500; and utilities, $1,500.**

Analysis: The asset cash is decreased; therefore, credit Cash for each of the three expense amounts. The following expenses are increased: Rent Expense, Salary Expense, and Utilities Expense. Each should be debited for the appropriate amount.

Journal Entry:

Rent Expense	2,700	
Salary Expense	4,500	
Utilities Expense	1,500	
Cash		8,700

Issued three cheques to pay cash for expenses.

Accounting Equation:

		OWNER'S		
ASSETS =	LIABILITIES +	EQUITY –	EXPENSES	

			Rent	Salary	Utilities
Cash			Expense	Expense	Expense
–8,700 =	0		–2,700	–4,500	–1,500

Note: In practice, the business would record these three transactions separately. To save space, we can record them together in a compound journal entry.

Ledger Accounts:

Cash					**Rent Expense**	
(1)	30,000	(5)	8,700		(5)	2,700
(2)	9,000					
(4)	900					

Salary Expense			**Utilities Expense**	
(5)	4,500		(5)	1,500

6. Transaction: Letourneau received a telephone bill for $360 and will pay this expense next week.

Analysis: Utilities expense is increased; therefore, debit this expense. The liability accounts payable is increased, so credit Accounts Payable.

Journal Entry:

Utilities Expense 360
    Accounts Payable 360
Received utility bill.

Accounting Equation:

ASSETS	=	LIABILITIES	+	OWNER'S EQUITY	–	EXPENSES
		Accounts Payable				Utilities Expense
0	=	+360			–	360

Ledger Accounts:

Accounts Payable			Utilities Expense		
	(6)	360	(5)	1,500	
			(6)	360	

LEARNING TIP

Recording an expense does not necessarily involve a credit to cash. In Transaction 6 the expense is recorded now, but the cash will be paid later. Likewise, a debit to cash does not always reflect revenue. Transaction 7 records cash collected on a receivable (the revenue was recorded in Transaction 3).

7. Transaction: Letourneau received $600 cash from HK Co., the client discussed in Transaction 3.

Analysis: The asset cash is increased; therefore, debit Cash. The asset accounts receivable is decreased; therefore, credit Accounts Receivable.

Journal Entry:

Cash 600
    Accounts Receivable 600
Received cash on account.

Accounting Equation:

ASSETS		=	LIABILITIES	+	OWNER'S EQUITY
	Accounts				
Cash	Receivable				
+600	–600	=	0	+	0

Note: This transaction has no effect on revenue; the related revenue is accounted for in Transaction 3.

Ledger Accounts:

Cash				Accounts Receivable			
(1)	30,000	(5)	8,700	(3)	1,500	(7)	600
(2)	9,000			(4)	1,200		
(4)	900						
(7)	600						

8. Transaction: Letourneau paid the telephone bill that was received and recorded in Transaction 6.

Analysis: The asset cash is decreased; credit Cash. The liability accounts payable is decreased; therefore, debit Accounts Payable.

Journal Entry:

Accounts Payable 360
    Cash 360
Paid cash on account.

Accounting Equation:	ASSETS	=	LIABILITIES	+	OWNER'S EQUITY
			Accounts		
	Cash		Payable		
	−360	=	−360	+	0

Note: This transaction has no effect on expense because the related expense was recorded in Transaction 6.

Ledger Accounts:

Cash					**Accounts Payable**			
(1)	30,000	(5)	8,700		(8)	360	(6)	360
(2)	9,000	(8)	360					
(4)	900							
(7)	600							

---

9. Transaction: Letourneau withdrew $3,300 cash for personal use.

Analysis: The asset cash decreased; credit Cash. The withdrawal decreased owner's equity; therefore, debit Jacob Letourneau, Withdrawals.

Journal Entry:

Jacob Letourneau, Withdrawals   3,300
       Cash   3,300
Withdrew cash for personal use.

Accounting Equation:	ASSETS	=	LIABILITIES	+	OWNER'S EQUITY
	Cash				Jacob Letourneau, Withdrawals
	−3,300	=	0		−3,300

Ledger Accounts:

Cash					**Jacob Letourneau, Withdrawals**	
(1)	30,000	(5)	8,700		(9)	3,300
(2)	9,000	(8)	360			
(4)	900	(9)	3,300			
(7)	600					

STOP & THINK

Review the chapter-opening story and concentrate on Frito-Lay Canada's need for financial statement information. How will the procedures you have applied in this chapter help Frito-Lay Canada convince potential investors that the business is financially stable?

Answer: The end product of the accounting process is a set of financial statements. Frito-Lay Canada's accounting records will generate the income statement, cash flow statement, and balance sheet that potential investors require of companies before investing.

Ledger Accounts after Posting

ASSETS		LIABILITIES		OWNER'S EQUITY		REVENUE		EXPENSES	

ASSETS

Cash

(1) 30,000		(5)	8,700
(2) 9,000		(8)	360
(4) 900		(9)	3,300
(7) 600			
Bal.28,140			

Accounts Receivable

(3) 1,500		(7)	600
(4) 1,200			
Bal. 2,100			

LIABILITIES

Accounts Payable

(8)	360	(6)	360
		Bal.	0

OWNER'S EQUITY

Jacob Letourneau, Capital

		(1)	30,000
		Bal.30,000	

J. Letourneau, Withdrawals

(9)	3,300		
Bal.	3,300		

REVENUE

Service Revenue

		(2)	9,000
		(3)	1,500
		(4)	2,100
		Bal.12,600	

EXPENSES

Rent Expense

(5)	2,700	
Bal. 2,700		

Salary Expense

(5)	4,500	
Bal. 4,500		

Utilities Expense

(5)	1,500	
(6)	360	
Bal. 1,860		

Trial Balance

To prepare the trial balance, we list and summarize the balances from the ledger accounts.

········ **THINKING IT OVER**

Which side of the trial balance is affected by a debit to accounts payable?

A: The credit side. (Students may want to say debit.) Illustration:

Accounts Payable

	Bal.	6,000

A debit to accounts payable reduces the *credit* balance of Accounts Payable.

Accounts Payable

	Bal.	6,000
1,000		
	Bal.	5,000

JACOB LETOURNEAU, LAWYER
Trial Balance
July 31, 2005

Account Title	Balance	
	Debit	Credit
Cash	$28,140	
Accounts receivable	2,100	
Accounts payable		$ 0
Jacob Letourneau, Capital		30,000
Jacob Letourneau, Withdrawals	3,300	
Service revenue		12,600
Rent expense	2,700	
Salary expense	4,500	
Utilities expense	1,860	
Total	$42,600	$42,600

Correcting Trial Balance Errors

In a trial balance, the total debits and total credits should always be equal. If they are not equal, then accounting errors exist. Computerized accounting systems eliminate most recording errors by often prohibiting unbalanced journal entries from being recorded. Computerized accounting systems also post journal amounts precisely as they have been journalized. But computers cannot *eliminate* all errors because humans sometimes input the wrong data.

Errors can be detected by computing the difference between total debits and total credits on the trial balance. Then perform one or more of the following actions:

1. Search the trial balance for a missing account. For example, suppose the accountant omitted Jacob Letourneau, Withdrawals from the trial balance above. The

total amount of the debits would be $39,300 ($42,600 – $3,300). Trace each account and its balance from the ledger to the trial balance, and you will locate the missing account.

2. Search the journal for the amount of the difference. For example, suppose the total credits on Jacob Letourneau, Lawyer's trial balance equal $42,600 and total debits equal $40,500. A $2,100 transaction may have been posted incorrectly to the ledger by omitting the debit entry. Search the journal for a $2,100 transaction and check its posting to the ledger.

3. Divide the difference between total debits and total credits by 2. A debit treated as a credit, or vice versa, doubles the amount of error. Suppose Jacob Letourneau, Lawyer paid $1,500 cash to pay the utilities expenses. This transaction was recorded correctly in the journal, but was posted as a debit to Cash and a debit to Utilities Expense. Thus, $3,000 appears on the debit side of the trial balance, and there is nothing on the credit side relating to this transaction. The out-of-balance amount is $3,000, and dividing by 2 identifies that the relevant transaction may have had a value of $1,500. Search the journal for a $1,500 transaction and check the posting to the ledger.

4. Divide the out-of-balance amount by 9. If the result is evenly divisible by 9, the error may be a *slide*, which is adding or deleting one or several zeroes in a figure (example: writing $61 as $610), or a *transposition* (example: treating $61 as $16). Suppose Jacob Letourneau, Lawyer listed the $3,300 balance in Jacob Letourneau, Withdrawals as $33,000 on the trial balance—a slide-type error. Total debits would differ from total credits by $29,700 (i.e., $33,000 – $3,300 = $29,700). Dividing $29,700 by 9 yields $3,300, the correct amount of the withdrawals. Trace this amount through the ledger until you reach the Jacob Letourneau, Withdrawals account with a balance of $3,300. Computer-based systems avoid such errors.

A warning: Do not confuse the trial balance with the balance sheet. A trial balance is an internal document seen only by the company's owners, managers, and accountants. The company reports its financial position—both inside the business and to the public—on the balance sheet, a formal financial statement. And remember that the financial statements are the focal point of the accounting process. The trial balance is merely a step in the preparation of the financial statements.

You have now seen how to record business transactions, post to the ledger accounts, and prepare a trial balance. Solidify your understanding of the accounting process by reviewing the Decision Guidelines feature, described on page 80.

Use of Accounting Information for Quick Decision Making

OBJECTIVE 7
Analyze transactions without a journal

Often business people make decisions without taking the time to follow all the steps in an accounting system. For example, suppose Intrawest Corporation, which owns a number of ski resorts, needs an additional ski lift at Blackcomb to meet skiers' demand. The company can either build an additional lift and increase revenues or not build the lift. The decision to build the lift will depend upon the different effects on the company.

Intrawest management does not need to record in the journal all the transactions that would be affected by its decision. After all, the company has not completed a transaction yet. But management does need to know how Intrawest will be affected by the decision. If the decision makers know accounting, they can skip the journal and go directly to the ledger accounts that would be affected. The following accounts summarize the immediate effects of building the lift and not building the lift.

LEARNING TIP

Assume that Don Smith, Withdrawals, $4,200, is erroneously listed as a credit amount on the trial balance in Exhibit 2-7.
(1) Recompute the trial balance totals.
(2) To find the mistake, calculate the difference between the column totals.
(3) Then divide the difference by two.
A: (1) Debit = $96,000; Credit = $104,400
(2) $104,400 – $96,000 = $8,400
(3) $8,400 ÷ 2 = $4,200

If you find that amount somewhere on the trial balance, you may have entered it in the wrong column. This is one easy way to find an error if your trial balance does not balance.

BUILD THE LIFT		DO NOT BUILD THE LIFT	
Cash	**Revenue**	**Cash**	**Revenue**
3,000,000	900,000 per year for ten years	No effect	No effect

Expenses
300,000 per year for ten years

Immediately Intrawest's management can see that building the additional lift will require more cash. But management can also see that Intrawest will generate more revenues if the lift is built. This may motivate Intrawest's management to use cash to build the lift.

Companies do not actually keep their records in this short-cut fashion. But a decision maker who needs information immediately can quickly analyze the effect of a set of transactions on the company's financial statements.

DECISION GUIDELINES — *Analyzing and Recording Transactions*

Decision	**Guidelines**
Has a transaction occurred?	If the event affects the entity's financial position and can be reliably recorded—*Yes* If either condition is absent—*No*
Where to record the transaction?	In the *journal*, the chronological record of transactions
What to record for each transaction?	Increases and/or decreases in all the accounts affected by the transaction (at cost)

How to record an increase/decrease in a(n)	Rules of debit and credit:	
	Increase	**Decrease**
Asset	Debit	Credit
Liability	Credit	Debit
Owner's equity	Credit	Debit
Revenue	Credit	Debit
Expense	Debit	Credit

Decision	**Guidelines**
Where to store all the information for each account?	In the *ledger*, the book of accounts and their balances
Where to list all the accounts and their balances?	In the *trial balance*
Where to report the results of operations?	In the income statement (revenues − expenses = net income or net loss)
Where to report the financial position?	In the balance sheet (assets = liabilities + owner's equity)

The trial balance of Michaels Computer Service Centre on March 1, 2006, lists the company's assets, liabilities, and owner's equity on that date.

Account Titles	Balance	
	Debit	Credit
Cash	$52,000	
Accounts receivable	9,000	
Accounts payable		$ 4,000
Jim Michaels, Capital		57,000
Total	$61,000	$61,000

During March the business engaged in the following transactions:

a. Borrowed $90,000 from the bank and signed a note payable in the name of the business.

b. Paid cash of $80,000 to a real estate company to acquire land.

c. Performed service for a customer and received cash of $10,000.

d. Purchased supplies on account, $600.

e. Performed customer service and earned revenue on account, $5,200.

f. Paid $2,400 of the Accounts Payable at March 1, 2006.

g. Paid the following cash expenses: salaries, $6,000; rent, $3,000; and interest, $800.

h. Received $6,200 of the Accounts Receivable at March 1, 2006.

i. Received a $400 utility bill that will be paid next week.

j. Michaels withdrew $3,600 for personal use.

Required

1. Open the following accounts, with the balances indicated, in the ledger of Michaels Computer Service Centre. Use the T-account format.
   Assets: Cash, $52,000; Accounts Receivable, $9,000; Supplies, no balance; Land, no balance
   Liabilities: Accounts Payable, $4,000; Notes Payable, no balance
   Owner's Equity: Jim Michaels, Capital, $57,000; Jim Michaels, Withdrawals, no balance
   Revenues: Service Revenue, no balance
   Expenses: Salary Expense, Rent Expense, Utilities Expense, Interest Expense (none have balances)

2. Journalize the preceding transactions. Key journal entries by transaction letter.

3. Post to the ledger.

4. Prepare the trial balance of Michaels Computer Service Centre at March 31, 2006.

5. Compute the net income or net loss of the entity during the month of March by producing an income statement. List expenses in alphabetical order.

Solution

Requirement 1

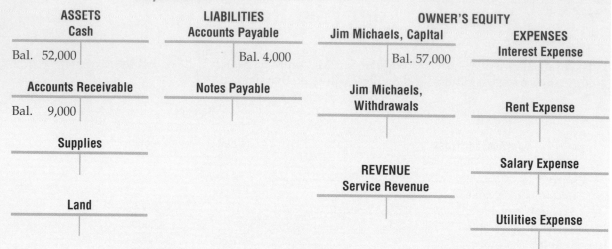

ASSETS

Cash

Bal. 52,000 |

Accounts Receivable

Bal. 9,000 |

Supplies

Land

LIABILITIES

Accounts Payable

| Bal. 4,000

Notes Payable

OWNER'S EQUITY

Jim Michaels, Capital

| Bal. 57,000

Jim Michaels, Withdrawals

REVENUE

Service Revenue

EXPENSES

Interest Expense

Rent Expense

Salary Expense

Utilities Expense

Requirement 2

	Accounts and Explanation	Debit	Credit
a.	Cash...	90,000	
	Notes Payable...		90,000
	Borrowed cash on note payable.		
b.	Land...	80,000	
	Cash		80,000
	Purchased land for cash.		
c.	Cash...	10,000	
	Service Revenue		10,000
	Performed service and received cash.		
d.	Supplies...	600	
	Accounts Payable.......................................		600
	Purchased supplies on account.		
e.	Accounts Receivable	5,200	
	Service Revenue		5,200
	Performed service on account.		
f.	Accounts Payable	2,400	
	Cash		2,400
	Paid cash to reduce accounts payable.		
g.	Salary Expense...	6,000	
	Rent Expense...	3,000	
	Interest Expense	800	
	Cash		9,800
	Issued three cheques to pay cash expenses.		
h.	Cash...	6,200	
	Accounts Receivable...................................		6,200
	Received cash on account.		
i.	Utilities Expense	400	
	Accounts Payable.......................................		400
	Received utility bill.		
j.	Jim Michaels, Withdrawals	3,600	
	Cash		3,600
	Withdrew cash for personal use.		

Requirement 3

ASSETS			LIABILITIES			OWNER'S EQUITY		EXPENSES	

ASSETS

Cash

Bal.	52,000	(b)	80,000
(a)	90,000	(f)	2,400
(c)	10,000	(g)	9,800
(h)	6,200	(j)	3,600
Bal.	62,400		

Accounts Receivable

Bal.	9,000	(h)	6,200
(e)	5,200		
Bal.	8,000		

Supplies

(d)	600	
Bal.	600	

Land

(b)	80,000	
Bal.	80,000	

LIABILITIES

Accounts Payable

(f)	2,400	Bal.	4,000
		(d)	600
		(i)	400
		Bal.	2,600

Notes Payable

	(a)	90,000
	Bal.	90,000

OWNER'S EQUITY

Jim Michaels, Capital

	Bal. 57,000

Jim Michaels, Withdrawals

(j)	3,600	
Bal.	3,600	

REVENUE

Service Revenue

	(c)	10,000
	(e)	5,200
	Bal.	15,200

EXPENSES

Interest Expense

(g)	800	
Bal.	800	

Rent Expense

(g)	3,000	
Bal.	3,000	

Salary Expense

(g)	6,000	
Bal.	6,000	

Utilities Expense

(i)	400	
Bal.	400	

Requirement 4

MICHAELS COMPUTER SERVICE CENTRE
Trial Balance
March 31, 2006

Account Title	Balance	
	Debit	Credit
Cash	$ 62,400	
Accounts receivable	8,000	
Supplies	600	
Land	80,000	
Accounts payable		$ 2,600
Notes payable		90,000
Jim Michaels, capital		57,000
Jim Michaels, withdrawals	3,600	
Service revenue		15,200
Interest expense	800	
Rent expense	3,000	
Salary expense	6,000	
Utilities expense	400	
Total	$164,800	$164,800

MICHAELS COMPUTER SERVICE CENTRE
Income Statement
For the Month Ended March 31, 2006

Revenues		
Service revenue		$15,200
Expenses:		
Interest expense..	$ 800	
Rent expense...	3,000	
Salary expense..	6,000	
Utilities expense...	400	
Total expenses		10,200
Net income..		$ 5,000

Cyber Coach

Visit the Study Guide on the Media Companion CD-ROM and the Student Resources area of the *Accounting* Companion Website for extra practice with the new material in Chapter 2.

www.pearsoned.ca/horngren

Summary

1. **Define and use key accounting terms: *account*, *ledger*, *debit*, and *credit*.** *Accounts* can be viewed in the form of the letter "T." The left side of each T-account is its *debit* side. The right side is its *credit* side. The *ledger*, which contains a record for each account, groups and numbers accounts by category in the following order: assets, liabilities, and owner's equity (and its subparts, revenues and expenses).

2. **Apply the rules of debit and credit.** *Assets* and *expenses* are increased by debits and decreased by credits. *Liabilities*, *owner's equity*, and *revenues* are increased by credits and decreased by debits. An account's *normal balance* is the side of the account—debit or credit—in which increases are recorded. Thus, the normal balance of assets and expenses is a debit, and the normal balance of liabilities, owner's equity, and revenues is a credit. The Withdrawals account, which decreases owner's equity, normally has a debit balance. *Revenues*, which are increases in owner's equity, have a normal credit balance. *Expenses*, which are decreases in owner's equity, have a normal debit balance.

3. **Record transactions in the journal.** The accountant begins the recording process by entering the transaction's information in the *journal*, a chronological list of all the entity's transactions.

4. **Post from the journal to the ledger.** Posting means transferring to the *ledger* accounts. Posting references are used to trace amounts back and forth between the journal and the ledger.

5. **Prepare and use a trial balance.** The *trial balance* is a summary of all the account balances in the ledger. When *double-entry accounting* has been done correctly, the total debits and the total credits in the trial balance are equal.

6. **Set up a chart of accounts for a business.** A *chart of accounts* lists all the accounts in the ledger and their account numbers.

7. **Analyze transactions without a journal.** Decision makers must often make decisions without a complete accounting system. They can analyze the transactions without a journal.

We can now trace the flow of accounting information through these steps:

Business Transaction ⟶ Source Documents

⟶ Journal Entry ⟶ Posting to Ledger

⟶ Trial Balance

Self-Study Questions

Test your understanding of the chapter by marking the correct answer for each of the following questions:

1. An account has two sides called the *(p. 55)*
   a. Debit and credit
   b. Asset and liability
   c. Revenue and expense
   d. Journal and ledger

2. Increases in liabilities are recorded by *(p. 56)*
   a. Debits
   b. Credits

3. Why do accountants record transactions in the journal? *(p. 58)*
   a. To ensure that all transactions are posted to the ledger
   b. To ensure that total debits equal total credits
   c. To have a chronological record of all transactions
   d. To help prepare the financial statements

4. Posting is the process of transferring information from the *(p. 60)*
   a. Journal to the trial balance
   b. Ledger to the trial balance
   c. Ledger to the financial statements
   d. Journal to the ledger

5. The purchase of land for cash is recorded by a *(p. 61)*
   a. Debit to Cash and a credit to Land
   b. Debit to Cash and a debit to Land
   c. Debit to Land and a credit to Cash
   d. Credit to Cash and a credit to Land

6. The purpose of the trial balance is to *(p. 64)*
   a. List all accounts with their balances
   b. Ensure that all transactions have been recorded

   c. Speed the collection of cash receipts from customers
   d. Increase assets and owner's equity

7. What is the normal balance of the Accounts Receivable, Office Supplies, and Rent Expense accounts? *(p. 65)*
   a. Debit
   b. Credit

8. A business has Cash of $3,000, Notes Payable of $2,500, Accounts Payable of $4,300, Service Revenue of $7,000 and Rent Expense of $1,800. Based on these data, how much are its total liabilities? *(p. 72)*
   a. $5,500
   b. $6,800
   c. $9,800
   d. $13,800

9. Smale Transport earned revenue on account. The earning of revenue on account is recorded by a *(pp. 73–77)*
   a. Debit to Cash and a credit to Revenue
   b. Debit to Accounts Receivable and a credit to Revenue
   c. Debit to Accounts Payable and a credit to Revenue
   d. Debit to Revenue and a credit to Accounts Receivable

10. The account credited for a receipt of cash on account is *(p. 76)*
   a. Cash
   b. Accounts Payable
   c. Service Revenue
   d. Accounts Receivable

Answers to the Self-Study Questions follow the Similar Accounting Terms.

Accounting Vocabulary

Account *(p. 52)*
Chart of accounts *(p. 69)*
Credit *(p. 55)*
Debit *(p. 55)*

Journal *(p. 58)*
Ledger *(p. 52)*
Posting *(p. 60)*
Trial balance *(p. 64)*

Similar Accounting Terms

Cr	Credit; right
Dr	Debit; left
The Ledger	The Books; the General Ledger
Entering the transaction in a journal	Making the journal entry; journalizing the transaction
Withdrawals by owner(s)	In a *proprietorship* or *partnership*, distributions from a company to its owner(s).

Answers to Self-Study Questions

1. a	3. c	5. c	7. a		9. b	
2. b	4. d	6. a	8. b ($6,800 = $2,500 + $4,300)		10. d	

Assignment Material

Questions

1. Name the basic shortcut device of accounting. What letter of the alphabet does it resemble? Name its two sides.

2. Is the following statement true or false? Debit means decrease and credit means increase. Explain your answer.

3. Write two sentences that use the term *debit* differently.

4. What are the three *basic* types of accounts? Name two additional types of accounts. To which one of the three basic types are these two additional types of accounts most closely related?

5. Suppose you are the accountant for Smith Courier Service. Keeping in mind double-entry bookkeeping, identify the *dual effects* of Mary Smith's investment of $10,000 cash in her business.

6. Briefly describe the flow of accounting information.

7. To what does the *normal balance* of an account refer?

8. Indicate the normal balance of the five types of accounts.

Account Type	Normal Balance
Assets	_____
Liabilities	_____
Owner's equity	_____
Revenues	_____
Expenses	_____

9. What does posting accomplish? Why is it important? Does it come before or after journalizing?

10. Label each of the following transactions as increasing owner's equity (+), decreasing owner's equity (–), or as having no effect on owner's equity (0). Write the appropriate symbol in the space provided.

    ___ Investment by owner
    ___ Bill customer for services
    ___ Purchase of supplies on credit
    ___ Pay expenses
    ___ Cash payment on account
    ___ Withdrawal by owner
    ___ Borrowing money on a note payable
    ___ Sale of services on account

11. What four steps does posting include? Which step is the fundamental purpose of posting?

12. Rearrange the following accounts in their logical sequence in the chart of accounts:

Notes Payable	Cash
Accounts Receivable	Jane East, Capital
Sales Revenue	Salary Expense

13. What is the meaning of the statement, Accounts Payable has a credit balance of $1,700?

14. Jack Brown Campus Cleaners launders the shirts of customer Bobby Baylor, who has a charge account at the cleaners. When Bobby picks up his clothes and is short of cash, he charges it. Later, when he receives his monthly statement from the cleaners, Bobby writes a cheque on his bank account and mails the cheque to the cleaners. Identify the two business transactions described here. Which transaction increases the business's owner's equity? Which transaction increases Jack Brown Campus Cleaners' cash?

15. Explain the difference between the ledger and the chart of accounts.

16. Why do accountants prepare a trial balance?

17. What is a compound journal entry?

18. The accountant for Bower Construction mistakenly recorded a $500 purchase of supplies on account as $5,000. He debited Supplies and credited Accounts Payable for $5,000. Does this error cause the trial balance to be out of balance? Explain your answer.

19. What is the effect on total assets of collecting cash on account from customers?

20. What is the advantage of analyzing and recording transactions without the use of a journal? Describe how this "journal-less" analysis works.

21. Briefly summarize the similarities and differences between manual and computer-based accounting systems in terms of journalizing, posting, and preparing a trial balance.

Exercises

Exercise 2-1 *Using accounting vocabulary* *(Obj. 1)*

Your employer, Prairie Tours, has just hired an office manager who does not understand accounting. The Prairie Tours trial balance lists Cash of $87,800. Write a short memo to the office manager, explaining the accounting process that produced this listing on the trial balance. Mention *debits, credits, journal, ledger, posting,* and *trial balance.*

Exercise 2-2 *Using debits and credits with the accounting equation* *(Obj. 1, 2)*

Link Back to Chapter 1 (Accounting Equation). Canadian National Railway Company (CN) (www.cn.ca) is one of North America's leading railways. At the end of 2002, CN had total assets of $18.9 billion and total liabilities of $12.3 billion.

Required

1. Write the company's accounting equation, and label each element as a debit amount or a credit amount.
2. CN's total revenues for 2002 were $6.1 billion, and total expenses for the year were $5.0 billion. How much was CN's net income (or net loss) for 2002? Write the equation to compute CN's net income, and indicate which element is a debit amount and which element is a credit amount. Does net income represent a net debit or a net credit? Does net loss represent a net debit or a net credit? Review Exhibit 1-8, page 22, if needed.
3. During 2002, the owners of CN were paid $170 million in the form of dividends (this is the same as owner's withdrawals). Did the dividends represent a debit amount or a credit amount?
4. Considering both CN's net income (or net loss) and dividends for 2002, by how much did the company's owner's equity increase or decrease during 2002? Was the change in owner's equity a debit amount or a credit amount?

Exercise 2-3 *Analyzing and journalizing transactions* *(Obj. 2, 3)*

Analyze the following transactions of Gregg Management Consulting in the manner shown for the December 1 transaction. Also, record each transaction in the journal.

| Dec. | 1 | Paid monthly utilities expense of $1,400. (Analysis: The expense, utilities expense, is increased; therefore, debit Utilities Expense. The asset, cash, is decreased; therefore, credit Cash.) |

| | 1 | Utilities Expense .... | 1,400 | |
| | | Cash .... | | 1,400 |

	4	Borrowed $16,000 cash, signing a note payable.
	8	Performed service on account for a customer, $3,200.
	12	Purchased office furniture on account, $2,000.
	19	Sold for $148,000 land that had cost this same amount.
	24	Purchased building for $280,000; signed a note payable.
	27	Paid the liability created on December 12.

Exercise 2-4 *Applying the rules of debit and credit* *(Obj. 2)*

Refer to Exercise 2-3 for the transactions of Gregg Management Consulting.

Required

1. Open the following T-accounts with their December 1 balances: Cash, debit balance $12,000; Land, debit balance $148,000; S. Gregg, Capital, credit balance $160,000.

2. Record the transactions of Exercise 2-3 directly in the T-accounts affected. Use dates as posting references in the T-accounts. Journal entries are not required.

3. Compute the December 31 balance for each account, and prove that total debits equal total credits.

Media Companion CD-ROM

Exercise 2-5   *Journalizing transactions*   *(Obj. 3)*

Frantic Fitness engaged in the following transactions during March 2005, its first month of operations:

Mar.   1   The business received $90,000 cash investment from Kim Honey to start Frantic Fitness.
   2   Purchased supplies for $1,000 on account.
   4   Paid $80,000 cash for building to use as an office.
   6   Presented a wellness seminar for a corporate customer and received cash, $5,000.
   9   Paid $200 on accounts payable.
   17   Performed wellness assessments for customers on account, $2,000.
   23   Received $1,600 cash from a customer on account.
   31   Paid the following expenses: salary, $2,400; rent, $1,000.

Required

Record the preceding transactions in the journal of Frantic Fitness. Key transactions by date and include an explanation for each entry, as illustrated in the chapter and Exhibit 2-4. Use the following accounts: Cash; Accounts Receivable; Office Supplies; Building; Accounts Payable; K. Honey, Capital; Service Revenue; Salary Expense; Rent Expense.

Exercise 2-6   *Posting to the ledger and preparing a trial balance*   *(Obj. 4, 5)*

Refer to Exercise 2-5 for the transactions of Frantic Fitness.

Required

1. After journalizing the transactions of Exercise 2-5, post the entries to the ledger, using T-account format. Key transactions by date. Date the ending balance of each account Mar. 31.

2. Prepare the trial balance of Frantic Fitness at March 31, 2005.

Exercise 2-7   *Describing transactions and posting*   *(Obj. 3, 4)*

The journal of Urban Skateboard for October 2006 is on page 89.

Required

1. Describe each transaction.

2. Post the transactions to the ledger using the following account numbers: Cash, 1000; Accounts Receivable, 1200; Supplies, 1400; Accounts Payable, 2000; Notes Payable, 2100; Tim Leggett, Capital, 3000; Sales Revenue, 4000; Advertising Expense, 5100; Rent Expense, 5600; Utilities Expense, 5800. Use dates, journal references, and posting references as illustrated in Exhibit 2-9. You may write the account numbers as posting references directly in your book unless directed otherwise by your instructor.

3. Compute the balance in each account after posting. Prepare Urban Skateboard's trial balance at October 31, 2006.

Date	Accounts and Explanation	Post Ref.	Debit	Credit
Oct. 2	Cash		36,000	
	Tim Leggett, Capital			36,000
5	Cash		30,000	
	Notes Payable...................................			30,000
9	Supplies...		540	
	Accounts Payable.............................			540
11	Accounts Receivable.........................		16,200	
	Sales Revenue...................................			16,200
14	Rent Expense		4,000	
	Cash			4,000
22	Cash		2,800	
	Accounts Receivable.........................			2,800
25	Advertising Expense		700	
	Cash..			700
27	Accounts Payable.............................		540	
	Cash			540
31	Utilities Expense		640	
	Accounts Payable.............................			640

Exercise 2-8   *Journalizing transactions*   **(Obj. 3)**

The first five transactions of Dale Carter Hockey School have been posted to the company's accounts as shown below:

Cash				Supplies		Hockey Equipment	
(1)	75,000	(3)	52,500	(2) 750		(5) 7,500	
(4)	13,750	(5)	7,500				

Land		Accounts Payable		Note Payable	
(3)	52,500		(2) 750		(4) 13,750

D. Carter, Capital

	(1) 75,000

Required

Prepare the journal entries that served as the sources for posting the five transactions. Date each entry April 30, 2005, and include an explanation for each entry as illustrated in the chapter.

Exercise 2-9   *Preparing a trial balance*   **(Obj. 5)**

Prepare the trial balance of Dale Carter Hockey School at April 30, 2005, using the account data from Exercise 2-8.

Exercise 2-10   *Preparing a trial balance*   **(Obj. 5)**

Media Companion CD-ROM

The accounts of Pervitz Consulting are listed on page 90 with their normal balances at October 31, 2005. The accounts are listed in no particular order.

Required

Prepare the company's trial balance at October 31, 2005, listing accounts in the sequence illustrated in the chapter. Supplies comes before Building and Land. List the expenses alphabetically.

Account	Balance
J. Pervitz, Capital	$29,280
Advertising expense	990
Accounts payable	3,180
Services revenue	16,200
Land	17,400
Notes payable	27,000
Cash	3,000
Salary expense	3,600
Building	39,000
Computer rental expense	4,200
J. Pervitz, withdrawals	3,600
Utilities expense	240
Accounts receivable	3,300
Supplies expense	180
Supplies	150

Exercise 2-11   *Correcting errors in a trial balance*   *(Obj. 5)*

The trial balance of Century Travel at February 28, 2006, does not balance.

Cash	$ 8,400	
Accounts receivable	5,800	
Supplies	1,200	
Land	132,000	
Accounts payable		$ 46,000
D. Tudin, capital		83,200
Service revenue		21,400
Rent expense	1,600	
Salary expense	3,600	
Utilities expense	600	
Total	$153,200	$150,600

Investigation of the accounting records reveals that the bookkeeper

a. Recorded a $800 cash revenue transaction by debiting Accounts Receivable. The credit entry was correct.

b. Posted a $2,000 credit to Accounts Payable as $200.

c. Did not record utilities expense or the related account payable in the amount of $400.

d. Understated D. Tudin, Capital by $800.

Required

Prepare the correct trial balance at February 28, 2006, complete with a heading. Journal entries are not required.

Exercise 2-12   *Recording transactions without a journal*   *(Obj. 7)*

Open the following T-accounts for Yoon Strategic Consulting at May 1, 2005: Cash; Accounts Receivable; Office Supplies; Office Furniture; Accounts Payable; Florence Yoon, Capital; Florence Yoon, Withdrawals; Consulting Revenue; Rent Expense; Salary Expense.

Record the following May transactions directly in the T-accounts of the business without using a journal. Use the letters to identify the transactions.

a. Florence Yoon opened a strategic consulting firm by investing $24,800 cash and office furniture valued at $10,800.

b. Paid monthly rent of $3,000.

c. Purchased office supplies on account, $1,200.

d. Paid employee salary, $2,000.

e. Paid $800 of the account payable credited in c.

f. Performed consulting service on account, $46,000.

g. Withdrew $4,000 for personal use.

Exercise 2-13   *Preparing a trial balance*   *(Obj. 5)*

After recording the transactions in Exercise 2-12, prepare the trial balance of Yoon Strategic Consulting at May 31, 2005.

Exercise 2-14   *Analyzing transactions without a journal*   *(Obj. 7)*

Sobey Nursing Services began when Nancy Sobey deposited $67,500 cash in the business bank account. During the first week, the business purchased supplies on credit for $7,500 and paid $12,000 cash for equipment. Sobey Nursing Services later paid $4,500 on account.

Required

1. Open the following T-accounts: Cash; Supplies; Equipment; Accounts Payable; N. Sobey, Capital.

2. Record the transactions described above directly in the T-accounts without using a journal.

3. Compute the balance in each account. Show that total debits equal total credits after you have recorded all the transactions.

Serial Exercise

Exercise 2-15 begins an accounting cycle that is completed in Chapter 5.

Exercise 2-15   *Recording transactions and preparing a trial balance*   *(Obj. 2, 3, 4, 5)*

Melanie Clark Engineers completed these transactions during early December 2005:

Dec. 2 Received $28,000 cash from Melanie Clark. The business gave owner's equity in the business to Clark.
  2 Paid monthly office rent, $1,000.
  3 Paid cash for a Dell computer, $6,000. The computer is expected to remain in service for five years.
  4 Purchased office furniture on account, $11,200. The furniture should last for five years.
  5 Purchased supplies on account, $600.
  9 Performed consulting services for a client and received cash for the full amount of $2,000.
  12 Paid utility expenses, $400.
  18 Performed consulting services for a client on account, $3,400.

Required

1. Open T-accounts in the ledger: Cash; Accounts Receivable; Supplies; Equipment; Furniture; Accounts Payable; Melanie Clark, Capital; Melanie Clark, Withdrawals; Service Revenue; Rent Expense; Salaries Expense; and Utilities Expense. (Some of these T-accounts will be used in later chapters.)

2. Journalize the transactions. Explanations are not required.

3. Post to the T-accounts. Key all items by date, and denote an account balance as *Bal*. Formal posting references are not required.

4. Prepare a trial balance at December 18, 2005. In the Serial Exercise of Chapter 3, we will add transactions for the remainder of December and will require a trial balance at December 31, 2005.

Challenge Exercises

Exercise 2-16   *Computing financial statement amounts without a journal*   (Obj. 7)

The owner of Wilkinson Technical Services is an architect with little understanding of accounting. She needs to compute the following summary information from the accounting records:

a. Net income for the month of March

b. Total cash paid during March

c. Cash collections from customers during March

d. Cash paid on a note payable during March

The quickest way to compute these amounts is to analyze the following accounts:

		Balance		Additional Information for the Month of March
Account		Feb. 28	Mar. 31	
a. B. Wilkinson, Capital		$14,400	$24,000	Withdrawals, $6,400
b. Cash.......................................		8,000	6,400	Cash receipts, $107,200
c. Accounts Receivable		38,400	41,600	Sales on account, $101,600
d. Notes Payable		20,800	25,600	New note borrowing, $10,080

The net income for March can be computed as follows:

B. Wilkinson, Capital

March Withdrawals	6,400	Feb. 28 Bal.	14,400
		March Net Income	x = $16,000
		March 31 Bal.	24,000

Use a similar approach to compute the other three items of summary information the shareholder needs.

Exercise 2-17   *Analyzing accounting errors*   (Obj. 2, 3, 4, 5)

Carol has trouble keeping her debits and credits equal. During a recent month she made the following errors:

a. In journalizing a cash receipt, Carol debited Cash for $1,000 instead of the correct amount of $1,900. She credited Service Revenue for $1,000, the incorrect amount.

b. Carol posted a $700 utility expense as $70. The credit posting to Cash was the correct amount of $700.

c. In preparing the trial balance, Carol omitted an $8,000 note payable.

d. Carol recorded a $120 purchase of supplies on account by debiting Supplies and crediting Accounts Payable for $210.

e. In recording a $700 payment on account, Carol debited Supplies and credited Accounts Payable.

Required

1. For each of these errors, state whether the total debits equal total credits on the trial balance.

2. Identify any accounts with misstated balances, and indicate the amount and direction of the error (account balance too high or too low).

Beyond the Numbers

Beyond the Numbers 2-1

Jim Gallacher asks your advice in setting up the accounting records for his new business, Jim's Photo Shoppe. The business will be a photography studio and will operate in a rented building. Jim's Photo Shoppe will need office equipment and cameras. The business will borrow money on notes payable to buy the needed equipment. Jim's Photo Shoppe will purchase on account photographic supplies and office supplies. Each asset has a related expense account, some of which have not yet been discussed. For example, equipment wears out (amortizes) and thus needs an amortization account. As supplies are used up, the business must record a supplies expense.

The business will need an office manager. This person will be paid a weekly salary of $1,800. Other expenses will include advertising and insurance. Since Jim's Photo Shoppe will want to know which aspects of the business generate the most and the least revenue, it will use separate service revenue accounts for portraits, school pictures, and weddings. Jim's Photo Shoppe's better customers will be allowed to open accounts receivable with the business.

Required

List all the accounts Jim's Photo Shoppe will need, starting with the assets and ending with the expenses. Indicate which accounts will be reported on the balance sheet and which accounts will appear on the income statement.

Ethical Issue

Associated Charities Inc., a charitable organization in Brandon, Manitoba, has a standing agreement with Prairie Trust. The agreement allows Associated Charities Inc. to overdraw its cash balance at the bank when donations are running low. In the past, Associated Charities Inc. managed funds wisely and rarely used this privilege. Greg Osadchuk has recently become the president of Associated Charities Inc. To expand operations, Osadchuk is acquiring office equipment and spending large amounts for fund-raising. During his presidency, Associated Charities Inc. has maintained a negative bank balance (a credit Cash balance) of approximately $14,000.

Required

What is the ethical issue in this situation? State why you approve or disapprove of Osadchuk's management of Associated Charities Inc.'s funds.

Problems (Group A)

Problem 2-1A   *Analyzing a trial balance*   *(Obj. 1)*

Link Back to Chapter 1 (Balance Sheet, Income Statement). Joan Stinson, the owner of Stinson Designs, is selling the business. She offers the trial balance on page 94 to prospective buyers.

Your best friend is considering buying Stinson Designs. She seeks your advice in interpreting this information. Specifically, she asks whether this trial balance is the same as a balance sheet and an income statement. She also wonders whether Stinson Designs is a sound company. She thinks it must be because the accounts are in balance.

Required

Write a short note to answer your friend's questions. To aid her decision, state how she can use the information on the trial balance to compute the Stinson Designs net income or net loss for the current period. State the amount of net income or net loss in your note.

STINSON DESIGNS
Trial Balance
December 31, 2006

Cash	$ 26,000	
Accounts receivable	30,000	
Prepaid expenses	4,000	
Land for future expansion	68,000	
Accounts payable		$ 62,000
Note payable		44,000
Joan Stinson, Capital		66,000
Joan Stinson, Withdrawals	30,000	
Service revenue		140,000
Advertising expense	16,000	
Rent expense	24,000	
Supplies expense	18,000	
Wage expense	96,000	
Total	$312,000	$312,000

Problem 2-2A *Analyzing and journalizing transactions* *(Obj. 2, 3)*

Angela Chong practises civil engineering under the business title Angela Chong Consulting. During April 2006 the company engaged in the following transactions:

Apr. 1   Chong deposited $21,000 cash in the business bank account. The business gave Chong owner's equity in the business.

5   Paid monthly rent on drafting equipment, $420.

9   Paid $13,200 cash to purchase land for an office site.

10   Purchased supplies on account, $900.

19   Paid $600 on account for supplies purchased on April 10.

22   Borrowed $12,000 from the bank for business use. Chong signed a note payable to the bank in the name of the business.

30   Revenues earned during the month included $3,600 cash and $4,200 on account.

30   Paid employee salaries of $1,440, office rent of $960, and utilities of $240.

30   Angela Chong withdrew $2,400 from the business for personal use.

Angela Chong Consulting uses the following accounts: Cash; Accounts Receivable; Supplies; Land; Accounts Payable; Notes Payable; A. Chong, Capital; A. Chong, Withdrawals; Service Revenue; Rent Expense; Salary Expense; Utilities Expense.

Required

1. Prepare an analysis of each business transaction of Angela Chong Consulting, as shown for the April 1 transaction:

Apr. 1   The asset cash is increased. Increases in assets are recorded by debits; therefore, debit Cash. The owner's equity is increased. Increases in owner's equity are recorded by credits; therefore, credit A. Chong, Capital.

2. Record each transaction in the journal, using the account titles given. Key each transaction by date. Explanations are not required.

Problem 2-3A *Journalizing transactions, posting to T-accounts, and preparing a trial balance* *(Obj. 2, 3, 4, 5)*

Ken Gilmour opened a translation business on January 2, 2005. During the first month of operations, the business completed the following transactions:

Jan. 2   The business received $60,000 cash from Ken Gilmour, which was deposited in a business bank account entitled Gilmour Translation Service.

3   Purchased supplies, $750, and furniture, $6,300, on account.

Jan. 3 Paid January rent expense, $1,350.
4 Performed translation services for a client and received cash, $2,250.
7 Paid $33,000 cash to acquire land for a future office site.
11 Translated a brochure for a client and billed the client $1,200.
15 Paid secretary salary, $975.
16 Paid for the furniture purchased January 3 on account.
18 Received partial payment from client on account, $600.
19 Translated legal documents for a client on account, $1,350.
22 Paid the water and electricity bills, $345.
29 Received $2,700 cash for translation for a client in an overseas business transaction.
31 Paid secretary salary, $975.
31 Ken Gilmour withdrew $2,250 for personal use.

Required

Open the following T-accounts: Cash; Accounts Receivable; Supplies; Furniture; Land; Accounts Payable; Ken Gilmour, Capital; Ken Gilmour, Withdrawals; Translation Revenue; Rent Expense; Salary Expense; Utilities Expense.

1. Record each transaction in the journal, using the account titles given. Key each transaction by date. Explanations are not required.

2. Post the transactions to the ledger using T-accounts, using transaction dates in the ledger. Label the balance of each account *Bal.* as shown in the chapter.

3. Prepare the trial balance of Gilmour Translation Service at January 31, 2005.

4. How will what you have learned in this problem help you manage a business?

Problem 2-4A *Journalizing transactions, posting to ledger accounts, and preparing a trial balance* **(Obj. 2, 3, 4, 5)**

The trial balance of the desktop publishing business of Tim Comrie at November 15, 2006, is shown below.

TIM COMRIE PUBLISHING
Trial Balance
November 15, 2006

Account Number	Account	Debit	Credit
1100	Cash..	$ 6,000	
1200	Accounts receivable	16,000	
1300	Supplies..	1,200	
1900	Land..	70,000	
2100	Accounts payable		$ 9,200
4000	T. Comrie, Capital................................		80,000
4100	T. Comrie, Withdrawals...........................	4,600	
5000	Service revenue...................................		14,200
6000	Rent expense	2,000	
6100	Salary expense....................................	3,600	
	Total...	$103,400	$103,400

During the remainder of November, the business completed the following transactions:

Nov. 16 Collected $8,000 cash from a client on account.
17 Performed publishing services for a client on account, $4,200.
21 Paid on account, $5,200.
22 Purchased supplies on account, $1,200.
23 Tim Comrie withdrew $4,200 for personal use.

Nov. 24 Was advised that Desk Top Inc. was prepared to buy all of Tim Comrie Publishing for $120,000.

26 Received $3,800 cash for design work just completed.

30 Paid employees' salaries, $4,800.

Required

1. Record the transactions that occurred during November 16 through 30 in *Page 6* of the journal. Include an explanation for each entry.

2. Post the transactions to the ledger, using dates, account numbers, journal references and posting references. Open the ledger accounts listed in the trial balance together with their balances at November 15. Use the three-column account format illustrated in the chapter. Enter *Bal.* (for previous balance) in the Item column, and place a check mark (✓) in the journal reference column for the November 15 balance of each account.

3. Prepare the trial balance of Tim Comrie Publishing at November 30, 2006.

Problem 2-5A *Correcting errors in a trial balance* *(Obj. 2, 5)*

Link Back to Chapter 1 (Income Statement). The trial balance for Sackville Copy Centre, shown below, does not balance. The following errors were detected:

a. The cash balance is overstated by $600.

b. Rent expense of $300 was posted as a credit rather than a debit.

c. The balance of Advertising Expense is $450, but it is listed as $600 on the trial balance.

d. A $900 debit to Accounts Receivable was posted as $90.

e. The balance of Utilities Expense is understated by $90.

f. A $1,950 debit to the S. Fawcett, Withdrawals account was posted as a debit to S. Fawcett, Capital.

g. A $150 purchase of supplies on account was neither journalized nor posted.

h. A $8,700 credit to Service Revenue was not posted.

i. Office furniture should be listed in the amount of $1,950.

SACKVILLE COPY CENTRE
Trial Balance
October 31, 2005

Cash	$ 5,700	
Accounts receivable	3,000	
Supplies	750	
Office furniture	3,450	
Land	69,000	
Accounts payable		$ 3,000
Notes payable		27,450
S. Fawcett, Capital		44,250
S. Fawcett, Withdrawals	5,550	
Service revenue		7,350
Salary expense	2,250	
Rent expense	900	
Advertising expense	600	
Utilities expense	300	
Total	$91,500	$82,050

Required

1. Prepare the correct trial balance at October 31, 2005. Journal entries are not required.

2. Prepare Sackville Copy Centre's income statement for the month ended October 31, 2005. Determine the company's net income or net loss for the month. Refer to Exhibit 1-8, page 22 if necessary.

Problem 2-6A   *Recording transactions directly in the ledger; preparing a trial balance*
(Obj. 2, 5, 7)

Dennis Huang started a catering service called Huang Catering in the province of Nova Scotia. During the first month of operations, January 2005, the business completed the following selected transactions:

a. Huang began the company with an investment of $30,000 cash and a van (automobile) valued at $26,000. The business gave Huang owner's equity in the business.

b. Borrowed $50,000 from the bank; signed a note payable.

c. Paid $6,000 for food service equipment.

d. Purchased supplies on account, $4,800.

e. Paid employee salary, $2,600.

f. Received $4,000 for a catering job.

g. Performed services at a wedding on account, $6,600.

h. Paid $2,000 of the account payable created in transaction d.

i. Received a $1,600 bill for advertising expense that will be paid in the near future.

j. Received cash on account, $2,200.

k. Paid the following cash expenses:

(1) Rent, $2,000.

(2) Insurance, $1,600.

l. Huang withdrew $2,000 for personal use.

Required

1. Open the following T-accounts: Cash; Accounts Receivable; Supplies; Food Service Equipment; Automobile; Accounts Payable; Notes Payable; D. Huang, Capital; D. Huang, Withdrawals; Service Revenue; Advertising Expense; Insurance Expense; Rent Expense; Salary Expense.

2. Record the transactions directly in the T-accounts without using a journal. Use the letters to identify the transactions.

3. Prepare the trial balance of Huang Catering at January 31, 2005.

Problem 2-7A   *Preparing the financial statements (Obj. 5)*

Link Back to Chapter 1 (Income Statement, Statement of Owner's Equity, Balance Sheet). Refer to Problem 2-6A. After completing the trial balance in Problem 2-6A, prepare the following financial statements for Huang Catering.

1. Income statement for the month ended January 31, 2005.

2. Statement of owner's equity for the month ended January 31, 2005.

3. Balance sheet at January 31, 2005.

Draw arrows linking the financial statements. If needed, use Exhibit 1-8, page 22, as a guide for preparing the financial statements.

Problem 2-8A   *Applying the rules of debit and credit, recording transactions in the journal*
(Obj. 2, 3)

Ryan Kessler operates a heavy equipment transport company, Kessler Transport. The company had the following transactions for the month of August 2005:

Aug.   1   Kessler Transport received $30,000 cash and a truck and trailer from Kessler. The truck had originally cost Kessler $300,000, but had a fair market value of $230,000 on August 1. The trailer had a fair market value of $30,000.

3   Purchased a new trailer by paying $16,000 cash and promising to pay another $60,000 in one week. The trailer had a list price of $94,000 and Kessler knew it was worth at least $86,000.

4   Paid parking space rental fees of $800 for the month of August. These fees covered three spaces—two for the trailers and one for the truck.

5   Hired an assistant at a rate of $750 per week.

9   Transported equipment for clients for $3,200. They paid $1,600 and promised to pay the balance in 30 days.

10   Paid $12,000 of the amount owing on the trailer purchase on August 3. Signed a promissory note for the balance, as the company was unable to pay the full amount that day.

20   Received $1,600 from the clients of August 9 as payment on the haulage.

26   Paid the assistant for three weeks' work.

29   Billed a client $7,500 for hauling equipment from Prince Albert to Saskatoon. The client, who was the owner of a service station, paid the bill by providing the company with $7,500 of repair parts that can be used on the truck.

30   Used $600 of repair parts on the truck.

Required

Record each transaction in the journal. Key each transaction by date. Explanations are not required.

Problem 2-9A   *Applying the rules of debit and credit, and recording transactions (Obj. 2, 3)*

Eagle Resort, owned by Trevor Kennedy, had the following account balances, in random order, on December 15, 2005 (all accounts have their "normal" balances):

Guest revenue	$209,000	Furniture	$57,800
Accounts receivable	8,800	Cash	3,800
Equipment rental expense	11,800	Notes receivable	26,000
T. Kennedy, Capital	93,800	Utilities expense	1,000
Supplies expense	2,800	Supplies inventory	5,800
Mortgage payable	30,000	Accounts payable	12,000
Salaries expense	81,000	Office equipment	10,200
Insurance expense	6,800	Boating equipment	96,800

The following events also took place during the final days of the year:

Dec.   16   The accountant discovered that an error had been made in posting an entry to the Guest Revenue account. The entry was correctly journalized but $4,200 was accidentally posted as $2,400 in the account.

17   Agreed to let a retired professor move in in the off season for a long stay, beginning today. The monthly rate is $3,200 payable in advance.

18   Collected a $12,000 note owed to Eagle Resort and collected interest of $1,200.

21   Purchased boating equipment for $14,000 from Boats Unlimited. Eagle Resort paid $3,000, provided room rentals for $1,600 to Boats Unlimited, and promised to pay the balance in 60 days.

23   Collected $2,400 for rooms for a conference held from December 16 to 23.

24   Eagle Resort paid $4,000 owing on the mortgage.

27   Trevor Kennedy withdrew $7,000 for personal use.

29   Provided meeting rooms to a lawyer for $2,000. The lawyer paid Eagle Resort $1,200 and provided legal work for the balance.

Required

Where appropriate, record each transaction from December 16 to 31 in the journal. Explanations are not required.

Problems (Group B)

Problem 2-1B *Analyzing a trial balance* *(Obj. 1)*

The owner of Olerud Communications, Nancy Olerud, is selling the business. She offers the trial balance shown below to prospective buyers.

Your best friend is considering buying Olerud Communications. He seeks your advice in interpreting this information. Specifically, he asks whether this trial balance is the same as a balance sheet and an income statement. He also wonders whether Olerud Communications is a sound company because all the accounts are in balance.

Required

Write a short note to answer your friend's questions. To aid his decision, state how he can use the information on the trial balance to compute Olerud Communications' net income or net loss for the current period. State the amount of net income or net loss in your note.

OLERUD COMMUNICATIONS
Trial Balance
December 31, 2006

Cash..	$ 18,000	
Accounts receivable	40,500	
Prepaid expenses...	6,000	
Land for future expansion	114,000	
Accounts payable...		$ 52,500
Note payable...		48,000
N. Olerud, Capital...		45,000
N. Olerud, Withdrawals....................................	72,000	
Sales revenue		201,000
Advertising expense...	4,500	
Rent expense...	39,000	
Supplies expense..	10,500	
Wage expense	42,000	
Totals...	$346,500	$346,500

Problem 2-2B *Analyzing and journalizing transactions* *(Obj. 2, 3)*

Westbank Theatres owns movie theatres in the shopping centres of a major metropolitan area. The business engaged in the following transactions in 2005:

Feb.	1	Received cash of $200,000 from the owner Tony Fonesca.
	1	Paid February rent on a theatre building, $4,000.
	2	Paid $100,000 cash to purchase land for a theatre site.
	5	Borrowed $440,000 from the bank to finance the first phase of construction of the new theatre. The business signed a note payable to the bank.
	7	Received $40,000 cash from ticket sales and deposited this amount in the bank. (Label the revenue as Sales Revenue.)
	10	Purchased theatre supplies on account, $3,400.
	15	Paid theatre employee salaries, $5,600.
	15	Paid property tax expense on a theatre building, $3,200.
	16	Paid $1,600 on account.
	17	The owner withdrew $13,000 for personal expenses.

Westbank Theatres uses the following accounts: Cash; Supplies; Land; Accounts Payable; Notes Payable; Tony Fonesca, Capital; Tony Fonesca, Withdrawals; Sales Revenue; Property Tax Expense; Rent Expense; Salary Expense.

Required

1. Prepare an analysis of each business transaction of Westbank Theatres as shown for the February 1 transaction:

    Feb. 1   The asset Cash is increased. Increases in assets are recorded by debits; therefore, debit Cash. The owner's equity of the entity is increased. Increases in owner's equity are recorded by credits; therefore, credit Tony Fonesca, Capital.

2. Record each transaction in the journal, using the account titles given. Key each transaction by date. Explanations are not required.

Problem 2-3B   *Journalizing transactions, posting to T-accounts, and preparing a trial balance   (Obj. 2, 3, 4, 5)*

Helen Boone opened a renovation business called Boone Renovations on September 3, 2006. During the first month of operations, the business completed the following transactions:

Sept.	3	Helen Boone deposited her cheque for $61,250 into the business bank account to start the business.
	4	Purchased supplies, $350, and furniture, $3,150, on account.
	5	Paid September rent expense, $875.
	6	Performed design services for a client and received $7,000 cash.
	7	Paid $26,250 cash to acquire land for a future office site.
	10	Designed a bathroom for a client, billed the client, and received her promise to pay the $1,750 within one week.
	14	Paid for the furniture purchased September 4 on account.
	15	Paid assistant's salary, $1,050.
	17	Received partial payment from client on account, $875.
	20	Prepared a recreation room design for a client on account, $3,150.
	28	Received $2,625 cash from a client for renovation of a cottage.
	30	Paid assistant's salary, $1,050.
	30	H. Boone withdrew $4,200 for personal use.

Required

Open the following T-accounts: Cash; Accounts Receivable; Supplies; Furniture; Land; Accounts Payable; H. Boone, Capital; H. Boone, Withdrawals; Service Revenue; Rent Expense; Salary Expense.

1. Record each transaction in the journal, using the account titles given. Key each transaction by date. Explanations are not required.

2. Post the transactions to the T-accounts, using transaction dates as posting references in the T-accounts. Label the balance of each account *Bal.*, as shown in the chapter.

3. Prepare the trial balance of Boone Renovations at September 30, 2006.

Problem 2-4B   *Journalizing transactions, posting to ledger accounts, and preparing a trial balance   (Obj. 2, 3, 4, 5)*

The trial balance of Sanchez Designs (see page 101) is dated February 14, 2006. During the remainder of February, Sanchez Designs completed the following transactions:

Feb.	15	Collected $6,000 cash from a client on account.
	16	Designed a system for a client on account, $5,800.
	20	Paid for items purchased on account, $3,200.
	21	Purchased supplies on account, $200.
	21	R. Sanchez withdrew $2,000 for personal use.
	21	Received a verbal promise of a $20,000 contract.
	22	Received cash of $6,200 for consulting work just completed.
	28	Paid employees' salaries, $3,200.

SANCHEZ DESIGNS
Trial Balance
February 14, 2006

Account Number	Account	Debit	Credit
1100	Cash..	$ 4,000	
1200	Accounts receivable	16,000	
1300	Supplies	1,600	
1600	Automobile	37,200	
2000	Accounts payable		$ 6,000
3000	R. Sanchez, Capital		50,000
3100	R. Sanchez, Withdrawals...............	2,400	
5000	Service revenue............................		14,400
6100	Rent expense	2,000	
6200	Salary expense	7,200	
	Total..	$70,400	$70,400

Required

1. Record the transactions that occurred during February 15 through 28 in *Page 3* of the journal. Include an explanation for each entry.

2. Open the ledger accounts listed in the trial balance, together with their balances at February 14. Use the three-column account format illustrated in the chapter. Enter *Bal.* (for previous balance) in the Item column, and place a check mark (✓) in the journal reference column for the February 14 balance in each account.

   Post the transactions to the ledger, using dates, account numbers, journal references, and posting references.

3. Prepare the trial balance of Sanchez Designs at February 28, 2006.

Problem 2-5B *Correcting errors in a trial balance* **(Obj. 2, 5)**

Link Back to Chapter 1 (Income Statement). The following trial balance does not balance:

RHODES LANDSCAPE CONSULTING
Trial Balance
June 30, 2005

Account	Debit	Credit
Cash..	$ 1,000	
Accounts receivable	5,000	
Supplies	450	
Office furniture....................................	1,800	
Land for future expansion	23,500	
Accounts payable.................................		$ 1,900
Notes payable		11,500
A. Rhodes, Capital		15,800
A. Rhodes, Withdrawals	1,000	
Consulting service revenue		3,250
Advertising expense..............................	250	
Rent expense..	500	
Salary expense	1,050	
Utilities expense	200	
Total..	$34,750	$32,450

The following errors were detected:

a. The cash balance is understated by $450.

b. The cost of the land was $22,300, not $23,500.

c. A $200 purchase of supplies on account was neither journalized nor posted.

d. A $1,900 credit to Consulting Service Revenue was not posted.

e. Rent Expense of $100 was posted as a credit rather than a debit.

f. The balance of Advertising Expense is $300, but it was listed as $250 on the trial balance.

g. A $150 debit to Accounts Receivable was posted as $15. The credit to Consulting Service Revenue was correct.

h. The balance of Utilities Expense is overstated by $35.

i. A $450 debit to the A. Rhodes, Withdrawals account was posted as a debit to A. Rhodes, Capital.

Required

1. Prepare the correct trial balance at June 30, 2005. Journal entries are not required.

2. Prepare the company's income statement for the month ended June 30, 2005. Use it to determine the Rhodes Landscape Consulting net income or net loss for the month.

Problem 2-6B *Recording transactions directly in the ledger; preparing a trial balance (Obj. 2, 5, 7)*

Carole Thibault started an investment counselling business, Thibault Consulting, in Montreal on June 1, 2006. During the first month of operations, the business completed the following selected transactions:

a. Thibault began the business with an investment of $40,000 cash, land valued at $40,000, and a building valued at $80,000. The business gave Thibault owner's equity in the business for the value of the cash, land, and building.

b. Thibault Consulting borrowed $60,000 from the bank; signed a note payable.

c. Purchased office supplies on account, $2,600.

d. Paid $36,000 for office furniture.

e. Paid employee salary, $4,400.

f. Performed consulting service on account for client, $10,200.

g. Paid $1,600 of the account payable created in transaction c.

h. Received a $4,000 bill for advertising expense that will be paid in the near future.

i. Performed consulting services for customers and received cash, $11,200.

j. Received cash on account, $2,400.

k. Paid the following cash expenses:
   (1) Rent of photocopier, $1,400.
   (2) Utilities, $800.

l. Carole Thibault withdrew $5,000 for personal use.

Required

1. Open the following T-accounts: Cash; Accounts Receivable; Office Supplies; Office Furniture; Land; Building; Accounts Payable; Notes Payable; Carole Thibault, Capital; Carole Thibault, Withdrawals; Service Revenue; Advertising Expense; Equipment Rental Expense; Salary Expense; Utilities Expense.

2. Record each transaction directly in the T-accounts without using a journal. Use the letters to identify the transactions.

3. Prepare the trial balance of Thibault Consulting at June 30, 2006.

Problem 2-7B   *Preparing the financial statements*   *(Obj. 5)*

Link Back to Chapter 1 (Income Statement, Statement of Owner's Equity, Balance Sheet).
Refer to Problem 2-6B. After completing the trial balance in Problem 2-6B, prepare
the following financial statements for Thibault Consulting:

1. Income statement for the month ended June 30, 2006.

2. Statement of owner's equity for the month ended June 30, 2006.

3. Balance sheet at June 30, 2006.

Draw arrows linking the financial statements. If needed, use Exhibit 1-8, page 22, as
a guide for preparing the financial statements.

Problem 2-8B   *Applying the rules of debit and credit, and recording transactions in the journal*   *(Obj. 2, 3)*

Ken Suzuki operated a fishing charter business, Pacific Charters. The business had
the following transactions in September 2005:

Sept. 1   Suzuki invested $30,000 cash and his 10-metre power boat in the charter busi-
ness. The business gave Suzuki owner's equity in the business. The boat had originally cost him $120,000, but had a fair market value of $75,000 on September 1,
2005.

3   Purchased a new boat by paying $21,000 cash and promising to pay another
$42,000 in one week. Suzuki felt that this was an excellent bargain as the boat had
a catalogue price of $90,000 and he knew it was worth at least $75,000.

4   Paid moorage fees of $4,200 for the month of September. These fees covered two
moorage slips—one for each charter boat.

5   Hired a deckhand at a rate of $1,200 per week.

9   Took clients out on a charter for $3,900. They paid $1,800 and promised to pay
the balance in 30 days.

10   Paid $3,000 of the amount owing on the boat purchased on September 3. Signed
a promissory note for the balance, as the company was unable to pay the full
amount that day.

15   Purchased $15,000 of equipment from a supplier. To pay for the equipment, Pacific
Charters took the supplier and her employees out on a day charter and also paid
the supplier $9,000 cash.

20   Received $900 from the clients of September 9 as payment on the charter.

26   Paid the deckhand for three weeks' work.

29   A client chartered the two boats for two days for $12,000. In payment, the client,
the owner of a service station, provided Pacific Charters with $6,000 of repair
parts that can be used on the boats, and cash.

30   Used $1,200 of repair parts on each of the two boats.

Required
Record each transaction in the journal. Key each transaction by date. Explanations
are not required.

Problem 2-9B   *Applying the rules of debit and credit, and recording transactions*   *(Obj. 2, 3)*

Portage Movers had the following account balances, in random order, on
December 15, 2005 (all accounts have their "normal" balances):

Moving fees earned	$130,800	Cash	$ 3,600
Accounts receivable	8,700	Storage fees earned	28,950
Rent expense	23,550	Notes receivable	22,500
H. Martinez, Capital	75,000	Utilities expense	1,200
Office supplies expense	1,050	Office supplies	4,800
Mortgage payable	19,500	Accounts payable	16,500
Salaries expense	80,550	Office equipment	6,150
Insurance expense	3,150	Moving equipment	116,100

The following events took place during the final days of the year:

Dec. 16 The accountant discovered that an error had been made in posting an entry to the Moving Fees Earned account. The entry was correctly journalized but $1,200 was accidentally posted as $2,100 in the account.

17 Moved a customer's goods to Portage's rented warehouse for storage. The moving fees were $1,500. Storage fees are $300 per month. The customer was billed for one month's storage.

18 Collected a $7,500 note owed to Portage Movers and collected interest of $900.

21 Purchased storage racks for $6,000. Paid $1,800, provided moving services for $750, and promised to pay the balance in 60 days.

23 Collected $1,500; $1,050 of this was for moving goods on December 15 (recorded as an accounts receivable at that time) and the balance was for storage fees for the period of December 16 to 23.

24 Portage Movers paid $9,000 owing on the mortgage.

27 Henry Martinez withdrew $3,000 for personal use.

29 Provided moving services to a lawyer for $1,200. The lawyer paid Portage Movers $750 and provided legal work for the balance.

31 Henry Martinez, the owner of Portage Movers, sold 1,000 shares he held in Brandon Haulage Inc. for $6,000.

Required

Where appropriate, record each transaction from December 16 to 31 in the journal. Explanations are not required.

Challenge Problems

Problem 2-1C   *Understanding the rules of debit and credit*   *(Obj. 2)*

Some individuals, for whatever reason, do not pay income tax or pay less than they should. Often their business transactions are cash transactions, so there is no paper trail to prove how much or how little they actually earned. Canada Customs and Revenue Agency, however, has a way of dealing with these individuals; they use a model (based on the accounting equation), to calculate how much the individual must have earned.

Canada Customs and Revenue Agency is about to audit Donna Wynn for the period January 1, 2004, to December 31, 2004. Donna buys and sells used cars for cash; the purchaser is responsible for having the car certified so it can be licensed and insured. Donna had $4,000 cash, and no other assets or liabilities at January 1, 2004.

Required

1. Use the accounting equation to explain how the Canada Customs and Revenue Agency model will be used to audit Donna.

2. What do you think are the accounting concepts underlying the model?

Problem 2-2C   *Using a formal accounting system. (Obj. 3, 4, 6)*

Over the years you have become friendly with a farmer, Jack Russell, who raises crops, which he sells, and has small herds of beef cattle and sheep. Jack maintains his basic herds and markets the calves and lambs each fall. His accounting system is quite simple; all his transactions are in cash. Jack pays tax each year on his income, which he estimates. He indicated to you once that he must be doing it right because Canada Customs and Revenue Agency audited him recently and assessed no additional tax.

You are taking your first accounting course and are quite impressed with the information one can gain from a formal accounting system.

Required

Explain to Jack Russell why it would be to his advantage to have a more formal accounting system with accounts, ledgers, and journals.

Extending Your Knowledge

Decision Problems

1. Recording transactions directly in the ledger, preparing a trial balance, and measuring net income or loss   (Obj. 2, 5, 7)

Your friend, Amin Akmali, has asked your advice about the effects that certain business transactions will have on his business. His business, Car Finders, finds the best deals on automobiles for clients. Time is short, so you cannot journalize transactions. Instead, you must analyze the transactions without the use of a journal. Akmali will continue in the business only if he can expect to earn monthly net income of $8,000. The business had the following transactions during March 2005:

a. Akmali deposited $20,000 cash in a business bank account.

b. The business borrowed $8,000 cash from the bank and issued a note payable due within one year.

c. Paid $600 cash for supplies.

d. Paid cash for advertising in the local newspaper, $1,200.

e. Paid the following cash expenses for one month: secretary (part-time) salary, $2,400; office rent, $800; utilities, $600; interest, $200.

f. Earned revenue on account, $10,600.

g. Earned $5,000 revenue and received cash.

h. Collected cash from customers on account, $2,400.

Required

1. Open the following T-accounts: Cash; Accounts Receivable; Supplies; Notes Payable; Amin Akmali, Capital; Service Revenue; Advertising Expense; Interest Expense; Rent Expense; Salary Expense; Utilities Expense.

2. Record the transactions directly in the T- accounts without using a journal. Key each transaction by letter.

3. Prepare a trial balance at March 31, 2005. List expenses alphabetically.

4. Compute the amount of net income or net loss for this first month of operations. Would you recommend Akmali continue in business?

2. Using the accounting equation   (Obj. 2)

Although all the following questions deal with the accounting equation, they are not related:

1. Explain the advantages of double-entry bookkeeping to a friend who is opening a used-book store.

2. When you deposit money in your bank account, the bank credits your account. Is the bank misusing the word *credit* in this context? Why does the bank use the term *credit* to refer to your deposit, and not *debit*?

3. Your friend asks, "When revenues increase assets and expenses decrease assets, why are revenues credits and expenses debits and not the other way around?" Explain to your friend why revenues are credits and expenses are debits.

Financial Statement Problem

Journalizing transactions   (Obj. 2, 3)

This problem helps to develop journalizing skill by using an actual company's account titles. Refer to the Intrawest Corporation financial statements (reported in

U.S. dollars) in Appendix A. Assume Intrawest completed the following selected transactions during November 2003:

Nov. 5 Earned ski and resort operations revenues on account, $6,000,000.
9 Borrowed $8,000,000 by signing a note payable (long-term other indebtedness).
12 Purchased ski and resort operations equipment on account, $9,000,000.
17 Paid $1,200,000, which represents payment of $1,000,000 on long-term debt plus interest expense of $200,000.
19 Earned resort revenues and immediately received cash of $500,000.
22 Collected the cash on account that was earned on November 5.
29 Received an electricity bill for $10,000 for Whistler and Blackcomb resorts, which will be paid in December. (This is a ski and resort operations expense.)
29 Paid half the account payable created on November 12.

Required

Journalize these transactions using the following account titles taken from the financial statements of Intrawest Corporation: Cash; Amounts Receivable; Ski and Resort Operations Assets; Amounts Payable; Long-Term Bank and Other Indebtedness; Ski and Resort Operations Revenue; Ski and Resort Operations Expenses; Interest. Explanations are not required.

CHAPTER

3

Measuring Business Income: The Adjusting Process

CHAPTER OBJECTIVES

After studying this chapter, you should be able to

1 Distinguish accrual-basis accounting from cash-basis accounting

2 Apply the revenue and matching principles

3 Make adjusting entries

4 Prepare an adjusted trial balance

5 Prepare the financial statements from the adjusted trial balance

A1 Account for a prepaid expense recorded initially as an expense

A2 Account for an unearned (deferred) revenue recorded initially as a revenue

 Media Companion CD-ROM

Visit the Media Companion CD-ROM that comes with this book for extra practice with the new material in Chapter 3.

WestJet Airlines Ltd. (www.westjet.com) is a Canadian success story. The company was started in 1996 by four Calgary entrepreneurs who saw an opportunity to provide low-fare air travel across western Canada. The company followed the format for success used by Southwest Airlines and Morris Air, two similar and successful operations. WestJet began with 220 employees and three aircraft. Its initial routes were solely in Western Canada, stretching from Vancouver to Winnipeg.

The airline industry in Canada changed significantly in 1999 when Canadian Airlines was acquired by Air Canada (www.aircanada.com). The merger provided WestJet with an opportunity to add routes to several Eastern-Canadian cities. Since that time, the company has continued to expand its operations and maintain its profitability. The *Toronto Star* recently reported that WestJet reported its 26th consecutive quarterly profit, with April–June 2003 earnings of $14.7 million, up 19.5% from the year before. Operating revenue rose by 25% to $205 million from $163.7 million. The second quarter profit, worth 19 cents per share, compared with year-earlier profit of $12.3 million, worth 16 cents per share.

In the article, Clive Beddoe, WestJet's president, CEO, and chairman, stated he was "thrilled" by the quarterly results, "achieved during one of the most challenging environments that our industry has experienced." He stated that WestJet expects to continue reducing costs as it adds more Boeing 737-700s to its fleet. It now has 21 of the latest 737s (half of its 42-plane fleet) and intends to add four more by year end while retiring two 200-series 737s.

Beddoe stated that, during the quarter, WestJet "truly became Canada's national low-fare airline with the launch of service to Gander and St. John's, Newfoundland. We now connect our nation's Atlantic and Pacific coasts through our network of 26 destinations."

Source: Based on Chris Sorensen, "WestJet Airlines Shares Soar on Big Profit Gain," *Toronto Star*, July 22, 2003, online at www.torontostar.ca, accessed on July 29, 2003.

WHAT do we mean when we say that WestJet earned $14.7 million in the

second quarter of the year ended December 31, 2003? The business earned net income, or profit, of $14.7 million in the quarter as reported on its income statement. WestJet's revenues consist of passenger revenue of $205 million. What are WestJet's expenses? They include advertising, salaries, costs of running the aircraft, administrative and other office costs, maintenance, and many others. WestJet operates in much the same way, except on a much larger scale, as EconoTravel, the travel business we studied in Chapters 1 and 2.

Whether the business is WestJet Airlines Ltd. or EconoTravel, the profit motive increases the owners' drive to carry on the business. As you study this chapter, consider how important net income is to a business.

At the end of each accounting period, the entity prepares its financial statements. The period may be a month, three months, six months, or a full year. WestJet is typical. The company reports on a quarterly basis—at the end of every three months—with audited financial statements at the end of its year.

Whatever the length of the period, the end accounting product is the set of financial statements. And the most important single amount in these statements is the net income or net loss—the profit or loss—for the period. Net income captures much information: total revenues minus total expenses for the period. A business that consistently earns net income adds value to its owners, its employees, its customers, and society.

An important step in financial statement preparation is the trial balance. The trial balance, introduced in Chapter 2 on page 64, lists the ledger accounts and their balances. The account balances in the trial balance include the effects of the transactions that occurred during the period—cash collections, purchases of assets, payments of bills, sales of assets, and so on. To measure its income, however, a business must do some additional accounting at the end of the period to bring the records up to date before preparing the financial statements. This process is called *adjusting the books* and it consists of making special entries called *adjusting entries*. This chapter focuses on these adjusting entries to show how to measure business income.

The accounting profession has concepts and principles to guide the measurement of business income. Chief among these are the concepts of accrual accounting, the accounting period, the revenue principle, and the matching principle. In this chapter, we apply these (and other) concepts and principles to measure the income and prepare the financial statements of EconoTravel for the month of April.

Accrual-Basis Accounting versus Cash-Basis Accounting

OBJECTIVE 1
Distinguish accrual-basis accounting from cash-basis accounting

There are two ways to do accounting:

- **Accrual-basis accounting**, frequently called simply *accrual accounting*, records the effect of every business transaction as it occurs. Most businesses use the accrual basis, and that is the method covered in this book.

- **Cash-basis accounting** records transactions only when cash receipts and cash payments occur. It ignores receivables, payables, and amortization. Only very small businesses tend to use cash-basis accounting.

Suppose Jamison Sporting Goods purchased $10,000 of supplies on account from Nike, the athletic wear products company. On the accrual basis, Jamison Sporting Goods records the asset supplies and the liability accounts payable as follows:

Supplies	10,000	
Accounts Payable		10,000
Purchased supplies on account.		

Under the accrual basis, Jamison's balance sheet reports the asset Supplies and the liability Accounts Payable.

In contrast, cash-basis accounting ignores this transaction because Jamison Sporting Goods paid no cash. The cash basis records only cash receipts and cash payments. *Cash receipts are treated as revenues, and cash payments are handled as expenses.* Therefore, under the cash basis, Jamison would record the $10,000 cash payment as an expense rather than as an asset. This is faulty accounting: Jamison acquired supplies, which are assets because they provide future benefit to the company.

Now let's see how differently the accrual basis and the cash basis account for a revenue. Suppose Jamison sold goods on account. Under the accrual basis, Jamison records a $20,000 sale as follows:

Accounts Receivable	20,000	
Sales Revenue		20,000
Sold goods on account.		

The balance sheet then reports the asset Accounts Receivable, and the income statement reports Sales Revenue. We have a complete picture of the transaction.

Under the cash basis, Jamison Sporting Goods would not record a sale *on account* because there is no cash receipt. Instead, it would wait until cash is received and then record the cash as revenue. As a result, cash-basis accounting never reports accounts receivable from customers. It shows the revenue in the wrong accounting period, when cash is received. Revenue should be recorded when it is earned, and that is how the accrual basis operates.

Exhibit 3-1 illustrates the difference between the accrual basis and the cash basis. Keep in mind that the accrual basis is the correct way to do accounting. As we saw in Exhibit 1-3 on page 8, the objective of financial statements is to communicate

EXHIBIT 3-1

Accrual-Basis Accounting
versus Cash-Basis
Accounting

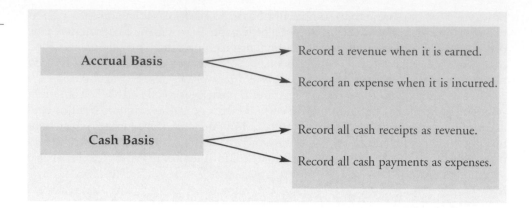

Accrual Basis	Record a revenue when it is earned.
	Record an expense when it is incurred.
Cash Basis	Record all cash receipts as revenue.
	Record all cash payments as expenses.

information that is useful to users. Clearly, accrual-basis accounting provides more complete information than does cash-basis accounting. This difference is important because the more complete the data, the better equipped decision makers are to reach accurate conclusions about the firm's financial health and future prospects. Four concepts used in accrual accounting are the accounting period, the revenue principle, the matching principle, and the time-period concept.

The Accounting Period

The only way to know for certain how successfully a business has operated is to close its doors, sell all its assets, pay the liabilities, and return any leftover cash to the owner. This process, called *liquidation*, is the same as going out of business. Obviously, it is not practical for accountants to measure business income in this manner. Instead, businesses need periodic reports on their progress. Accountants slice time into small segments and prepare financial statements for specific periods.

The most basic accounting period is one year, and virtually all businesses prepare annual financial statements. For about 60 percent of companies in a recent Canadian survey, the annual accounting period is the calendar year from January 1 through December 31. The other companies in the survey use a *fiscal year* ending on some date other than December 31. The year-end date is usually the low point in business activity for the year. Retailers are a notable example. Traditionally, their fiscal year ends on January 31, because the low point in their business activity has followed the after-Christmas sales in January; the Forzani Group (www.forzanigroup.com) and the Hudson's Bay Co. (www.hbc.com/bay) are two examples. Eight percent of the companies in the survey mentioned above have a January 31 year-end date like the Hudson's Bay Co.

Managers and investors cannot wait until the end of the year to gauge a company's progress. Companies therefore prepare financial statements for *interim* periods, which are less than a year. Managers want financial information more often, so monthly financial statements are common. A series of monthly statements can be combined for quarterly and semiannual periods. Most of the discussions in this book are based on an annual accounting period, but the procedures and statements can be applied to interim periods as well.

Revenue Principle

The **revenue principle** tells accountants (1) *when* to record revenue, and (2) the *amount* of revenue to record. Revenue, defined in Chapter 1, page 12, is the increase in owner's equity from delivering goods and services to customers in the course of operating a business. When we speak of "recording" something in accounting, we mean to make an entry in the journal. That is where the accounting process starts.

The general principle guiding *when* to record revenue is that revenue should be recorded as it has been earned—but not before. In *most* cases, revenue is earned when the business has delivered a completed good or service to the customer. The business has done everything required by the agreement, including transferring the item to the customer. Exhibit 3-2 shows two situations that provide guidance on when to record revenue. The first situation illustrates when *not* to record revenue, because the client merely states her plans. Situation 2 illustrates when revenue should be recorded—after EconoTravel has performed the service for the client.

The general principle guiding the *amount* of revenue to record is record revenue equal to the cash value of the goods or the service transferred to the customer. Suppose that, in order to obtain a new client, EconoTravel performs travel service for the price of $1,000. Ordinarily, the business would have charged $1,200 for this service. How much revenue should the business record? The answer is $1,000 because that was the cash value of the transaction. EconoTravel will not receive the full value of $1,200, so that is not the amount of revenue to record. The business will receive only $1,000 cash, and that pinpoints the amount of revenue earned.

The Matching Principle

The **matching principle** is the basis for recording expenses. Recall that expenses— such as rent, utilities, and advertising—are the costs of assets and services that are consumed in the earning of revenue. The matching principle directs accountants to (1) identify all expenses incurred during the accounting period, (2) measure the expenses, and (3) match the expenses related to the revenues earned during that same span of time. To match expenses against revenues means to subtract the related expenses from the revenues in order to compute net income or net loss. Exhibit 3-3 illustrates the matching principle.

There is a natural link between revenues and some types of expenses. Accountants follow the matching principle by first identifying the revenues of a period and then the expenses that can be linked to particular revenues. For example, a business that pays sales commissions to its sales persons will have commission expense if the employees make sales. If they make no sales, the business has no commission expense. *Cost of goods sold* is another example. If there are no sales of personal watercraft, Bombardier reports no cost of goods sold.

Other expenses are not so easy to link with particular sales. Monthly rent expense occurs, for example, regardless of the revenues earned during the period. The matching principle directs accountants to identify these types of expenses with a particular time period, such as a month or a year. If EconoTravel employs a secretary at a monthly salary of $2,300, the business will record salary expense of $2,300 each month.

EXHIBIT 3-2

Recording Revenue

No transaction has occurred.
Situation 1—Do Not Record Revenue

I plan to have you make my travel arrangements.

EconoTravel
MARCH
12

The client has taken a trip arranged by EconoTravel.
Situation 2—Record Revenue

EconoTravel
APRIL
2

EXHIBIT 3-3

The Matching Principle

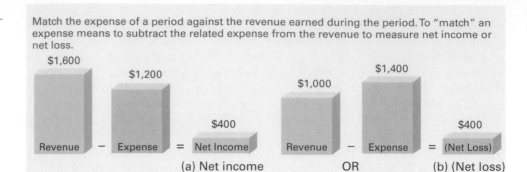

Match the expense of a period against the revenue earned during the period. To "match" an expense means to subtract the related expense from the revenue to measure net income or net loss.

(a) Net income OR (b) (Net loss)

EconoTravel prepares a monthly statement for the business at April 30. How does the company account for a transaction that begins in April but ends in May? How does it bring the accounts up to date for preparing the financial statements? To answer these questions, accountants use the time-period concept.

Time-Period Concept

Managers, investors, and creditors make decisions daily and need periodic readings on the business's progress. Therefore, accountants prepare financial statements at regular intervals.

The **time-period concept** ensures that accounting information is reported at regular intervals. It interacts with the accounting period, revenue principle, and matching principle to underlie the use of accruals. To measure income accurately, companies update the revenue and expense accounts immediately prior to the end of the period. The Royal Bank (www.royalbank.ca) provides a real example of an expense accrual. The Royal Bank has an October 31 year end. When October 31 falls during a pay period (say, October 31, 2006, which is on a Tuesday, and the Royal Bank pays its employees bi-weekly on Fridays), the company must record the employee compensation owed to the workers for unpaid services performed up to and including October 31. Assume weekly salary and wages expense for the Royal Bank's B.C. Division is $4,600,000; the entry to accrue the expense would be ($\frac{2}{5} \times \$4,600,000 = \$1,840,000$):

```
2003
Oct. 31   Salary and Wages Expense ....................................   1,840,000
              Salary and Wages Payable ...........................                    1,840,000
          Accrued salary and wages expense for October 30 and 31, 2006.
```

This entry serves two purposes. First, it assigns the expense to the proper period. Without the accrual entry at October 31, total expenses for 2006 would be understated, and, as a result, net income would be overstated. Incorrectly, the expense would fall in the 2007 fiscal year when the Royal Bank makes the next payroll disbursement. Second, the accrual entry also records the liability for reporting on the balance sheet at October 31, 2006. Without the accrual entry, total liabilities would be understated.

At the end of the accounting period, companies also accrue revenues that have been earned but not collected. The remainder of the chapter discusses how to make the adjusting entries to bring the accounts up to date.

Adjusting the Accounts

At the end of the period, the accountant prepares the financial statements. This end-of-the-period process begins with the trial balance that lists the accounts and their balances after the period's transactions have been recorded in the journal and posted to the accounts in the ledger. We prepared trial balances in Chapter 2.

Exhibit 3-4 is the trial balance of EconoTravel at April 30, 2006. (Accounts and balances differ from those in Chapter 2. Assume the company has been in business for one year.) This *unadjusted trial balance* includes some new accounts that will be explained here. It lists most, but not all, of the revenue accounts and the expenses of the travel agency for the month of April. These trial balance amounts are incomplete because they omit certain revenue and expense transactions that affect more than one accounting period. That is why the trial balance is *unadjusted*. In most cases, however, we refer to it simply as the trial balance, without the label "unadjusted."

Under cash-basis accounting, there would be no need for adjustments to the accounts because all April cash transactions would have been recorded. However, the accrual basis requires adjusting entries at the end of the period in order to produce correct balances for the financial statements. To see why, consider the Supplies account in Exhibit 3-4.

EconoTravel uses supplies in providing travel services for clients during the month. This use reduces the quantity of supplies on hand and thus constitutes an expense, just like salary expense or rent expense. The business does not bother to record this expense daily, and it is not worth the effort to record supplies expense more than once a month. It is time-consuming to make hourly, daily, or even weekly journal entries to record the expense incurred by the use of supplies. So how does the business account for supplies expense?

By the end of the month, the Supplies balance of $1,400 on the unadjusted trial balance (Exhibit 3-4) is not correct. The unadjusted balance represents the amount of supplies on hand at the start of the month plus any supplies purchased during the month. This balance fails to take into account the supplies used (*supplies expense*) during the accounting period. It is necessary, then, to subtract the month's expenses from the amount of supplies listed on the trial balance. The resulting new adjusted balance measures the cost of supplies that are still on hand at April 30, say $800, based on a physical count of supplies remaining on hand. This is the correct amount of supplies to report on the balance sheet—$800. The adjusting entry will, in this way, bring the supplies accounts up to date.

Adjusting entries assign revenues to the period in which they are earned and expenses to the period in which they are incurred. Adjusting entries also update the asset and liability accounts. They are needed to (1) measure properly the period's income on the income statement, and (2) bring related asset and liability accounts to correct balances for the balance sheet. For example, an adjusting entry

EXHIBIT 3-4

Unadjusted Trial Balance

ECONOTRAVEL
Unadjusted Trial Balance
April 30, 2006

Cash	$ 49,600	
Accounts receivable	4,500	
Supplies	1,400	
Prepaid insurance	4,200	
Furniture	33,000	
Accounts payable		$ 26,200
Unearned service revenue		900
Don Smith, capital		62,500
Don Smith, withdrawals	6,400	
Service revenue		14,000
Rent expense	1,800	
Salary expense	1,900	
Utilities expense	800	
Total	$103,600	$103,600

is needed to transfer the amount of supplies used during the period from the asset account Supplies to the expense account Supplies Expense. The adjusting entry updates both the Supplies asset account and the Supplies Expense account. This achieves accurate measures of assets and expenses. Adjusting entries, which are the key to accrual-basis accounting, are made before the financial statements are prepared. The end-of-period process of updating the accounts is called *adjusting the accounts*, *making the adjusting entries*, or *adjusting the books*.

A large company would use accounting software to print out a trial balance. For example, at Nexen Inc. (www.nexeninc.com), a multidivisional company that locates, produces, and transports oil and natural gas, each division has its own accounting software that prints a monthly trial balance. The accountants then analyze the amounts on the trial balance. This analysis results in the adjusting entries. Nexen posts the adjusting entries to update its ledger accounts. The trial balance has now become the company's *adjusted* trial balance. At Nexen, the adjusted trial balances from all divisions are consolidated, or grouped. This chapter shows the adjusting process as it moves from the trial balance to the adjusted trial balance.

Two basic types of adjustments are *prepaids* and *accruals*.

Prepaids (Deferrals) and Accruals

In a *prepaid*-type adjustment, the cash transaction occurs before the related expense or revenue is recorded. Prepaids are also called *deferrals* because the recording of the expense or the revenue is deferred to periods after cash is paid or received. *Accrual*-type adjustments are the opposite of prepaids. For accruals we record the expense or revenue before the related cash is paid or received.

Adjusting entries can be further divided into five categories:

1. Prepaid expenses
2. Amortization of capital assets
3. Accrued expenses
4. Accrued revenues
5. Unearned revenues

The core of this chapter is the discussion of these five types of adjusting entries on pages 114–123. Study this material carefully because it is the most challenging topic in all of introductory accounting.

Prepaid Expenses

Prepaid expenses are advance payments of expense. The category includes miscellaneous assets that typically expire or are used up in the near future. Prepaid rent and prepaid insurance are examples of prepaid expenses. They are called "prepaid" expenses because they are expenses that are paid in advance. Salary expense and utilities expense, among others, are typically *not* prepaid expenses because they are not paid in advance. All companies, large and small, must make adjustments regarding prepaid expenses. For example, Swiss Chalet must contend with such prepayments as rents, packaging supplies, and insurance.

Prepaid Insurance   Automobile insurance is usually paid in advance. This prepayment creates an asset for the policyholder, because that person has purchased the future benefit of insurance protection. Suppose EconoTravel purchases insurance on April 1, 2006, for two automobiles. The cost of the insurance is $4,200. The entry to record the payment is a debit to the asset account, Prepaid Insurance, as follows:

Apr. 1	Prepaid Insurance	4,200	
	Cash		4,200
	Paid annual premium for automobile insurance.		

After posting, Prepaid Insurance appears as follows:

ASSETS
Prepaid Insurance

Apr. 1	4,200

The trial balance at April 30, 2006, lists Prepaid Insurance as an asset with a debit balance of $4,200. Throughout April, the Prepaid Insurance account maintains this beginning balance, as shown in Exhibit 3-4 (page 113). But $4,200 is *not* the amount to report for Prepaid Insurance on EconoTravel's balance sheet at April 30. Why?

At April 30, Prepaid Insurance should be adjusted to remove from its balance the amount of the asset that has been used up, which is one month's worth of the prepayment. By definition, the amount of an asset that has been used, or has expired, is *expense*. The adjusting entry transfers one-twelfth, or $350 ($4,200 × $\frac{1}{12}$), of the debit balance from Prepaid Insurance to Insurance Expense. The debit side of the entry records an increase in Insurance Expense and the credit records a decrease in the asset Prepaid Insurance.

Apr. 30	Insurance Expense..	350	
	Prepaid Insurance..		350
	To record insurance expense ($4,200 × $\frac{1}{12}$).		

After posting, Prepaid Insurance and Insurance Expense appear as follows:

ASSETS
Prepaid Insurance

Apr. 1	4,200	**Apr. 30**	**350**
Bal.	3,850		

EXPENSES
Insurance Expense

Apr. 30	**350**	
Bal.	350	

Correct asset amount, **$3,850** → Total accounted for, **$4,200** ← Correct expense amount, **$350**

The full $4,200 has been accounted for. Eleven-twelfths measures the asset, and one twelfth measures the expense. Recording this expense illustrates the matching principle.

The same analysis applies to a prepayment of twelve months' rent. The only difference is in the account titles, which would be Prepaid Rent and Rent Expense instead of Prepaid Insurance and Insurance Expense. In a computerized system, the adjusting entry crediting the prepaid account and debiting the expense account could be established to recur automatically in each subsequent accounting period until the prepaid account has a zero balance.

The chapter appendix shows an alternative treatment of prepaid expenses. The end result on the financial statements is the same as that for the method given here.

Supplies Supplies are accounted for the same way as prepaid expenses. On April 2, EconoTravel paid cash of $1,400 for office supplies.

Apr. 2	Supplies...	1,400	
	Cash...		1,400
	Paid cash for supplies.		

Assume that the business purchased no additional supplies during April. The April 30 trial balance, therefore, lists Supplies with a $1,400 debit balance as shown in Exhibit 3-4. But EconoTravel's April 30 balance sheet should *not* report supplies of $1,400. Why?

During April, EconoTravel used supplies in performing services for clients. The cost of the supplies used is the measure of *supplies expense* for the month. To measure the business's supplies expense during April, Don Smith counts the supplies on hand at the end of the month. This is the amount of the asset still available to the business. Assume the count indicates that supplies costing $800 remain. Subtracting the entity's $800 of supplies on hand at the end of April from the cost of supplies available during April ($1,400) measures supplies expense during the month ($600).

Cost of asset available during the period	–	Cost of asset on hand at the end of the period	=	Cost of asset used (expense) during the period
$1,400	–	$800	=	$600

The April 30 adjusting entry to update the Supplies account and to record the supplies expense for the month debits the expense and credits the asset:

Apr. 30	Supplies Expense...	600	
	Supplies		600
	To record supplies expense ($1,400 – $800).		

After posting, the Supplies and Supplies Expense accounts appear as follows:

ASSETS Supplies				EXPENSES Supplies Expense	
Apr. 2	1,400	Apr. 30 600		Apr. 30	600
Bal.	800			Bal.	600

Correct asset amount, $800	→	Total accounted for, $1,400	←	Correct expense amount, $600

The Supplies account enters the month of May with an $800 balance, and the adjustment process is repeated each month.

Amortization of Capital Assets

The logic of the accrual basis of accounting is best illustrated by how businesses account for capital assets. **Capital assets** are long-lived tangible assets, such as land, buildings, furniture, machinery, and equipment. All capital assets but land decline in usefulness as they age. This decline is an *expense* to the business. Accountants systematically spread the cost of each capital asset, except land, over the years of its useful life. The *CICA Handbook* calls this process of allocating the cost of a long-lived or capital asset to expense over its life **amortization**. Another term in common usage is *depreciation*.

Similarity to Prepaid Expenses The concept underlying accounting for capital assets and amortization expense is the same as for prepaid expenses. In a sense, capital assets are large prepaid expenses that expire over a number of periods. For both prepaid expenses and capital assets, the business purchases an asset that wears out or is used up. As the asset is used, more and more of its cost is transferred from the asset account to the expense account. The major difference between prepaid expenses and capital assets is the length of time it takes for the asset to lose its usefulness (or expire). Prepaid expenses usually expire within a year, whereas most capital assets remain useful for a number of years.

Consider EconoTravel's operations. Suppose that, on April 3, the business purchased furniture on account for $33,000 and made this journal entry:

Apr. 3	Furniture..	33,000	
	Accounts Payable...		33,000
	Purchased office furniture on account.		

After posting, the Furniture account appears as follows:

ASSETS
Furniture

Apr. 3	33,000

In accrual-basis accounting, an asset is recorded when the furniture is acquired. Then, a portion of the asset's cost is transferred from the asset account to Amortization Expense each period that the asset is used. This method matches the asset's expense to the revenue of the period, which is an application of the matching principle. In many computerized systems, the adjusting entry for amortization is programmed to occur automatically each month for the duration of the asset's life.

Don Smith believes the furniture will remain useful for five years and be virtually worthless at the end of its life. One way to compute the amount of amortization for each year is to divide the cost of the asset ($33,000 in our example) by its useful life (5 years). This procedure—called the straight-line method—gives annual amortization of $6,600 ($33,000/5 years = $6,600 per year). Amortization for the month of April is $550 ($6,600/12 months = $550 per month).

The Accumulated Amortization Account Amortization expense for April is recorded by the following entry:

Apr. 30	Amortization Expense—Furniture	550	
	Accumulated Amortization—Furniture		550
	To record monthly amortization expense on furniture.		

Accumulated Amortization is credited instead of Furniture, because the original cost of the capital asset should remain in the asset account as long as the business uses the asset. Accountants and managers may refer to the Furniture account to see how much the asset cost. This information is useful in a decision about whether to replace the furniture and the amount to pay.

The amount of amortization, however, is an *estimate*. Accountants use the **Accumulated Amortization** account to show the cumulative sum of all amortization expense from the date of acquiring the asset. Therefore, the balance in this account increases over the life of the asset.

Accumulated Amortization is a *contra asset* account, which means an asset account with a normal credit balance. [Recall from Chapter 2, page 65, that the normal balance on an account marks the side of the account where increases are recorded.] A **contra account** has two distinguishing characteristics:

- A contra account has a companion account.

- A contra account's normal balance (debit or credit) is the opposite of that of the companion account.

In this case, Accumulated Amortization is the contra account that accompanies Furniture. It appears in the ledger directly after Furniture. Furniture has a debit balance, and therefore Accumulated Amortization, a contra asset, has a credit balance. *All contra asset accounts have credit balances.*

A business carries an accumulated amortization or depreciation account for each depreciable asset. If a business has a building and a machine, for example, it will carry the accounts Accumulated Amortization—Building, and Accumulated Amortization—Machine.

After the amortization entry has been posted, the Furniture, Accumulated Amortization—Furniture, and Amortization Expense accounts of EconoTravel are

KEY POINT

Use a separate Amortization Expense account and Accumulated Amortization account for each type of asset (Amortization Expense—Furniture, Amortization Expense—Buildings, and so on). You must know the amount of amortization recorded for each asset.

THINKING IT OVER

Describe one similarity and one difference between
(1) prepaid expenses and
(2) capital assets and the related amortization.

A: Similarity: For both prepaid expenses and capital assets, the business first records the purchase as an asset. The business then records the expense later. Difference: Prepaid expenses cover a shorter time period than capital assets and the related amortization.

ASSETS Furniture		CONTRA ASSET Accumulated Amortization— Furniture		EXPENSES Amortization Expense— Furniture	
Apr. 3 33,000			Apr. 30 550	Apr. 30 550	
Bal. 33,000			Bal. 550	Bal. 550	

Carrying Value   The balance sheet shows the relationship between Furniture and Accumulated Amortization—Furniture. The balance of Accumulated Amortization—Furniture is subtracted from the balance of Furniture. This net amount of a capital asset (cost minus accumulated amortization) is called its **carrying value**, or *net carrying value*, or *book value*, as shown below for Furniture:

Furniture..	$33,000
Less: Accumulated Amortization—Furniture	550
Carrying Value	$32,450

Suppose the travel agency owns a building that cost $96,000, on which annual amortization is $4,800. The amount of amortization for one month would be $400 ($4,800/12), and the following entry records amortization for April.

Apr. 30	Amortization Expense—Building	400	
	Accumulated Amortization—Building		400
	To record monthly amortization on building.		

The balance sheet at April 30 would report EconoTravel's capital assets as shown in Exhibit 3-5.

Exhibit 3-6 shows how Inco Limited (www.inco.com)—producers of nickel, copper, alloys, and other primary metal products—displayed capital assets in a recent annual report. Inco has mines and mining plants located around the world; these mines and plants are displayed in line 1 of Exhibit 3-6. Lines 2, 3, 4, and 5 list the costs of processing facilities and other buildings used for offices, production, and research, as well as air conditioners, computers, plumbing, and so on, in those facilities and buildings. In addition, trucks, automobiles, and other such

EXHIBIT 3-5

Capital Assets on the
Balance Sheet of
EconoTravel (April 30)

Capital Assets		
Furniture	$33,000	
Less: Accumulated Amortization—Furniture	550	$ 32,450
Building	96,000	
Less: Accumulated Amortization—Building	400	95,600
Capital Assets, Net		$128,050

EXHIBIT 3-6

Inco Limited's Reporting of
Capital Assets (Amounts in
Millions)

(1) Mines and mining plants	$ 2,745	
(2) Processing facilities	3,281	
(3) Voisey's Bay project	3,338	
(4) Goro project	637	
(5) Other	595	
(6) Total property, plant and equipment, at cost	10,596	
(7) Accumulated depreciation	3,095	
(8) Accumulated depletion	1,156	
(9) Total accumulated depreciation and depletion	4,251	
(10) Property, plant and equipment, net	$ 6,345	

vehicles would be included. Note that Inco uses the terms *depreciation* and *depletion* in lines 7, 8, and 9; they are other words for amortization. Amortization is discussed more fully in Chapter 10.

Let's now return to EconoTravel's situation.

Accrued Expenses

Businesses incur many expenses before they pay cash. Payment is not due until later. Consider an employee's salary. The employer's salary expense and salary payable grow as the employee works, so the liability is said to *accrue*. Another example is interest expense on a note payable. Interest accrues as time passes. The term **accrued expense** refers to an expense that the business has incurred but has not yet paid. Therefore, accrued expenses can be viewed as the opposite of prepaid expenses.

It is time-consuming to make hourly, daily, or even weekly journal entries to accrue expenses. Consequently, the accountant waits until the end of the period. Then an adjusting entry brings each expense (and related liability) up to date just before the financial statements are prepared.

LEARNING TIP

A prepaid expense is paid first and expensed later. An accrued expense is expensed first and paid later. Prepaids and accruals are opposites.

Salary Expense Most companies pay their employees at predetermined times. Suppose EconoTravel pays its employee a monthly salary of $3,800, half on the 15th and half on the last day of the month. Here is a calendar for April with the two paydays circled:

			APRIL			
S	M	T	W	T	F	S
					1	2
3	4	5	6	7	8	9
10	11	12	13	14	(15)	16
17	18	19	20	21	22	23
24	25	26	27	28	29	(30)

Assume that, if either payday falls on a weekend, EconoTravel pays the employee on the following Monday. During April, the travel agency paid its employee's first half-month salary of $1,900 on Friday, April 15, and recorded the following entry:

Apr. 15	Salary Expense..	1,900	
	Cash...		1,900
	To pay salary.		

After posting, the Salary Expense account is

EXPENSES
Salary Expense
Apr. 15	1,900	

The trial balance at April 30 (Exhibit 3-4, page 113) includes Salary Expense, with its debit balance of $1,900. Because April 30, the second payday of the month, falls on a Saturday, the second half-month amount of $1,900 will be paid on Monday, May 2. Without an adjusting entry, this second $1,900 amount is not included in the April 30 trial balance amount for Salary Expense. Therefore, at April 30, the business adjusts for additional *salary expense* and *salary payable* of $1,900 by recording an increase in each of these accounts as follows:

Apr. 30	Salary Expense..	1,900	
	Salary Payable...		1,900
	To accrue salary expense.		

After posting, the Salary Expense and Salary Payable accounts are updated to April 30:

EXPENSES				LIABILITIES		
Salary Expense				**Salary Payable**		
Apr.15	1,900				Apr. 30	1,900
Apr. 30	**1,900**				Bal.	1,900
Bal.	3,800					

The accounts at April 30 now contain the complete salary information for the month of April. The expense account has a full month's salary, and the liability account shows the portion that the business still owes at April 30. EconoTravel will record the payment of this liability on Monday, May 2.

This payment entry does not affect April or May expenses because the April expense was recorded on April 15 and April 30. May expense will be recorded in a like manner, starting on May 15. All accrued expenses are recorded with similar entries—a debit to the appropriate expense account and a credit to the related liability account.

Many computerized systems contain a payroll module. The adjusting entry for accrued weekly and monthly salaries is automatically journalized and posted at the end of each accounting period.

Accrued Revenues

Businesses often earn revenue before they collect the cash. Collection occurs later. A revenue that has been earned but not yet collected is called an **accrued revenue**.

Assume EconoTravel is hired on April 15 by Rutledge Tours Co. to make travel arrangements on a monthly basis. Under this agreement, Rutledge will pay EconoTravel $1,000 monthly, with the first payment on May 15. During April, EconoTravel will earn half a month's fee, $500, for work performed April 15 through April 30. On April 30, EconoTravel makes the following adjusting entry to record an increase in Accounts Receivable and Service Revenue:

Apr. 30	Accounts Receivable	500	
	Service Revenue		500
	To accrue service revenue ($1,000 × ½).		

We see from the unadjusted trial balance in Exhibit 3-4 (page 113) that Accounts Receivable has an unadjusted balance of $4,500. The Service Revenue unadjusted balance is $14,000. Posting the April 30 adjustment has the following effects on these two accounts:

ASSETS				REVENUES		
Accounts Receivable				**Service Revenue**		
	4,500					14,000
Apr. 30	**500**				**Apr. 30**	**500**
Bal.	5,000				Bal.	14,500

This adjusting entry illustrates the revenue principle. Without the adjustment, the travel agency's financial statements would be misleading—they would understate Accounts Receivable and Service Revenue by $500 each. All accrued revenues are accounted for similarly—by debiting a receivable and crediting a revenue.

We now turn to a different category of adjusting entries.

Unearned Revenues

Some businesses collect cash from customers in advance of doing work for them. Receiving cash in advance creates a liability called **unearned revenue** or **deferred revenue**. This obligation arises from receiving cash in advance of providing a product or service. Only when the job is completed will the business have earned the revenue.

Suppose Baldwin Investments engages EconoTravel's services, agreeing to pay the travel agency $900 monthly, beginning immediately. Suppose Baldwin makes the first payment on April 20. EconoTravel records the cash receipt and the related increase in the business's liabilities as follows:

Apr. 20   Cash... 900
        Unearned Service Revenue   900
      Received revenue in advance.

After posting, the liability account appears as follows:

LIABILITIES
Unearned Service Revenue

	Apr. 20	900

Unearned Service Revenue is a liability because it represents EconoTravel's obligation to perform service for the client. The April 30 unadjusted trial balance (Exhibit 3-4) lists Unearned Service Revenue with a $900 credit balance prior to the adjusting entries. During the last 10 days of the month—April 21 through April 30—the travel agency will have *earned* one-third (10 days divided by April's total 30 days) of the $900, or $300. Therefore, the accountant makes the following adjustment to decrease the liability, Unearned Service Revenue, and to record an increase in Service Revenue as follows:

Apr. 30   Unearned Service Revenue.. 300
        Service Revenue   300
      To record service revenue that was collected in advance ($900 × $\frac{1}{3}$).

This adjusting entry shifts $300 of the total amount of unearned service revenue from the liability account to the revenue account. After posting, the balance of Service Revenue is increased by $300 and the balance of Unearned Service Revenue has been reduced by $300 to $600. Now, both accounts have their correct balances at April 30, as follows:

LIABILITIES				REVENUES		
Unearned Service Revenue				**Service Revenue**		
Apr. 30	**300**	Apr. 20	900			14,000
		Bal.	600	Apr. 30		500
				Apr. 30		**300**
				Bal.		14,800

Correct liability amount, $600 → Total accounted for, $900 ← Correct revenue amount, $300

All types of revenues that are collected in advance are accounted for similarly.

An unearned revenue to one company can be a prepaid expense to the company that made the payment. For example, suppose that two months in advance IBM Canada Ltd. (www.ibm.com/ca/en) paid WestJet $1,800 for the airfare of IBM executives. To IBM, the payment is Prepaid Travel Expense. To WestJet, the receipt of cash creates Unearned Service Revenue. After the executives take the trip, WestJet records the revenue by reducing Unearned Service Revenue.

Exhibit 3-7 diagrams the timing of prepaid-type and accrual-type adjusting entries. The chapter appendix shows an alternate treatment of unearned revenues and prepaid expenses.

EXHIBIT 3-7

Prepaid-Type and Accrual-Type Adjustments*

PREPAIDS—The cash transaction occurs initially.

	Initially				Later		
Prepaid expenses	Pay cash and record an asset: Prepaid Expense	XXX		→	Record an expense and decrease the asset: Expense	XXX	
	Cash		XXX		Prepaid Expense		XXX
Unearned revenues	Receive cash and record unearned revenue: Cash	XXX		→	Record a revenue and decrease unearned revenue: Unearned Revenue	XXX	
	Unearned Revenue		XXX		Revenue		XXX

ACCRUALS—The cash transaction occurs later.

	Initially				Later		
Accrued expenses	Record (accrue) an expense and the related payable: Expense	XXX		→	Pay cash and decrease the payable: Payable	XXX	
	Payable		XXX		Cash		XXX
Accrued revenues	Record (accrue) a revenue and the related receivable: Receivable	XXX		→	Receive cash and decrease the receivable: Cash	XXX	
	Revenue		XXX		Receivable		XXX

The authors thank Darrel Davis and Alfonso Oddo for suggesting this exhibit.

*See the Appendix of this chapter for an alternative treatment of accounting for prepaids and accruals.

Consider the tuition you pay. Assume that one semester's tuition costs $2,000 and that you make a single payment at the start of the term. Can you make the journal entries to record the tuition transaction on your own books and on the books of your college or university?

Answer:

Start of semester:

Your Entries			**Your College's Entries**		
Prepaid Tuition	2,000		Cash	2,000	
Cash		2,000	Unearned Tuition		
Paid semester tuition.			Revenue		2,000
			Received revenue in advance.		

End of semester:

Tuition Expense	2,000		Unearned Tuition Revenue	2,000	
Prepaid Tuition		2,000	Tuition Revenue		2,000
To record tuition expense.			To record unearned tuition revenue that has been earned.		

Summary of the Adjusting Process

One purpose of the adjusting process is to measure business income accurately. The other purpose of the adjusting process is to update the balance sheet accounts. All adjusting entries debit or credit:

- At least one *income statement* account, either a **Revenue** or an **Expense**

and

- At least one *balance sheet* account, either an **Asset** or a **Liability**

No adjusting entry debits or credits Cash because the cash transactions are recorded at other times. (The exception to this rule is when an adjusting entry is made to correct an error involving Cash.) Exhibit 3-8 summarizes the adjusting entries.

Exhibit 3-9 on page 124 summarizes the adjusting entries of EconoTravel at April 30. Panel A of the exhibit briefly describes the data for each adjustment, Panel B gives the adjusting entries, and Panel C shows the accounts after they have been posted. (Recall from Chapter 2, page 60, that posting is the process of transferring amounts from the journal to the ledger.) The adjustments are keyed by letter.

EXHIBIT 3-8

Summary of Adjusting Entries

	Type of Account	
Category of Adjusting Entry	**Debited**	**Credited**
Prepaid expense	Expense	Asset
Amortization	Expense	Contra asset
Accrued expense	Expense	Liability
Accrued revenue	Asset	Revenue
Unearned revenue	Liability	Revenue

Adapted from material provided by Beverly Terry.

EXHIBIT 3-9

Journalizing and Posting the Adjusting Entries

Panel A: Information for Adjustments at April 30, 2006

a. Prepaid insurance expired during April, $350.
b. Supplies remaining on hand at April 30, 2006, $800.
c. Amortization on furniture for the month of April, $550.
d. Accrued salary expense, $1,900.
e. Accrued service revenue, $500.
f. Amount of unearned service revenue that was earned during April, $300.

Panel B: Adjusting Entries

a. Insurance Expense	350	
Prepaid Insurance		350
To record insurance expense.		
b. Supplies Expense	600	
Supplies		600
To record supplies used.		
c. Amortization Expense—Furniture	550	
Accumulated Amortization—Furniture		550
To record amortization on furniture.		
d. Salary Expense	1,900	
Salary Payable		1,900
To accrue salary expense.		
e. Accounts Receivable	500	
Service Revenue		500
To accrue service revenue.		
f. Unearned Service Revenue	300	
Service Revenue		300
To record unearned revenue that has been earned.		

Panel C: Ledger Accounts

ASSETS

Cash

Bal. 49,600	

Accounts Receivable

Bal. 4,500	
(e) 500	
Bal. 5,000	

Supplies

Bal. 1,400	(b) 600
Bal. 800	

Prepaid Insurance

Bal. 4,200	(a) 350
Bal. 3,850	

Furniture

Bal. 33,000	

Accumulated Amortization—Furniture

	(c) 550
	Bal. 550

LIABILITIES

Accounts Payable

	Bal. 26,200

Salary Payable

	(d) 1,900
	Bal. 1,900

Unearned Service Revenue

(f) 300	Bal. 900
	Bal. 600

OWNER'S EQUITY

Don Smith, Capital

	Bal. 62,500

Don Smith, Withdrawals

Bal. 6,400	

REVENUES

Service Revenue

	Bal. 14,000
	(e) 500
	(f) 300
	Bal. 14,800

EXPENSES

Insurance Expense

(a) 350	
Bal. 350	

Salary Expense

Bal. 1,900	
(d) 1,900	
Bal. 3,800	

Supplies Expense

(b) 600	
Bal. 600	

Rent Expense

1,800	

Amortization Expense—Furniture

(c) 550	
Bal. 550	

Utilities Expense

Bal. 800	

Accounting and the *e*-World

"Grossing Up" the Revenue by Dot.com Companies

Suppose you have decided to take a trip to Mexico. You want the cheapest package possible for air travel and hotels. You log on to expedia.ca and begin to plan your trip. You submit a request to Expedia, Inc. based on when you want to leave and return, the type of hotel you would like to stay in, and other amenities you are interested in. Expedia then searches its database and offers you a price for the trip. Once you accept the offer and pay with your credit card, you can start dreaming about your Mexican vacation.

Expedia does some work on your behalf. It will pay the airline company for your plane tickets and pay the hotel for your accommodation. Expedia also earns a fee for putting together your travel package.

Should Expedia record revenue for the full price of your ticket and accommodation or only for the fee it earns? This question has been subject to intense debate over the past few years. Most Internet companies record as revenue the full value of the products sold through their sites. Those recording the full value argue that they buy the product and take full ownership, and they control the amount of profit on each sale. The Accounting Standards Board in Canada refers to this practice as "grossing up" revenue. In some cases, dot.com companies gross up revenue to show a profit when they are actually operating at a loss.

This issue has become so important that the Accounting Standards Board, through its Emerging Issues Committee, has issued an abstract, EIC-123, on this topic. In it, the Committee states that an enterprise should recognize revenue based on the gross amount billed if it is the "primary obligator," the company primarily responsible for ensuring the good or service is provided. If the supplier (for example, the airline company) is the primary obligator, the enterprise should recognize revenue based on the net amount retained, which is the fee earned on each sale. Accountants have to use their professional judgment in applying these rules of revenue recognition.

Sources: Based on: Elizabeth McDonald, "Plump from Web Sales, Some Dot.Coms Face Crash Diet of Restriction of Booking Revenue," *Wall Street Journal*, February 28, 2000, p.C4. Jeremy Kahn, "Presto Chango! Sales are huge!" *Fortune*, March 21, 2000, pp 90–96. EIC-123, Emerging Issues Committee of the Accounting Standards Board, Canadian Institute of Chartered Accountants.

The Adjusted Trial Balance

This chapter began with the trial balance before any adjusting entries—the unadjusted trial balance (Exhibit 3-4). After the adjustments are journalized and posted, the accounts appear as shown in Exhibit 3-9, Panel C. A useful step in preparing the financial statements is to list the accounts, along with their adjusted balances, on an **adjusted trial balance**. This document has the advantage of listing all the accounts and their adjusted balances in a single place. Exhibit 3-10 on page 126 shows the preparation of the adjusted trial balance.

Exhibit 3-10 shows the first six columns of a *work sheet*. We will consider the complete work sheet in Chapter 4. For now, simply note how clearly this format presents the data. The information in the Account Title column and in the Trial Balance columns is drawn directly from the ledger. The two Adjustments columns list the debit and credit adjustments directly across from the appropriate account title. Each adjusting debit is identified by a letter in parentheses that refers to the adjusting entry. For example, the debit labelled (a) on the work sheet refers to the debit adjusting entry of $350 to Insurance Expense in Panel B of Exhibit 3-9. Similarly, for credit-adjusting entries, the corresponding credit—labelled (a)— refers to the $350 credit to Prepaid Insurance.

OBJECTIVE 4
Prepare an adjusted trial balance

KEY POINT

The differences between the amounts in the trial balance in Exhibit 3-4 and in the adjusted trial balance of Exhibit 3-10 result from the adjusting entries. If the adjusting entries were not given, you could determine them by computing the differences between the adjusted and unadjusted amounts.

EXHIBIT 3-10

Preparation of Adjusted Trial Balance

ECONOTRAVEL
Preparation of Adjusted Trial Balance
April 30, 2006

Account Title	Trial Balance Debit	Trial Balance Credit	Adjustments Debit		Adjustments Credit		Adjusted Trial Balance Debit	Adjusted Trial Balance Credit
Cash	49,600						49,600	
Accounts receivable	4,500		(e)	500			5,000	
Supplies	1,400				(b)	600	800	
Prepaid insurance	4,200				(a)	350	3,850	
Furniture	33,000						33,000	
Accumulated amortization		0			(c)	550		550
Accounts payable		26,200						26,200
Salary payable		0			(d)	1,900		1,900
Unearned service revenue		900	(f)	300				600
Don Smith, capital		62,500						62,500
Don Smith, withdrawals	6,400						6,400	
Service revenue		14,000			(e)	500		14,800
					(f)	300		
Insurance expense	0		(a)	350			350	
Salary expense	1,900		(d)	1,900			3,800	
Rent expense	1,800						1,800	
Supplies expense	0		(b)	600			600	
Amortization expense	0		(c)	550			550	
Utilities expense	800						800	
	103,600	103,600		4,200		4,200	106,550	106,550

EXHIBIT 3-11

Preparing the Financial Statements of EconoTravel from the Adjusted Trial Balance

Account Title	Adjusted Trial Balance Debit	Adjusted Trial Balance Credit	
Cash	49,600		
Accounts receivable	5,000		
Supplies	800		
Prepaid insurance	3,850		
Furniture	33,000		
Accumulated amortization		550	Balance Sheet (Exhibit 3-14)
Accounts payable		26,200	
Salary payable		1,900	
Unearned service revenue		600	
Don Smith, Capital		62,500	Statement of
Don Smith, Withdrawals	6,400		Owner's Equity (Exhibit 3-13)
Service revenue		14,800	
Insurance expense	350		
Salary expense	3,800		
Rent expense	1,800		
Supplies expense	600		Income Statement (Exhibit 3-12)
Amortization expense	550		
Utilities expense	800		
	106,550	106,550	

The Adjusted Trial Balance columns give the adjusted account balances. Each amount on the adjusted trial balance of Exhibit 3-10 is computed by combining the amounts from the unadjusted trial balance plus or minus the adjustments. For example, Accounts Receivable starts with a debit balance of $4,500. Adding the $500 debit amount from adjusting entry (e) gives Accounts Receivable an adjusted balance of $5,000. As we discussed at the outset of the chapter, Supplies begins with a debit balance of $1,400. After the $600 credit adjustment, its adjusted balance is $800. More than one entry may affect a single account, as is the case for Service Revenue. If an account is unaffected by the adjustments, it will show the same amount on both the adjusted and unadjusted trial balances. This is true for the Cash, Furniture, Accounts Payable, and Don Smith, Withdrawals accounts, to name a few.

Preparing the Financial Statements from the Adjusted Trial Balance

OBJECTIVE 5
Prepare the financial statements from the adjusted trial balance

The April financial statements of EconoTravel can be prepared from the adjusted trial balance. Exhibit 3-11 (page 126) shows how the accounts are distributed from the adjusted trial balance to three of the four main financial statements. The income statement (Exhibit 3-12) comes from the revenue and expense accounts. The statement of owner's equity (Exhibit 3-13) shows the reasons for the change in the owner's capital account during the period. The balance sheet (Exhibit 3-14) reports the assets, liabilities, and owner's equity. You learned these relationships in Chapter 1.

The financial statements are best prepared in the order shown: the income statement first, followed by the statement of owner's equity, and then the balance sheet. The essential features of all financial statements are:

Heading:
- Name of the entity
- Title of the statement
- Date, or period, covered by the statement

Body of the statement

It is customary to list expenses in descending order by amount, as shown in Exhibit 3-12, or in alphabetical order. However, Miscellaneous Expense, a catch-all account for expenses that do not fit another category, is usually reported last. Miscellaneous Expense should be a relatively low dollar amount. If it is not, new expense accounts should be created.

Relationships among the Three Financial Statements

The arrows in Exhibits 3-12, 3-13, and 3-14, illustrate the relationship among the income statement, the statement of owner's equity, and the balance sheet. (The relationships among the financial statements were introduced in Chapter 1, page 21.) Consider why the income statement is prepared first and the balance sheet last.

1. The income statement reports net income or net loss, calculated by subtracting expenses from revenues. Because revenues and expenses are owner's equity accounts, their net figure is then transferred to the statement of owner's equity. Note that net income in Exhibit 3-12, $6,900, increases owner's equity in Exhibit 3-13. A net loss would decrease owner's equity.

2. Capital is a balance sheet account, so the ending balance in the statement of owner's equity is transferred to the balance sheet. This amount is the final balancing element of the balance sheet. To solidify your understanding of this relationship, trace the $63,000 figure from Exhibit 3-13 to Exhibit 3-14.

EXHIBIT 3-12

Income Statement

ECONOTRAVEL
Income Statement
For the Month Ended April 30, 2006

Revenue:		
Service revenue		$14,800
Expenses:		
Salary expense	$3,800	
Rent expense	1,800	
Utilities expense	800	
Supplies expense	600	
Amortization expense	550	
Insurance expense	350	
Total expenses		7,900
Net income		$6,900

EXHIBIT 3-13

Statement of Owner's Equity

①

ECONOTRAVEL
Statement of Owner's Equity
For the Month Ended April 30, 2006

Don Smith, capital, April 1, 2006	$62,500
Add: Net income	6,900
	69,400
Less: Withdrawals	6,400
Don Smith, capital, April 30, 2006	$63,000

EXHIBIT 3-14

Balance Sheet

②

ECONOTRAVEL
Balance Sheet
April 30, 2006

Assets			Liabilities		
Cash		$49,600	Accounts payable		$26,200
Accounts receivable		5,000	Salary payable		1,900
Supplies		800	Unearned service		
Prepaid insurance		3,850	revenue		600
Furniture	$33,000		Total liabilities		28,700
Less: Accumulated					
amortization	550	32,450	**Owner's Equity**		
			Don Smith, capital		63,000
			Total liabilities and		
Total assets		$91,700	owner's equity		$91,700

You may be wondering why the total assets on the balance sheet ($91,700 in Exhibit 3-14) do not equal the total debits on the adjusted trial balance ($106,550 in Exhibit 3-11). Likewise, the total liabilities and owner's equity do not equal the total credits on the adjusted trial balance ($106,550 in Exhibit 3-11). The reason for these differences is that Accumulated Amortization and Don Smith, Withdrawals are contra accounts. Recall that contra accounts are *subtracted* from their companion accounts on the balance sheet. However, on the adjusted trial balance, contra accounts are *added* as a debit or credit in their respective columns.

Ethical Issues in Accrual Accounting

Like most other aspects of life, accounting poses ethical challenges. At the most basic level, accountants must be honest in their work. Only with honest and complete information, including accounting data, can people expect to make wise decisions. An example will illustrate the importance of ethics in accrual accounting.

Furniture Unlimited is a small business started three years ago by Claudia Cattenco and Ian Korleff in Regina. The company sells inexpensive furniture; its target market is college and university students. The company has been quite successful and so the two owners decide to open a branch in Saskatoon. They need to borrow $200,000 for inventory and for prepaid rent on a store they have found. Assume that Furniture Unlimited understated expenses purposely in order to inflate net income as reported on the company's income statement. A banker could be tricked into lending money to Furniture Unlimited. Then if Furniture Unlimited could not repay the loan, the bank would lose money—all because the banker relied on incorrect accounting information.

Accrual accounting provides several opportunities for unethical accounting. Recall from earlier in this chapter that amortization expense is an estimated figure. No business can foresee exactly how long its buildings and equipment will last, so accountants must estimate these assets' useful lives. Accountants then record amortization on capital assets over their *estimated* useful lives. A dishonest proprietor could buy a five-year asset and amortize it over 10 years. For each of the first five years, the company will report less amortization expense, and more net income, than it should. People who rely on the company's financial statements, such as bank lenders, can be deceived into doing business with the company. You may reply, "But the company will be recording amortization for the full 10 years, including the last five years after the asset is worn out. Net income will be lower in the last five years, and this lower net income will offset the higher net income reported during the first five years." This is true, but the damage to the company's reputation from reporting too much net income too quickly will remain. Accounting information must be honest and complete—completely ethical—to serve its intended purpose. As you progress through introductory accounting, you will see other situations that challenge the ethics of accountants.

The cash basis of accounting poses fewer ethical challenges because cash is not an estimated figure. Either the company has the cash, or it does not. Therefore, the amount of cash a company reports is rarely disputed. By contrast, adjusting entries for accrued expenses, accrued revenues, and amortization often must be estimated. Whenever there is an estimate, the accountant must often deal with pressure from managers or owners of the business to use the adjusting process to make the company look different from its true condition. The rules of conduct of the various professional accounting associations (discussed in Chapter 1) prohibit accountants from being associated with false or misleading financial information. Even with added ethical challenges, the accrual basis provides more complete accounting information than the cash basis. That is why accounting rests on the accrual basis.

The Decision Guidelines feature provides a map of the adjusting process that leads up to the adjusted trial balance.

DECISION GUIDELINES — Measuring Business Income: The Adjusting Process

Decision	Guidelines
Which basis of accounting better measures income (revenues – expenses)?	*Accrual basis*, because it provides more complete reports of operating performance
How to measure Revenues? Expenses?	 Revenue principle Matching principle
Where to start with the measurement of income at the end of the period?	Unadjusted trial balance, usually referred to simply as the *trial balance*
How to update the accounts for preparation of the financial statements?	*Adjusting entries* at the end of the accounting period
What are the categories of adjusting entries?	Prepaid expenses Amortization of capital assets Accrued expenses Accrued revenues Unearned revenues
How do the adjusting entries differ from other journal entries?	1. Adjusting entries are usually made at the end of the accounting period. 2. Adjusting entries never affect cash (except to correct errors). 3. All adjusting entries debit or credit • At least one *income statement* account (a **Revenue** or an **Expense**) and • At least one *balance sheet* account (an **Asset** or a **Liability**)
Where are the accounts with their adjusted balances summarized?	*Adjusted trial balance*, which becomes the basis for preparing the financial statements

The trial balance of Dobrowski Service Company pertains to December 31, 2006, which is the end of its year-long accounting period.

DOBROWSKI SERVICE COMPANY
Trial Balance
December 31, 2006

Cash	$ 297,000	
Accounts receivable	555,000	
Supplies	9,000	
Furniture and fixtures	150,000	
Accumulated amortization—furniture and fixtures		$ 60,000
Building	315,000	
Accumulated amortization—building		195,000
Land	75,000	
Accounts payable		570,000
Salary payable		
Unearned service revenue		67,500
D. Dobrowski, capital		439,500
D. Dobrowski, withdrawals	97,500	
Service revenue		429,000
Salary expense	258,000	
Supplies expense		
Amortization expense—furniture and fixtures		
Amortization expense—building		
Miscellaneous expense	4,500	
Total	$1,761,000	$1,761,000

Data needed for the adjusting entries include:

a. A count of supplies shows $3,000 of unused supplies on hand on December 31.

b. Amortization for the year on furniture and fixtures, $30,000.

c. Amortization for the year on building, $15,000.

d. Salaries owed but not yet paid, $7,500.

e. Accrued service revenue, $18,000.

f. Of the $67,500 balance of unearned service revenue, $48,000 was earned during the year.

Required

1. Open the ledger accounts with their unadjusted balances using T-account format.

2. Journalize Dobrowski Service Company's adjusting entries at December 31, 2006. Key entries by letter as in Exhibit 3-9 (page 124).

3. Post the adjusting entries into the T-accounts.

4. Write the trial balance on a work sheet, enter the adjusting entries, and prepare an adjusted trial balance, as shown in Exhibit 3-10.

5. Prepare the income statement, the statement of owner's equity, and the balance sheet. Draw the arrows linking these three statements.

Solution

Requirements 1 and 3

ASSETS

Cash

Bal. 297,000	

Accounts Receivable

Bal. 555,000	
(e) 18,000	
Bal. 573,000	

Supplies

Bal. 9,000	(a)	6,000	
Bal. 3,000			

Furniture and Fixtures

Bal. 150,000	

Accumulated Amortization—Furniture and Fixtures

	Bal. 60,000
	(b) 30,000
	Bal. 90,000

Building

Bal. 315,000	

Accumulated Amortization—Building

	Bal. 195,000
	(c) 15,000
	Bal. 210,000

Land

Bal. 75,000	

LIABILITIES

Accounts Payable

	Bal. 570,000

Salary Payable

	(d) 7,500
	Bal. 7,500

Unearned Service Revenue

(f)	48,000	Bal. 67,500	
		Bal. 19,500	

OWNER'S EQUITY

D. Dobrowski, Capital

	Bal. 439,500

D. Dobrowski, Withdrawals

Bal. 97,500	

REVENUE

Service Revenue

	Bal. 429,000
	(e) 18,000
	(f) 48,000
	Bal. 495,000

EXPENSES

Salary Expense

Bal. 258,000	
(d) 7,500	
Bal. 265,500	

Supplies Expense

(a)	6,000	
Bal.	6,000	

Amortization Expense—Furniture and Fixtures

(b)	30,000	
Bal.	30,000	

Amortization Expense—Building

(c)	15,000	
Bal.	15,000	

Miscellaneous Expense

Bal. 4,500	

Requirement 2

2006

a. Dec. 31 Supplies Expense.. 6,000
              Supplies... 6,000
              To record supplies used ($9,000 – $3,000).

b. Dec. 31 Amortization Expense—Furniture and Fixtures 30,000
              Accumulated Amortization—Furniture
              and Fixtures... 30,000
              To record amortization expense on furniture and
              fixtures.

c. Dec. 31 Amortization Expense—Building........................... 15,000
              Accumulated Amortization—Building.............. 15,000
              To record amortization expense on building.

d. Dec. 31 Salary Expense.. 7,500
              Salary Payable... 7,.500
              To accrue salary expense.

e. Dec. 31 Accounts Receivable 18,000
              Service Revenue.. 18,000
              To accrue service revenue.

f. Dec. 31 Unearned Service Revenue 48,000
              Service Revenue.. 48,000
              To record unearned service revenue that has been
              earned.

Requirement 4

DOBROWSKI SERVICE COMPANY
Preparation of Adjusted Trial Balance
December 31, 2006

Account Title	Trial Balance Debit	Trial Balance Credit	Adjustments Debit	Adjustments Credit	Adjusted Trial Balance Debit	Adjusted Trial Balance Credit
Cash	297,000				297,000	
Accounts receivable	555,000		(e) 18,000		573,000	
Supplies	9,000			(a) 6,000	3,000	
Furniture and fixtures	150,000				150,000	
Accumulated amortization —furniture and fixtures		60,000		(b) 30,000		90,000
Building	315,000				315,000	
Accumulated amortization —building		195,000		(c) 15,000		210,000
Land	75,000				75,000	
Accounts payable		570,000				570,000
Salary payable	0			(d) 7,500		7,500
Unearned service revenue		67,500	(f) 48,000			19,500
D. Dobrowski, capital		439,500				439,500
D. Dobrowski, withdrawals	97,500				97,500	
Service revenue		429,000		(e) 18,000		495,000
				(f) 48,000		
Salary expense	258,000		(d) 7,500		265,500	
Supplies expense	0		(a) 6,000		6,000	
Amortization expense —furniture and fixtures	0		(b) 30,000		30,000	
Amortization expense —building	0		(c) 15,000		15,000	
Miscellaneous expense	4,500				4,500	
	1,761,000	1,761,000	124,500	124,500	1,831,500	1,831,500

DOBROWSKI SERVICE COMPANY
Income Statement
For the Year Ended December 31, 2006

Revenues:		
Service revenue		$495,000
Expenses:		
Salary expense	$265,500	
Amortization expense—furniture and fixtures	30,000	
Amortization expense—building	15,000	
Supplies expense	6,000	
Miscellaneous expense	4,500	
Total expenses		321,000
Net income		$174,000

DOBROWSKI SERVICE COMPANY
Statement of Owner's Equity
For the Year Ended December 31, 2006

D. Dobrowski, capital, January 1, 2006	$439,500
Add: Net income	174,000
	613,500
Less: Withdrawals	97,500
D. Dobrowski, capital, December 31, 2006	$516,000

DOBROWSKI SERVICE COMPANY
Balance Sheet
December 31, 2006

Assets			Liabilities		
Cash		$ 297,000	Accounts payable		$ 570,000
Accounts			Salary payable		7,500
receivable		573,000	Unearned service revenue		19,500
Supplies		3,000	Total liabilities		597,000
Furniture					
and fixtures	$150,000		**Owner's Equity**		
Less: Accumulated			D. Dobrowski, capital		516,000
amortization	90,000	60,000			
Building	$315,000				
Less: Accumulated					
amortization	210,000	105,000			
Land		75,000			
			Total liabilities and		
Total assets		$1,113,000	owner's equity		$1,113,000

1

2

Cyber Coach

Visit the Study Guide on the Media Companion CD-ROM and the Student Resources area of the *Accounting* Companion Website for extra practice with the new material in Chapter 3.

www.pearsoned.ca/horngren

Summary

1. **Distinguish accrual-basis accounting from cash-basis accounting.** In *accrual accounting*, business events are recorded as they occur. In *cash-basis accounting*, only those events that affect cash are recorded. The cash basis omits important events such as purchases and sales of assets on account. It also distorts the financial statements by labelling as expenses those cash payments that have long-term effects, such as the purchases of buildings and equipment. Some small organizations use cash-basis accounting, but the generally accepted method is the accrual basis.

2. **Apply the revenue and matching principles.** Businesses divide time into definite periods—such as a month, a quarter, and a year—to report the entity's financial statements. The year is the basic *accounting period*, but companies prepare financial statements as often as they need the information. Accountants have developed the *revenue principle* to determine when to record revenue and the amount of revenue to record. The *matching principle* guides the accounting for expenses. It directs accountants to match expenses against the revenues earned during a particular period of time.

3. **Make adjusting entries.** *Adjusting entries* are a result of the accrual basis of accounting. Made at the end of the period, these entries update the accounts for preparation of the financial statements. Adjusting entries can be divided into five categories: *prepaid expenses, amortization, accrued expenses, accrued revenues,* and *unearned revenues.*

4. **Prepare an adjusted trial balance.** To prepare the *adjusted trial balance*, enter the adjusting entries next to the *unadjusted trial balance* and compute each account's balance.

5. **Prepare the financial statements from the adjusted trial balance.** The adjusted trial balance can be used to prepare the financial statements. The three financial statements are related as follows: Income, shown on the *income statement*, increases the owner's capital, which also appears on the *statement of owner's equity*. The ending balance of capital is the last amount reported on the *balance sheet*.

Self-Study Questions

Test your understanding of the chapter by marking the correct answer for each of the following questions:

1. Accrual accounting (*pp. 109–110*)
   a. Results in higher income than cash-basis accounting
   b. Leads to the reporting of more complete information than does cash-basis accounting
   c. Is not acceptable under GAAP
   d. Omits adjusting entries at the end of the period

2. Under the revenue principle, revenue is recorded (*p. 110*)
   a. At the earliest acceptable time
   b. At the latest acceptable time
   c. After it has been earned, but not before
   d. At the end of the accounting period

3. The matching principle provides guidance in accounting for (*pp. 111–112*)
   a. Expenses   c. Assets
   b. Owner's equity   d. Liabilities

4. Adjusting entries (*pp. 112–114*)
   a. Assign revenues to the period in which they are earned
   b. Help to properly measure the period's net income or net loss
   c. Bring asset and liability accounts to correct balances
   d. All of the above

5. A building-cleaning firm began November with supplies of $160. During the month, the firm purchased supplies of $290. At November 30, supplies on hand total $210. Supplies expense for the period is (*pp. 115–116*)
   a. $210   c. $290
   b. $240   d. $450

6. A building that cost $120,000 has accumulated amortization of $50,000. The carrying value of the building is (*pp. 118–119*)
   a. $50,000   c. $120,000
   b. $70,000   d. $170,000

7. The adjusting entry to accrue salary expense (*pp. 119–120*)
   a. Debits Salary Expense and credits Cash
   b. Debits Salaries Payable and credits Salary Expense
   c. Debits Salaries Payable and credits Cash
   d. Debits Salary Expense and credits Salaries Payable

8. A business received cash of $3,000 in advance for service that will be provided later. The cash receipt entry debited Cash and credited Unearned Revenue for $3,000. At the end of the period, $1,100 is still unearned. The adjusting entry for this situation will (*pp. 121–122*)
   a. Debit Unearned Revenue and credit Revenue for $1,900
   b. Debit Unearned Revenue and credit Revenue for $1,100
   c. Debit Revenue and credit Unearned Revenue for $1,900

d. Debit Revenue and credit Unearned Revenue for $1,100

9. The links among the financial statements are (pp. 127–129)
   a. Net income from the income statement to the statement of owner's equity
   b. Ending capital from the statement of owner's equity to the balance sheet
   c. Both a and b above

d. None of the above

10. Accumulated Amortization is reported on the (p. 128)
    a. Balance sheet
    b. Income statement
    c. Statement of owner's equity
    d. Both a and b

Answers to the Self-Study Questions follow the Similar Accounting Terms.

Accounting Vocabulary

Accrual accounting *(p. 109)*
Accrued expense *(p. 119)*
Accrued revenue *(p. 120)*
Accumulated amortization *(p. 117)*
Adjusted trial balance *(p. 125)*
Adjusting entry *(p. 113)*
Amortization *(p. 116)*
Capital asset *(p. 116)*
Carrying value (of a capital asset) *(p. 118)*

Cash-basis accounting *(p. 109)*
Contra account *(p. 117)*
Deferred revenue *(p. 121)*
Matching principle *(p. 111)*
Prepaid expense *(p. 114)*
Revenue principle *(p. 110)*
Time-period concept *(p. 112)*
Unearned revenue *(p. 121)*

Similar Accounting Terms

Accrual accounting	Accrual-basis accounting
Amortization	Depreciation; depletion
Capital asset	Plant asset; fixed asset
Carrying value	Book value
Deferred	Unearned

Answers to Self-Study Questions

1. b
2. c
3. a
4. d
5. b ($160 + $290 − $210 = $240)
6. b ($120,000 − $50,000 = $70,000)
7. d
8. a ($3,000 received − $1,100 unearned = $1,900 earned)
9. c
10. a

Assignment Material

Questions

1. Distinguish accrual accounting from cash-basis accounting.

2. How long is the basic accounting period? What is a fiscal year? What is an interim period?

3. What two questions does the revenue principle help answer?

4. Briefly explain the matching principle.

5. What is the purpose of making adjusting entries?

6. Why are adjusting entries usually made at the end of the accounting period, not during the period?

7. Name five categories of adjusting entries and give an example of each.

8. Do all adjusting entries affect the net income or net loss of the period? Include the definition of an adjusting entry.

9. Why must the balance of Supplies be adjusted at the end of the period?

10. Manning Supply Company pays $3,600 for an insurance policy that covers three years. At the end of the first year, the balance of its Prepaid Insurance account contains two elements. What are the two elements, and what is the correct amount of each?

11. The title Prepaid Expense suggests that this type of account is an expense. If it is, explain why. If it is not, what type of account is it?

12. What is a contra account? Identify the contra

account introduced in this chapter, along with the account's normal balance.

13. The manager of Quickie-Pickie, a convenience store, presents the company's balance sheet to a banker to obtain a loan. The balance sheet reports that the company's capital assets have a carrying value of $135,000 and accumulated amortization of $65,000. What does *carrying value* of a capital asset mean? What was the cost of the capital assets?

14. Give the entry to record accrued interest revenue of $800.

15. Why is an unearned revenue a liability? Give an example.

16. Identify the types of accounts (assets, liabilities, and so on) debited and credited for each of the five types of adjusting entries.

17. What purposes does the adjusted trial balance serve?

18. Explain the relationship among the income statement, the statement of owner's equity, and the balance sheet.

19. Bellevue Company failed to record the following adjusting entries at December 31, the end of its fiscal year: (a) accrued expenses, $1,000; (b) accrued revenues, $1,700; and (c) amortization, $2,000. Did these omissions cause net income for the year to be understated or overstated and by what overall amount?

Exercises

Exercise 3-1   *Cash-basis versus accrual accounting*   **(Obj. 1)**

Sheridan Lake Lodge had the following selected transactions during January:

Jan.		
	1	Paid cash for rent for January, February, and March, $7,800.
	5	Paid electricity expenses, $1,200.
	9	Received cash for the day's room rentals, $4,200.
	14	Paid cash for six television sets, $9,000. They will last three years.
	23	Served a banquet, receiving a note receivable, $3,600.
	31	Made an adjusting entry for January's rent (from January 1).
	31	Accrued salary expense, $2,700.

Show how each transaction would be handled using the cash basis and the accrual basis of accounting. Under each column give the amount of revenue or expense for January. Journal entries are not required. Use the following format for your answer, and show your computations:

Sheridan Lake Lodge—Amount of Revenue or Expense for January

Date	Cash Basis	Accrual Basis

Exercise 3-2   *Applying accounting concepts and principles*   **(Obj. 2)**

Identify the accounting concept or principle that gives the most direction on how to account for each of the following situations:

a. Expenses of the period total $9,000. This amount should be subtracted from revenue to compute the period's income.

b. Expenses of $3,000 must be accrued at the end of the period to measure income properly.

c. A customer states her intention to switch travel agencies. Should the new travel agency record revenue based on this intention?

d. The owner of a business desires monthly financial statements to measure the financial progress of the entity on an ongoing basis.

Exercise 3-3   *Applying the revenue and matching principles; accrual basis versus cash basis*   **(Obj. 1, 2)**

National Storage operates approximately 300 miniwarehouses across Canada. The company's headquarters are in Lethbridge, Alberta. During 2006, National earned rental revenue of $24.0 million and collected cash of $25.6 million from customers. Total expenses for 2006 were $14.4 million, of which National paid $13.6 million.

Required

1. Apply the revenue principle and the matching principle to compute National Storage's net income for 2006.

2. Identify the information that you did not use to compute National Storage's net income. Give the reason for not using the information.

Exercise 3-4 *Applying accounting concepts* *(Obj. 2)*

Write a memo to your supervisor explaining in your own words the concept of amortization as it is used in accounting. Use the following format:

Date: (fill in) _____

To: Supervisor

From: (Student Name) _____

Subject: The concept of amortization

Media Companion CD-ROM

Exercise 3-5 *Allocating prepaid expense to the asset and expense* *(Obj. 2, 3)*

Compute the amounts indicated by question marks for each of the following Prepaid Insurance situations. For situations 1 and 2, journalize the needed entry. Consider each situation separately.

	Situation			
	1	2	3	4
Beginning Prepaid Insurance..	$1,800	$3,000	$5,400	$3,600
Payments for Prepaid Insurance during the year	8,400	?	6,600	?
Total amount to account for..	?	?	12,000	7,800
Ending Prepaid Insurance..	6,200	2,400	?	3,000
Insurance Expense..	$?	$4,200	$8,400	$4,800

Exercise 3-6 *Journalizing adjusting entries* *(Obj. 3)*

Journalize the entries for the following adjustments at December 31, the end of the accounting period:

a. Employee salaries owed for Monday and Tuesday of a five-day workweek; weekly payroll, $30,000.

b. Prepaid insurance expired, $1,200.

c. Interest revenue accrued, $8,000.

d. Unearned service revenue that becomes earned, $3,200.

e. Amortization, $9,600.

Exercise 3-7 *Analyzing the effects of adjustments on net income* *(Obj. 3)*

Suppose the adjustments required in Exercise 3-6 were not made. Compute the overall overstatement or understatement of net income as a result of the omission of these adjustments.

Exercise 3-8 *Journalizing adjusting entries* **(Obj. 3)**

Journalize the adjusting entry needed at December 31 for each of the following independent situations.

a. On July 1, when we collected $18,000 rent in advance, we debited Cash and credited Unearned Rent Revenue. The tenant was paying for one year's rent in advance.

b. The business owes interest expense of $2,700 that it will pay early in the next period.

c. Interest revenue of $2,100 has been earned but not yet received on a $30,000 note receivable held by the business.

d. Salary expense is $3,000 per day—Monday through Friday—and the business pays employees each Friday. This year December 31 falls on a Wednesday.

e. The unadjusted balance of the Supplies account is $6,750. The total cost of supplies remaining on hand on December 31 is $2,250.

f. Equipment was purchased last year at a cost of $75,000. The equipment's useful life is four years. It will have no value after four years.

g. On September 1, when we paid $2,700 for a one-year insurance policy, we debited Prepaid Insurance and credited Cash.

Exercise 3-9 *Recording adjustments in T-accounts* **(Obj. 3)**

The accounting records of Event Planners include the following unadjusted balances at May 31: Accounts Receivable, $3,600; Supplies, $1,800; Salary Payable, $0; Unearned Service Revenue, $1,600; Service Revenue, $58,800; Salary Expense, $4,800; and Supplies Expense, $0.

The company's accountant develops the following data for the May 31 adjusting entries:

a. Supplies on hand, $300

b. Salary owed to employee, $1,800

c. Service revenue accrued, $1,050

d. Unearned service revenue that has been earned, $600

Open T-accounts as needed and record the adjustments directly in the accounts, keying each adjustment amount by letter. Show each account's adjusted balance. Journal entries are not required.

Exercise 3-10 *Explaining unearned revenues* **(Obj. 3)**

Write a paragraph to explain why unearned revenues are liabilities rather than revenues. In your explanation use the following actual example: *Maclean's Magazine* collects cash from subscribers in advance and later mails the magazines to subscribers over a one-year period. Explain what happens to the unearned subscription revenue over the course of a year as the magazines are mailed to subscribers. Into what other account does the unearned subscription revenue go? Give the adjusting entry that *Maclean's Magazine* would make to record the earning of $50,000 of subscription revenue. Include an explanation for the entry.

Exercise 3-11 *Adjusting the accounts* **(Obj. 3, 4)**

The adjusted trial balance (on the next page) of Morton Consulting is incomplete. Enter the adjustment amounts directly in the adjustment columns of the text. Service Revenue is the only account affected by more than one adjustment.

**Media Companion
CD-ROM**

	MORTON CONSULTING						
	Preparation of Adjusted Trial Balance						
	May 31, 2006						
Account Title	Trial Balance		Adjustments		Adjusted Trial Balance	
	Debit	Credit	Debit	Credit	Debit	Credit
Cash	18,000				18,000	
Accounts receivable	39,000				42,600	
Supplies	6,240				4,800	
Office furniture	193,800				193,800	
Accumulated amortization		84,240				86,400
Salary payable		0				5,400
Unearned revenue		5,400				4,140
T. Morton, capital		158,160				158,160
T. Morton, withdrawals	36,000				36,000	
Service revenue		69,780				74,640
Salary expense	16,140				21,540	
Rent expense	8,400				8,400	
Amortization expense	0				2,160	
Supplies expense	0				1,440	
	317,580	317,580			328,740	328,740

Exercise 3-12 *Journalizing adjustments* *(Obj. 3, 4)*

Make journal entries for the adjustments that would complete the preparation of the adjusted trial balance in Exercise 3-11. Date the entries and include explanations.

Exercise 3-13 *Explaining the adjusted trial balance* *(Obj. 4)*

Write a business memorandum to your supervisor explaining the difference between the unadjusted amounts and the adjusted amounts in Exhibit 3-10, page 126. Use Accounts Receivable in your explanation. If necessary, refer back to the discussion of Accrued Revenues that begins on page 120.

Business memos are formatted as follows:

Date: (fill in) _____

To: Supervisor

From: (Student Name) _____

Subject: Difference between the *unadjusted* and the *adjusted* amounts on an adjusted trial balance.

Media Companion CD-ROM

Exercise 3-14 *Preparing the financial statements* *(Obj. 5)*

Refer to the adjusted trial balance in Exercise 3-11. Prepare Morton Consulting's income statement and statement of owner's equity for the month ended May 31, 2006, and its balance sheet on that date. Draw the arrows linking the three statements.

Exercise 3-15 *Preparing the financial statements* *(Obj. 5)*

The accountant for Sandra Rubin's business, Rubin Technologies has posted adjusting entries (a) through (e) to the accounts at December 31, 2006. Selected balance sheet accounts and all the revenues and expenses of the entity follow in T-account form:

Accounts Receivable		Supplies		Accumulated Amortization —Furniture	
103,500		18,000	(a) 4,500		22,500
(e) 29,250					(b) 9,000

Accumulated Amortization —Electronic Equipment		Salaries Payable		Service Revenue	
	148,500		(d) 6,750		607,500
	(c) 22,500				(e) 20,250

Salary Expense		Supplies Expense		Amortization Expense— Furniture		Amortization Expense— Electronic Equipment	
126,000		(a) 4,500		(b) 9,000		(c) 22,500	
(d) 6,750							

Required

1. Prepare the income statement of Rubin Technologies for the year ended December 31, 2006. List expenses in order from the largest to the smallest.
2. Were the company's 2006 operations successful? Give the reason for your answer.

Exercise 3-16 *Preparing the statement of owner's equity* *(Obj. 5)*

Gibbens Consulting began the year on January 1, 2006, with capital of $52,500. On July 12, 2006, Eric Gibbens (the owner) invested $6,000 cash in the business. On September 26, 2006, he transferred to the company land valued at $35,000. The income statement for the year ended December 31, 2006, reported a net loss of $14,000. During this fiscal year, Gibbens withdrew $750 monthly for personal use.

Required

1. Prepare the company's statement of owner's equity for the year ended December 31, 2006.
2. Did the owner's equity of the business increase or decrease during the year? What caused this change?

Serial Exercise

Exercise 3-17 continues the Melanie Clark Engineers situation begun in Exercise 2-15 of Chapter 2.

Exercise 3-17 *Adjusting the accounts, preparing an adjusted trial balance, and preparing the financial statements* *(Obj. 3, 4, 5)*

Refer to Exercise 2-15 of Chapter 2. Start from the trial balance and the posted T-accounts that Melanie Clark Engineers prepared for this engineering practice at December 18. Make sure the account balances in your trial balance and T-accounts match those in the trial balance at December 18, 2005, shown on the next page.

MELANIE CLARK ENGINEERS
Trial Balance
December 18, 2005

Cash	$22,600	
Accounts receivable	3,400	
Supplies	600	
Equipment	6,000	
Furniture	11,200	
Accounts payable		$11,800
Melanie Clark, capital		28,000
Melanie Clark, withdrawals	0	
Service revenue		5,400
Rent expense	1,000	
Utilities expense	400	
Salary expense	0	
Total	$45,200	$45,200

Later in December, the business completed these transactions:

Dec. 21   Received $2,400 in advance for engineering work to be performed evenly over the next 30 days.
   21   Hired a secretary to be paid $4,200 salary on the 21st day of each month.
   26   Paid for the supplies purchased on December 5.
   28   Collected $1,200 from the consulting client of December 18.
   30   Melanie Clark withdrew $3,200 cash for personal use.

Required

1. Open these T-accounts: Accumulated Amortization—Equipment; Accumulated Amortization—Furniture; Salaries Payable; Unearned Service Revenue; Amortization Expense—Equipment; Amortization Expense—Furniture; Supplies Expense.

2. Journalize the transactions of December 21 through 30.

3. Post to the T-accounts, keying all items by date.

4. Prepare a trial balance at December 31. Also set up columns for the adjustments and for the adjusted trial balance, as illustrated in Exhibit 3-10.

5. At December 31, the company gathers the following information for the adjusting entries:

   a. Accrued service revenue, $1,200

   b. Earned a portion of the service revenue collected in advance on December 21.

   c. Supplies remaining on hand at December 31, $200

   d. Amortization expense—equipment, $100; furniture, $120

   e. Accrued $1,400 expense for secretary's salary

   Make these adjustments directly in the adjustments columns, and complete the adjusted trial balance at December 31.

6. Journalize and post the adjusting entries. Denote each adjusting amount as *Adj*. and an account balance as *Bal*.

7. Prepare the income statement and statement of owner's equity of Melanie Clark Engineers for the month ended December 31, 2005 and prepare the balance sheet at that date.

Challenge Exercises

Exercise 3-18 *Computing the amount of revenue*   *(Obj. 3)*

Taylor Enterprises aids international students upon their arrival in Canada from China. Paid by the Chinese government, Irene Taylor collects some service revenue in advance. In other cases Taylor Enterprises receives cash after performing relocation services. At the end of August—a particularly busy period—Taylor's books show the following:

	July 31	August 31
Accounts receivable...	$8,800	$10,000
Unearned service revenue............................	4,800	1,600

During August, Taylor Enterprises received cash of $16,000 from the Chinese government. How much service revenue did the business earn during August? Show your work.

Exercise 3-19 *Computing cash amounts*   *(Obj. 3)*

For the situation of Exercise 3-18, assume the service revenue of Taylor Enterprises was $23,600 during August. How much cash did the business collect from the Chinese government that month? Show your work.

Beyond the Numbers

Beyond the Numbers 3-1

Suppose a new management team is in charge of Alpine Waters Inc., a microbrewery. Assume Alpine Waters Inc.'s new top executives rose through the company ranks in the sales and marketing departments and have little appreciation for the details of accounting. Consider the following conversation between two executives:

John Ramsay, President: "I want to avoid the hassle of adjusting the books every time we need financial statements. Sooner or later we receive cash for all our revenues, and we pay cash for all our expenses. I can understand cash transactions, but all these accruals confuse me. If I cannot understand *our own* accounting, I'm fairly certain the average person who invests in our company cannot understand it either. Let's start recording only our cash transactions. I bet it won't make any difference to anyone."

Kate McNamara, Chief Financial Officer: "Sounds good to me. This will save me lots of headaches. I'll implement the new policy immediately."

Write a business memo to the company president giving your response to the new policy. Identify at least five individual items (such as specific accounts) in the financial statements that will be reported incorrectly. Will outside investors care? Use the format of a business memo given with Exercise 3-13 on page 140.

Ethical Issue

The net income of Corcorran's, a specialty store, decreased sharply during 2006. Mary Corcorran, owner of the store, anticipates the need for a bank loan in 2007. Late in 2006, she instructs the accountant to record a $24,600 sale of furniture to the Corcorran family, even though the goods will not be shipped from the manufacturer until January 2007. Corcorran also tells the accountant not to make the following December 31, 2006 adjusting entries:

| Salaries owed to employees.................................... | $27,000 |
| Prepaid insurance that has expired .... | 1,200 |

Required

1. Compute the overall effect of these transactions on the store's reported income for 2006.

2. Why did Corcorran take this action? Is this action ethical? Give your reason, identifying the parties helped and the parties harmed by Corcorran's action.

3. As a personal friend, what advice would you give *the accountant*?

Problems (Group A)

Problem 3-1A   *Cash-basis versus accrual-basis accounting*   *(Obj. 1, 2)*

Highlands Speech and Hearing Clinic experienced the following selected transactions during March:

Mar. 1   Paid for insurance for March through May, $2,700.
      4   Paid gas bill, $1,200.
      5   Performed services on account, $3,000.
      9   Purchased office equipment for cash, $4,200.
    12   Received cash for services performed, $2,700.
    14   Purchased office equipment on account, $900.
    28   Collected $1,500 on account from March 5.
    31   Paid salary expense, $3,300.
    31   Paid account payable from March 14.
    31   Recorded adjusting entry for March insurance expense (see March 1).
    31   Debited unearned revenue and credited revenue to adjust these accounts, $2,100.

Required

1. Show how each transaction would be accounted for using the cash basis and the accrual basis. Use the format below for your answer, and show your computations. Under each column give the amount of revenue or expense for March. Journal entries are not required.

Highlands Speech and Hearing Clinic—Amount of Revenue or Expense for March

Date	Cash Basis	Accrual Basis

2. Compute March net income or net loss under each method.

3. Indicate which measure of net income or net loss is preferable. Give your reason.

Problem 3-2A   *Applying accounting principles*   *(Obj. 1, 2)*

Write a business memo to a new bookkeeper to explain the difference between the cash basis of accounting and the accrual basis. Mention the roles of the revenue principle and the matching principle in accrual-basis accounting.
    This is the format of a business memo:

Date:	(fill in)
To:	New Bookkeeper
From:	(Student Name)
Subject:	Difference between cash-basis and accrual-basis accounting

Problem 3-3A   *Journalizing adjusting entries*   *(Obj. 3)*

Journalize the adjusting entry needed on December 31, the company's year end, for each of the following independent cases affecting Woodside Contractors:

a. Details of Prepaid Rent are shown in the account:

Prepaid Rent

Jan. 1	Bal.	6,000
Mar. 31		12,000
Sept. 30		12,000

Woodside Contractors pays office rent semiannually on March 31 and September 30. At December 31, part of the last payment is still available to cover January to March of the next year.

b. Woodside Contractors pays its employees each Friday. The amount of the weekly payroll is $24,000 for a five-day workweek, and the daily salary amounts are equal. The current accounting period ends on Monday.

c. Woodside Contractors has lent money to help employees find housing, receiving notes receivable in return. During the current year the entity has earned interest revenue of $4,500, which it will receive next year.

d. The beginning balance of Supplies was $12,060. During the year the company purchased supplies costing $37,080, and at December 31 the inventory of supplies remaining on hand is $12,900.

e. Woodside Contractors is installing cable in a large building, and the owner of the building paid Woodside Contractors $75,000 as the annual service fee. Woodside Contractors recorded this amount as Unearned Service Revenue. Robin Zweig, the general manager, estimates that the company has earned one-fourth of the total fee during the current year.

f. Amortization for the current year includes: Equipment, $23,100; and Trucks, $61,920. Make a compound entry.

Problem 3-4A   *Analyzing and journalizing adjustments*   *(Obj. 3)*

Perry Construction's unadjusted and adjusted trial balances at April 30, 2006, are shown on the top of the next page.

Required

Journalize the adjusting entries that account for the differences between the two trial balances.

Problem 3-5A   *Journalizing and posting adjustments to T-accounts; preparing the adjusted trial balance*   *(Obj. 3, 4)*

The trial balance of Selkirk Realty at October 31, 2007, appears on the bottom of the next page. The data needed for the month-end adjustments follow:

Adjustment data:

a. Prepaid rent still available at October 31, $1,200.

b. Supplies used during the month, $1,920.

c. Amortization for the month, $2,700.

d. Accrued advertising expense at October 31, $960. (Credit Accounts Payable.)

e. Accrued salary expense at October 31, $540.

f. Unearned commission revenue still remaining to be earned at October 31, $6,000.

PERRY CONSTRUCTION
Adjusted Trial Balance
April 30, 2006

Account Title	Trial Balance Debit	Trial Balance Credit	Adjusted Trial Balance Debit	Adjusted Trial Balance Credit
Cash	24,720		24,720	
Accounts receivable	25,440		26,800	
Interest receivable	0		800	
Notes receivable	16,400		16,400	
Supplies	3,920		1,160	
Prepaid rent	9,920		2,880	
Equipment	265,800		265,800	
Accumulated amortization—equipment		64,040		69,160
Accounts payable		27,680		27,680
Wages payable		0		1,280
Unearned service revenue		2,680		440
H. Owner, capital		235,160		235,160
H. Owner, withdrawals	14,400		14,400	
Service revenue		39,760		43,360
Interest revenue		0		800
Wage expense	6,400		7,680	
Rent expense	0		7,040	
Amortization expense—equipment	0		5,120	
Insurance expense	1,480		1,480	
Supplies expense	0		2,760	
Utilities expense	840		840	
	369,320	369,320	377,880	377,880

SELKIRK REALTY
Trial Balance
October 31, 2007

Cash	$ 13,300	
Accounts receivable	44,250	
Prepaid rent	9,300	
Supplies	2,340	
Furniture	68,130	
Accumulated amortization—furniture		$ 34,920
Accounts payable		5,820
Salary payable		0
Unearned commission revenue		6,870
I. Jarvis, capital		75,180
I. Jarvis, withdrawals	2,000	
Commission revenue		25,200
Salary expense	6,480	
Rent expense	0	
Amortization expense—furniture	0	
Advertising expense	2,190	
Supplies expense	0	
Total	$147,990	$147,990

Required

1. Open T-accounts for the accounts listed in the trial balance, inserting their October 31 unadjusted balances.

2. Journalize the adjusting entries and post them to the T-accounts. Key the journal entries and the posted amounts by letter.

3. Prepare the adjusted trial balance.

4. How will the company use the adjusted trial balance?

Problem 3-6A *Preparing the financial statements from an adjusted trial balance* *(Obj. 5)*

Media Companion CD-ROM

The adjusted trial balance of Belford Systems at December 31, 2006, is shown below.

Required

1. Prepare Belford Systems' 2006 income statement, statement of owner's equity, and balance sheet. List expenses in decreasing order on the income statement and show total liabilities on the balance sheet. If your three financial statements appear on one page, draw the arrows linking the three financial statements. If they are on separate pages, write a short paragraph describing how the three financial statements are linked. How will what you have learned in this problem help you manage a business?

2. a. Which financial statement reports Belford Systems' results of operations? Were operations successful during 2006? Cite specifics from the financial statements to support your evaluation.

   b. Which statement reports the company's financial position? Does Belford Systems' financial position look strong or weak? Give the reason for your evaluation.

BELFORD SYSTEMS
Adjusted Trial Balance
December 31, 2006

Cash	$ 3,960	
Accounts receivable	26,760	
Supplies	6,900	
Prepaid rent	4,800	
Equipment	60,540	
Accumulated amortization —equipment		$ 13,050
Office furniture	113,130	
Accumulated amortization —office furniture		14,610
Accounts payable		14,220
Interest payable		2,490
Unearned service revenue		1,860
Notes payable		40,500
J. Belford, capital		78,270
J. Belford, withdrawals	87,000	
Service revenue		374,730
Amortization expense—equipment	20,040	
Amortization expense—office furniture	7,110	
Salary expense	119,700	
Rent expense	52,200	
Interest expense	9,300	
Utilities expense	8,010	
Insurance expense	11,430	
Supplies expense	8,850	
Total	$539,730	$539,730

Problem 3-7A *Preparing an adjusted trial balance and the financial statements*
(Obj. 3, 4, 5)

The unadjusted trial balance of Quest Data at July 31, 2007, and the related month-end adjustment data appear below:

QUEST DATA Trial Balance July 31, 2007		
Cash...	$ 16,800	
Accounts receivable...	34,800	
Prepaid rent	10,800	
Supplies	2,400	
Furniture...	86,400	
Accumulated amortization—furniture............		$ 10,500
Accounts payable..		10,350
Salary payable		0
M. Wong, capital		115,950
M. Wong, withdrawals.......................................	12,000	
Consulting revenue..		35,250
Salary expense	7,200	
Rent expense...	0	
Utilities expense	1,650	
Amortization expense—furniture	0	
Supplies expense...	0	
Total...	$172,050	$172,050

Adjustment data:

a. Accrued consulting revenue at July 31, $2,700.

b. Prepaid rent had expired during the month. The unadjusted prepaid balance of $10,800 relates to the period July through October.

c. Supplies remaining on hand at July 31, $1,200.

d. Amortization on furniture for the month. The estimated useful life of the furniture is four years, it will have no value at the end of the four years, and the straight-line method of amortization is used.

e. Accrued salary expense at July 31 for one day only. The five-day weekly payroll is $3,000.

Required

1. Using Exhibit 3-10 (page 126) as an example, recopy the trial balance and prepare the adjusted trial balance of Quest Data at July 31, 2007. Key each adjusting entry by letter.

2. Prepare the income statement, the statement of owner's equity, and the balance sheet. Draw the arrows linking the three financial statements, or write a short description of how they are linked.

Problem 3-8A *Applying the revenue and matching principles, making adjusting entries, preparing an adjusted trial balance and income statement* *(Obj. 2, 3, 4, 5)*

Sutanto Logistics provides telecommunications consulting services. On December 31, 2007, the end of its first year of operations, the business had the following account balances (in alphabetical order):

Accounts payable	$12,000
Accounts receivable	11,400
Accumulated amortization—equipment..............	0

Accumulated amortization—furniture	$ 0
Cash	6,000
Computer equipment	36,000
Consulting revenue	213,000
Furniture	120,000
G. Sutanto, capital	96,000
G. Sutanto, withdrawals	45,000
Prepaid consulting expense	7,500
Salaries expense	54,900
Supplies	2,700
Supplies expense	11,700
Travel expense	25,800

The following information was available on December 31, 2007:

a. A physical count shows $3,000 of supplies remaining on hand on December 31.

b. The computer equipment has an expected useful life of four years, with no expected value after four years. The computers were purchased on January 2, and the straight-line method of amortization is used.

c. The furniture, purchased on January 2, is expected to be used for 10 years, with no expected value after 10 years. The straight-line method of amortization is used.

d. On October 1, Sutanto Logistics hired a consultant to prepare a business plan and agreed to pay her $1,500 per month. The business paid her for five months' work in advance.

e. The company's office manager, who earns $300 per day, worked the last five days of the year and will be paid on January 5, 2008.

f. On December 30, Sutanto Logistics provided consulting for a client for $3,000 to be paid in 30 days.

Required

1. Journalize the adjusting entries required on December 31, 2007. Key the journal entries by letter.

2. Prepare, with accounts in the correct sequence, an adjusted trial balance on December 31, 2007.

3. Prepare an income statement for the year ended December 31, 2007.

Problems (Group B)

Problem 3-1B   *Cash basis versus accrual basis (Obj. 1, 2)*

Thompson Office Design had the following selected transactions during October:

Oct.	1	Paid for insurance for October through December, $1,800.
	4	Performed design service on account, $3,000.
	5	Purchased office furniture on account, $450.
	8	Paid advertising expense, $900.
	11	Purchased office equipment for cash, $2,400.
	19	Performed design services and received cash, $2,100.
	24	Collected $1,200 on account for the October 4 service.
	26	Paid account payable from October 5.
	29	Paid salary expense, $3,100.
	31	Recorded adjusting entry for October insurance expense (see Oct. 1).
	31	Debited unearned revenue and credited revenue to adjust these accounts, $1,800.

Required

1. Show how each transaction would be accounted for using the cash basis and

the accrual basis. Use the format below for your answer, and show your computations. Under each column give the amount of revenue or expense for October. Journal entries are not required.

Thompson Office Design—Amount of Revenue or Expense for October

Date	Cash Basis	Accrual Basis

2. Compute October net income or net loss under each method.

3. Indicate which measure of net income or net loss is preferable. Give your reason.

Problem 3-2B *Applying accounting principles* *(Obj. 2, 3)*

As the controller of Chow Security Systems, you have hired a new bookkeeper, whom you must train. She objects to making an adjusting entry for accrued salaries at the end of the period. She reasons, "We will pay the salaries soon. Why not wait until payment to record the expense? In the end, the result will be the same." Write a business memo to explain to the bookkeeper why the adjusting entry for accrued salary expense is needed.

This is the format of the business memo:

Date: (fill in) _____

To: New Bookkeeper

From: (Student Name) _____

Subject: Why the adjusting entry for salary expense is needed

Problem 3-3B *Journalizing adjusting entries* *(Obj. 3)*

Journalize the adjusting entry needed on December 31, the company's year end, for each of the following independent cases affecting Huff Telecommunications:

a. Each Friday the company pays its employees for the current week's work. The amount of the payroll is $18,000 for a five-day workweek. The current accounting period ends on Thursday.

b. Huff Telecommunications has received notes receivable from some clients for professional services. During the current year, Huff Telecommunications has earned interest revenue of $1,020, which will be received next year.

c. The beginning balance of Supplies was $10,800. During the year the company purchased supplies costing $15,180, and at December 31 the inventory of supplies remaining on hand is $5,820.

d. The company is developing a wireless communication system for a large company, and the client paid Huff $216,000 at the start of the project. Huff recorded this amount as Unearned Consulting Revenue. The development will take several months to complete. Huff executives estimate that the company has earned three-fourths of the total fee during the current year.

e. Amortization for the current year includes: Office Furniture, $33,000, and Design Equipment, $38,160. Make a compound entry.

f. Details of Prepaid Insurance are shown in the account:

Prepaid Insurance

Jan. 1	Bal.	1,800	
Apr. 30		2,700	
Oct. 31		2,700	

Huff Telecommunications pays semiannual insurance premiums (the payment for insurance coverage is called a *premium*) on April 30 and October 31. At December 31, part of the last payment is still available to cover January to April of the next year.

Problem 3-4B *Analyzing and journalizing adjustments* *(Obj. 3)*

Yaskiel Consulting's unadjusted and adjusted trial balances at December 31, 2007, follow:

YASKIEL CONSULTING
Adjusted Trial Balance
December 31, 2007

Account Title	Trial Balance Debit	Trial Balance Credit	Adjusted Trial Balance Debit	Adjusted Trial Balance Credit
Cash	10,990		10,990	
Accounts receivable	8,260		14,090	
Supplies	1,090		280	
Prepaid insurance	2,600		2,330	
Office furniture	21630		21,630	
Accumulated amortization—				
office furniture		8,220		10,500
Accounts payable		6,310		6,310
Salary payable		0		960
Interest payable		0		480
Note payable		12,000		12,000
Unearned consulting revenue		1,840		1,160
Ava Yaskiel, capital		13,510		13,510
Ava Yaskiel, withdrawals	22,500		22,500	
Consulting revenue		69,890		76,400
Amortization expense—furniture	0		2,280	
Supplies expense	0		810	
Utilities expense	4,960		4,960	
Salary expense	26,660		27,620	
Rent expense	12,200		12,200	
Interest expense	880		1,360	
Insurance expense	0		270	
	111,770	111,770	121,320	121,320

Required
Journalize the adjusting entries that account for the differences between the two trial balances.

Problem 3-5B *Journalizing and posting adjustments to T-accounts; preparing and using the adjusted trial balance and the financial statements* *(Obj. 3, 4)*

The trial balance of Vella Printing at December 31, 2006, appears on the next page. The data needed for the month-end adjustments appear below.

Adjustment data:

a. Unearned printing revenue still remaining to be earned at December 31, $1,250.

b. Prepaid rent still available at December 31, $465.

c. Supplies used during the month, $525.

d. Amortization for the month, $300.

e. Accrued advertising expense at December 31, $460. (Credit Accounts Payable.)

f. Accrued salary expense at December 31, $400.

VELLA PRINTING
Trial Balance
December 31, 2006

Cash..	$ 5,325	
Accounts receivable...	17,835	
Prepaid rent	1,815	
Supplies	885	
Furniture and equipment	14,805	
Accumulated amortization—		
furniture and equipment		$ 2,725
Accounts payable...		2,480
Salary payable		0
Unearned printing revenue................................		2,100
S. Vella, capital..		29,630
S. Vella, withdrawals	4,000	
Printing revenue..		11,780
Salary expense	2,850	
Rent expense..	0	
Amortization expense—		
furniture and equipment	0	
Advertising expense...	1,200	
Supplies expense..	0	
Total...	$48,715	$48,715

Required

1. Open T-accounts for the accounts listed in the trial balance, inserting their December 31 unadjusted balances.

2. Journalize the adjusting entries on December 31, and post them to the T-accounts. Key the journal entries and posted amounts by letter.

3. Prepare the adjusted trial balance.

4. How will the company use the adjusted trial balance?

Media Companion CD-ROM

Problem 3-6B *Preparing the financial statements from an adjusted trial balance* *(Obj. 3, 4, 5)*

The adjusted trial balance of Renaud Antique Auctioneers at the end of its year, December 31, 2007, is shown on the next page.

Required

1. Prepare Renaud Antique Auctioneer's 2007 income statement, statement of owner's equity, and balance sheet. List expenses in decreasing order on the income statement and show total liabilities on the balance sheet. If your three financial statements appear on one page, draw the arrows linking the three financial statements. If they are on separate pages, write a short paragraph describing how the three financial statements are linked. How will what you have learned in this problem help you manage a business?

2. a. Which financial statement reports Renaud's results of operations? Were 2007 operations successful? Cite specifics from the financial statements to support your evaluation.

   b. Which statement reports the company's financial position? Does Renaud's financial position look strong or weak? Give the reason for your evaluation.

RENAUD ANTIQUE AUCTIONEERS
Adjusted Trial Balance
December 31, 2007

Cash...	$ 9,360	
Accounts receivable	165,960	
Prepaid rent	5,400	
Supplies	3,880	
Equipment..	302,760	
Accumulated amortization—equipment.........		$ 88,960
Office furniture..	96,400	
Accumulated amortization—office furniture		14,680
Accounts payable...		54,400
Unearned service revenue		18,080
Interest payable		8,520
Salary payable		3,720
Notes payable..		180,000
M. Renaud, capital..		129,520
M. Renaud, withdrawals	192,000	
Service revenue		783,160
Amortization expense—equipment	45,200	
Amortization expense—office furniture..........	9,640	
Salary expense	351,200	
Rent expense...	48,000	
Interest expense..	16,800	
Utilities expense	15,080	
Insurance expense...	12,600	
Supplies expense...	6,760	
Total...	$1,281,040	$1,281,040

Problem 3-7B *Preparing an adjusted trial balance and the financial statements*
(Obj. 3, 4, 5)

Consider the unadjusted trial balance of Hutton Landscaping at October 31, 2006, and the related month-end adjustment data.

HUTTON LANDSCAPING
Trial Balance
October 31, 2006

Cash...	$ 14,175	
Accounts receivable	18,000	
Prepaid rent	9,000	
Supplies	1,350	
Equipment..	60,750	
Accumulated amortization— equipment		$ 6,750
Accounts payable...		6,300
Salary payable		0
T. Mack, capital...		81,000
T. Mack, withdrawals..	8,100	
Landscaping design revenue		21,150
Salary expense	3,150	
Rent expense...	0	
Utilities expense	675	
Amortization expense— equipment	0	
Supplies expense...	0	
Total...	$115,200	$115,200

Adjustment data:

a. Accrued landscaping design revenue at October 31, $4,500.

b. Some of the prepaid rent had expired during the month. The unadjusted prepaid balance of $4,000 relates to the period October 1, 2006, through January 31, 2007.

c. Supplies remaining on hand at October 31, $450.

d. Amortization on equipment for the month. The equipment's expected useful life is five years; it will have no value at the end of its useful life, and the straight-line method of amortization is used.

e. Accrued salary expense at October 31 should be for one day only. The five-day weekly payroll is $4,500.

Required

1. Recopy the trial balance using the format in Exhibit 3-10 (page 126), and prepare the adjusted trial balance of Hutton Landscaping at October 31, 2006. Key each adjusting entry by letter.

2. Prepare the income statement, the statement of owner's equity, and the balance sheet. Draw the arrows linking the three financial statements, or write a short description of how they are linked.

Problem 3-8B *Applying the revenue and matching principles, making adjusting entries, preparing an adjusted trial balance and income statement* **(Obj. 2, 3, 4, 5)**

Vineberg Employment Counsellors provides counselling services to employees of companies that are downsizing. On December 31, 2006, the end of its first year of operations, the business had the following account balances (in alphabetical order):

Accounts payable	$ 78,000
Accounts receivable	16,800
Accumulated amortization—building	0
Accumulated amortization—computer equipment	0
Building	240,000
Cash	7,200
Computer equipment	57,600
Consulting revenue	306,000
K. Vineberg, capital	276,000
K. Vineberg, withdrawals	66,000
Land	120,000
Prepaid consulting expense	9,600
Salaries expense	100,800
Supplies	4,200
Supplies expense	20,400
Utilities expense	17,400

The following information was available on December 31, 2006:

a. A physical count shows $7,200 of supplies remaining on hand on December 31.

b. The building has an expected useful life of 10 years, with no expected value after 10 years. The building was purchased on January 2, and the straight-line method of amortization is used.

c. The computer equipment, purchased on January 2, is expected to be used for four years with no expected value after four years. The straight-line method of amortization is used.

d. On November 1, the company hired a pension consultant and agreed to pay her $2,400 per month. The company paid her for four months' work, in advance.

e. The company's assistant, who earns $400 per day, worked the last six days of the year and will be paid on January 4, 2007.

f. On December 29, the company provided counselling services to a customer for $12,000, to be paid in 30 days.

Required

1. Journalize the adjusting entries required on December 31, 2006.
2. Prepare, with accounts in the correct sequence, an adjusted trial balance on December 31, 2006.
3. Prepare an income statement for the year ended December 31, 2006.

Challenge Problems

Problem 3-1C   *Understanding accrual-basis accounting*   **(Obj. 1, 2, 3)**

The basic accounting period is one year and all organizations report on an annual basis. It is common for large companies to report on a semiannual basis, and some even report monthly. Interim reporting has a cost, however.

You are working part-time as an accounting clerk for Paradise Corp. The company was private and prepared only annual financial statements for its shareholders. Paradise has gone public and now must report quarterly. Samantha Fleming, your supervisor in the accounting department, is concerned about all the additional work that will be required to produce the quarterly statements.

Required

What does Samantha mean when she talks about "additional work"?

Problem 3-2C   *Application of the matching principle*   **(Obj. 2)**

The matching principle is well established as a basis for recording expenses.

Required

1. New accountants sometimes state the principle as matching revenues against expenses. Explain to a new accountant why matching revenues against expenses is incorrect.
2. It has been suggested that not-for-profit organizations, such as churches and hospitals, should flip their income statements and show revenues as a deduction from expenses. Why do you think that the suggestion has been made?

Extending Your Knowledge

Decision Problems

1. Valuing a business on the basis of its net income   *(Obj. 4, 5)*

Cameron Masson has owned and operated Alberta Biotech, a management consulting firm, since its beginning 10 years ago. From all appearances the business has prospered. Masson lives in the fast lane—flashy car, home located in an expensive suburb, frequent trips abroad, and other signs of wealth. In the past few years, you have become friends with him through weekly rounds of golf at the country club. Recently, he mentioned that he has lost his zest for the business and would consider selling it for the right price. He claims that his clientele is firmly established, and that the business "runs on its own." According to Masson, the consulting procedures are fairly simple, and anyone could perform the work.

Assume you are interested in buying this business. You obtain its most recent monthly trial balance, which follows. Assume that revenues and expenses vary little from month to month and April is a typical month.

Your investigation reveals that the trial balance does not include the effects of monthly revenues of $3,300 and expenses totalling $6,200. If you were to buy Alberta Biotech, you would hire a manager so you could devote your time to other duties. Assume that this person would require a monthly salary of $6,000.

ALBERTA BIOTECH
Trial Balance
April 30, 2007

Cash..	$ 29,100	
Accounts receivable	44,700	
Prepaid expenses	7,800	
Capital assets	723,900	
Accumulated amortization...................		$568,800
Land for future expansion...................	144,000	
Accounts payable.................................		41,400
Salaries payable...................................		0
Unearned consulting revenue..............		170,100
C. Masson, capital................................		172,200
C. Masson, withdrawals	27,000	
Consulting revenue..............................		36,900
Salary expense.....................................	10,200	
Rent expense..	0	
Utilities expense..................................	2,700	
Amortization expense	0	
Supplies expense.................................	0	
Total..	$989,400	$989,400

Required

1. Is this an unadjusted or adjusted trial balance? How can you tell?
2. Assume that the most you would pay for the business is 40 times the monthly net income you could expect to earn from it. Compute this possible price.
3. Masson states that the lowest price he will accept for the business is $225,000 plus the balance in owner's equity on April 30. Compute this amount.
4. Under these conditions, how much should you offer Masson? Give your reasons.

2. Understanding the concepts underlying the accrual basis of accounting (Obj. 1, 2)

The following independent questions relate to the accrual basis of accounting:

1. It has been said that the only time a company's financial position is known for certain is when the company is wound up and its only asset is cash. Why is this statement true?
2. A friend suggests that the purpose of adjusting entries is to correct errors in the accounts. Is your friend's statement true? What is the purpose of adjusting entries if the statement is wrong?
3. The text suggested that furniture (and each other capital asset that is amortized) is a form of prepaid expense. Do you agree? Why do you think some accountants view capital assets this way?

Financial Statement Problems

1. Journalizing and posting transactions, and tracing account balances to the financial statements   (Obj. 3, 4, 5)

Intrawest Corporation—like all other businesses—makes adjusting entries prior to year end in order to measure assets, liabilities, revenues, and expenses properly.

Examine Intrawest's balance sheet and pay particular attention to Prepaid Expenses and Other (Hint: Note 8(a)) and Amounts Payable (which includes Salary Payable and Interest Payable) and Deferred Revenue (another name for unearned revenue).

Required

1. Open T-accounts for: Prepaid Expenses and Other; Amounts Payable; and Season Pass Revenue (see Deferred Revenue and include current and long-term). Insert Intrawest's balances (in thousands) at June 30, 2002.

2. Journalize the following for the current year, ended June 30, 2003. Key entries by letter. Explanations are not required.

   Cash transactions (amounts in thousands of U.S. dollars):

   a. Paid prepaid expenses, $12,990.

   b. Paid the June 30, 2002, accounts payable.

   c. Received $52,600 cash for customers' advance season's pass payments.

   Adjustments at June 30, 2003 (amounts in thousands of U.S. dollars):

   d. Prepaid expenses expired, $4,613. (Debit Ski and Resort Operations Expense.)

   e. Amounts Payable, $218,444. (Debit Ski and Resort Operations Expense.)

   f. Earned sales revenue for which cash has been received from customers in advance for season's passes, $17,206.

3. After these entries are posted, show that the balance in the Prepaid Expenses and Other account agrees with the corresponding amount reported in the June 30, 2003, balance sheet.

Appendix

OBJECTIVE A1
Account for a prepaid expense
recorded initially as an expense

Alternative Treatment of Accounting for Prepaid Expenses and Unearned Revenues

Chapters 1 through 3 illustrate the most popular way to account for prepaid expenses and unearned revenues. This appendix illustrates an alternative—and equally appropriate—approach to handling prepaid expenses and unearned revenues.

···············
THINKING IT OVER

How does a business record
(1) prepayment of monthy rent in
an expense account;
(2) utilities expense;
(3) the prepayment of three
months' rent?

A:
(1) Rent Expense   XX
    Cash   XX
(2) Utilities Expense   XX
    Cash   XX
(3) Rent Expense   XX
    Cash   XX
It is easier to record the payment
as an expense than as an asset,
like most payments.

Prepaid Expenses

Prepaid expenses are advance payments of expenses. Prepaid Insurance, Prepaid Rent, Prepaid Advertising, and Prepaid Legal Cost are prepaid expenses. Supplies that will be used up in the current period or within one year are also accounted for as prepaid expenses.

When a business prepays an expense—insurance, for example—it can debit an *asset* account (Prepaid Insurance) as illustrated on page 114 as follows:

Aug. 1	Prepaid Insurance..........................	XXX	
	Cash...		XXX

Alternatively, it can debit an *expense* account in the entry to record this cash payment:

Aug. 1	Insurance Expense..........................	XXX	
	Cash...		XXX

Regardless of the account debited, the business must adjust the accounts at the end of the period to report the correct amounts of the expense and the asset.

Prepaid Expense Recorded Initially as an Expense

Prepaying an expense creates an asset, as explained under the "Prepaid Insurance" heading on page 114. However, the asset may be so short-lived that it will expire in the current accounting period—within one year or less. Thus the accountant may decide to debit the prepayment to an expense account at the time of payment. A $4,200 cash payment for insurance coverage (for one year, in advance) on August 1, 2006, may be debited to Insurance Expense:

2006			
Aug. 1	Insurance Expense..........................	4,200	
	Cash...		4,200

At December 31, 2006, only five months' prepayment has expired, leaving seven months' insurance still prepaid. In this case, the accountant must transfer $7/12$ of the original prepayment of $4,200, or $2,450, to Prepaid Insurance. At December 31, 2006, the business still has the benefit of the prepayment for January through July of 2007. The December 31 adjusting entry is

Adjusting Entries

2006			
Dec. 31	Prepaid Insurance.................................	2,450	
	Insurance Expense............................		2,450
	Prepaid insurance is $2,450 ($4,200 × $7/12$).		

After posting, the two accounts appear as follows:

ASSETS		EXPENSES	
Prepaid Insurance		**Insurance Expense**	

2006			2006		2006	
Dec. 31	Adj. 2,450		Aug. 1	CP 4,200	Dec. 31	Adj. 2,450
Dec. 31	Bal. 2,450		Dec. 31	Bal. 1,750		

CP = Cash payment entry   Adj. = Adjusting entry

The balance sheet for 2006 reports Prepaid Insurance of $2,450, and the income statement for 2006 reports Insurance Expense of $1,750, regardless of whether the business initially debits the prepayment to an asset account or to an expense account.

Unearned (Deferred) Revenues

Unearned (deferred) revenues arise when a business collects cash in advance of earning the revenue. The recognition of revenue is *deferred* until later when it is earned. Unearned revenues are liabilities because the business that receives cash owes the other party goods or services to be delivered later.

Unearned (Deferred) Revenue Recorded Initially as a Revenue

OBJECTIVE A2
Account for an unearned (deferred) revenue recorded initially as a revenue

Receipt of cash in advance of earning the revenue creates a liability, as recorded on page 121. Another way to account for the initial transaction is to credit a *revenue* account. If the business has earned all the revenue within the period during which it received the cash, no adjusting entry is needed at the end of the period. However, if the business earns only a part of the revenue during the period, it must make adjusting entries.

Suppose on October 1, 2007, a consulting firm records the receipt of cash for a nine-month advance fee of $14,400 as revenue. The cash receipt entry is

2007			
Oct. 1	Cash	14,400	
	Consulting Revenue.........................		14,400

THINKING IT OVER

The required adjusting entry depends on the way the transaction was originally recorded.
(1) If the receipt of cash is recorded as a liability before it is earned, what adjusting entry is required?
(2) If the receipt of cash is originally recorded as revenue, what adjusting entry is required?

A:
(1) Unearned Revenue XX
    Revenue   XX
(2) Revenue   XX
    Unearned Revenue   XX
These entries are not interchangeable.

At December 31 the firm has earned only 3/9 of the $14,400, or $4,800. Accordingly, the firm makes an adjusting entry to transfer the unearned portion (6/9 of $14,400, or $9,600) from the revenue account to a liability account as follows:

Adjusting Entries

2007			
Dec. 31	Consulting Revenue..............................	9,600	
	Unearned Consulting Revenue......		9,600
	Consulting revenue earned in advance.		

The adjusting entry leaves the unearned portion (6/9, or $9,600) of the original amount in the liability account because the consulting firm still owes consulting service to the client during January through June of 2008. After posting, the total amount ($14,400) is properly divided between the liability account ($9,600) and the revenue account ($4,800), as follows:

LIABILITIES		REVENUE	
Unearned Consulting Revenue		**Consulting Revenue**	

	2007		2007		2007	
	Dec. 31	Adj. 9,600	Dec. 31	Adj. 9,600	Oct. 1	CR 14,400
	Dec. 31	Bal. 9,600			Dec. 31	Bal. 4,800

CR = Cash receipt entry   Adj. = Adjusting entry

The firm's 2007 income statement reports consulting revenue of $4,800, and the balance sheet at December 31, 2007, reports as a liability the unearned consulting revenue of $9,600, regardless of whether the business initially credits a liability account or a revenue account.

Appendix Exercises

Exercise 3A-1 *Recording supplies transactions two ways* *(Obj. A1)*

At the beginning of the year, supplies of $3,380 were on hand. During the year, the business paid $10,800 cash for supplies. At the end of the year, the count of supplies indicates the ending balance is $2,720.

Required

1. Assume that the business records supplies by initially debiting an *asset* account. Therefore, place the beginning balance in the Supplies T-account, and record the above entries directly in the accounts without using a journal.
2. Assume that the business records supplies by initially debiting an *expense* account. Therefore, place the beginning balance in the Supplies Expense T-account, and record the above entries directly in the accounts without using a journal.
3. Compare the ending account balances under both approaches. Are they the same? Explain.

Exercise 3A-2 *Recording unearned revenues two ways* *(Obj. A2)*

At the beginning of the year, the company owed customers $5,500 for unearned service revenue collected in advance. During the year, the business received advance cash receipts of $20,000. At year end, the unearned revenue liability is $7,400.

Required

1. Assume that the company records unearned revenues by initially crediting a *liability* account. Open T-accounts for Unearned Service Revenue and Service Revenue, and place the beginning balance in Unearned Service Revenue. Journalize the cash collection and adjusting entries, and post their dollar amounts. As references in the T-accounts, denote a balance by *Bal.*, a cash receipt by *CR*, and an adjustment by *Adj.*
2. Assume that the company records unearned revenues by initially crediting a *revenue* account. Open T-accounts for Unearned Service Revenue and Service Revenue, and place the beginning balance in Service Revenue. Journalize the cash collection and adjusting entries, and post their dollar amounts. As references in the T-accounts, denote a balance by *Bal.*, a cash receipt by *CR*, and an adjustment by *Adj.*
3. Compare the ending balances in the two accounts. Explain why they are the same or different.

Appendix Problems

Problem 3A-1 *Recording prepaid rent and rent revenue collected in advance two ways*
(Obj. A1, A2)

Johal Sales and Service completed the following transactions during 2006:

Aug. 31   Paid $6,000 store rent covering the six-month period ending February 28, 2007.
Dec. 1   Collected $6,400 cash in advance from customers. The service revenue will be earned $1,600 each month over the period ending March 31, 2007.

Required

1. Journalize these entries by debiting an asset account for Prepaid Rent and by crediting a liability account for Unearned Service Revenue. Explanations are not required.

2. Journalize the related adjustments at December 31, 2006.

3. Post the entries to the ledger accounts, and show their balances at December 31, 2006. Posting references are not required.

4. Repeat Requirements 1 through 3. This time debit Rent Expense for the rent payment and credit Service Revenue for the collection of revenue in advance.

5. Compare the account balances in Requirements 3 and 4. They should be equal.

Problem 3A-2 *Applying the revenue and matching principles, making adjusting entries, accounting for prepaid expenses recorded initially as an expense, accounting for unearned revenue recorded initially as a revenue* **(Obj. 2, 3, A1, A2)**

Fazelli Consulting develops custom software for clients in the construction business. Fazelli Consulting had the following information available at the close of its first year of business, June 30, 2006:

1. Insurance payments during the year were debited to Insurance Expense. An examination of the policies showed the following:
   - Policy 1: a two-year policy purchased on March 31, 2006, for $4,800.
   - Policy 2: a one-year policy purchased on July 2, 2005, for $1,200.

2. On July 2, 2005, the company purchased $1,000 of supplies and recorded the purchase as a debit to Supplies Expense. Throughout the year the company purchased additional supplies for $2,400, recording the purchase the same way. An inventory count on June 30, 2006, showed that $1,600 of supplies remained on hand.

3. Computer equipment was purchased on January 2, 2006 for $32,000. The equipment was expected to be used for four years and then discarded.

4. The six employees each earn an average of $600 per day for a five-day week and are paid each Thursday. June 30, 2006, was a Friday.

5. An examination of the contracts signed with clients showed the following:
   - Customer A signed a contract on September 1, 2005 and paid $48,000 to Fazelli Consulting. The contract was for software that was to be completed in twelve months from the date of signing.
   - Customer B signed a contract on October 30, 2005, and was to make progress payments of $2,000 each month commencing November 1. The contract was for 30 months. Revenue was recognized on a monthly basis.

All money received to date on the two contracts was credited to Development Fees Earned. Any change to the contract amount will be made at the end of the contract.

Required

1. Journalize the adjusting entries on June 30, 2006.

2. Give the journal entry required to record the payment of wages on July 6, 2006. Since all employees are paid for the July 1 holiday, each was paid for five working days on July 6.

3. Calculate the *total effects* of the adjusting entries (parts 1 to 5) on each of the:
   a. Income statement
   b. Balance sheet.

Completing the Accounting Cycle

CHAPTER OBJECTIVES

After studying this chapter, you should be able to

1 Prepare an accounting work sheet

2 Use the work sheet to complete the accounting cycle

3 Close the revenue, expense, and withdrawal accounts

4 Correct typical accounting errors

5 Classify assets and liabilities as current or long-term

6 Use the current ratio and debt ratio to evaluate a company

 Media Companion CD-ROM

Visit the Media Companion CD-ROM that comes with this book for extra practice with the new material in Chapter 4.

It's a beautiful day in late spring in Vancouver, but you are still immersed in hockey as you watch the Vancouver Canucks play the Toronto Maple Leafs in the sixth game of the Stanley Cup Championship. The teams are playing a best-of-seven series and the Leafs lead the series three games to two. The Canucks need to win this game or Toronto will win the Stanley Cup.

The game is close. After the first period, the score is tied at 1-1. There is no scoring in the second, but Toronto scores early in the third period to take a 2-1 lead. The Canucks fight back and score the tying goal with two minutes to go. There is no more scoring in regulation time and the final result will be decided in overtime.

The game goes back and forth in overtime, before Todd Bertuzzi finally scores to give the Canucks the game and force a seventh game back in Toronto.

When the teams return to Toronto to play the seventh game, what will the scoreboard say at the start of the game? Will it be 3-2 to carry over the score from the previous game? Or will the scoreboard be set back to zero? The answer is obvious: After a game is completed, the scoreboard is always set back to zero.

In the same way, the accounting process sets the scoreboard back to zero at the end of each fiscal period. The process is called "closing the books," and that is the main topic in this chapter. The logic behind the closing process in accounting is the same as setting the scoreboard back to zero after a game. The final step in the process is reporting the financial statements to the public.

THUS FAR, we have prepared the financial statements from an adjusted trial balance. That approach works well for quick decision making, but organizations of all sizes take the accounting process a step further. Whether it's General Motors or EconoTravel, the closing process follows the basic pattern outlined in this chapter. It marks the end of the *accounting cycle* for a given period.

The accounting process often uses a document known as the accountant's *work sheet*. There are many different types of work sheets in business—as many as there are needs for summary data. Work sheets are useful because they aid decision making.

The Accounting Cycle

The **accounting cycle** is the process by which companies produce their financial statements for a specific period of time. For a new business, the cycle begins with setting up (opening) the ledger accounts. Don Smith started EconoTravel on April 2, 2005, so the first step in the cycle was to open the accounts. After a business has operated for one period, however, the account balances carry over from period to period. Therefore, the accounting cycle usually starts with the account balances at the beginning of the period. Exhibit 4-1 outlines the complete accounting cycle. The boldface items in Panel A indicate the new steps that we will be discussing in this chapter.

The accounting cycle includes work performed at two different times:

- During the period—Journalizing transactions
  Posting to the ledger
- End of the period—Adjusting the accounts, including journalizing and posting the adjusting entries
  Closing the accounts, including journalizing and posting the closing entries
  Preparing the financial statements (income statement, statement of owner's equity, and balance sheet)

> **KEY POINT**
>
> The accounting cycle is repeated each accounting period. The goal of the cycle is the financial statements.

The end-of-period work also readies the accounts for the next period. In Chapters 3 and 4, we cover the end-of-period accounting for a service business such as EconoTravel. Chapter 5 then shows how a merchandising entity adjusts and closes its books.

Companies prepare financial statements on a monthly or a quarterly basis, and steps 1 to 6a in Exhibit 4-1 are adequate for statement preparation. Steps 6b through 7 can be performed monthly or quarterly but are necessary only at the end of the year.

EXHIBIT 4-1

The Accounting Cycle

PANEL A

During the Period	End of the Period

1. Start with the account balances in the ledger at the beginning of the period.
2. Analyze and journalize transactions as they occur.
3. Post journal entries to the ledger accounts.
	4. Compute the unadjusted balance in each account at the end of the period.
	5. **Enter the trial balance on the work sheet, and complete the work sheet. (Optional)**
	6. Using the adjusted trial balance or the full work sheet as a guide,
	   a. Prepare the financial statements.
	   b. Journalize and post the adjusting entries.
	   c. **Journalize and post the closing entries.**
	7. **Prepare the postclosing trial balance. This trial balance becomes step 1 for the next period.**

PANEL B

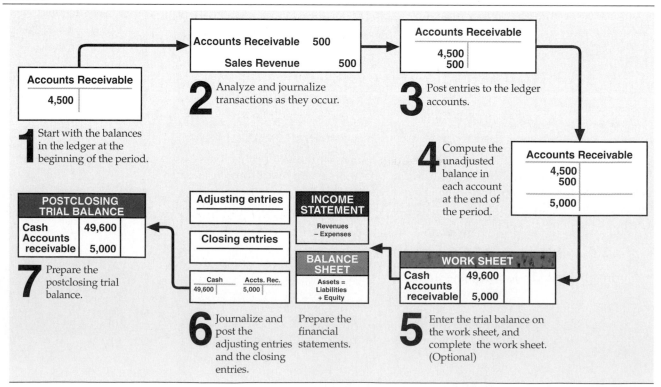

The Work Sheet

OBJECTIVE 1
Prepare an accounting work sheet

Accountants often use a **work sheet**, a document with many columns, to help summarize data for the financial statements. Listing all the accounts and their unadjusted balances helps identify the accounts that need adjustment. The work sheet aids the closing process by listing the ending adjusted balances of all the accounts.

The work sheet is not part of the ledger or the journal, nor is it a financial statement. Therefore, it is not part of the formal accounting system. Instead, it is a summary device that exists for the accountant's convenience.

Exhibits 4-2 through 4-6 illustrate the development of a typical work sheet for EconoTravel. The heading at the top names the business, identifies the document, and states the accounting period. A step-by-step description of its preparation follows.

Steps introduced in Chapter 3 to prepare the adjusted trial balance:

1. Print the account titles and their unadjusted ending balances in the Trial Balance columns of the work sheet, and total the amounts (Exhibit 4-2).

2. Enter the adjustments in the Adjustments columns, and total the amounts (Exhibit 4-3).

3. Compute each account's adjusted balance by combining the trial balance and adjustment figures. Enter the adjusted amounts in the Adjusted Trial Balance columns (Exhibit 4-4).

New steps introduced in this chapter:

4. Extend the asset, liability, and owner's equity amounts from the Adjusted Trial Balance to the Balance Sheet columns. Extend the revenue and expense amounts to the Income Statement columns. Total the statement columns (Exhibit 4-5).

5. Compute net income or net loss as the difference between total revenues and total expenses on the income statement. Enter net income or net loss as a balancing amount on the income statement and the balance sheet, and compute the adjusted column totals (Exhibit 4-6).

Let's examine these steps in greater detail.

1. Print the account titles and their unadjusted ending balances in the Trial Balance columns of the work sheet, and total the amounts. Total debits must equal total credits, as shown in Exhibit 4-2. The account titles and balances come directly from the ledger accounts before the adjusting entries are prepared. Accounts are grouped on the work sheet by category (assets, liabilities, owner's equity, revenues, expenses) and are usually listed in the order in which they appear in the ledger (Cash first, Accounts Receivable second, and so on).

Accounts may have zero balances (for example, Amortization Expense). All accounts are listed on the trial balance because they appear in the ledger. Electronically prepared work sheets list all the accounts, not just those with a balance.

2. Enter the adjusting entries in the Adjustments columns, and total the amounts. Exhibit 4-3 includes the April adjusting entries. These are the same adjustments as those we used in Chapter 3 to prepare the adjusted trial balance.

We can identify the accounts that need to be adjusted by scanning the trial balance. Cash needs no adjustment because all cash transactions are recorded as they occur during the period. Consequently, Cash's balance is up to date.

Accounts Receivable is listed next. Has EconoTravel earned revenue that it has not yet recorded? The answer is yes. At April 30, the business has earned $500, which must be accrued because the cash will be received during May. EconoTravel debits Accounts Receivable and credits Service Revenue on the work sheet in Exhibit 4-3. A letter is used to link the debit and the credit of each adjusting entry.

EXHIBIT 4-2

Trial Balance

	ECONOTRAVEL Accounting Work Sheet For the Month Ended April 30, 2006									
	Trial Balance		Adjustments		Adjusted Trial Balance		Income Statement		Balance Sheet	
Account Title	Dr.	Cr.	Dr.	Cr.	Dr.	Cr.	Dr.	Cr.	Dr.	Cr.
Cash	49,600									
Accounts receivable	4,500									
Supplies	1,400									
Prepaid rent	6,000									
Furniture	33,000									
Accumulated amortization		0								
Accounts payable		26,200								
Salary payable		0								
Unearned service revenue		900								
Don Smith, capital		62,500								
Don Smith, withdrawals	6,400									
Service revenue		14,000								
Rent expense	0									
Salary expense	1,900									
Supplies expense	0									
Amortization expense	0									
Utilities expense	800									
	103,600	103,600								
Net income										

Print the account titles and their un-adjusted ending balances in the Trial Balance columns of the work sheet, and total the amounts.

By moving down the trial balance, the accountant identifies the remaining accounts that need adjustment. Supplies is next. The business has used supplies during April, so it debits Supplies Expense and credits Supplies. The other adjustments are analyzed and entered on the work sheet as you learned in Chapter 3.

Listing the accounts in their proper sequence aids the process of identifying accounts that need to be adjusted. But suppose that one or more accounts are omitted from the trial balance. This account can always be written below the first column totals—$103,600. Assume that Supplies Expense was accidentally omitted and thus did not appear on the trial balance. When the accountant identifies the need to update the Supplies account, he or she knows that the debit in the adjusting entry is to Supplies Expense. In this case, the accountant can write Supplies Expense on the line beneath the amount totals and enter the debit adjustment—$600—on the Supplies Expense line. Keep in mind that the work sheet is not the finished version of the financial statements, so the order of the accounts on the work sheet is not critical. Supplies Expense should preferably be listed in its proper sequence on the income statement. After the adjustments are entered on the work sheet, the amount columns are totalled.

3. Compute each account's adjusted balance by combining the trial balance and adjustment figures. Enter the adjusted amounts in the Adjusted Trial Balance columns. Exhibit 4-4 shows the work sheet with the adjusted trial balance columns completed. Accountants perform this step as illustrated in Chapter 3. For example, the Cash balance is up to date, so it receives no adjustment. Accounts Receivable's adjusted balance of $5,000 is computed by adding the $500 debit adjustment to the trial balance amount of $4,500. Supplies' adjusted balance of $800 is determined by subtracting the $600 credit adjustment from the unadjusted debit balance of $1,400. An account may receive more than one adjustment, as does Service Revenue. The column totals must maintain the equality of debits and credits.

4. Extend (that is, transfer) the asset, liability, and owner's equity amounts from the Adjusted Trial Balance to the Balance Sheet columns. Extend the revenue and expense amounts to the Income Statement columns. Total the statement columns. Every account is either a balance sheet account or an income statement account. The asset, liability, and owner's equity accounts go to the balance sheet, and the revenues and expenses go to the income statement. Debits on the adjusted trial balance remain debits in the statement columns, and credits remain credits. Generally, each account's adjusted balance should appear in only one statement column, as shown in Exhibit 4-5.

Total the *income statement columns first*, as follows:

Income Statement
- Debits (Dr.)   Total expenses   = $7,750 ⎤
                                                  Difference = $7,050
- Credits (Cr.)   Total revenues   = $14,800 ⎦

Then total the *balance sheet* columns:

Balance Sheet
- Debits (Dr.)   Total assets   = $98,800 ⎤
                                                  Difference = $7,050
- Credits (Cr.)   Total liabilities and owner's equity   = $91,750 ⎦

5. Compute net income or net loss as the difference between total revenues and total expenses on the income statement. Enter net income as a debit balancing amount on the income statement and as a credit amount on the balance sheet. Then compute the adjusted column totals. Exhibit 4-6 presents the completed accounting work sheet, which shows net income of $7,050, computed as follows:

KEY POINT

Remember, from Chapter 3, how posting references help track data from the journal to the ledger. These identifiers are equally important for organizing the adjusting entries on the work sheet.

KEY POINT

Net income is the difference between the debit and credit Income Statement columns.

Revenue (total credits on the income statement)	$14,800
Expenses (total debits on the income statement)	7,750
Net income	$ 7,050

Net income of $7,050 is entered in the debit column of the income statement. This brings total debits on the income statement up to the total for credits on the income statement. The net income amount is then extended to the credit column of the balance sheet because an excess of revenues over expenses increases capital, and increases in capital are recorded by a credit. In the closing process, net income will find its way into the Capital account, as we shall soon see. After completion, total debits equal total credits in the Income Statement columns and in the Balance Sheet columns. The balance sheet columns are totalled at $98,800.

If expenses exceed revenues, the result is a net loss. In that event, *Net loss* is printed on the work sheet. The loss amount should be entered in the *credit* column of the income statement and in the *debit* column of the balance sheet, because an excess of expenses over revenue decreases capital, and decreases in capital are recorded by a debit.

Mid-Chapter Summary Problem
for Your Review

The trial balance of Curry's Service Company at December 31, 2006, the end of its fiscal year, is presented below:

CURRY'S SERVICE COMPANY
Trial Balance
December 31, 2006

Cash	$132,000	
Accounts receivable	246,667	
Supplies	4,000	
Furniture and fixtures	66,667	
Accumulated amortization —furniture and fixtures		$ 26,667
Building	140,000	
Accumulated amortization—building		86,667
Land	33,333	
Accounts payable		253,333
Salary payable		0
Unearned service revenue		30,000
Bill Curry, capital		195,333
Bill Curry, withdrawals	43,333	
Service revenues		190,667
Salary expense	114,667	
Supplies expense	0	
Amortization expense —furniture and fixtures	0	
Amortization expense—building	0	
Miscellaneous expense	2,000	
Total	$782,667	$782,667

Data needed for the adjusting entries include:

a. Supplies remaining on hand at year end, $1,333
b. Amortization on furniture and fixtures, $13,333
c. Amortization on building, $6,667
d. Salaries owed but not yet paid, $3,333
e. Service revenues to be accrued, $8,000
f. Of the $30,000 balance of Unearned Service Revenue, $21,333 was earned during 2006.

Required

Prepare the work sheet of Curry's Service Company for the year ended December 31, 2006. Key each adjusting entry by the letter corresponding to the data given.

Solution

CURRY'S SERVICE COMPANY
Work Sheet
For the Year Ended December 31, 2006

Account Title	Trial Balance Debit	Trial Balance Credit	Adjustments Debit	Adjustments Credit	Adjusted Trial Balance Debit	Adjusted Trial Balance Credit	Income Statement Debit	Income Statement Credit	Balance Sheet Debit	Balance Sheet Credit
Cash	132,000				132,000				132,000	
Accounts receivable	246,667		(e) 8,000		254,667				254,667	
Supplies	4,000			(a) 2,667	1,333				1,333	
Furniture and fixtures	66,667				66,667				66,667	
Accumulated amortization —furniture and fixtures		26,667		(b)13,333		40,000				40,000
Building	140,000				140,000				140,000	
Accumulated amortization —building		86,667		(c) 6,667		93,334				93,334
Land	33,333				33,333				33,333	
Accounts payable		253,333				253,333				253,333
Salary payable		0		(d) 3,333		3,333				3,333
Unearned service revenue		30,000	(f) 21,333			8,667				8,667
Bill Curry, capital		195,333				195,333				195,333
Bill Curry, withdrawals	43,333				43,333				43,333	
Service revenues		190,667		(e) 8,000		220,000		220,000		
				(f) 21,333						
Salary expense	114,667		(d) 3,333		118,000		118,000			
Supplies expense	0		(a) 2,667		2,667		2,667			
Amortization expense —furniture and fixtures	0		(b) 13,333		13,333		13,333			
Amortization expense—building	0		(c) 6,667		6,667		6,667			
Miscellaneous expense	2,000				2,000		2,000			
	782,667	782,667	55,333	55,333	814,000	814,000	142,667	220,000	671,333	594,000
Net income							77,333			77,333
							220,000	220,000	671,333	671,333

OBJECTIVE 2
Use the work sheet to complete the accounting cycle

Completing the Accounting Cycle

The work sheet helps organize accounting data and compute the net income or net loss for the period. It also helps accountants prepare the financial statements, record the adjusting entries, and close the accounts.

Preparing the Financial Statements

The work sheet shows the amount of net income or net loss for the period, but it is still necessary to prepare the financial statements. (The financial statements can be prepared directly from the adjusted trial balance; see page 126. This is why completion of the work sheet is optional.) The sorting of accounts to the balance sheet and income statement eases the preparation of the statements. The work sheet also provides the data for the statement of owner's equity. Exhibit 4-7 presents the April financial statements for EconoTravel (based on the data from the work sheet in Exhibit 4-6).

Recording the Adjusting Entries

The adjusting entries are a key element of accrual-basis accounting. The work sheet helps identify the accounts that need adjustments. But, actual adjustment of the accounts requires journal entries that are posted to the ledger accounts; see Panel A of Exhibit 4-8. Panel B shows the postings to the accounts, with "Adj." denoting an amount posted from an adjusting entry. Only the revenue and expense accounts are presented in the exhibit in order to focus on the closing process, which is discussed in the next section.

The adjusting entries can be recorded in the journal as they are entered on the work sheet, but it is not necessary to journalize them at the same time. Most accountants prepare the financial statements immediately after completing the work sheet. They can wait to journalize and post the adjusting entries before they make the closing entries.

Delaying the journalizing and posting of the adjusting entries illustrates another use of the work sheet. Many companies journalize and post the adjusting entries—as in Exhibit 4-8—only once annually—at the end of the year. The need for monthly and quarterly financial statements, however, requires a tool like the work sheet. The entity can use the work sheet to aid in preparing interim statements without journalizing and posting the adjusting entries.

OBJECTIVE 3
Close the revenue, expense, and withdrawal accounts

Closing the Accounts

Closing the accounts refers to the step at the end of the period that prepares the accounts for recording the transactions of the next period. Closing the accounts consists of journalizing and posting the closing entries. Closing results in the balances of the revenue and expense accounts becoming zero in order to clearly measure the net income of each period separately from all other periods.

Recall that the income statement reports only one period's income. For example, net income for Molson Breweries (www.molson.com) for the year ended March 31, 2004, relates exclusively to the twelve months ended on that date. At March 31, 2004, Molson accountants close the company's revenue and expense accounts for that year. Because these accounts' balances relate to a particular accounting period (2004

EXHIBIT 4-7

April Financial Statements of
EconoTravel

ECONOTRAVEL
Income Statement
For the Month Ended April 30, 2006

Revenues:		
Service revenue		$14,800
Expenses:		
Salary expense..	$3,800	
Rent expense..	2,000	
Utilities expense..	800	
Supplies expense	600	
Amortization expense—furniture...............................	550	
Total expenses..		7,750
Net income		$ 7,050

ECONOTRAVEL
Statement of Owner's Equity
For the Month Ended April 30, 2006

Don Smith, capital, April 1, 2006...	$62,500
Add: Net income	7,050
	69,550
Less: Withdrawals	6,400
Don Smith, capital, April 30, 2006...	$63,150

ECONOTRAVEL
Balance Sheet
April 30, 2006

Assets			**Liabilities**		
Cash		$49,600	Accounts payable		$26,200
Accounts receivable...		5,000	Salary payable............................		1,900
Supplies......................		800	Unearned service revenue.........		600
Prepaid rent		4,000	Total liabilities........................		28,700
Furniture	$33,000				
Less: Accumulated			**Owner's Equity**		
amortization........	550	32,450	Don Smith, capital.....................		63,150
			Total liabilities and		
Total assets		$91,850	owner's equity		$91,850

in this case) and are therefore closed at the end of the period (March 31, 2004), the revenue and expense accounts are called **temporary (nominal) accounts**. For example, assume EconoTravel's year end is April 30, 2006. The balance of Service Revenue at April 30, 2006, is $14,800. This balance relates exclusively to the month of April and must be zeroed out before EconoTravel starts accounting for the revenue the business will earn during the next year, beginning May 1, 2006.

The Withdrawals account—although not a revenue or an expense—is also a temporary account, because it measures withdrawals taken during a specific period. The closing process applies only to temporary accounts.

To better understand the closing process, contrast the nature of the temporary accounts with the nature of the **permanent (real) accounts**—the asset, liability, and owner's capital accounts. The asset, liability, and owner's capital accounts are *not*

EXHIBIT 4-8

Journalizing and Posting the
Adjusting Entries

Panel A: Journalizing Adjusting Entries

Page 4

Apr. 30	Accounts Receivable	500	
	Service Revenue		500
30	Supplies Expense	600	
	Supplies		600
30	Rent Expense	2,000	
	Prepaid Rent		2,000
30	Amortization Expense—Furniture	550	
	Accumulated Amortization—Furniture		550
30	Salary Expense	1,900	
	Salaries Payable		1,900
30	Unearned Service Revenue	300	
	Service Revenue		300

Panel B: Posting the Adjustments to the Revenue and Expense Accounts

REVENUE

Service Revenue

		14,000
Adj.		500
Adj.		300
Bal.		14,800

EXPENSES

Rent Expense

| Adj. | 2,000 | |
| Bal. | 2,000 | |

Salary Expense

	1,900	
Adj.	1,900	
Bal.	3,800	

Amortization Expense— Furniture

| Adj. | 550 | |
| Bal. | 550 | |

Utilities Expense

| | 800 | |
| Bal. | 800 | |

Supplies Expense

| Adj. | 600 | |
| Bal. | 600 | |

Adj. = Amount posted from an adjusting entry   Bal. = Balance

········ **THINKING IT OVER**

Where is each account
extended—Income Statement,
debit column; Income Statement,
credit column; Balance Sheet,
debit column; or Balance Sheet,
credit column?

1. Cash.
   A: Balance Sheet, debit

2. Supplies.
   A: Balance Sheet, debit

3. Supplies Expense.
   A: Income Statement, debit

4. Unearned Revenue.
   A: Balance Sheet, credit

5. Service Revenue.
   A: Income Statement, credit

6. Owner's Equity.
   A: Balance Sheet, credit

closed at the end of the period because their balances are not used to measure income. Consider Cash, Accounts Receivable, Supplies, Buildings, Accounts Payable, Notes Payable, and Capital. These accounts do not represent *business activity* for a single period, as do revenues and expenses, which relate exclusively to one accounting period. Instead the permanent accounts represent assets, liabilities, and capital that are on hand at a specific time. This is why their balances at the end of one accounting period carry over to become the beginning balances of the next period. For example, the Cash balance at December 31, 2005 is also the beginning balance for 2006.

Closing entries transfer the revenue, expense, and withdrawal balances from their respective accounts to the Capital account. As you know,

| REVENUES | *increase* | owner's equity |
| EXPENSES and WITHDRAWALS | *decrease* | owner's equity |

It is when we post the closing entries that the Capital account absorbs the impact of the balances in the temporary accounts.

As an intermediate step, however, the revenues and the expenses are transferred first to an account entitled **Income Summary**. This temporary account collects in one place the sum of all the expenses (a debit) and the sum of all the revenues (a credit). The Income Summary account is like a temporary "holding tank" that is used only in the closing process. The balance of Income Summary is then transferred to the Capital account. Exhibit 4-9 gives a picture of the closing process. Observe that Owner's Capital is the final account in the closing process.

EXHIBIT 4-9

The Closing Process

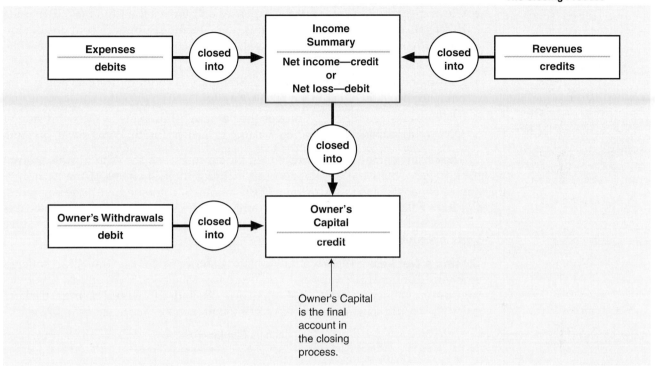

The steps in closing the accounts of a corporation like EconoTravel are as follows (the circled numbers are keyed to Exhibit 4–10 on page 173):

① Debit each *revenue* account for the amount of its credit balance. Credit Income Summary for the sum of the revenues. This entry transfers the sum of the revenues to the *credit* side of the Income Summary.

② Credit each *expense* account for the amount of its debit balance. Debit Income Summary for the sum of the expenses. This entry transfers the sum of the expenses to the *debit* side of the Income Summary. It is not necessary to make a separate closing entry for each expense. In one closing entry, record one debit to Income Summary and a separate credit to each expense account.

③ To close net income, debit Income Summary for the amount of its *credit balance* (*net income* equals revenues minus expenses) and credit the Capital account. If there is a *net loss*, Income Summary has a *debit balance*. In that case, credit Income Summary for this amount and debit Capital. This entry transfers the net income or loss from Income Summary to the Capital account.

④ Credit the *Withdrawals* account for the amount of its debit balance. Debit the Capital account. This entry transfers the Withdrawals amount to the *debit* side of the Capital account. Withdrawals are not expenses and do not affect net income or net loss.

These steps are best illustrated with an example. Suppose EconoTravel closes the books at the end of April. Exhibit 4-10 presents the complete closing process

KEY POINT

There is no account for Net Income, which is the net result of all revenue and expense accounts. The Income Summary combines all revenue and expense amounts into one account.

THINKING IT OVER

(1) Would the Income Summary have a debit or a credit balance if the company suffers a net loss? (2) In the event of a loss, how is Income Summary closed?

A: (1) Expenses would exceed revenues, and Income Summary would have a debit balance. (2) Income Summary is credited, and Capital is debited.

for the business. Panel A gives the closing journal entries, and Panel B shows the accounts after the closing entries have been posted.

The amount in the debit side of each expense account is its adjusted balance. For example, Rent Expense has a $2,000 debit balance. Also note that Service Revenue has a credit balance of $14,800 before closing. These amounts come directly from the adjusted balances in Exhibit 4-8, Panel B.

- Closing entry ① , denoted in the Service Revenue account by *Clo.*, transfers Service Revenue's balance to the Income Summary account. This entry zeroes out Service Revenue for April and places the revenue on the credit side of Income Summary.

- Closing entry ② zeroes out the expenses and moves their total ($7,750) to the debit side of Income Summary. At this point, Income Summary contains the impact of April's revenues and expenses; hence Income Summary's balance is the month's net income ($7,050).

- Closing entry ③ closes the Income Summary account by transferring net income to the credit side of Don Smith, Capital.[1]

- The last closing entry, ④ , moves the owner withdrawals to the debit side of Don Smith, Capital, leaving a zero balance in the Don Smith, Withdrawals account.

The closing entries set all the revenues, the expenses, and the Withdrawals account back to zero. Now the Capital account includes the full effects of the April revenues, expenses, and withdrawals. These amounts, combined with the beginning Capital's balance, give the Capital account an ending balance of $63,150. Trace this ending Capital balance to the statement of owner's equity and also to the balance sheet in Exhibit 4-7.

Closing a Net Loss   What would the closing entries be if EconoTravel had suffered a net *loss* during April? Suppose April expenses totalled $15,400 and all other factors were unchanged. Only closing entries ② and ③ would change. Closing entry ② would transfer expenses of $15,400 to Income Summary, as follows:

Income Summary

Clo.	15,400	Clo.	14,800
Bal.	600		

Closing entry ③ would then credit Income Summary to close its debit balance and to transfer the net loss to Don Smith, Capital:

③   Apr. 30   Don Smith, Capital 600
                    Income Summary 600

After posting, these two accounts would appear as follows:

Income Summary					**Don Smith, Capital**		
Clo.	15,400	Clo.	14,800	→ Clo.	600		62,500
Bal.	600	Clo.	600				

Finally, the Withdrawals balance would be closed to Capital, as before. The double line in an account means that the account has a zero balance; nothing more will be posted to it in the current period.

---

[1] The Income Summary account is a convenience for combining the effects of the revenues and expenses prior to transferring their income effect to Capital. It is not necessary to use the Income Summary account in the closing process. Another way of closing the revenues and expenses makes no use of this account. In this alternative procedure, the revenues and expenses are closed directly to Capital.

Exhibit 4-10

Journalizing and Posting the Closing Entries

Panel A: Journalizing

Closing Entries   Page 5

1 Apr. 30   Service Revenue   14,800
                  Income Summary.............................   14,800
              To close the revenue account and
              create the Income Summary account.

2   30   Income Summary   7,750
                  Rent Expense   2,000
                  Salary Expense   3,800
                  Supplies Expense   600
                  Amortization Expense......................   550
                  Utilities Expense   800
              To close the expense accounts.

3   30   Income Summary...................................   7,050
                  Don Smith, Capital   7,050
              To close the Income Summary
              account and transfer net income to
              the Capital account.
              (Income Summary balance
              = $14,800 – $7,750).

4   30   Don Smith, Capital...............................   6,400
                  Don Smith, Withdrawals   6,400
              To close the Withdrawals account and
              transfer the Withdrawals amount to
              the Capital account.

Panel B: Posting

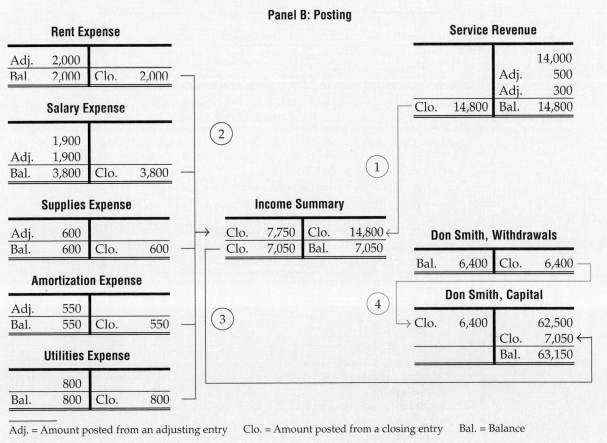

Adj. = Amount posted from an adjusting entry   Clo. = Amount posted from a closing entry   Bal. = Balance

The closing process is fundamentally mechanical and is completely automated in a computerized system. Accounts are identified as either temporary or permanent. The temporary accounts are closed automatically by selecting that option from the software's menu. Posting also occurs automatically.

Postclosing Trial Balance

The accounting cycle ends with the **postclosing trial balance** (Exhibit 4-11). The postclosing trial balance is the final check on the accuracy of journalizing and posting the adjusting and closing entries. It lists the ledger's accounts and their adjusted balances after closing. This step shows where the business stands as it moves into the next accounting period. The postclosing trial balance is dated as of the end of the period for which the statements have been prepared.

The postclosing trial balance resembles the balance sheet. It contains the ending balances of the permanent accounts—the balance sheet accounts: the assets, liabilities, and owner's equity. No temporary accounts—revenues, expenses, or withdrawal accounts—are included because their balances have been closed. The ledger is up to date and ready for the next period's transactions.

OBJECTIVE 4
Correct typical accounting errors

Correcting Journal Entries

In Chapter 2 we discussed errors that affect the trial balance: treating a debit as a credit and vice versa; transpositions; and slides. Here we show how to correct errors in journal entries.

When a journal entry contains an error and the error is detected before posting, the entry can be corrected.

If the error is detected after posting, the accountant makes a *correcting entry*. Suppose EconoTravel paid $10,000 cash for furniture and erroneously debited Supplies as follows:

Incorrect Entry

May 13	Supplies...	10,000	
	Cash...		10,000
	Bought supplies.		

The debit to Supplies is incorrect, so it is necessary to make the following correcting entry:

Correcting Entry

May 15	Furniture...	10,000	
	Supplies...		10,000
	To correct May 13 entry.		
	Furniture was purchased.		

EXHIBIT 4-11

Postclosing Trial Balance

ECONOTRAVEL Postclosing Trial Balance April 30, 2006		
Cash..	$49,600	
Accounts receivable	5,000	
Supplies	800	
Prepaid rent	4,000	
Furniture..	33,000	
Accumulated amortization—Furniture		$ 550
Accounts payable..		26,200
Salary payable		1,900
Unearned service revenue		600
Don Smith, Capital		63,150
Total	$92,400	$92,400

The credit to Supplies in the second entry offsets the incorrect debit of the first entry. The debit to Furniture in the correcting entry places the furniture's cost in the correct account. Now both Supplies and Furniture are correct. Cash was unaffected by the error because Cash was credited correctly in the entry on May 13.

Classification of Assets and Liabilities

OBJECTIVE 5
Classify assets and liabilities as current or long-term

On the balance sheet, assets and liabilities are classified as either *current* or *long-term* to indicate their relative liquidity. **Liquidity** is a measure of how quickly an item can be converted to cash. Cash is the most liquid asset. Accounts receivable is a relatively liquid asset because the business expects to collect the amount in cash in the near future. Supplies are less liquid than accounts receivable, and furniture and buildings are even less so.

Users of financial statements are interested in liquidity because business difficulties often arise because of a shortage of cash. How quickly can the business convert an asset to cash and pay a debt? How soon must a liability be paid? These are questions of liquidity. Balance sheets list assets and liabilities in the order of their relative liquidity.

Assets

Current Assets   **Current assets** are assets that are expected to be converted to cash, sold, or consumed during the next 12 months or within the business's normal operating cycle if longer than a year. The **operating cycle** is the time span during which (1) cash is used to acquire goods and services, and (2) those goods and services are sold to customers, who in turn pay for their purchases with cash. For most businesses, the operating cycle is a few months. A few types of business have operating cycles longer than a year. Cash, Accounts Receivable, Notes Receivable due within a year or less, and Prepaid Expenses are current assets. Merchandising entities such as The Bay (www.hbc.com/bay) and Canadian Tire (www.canadiantire.ca), and manufacturing entities such as Magna International Inc. (www.magna.com) and Bombardier Inc. (www.bombardier.com), have an additional current asset, Inventory. This account shows the cost of goods that are held for sale to customers.

Long-Term Assets   **Long-term assets** are all assets other than current assets. One category of long-term assets is **capital assets**. Land, Buildings, Furniture and Fixtures, and Equipment are capital assets. Of these, EconoTravel has only Furniture.

Other categories of long-term assets include Investments and Other Assets (a catchall category for assets that are not classified more precisely). We discuss these categories in more detail in later chapters.

Liabilities

Financial statement users (such as creditors) are interested in the due dates of an entity's liabilities. Liabilities that must be paid the soonest create the greatest strain on cash. Therefore, the balance sheet lists liabilities in the order in which they are due to be paid. Knowing how many of a business's liabilities are current and how many are long-term helps creditors assess the likelihood of collecting from the entity. Balance sheets usually have at least two liability classifications, *current liabilities* and *long-term liabilities*.

Current Liabilities   **Current liabilities** are debts that are due to be paid within one year or one of the entity's operating cycles if the cycle is longer than a year. Accounts Payable, Notes Payable due within one year, Salaries Payable, Unearned Revenue, Goods and Services Tax Payable, and Interest Payable owed on notes payable are current liabilities.

Long-Term Liabilities All liabilities that are not current are classified as **long-term liabilities**. Many notes payable are long-term—payable after the longer of one year or the entity's operating cycle. Some notes payable are paid in installments, with the first installment due within one year, the second installment due the second year, and so on. In this case, the first installment would be a current liability and the remainder long-term liabilities. For example, a $200,000 note payable to be paid $20,000 per year over ten years would include a current liability of $20,000 for next year's payment and a long-term liability of $180,000.

Thus far in this book we have presented the *unclassified* balance sheet of EconoTravel. Our purpose was to focus on the main points of assets, liabilities, and owner's equity without the details of *current* assets, *current* liabilities, and so on. Exhibit 4-12 presents EconoTravel's classified balance sheet. (Notice that EconoTravel has no long-term liabilities. Suppose the company had incurred a debt for its furniture and the debt would not be repaid during the coming year. This debt would have appeared as a long-term liability on the balance sheet.)

Compare EconoTravel's *classified* balance sheet in Exhibit 4-12 with the *unclassified* balance sheet in Exhibit 4-7. The classified balance sheet reports totals for current assets and current liabilities, which do not appear on the unclassified balance sheet. Also, EconoTravel has no long-term liabilities, so there are none to report on either balance sheet.

The classified balance sheet of Ivaco Products Company, a fictitious company, is shown in Exhibit 4-13. It shows how a company with many different accounts could present its data on a classified balance sheet.

Now let's examine an actual company's classified balance sheet.

EXHIBIT 4-12

Classified Balance Sheet of
EconoTravel

ECONOTRAVEL
Balance Sheet
April 30, 2006

Assets		Liabilities	
Current assets:		Current liabilities:	
Cash	$49,600	Accounts payable	$26,200
Accounts receivable	5,000	Salary payable	1,900
Supplies	800	Unearned service revenue	600
Prepaid rent	4,000	Total current liabilities	28,700
Total current assets	59,400		
		Owner's Equity	
Capital assets:		Don Smith, capital	63,150
Furniture $33,000			
Less: Accumulated			
amortization 550			
Total capital assets	32,450	Total liabilities and	
Total assets	$91,850	owner's equity	$91,850

STOP & THINK

Why is the classified balance sheet in Exhibit 4-12 more useful than an unclassified balance sheet (Exhibit 4-7) to a banker considering whether to lend $10,000 to EconoTravel?

Answer: A classified balance sheet indicates

- which of EconoTravel's liabilities, and the dollar amounts, that the company must pay within the next year.
- which of EconoTravel's assets are the most liquid and thus available to pay the liabilities.
- which assets and liabilities (and amounts) are long-term.

EXHIBIT 4-13

Classified Balance Sheet of
Ivaco Products Company

IVACO PRODUCTS COMPANY
Balance Sheet
June 30, 2007

Assets

Current assets:

Cash	$ 26,400	
Investments	57,000	
Accounts receivable	235,000	
Interest receivable	26,800	
Current portion of note receivable	51,600	
Inventory	847,800	
Supplies	5,200	
Prepaid insurance	24,600	
Prepaid rent	27,000	
Total current assets		$1,301,400

Other assets:

Note receivable	100,000	
Less: Current portion of note receivable	51,600	
Total other assets		48,400

Capital assets:

Equipment	$ 60,000		
Less: accumulated amortization	18,000	42,000	
Furniture and fixtures	70,000		
Less: accumulated amortization	30,000	40,000	
Buildings	240,000		
Less: accumulated amortization	160,000	80,000	
Land		70,000	
Total capital assets			232,000
Total assets			$1,581,800

Liabilities

Current liabilities:

Accounts payable	$357,000	
Salaries and wages payable	22,400	
Interest payable	24,600	
Current portion of notes payable	60,000	
Goods and services tax payable	64,600	
Current portion of mortgage payable	72,200	
Other current liabilities	23,600	
Total current liabilities		$ 624,400

Long-term liabilities:

Notes payable	$340,000		
Less current portion of notes payable	60,000	280,000	
Mortgage payable	220,000		
Less current portion of mortgage payable	72,200	147,800	
Total long-term liabilities			427,800
Total liabilities			1,052,200

Owner's Equity

Ivan Hanley, capital	529,600
Total liabilities and owner's equity	$1,581,800

An Actual Classified Balance Sheet

Exhibit 4-14 is an adapted classified balance sheet of Noranda Inc. (www. noranda.com), a Canadian mining company. The statement is labelled Consolidated because it reports the accounts of Noranda and its component companies as well. Dollar amounts are reported in millions to avoid clutter. Noranda Inc.'s year end is December 31. It is customary to present two or more years' statements together to allow people to compare one year with the other—2002 and 2001 in this case.

You should be familiar with all but a few of Noranda Inc.'s account titles. Titles you might not be familiar with are Deferred Credits, Minority Interest in Subsidiaries, and Shareholders' Equity. In Noranda Inc.'s case, Deferred Credits include the accrued costs of closing down mines owned by the company and the accrued costs of future pensions payable. *Minority Interest in Subsidiaries* includes the preferred and common shares of stock of companies in which Noranda Inc. has a significant investment. *Shareholders' Equity* is the owners' equity of a corporation, and includes shareholders' investment in shares of Noranda Inc. stock and the results of ongoing operations.

Note that Noranda Inc. provides labels only for current assets and current liabilities; the remaining assets and liabilities are long-term because they are not labelled "current."

Formats of Balance Sheets

The balance sheets of Ivaco Products Company shown in Exhibit 4-13 and of Noranda Inc. shown in Exhibit 4-14 list the assets at the top, with the liabilities and owner's eq-

EXHIBIT 4-14

Consolidated Balance Sheet

NORANDA INC.
Consolidated Balance Sheet
December 31, 2002

($ millions)	2002	2001
ASSETS		
Current assets		
Cash and cash equivalents	$ 463	$ 285
Accounts receivable	752	829
Inventories	1,415	1,463
	2,630	2,577
Capital assets	8,073	9,208
Investment and other assets	408	247
Future tax asset	266	109
	$11,377	$12,141
LIABILITIES AND SHAREHOLDERS' EQUITY		
Current liabilities		
Bank advances and short-term notes	$ 39	$ 5
Accounts and taxes payable	1,137	1,185
Debt due within one year	490	512
	1,666	1,702
Long-term debt	4,762	4,403
Future tax liability	306	429
Deferred credits	579	590
Minority interest in subsidiaries	1,136	1,220
Shareholders' equity	2,928	3,797
	$11,377	$12,141

uity below. This is the *report format*. The balance sheet of EconoTravel presented in Exhibit 4-7 lists the assets at the left, with the liabilities and the owner's equity at the right. That is the *account format*.

Either format is acceptable. The report format is more extensively used by Canadian companies.

Accounting Ratios

OBJECTIVE 6
Use the current ratio and debt ratio to evaluate a company

The purpose of accounting is to provide information for decision making. Chief users of accounting information include managers, investors, and creditors. A creditor considering lending money must predict whether the borrower can repay the loan. If the borrower already has a large amount of debt, the probability of repayment is lower than if the borrower has a small amount of liabilities. To assess financial position, decision makers use ratios computed from a company's financial statements.

Current Ratio

One of the most common ratios is the **current ratio**, which is the ratio of an entity's current assets to its current liabilities:

$$\text{Current Ratio} = \frac{\text{Total current assets}}{\text{Total current liabilities}}$$

The current ratio measures the ability to pay current liabilities with current assets. A company prefers a high current ratio, which means the business has sufficient current assets to pay current liabilities when they come due, plus a cushion of additional current assets. An increasing current ratio from period to period generally indicates improvement in financial position.

A rule of thumb: A strong current ratio would be in the range of 2.00; it would indicate that the company has approximately $2.00 in current assets for every $1.00 in current liabilities. A company with a current ratio of 2.00 would probably have little trouble paying its current liabilities. Most successful businesses operate with current ratios between 1.30 and 2.00. A current ratio of 1.00 is considered quite low. Lenders and investors would view a company with a current ratio of 1.50 to 2.00 as substantially less risky. Such a company could probably borrow money on better terms and also attract more investors.

Debt Ratio

A second aid to decision making is the **debt ratio**, which is the ratio of total liabilities to total assets:

$$\text{Debt ratio} = \frac{\text{Total liabilities}}{\text{Total assets}}$$

The debt ratio indicates the proportion of a company's assets that are financed with debt. This ratio measures a company's ability to pay both current and long-term debts—total liabilities.

A *low* debt ratio is safer than a high debt ratio. Why? Because a company with low liabilities has low required payments. Such a company is unlikely to get into financial difficulty. By contrast, a company with a high debt ratio may have trouble paying its liabilities, especially when sales are low and cash is scarce. When a company fails to pay its debts on a timely basis, the creditors can take the business away from its owners. The largest retail bankruptcy in history, Federated Department Stores (owned at the time by the Canadian company Campeau Corporation) was due largely to high debt during a retail-industry recession. Campeau was unable to weather the downturn and had to declare bankruptcy.

········ **THINKING IT OVER**

A company has current assets of $100,000 and current liabilities of $50,000. How will the payment of a $10,000 account payable affect the current ratio?

A: The payment of an account payable would cause both cash and accounts payable to decrease and thus would increase the current ratio from 2.00 to 2.25. In other words, payment of the liability would make the company look better.

Managing Both the Current Ratio and the Debt Ratio In general, a *high* current ratio is preferred over a low current ratio. *Increases* in the current ratio indicate improving financial position. By contrast, a *low* debt ratio is preferred over a high debt ratio. Improvement is indicated by a *decrease* in the debt ratio.

DECISION GUIDELINES   *Completing the Accounting Cycle*

Decision	Guidelines
How (where) to summarize the effects of all the company's transactions and adjustments throughout the period?	Accountant's *work sheet* with columns for: • Trial balance • Adjustments • Adjusted trial balance • Income statement • Balance sheet
What is the last *major* step in the accounting cycle?	*Closing entries* for the *temporary accounts:* Revenues $\left.\begin{array}{l}\\\\\end{array}\right\}$ Income statement accounts Expenses Owner's withdrawals
Why close revenues, expenses, and owner's withdrawals?	Because the *temporary accounts* have balances that relate only to one accounting period (fiscal year) and do *not* carry over to the next accounting period (fiscal year).
Which accounts do not get closed?	*Permanent (balance sheet) accounts:* • Assets • Liabilities • Owner's capital The balances of these accounts *do* carry over to the next accounting period.
How do businesses classify their assets and liabilities for reporting on the balance sheet?	*Current* (within one year or the company's operating cycle if longer than a year) or *Long-term* (not current)
How do decision makers evaluate a company?	There are many ways, such as the company's net income or net loss on the income statement, and the trend of net income from year to year. Another way to evaluate a company is based on the company's *financial ratios*. Two key ratios: Current ratio $= \dfrac{\text{Total current assets}}{\text{Total current liabilities}}$ The current ratio measures the company's ability to pay its current liabilities with its current assets. Debt ratio $= \dfrac{\text{Total liabilities}}{\text{Total assets}}$ The debt ratio measures the entity's overall ability to pay its liabilities. The debt ratio shows the proportion of the entity's assets that are financed with debt.

A rule of thumb: A debt ratio below 0.60, or 60%, is considered safe for most businesses. A debt ratio above 0.80, or 80%, borders on high risk. Most companies have debt ratios in the range of 0.60 to 0.80.

Financial ratios are an important aid to decision makers. However, it is unwise to place too much confidence in a single ratio or group of ratios. For example, a company may have a high current ratio, which indicates financial strength. It may also have a high debt ratio, which suggests weakness. Which ratio gives the more reliable signal about the company? Experienced managers, lenders, and investors evaluate a company by examining a large number of ratios over several years to spot trends and turning points. These people also consider other facts, such as the company's cash position and its trend in net income. No single ratio gives the whole picture about a company.

As you progress through the study of accounting, we will introduce key ratios used for decision making. Chapter 18 (in Volume II) then summarizes all the ratios discussed in this book and provides a good overview of ratios used in decision making.

Accounting Around the Globe

Dell Computer Corporation: Where Customer Focus Equals Solid Financials

Michael Dell dropped out of the University of Texas in 1984 to start Dell Computer, and, as he puts it, "my parents were upset, until I showed them my first financial statement." Dell began with $1,000, and Dell Computer Corporation was profitable from day one.

Today Dell is Number 1 in desktop PCs, Number 1 in the United States in low-end servers, and North America's Number 1 Internet retailer. Even with the PC industry in a slump, the company is on track to earn $2 billion net income in 2003. And while many technology shares fell 80% from their 2000 peak, Dell's shares were down just 8% in 2002.

One of the main reasons Michael Dell was featured in *Business Week*'s January 13, 2003, issue as one of "The Best Managers of the Year" is that he does not let the market valuation of his business cloud his vision. "There are two pieces of financials," says Dell. "One is the market's interpretation, . . . stock price [and] credit ratings. Another is financial results. We don't have control of the market's reaction. We can focus on [keeping] our costs in line and [on having] the right mix of product." This focus fits with the company's mandate: " . . . The most important thing is to satisfy our customers. The second most important thing is to be profitable. If we don't do the first one well, the second one won't happen."

Dell has made a science of shaving costs from the PC-assembly process. Its process is so efficient that it rarely needs more than two hours' worth of parts inventory. Parts storage takes up a space no larger than your bedroom. Operating costs are only 10% of Dell's $35 billion revenue in 2002—compared with 21% at Hewlett-Packard, 25% at Gateway, and 46% at Cisco.

The direct-to-customer model has worked so well in PCs that Michael Dell wants to expand it into several other product lines, such as handhelds, servers, and storage systems. He knows that PCs alone will not keep his profit machine growing. Hewlett-Packard, Gateway, Cisco, and IBM: Watch out!

Based on: Kathryn Jones, "The Dell Way," *Business 2.0*, February 2003, www.business2.com/articles/mag/. Anonymous, "Michael Dell, Dell Computer," *Business Week*, January 13, 2003, p. 62. Del Jones, "Dell, Take Time to Build: Computer Chief Says Company Puts Its Focus on Customers," *USA Today*, October 10, 2002, p. B.06.

Summary Problem
for Your Review

Refer to the data in the Mid-Chapter Summary Problem for Your Review, presented on pages 166–167.

Required

1. Journalize and post the adjusting entries. (Before posting to the accounts, enter into each account its balance as shown in the trial balance. For example, enter the $246,667 balance in the Accounts Receivable account before posting its adjusting entry.) Key adjusting entries by *letter*, as shown in the work sheet solution to the mid-chapter review problem. You can take the adjusting entries straight from the work sheet on p. 167. Explanations are not required. Find the ending balances of the permanent accounts.

2. Journalize and post the closing entries. (Each account should carry its balance as shown in the adjusted trial balance.) Provide explanations. To distinguish closing entries from adjusting entries, key the closing entries by *number*. Draw the arrows to illustrate the flow of data, as shown in Exhibit 4-10, page 173. Indicate the balance of the Capital account after the closing entries are posted.

3. Prepare the income statement for the year ended December 31, 2006. List Miscellaneous Expense last among the expenses, a common practice.

4. Prepare the statement of owner's equity for the year ended December 31, 2006. Draw the arrow that links the income statement to the statement of owner's equity, if both statements are on the same page. Otherwise, explain how they are linked.

5. Prepare the classified balance sheet at December 31, 2006. Use the report form. All liabilities are current. Draw the arrow that links the statement of owner's equity to the balance sheet, if both statements are on the same page. Otherwise, explain how they are linked.

Solution

Requirement 1

a. Dec. 31	Supplies Expense..	2,667	
	Supplies..		2,667
b. Dec. 31	Amortization Expense—Furniture and Fixtures.......	13,333	
	Accumulated Amortization		
	—Furniture and Fixtures....................................		13,333
c. Dec. 31	Amortization Expense—Building.............................	6,667	
	Accumulated Amortization—Building.................		6,667
d. Dec. 31	Salary Expense	3,333	
	Salary Payable...		3,333
e. Dec. 31	Accounts Receivable	8,000	
	Service Revenue..		8,000
f. Dec. 31	Unearned Service Revenue	21,333	
	Service Revenue..		21,333

Accounts Receivable

246,667	
(e) 8,000	
Bal. 254,667	

Supplies

4,000	(a)	2,667	
Bal. 1,333			

Accumulated Amortization —Furniture and Fixtures

	26,667
	(b) 13,333
	Bal. 40,000

Accumulated Amortization —Building

	86,667
	(c) 6,667
	Bal. 93,334

Salary Payable

	(d) 3,333
	Bal. 3,333

Unearned Service Revenue

(f) 21,333	30,000
	Bal. 8,667

Service Revenue

	190,667
	(e) 8,000
	(f) 21,333
	Bal. 220,000

Salary Expense

114,667	
(d) 3,333	
Bal. 118,000	

Supplies Expense

(a) 2,667	
Bal. 2,667	

Amortization Expense —Furniture and Fixtures

(b) 13,333	
Bal. 13,333	

Amortization Expense —Building

(c) 6,667	
Bal. 6,667	

Requirement 2

a. Dec. 31	Service Revenue..	220,000	
	Income Summary		220,000
	To close the revenue account and create the Income Summary account.		
b. Dec. 31	Income Summary	142,667	
	Salary Expense..		118,000
	Supplies Expense..		2,667
	Amortization Expense —Furniture and Fixtures.......................		13,333
	Amortization Expense—Building..............		6,667
	Miscellaneous Expense................................		2,000
	To close the expense accounts.		
c. Dec. 31	Income Summary	77,333	
	Bill Curry, Capital		77,333
	To close the Income Summary account. (Income Summary balance = $220,000 − $142,667).		
d. Dec. 31	Bill Curry, Capital	43,333	
	Bill Curry, Withdrawals..............................		43,333
	To close the Withdrawals account and transfer the Withdrawals amount to the Capital account.		

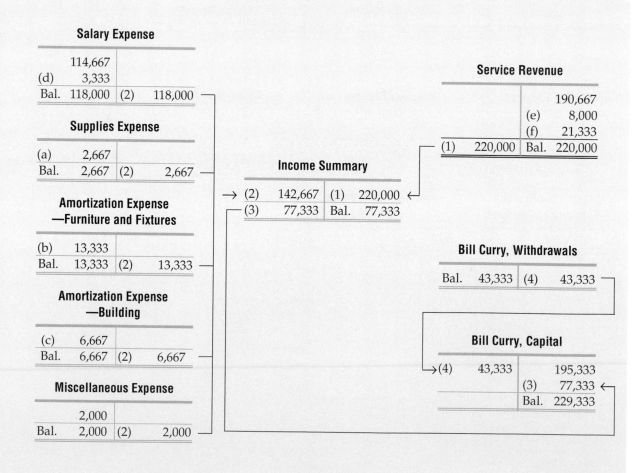

Requirement 3

CURRY'S SERVICE COMPANY
Income Statement
For the Year Ended December 31, 2006

Revenues:		
Service revenue		$220,000
Expenses:		
Salary expense	$118,000	
Amortization expense—furniture and fixtures	13,333	
Amortization expense—building	6,667	
Supplies expense	2,667	
Miscellaneous expense	2,000	
Total expenses		142,667
Net Income		$77,333

Requirement 4

CURRY'S SERVICE COMPANY
Statement of Owner's Equity
For the Year Ended December 31, 2006

Bill Curry, Capital, January 1, 2006	$195,333
Add: Net income	77,333
	272,666
Less: Withdrawals	43,333
Bill Curry, Capital, December 31, 2006	$229,333

Requirement 5

CURRY'S SERVICE COMPANY
Balance Sheet
December 31, 2006

Assets		
Current assets:		
Cash		$132,000
Accounts receivable		254,667
Supplies		1,333
Total current assets		388,000
Capital assets:		
Furniture and fixtures	$66,667	
Less: Accumulated amortization	40,000	26,667
Building	140,000	
Less: Accumulated amortization	93,334	46,666
Land		33,333
Total capital assets		106,666
Total assets		$494,666
Liabilities		
Current liabilities:		
Accounts payable		$253,333
Unearned service revenue		8,667
Salary payable		3,333
Total current liabilities		265,333
Owner's Equity		
Bill Curry, capital		229,333
Total liabilities and owner's equity		$494,666

Summary

1. **Prepare an accounting work sheet.** The *accounting cycle* is the process by which accountants produce the financial statements for a specific period of time. The cycle starts with the beginning account balances. During the period, the business journalizes transactions and posts them to the ledger accounts. At the end of the period, the trial balance is prepared, and the accounts are adjusted in order to measure the period's net income or net loss. Completion of the accounting cycle is aided by use of a *work sheet*. This multicolumned document summarizes the effects of all the period's activity.

2. **Use the work sheet to complete the accounting cycle.** The work sheet is neither a journal nor a ledger but merely a convenient device for completing the accounting cycle. It has columns for the trial balance, the adjustments, the adjusted trial balance, the income statement, and the balance sheet. It aids the adjusting process, and it is the place where the period's net income or net loss is first computed. The work sheet also provides the data for the financial statements and the *closing entries*. It is not, however, a necessity. The accounting cycle can be completed from the less elaborate adjusted trial balance.

3. **Close the revenue, expense, and withdrawal accounts.** Revenues, expenses, and withdrawals represent increases and decreases in the capital account for a specific period. At the end of the period, their balances are closed out to zero, and, for this reason, they are called *temporary accounts*. Assets, liabilities, and capital accounts are not closed out to zero because they are the *permanent accounts*. Their balances at the end of one period become the beginning balances of the next period. The final accuracy check of the period is the *postclosing trial balance*.

4. **Correct typical accounting errors.** Accountants correct errors by making correcting journal entries.

5. **Classify assets and liabilities as current or long-term.** The balance sheet reports *current* and *long-term assets* and *current* and *long-term liabilities*. It can be presented in *report format* or *account format*.

6. **Use the current ratio and debt ratio to evaluate a company.** Two decision-making aids are the *current ratio* (total current assets divided by total current liabilities) and the *debt ratio* (total liabilities divided by total assets).

Self-Study Questions

Test your understanding of the chapter by marking the correct answer to each of the following questions:

1. The focal point of the accounting cycle is the (*p. 163*)
   a. Financial statements   c. Adjusted trial balance
   b. Trial balance   d. Work sheet

2. Arrange the following accounting cycle steps in their proper order (*p. 164*)
   a. Complete the work sheet
   b. Journalize and post adjusting entries
   c. Prepare the postclosing trial balance
   d. Journalize and post cash transactions
   e. Prepare the financial statements
   f. Journalize and post closing entries

3. The work sheet is a (*p. 164a*)
   a. Journal   c. Financial statement
   b. Ledger   d. Convenient device for completing the accounting cycle

4. The usefulness of the work sheet is (*pp. 164–164a*)
   a. Identifying the accounts that need to be adjusted

   b. Summarizing the effects of all the transactions of the period
   c. Aiding the preparation of the financial statements
   d. All of the above

5. Which of the following accounts is not closed? (*pp. 168–171*)
   a. Supplies Expense   c. Interest Revenue
   b. Prepaid Insurance   d. Withdrawals

6. The closing entry for Salary Expense, with a balance of $322,000, is (*pp. 168–171*)

   a. Salary Expense   322,000
        Income Summary   322,000
   b. Salary Expense   322,000
        Salary Payable   322,000
   c. Income Summary   322,000
        Salary Expense   322,000
   d. Salary Payable   322,000
        Salary Expense   322,000

7. The purpose of the postclosing trial balance is to (p. 174)
   a. Provide the account balances for preparation of the balance sheet
   b. Ensure that the ledger is in balance for the start of the next period
   c. Aid the journalizing and posting of the closing entries
   d. Ensure that the ledger is in balance for completion of the work sheet

8. A payment on account was recorded by debiting Supplies and crediting Cash. This entry was posted. The correcting entry is (pp. 174–175)
   a. Accounts Payable   X
          Supplies   X
   b. Supplies   X
          Accounts Payable   X
   c. Cash   X
          Accounts Payable   X
   d. Cash   X
          Supplies   X

9. The classification of assets and liabilities as current or long-term depends on (p. 175)
   a. Their order of listing in the ledger
   b. Whether they appear on the balance sheet or the income statement
   c. The relative liquidity of the item
   d. The format of the balance sheet—account format or report format

10. Suppose in 2006, EconoTravel debited Amortization Expense for the cost of a computer used in the business. For 2006, this error (pp. 174–175)
   a. Overstated net income
   b. Understated net income
   c. Either a or b, depending on the circumstances
   d. Had no effect on net income

Answers to the Self-Study Questions follow the Similar Accounting Terms.

Accounting Vocabulary

Accounting cycle (p. 163)
Capital asset (p. 175)
Closing entries (p. 170)
Closing the accounts (p. 168)
Current asset (p. 175)
Current liability (p. 175)
Current ratio (p. 179)
Debt ratio (p. 179)
Income Summary (p. 171)
Liquidity (p. 175)
Long-term asset (p. 175)

Long-term liability (p. 176)
Nominal account (p. 169)
Operating cycle (p. 175)
Permanent account (p. 169)
Postclosing trial balance (p. 174)
Real account (p. 169)
Reversing entry (p. 213)
Temporary account (p. 169)
Work sheet (p. 164a)

Similar Accounting Terms

Capital assets	Fixed assets; Plant and equipment; Property, plant, and equipment; Plant assets
Current ratio	Working capital ratio
Permanent account	Real account
Temporary account	Nominal account

Answers to Self-Study Questions

1. a	3. d	5. b	7. b	9. c
2. d, a, e, b, f, c	4. d	6. c	8. a	10. b

Assignment Material

Questions

1. Identify the steps in the accounting cycle; distinguish those that occur during the period from those that are performed at the end of the period.

2. Why is the work sheet a valuable accounting tool?

3. Name two advantages the work sheet has over the adjusted trial balance.

4. Why must the adjusting entries be journalized and posted if they have already been entered on the work sheet?

5. Why should the adjusting entries be journalized and posted before the closing entries are made?

6. Which types of accounts are closed?

7. What purpose is served by closing the accounts?

8. State how the work sheet helps with recording the closing entries.

9. Distinguish between permanent accounts and temporary accounts; indicate which type is closed at the end of the period. Give five examples of each type of account.

10. Is Income Summary a permanent account or a temporary account? When and how is it used?

11. Give the closing entries for the following accounts (balances in parentheses): Service Revenue ($4,700), Salary Expense ($1,100), Income Summary (credit balance of $2,000), Withdrawals ($2,300).

12. Why are assets classified as current or long-term?

On what basis are they classified? Where do the classified amounts appear?

13. Indicate which of the following accounts are current assets and which are long-term assets: Prepaid Rent, Building, Furniture, Accounts Receivable, Merchandise Inventory, Cash, Note Receivable (due within one year), Note Receivable (due after one year).

14. In what order are assets and liabilities listed on the balance sheet?

15. Name an outside party that is interested in whether a liability is current or long-term. Why would this party be interested in this information?

16. A friend tells you that the difference between a current liability and a long-term liability is that they are payable to different types of creditors. Is your friend correct? Include in your answer the definitions of these two categories of liabilities.

17. Show how to compute the current ratio and the debt ratio. Indicate what ability each ratio measures, and state whether a high value or a low value is safer for each.

18. Capp Company purchased supplies of $120 on account. The accountant debited Inventory and credited Accounts Payable for $120. A week later, after this entry has been posted to the ledger, the accountant discovers the error. How should he correct the error?

Exercises

Media Companion CD-ROM

Exercise 4-1 *Preparing a work sheet* *(Obj. 1)*

The trial balance of Brieger Testing Services appears on the following page.

Additional information at September 30, 2007:

a. Accrued service revenue, $420.

b. Amortization, $80.

c. Accrued salary expense, $1,000.

d. Prepaid rent expired, $1,200.

e. Supplies used, $3,300.

BRIEGER TESTING SERVICES
Trial Balance
September 30, 2007

Cash..	$ 7,120	
Accounts receivable	6,880	
Prepaid rent.......................................	2,400	
Supplies	6,780	
Equipment...	65,200	
Accumulated amortization..................		$ 5,680
Accounts payable...............................		3,200
Salary payable....................................		0
J. Brieger, capital..............................		72,060
J. Brieger, withdrawals	6,000	
Service revenue..................................		18,600
Amortization expense	0	
Salary expense	3,600	
Rent expense......................................	0	
Utilities expense	1,560	
Supplies expense................................	0	
Total...	$99,540	$99,540

Required

Complete the Brieger Testing Services work sheet for September 2007.

Exercise 4-2 *Journalizing adjusting and closing entries* *(Obj. 2)*

Journalize the adjusting and closing entries for the company in Exercise 4-1.

Exercise 4-3 *Posting adjusting and closing entries* *(Obj. 2)*

Set up T-accounts for those accounts affected by the adjusting and closing entries in Exercise 4-1. Post the adjusting and closing entries to the accounts, denoting adjustment amounts by *Adj.*, closing amounts by *Clo.*, and balances by *Bal.* Double underline the accounts with zero balances after you close them and show the ending balance in each account.

Exercise 4-4 *Preparing a postclosing trial balance* *(Obj. 2)*

Prepare the postclosing trial balance for the company in Exercise 4-1.

Exercise 4-5 *Identifying and journalizing closing entries* *(Obj. 3)*

Bombardier Inc. (www.bombardier.com), the transporation, motorized consumer products, aerospace, and financial and real estate services company, reported the following items adapted from a recent financial report (amounts in millions):

Cash and term deposits...........	$ 896	Amortization expense	$ 166	
Revenues....................................	7,976	Other assets..................................	230	
Accounts payable	2,125	Interest expense...........................	160	
Accounts receivable	358	Long-term liabilities	1,355	

Prepare Bombardier Inc.'s closing entries for the above accounts.

Exercise 4-6 *Identifying and journalizing closing entries* *(Obj. 3)*

From the selected accounts (on the next page) that Viera Printers reported in its June 30, 2006, annual financial statements, prepare the company's closing entries.

Dan Viera, Capital	$118,400	Interest expense	$ 8,800
Service revenue	336,400	Accounts receivable	56,000
Unearned revenues	5,400	Salaries payable	3,400
Salary expense	50,000	Amortization expense	40,800
Accumulated amortization	140,000	Rent expense	23,600
Supplies expense	6,800	Dan Viera, Withdrawals	120,000
Interest revenue	2,800	Supplies	5,600

Exercise 4-7 *Identifying and journalizing closing entries* *(Obj. 3)*

The accountant for Decker Environmental Consulting has posted adjusting entries (a) through (e) to the accounts at December 31, 2007. All the revenue, expense, and owner's equity accounts of the entity are listed here in T-account form.

Accounts Receivable

	39,000	
(a)	5,250	

Supplies

	6,000	(b)	3,000	

Accumulated Amortization —Furniture

			9,000
		(c)	1,650

Accumulated Amortization —Building

			49,500
		(d)	9,000

Salaries Payable

		(e)	1,050

B. Decker, Capital

			78,600

B. Decker, Withdrawals

92,100	

Service Revenue

		166,500	
	(a)	5,250	

Salary Expense

	39,000		
(e)	1,050		

Supplies Expense

(b)	3,000

Amortization Expense —Furniture

(c)	1,650

Amortization Expense —Building

(d)	9,000

Required

1. Journalize Decker Environmental Consulting's closing entries at December 31, 2007.
2. Determine Decker Environmental Consulting's ending capital balance at December 31, 2007.

Exercise 4-8 *Preparing a statement of owner's equity* *(Obj. 3)*

From the following accounts of Johnson Consulting prepare the entity's statement of owner's equity for the year ended December 31, 2007.

J. Johnson, Capital

Dec. 31	8,000	Jan. 1	9,000	
		Dec. 31	10,750	

J. Johnson, Withdrawals

Mar. 31	2,250	Dec. 31	8,000
Jun. 30	1,750		
Sept. 30	2,250		
Dec. 31	1,750		

Income Summary

Dec. 31	21,250	Dec. 31	32,000
Dec. 31	10,750		

Exercise 4-9 *Identifying and recording adjusting and closing entries* **(Obj. 2, 3)**

The trial balance and income statement amounts from the March work sheet of O'Neill Systems follow:

Account Title	Trial Balance		Income Statement	
Cash	$ 12,400			
Supplies	9,600			
Prepaid rent	4,400			
Office equipment	200,400			
Accumulated amortization...................................		$ 24,800		
Accounts payable...		18,400		
Salaries payable..		0		
Unearned service revenue		17,600		
P. O'Neill, capital..		143,200		
P. O'Neill, withdrawals	4,000			
Service revenue		46,800		$52,000
Salary expense...	12,000		$15,200	
Rent expense..	4,800		5,600	
Amortization expense	0		1,200	
Supplies expense..	0		1,600	
Utilities expense..	3,200		3,200	
	$250,800	$250,800	$26,800	$52,000
Net income...			25,200	
			$52,000	$52,000

Required

Journalize the adjusting and closing entries of O'Neill Systems at March 31.

Exercise 4-10 *Making correcting entries* **(Obj. 4)**

1. Suppose EconoTravel paid an account payable of $1,200 and erroneously debited Supplies. Make the journal entry to correct this error.

2. Suppose EconoTravel made the following adjusting entry to record amortization at April 30.

   Amortization Expense—Furniture...... 1,100

      Furniture   1,100

   Make the journal entry to correct this error.

3. Suppose, in closing the books, EconoTravel made this closing entry:

   Income Summary................................... 29,600

      Service Revenue   29,600

   Make the journal entry to correct this error.

Exercise 4-11 *Preparing a classified balance sheet* **(Obj. 5, 6)**

Refer to Exercise 4-9.

Required

1. After solving Exercise 4-9, use the data in that exercise to prepare O'Neill Systems' classified balance sheet at March 31, 2007. Use the report format.

2. Compute O'Neill Systems' current ratio and debt ratio at March 31, 2007. One year ago, the current ratio was 1.20 and the debt ratio was 0.30. Indicate whether O'Neill Systems' ability to pay its debts has improved or deteriorated during the current year.

Exercise 4-12 *Correcting accounting errors* *(Obj. 4)*

Prepare a correcting entry for each of the following accounting errors:

a. Debited Supplies and credited Accounts Payable for a $4,500 purchase of office equipment on account.

b. Accrued interest revenue of $1,500 by a debit to Accounts Receivable and a credit to Interest Revenue.

c. Adjusted prepaid rent by debiting Prepaid Rent and crediting Rent Expense for $3,000. This adjusting entry should have debited Rent Expense and credited Prepaid Rent for $3,000.

d. Debited Salary Expense and credited Accounts Payable to accrue salary expense of $6,000.

e. Recorded the earning of $3,900 service revenue collected in advance by debiting Accounts Receivable and crediting Service Revenue.

Exercise 4-13 *Classifying assets and liabilities as current or long-term* *(Obj. 5)*

Wu Corporation had sales of $3,400 million during 2006, and total assets of $800 million at December 31, 2006, the end of the company's fiscal year. Wu Corporation's financial statements reported the following (all amounts in millions):

Sales revenue	$2,400	Prepaid expenses	$ 30
Inventory	300	Land and buildings	160
Long-term debt	2	Accounts payable	170
Receivables	18	Operating expenses	1,000
Interest expense	2	Accumulated amortization	150
Equipment	400	Accrued liabilities	
		(such as Salaries payable)	60

While some of these account titles may be new to you, they are similar to those you have seen already.

Required

1. Identify the assets (including contra assets) and liabilities.
2. Classify each asset and each liability as current or long-term.

Serial Exercise

This exercise continues the Melanie Clark Engineers situation begun in Exercise 2-15 of Chapter 2 and extended to Exercise 3-17 of Chapter 3.

Exercise 4-14 *Closing the books, preparing a classified balance sheet, and evaluating a business* *(Obj. 3, 5, 6)*

Refer to Exercise 3-17 of Chapter 3. Start from the posted T-accounts and the adjusted trial balance on the next page that Melanie Clark Engineers prepared at December 31.

Required

1. Journalize and post the closing entries at December 31, 2005. Denote each closing amount as *Clo.* and an account balance as *Bal.*
2. Prepare a classified balance sheet at December 31, 2005.
3. Compute the current ratio and the debt ratio of Melanie Clark Engineers and evaluate these ratio values as indicative of a strong or weak financial position.
4. If your instructor assigns it, complete the accounting work sheet at December 31, 2005.

MELANIE CLARK ENGINEERS
Adjusted Trial Balance
December 31, 2005

Cash	$22,400	
Accounts receivable	3,400	
Supplies	200	
Equipment	6,000	
Accumulated amortization—equipment		$ 100
Furniture	11,200	
Accumulated amortization—furniture		120
Accounts payable		11,200
Salaries payable		1,400
Unearned service revenue		1,600
Melanie Clark, capital		28,000
Melanie Clark, withdrawals	3,200	
Service revenue		7,400
Rent expense	1,000	
Utilities expense	400	
Salary expense	1,400	
Amortization expense—equipment	100	
Amortization expense—furniture	120	
Supplies expense	400	
Total	$49,820	$49,820

Challenge Exercise

Exercise 4-15   *Computing financial statement amounts*   **(Obj. 2, 5)**

The unadjusted accounts balance of Stinson Consulting follow:

Cash	$ 1,900	Unearned service revenue	$ 5,300
Accounts receivable	7,200	Scott Stinson, capital	90,200
Supplies	1,100	Scott Stinson, withdrawals	46,200
Prepaid Insurance	2,200	Service revenue	93,600
Furniture	8,400	Salary expense	32,700
Accumulated amortization—		Amortization expense—	
furniture	1,300	furniture	0
Building	57,800	Amortization expense—	
Accumulated amortization—		building	0
building	14,900	Supplies expense	0
Land	51,200	Insurance expense	0
Accounts payable	6,100	Utilities expense	2,700
Salaries payable	0		

Adjusting data at the end of the year included the following:

a. Unearned service revenue that has been earned, $3,600.

b. Accrued service revenue, $1,700.

c. Supplies used in operations, $600.

d. Accrued salary expense, $1,400.

e. Insurance expense, $1,800.

f. Amortization expense—furniture, $800; building, $2,100.

Scott Stinson, the proprietor of Stinson Consulting, has received an offer to sell his company. He needs to know the following information as soon as possible:

1. Net income for the year covered by these data.

2. Total assets.

3. Total liabilities.

4. Total owner's equity.

5. Proof that total assets equal total liabilities plus total owner's equity after all items are updated.

Required

Without opening any accounts, making any journal entries, or using a work sheet, provide Scott Stinson with the requested information. Show all computations.

Ethical Issue

Discount Hardware wishes to expand its business and has borrowed $200,000 from The Toronto-Dominion Bank (www.tdcanadatrust.com). As a condition for making this loan, the bank required Discount Hardware to maintain a current ratio of at least 1.50 and a debt ratio of no more than 0.50, and to submit annual financial statements to the bank.

Business during the third year has been good but not great. Expansion costs have brought the current ratio down to 1.40 and the debt ratio up to 0.51 at December 15. The managers of Discount Hardware are considering the implication of reporting this current ratio to TD Canada Trust. One course of action that the managers are considering is to record in December of the third year some revenue on account that Discount Hardware will earn in January of next year. The contract for this job has been signed, and Discount Hardware will deliver the materials during January.

Required

1. Journalize the revenue transaction using your own numbers, and indicate how recording this revenue in December would affect the current ratio and the debt ratio.

2. State whether it is ethical to record the revenue transaction in December. Identify the accounting principle relevant to this situation.

3. Propose an ethical course of action for Discount Hardware.

Problems (Group A)

Media Companion CD-ROM

Problem 4-1A   *Preparing a work sheet*   *(Obj. 1)*

The trial balance of John Alagia Design at May 31, 2006, follows on the next page.

Additional data at May 31, 2006:

a. Amortization: furniture, $480; building, $460.

b. Accrued salary expense, $600.

c. A count of supplies showed that unused supplies amounted to $410.

d. During May, $390 of prepaid insurance coverage expired.

e. Accrued interest expense, $220.

f. Of the $8,800 balance of Unearned Revenue, $4,400 was earned during May.

g. Accrued advertising expense, $60. (Credit Accounts Payable.)

h. Accrued interest revenue, $170.

Required

Complete John Alagia Design's work sheet for May.

JOHN ALAGIA DESIGN
Trial Balance
May 31, 2006

Cash	$ 8,670	
Notes receivable	10,340	
Interest receivable	0	
Supplies	560	
Prepaid insurance	1,790	
Furniture	27,410	
Accumulated amortization—furniture		$ 1,480
Building	53,900	
Accumulated amortization—building		34,560
Land	18,700	
Accounts payable		14,730
Interest payable		0
Salary payable		0
Unearned design services revenue		8,800
Notes payable, long-term		18,700
John Alagia, capital		34,290
John Alagia, withdrawals	3,800	
Design services revenue		16,970
Interest revenue		0
Amortization expense—furniture	0	
Amortization expense—building	0	
Salary expense	2,170	
Insurance expense	0	
Interest expense	0	
Utilities expense	1,130	
Advertising expense	1,060	
Supplies expense	0	
Total	$129,530	$129,530

Problem 4-2A *Preparing financial statements from an adjusted trial balance; journalizing adjusting and closing entries; evaluating a business* **(Obj. 2, 5, 6)**

The adjusted trial balance of Muskoka Golf School at April 30, 2007, the end of the company's fiscal year, follows on the next page.

Adjusting data at April 30, 2007, which have all been incorporated into the trial balance figures above, consist of:

a. Of the balance of Unearned Teaching Revenue at the beginning of the year, $16,720 was earned during the year.

b. Supplies used during the year, $23,520.

c. During the year, $21,480 of prepaid insurance coverage expired.

d. Accrued interest expense, $5,120.

e. Accrued teaching revenue, $8,800.

f. Amortization for the year: equipment, $27,600; building, $14,840.

g. Accrued wages expense, $3,320.

Required

1. Journalize the adjusting entries that would lead to the adjusted trial balance shown here. Also journalize the closing entries.

2. Prepare Muskoka Golf School's income statement and statement of owner's equity for the year ended April 30, 2007, and the classified balance sheet on that date. Use the account format for the balance sheet.

3. Compute Muskoka Golf School's current ratio and debt ratio at April 30, 2007. One year ago, the current ratio stood at 1.21, and the debt ratio was 0.82. Did Muskoka Golf School's ability to pay debts improve or deteriorate during 2007?

MUSKOKA GOLF SCHOOL
Adjusted Trial Balance
April 30, 2007

Cash	$ 5,480	
Accounts receivable	174,960	
Supplies	14,760	
Prepaid insurance	9,160	
Equipment	255,720	
Accumulated amortization—equipment		$ 113,720
Building	297,320	
Accumulated amortization—building		73,040
Land	80,000	
Accounts payable		78,200
Interest payable		9,120
Wages payable		3,320
Unearned teaching revenue		14,640
Notes payable, long-term		279,600
J. Wilson, capital		256,800
J. Wilson, withdrawals	110,000	
Teaching revenue		394,200
Amortization expense—equipment	27,600	
Amortization expense—building	14,840	
Wages expense	131,240	
Insurance expense	21,480	
Interest expense	32,680	
Utilities expense	19,880	
Supplies expense	27,520	
Total	$1,222,640	$1,222,640

Problem 4-3A   *Taking the accounting cycle through the closing entries*   *(Obj. 2, 3)*

The unadjusted T-accounts of Morowitz Media at December 31, 2006 follow on the next page. The related year-end adjustment data appear below.

Adjustment data at December 31, 2006, include:

a. Amortization for the year, $15,000.

b. Supplies still unused at the year end, $6,000.

c. Accrued service revenue, $12,000.

d. Of the $6,000 balance of Unearned Service Revenue at the beginning of the year, the entire amount was earned during the year.

e. Accrued salary expense, $12,000.

Cash	Accounts Receivable	Supplies
Bal. 87,000	Bal. 132,000	Bal. 18,000

Equipment	Accumulated Amortization	Accounts Payable
Bal. 171,000	Bal. 36,000	Bal. 48,000

Salary Payable	Unearned Service Revenue	Notes Payable, Long-Term
0	Bal. 6,000	Bal. 120,000

W. Morowitz, Capital	W. Morowitz, Withdrawals	Service Revenue
Bal. 123,000	Bal. 162,000	Bal. 390,000

Supplies Expense	Salary Expense	Insurance Expense
0	Bal. 108,000	Bal. 30,000

Amortization Expense	Interest Expense
0	Bal. 15,000

Required

1. Write the trial balance on a work sheet and complete the work sheet. Key each adjusting entry by the letter corresponding to the data given.
2. Prepare the income statement, the statement of owner's equity, and the classified balance sheet in account format.
3. Journalize the adjusting and closing entries.
4. Did Morowitz Media have a profitable year or a bad year during 2006? Give the reason for your answer.

Problem 4-4A   *Completing the accounting cycle*   *(Obj. 2, 3)*

This problem should be used only in conjunction with Problem 4-3A. It completes the accounting cycle by posting to T-accounts and preparing the postclosing trial balance.

Required

1. Using the Problem 4-3A data, post the adjusting and closing entries to the T-accounts, denoting adjusting amounts by *Adj.*, closing amounts by *Clo.*, and account balances by *Bal.*, as shown in Exhibit 4-10 (page 173). Double underline all accounts with a zero ending balance.
2. Prepare the postclosing trial balance.

Problem 4-5A   *Completing the accounting cycle*   *(Obj. 2, 3, 5)*

The trial balance of Featherstone Environmental Services at October 31, 2007, and the data needed for the month-end adjustments are as follows on the next page.

FEATHERSTONE ENVIRONMENTAL SERVICES
Trial Balance
October 31, 2007

Account Title	Debit	Credit
Cash	$ 22,050	
Accounts receivable	68,895	
Prepaid rent	9,900	
Supplies	3,780	
Furniture	120,735	
Accumulated amortization—furniture		$ 15,300
Building	307,350	
Accumulated amortization—building		54,450
Land	81,000	
Accounts payable		32,805
Salary payable		0
Unearned consulting revenue		23,850
K. Featherstone, capital		461,205
K. Featherstone, withdrawals	17,550	
Consulting revenue		56,520
Salary expense	8,280	
Rent expense	0	
Utilities expense	4,590	
Amortization expense—furniture	0	
Amortization expense—building	0	
Supplies expense	0	
Total	$644,130	$644,130

The data needed for the month-end adjustments are as follows:

a. Unearned consulting revenue that still had not been earned at October 31, $22,050.
b. Rent still prepaid at October 31, $9,000.
c. Supplies used during the month, $3,465.
d. Amortization on furniture for the month, $1,125.
e. Amortization on building for the month, $2,610.
f. Accrued salary expense at October 31, $1,395.

Required

1. Open ledgers for the accounts listed in the trial balance, inserting their October 31 unadjusted balances. Also open the Income Summary account. Date the balances of the following accounts October 1: Prepaid Rent, Supplies, Building, Accumulated Amortization—Building, Furniture, Accumulated Amortization—Furniture, Unearned Consulting Revenue, and K. Featherstone, Capital.

2. Write the trial balance on a work sheet and complete the work sheet of Featherstone Environmental Services for the month ended October 31, 2007.

3. Using the completed work sheet, prepare the income statement, the statement of owner's equity, and the classified balance sheet in account format.

4. Using the work sheet data, journalize and post the adjusting and closing entries. Use dates and posting references. Use 12 as the number of the journal page.

5. Prepare a postclosing trial balance.

Problem 4-6A *Preparing a classified balance sheet in report format; evaluating a business* *(Obj. 5, 6)*

The accounts of Wolford Financial Services at March 31, 2006, are listed in alphabetical order.

Accounts payable	$11,760	Interest receivable	$ 720
Accounts receivable	9,200	Land	8,000
Accumulated amortization		Notes payable, long-term	2,560
—building	37,840	Notes receivable, long-term	5,520
Accumulated amortization		Other assets	1,840
—furniture	6,160	Other current liabilities	880
Advertising expense	720	Prepaid insurance	480
Amortization expense	1,520	Prepaid rent	3,760
A. Wolford, capital	40,560	Salary expense	14,240
A. Wolford, withdrawals	24,960	Salaries payable	1,920
Building	44,720	Service revenue	56,880
Cash	2,720	Supplies	3,040
Furniture	34,560	Supplies expense	3,680
Insurance expense	480	Unearned service revenue	1,360
Interest payable	240		

Required

1. All adjustments have been journalized and posted, but the closing entries have not yet been made. Prepare the company's classified balance sheet in report format at March 31, 2006. Use captions for total assets, total liabilities, and total liabilities and owner's equity.

2. Compute Wolford Financial Services' current ratio and debt ratio at March 31, 2006. At March 31, 2005, the current ratio was 1.28, and the debt ratio was 0.32. Did Wolford Financial Services' ability to pay debts improve or deteriorate during 2006?

Problem 4-7A *Analyzing and journalizing corrections, adjustments, and closing entries (Obj. 3, 4)*

Link Back to Chapter 2 (Accounting Errors).

The auditors of Cohen Logistics encountered the following situations while adjusting and closing the books at February 28. Consider each situation independently.

a. The company bookkeeper made the following entry to record a $620 credit purchase of supplies:

Feb. 26	Equipment	620	
	Accounts Payable		620

Prepare the correcting entry, dated February 28.

b. A $270 debit to Accounts Receivable was posted as $720.

(1) At what stage of the accounting cycle will this error be detected?

(2) Describe the technique for identifying the amount of the error.

c. The $1,740 balance of Utilities Expense was entered as $17,400 on the trial balance.

(1) What is the name of this type of error?

(2) Assume this is the only error in the trial balance. Which will be greater, the total debits or the total credits, and by how much?

(3) How can this type of error be identified?

d. The accountant failed to make the following adjusting entries at February 28:

(1) Accrued service revenue, $2,700.

(2) Insurance expense, $1,080.

(3) Accrued interest expense on a note payable, $1,560.

(4) Amortization of equipment, $11,100.

(5) Earned service revenue that had been collected in advance, $8,100.

Compute the overall net income effect of these omissions.

e. Record each of the adjusting entries identified in item d.

f. The revenue and expense accounts *after* the adjusting entries had been posted were Service Revenue, $179,995; Wage Expense, $78,325; Amortization Expense, $15,270; and Insurance Expense, $1,860. Two balances prior to closing were Capital, $137,725, and Withdrawals, $91,000. Journalize the closing entries.

Problem 4-8A *Preparing a work sheet, journalizing adjusting entries, closing the accounts (Obj. 1, 3)*

Eagle Ridge Marina performs overhauls and repairs to boats and motors at the marina and at the customer's location. The company's trial balance for the year ended June 30, 2007, follows.

EAGLE RIDGE MARINA
Trial Balance
June 30, 2007

Cash	$ 6,900	
Accounts receivable	36,600	
Repair supplies	59,400	
Prepaid insurance	14,100	
Equipment	180,000	
Accumulated amortization—equipment		$ 72,000
Building	264,000	
Accumulated amortization—building		52,800
Land	165,000	
Accounts payable		19,500
Unearned repair revenues		6,000
Property taxes payable		3,000
Notes payable, long-term		27,000
Mortgage payable		180,000
J. Alexander, capital		172,800
J. Alexander, withdrawals	141,000	
Repair fees earned		517,500
Wages expense	133,800	
Utilities expense	2,400	
Travel expenses	47,400	
Total	$1,050,600	$1,050,600

Additional information:

a. On June 30, repair supplies costing $6,600 were still on hand.

b. An examination of the insurance policies showed $8,700 of insurance coverage had expired in the year ended June 30, 2007.

c. An examination of the equipment and the building showed the following:

	Equipment	Building
Estimated useful life	5 years	10 years
Estimated value at the end of the useful life	$0	$0

Amortization is calculated on a straight-line basis over the asset's life.

d. The company had performed $3,000 of services for a client who had paid $6,000 in advance.

e. Accrued interest on the mortgage at June 30, $2,400.

f. Accrued wages at June 30, $3,600.

Required

1. Complete a work sheet for the year ended June 30, 2007.
2. Journalize the adjusting entries required on June 30, 2007.
3. Journalize the closing entries that would be required on June 30, 2007.
4. Prepare a postclosing trial balance for June 30, 2007.

Problem 4-9A *Preparing a work sheet, closing the accounts, classifying the assets and liabilities, evaluating the current and debt ratios* ***(Obj. 1, 3, 4, 6)***

Mark Hanson, the accountant for Botwin Graphics had prepared the work sheet shown on the next page on a computer spreadsheet but has lost much of the data. The only particular item the accountant can recall is that there was an adjustment made to correct an error made where $900 of supplies, purchased on credit, had been incorrectly recorded as $9,000 of equipment.

Required

1. Complete the work sheet by filling in the missing data.
2. Journalize the closing entries that would be required on December 31, 2006.
3. Prepare the company's classified balance sheet as of December 31, 2006.
4. Compute Botwin Graphics' current ratio and debt ratio for December 31, 2006. On December 31, 2005, the current ratio was 2.25 and the debt ratio was 0.41. Comment on the changes in the ratios.

Problems (Group B)

Problem 4-1B *Preparing a work sheet* ***(Obj. 1)***

The trial balance of Cranbrook Construction at July 31, 2006, appears on page 203.

Additional data at July 31, 2006:

a. Amortization: equipment, $1,020; building, $1,110.
b. Accrued wages expense, $720.
c. A count of supplies showed that unused supplies amounted to $44,220.
d. During July, $1,500 of prepaid insurance coverage expired.
e. Accrued interest expense, $540.
f. Of the $31,680 balance of Unearned Service Revenue, $14,910 was earned during July.
g. Accrued advertising expense, $300. (Credit Accounts Payable.)
h. Accrued service revenue, $3,300.

Required

Complete Cranbrook Construction's work sheet for July.

BOTWIN GRAPHICS
Accounting Work Sheet
For the Year Ended December 31, 2006

Account Title	Trial Balance Debit	Trial Balance Credit	Adjustments Debit	Adjustments Credit	Adjusted Trial Balance Debit	Adjusted Trial Balance Credit	Income Statement Debit	Income Statement Credit	Balance Sheet Debit	Balance Sheet Credit
Cash	3,000								3,000	
Accounts receivable	34,050				34,200					
Supplies	2,100			(b) 1,050	2,100					
Prepaid insurance	2,400									
Equipment	39,000				30,000					
Accumulated amortization—equipment		4,500				6,750				
Building	129,000				129,000					
Accumulated amortization—building		36,900		(e) 3,450						
Land	36,000				36,000					
Accounts payable		24,000								
Wages payable		1,350								
Interest payable		3,000		(f) 600						
Unearned revenues		4,050	(g) 600							
Mortgage payable		60,000								60,000
W. Botwin, capital		88,500								88,500
W. Botwin, withdrawals	27,000				27,000				27,000	
Graphics fees earned		142,650						143,400		
Wages expense	85,050				85,650					
Insurance expense	3,300									
Interest expense	3,000									
Utilities expense	1,050				1,050					
Supplies expense			(b) 1,050				1,050			
Amortization expense—equipment			(d) 2,250				2,250			
Amortization expense—building										
Totals	364,950	364,950								

202

CRANBROOK CONSTRUCTION
Trial Balance
July 31, 2006

Cash	$ 63,600	
Accounts receivable	113,460	
Supplies	52,980	
Prepaid insurance	6,900	
Equipment	98,070	
Accumulated amortization—equipment		$ 78,720
Building	128,670	
Accumulated amortization—building		31,500
Land	84,900	
Accounts payable		68,070
Interest payable		0
Wages payable		0
Unearned service revenue		31,680
Notes payable, long-term		67,200
T. Jackson, capital		237,390
T. Jackson, withdrawals	12,600	
Service revenue		60,570
Amortization expense—equipment	0	
Amortization expense—building	0	
Wages expense	9,600	
Insurance expense	0	
Interest expense	0	
Utilities expense	3,330	
Advertising expense	1,020	
Supplies expense	0	
Total	$575,130	$575,130

Problem 4-2B *Preparing financial statements from an adjusted trial balance; journalizing adjusting and closing entries; evaluating a business* **(Obj. 2, 5, 6)**

The *adjusted* trial balance of Alan Wood Design at June 30, 2005, the end of the company's fiscal year, appears on the following page.

Adjusting data at June 30, 2005, which *have been incorporated* into the trial balance figures on page 204, consist of:

a. Amortization for the year: equipment, $8,760; building, $4,764.

b. Supplies used during the year, $4,296.

c. During the year, $3,920 of prepaid insurance coverage expired.

d. Accrued interest expense, $828.

e. Accrued service revenue, $1,128.

f. Of the balance of Unearned Service Revenue at the beginning of the year, $9,348 was earned during the year.

g. Accrued wages expense, $924.

Required

1. Journalize the adjusting entries that would lead to the adjusted trial balance shown on page 204. Also journalize the closing entries.

2. Prepare the income statement and statement of owner's equity for the year ended June 30, 2005, and the classified balance sheet on that date. Use the account format for the balance sheet.

3. Compute Alan Wood Design's current ratio and debt ratio at June 30, 2005. One

year ago, the current ratio stood at 1.01, and the debt ratio was 0.71. Did Alan Wood Design's ability to pay debts improve or deteriorate during the year?

ALAN WOOD DESIGN
Adjusted Trial Balance
June 30, 2005

Cash..	$ 23,220	
Accounts receivable	31,764	
Supplies	37,548	
Prepaid insurance	3,840	
Equipment..	66,960	
Accumulated amortization—equipment.........		$ 19,776
Building	137,880	
Accumulated amortization—building.............		20,220
Land	36,000	
Accounts payable		46,080
Interest payable		1,788
Wages payable		924
Unearned service revenue		2,760
Notes payable, long-term.................................		116,400
Alan Wood, capital..		82,068
Alan Wood, withdrawals	54,360	
Service revenue...		167,832
Amortization expense—equipment	8,760	
Amortization expense—building	4,764	
Wages expense..	25,764	
Insurance expense...	3,720	
Interest expense..	13,812	
Utilities expense	5,160	
Supplies expense...	4,296	
Total...	$457,848	$457,848

Problem 4-3B   *Taking the accounting cycle through the closing entries*   *(Obj. 2, 3)*

The unadjusted T-accounts of Zhang Systems at December 31, 2007, appear on the next page and the related year-end adjustment data are given below.

Adjustment data at December 31, 2007, include:

a. Of the $15,000 balance of Unearned Service Revenue at the beginning of the year, all of it was earned during the year.

b. Supplies still unused at year end, $3,000.

c. Amortization for the year, $27,000.

d. Accrued salary expense, $3,000.

e. Accrued service revenue, $6,000.

Required

1. Write the trial balance on a work sheet, and complete the work sheet. Key each adjusting entry by the letter corresponding to the data given.

2. Prepare the income statement, the statement of owner's equity, and the classified balance sheet in account format.

3. Journalize the adjusting and closing entries.

4. Did Zhang Systems have a profitable year or a bad year during 2007? Give the reason for your answer.

Cash		Accounts Receivable		Supplies	
Bal. 15,000		Bal. 108,000		Bal. 27,000	

Equipment		Accumulated Amortization		Accounts Payable	
Bal. 297,000			Bal. 108,000		Bal. 18,000

Salary Payable		Unearned Service Revenue		Note Payable, Long-Term	
	0		Bal. 15,000		Bal. 180,000

Y. Zhang, Capital		Y. Zhang, Withdrawals		Supplies Expense	
	Bal. 108,000	Bal. 186,000		0	

Service Revenue		Salary Expense		Rent Expense	
	Bal. 447,000	Bal. 159,000		Bal. 45,000	

Amortization Expense		Interest Expense	
0		Bal. 18,000	

Insurance Expense	
Bal. 21,000	

Problem 4-4B *Completing the accounting cycle* **(Obj. 2, 3)**

This problem should be used only in conjunction with Problem 4-3B. It completes the accounting cycle by posting to T-accounts and preparing the postclosing trial balance.

Required

1. Using the Problem 4-3B data, post the adjusting and closing entries to the T-accounts, denoting adjusting amounts by *Adj.*, closing amounts by *Clo.*, and account balances by *Bal.*, as shown in Exhibit 4-10 (page 173). Double underline all accounts with a zero ending balance.
2. Prepare the postclosing trial balance.

Problem 4-5B *Completing the accounting cycle* **(Obj. 2, 3, 5)**

The trial balance of Breitman Insurance Agency at August 31, 2007, appears on page 206. The data needed for the month-end adjustments follow.

Adjustment data:

a. Commission revenue received in advance that had not been earned at August 31, $20,250.

b. Rent still prepaid at August 31, $3,150.

c. Supplies used during the month, $1,020.

d. Amortization on furniture for the month, $1,110.

e. Amortization on building for the month, $390.

f. Accrued salary expense at August 31, $1,380.

**Media Companion
CD-ROM**

BREITMAN INSURANCE AGENCY
Trial Balance
August 31, 2007

Account Title	Debit	Credit
Cash	$ 71,400	
Accounts receivable	46,680	
Prepaid rent	3,870	
Supplies	2,700	
Furniture	46,050	
Accumulated amortization—furniture		$ 38,400
Building	224,700	
Accumulated amortization—building		85,800
Land	45,000	
Accounts payable		12,720
Salaries payable		0
Unearned commission revenue		26,700
O. Breitman, capital		215,760
O. Breitman, withdrawals	14,400	
Commission revenue		81,900
Salary expense	3,300	
Rent expense	0	
Utilities expense	1,230	
Amortization expense—furniture	0	
Amortization expense—building	0	
Advertising expense	1,950	
Supplies expense	0	
Total	$461,280	$461,280

Required

1. Open the accounts listed in the trial balance and insert their August 31 unadjusted balances. Also open the Income Summary account. Date the balances of the following accounts as of August 1: Prepaid Rent, Supplies, Furniture, Accumulated Amortization—Furniture, Building, Accumulated Amortization—Building, Unearned Commission Revenue, and O. Breitman, Capital.

2. Write the trial balance on a work sheet and complete the work sheet of Breitman Insurance Agency for the month ended August 31, 2007.

3. Using the completed work sheet, prepare the income statement, the statement of owner's equity, and the classified balance sheet in account format.

4. Using the work sheet data, journalize and post the adjusting and closing entries. Use dates and posting references. Use page 7 as the number of the journal page.

5. Prepare a postclosing trial balance.

Problem 4-6B *Preparing a classified balance sheet in report format; evaluating a business (Obj. 5, 6)*

The accounts of Mayer Travel at December 31, 2006, are listed in alphabetical order on the following page.

Required

1. *All adjustments have been journalized and posted, but the closing entries have not yet been made.* Prepare the company's classified balance sheet in report format at December 31, 2007. Use captions for total assets, total liabilities, and owner's equity.

2. Compute Mayer Travel's current ratio and debt ratio at December 31, 2007. At December 31, 2006, the current ratio was 1.52 and the debt ratio was 0.37. Did Mayer Travel's ability to pay debts improve or deteriorate during 2007?

Accounts payable	$ 30,600	Interest payable	$ 3,600
Accounts receivable	39,600	Interest receivable	1,200
Accumulated amortization		Land	120,000
—building	226,800	Notes payable, long-term	166,800
Accumulated amortization		Notes receivable, long-term	24,000
—furniture	69,600	Other assets	21,600
Advertising expense	13,200	Other current liabilities	28,200
Amortization expense	7,800	Prepaid insurance	6,600
Building	626,400	Prepaid rent	39,600
Cash	39,000	Salary expense	147,600
Commission revenue	561,000	Salary payable	23,400
E. Mayer, capital	418,800	Supplies	15,000
E. Mayer, withdrawals	284,400	Supplies expense	34,200
Furniture	136,200	Unearned commission	
Insurance expense	4,800	revenue	32,400

Problem 4-7B *Analyzing and journalizing corrections, adjustments, and closing entries (Obj. 3, 4)*

Link Bank to Chapter 2 (Accounting Errors).

Accountants for Mainland Catering Service encountered the following situations while adjusting and closing the books at December 31. Consider each situation independently.

a. The company bookkeeper made the following entry to record a $4,500 credit purchase of office equipment:

Nov. 12 Office Supplies	4,500	
Accounts Payable		4,500

   Prepare the correcting entry, dated December 31.

b. A $2,250 credit to Cash was posted as a debit.

   (1) At what stage of the accounting cycle will this error be detected?

   (2) Describe the technique for identifying the amount of the error.

c. The $88,500 balance of Equipment was entered as $8,850 on the trial balance.

   (1) What is the name of this type of error?

   (2) Assume this is the only error in the trial balance. Which will be greater, the total debits or the total credits, and by how much?

   (3) How can this type of error be identified?

d. The accountant failed to make the following adjusting entries at December 31:

   (1) Accrued property tax expense, $600.

   (2) Supplies expense, $3,270.

   (3) Accrued interest revenue on a note receivable, $1,950.

   (4) Amortization of equipment, $12,000.

   (5) Earned service revenue that had been collected in advance, $15,300.

   Compute the overall net income effect of these omissions.

e. Record each of the adjusting entries identified in item d.

f. The revenue and expense accounts, *after* the adjusting entries had been posted, were Service Revenue, $57,600; Interest Revenue, $1,500; Salary Expense, $12,690; Rent Expense, $3,825; and Amortization Expense, $4,160. Two balances prior to closing were Capital, $36,450, and Withdrawals, $22,500. Journalize the closing entries.

Problem 4-8B *Preparing a work sheet, journalizing the adjustments, closing the accounts*
(Obj. 1, 3)

Slee Truck Services performs overhauls and repairs to trucks on the road and at the customer's location. The company's trial balance for the year ended March 31, 2006, is shown below.

SLEE TRUCK SERVICES
Trial Balance
March 31, 2006

Cash	$ 10,200	
Accounts receivable	63,600	
Repair supplies	26,700	
Prepaid insurance	11,700	
Equipment	210,000	
Accumulated amortization—equipment		$ 84,000
Building	282,000	
Accumulated amortization—building		56,400
Land	195,000	
Accounts payable		21,600
Unearned repair revenues		4,500
Employee withholdings payable		6,000
Notes payable, long-term		24,000
Mortgage payable		180,000
J. Slee, capital		287,100
J. Slee, withdrawals	27,000	
Repair fees earned		282,900
Wages expense	94,200	
Utilities expense	3,300	
Travel expenses	22,800	
Total	$946,500	$946,500

Additional information:

a. On March 31, supplies costing $3,900 were still on hand.

b. An examination of the insurance policies showed $6,300 of insurance coverage had expired during the year ended March 31, 2006.

c. An examination of the equipment and the building showed the following:

	Equipment	Building
Estimated useful life	5 years	10 years
Estimated value at the end of the useful life	$0	$0

Amortization is calculated on a straight-line basis over the asset's life.

d. The company had performed $2,400 of services for a client who had paid $4,500 in advance.

e. Accrued interest on the mortgage at March 31, $1,800.

f. Accrued wages at March 31, $2,700.

Required

1. Complete a work sheet for the year ended March 31, 2006.

2. Journalize the adjusting entries required on March 31, 2006.

3. Journalize the closing entries that would be required on March 31, 2006.

4. Prepare a postclosing trial balance for March 31, 2006.

Problem 4-9B *Preparing a work sheet, closing the accounts, classifying the assets and liabilities, evaluating the current and debt ratios* **(Obj. 1, 3, 4, 6)**

Shawn Venne, the accountant for Sherwood Consulting, prepared the work sheet shown on the next page on a computer spreadsheet but has lost much of the data. The only particular item Venne can recall is that there was an adjustment made to correct an error made where $1,200 of supplies, purchased on credit, had been incorrectly recorded as $12,000 of equipment.

Required:

1. Complete the work sheet by filling in the missing data.
2. Journalize the closing entries that would be required on December 31, 2007.
3. Prepare the company's classified balance sheet at December 31, 2007.
4. Compute Sherwood Consulting's current ratio and debt ratio for December 31, 2007. On December 31, 2006, the current ratio was 2.14 and the debt ratio was 0.47. Comment on the changes in the ratios.

Challenge Problems

Problem 4-1C *Closing the revenue and expense accounts* **(Obj. 3)**

Small businesses used to use a simplified journal called a "synoptic" journal to account for their businesses. The synoptic journal usually had columns for cash, accounts receivable, other assets, accounts payable, revenues, expenses, and so on. It required double-entry bookkeeping and the columns were usually totalled every month. None of the accounts in the synoptic journal were ever closed; each year flowed into the next year. The column totals for revenues and expenses grew ever larger.

Required

1. Explain why the synoptic journal was used by small businesses. What was the advantage it provided?
2. What do you think was the principal disadvantage of the synoptic journal? Why is it a disadvantage?

Problem 4-2C *Understanding the current ratio* **(Obj. 6)**

It is July 15, 2007. A friend, who works in the office of a local company that has four fast-food restaurants, has come to you with a question. He knows you are studying accounting and asks if you could help him sort something out. He acknowledges that although he has worked for the company for three years as a general clerk, he really does not understand the accounting work he is doing.

The company has a large bank loan and, as your friend understands it, the company has agreed with the bank to maintain a current ratio (he thinks that is what it is called) of 1.8 to 1 (1.8:1). The company's year end is June 30. The owner came to him on July 7, 2007, and asked him to issue a batch of cheques to suppliers but to date them June 30. Your friend recognizes that the cheques will have an effect on the June 30, 2007, financial statements but doesn't think the effect will be too serious.

Required

Explain to your friend what the effect of paying invoices after June 30 but dating the cheques prior to June 30 has on the current ratio. Provide an example to illustrate your explanation.

SHERWOOD CONSULTING
Accounting Work Sheet
For the Year Ended December 31, 2007

Account Title	Trial Balance Debit	Trial Balance Credit	Adjustments Debit	Adjustments Credit	Adjusted Trial Balance Debit	Adjusted Trial Balance Credit	Income Statement Debit	Income Statement Credit	Balance Sheet Debit	Balance Sheet Credit
Cash	33,000								33,000	
Accounts receivable	40,800			(b) 2,400	41,400					
Supplies	5,700									
Prepaid insurance	6,000				4,800					
Equipment	82,500				70,500					
Accumulated amortization—equipment		7,200				10,800				
Building	180,000			(e) 6,000	180,000					
Accumulated amortization—building		12,000								
Land	90,000			(f) 1,800	90,000					
Accounts payable		15,000								
Interest payable		9,000								
Wages payable		3,600								
Unearned consulting fees		10,500	(g) 1,500							
Mortgage payable		150,000			18,000					150,000
L. Sherwood, capital		123,000			102,300					123,000
L. Sherwood, withdrawals	18,000								18,000	
Consulting fees earned		249,900			1,500			252,000		
Wages expense	100,500									
Insurance expense	13,200									
Interest expense	9,000		(b) 2,400				2,400			
Utilities expense	1,500		(d) 3,600				3,600			
Supplies expense										
Amortization expense—equipment										
Amortization expense—building										
Totals	580,200	580,200								

Extending Your Knowledge

Decision Problems

1. Completing the accounting cycle to develop the information for a bank loan (Obj. 4, 6)

One year ago, your friend Don Jenner founded Jenner Consulting Services. The business has prospered. Jenner, who remembers that you took an accounting course while in college, comes to you for advice. He wishes to know how much net income his business earned during the past year. He also wants to know what the entity's total assets, liabilities, and owner's equity are. The accounting records consist of the T-accounts of the company's ledger, which were prepared by a bookkeeper who moved to another city. The ledger at December 31 of the fiscal year appears as follows:

Cash	Accounts Receivable	Prepaid Rent
Dec. 31 17,490	Dec. 31 37,080	Jan. 2 8,400

Supplies	Computer Equipment	Accumulated Amortization
Jan. 2 7,800	Jan. 2 130,800	0

Accounts Payable	Unearned Service Revenue	Salaries Payable
Dec. 31 55,620	Dec. 31 12,390	0

D. Jenner, Capital	D. Jenner, Withdrawals	Service Revenue
Jan. 2 75,000	Dec. 31 130,260	Dec. 31 242,220

Amortization Expense	Salary Expense	Supplies Expense
0	Dec. 31 51,000	0

Rent Expense	Utilities Expense
0	Dec. 31 2,400

Jenner indicates that at the year's end customers owe the company $4,800 accrued service revenue, which he expects to collect early next year. These revenues have not been recorded. During the year the company collected $12,390 service revenue in advance from customers, but the company earned only $1,800 of that amount. Rent expense for the year was $7,200, and the company used up $6,300 in supplies. Jenner estimates that amortization on the equipment was $17,700 for the year. At December 31, Jenner Consulting owes an employee $3,600 accrued salary.

Jenner expresses concern that his withdrawals during the year might have exceeded the business's net income. To get a loan to expand the business, Jenner must show the bank that Jenner Consulting's owner's equity has grown from its original $75,000 balance. Has it? You and Jenner agree that you will meet again in one week. You perform the analysis and prepare the financial statements to answer his questions.

2. Finding an error in the work sheets (Obj. 1, 4)

You are preparing the financial statements for the year ended October 31, 2006, for Cusik Publishing Company, a weekly newspaper. You began with the trial balance of the ledger, which balanced, and then made the required adjusting entries. To save time, you omitted preparing an adjusted trial balance. After making the adjustments on the work sheet, you extended the balances from the trial balance, adjusted for the adjusting entries, and computed amounts for the income statement and balance sheet columns.

a. When you added the debits and credits in the income statement columns, you found that the credits exceeded the debits by $30,000. According to your finding, did Cusik Publishing Company have a profit or a loss?

b. You took the balancing amount from the income statement columns to the debit column of the balance sheet and found that the total debits exceeded the total credits in the balance sheet. The difference between the total debits and the total credits on the balance sheet is $60,000, which is two times the amount of the difference you calculated for the income statement columns. What is the cause of this difference? (Except for these errors, everything else is correct.)

Financial Statement Problem

Using an actual balance sheet   (Obj. 6)

This problem, based on Intrawest Corporation's balance sheet in Appendix A, will familiarize you with some of the assets and liabilities of this actual company. Answer these questions, using Intrawest's balance sheet:

a. Which balance sheet format does Intrawest use?

b. What currency does Intrawest use to report financial results in its financial statements?

c. Name the company's largest current asset and largest current liability at June 30, 2003.

d. How much were total current assets and total current liabilities at June 30, 2002? Which had changed by the greater percentage during the year ended June 30, 2003: total current assets or total current liabilities? What were the percent changes?

e. Compute Intrawest Corporation's current ratio at June 30, 2003, and June 30, 2002. Also compute the debt ratios at these dates. Did the ratio values improve or deteriorate during 2003?

f. What is the cost of the company's capital assets at June 30, 2003? What is the book value of these assets? To answer this question, refer to the Ski and Resort Operations note.

Appendix

Reversing Entries: An Optional Step

Reversing entries are special types of entries that ease the burden of accounting after adjusting and closing entries have been made at the end of a period. Reversing entries are used most often in conjunction with accrual-type adjustments such as an accrued salary expense and accrued service revenue. Reversing entries are *not* used for adjustments to record amortization and prepayments. *GAAP do not require reversing entries. They are used only for convenience and to save time.*

Accounting for Accrued Expenses   To see how reversing entries work, return to EconoTravel's unadjusted trial balance at April 30, 2006 (Exhibit 4-2, page 164b). Salary Expense has a debit balance of $1,900 from salaries paid during April. At April 30, the company owes employees an additional $1,900 for the last part of the month.

Assume for this illustration that on May 5, the next payroll date, EconoTravel will pay $1,900 of accrued salary plus $200 in salary that the employee has earned in the first few days of May. EconoTravel's next payroll payment will be $2,100 ($1,900 + $200). But EconoTravel must include the $1,900 in salary expense for April. To do so, EconoTravel makes the following adjusting entry on April 30:

Adjusting Entries

April 30	Salary Expense	1,900	
	Salary Payable		1,900

After posting, the Salary Payable and Salary Expense accounts appear as follows:

Salary Payable

	Apr. 30 Adj.[1] 1,900
	Apr. 30 Bal. 1,900

Salary Expense

Paid during	
April CP 1,900	
Apr. 30 Adj. 1,900	
Apr. 30 Bal. 3,800	

After the adjusting entry,

- The April income statement reports salary expense of $3,800.
- The April 30 balance sheet reports salary payable of $1,900.

The $3,800 debit balance of Salary Expense is eliminated by this closing entry at April 30, 2006, as follows:

Closing Entries

April 30	Income Summary	3,800	
	Salary Expense		3,800

---

[1] Entry explanations used throughout this discussion are

Adj. = Adjusting entry	CP = Cash payment entry—includes a credit to Cash
Bal. = Balance	CR = Cash receipt entry—includes a debit to Cash
Clo. = Closing entry	Rev. = Reversing entry

After posting, Salary Expense has a zero balance as follows:

Salary Expense

Paid during		
April CP	1,900	
Apr. 30 Adj.	1,900	
Apr. 30 Bal.	3,800	Apr. 30 Clo. 3,800

Accounting without a Reversing Entry   On May 5, the next payday, EconoTravel pays the payroll of $2,100 and makes this journal entry:

May 5	Salary Payable	1,900	
	Salary Expense	200	
	Cash		2,100

This method of recording the cash payment is correct. However, it wastes time because the company's accountant must refer to the adjusting entries of April 30. Otherwise, EconoTravel does not know the amount of the debit to Salary Payable (in this example, $1,900). Searching the preceding period's adjusting entries takes time and, in business, time is money. To save time, accountants use reversing entries.

Making a Reversing Entry   A *reversing entry* switches the debit and the credit of a previous adjusting entry. *A reversing entry, then, is the exact opposite of a prior adjusting entry.* The reversing entry is dated the first day of the period following the adjusting entry.

To illustrate reversing entries, recall that on April 30, 2006, EconoTravel made the following adjusting entry to accrue Salary Payable:

Adjusting Entries

Apr. 30	Salary Expense	1,900	
	Salary Payable		1,900

The reversing entry simply reverses the position of the debit and the credit:

Reversing Entries

May 1	Salary Payable...	1,900	
	Salary Expense		1,900

Observe that the reversing entry is dated the first day of the new period. It is the exact opposite of the April 30 adjusting entry. Ordinarily, the accountant who makes the adjusting entry also prepares the reversing entry at the same time. EconoTravel dates the reversing entry as of the first day of the next period, however, so that it affects only the new period. Note how the accounts appear after the company posts the reversing entry:

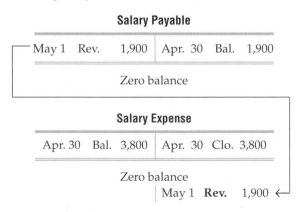

Salary Payable

May 1 Rev. 1,900	Apr. 30 Bal. 1,900

Zero balance

Salary Expense

Apr. 30 Bal. 3,800	Apr. 30 Clo. 3,800

Zero balance

May 1 **Rev.** 1,900

The arrow shows the transfer of the $1,900 credit balance from Salary Payable to Salary Expense. This credit balance in Salary Expense does not mean that the entity has negative salary expense, as you might think. Instead, the odd credit balance is merely a temporary result of the reversing entry. The credit balance is eliminated on May 5 when the $2,100 cash payment for salaries is debited to Salary Expense in the customary manner:

May 5   Salary Expense 2,100
               Cash...   2,100

Then this cash payment entry is posted as follows:

Salary Expense

May 5	CP	2,100	May 1	Rev.	1,900
May 5	Bal.	200			

Now Salary Expense has its correct debit balance of $200, which is the amount of salary expense incurred thus far in May. The $2,100 cash disbursement also pays the liability for Salary Payable so that Salary Payable has a zero balance, which is correct.

Accounting for Accrued Revenues   While most reversing entries are made to accrue expenses, reversing entries may be made to accrue revenues. For example, if EconoTravel had completed some consulting work for a client, an entry would be made to debit Fees Receivable and credit Fee Revenue at April 30, 2006. Fee Revenue would be closed to the Income Summary in the usual way. A reversing entry on May 1, 2006, would reduce the Fees Receivable and temporarily create a debit balance in the Fee Revenue account. When the payment is received, the accountant would debit Cash and credit Fee Revenue.

Appendix Problem

Problem 4A-1   *Using reversing entries*

Refer to the data in Problem 4-5B, pages 205–206.

Required

1. Open ledger accounts for Salaries Payable and Salary Expense. Insert their unadjusted balances at August 31, 2007.
2. Journalize adjusting entry *f* and the closing entry for Salary Expense at August 31. Post to the accounts.
3. On September 5, Breitman Insurance Agency paid the next payroll amount of $1,740. Journalize this cash payment, and post to the accounts. Show the balance in each account.
4. Repeat Requirements 1 through 3 using a reversing entry. Compare the balances of Salaries Payable and Salary Expense computed by using a reversing entry with those balances computed without using a reversing entry (as they appear in your answer to Requirement 3).

Merchandising Operations and the Accounting Cycle

CHAPTER OBJECTIVES

After studying this chapter, you should be able to

1 Use sales and gross margin to evaluate a company

2 Account for the purchase and sale of inventory under the perpetual inventory system

3 Adjust and close the accounts of a merchandising business under the perpetual inventory system

4 Prepare a merchandiser's financial statements under the perpetual inventory system

5 Use the gross margin percentage and the inventory turnover ratio to evaluate a business

6 Compute the cost of goods sold under the periodic inventory system

Supplement Learning Objectives

S2 Account for the purchase and sale of inventory under the periodic inventory system

S3 Compute the cost of goods sold under the periodic inventory system

S4 Adjust and close the accounts of a merchandising business under the periodic inventory system

S5 Prepare a merchandiser's financial statements under the periodic inventory system

 Media Companion CD-ROM

Visit the Media Companion CD-ROM that comes with this book for extra practice with the new material in Chapter 5.

Danier Leather Inc. (www.danier.com) is a leading designer, manufacturer, and retailer of high-quality leather and suede clothing and accessories. The company was founded in 1972 and has been a recognized leader in leather and suede design. The company now has approximately 100 stores (mainly in Canada, but also in Long Island, New York). It is the second-largest outerwear retailer in Canada.

How did this company grow? Danier cultivated a brand image, successfully differentiating its brand so that it became recognized as the Canadian leader in its market. Danier relies on high-quality, fashionable leather and modern styling to attract customers. The company's strategy is to develop a product line that is neither at the "high end" nor the "low end" of the market it serves. In terms of price, it's the middle segment of the market.

Danier has been successful in its approach. Including fiscal 2003, the company has been profitable for 29 consecutive years. Sales have grown to approximately $175 million per year, up from $108 million five years ago.

However, there is competition. Danier Leather has responded by developing a growth strategy that includes opening more retail stores in Canada and the United States, and exploring possibilities to expand further abroad. The company is also active in online retailing through its website, www.danier.com. In addition, Danier is expanding its product line to include accessories such as handbags, gloves, and belts, and has a goal of having these products account for 30 percent of total sales. Finally, the company has targeted a new market—corporate sales. Danier Leather Inc. hopes to sell products to corporations and other organizations to use as premiums and incentives for employees, suppliers, and customers.

Source: Danier Leather Inc. 2003 Annual Report

WHAT comes to mind when you think of *merchandising?* You probably think of the clothing that you purchase from a department store, the bread you buy at the grocery store, or the gas you purchase at your local service station. In addition to Danier Leather, merchandisers include Zellers (www.hbc.com/zellers), The Bay (www.hbc.com/bay), Canadian Tire (www.canadiantire.ca), Petro-Canada (www.petro-canada.ca), and Shoppers Drug Mart (www.shoppersdrugmart.ca).

How do the operations of Danier Leather and other merchandisers differ from those of the businesses we have studied so far? In the first four chapters, EconoTravel provided an illustration of a business that earns revenue by selling its services. Service enterprises include Marriott Hotels (www.marriott.com), WestJet (www.westjet.com), physicians, lawyers, public accountants, the Montreal Canadiens (www.canadiens.com) hockey club, and the twelve-year-old who cuts lawns in your neighbourhood. A *merchandising entity* earns its revenue by selling products, called *merchandise inventory* or, simply, *inventory.*

This chapter demonstrates the central role of inventory in a business that sells merchandise. **Inventory** includes all goods that the company owns and expects to sell in the normal course of operations. Some businesses, such as Wal-Mart (www.walmart.com) department stores, Esso (www.imperialoil.ca) gas stations, and Safeway grocery stores (www.safeway.com), buy their inventory in finished form ready for sale to customers. Others, such as EA Sports (www.easports.com) and Labatt Breweries (www.beer.com/ca/), manufacture their own products. Both groups sell products rather than services.

We illustrate accounting for the purchase and sale of inventory, how to adjust and close the books of a merchandiser, and how to prepare financial statements for a merchandiser. The chapter illustrates both the perpetual and periodic inventory methods. The chapter covers two ratios that investors and creditors use to evaluate companies. Before launching into merchandising, let's compare service entities, with which you are familiar, with merchandising companies. The following summarized financial statements will show how the two types of companies are similar and different:

SERVICE CO.* Income Statement For the Year Ended June 30, 2005		MERCHANDISING CO.** Income Statement For the Year Ended June 30, 2005	
Service revenue	$XXX →	*Sales* revenue	$XXX
Expenses ———		*Cost of goods sold*	X
Salary expense	X	*Gross margin*	XX
Amortization expense	X →	*Operating expenses*	
Net income	$ X	Salary expense	X
		Amortization expense	X
		Income tax expense	X
		Net income	$ X

SERVICE CO. Balance Sheet June 30, 2005		MERCHANDISING CO. Balance Sheet June 30, 2005	
Assets		**Assets**	
Current assets:		Current assets:	
Cash	$X	Cash	$X
Short-term investments	X	Short-term investments	X
Accounts receivable, net	X	Accounts receivable, net	X
Prepaid expenses	X	*Inventory*	X
		Prepaid expenses	X

* Such as EconoTravel

** Such as Danier Leather Inc., a corporation

What Are Merchandising Operations?

Exhibit 5-1 shows the income statement of Danier Leather Inc. for two recent years. Danier Leather's income statement differs from those of the service business discussed in previous chapters. For comparison, Exhibit 5-1 also provides the income statement for EconoTravel. The bolded items in the Daniel Leather statement are unique to merchandising operations.

The selling price of merchandise sold by a business is called **sales revenue**, often abbreviated as **sales**. (**Net sales** equals sales revenue minus any sales returns and sales discounts.) The major revenue of a merchandising entity, sales revenue, results in an increase in capital from delivering inventory to customers. The major expense of a merchandiser is **cost of goods sold**, also called **cost of sales**. It represents the entity's cost of the goods (the inventory) it sold to customers. While inventory is held by a business, the inventory is an asset because the goods are an economic resource with future value to the company. When the inventory is sold, however, the inventory's cost becomes an expense to the seller because the goods are no longer available. When one of the Danier Leather stores sell a leather jacket to a customer, the jacket's cost is expensed as cost of goods sold on Danier Leather's books.

Net sales revenue minus cost of goods sold is called **gross margin** or **gross profit**.

Net sales revenue (sometimes abbreviated as Sales)	–	Cost of goods sold (same as Cost of sales)	=	Gross margin (same as Gross profit)

or, more simply,

Sales	–	Cost of sales	=	Gross margin

DANIER LEATHER INC.
Consolidated Statement of Earnings (adapted)
For the Years Ended June 28, 2003 and June 29, 2002

	(In thousands of dollars)	
	2003	2002
Revenue	$175,487	$179,977
Cost of sales	88,788	92,098
Gross margin (gross profit)	86,699	87,879
Selling, general, and administrative expenses	77,390	69,264
Earnings before interest and income taxes	9,309	18,615
Interest expense—net	66	461
Earnings before income taxes	9,243	18,154
Income taxes expense	3,849	7,429
Net earnings	$ 5,394	$ 10,725

ECONOTRAVEL
Income Statement
For the Year Ended December 31, 2006

Service revenue	$226,000
Expenses (listed individually)	84,000
Net earnings	$142,000

Gross margin is a measure of business success. A sufficiently high gross margin is vital to a merchandiser, since all other expenses of the company are deducted from this gross margin. Danier Leather's operations were more successful during the year ended June 29, 2002 because net income was higher than in fiscal 2003.

The following example will clarify the nature of gross margin. Suppose Danier Leather's cost for a certain jacket is $100 and Danier sells the jacket to a customer in Halifax for $180. Danier's gross margin on the jacket is $80 ($180 – $100). The gross margin reported on Danier's income statement, $86,699,000, is the sum of the gross margins on all the products the company sold during its 2003 fiscal year.

What Goes into Inventory Cost?

The $37,029,000 cost of inventory on Danier Leather Inc.'s balance sheet represents all the costs Danier incurred to bring the merchandise to the point of sale. Suppose Danier purchases handbags from a manufacturer in Singapore. Danier's cost of a handbag would include

- Cost of the handbag—say $40.00 per bag.
- Customs duties paid to the Canadian government in order to import the handbags—say $4.00, added to the cost of each handbag.
- Shipping cost from the manufacturer in Singapore to Danier's location in Saskatchewan. This cost is called *freight* or *freight in*. Assume freight adds $2.00 of cost to each handbag.
- Insurance on the handbags while in transit—say $1.00 per handbag.

In total, Danier Leather's cost of this handbag totals $47.00 ($40.00 + $4.00 + $2.00 + $1.00). The cost principle applies to all assets, as follows:

The cost of any asset is the sum of all the costs
incurred to bring the asset to its intended use.

For merchandise inventory, the intended use is readiness for sale. After the goods are offered for sale, then other costs, such as advertising, display, and sales commissions, are expensed. Thus these costs are *not* included as the cost of inventory.

The Operating Cycle for a Merchandising Business

Some merchandising entities buy inventory, sell the inventory to their customers, and use the cash to purchase more inventory to repeat the cycle. Other merchandisers, like Cedar Creek Estate Winery (www.cedarcreek.bc.ca) or Motorola Canada Limited (www.motorola.ca), manufacture their products and sell them to customers. Danier Leather manufactures some of the products it sells. The balance of this chapter considers the first group of merchandisers that buy products and resell them. Exhibit 5-2 diagrams the operating cycle for *cash sales* and for *sales on account*. For a cash sale—Panel A—the cycle is from cash to inventory, which is purchased for resale, and back to cash. For a sale on account—Panel B—the cycle is from cash to inventory to accounts receivable and back to cash. In all lines of business, managers strive to shorten the cycle in order to keep assets active. The faster the sale of inventory and the collection of cash, the higher the profits, assuming cost and selling price stay the same.

Inventory Systems: Perpetual and Periodic

There are two main types of inventory accounting systems: the periodic system and the perpetual system.

The **periodic inventory system** is used by businesses that sell relatively inexpensive goods. A very small grocery store without an optical-scanning cash register to read UPC codes does not keep a daily running record of every loaf of bread and package of bacon that it buys and sells. The cost of record keeping would be overwhelming. Instead, grocers count their inventory periodically—at least once a year—to determine the quantities on hand. The inventory amounts are used to prepare the annual financial statements. Businesses such as restaurants and small retail stores also use the periodic inventory system. The end-of-chapter supplement covers the periodic inventory system. That system is being used less and less as more businesses keep their inventory records by computer.

Under the **perpetual inventory system**, the business maintains a running record of inventory and cost of goods sold. This system achieves control over expensive goods such as automobiles, jewellery, and furniture. Recently, the low cost of computer information systems has increased the use of perpetual systems. Computers

EXHIBIT 5-2

Operating Cycle of a
Merchandiser

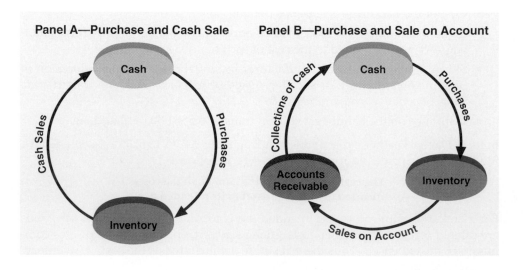

reduce the time required to manage inventory and thus increase a company's ability to control its merchandise. But even under a perpetual system the business counts the inventory on hand at least once a year. The physical count establishes the correct amount of ending inventory, which may have been affected by pilferage or spoilage, and serves as a check on the perpetual records.

The following chart compares the perpetual and periodic systems:

Perpetual Inventory System
- Keeps a running record of all goods bought and sold (units and price)
- Inventory counted at least once a year
- Used for all types of goods

Periodic Inventory System
- Does *not* keep a running record of all goods bought and sold
- Inventory counted at least once a year
- Used for *inexpensive* goods

Computerized Inventory Systems

A computerized inventory system can keep accurate, up-to-date records of the number and cost of units purchased, the number and cost of units sold, and the quantities and cost on hand. Inventory systems are often integrated with accounts receivable and sales. The computer can keep up-to-the-minute records, so managers can call up current inventory information at any time. For example, in a perpetual system the "cash register" at IKEA or Mark's Work Wearhouse is a computer terminal that records the sale and also updates the inventory records. Bar codes, which are scanned by a laser, are part of the perpetual inventory system. The lines of the bar code represent coded data that keep track of each item. Because most businesses use bar codes, we base our inventory discussions on the perpetual system.[1]

Accounting for Inventory in the Perpetual Inventory System

OBJECTIVE 2
Account for the purchase and sale of inventory under the perpetual inventory system

The cycle of a merchandising entity begins with the purchase of inventory, as Exhibit 5-2 shows. For example, an electronics store records the purchase of DVD players, MP3 players, and other items of inventory acquired for resale by debiting the Inventory account. A $10,000 purchase on account is recorded as follows:

June 14	Inventory	10,000	
	Accounts Payable...		10,000
	Purchased inventory on account.		

LEARNING **TIP**

The Inventory account should be used only for purchases of merchandise for resale. Purchases of any other assets are recorded in a different asset account. For example, the purchase of supplies is debited to Supplies, not to Inventory.

The Purchase Invoice: A Basic Business Document

Business documents are the tangible evidence of transactions. In this section, we trace the steps that Austin Sound Centre, in Kingston, Ontario, takes to order, receive, and pay for inventory. Many companies buy and sell their goods electronically—with no invoices, no cheques, and so on. Here we use actual documents to illustrate what takes place behind the scenes.

1. Suppose Austin Sound Centre wants to stock JVC brand CD players, DVD players, and speakers. Austin prepares a *purchase order* and transmits it to JVC Canada Inc. (www.jvc.ca).

2. On receipt of the purchase order, JVC searches its warehouse for the inventory that Austin Sound Centre ordered. JVC ships the equipment and sends the invoice to Austin Sound on the same day. The **invoice** is the seller's request for payment from the purchaser. It is also called the *bill*.

---

[1]For instructors who prefer to concentrate on the periodic inventory system, an overview starts on page 241 and a comprehensive treatment of that system begins on page 273. Follow Chapter Objectives S2 through S5 instead of Chapter Objectives 2 through 4.

3. Often the purchaser receives the invoice before the inventory arrives. Austin Sound does not pay immediately. Instead, Austin Sound waits until the inventory arrives in order to ensure that it is the correct type and quantity ordered, and in good condition. After the inventory is inspected and approved, Austin Sound pays JVC the invoice amount according to the terms of payment previously negotiated.

Exhibit 5-3 is a copy of an invoice from JVC Canada Inc. to Austin Sound Centre. From Austin Sound's perspective, this document is a *purchase invoice* (it is being used to purchase goods). To JVC it is a *sales invoice* (it is being used to sell goods).

Discounts from Purchase Prices

There are two major types of discounts from purchase prices: quantity discounts and cash discounts (called *purchase discounts*).

Quantity Discounts A *quantity discount* works this way. The larger the quantity purchased, the lower the price per item. For example, JVC may offer no quantity discount for the purchase of only one or two CD players, and charge the *list* price—the full price—of $200 per unit. However, JVC may offer the following quantity discount terms in order to persuade customers to buy more CD players:

Quantity	Quantity Discount	Net Price per Unit
Buy minimum quantity, 3 CD players	5%	$190 [$200 − 0.05($200)]
Buy 4–9 CD players	10%	$180 [$200 − 0.10($200)]
Buy more than 9 CD players	20%	$160 [$200 − 0.20($200)]

EXHIBIT 5-3

Business Invoice

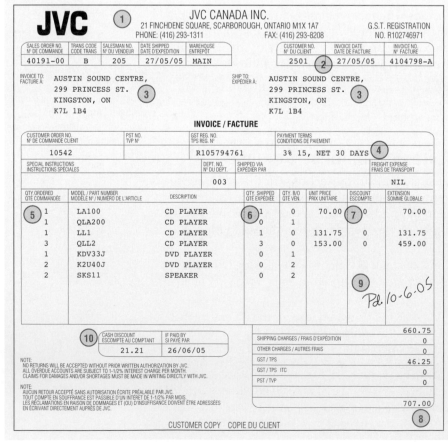

(1) The seller

(2) The invoice date, needed for determining whether the purchaser gets a discount for prompt payment (see 4)

(3) The purchaser. This inventory is invoiced (billed) and shipped to the same address.

(4) Credit terms of the transaction: If it pays within 15 days of the invoice date, Austin Sound may deduct 3% of the total amount. Otherwise, the full amount—net—is due in 30 days.*

(5) Austin ordered 6 CD players, 3 DVD players, and 2 speakers.

(6) JVC shipped 5 CD players, no DVD players, and no speakers.

(7) Quantity discount offered by JVC

(8) Total invoice amount

(9) Austin's payment date. How much did Austin pay? (See 10.)

(10) Payment occurred 14 days after the invoice date—within the discount period—so Austin paid $685.79 ($707 − 3% discount). We will disregard GST for now.

*A full discussion of discounts appears in the next section.

Suppose Austin Sound Centre purchases five CD players from this manufacturer. The cost of each CD player is, therefore, $180. Purchase of five units on account would be recorded by debiting Inventory and crediting Accounts Payable for the total price of $900 ($180 per unit × 5 items purchased).

There is no Quantity Discount account and no special accounting entry for a quantity discount. Instead, all accounting entries are based on the net price of a purchase after the quantity discount has been subtracted, as shown on the invoice.

Purchase Discounts   Many businesses also offer purchase discounts to their customers. A purchase discount is totally different from a quantity discount. A *purchase discount* is a reward for prompt payment. If a quantity discount is also offered, the purchase discount is computed on the net purchase amount after the quantity discount has been subtracted, further reducing the cost of the inventory to the purchaser.

JVC's credit terms of 3% 15, NET 30 DAYS can also be expressed as 3/15 n/30. This means that Austin Sound Centre may deduct 3 percent of the total amount due if Austin pays within 15 days of the invoice date. Otherwise, the full amount— NET—is due in 30 days. Terms of simply n/30 indicate that no discount is offered, and that payment is due 30 days after the invoice date. Terms of *eom* mean that payment is due by the end of the current month. However, a purchase after the 25th of the current month on terms of *eom* can be paid at the end of the next month.

Many businesses that have computerized accounting systems program their system to flag invoices as the date for taking the discount approaches so the business can take advantage of the purchase discount.

Let's use the Exhibit 5-3 transaction to illustrate accounting for a purchase discount. For the moment, disregard GST and use the invoice total of $707.00 when recording purchases and purchase discounts. GST is discussed on page 229. Austin Sound Centre records the purchase on account as follows:

May 27	Inventory	707.00	
	Accounts Payable..		707.00
	Purchased inventory on account.		

The accounting equation shows that a credit purchase of inventory increases both assets (Inventory) and liabilities (Accounts Payable), as follows:

ASSETS	=	LIABILITIES	+	OWNER'S EQUITY
Inventory	=	Accounts Payable		
$707	=	$707	+	0

Austin paid within the discount period so its cash payment entry is

June 10	Accounts Payable	707.00	
	Cash		685.79
	Inventory..		21.21
	Paid on account within discount period.		
	The discount is $21.21 [707.00 × 0.03]		

After paying the account, Austin Sound's assets and liabilities both decrease, as follows:

ASSETS			=	LIABILITIES	+	OWNER'S EQUITY
Cash	+	Inventory	=	Accounts Payable		
−$685.29		−$21.21	=	−$707	+	0

−$707

Note the credit to Inventory. After Austin Sound has taken its discount, Austin Sound must adjust the Inventory account to reflect its true cost of the goods. In effect, this inventory cost Austin Sound $685.79 ($707.00 minus the purchase discount of $21.21 [3% of $707.00]), as shown in the following Inventory account:

Inventory

May 27	707.00	June 10	21.21
Bal.	685.79		

However, if Austin Sound pays this invoice after the discount period, it must pay the full invoice amount. In this case, the payment entry is

June 29	Accounts Payable...	707.00	
	Cash		707.00
	Paid on account after discount period.		

Without the discount, Austin Sound's cost of the inventory is the full amount of $707, as shown in the following T-account:

Inventory

May 27	707.00

Purchase Returns and Allowances

Most businesses allow their customers to *return* merchandise that is defective, damaged in shipment, or otherwise unsuitable. Or, if the buyer chooses to keep damaged goods, the seller may deduct an *allowance* from the amount the buyer owes. Both purchase returns and purchase allowances decrease the amount that the buyer must pay the seller.

Suppose the $70 CD player (model LA100) purchased by Austin Sound Centre (in Exhibit 5-3) was not the CD player ordered. Austin Sound returns the merchandise to the seller and records the purchase return as follows:

June 3	Accounts Payable...	70.00	
	Inventory..		70.00
	Returned inventory to seller.		

Now assume that one of the JVC CD players was damaged in shipment to Austin Sound Centre. The damage is minor, and Austin decides to keep the CD player in exchange for a $15 allowance from JVC. To record this purchase allowance, Austin Sound Centre makes this entry:

June 4	Accounts Payable...	15.00	
	Inventory..		15.00
	Received a purchase allowance.		

The return and the allowance had two effects:

(1) They decreased Austin Sound's liability, which is why we debit Accounts Payable.

(2) They decreased the net cost of the inventory, which is why we credit Inventory.

Assume that Austin Sound has not yet paid its liability to JVC. After these return ($70) and allowance ($15) transactions are posted, Austin Sound's accounts will show these balances:

Inventory					**Accounts Payable**			
May 27	707.00	June 3	70.00		June 3	70.00	May 27	707.00
		June 4	15.00		June 4	15.00		
Bal.	622.00						Bal.	622.00

Austin Sound's cost of *inventory* is $622, and Austin Sound owes JVC $622 on *account payable*. If Austin Sound pays within the discount period, 3 percent will be deducted from the $622.00 balance.

Transportation Costs: Who Pays?

The transportation cost of moving inventory from seller to buyer can be significant. The purchase agreement specifies FOB terms to indicate who pays the shipping charges. *FOB* means *free on board*. FOB governs

(1) when legal title passes from the seller to buyer, and

(2) who pays the freight.

- Under FOB *shipping point* terms, title passes when the inventory leaves the seller's place of business—the shipping point. The buyer owns the goods while they are in transit, and therefore the buyer pays the transportation cost.

- Under FOB *destination* terms, title passes when the goods reach the destination, so the seller pays transportation cost.

Exhibit 5-4 summarizes FOB.

Freight In   FOB shipping point terms are the most common, so the buyer generally pays the shipping cost. A freight cost that the buyer pays on an inventory purchase is called *freight in*. In accounting, the cost of an asset includes all costs incurred to bring the asset to its intended use. For inventory, cost therefore includes the

- *Net cost* after all discounts, returns, and allowances have been subtracted, plus

- *Freight* (transportation, or shipping) costs to be paid

To record the payment for freight in, the buyer debits Inventory and credits Cash or Accounts Payable for the amount. Suppose Austin Sound receives a $70 shipping bill directly from the freight company. Austin's entry to record payment of the freight charge is:

June 1	Inventory	70.00	
	Cash		70.00
	Paid a freight bill.		

The freight charge increases the cost of the inventory to $692.00 as follows:

Inventory

(Purchase)	May 27	707.00	June 3	70.00	(Return)
(Freight)	June 1	70.00	June 4	15.00	(Allowance)
(Net cost)	Bal.	692.00			

Any discounts would be computed only on the account payable to the seller, not on the transportation costs, because the freight company usually offers no discount.

Under FOB shipping point terms, the seller sometimes prepays the transportation cost as a convenience, and adds this cost on the invoice. The buyer can debit Inventory for the combined cost of the inventory and the shipping cost because both costs apply to the merchandise. A $10,000 purchase of goods, coupled with a related freight charge of $800, would be recorded as follows:

March 12	Inventory	10,800	
	Accounts Payable		10,800
	Purchased inventory on account, including freight of $800.		

	FOB Shipping Point	FOB Destination
When does title pass to buyer?	At the shipping point	At the destination
Who pays transportation cost?	Buyer	Seller

EXHIBIT 5-4

FOB Terms

If the buyer pays within the discount period, the discount will be computed on the $10,000 merchandise cost, not on the $10,800. No discount is offered on transportation cost.

Freight Out   The cost of freight charges paid to ship goods sold to customers is called *freight out*. Freight out is a delivery expense. Delivery expense is an operating expense for the seller. It is debited to the Delivery Expense account.

Selling Inventory and Recording Cost of Goods Sold

After a company buys inventory, the next step in the operating cycle is to sell the goods. We shift now to the selling side and follow Austin Sound Centre through a sequence of selling transactions. A sale earns a reward, Sales Revenue. A sale also requires a sacrifice in the form of an expense, Cost of Goods Sold, as the seller gives up the asset Inventory.

After making a sale on account, Austin Sound Centre may experience any of the following:

- A sales return: The customer may return goods to Austin Sound.
- A sales allowance: For one reason or another, Austin Sound may grant a sales allowance to reduce the amount of cash collectible from the customer.
- A sales discount: If the customer pays within the discount period—under terms such as 2/10 n/30—Austin Sound collects the discounted amount.
- Freight out: Austin Sound may have to pay Delivery Expense to transport the goods to the buyer's location.

The sale of inventory may be for cash or on account, as Exhibit 5-2 shows.

Cash Sale   Sales of retailers, such as grocery stores and restaurants, are often for cash. Cash sales of $5,000 would be recorded by debiting Cash and crediting Sales Revenue as follows:

Jan. 9	Cash..	5,000	
	Sales Revenue		5,000
	Cash sale.		

To update the inventory records, the business also must decrease the Inventory balance. Suppose these goods cost the seller $3,200. An accompanying entry is needed to transfer the $3,200 cost of the goods—*not their selling price of $5,000*—from the Inventory account to the Cost of Goods Sold account as follows:

Jan. 9	Cost of Goods Sold..	3,200	
	Inventory..		3,200
	Recorded the cost of goods sold.		

Cost of goods sold (also called cost of sales) is the largest single expense of most businesses that sell merchandise, such as Future Shop (www.futureshop.ca), JVC, and Austin Sound. It is the cost of the inventory that the business has sold to customers. The Cost of Goods Sold account keeps a current balance as transactions are journalized and posted.

KEY POINT

The recording of cost of goods sold along with sales revenue is an example of the matching principle (Chapter 3, page 111)—matching expense against revenue to measure net income.

After posting, the Cost of Goods Sold account holds the cost of the merchandise sold ($3,200 in this case):

Inventory				Cost of Goods Sold		
Purchases (amount assumed)	60,000	Jan. 9	3,200	Jan. 9	3,200	

The computer automatically records this entry when the cashier keys in the code number of the inventory that is sold. Optical scanners at cash registers perform this task in most stores.

Sale on Account   Most sales in Canada are made on account (on credit), using either the seller's credit facility or a credit card such as Visa (www.visa.com) or MasterCard (www.mastercard.com/canada). To simplify the discussion, we will assume the seller records the receivable as a regular account receivable rather than a special receivable from the credit card company. An $8,000 sale on account is recorded by a debit to Accounts Receivable and a credit to Sales Revenue, as follows:

Jan. 11	Accounts Receivable	8,000	
	Sales Revenue		8,000
	Sale on account.		

If we assume that these goods cost the seller $4,800, the accompanying cost of goods sold and inventory entry is

Jan. 11	Cost of Goods Sold	4,800	
	Inventory		4,800
	Recorded the cost of goods sold.		

After recording the January 9 and 11 transactions, sales revenue is $13,000 ($5,000 + $8,000). Cost of goods sold totals $8,000 ($3,200 + $4,800).

The seller records the related cash receipt on account as follows:

Jan. 19	Cash	8,000	
	Accounts Receivable		8,000
	Collection on account.		

STOP & THINK

Why is there no January 19 entry to Sales Revenue, Cost of Goods Sold, or Inventory?

Answer: On January 19 the seller merely receives one asset—Cash—in place of another asset—Accounts Receivable. The sales revenue, the related cost of goods sold, and the decrease in inventory for the goods sold were recorded on January 11. Examine the two entries on January 11.

Offering Sales Discounts and Sales Returns and Allowances

We just saw that purchase discounts and purchase returns and allowances decrease the cost of inventory purchases. In the same way, **sales discounts** and **sales returns and allowances**, which are contra accounts to Sales Revenue, decrease the revenue earned on sales.

KEY POINT

A contra account always has a companion account with the opposite balance. Thus, both Sales Discounts and Sales Returns and Allowances (debit balances) are reported with Sales Revenue (credit balance) on the income statement.

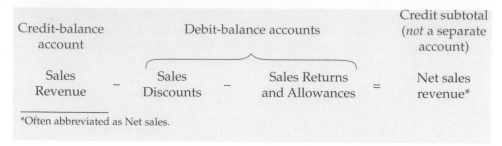

Credit-balance account		Debit-balance accounts		Credit subtotal (*not* a separate account)
Sales Revenue	− Sales Discounts	−	Sales Returns and Allowances	= Net sales revenue*

*Often abbreviated as Net sales.

This equation calculates net sales. Note that sales discounts can be given on both goods and services.

Companies keep close watch on their customers' paying habits and on their own sales of defective and unsuitable merchandise. They maintain separate accounts for Sales Discounts and Sales Returns and Allowances. Let's examine a sequence of the sale transactions of JVC. Assume JVC is selling to Austin Sound Centre.

On July 7, JVC sells stereo components for $10,800 on credit terms of 3/15 n/30. These goods cost JVC $7,050. JVC's entries to record this credit sale and the related cost of goods sold are:

July 7	Accounts Receivable	$10,800	
	Sales Revenue		$10,800
	Sale on account.		

July 7	Cost of Goods Sold	$7,050	
	Inventory...		$7,050
	Recorded the cost of goods sold.		

KEY POINT

The sale of inventory and the return of goods by customers require two separate journal entries.

Assume the buyer, Austin Sound Centre, returns goods that were sold by JVC for $900. These goods are not damaged and can be resold. JVC records the sales return and the related decrease in Accounts Receivable as follows:

July 12	Sales Returns and Allowances..................................	900	
	Accounts Receivable...		900
	Received returned goods.		

JVC receives the returned merchandise and updates the inventory records. JVC must also decrease cost of goods sold as follows (these goods cost JVC $600):

July 12	Inventory	600	
	Cost of Goods Sold		600
	Returned goods to inventory.		

Suppose JVC grants to the buyer a $150 sales allowance for damaged goods. Austin Sound then subtracts $150 from the amount it will pay JVC. JVC journalizes this transaction by debiting Sales Returns and Allowances and crediting Accounts Receivable as follows:

July 15	Sales Returns and Allowances..................................	150	
	Accounts Receivable...		150
	Granted a sales allowance for damaged goods.		

No inventory entry is needed for a sales allowance transaction because the seller, JVC, receives no returned goods from the customer. Instead, JVC will simply receive less cash from the customer.

After the preceding entries are posted, all the accounts have up-to-date balances. JVC's Accounts Receivable has a $9,750 debit balance, as follows:

Accounts Receivable

(Sale)	July 7	10,800	July 12	900	(Return)
			15	150	(Allowance)
	Bal.	9,750			

On July 22, the last day of the discount period, JVC collects $6,000 of this accounts receivable. Assume JVC allows customers to take discounts on all amounts JVC receives within the discount period. JVC's cash receipt is $5,820 [calculated as $6,000 − (0.03 × $6,000)], and the collection entry is

July 22	Cash..	5,820	
	Sales Discounts.	180	
	Accounts Receivable..		6,000
	Cash collection within the discount period.		
	Sales discount is $180 (0.03 × $6,000).		

Suppose JVC collects the remainder of $3,750 on July 28. That date is after the discount period, so there is no sales discount. To record this collection on account, JVC debits Cash and credits Accounts Receivable for the same amount, as follows:

July 28	Cash..	3,750	
	Accounts Receivable..		3,750
	Cash collection after the discount period.		

In Exhibit 5-1, Danier Leather Inc.—like most other businesses—reports to the public only the net sales figure. But Danier managers use the return and allowance data to track customer satisfaction and product quality.

Goods and Services Tax

This topic is introduced here to make you aware of the goods and services tax because most goods and services sold today in Canada have the Goods and Services Tax (GST) levied on them by the federal government at the time of sale. However, it was decided to omit consideration of the GST from the discussion and examples in the early chapters to avoid making the material overly complicated. The following discussion provides a brief introduction to the topic; GST is dealt with more fully in Chapter 11.

The manufacturer, wholesaler, and retailer pay the GST on the cost of their purchases, and then pass it on to the next link in the economic chain by charging and collecting it on their respective sales. The consumer, the last link in the chain, pays the final tax. Each entity that collects the GST remits the net tax collected to the Receiver General at the Canada Customs and Revenue Agency (CCRA).

The GST is designed to be a consumption tax and, as was suggested above, the entity ultimately paying the tax is the final purchaser of the product or service. Earlier links in the chain (for example, the retailer) pay tax on their purchases, but are then allowed to deduct (or recover) that tax from the tax they themselves collect on their sales. Therefore the GST paid on purchases does not really affect the cost of the purchase. For example, Austin Sound Centre paid the GST of 7 percent, or $4.90 ($70 × 0.07), on the LA100 purchased in Exhibit 5-3. The entry to record the purchase of the single CD player would have been:

May 27	Inventory	70.00	
	GST Recoverable	4.90	
	Accounts Payable...		74.90
	Purchased JVC LA100 CD player on account.		

Assume Austin Sound sold the JVC LA100 CD player for $110.00 to a customer; the GST on the sale would be $7.70 ($110.00 × 0.07). The entry to record the sale would be

June 10	Cash	117.70	
	GST Payable..		7.70
	Sales		110.00
	Sold JVC LA100 CD player for cash.		

Subsequently, Austin Sound would have to remit to the Receiver General at the CCRA the difference between the GST paid and the GST collected, the net GST.

The entry would be

July 31	GST Payable	7.70	
	GST Recoverable		4.90
	Cash		2.80

Payment of GST collected net of GST paid
(recoverable) on purchases ($7.70 – $4.90).

The discussion of GST above is greatly simplified for the purposes of this text. The actual GST is more complicated than as presented for two major reasons:

1. Supplies and services are divided into three classes and each class is taxed differently. The three classes are (1) Taxable supplies and services; (2) Zero-rated supplies and services; (3) Exempt supplies and services.

2. Some provinces (Quebec, Nova Scotia, New Brunswick, and Newfoundland and Labrador) have harmonized, or combined, their provincial sales tax with the GST to some degree.

Discussion of the GST beyond the level above is beyond the scope of this chapter.

Mid-Chapter Summary Problem
for Your Review

Vincent Sales Company engaged in the following transactions during September of the current year:

Sept.	3	Purchased inventory on credit terms of 1/10 net eom, $3,220.
	9	Returned 40 percent of the inventory purchased on September 3. It was defective.
	12	Sold goods for cash, $1,840 (cost, $1,100).
	15	Purchased goods of $10,200, less a $200 quantity discount. Credit terms were 3/15 n/30.
	16	Paid a $520 freight bill on goods purchased.
	18	Sold inventory for $4,000 on credit terms of 2/10 n/30 (cost, $2,360).
	22	Received merchandise returned from the customer from the September 18 sale, $1,600 (cost, $960). Merchandise was the wrong size.
	24	Borrowed exactly enough money from the bank to pay for the September 15 purchase in time to take advantage of the discount offered. Signed a note payable to the bank for the net amount.
	24	Paid supplier for goods purchased on September 15, less all returns and discounts.
	28	Received cash in full settlement of the account from the customer who purchased inventory on September 18.
	29	Paid the amount owed on account from the purchase of September 3, less the September 9 return.
	30	Purchased inventory for cash, $1,800, less a quantity discount of $70.

Required

1. Journalize the transactions above. Explanations are not required.

2. Set up T-accounts and post the journal entries to show the ending balances in the Inventory and Cost of Goods Sold accounts.

3. Assume that the note payable signed on September 24 requires the payment of $190 interest expense. Was the decision to borrow funds to take advantage of the cash discount wise or unwise?

Solution

Requirement 1

Note: To save space, calculations have been included in the journal entries. Normally, they would be included in the explanations and space would be left between each journal entry.

Sept.	3	Inventory	3,220	
		Accounts Payable		3,220
	9	Accounts Payable ($3,220 × 0.40)	1,288	
		Inventory		1,288
	12	Cash	1,840	
		Sales Revenue		1,840
	12	Cost of Goods Sold	1,100	
		Inventory		1,100
	15	Inventory ($10,200 – $200)	10,000	
		Accounts Payable		10,000
	16	Inventory	520	
		Cash		520
	18	Accounts Receivable	4,000	
		Sales Revenue		4,000
	18	Cost of Goods Sold	2,360	
		Inventory		2,360
	22	Sales Returns and Allowances	1,600	
		Accounts Receivable		1,600
	22	Inventory	960	
		Cost of Goods Sold		960
	24	Cash [$10,000 – 0.03($10,000)]	9,700	
		Note Payable		9,700
	24	Accounts Payable	10,000	
		Inventory ($10,000 × 0.03)		300
		Cash ($10,000 × 0.97)		9,700
	28	Cash [($4,000 – $1,600) × 0.98]	2,352	
		Sales Discounts [($4,000 – $1,600) × 0.02]	48	
		Accounts Receivable ($4,000 – $1,600)		2,400
	29	Accounts Payable ($3,220 – $1,288)	1,932	
		Cash		1,932
	30	Inventory ($1,800 – $70)	1,730	
		Cash		1,730

Requirement 2

Inventory					**Cost of Goods Sold**			
Sept. 3	3,220	Sept. 9	1,288		Sept. 12	1,100	Sept. 22	960
15	10,000	12	1,100		18	2,360		
16	520	18	2,360		Bal.	2,500		
22	960	24	300					
30	1,730							
Bal.	11,382							

Requirement 3

The decision to borrow funds was wise, because the discount ($300) exceeded the interest paid on the amount borrowed ($190). Thus the entity was $110 better off as a result of its decision.

Cyber Coach

Visit the Study Guide on the Media Companion CD-ROM and the Student Resources area of the *Accounting* Companion Website for extra practice with the new material in Chapter 5.

www.pearsoned.ca/horngren

OBJECTIVE 3
Adjust and close the accounts of a merchandising business under the perpetual inventory system

Adjusting and Closing the Accounts of a Merchandising Business

A merchandising business adjusts and closes the accounts the same way a service entity does. If a work sheet is used, the trial balance is entered and the work sheet is completed to determine net income or net loss. The work sheet provides the data for journalizing the adjusting and closing entries and for preparing the financial statements.

Adjusting Inventory Based on a Physical Count

KEY POINT

If book inventory exceeds physical inventory, book inventory would be adjusted downwards. As a result of this inventory adjustment, cost of goods sold is higher and gross margin is lower. The cost associated with buying these missing units is not accompanied by the revenue from a sale. Therefore gross margin shrinks by this amount (cost).

In theory, the Inventory account remains up to date at all times. However, the actual amount of inventory on hand may differ from what the books show. Losses due to theft and damage can be significant. Also, accounting errors can cause Inventory's balance to need adjustment either upwards or, more often, downwards. For this reason virtually all businesses, such as the grocery chain Loblaws, take a physical count of inventory at least once each year. The most common time for a business to count its inventory is at the end of the fiscal year, before the financial statements are prepared. The business then adjusts the Inventory account to the correct amount on the basis of the physical count.

Exhibit 5-5, Austin Sound Centre's trial balance at December 31, 2007, lists an $81,000 balance for inventory. With no shrinkage—due to theft or error—the business should have on hand inventory costing $81,000. But on December 31, when Steve Austin, the owner of Austin Sound, counts the merchandise in the store, the total cost of the goods on hand comes to only $80,400. Austin Sound would record the inventory shrinkage of $600 (which is $81,000 – $80,400) with this adjusting entry:

Dec. 31	Cost of Goods Sold...	600	
	Inventory...		600

This entry brings Inventory and Cost of Goods Sold to their correct balances. Austin Sound's December 31, 2007, adjustment data, including this inventory information [item (b)], are given at the bottom of Exhibit 5-5 as additional data.

The physical count can indicate that more inventory is present than the books show. A search of the records may reveal that Austin Sound received inventory but did not record the corresponding purchase entry. This would be entered the standard way: debit Inventory and credit Cash or Accounts Payable. If the reason for the excess inventory could not be identified, the business adjusts the accounts by debiting Inventory and crediting Cost of Goods Sold. To illustrate a merchandiser's adjusting and closing process, let's use Austin Sound's December 31, 2007, trial balance in Exhibit 5-5. All the new accounts—Inventory, Cost of Goods Sold, and the contra accounts—are highlighted for emphasis. The additional data item (b) gives the ending inventory figure as $80,400.

Preparing and Using the Work Sheet of a Merchandising Business

The Exhibit 5-6 work sheet is similar to the work sheets we have seen so far, but there are a few differences. This work sheet does not include adjusted trial balance columns. In most accounting systems, a single operation combines trial balance

EXHIBIT 5-5

Trial Balance

AUSTIN SOUND CENTRE
Trial Balance
December 31, 2007

Cash	$ 5,700	
Accounts receivable	9,200	
Note receivable, current	16,000	
Interest receivable	0	
Inventory	**81,000**	
Supplies	1,300	
Prepaid insurance	2,400	
Furniture and fixtures	66,400	
Accumulated amortization		$ 4,800
Accounts payable		94,000
Unearned sales revenue		4,000
Wages payable		0
Interest payable		0
Note payable, long-term		25,200
Steve Austin, capital		51,800
Steve Austin, withdrawals	108,200	
Sales revenue		**336,000**
Sales discounts	**2,800**	
Sales returns and allowances	**4,000**	
Interest revenue		1,200
Cost of goods sold	**181,000**	
Wages expense	19,600	
Rent expense	16,800	
Amortization expense	0	
Insurance expense	0	
Supplies expense	0	
Interest expense	2,600	
Total	$517,000	$517,000

Additional data at December 31, 2007:

a. Interest revenue earned but not yet collected, $800.

b. Inventory on hand, $80,400.

c. Supplies on hand, $200.

d. Prepaid insurance expired during the year, $2,000.

e. Amortization, $1,200.

f. Unearned sales revenue earned during the year, $2,600.

g. Accrued wages expense, $800.

h. Accrued interest expense, $400.

amounts with the adjustments and extends the adjusted balances directly to the income statement and balance sheet columns. Therefore, to reduce clutter, the adjusted trial balance columns are omitted so that the work sheet contains four pairs of columns, not five.

Account Title Column   The trial balance lists a number of accounts without balances. Ordinarily, these accounts are affected by the adjusting process. Examples include Interest Receivable, Wages Payable, and Amortization Expense. The accounts are listed in order by account number, the order in which they appear in the ledger. If additional accounts are needed, they can be written in at the bottom of the work sheet above the net income amount.

Trial Balance Columns   Examine the Inventory account in the Trial Balance. Inventory has a balance of $81,000 before the physical count at the end of the year.

EXHIBIT 5-6

Work Sheet

	AUSTIN SOUND CENTRE Accounting Work Sheet For the Year Ended December 31, 2007							
	Trial Balance		Adjustments		Income Statement		Balance Sheet	
Account Title	Debit	Credit	Debit	Credit	Debit	Credit	Debit	Credit
Cash	5,700						5,700	
Accounts receivable	9,200						9,200	
Note receivable, current	16,000						16,000	
Interest receivable	0		(a) 800				800	
Inventory	**81,000**			**(b) 600**			**80,400**	
Supplies	1,300			(c) 1,100			200	
Prepaid insurance	2,400			(d)2,000			400	
Furniture and fixtures	66,400						66,400	
Accumulated amortization		4,800		(e) 1,200				6,000
Accounts payable		94,000						94,000
Unearned sales revenue		4,000	(f) 2,600					1,400
Wages payable		0		(g) 800				800
Interest payable		0		(h) 400				400
Note payable, long-term		25,200						25,200
Steve Austin, capital		51,800						51,800
Steve Austin, withdrawals	108,200						108,200	
Sales revenue		336,000		(f) 2,600		338,600		
Sales discounts	2,800				2,800			
Sales returns and allowances	4,000				4,000			
Interest revenue		1,200		(a) 800		2,000		
Cost of goods sold	**181,000**		**(b) 600**		**181,600**			
Wages expense	19,600		(g) 800		20,400			
Rent expense	16,800				16,800			
Amortization expense	0		(e) 1,200		1,200			
Insurance expense	0		(d) 2,000		2,000			
Supplies expense	0		(c) 1,100		1,100			
Interest expense	2,600		(h) 400		3,000			
	517,000	517,000	9,500	9,500	232,900	340,600	287,300	179,600
Net income					107,700			107,700
					340,600	340,600	287,300	287,300

Cost of Goods Sold's balance is $181,000 before any adjustment based on the physical count. We shall assume that any difference between the Inventory amount on the trial balance ($81,000) and the correct amount based on the physical count ($80,400) is unexplained and should be debited or credited directly to Cost of Goods Sold.

Adjustments Columns The adjustments are similar to those discussed in Chapters 3 and 4. They may be entered in any order desired. The debit amount of each entry should equal the credit amount, and total debits should equal total credits. You should review the adjusting data in Exhibit 5-5 to reassure yourself that the adjustments are correct.

Income Statement Columns The income statement columns contain adjusted amounts for the revenues and expenses. Sales Revenue, for example, has an adjusted balance of $338,600.

The *income statement* column subtotals indicate whether the business had a net income or a net loss.

- Net income: Total credits > Total debits
- Net loss: Total debits > Total credits

Austin Sound's total credits of $340,600 exceed the total debits of $232,900, so the company earned a net income.

Insert the net *income* amount in the debit column to bring total debits into agreement with total credits. Insert a net *loss* amount in the credit column to equalize total debits and total credits. Net income or net loss is then extended to the opposite column of the balance sheet, so that total debits equal total credits.

Balance Sheet Columns   The only new item on the balance sheet is Inventory. The balance listed in Exhibit 5-6 is the ending amount of $80,400, as determined by the physical count of goods on hand at the end of the period.

Preparing a Merchandiser's Financial Statements

OBJECTIVE 4
Prepare a merchandiser's financial statements under the perpetual inventory system

Exhibit 5-7 presents Austin Sound Centre's financial statements.

To solidify your understanding of how the financial statements are prepared, you should trace the amounts in the work sheet (Exhibit 5-6) to the financial statements in Exhibit 5-7.

Income Statement   The income statement reports **operating expenses**, which are those expenses other than cost of goods sold incurred in the entity's major line of business—merchandising. Austin Sound's operating expenses include wages expense, rent, insurance, amortization of furniture and fixtures, and supplies expense. In Exhibit 5-1, Danier Leather Inc.'s total operating expenses are $77,390,000 for the year ended June 28, 2003.

Many companies report their operating expenses in two categories:

- *Selling expenses* are those expenses related to marketing the company's products—sales salaries; sales commissions; advertising; amortization, rent, utilities, and property taxes on store buildings; amortization on store furniture; delivery expense; and so on.
- *General expenses* include office expenses, such as the salaries of the company president and office employees; amortization, rent, utilities, property taxes on the home office building; and office supplies.

Danier Leather Inc. (Exhibit 5-1) combines selling and general and administrative expenses for reporting on the income statement.

Gross margin minus operating expenses equals **income from operations**, or **operating income**. Many people view operating income as an important indicator of a business's performance because it measures the results of the entity's major ongoing activities.

The last section of Austin Sound's income statement is **other revenue and expense**. This category reports revenues and expenses that are outside the main operations of the business. Examples include gains and losses on the sale of capital assets (not inventory) and gains and losses on lawsuits. Accountants have traditionally viewed Interest Revenue and Interest Expense as "other" items, because they arise from loaning money and borrowing money. These are financing activities that are outside the operating scope of selling merchandise. Danier Leather Inc.'s income statement in Exhibit 5-1 shows interest expense and income tax expenses as separate expenses.

The bottom line of the income statement is net income:

Net income   =   Total revenues and gains   –   Total expenses and losses

We often hear the term *bottom line* used to refer to a final result. *Bottom line* originated in the position of net income on the income statement.

EXHIBIT 5-7

Financial Statements of Austin Sound Centre

AUSTIN SOUND CENTRE
Income Statement
For the Year Ended December 31, 2007

Sales revenue		$338,600
Less: Sales discounts	$2,800	
Sales returns and allowances	4,000	6,800
Net sales revenue		$331,800
Cost of goods sold		181,600
Gross margin		150,200
Operating expenses:		
Wages expense	20,400	
Rent expense	16,800	
Insurance expense	2,000	
Amortization expense	1,200	
Supplies expense	1,100	41,500
Income from operations		108,700
Other revenue and (expense):		
Interest revenue	2,000	
Interest expense	(3,000)	(1,000)
Net income		$107,700

AUSTIN SOUND CENTRE
Statement of Owner's Equity
For the Year Ended December 31, 2007

Steve Austin, capital, January 1, 2007	$ 51,800
Add: Net income	107,700
	159,500
Less: Withdrawals	108,200
Steve Austin, capital, December 31, 2007	$ 51,300

AUSTIN SOUND CENTRE
Balance Sheet
December 31, 2007

Assets

Current assets:

Cash	$ 5,700
Accounts receivable	9,200
Note receivable	16,000
Interest receivable	800
Inventory	80,400
Prepaid insurance	400
Supplies	200
Total current assets	112,700

Capital assets:

Furniture and fixtures	$66,400	
Less: Accumulated amortization	6,000	60,400
Total assets		$173,100

Liabilities

Current liabilities:

Accounts payable	$ 94,000
Unearned sales revenue	1,400
Wages payable	800
Interest payable	400
Total current liabilities	96,600
Long-term liability:	
Note payable	25,200
Total liabilities	121,800

Owner's Equity

S. Austin, capital	51,300
Total liabilities and owner's equity	$173,100

Statement of Owner's Equity   A merchandiser's statement of owner's equity looks exactly like that of a service business. In fact, you cannot determine whether the entity sells merchandise or services from looking at the statement of owner's equity.

Balance Sheet   If the business is a merchandiser, the balance sheet shows inventory as a major current asset. In contrast, service businesses usually have no inventory at all or minor amounts of inventory.

Journalizing the Adjusting and Closing Entries for a Merchandising Business

Exhibit 5-8 presents Austin Sound Centre's adjusting entries, which are similar to those you have seen previously, except for the inventory adjustment [entry (b)]. The closing entries in the exhibit also follow the pattern illustrated in Chapter 4.

The *first closing entry* debits the revenue accounts for their ending balances. The offsetting credit of $340,600 transfers their sum to Income Summary. This amount comes directly from the credit column of the income statement on the work sheet (Exhibit 5-6).

LEARNING TIP

The adjusting and closing entries here are very similar to those discussed in Chapter 4, pages 162–215. The closing entries also clear the Cost of Goods Sold expense account for accumulating costs in the next period.

EXHIBIT 5-8

Adjusting and Closing Entries for a Merchandiser

Journal

Adjusting Entries

a.	Dec. 31	Interest receivable	800	
		Interest revenue		800
b.	Dec. 31	Cost of goods sold	600	
		Inventory		600
c.	Dec. 31	Supplies expense ($1,300 – $200)	1,100	
		Supplies		1,100
d.	Dec. 31	Insurance expense	2,000	
		Prepaid insurance		2,000
e.	Dec. 31	Amortization expense	1,200	
		Accumulated amortization		1,200
f.	Dec. 31	Unearned sales revenue	2,600	
		Sales revenue		2,600
g.	Dec. 31	Wages expense	800	
		Wages payable		800
h.	Dec. 31	Interest expense	400	
		Interest payable		400

Closing Entries

Dec. 31	Sales revenue	338,600	
	Interest revenue	2,000	
	Income summary		340,600
Dec. 31	Income summary	232,900	
	Cost of goods sold		181,600
	Sales discounts		2,800
	Sales returns and allowances		4,000
	Wages expense		20,400
	Rent expense		16,800
	Amortization expense		1,200
	Insurance expense		2,000
	Supplies expense		1,100
	Interest expense		3,000
Dec. 31	Income summary ($340,600 – $232,900)	107,700	
	Steve Austin, Capital		107,700
Dec. 31	Steve Austin, Capital	108,200	
	Steve Austin, Withdrawals		108,200

The *second closing entry* includes credits to Cost of Goods Sold, to the contra revenue accounts (Sales Discounts, Sales Returns and Allowances), and to the expense accounts. The offsetting $232,900 debit to Income Summary represents the amount of total expenses plus the contra revenue accounts, which come from the debit column of the income statement on the work sheet.

The *last two closing entries* close net income from Income Summary and also close the owner withdrawals into the Capital account.

Study Exhibits 5-6, 5-7, and 5-8 carefully because they illustrate the entire end-of-period process that leads to the financial statements. As you progress through this book, you may want to refer to these exhibits to refresh your understanding of the adjusting and closing process for a merchandising business.

Learning Tip Here is an easy way to remember the closing process. First, look at the work sheet. Then:

1. Debit all income statement accounts that have a credit balance. Credit Income Summary for the total of all these debits.
2. Credit all income statement accounts that have a debit balance. Debit Income Summary for the total of all these credits.
3. Calculate the balance in the Income Summary account. If the account has a debit balance, there is a net loss; credit Income Summary for that amount, and debit Capital. If Income Summary has a credit balance, there is a net income; debit Income Summary for that amount, and credit Capital.
4. Look at the debit balance of Withdrawals in the balance sheet column. Credit Withdrawals for its balance, and debit Capital for the same amount.

Income Statement Formats: Multi-Step and Single-Step

For a review of balance sheet formats see Chapter 4, page 178.

We have seen that the balance sheet appears in two formats: the report format (assets on top, owner's equity at the bottom) and the account format (assets at left, liabilities and owner's equity at right). There are also two basic formats for the income statement: *multi-step* and *single-step*. A recent survey indicated the multi-step format was used by 98 percent of the companies surveyed; the remainder used the single-step format.[2]

Multi-Step Income Statement

The **multi-step format** shows subtotals to highlight significant relationships. In addition to net income, it also presents gross margin and operating income, or income from operations. This format communicates a merchandiser's results of operations especially well, because gross margin and income from operations are two key measures of operating performance. Danier Leather Inc. uses the multi-step format. The income statements presented thus far in this chapter have been multi-step income statements. Austin Sound Centre's multi-step income statement for the year ended December 31, 2007, appears in Exhibit 5-7.

Single-Step Income Statement

The **single-step format** groups all revenues together, and then lists and deducts all expenses together without drawing any subtotals. Maple Leaf Foods Inc. (www.mapleleaf.com) uses this format. The single-step format has the advantage of listing all revenues together and all expenses together, as shown in Exhibit 5-9. Thus

---

[2]Byrd, C., I. Chen, and H. Chapman, *Financial Reporting in Canada 2001*, Twenty-Sixth Edition. (Toronto: Canadian Institute of Chartered Accountants, 2001), p. 91.

EXHIBIT 5-9

Single-Step Income
Statement

AUSTIN SOUND CENTRE
Income Statement
For the Year Ended December 31, 2007

Revenues:	
Net sales..	$331,800
Interest revenue	2,000
Total revenues	333,800
Expenses:	
Cost of goods sold	$181,600
Wages expense	20,400
Rent expense	16,800
Interest expense	3,000
Insurance expense	2,000
Amortization expense.....................................	1,200
Supplies expense	1,100
Total expenses..	226,100
Net income..	$107,700

it clearly distinguishes revenues from expenses. The income statements in Chapters 1 through 4 were single-step. This format works well for service entities, because they have no gross margin to report, and for companies that have several types of revenues.

Most published financial statements are highly condensed. Appendix A at the end of the book gives the income statement for Intrawest Corporation. Of course, condensed statements can be supplemented with desired details in the notes to the financial statements.

Two Key Ratios for Decision Making

Merchandise inventory is the most important asset to a merchandising business because it captures the essence of the entity. To manage the business, owners and managers focus on the best way to sell the inventory. They use several ratios to evaluate operations, among them *gross margin percentage* and *rate of inventory turnover.*

The Gross Margin Percentage

A key decision tool for a merchandiser is related to gross margin, which is net sales minus cost of goods sold. Merchandisers strive to increase the **gross margin percentage**, which is computed as follows:

EXHIBIT 5-10

Gross Margin on $1.00 of
Sales for Two Merchandisers

For Austin Sound Centre
(Exhibit 5-7)

$$\text{Gross margin percentage} = \frac{\text{Gross margin}}{\text{Net sales revenue}} = \frac{\$150,200}{\$331,800} = 0.453 = 45.3\%$$

The gross margin percentage (also called the *gross profit percentage*) is one of the most carefully watched measures of profitability. A 45-percent gross margin means that each dollar of sales generates 45 cents of gross profit. On average, the goods cost the seller 55 cents. A small increase in the gross margin percentage may signal an important rise in income, and vice versa for a decrease.

Exhibit 5-10 compares Austin Sound Centre's gross margin to Wal-Mart's gross margin.

The Rate of Inventory Turnover

Owners and managers strive to sell inventory as quickly as possible because it generates no profit until it is sold. The faster the sales occur, the higher the income. The slower the sales, the lower the income. Ideally, a business could operate with zero inventory. Most businesses, however, including retailers such as Austin Sound Centre, must keep goods on hand for customers. Successful merchandisers purchase carefully to keep the goods moving through the business at a rapid pace. **Inventory turnover**, the ratio of cost of goods sold to average inventory, indicates how rapidly inventory is sold. Its computation follows:

For Austin Sound Centre (Exhibit 5-7)

$$\text{Inventory turnover} = \frac{\text{Cost of goods sold}}{\text{Average inventory}} = \frac{\text{Cost of goods sold}}{(\text{Beginning inventory} + \text{ending inventory})/2} = \frac{\$181{,}600}{(\$77{,}200^* + \$80{,}400)/2}$$

$$= \text{2.3 times per year (about every 159 days)}$$

*Taken from the balance sheet at the end of the preceding period.

Accounting and the e-World

Amazon.ca: For E-Tailers, Free Shipping Isn't Free, But It's Not a Cost, Either

Online shopping is becoming more popular as people become familiar with the advantages of Internet shopping and as payment methods for online purchases become more secure. It is an efficient way for many students to shop, since Internet stores are open 24 hours a day, 7 days a week, 365 days a year!

A major online retailer is amazon.ca. In an effort to entice customers to use its services and buy more products, amazon.ca offers free shipping on orders over $39.00, shipped at one time to a Canadian address. Amazon views shipping as a key factor in boosting its growth.

Amazon has to pay freight companies to deliver the products its customers have ordered. How do Amazon and other e-tailers account for shipping and handling costs?

It appears that Amazon and other e-tailers have been able to bend certain accounting rules. One such rule is that the cost of products sold to customers is usually recorded as Cost of Goods Sold, a merchandiser's major expense. Online companies count some of this cost as "sales and marketing expenses." By listing these "fulfillment costs" as marketing expenses, both e-tailers and catalogue houses don't have to subtract the expense in calculating gross margin.

E-commerce has caused the Accounting Standards Board in Canada to re-think some generally accepted accounting policies. It would appear, however, that at the time of writing, the Accounting Standards Board has taken no definitive position on these "fulfillment costs." (The same is true of the Financial Accounting Standards Board in the United States.) Consequently, e-tailers are free to choose a policy that excludes these costs from the calculation of gross margin.

Based on: Nick Winfield, "Survival Strategy: Amazon Takes Page from Wal-Mart to Prosper on Web—Internet Retailer Cuts Prices and Keeps Eye on Costs in Bid for High Volumes—Betting Big on Free Shipping," *Wall Street Journal*, November 22, 2002, p. A1. Saul Hansell, "Amazon's Loss in Quarter Shows a Sharp Decrease," *The New York Times*, October 25, 2002, p. 8. Katherine Hobson, "Silver Lining: FASB Spares E-Tailers in Cost Ruling," *The Street.com*, August 8, 2000.

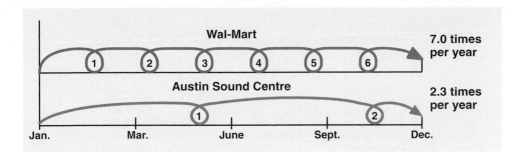

Exhibit 5-11

Rate of Inventory Turnover for Two Merchandisers

Inventory turnover is usually computed for an annual period, and the relevant cost-of-goods sold figure is the amount from the entire year. Average inventory is computed from the beginning and ending balances of the annual period. Austin Sound Centre's beginning inventory would be taken from the business's balance sheet at the end of the preceding year. The resulting inventory turnover statistic shows how many times the average level of inventory was sold during the year. A high rate of turnover is preferable to a low turnover rate. An increase in turnover rate usually means higher profits, but may sometimes lead to a shortage of inventory to sell.

Inventory turnover varies from industry to industry. Grocery stores, for example, turn their goods over faster than automobile dealers do. Drug stores have a higher turnover than furniture stores do. Retailers of electronic products, such as Austin Sound Centre, have an average turnover of 3.6 times per year. Austin Sound's turnover rate of 2.3 times per year suggests that Austin Sound is not very successful. Exhibit 5-11 compares the inventory turnover rate of Austin Sound and Wal-Mart Stores, Inc.

Exhibits 5-10 and 5-11 tell an interesting story. Wal-Mart sells lots of inventory at a relatively low gross profit margin. Wal-Mart earns its profits by turning its inventory over rapidly—7.0 times during the year. Austin Sound Centre, a small business, prices inventory to earn a higher gross margin on each dollar of sales and only turns over its inventory 2.3 times during the year.

Gross margin percentage and rate of inventory turnover do not provide enough information to yield an overall conclusion about a merchandiser, but this example shows how owners and managers may use accounting information to evaluate a company.

REAL WORLD EXAMPLE

Many businesses use the gross margin percentage (also known as the markup percentage) as a means of determining how well inventory is selling. If too much inventory is purchased and it must be marked down, the gross margin percentage will decline. By monitoring the gross margin percentage, problems can be corrected quickly.

Measuring Cost of Goods Sold and Inventory Purchases in the Periodic Inventory System

OBJECTIVE 6
Compute the cost of goods sold under the periodic inventory system

The perpetual inventory accounting system that we have illustrated is designed to produce up-to-date records of inventory and cost of goods sold. Of course, adjustments are made to these records as a result of spoilage and theft; this is typically done after the physical count of inventory. The perpetual inventory system provides the data for many day-to-day decisions and for preparation of the financial statements. However, managers have other information needs that the perpetual inventory system does not meet. For example, the buyers for Danier Leather Inc. and Austin Sound Centre must know how much inventory to purchase in order to reach their sales goals.

Another computation of cost of goods sold—from the periodic inventory system—helps managers plan their purchases of inventory. This alternative computation of cost of goods sold is used so often in accounting that your education would be incomplete without it. (The supplement at the end of the chapter covers the periodic inventory system in more detail.)

EXHIBIT 5-12

Beginning inventory..	$ 77,200
+ **Net purchases**	174,400*
+ Freight in	10,400
= Cost of goods available for sale	262,000
− Ending inventory	(80,400)
= Cost of goods sold.......................................	$181,600

*Computation of **Net purchases**:

Purchases..	$182,800
− Purchase discounts	(6,000)
− Purchase returns and allowances	(2,400)
= Net purchases..	$174,400

Exhibit 5-12 gives the alternative computation of Austin Sound Centre's cost of goods sold for 2007. Austin Sound began the year with inventory of $77,200. During the year, Austin Sound purchased more goods, also paying freight charges. The sum of these amounts makes up Austin Sound's cost of goods available for sale. Note that **net purchases** equals purchases minus purchase discounts and purchase returns and allowances. Subtract ending inventory, and the result is cost of goods sold for the period. Exhibit 5-13 diagrams the alternative computation of cost of goods sold, with Austin Sound Centre amounts used for the illustration.

The Decision Guidelines feature summarizes some key decisions of a merchandising business. One key decision is how much inventory the business should purchase in order to achieve its goals.

Here is how Steve Austin, the owner of Austin Sound Centre, would decide how much inventory to buy (all numbers based on Exhibit 5-13):

1. Owner predicts Cost of goods sold for the period...................... $181,600
2. Owner predicts Ending inventory at the end of the period 80,400
3. Cost of goods available for sale = Sum of Ending inventory
   + Cost of goods sold... 262,000
4. Subtract the period's beginning inventory .... (77,200)
5. The difference is the amount of inventory to purchase
   (including Freight in) during the coming year........................... $184,800

EXHIBIT 5-13

Relationship between the
Inventory Account and Cost
of Goods Sold in the Periodic
Inventory System (Amounts
for Austin Sound Centre)

Inventory

Beginning balance	77,200	
Net purchases	174,400	
Freight in	10,400	Cost of goods sold 181,600
Ending balance	80,400	

This T-account shows that the *perpetual* and the *periodic* inventory systems compute the same amounts for ending inventory and for cost of goods sold:

- The *perpetual* system accumulates the balances of Inventory and Cost of Goods Sold throughout the period.
- The *periodic* system determines the correct amounts for Inventory and Cost of Goods Sold only at the end of the period.
- Both systems present the correct amounts for Inventory and Cost of Goods Sold at the *beginning* of the period.

The authors thank Betsy Willis and David Sale for suggesting this exhibit.

Decision	Guidelines
How do merchandising operations differ from service operations?	• Merchandisers buy and sell *merchandise inventory* (often called inventory, or goods). • Service entities perform a *service*.
How do a merchandiser's financial statements differ from the financial statements of a service business?	Balance sheet: • Merchandiser has *inventory*, an asset. • Service business has no inventory.

Income statement:

Merchandiser

	Sales revenue	$XXX
–	Cost of goods sold	(X)
=	Gross margin	$ XX
–	Operating expenses	(X)
=	Net income	$ X

Service Business

	Service revenue	$XX
–	Operating expense	(X)
=	Net income	$ X

Statements of owner's equity:
No difference

Decision	Guidelines
What types of inventory systems are there?	• *Perpetual system* shows the amount of inventory on hand (the asset) and the cost of goods sold (the expense) at all times. • *Periodic system* shows the correct balances of inventory and cost of goods sold only after a physical count of the inventory and adjustment of the books to reflect that count, which occurs at least once each year.
How do the adjusting and closing processes of merchandisers and service entities differ?	Very little. The merchandiser may have to *adjust* the Inventory account for spoilage and theft. The merchandiser must *close* the Cost of Goods Sold account. Service entities have no inventory to adjust or cost of goods sold to close.

How to format the merchandiser's income statement?

Multi-step format

	Sales revenue	$XXX
–	Cost of goods sold	(X)
=	Gross margin	$ XX
–	Operating expenses	(X)
=	Income from operations	$ X
+	Other revenues	X
–	Other expenses	(X)
=	Net income	$ XX

Single-step format

Revenues:

Sales revenue	$ XXX
Other revenues	X
Total revenues	$ XXX

Expenses:

Cost of goods sold	(X)
Operating expenses	(X)
Other expenses	(X)
Total expenses	$ XX
Net income	$ XX

Decision	Guidelines
How to evaluate inventory operations?	Two key ratios: $$\text{Gross margin percentage}^* = \frac{\text{Gross margin}}{\text{Net sales revenue}}$$ $$\text{Inventory turnover}^* = \frac{\text{Cost of goods sold}}{\text{Average inventory}}$$ *In most cases—the higher, the better

How to determine the amount of cost of goods sold?

Can use the *cost of goods sold* model from the periodic system (assumed amounts):

	Beginning inventory	$100
+	Net purchases and freight in	800
=	Cost of goods available	900
–	Ending inventory	(200)
=	Cost of goods sold	$700

Cost of goods sold is computed automatically in the perpetual inventory system.

Summary Problem

for Your Review

The following trial balance and additional data are related to Kathy Pittman Distributing Company.

KATHY PITTMAN DISTRIBUTING COMPANY
Trial Balance
December 31, 2006

Cash	$ 8,505	
Accounts receivable	55,650	
Inventory	90,750	
Supplies	5,895	
Prepaid rent	9,000	
Furniture and fixtures	39,750	
Accumulated amortization		$ 31,800
Accounts payable		69,510
Salaries payable		0
Interest payable		0
Unearned sales revenue		5,250
Notes payable, long-term		52,500
Kathy Pittman, capital		35,520
Kathy Pittman, withdrawals	72,000	
Sales revenue		520,050
Sales discounts	15,450	
Sales returns and allowances	12,300	
Cost of goods sold	257,655	
Salary expense	124,125	
Rent expense	10,500	
Amortization expense	0	
Utilities expense	8,700	
Supplies expense	0	
Interest expense	4,350	
Total	$714,630	$714,630

Additional data at December 31, 2006:

a. Supplies used during the year, $3,870.

b. Prepaid rent remaining in force, $1,500.

c. Unearned sales revenue still not earned, $3,600. The company expects to earn this amount during the next few months.

d. Amortization. The furniture and fixtures' estimated useful life is ten years, and they are expected to have no value when they are retired from service.

e. Accrued salaries, $1,950.

f. Accrued interest expense, $900.

g. Inventory still remaining on hand, $98,700.

Required

1. Enter the trial balance on a work sheet and complete the work sheet.

2. Journalize the adjusting and closing entries at December 31, 2006. Post to the Income Summary account as an accuracy check on the entries affecting that account. The credit balance closed out of Income Summary should equal net income computed on the work sheet.

3. Prepare the company's multi-step income statement, statement of owner's equity, and balance sheet in account format. Draw arrows connecting the statements, or state how the statements are linked.

4. Compute the inventory turnover for 2006. Inventory at December 31, 2005, was $89,250. Turnover for 2005 was 2.1 times. Would you expect Kathy Pittman Distributing Company to be more or less profitable in 2006 than in 2005? Give your reason.

Solution

Requirement 1

KATHY PITTMAN DISTRIBUTING COMPANY
Work Sheet
For the Year Ended December 31, 2006

Account Title	Trial Balance Debit	Trial Balance Credit	Adjustments Debit	Adjustments Credit	Income Statement Debit	Income Statement Credit	Balance Sheet Debit	Balance Sheet Credit
Cash	8,505						8,505	
Accounts receivable	55,650						55,650	
Inventory	90,750		(g)7,950				98,700	
Supplies	5,895			(a) 3,870			2,025	
Prepaid rent	9,000			(b)7,500			1,500	
Furniture and fixtures	39,750						39,750	
Accumulated amortization		31,800		(d)3,975				35,775
Accounts payable		69,510						69,510
Salary payable		0		(e) 1,950				1,950
Interest payable		0		(f) 900				900
Unearned sales revenue		5,250	(c)1,650					3,600
Note payable, long-term		52,500						52,500
Kathy Pittman, capital		35,520						35,520
Kathy Pittman, withdrawals	72,000						72,000	
Sales revenue		520,050		(c) 1,650		521,700		
Sales discounts	15,450				15,450			
Sales returns and allowances	12,300				12,300			
Cost of goods sold	257,655			(g) 7,950	249,705			
Salary expense	124,125		(e)1,950		126,075			
Rent expense	10,500		(b)7,500		18,000			
Amortization expense	0		(d)3,975		3,975			
Utilities expense	8,700				8,700			
Supplies expense	0		(a)3,870		3,870			
Interest expense	4,350		(f) 900		5,250			
	714,630	714,630	27,795	27,795	443,325	521,700	278,130	199,755
Net income					78,375			78,375
					521,700	521,700	278,130	278,130

Adjusting entries

2006

Dec. 31	Supplies expense..	3,870	
	Supplies...		3,870
Dec. 31	Rent expense...	7,500	
	Prepaid rent		7,500
Dec. 31	Unearned sales revenue ($5,250 – $3,600)	1,650	
	Sales revenue...		1,650
Dec. 31	Amortization expense ($39,750/10)....................	3,975	
	Accumulated amortization		3,975
Dec. 31	Salary expense..	1,950	
	Salary payable..		1,950
Dec. 31	Interest expense	900	
	Interest payable..		900
Dec. 31	Inventory ($98,700 – $90,750).............................	7,950*	
	Cost of goods sold		7,950

Closing entries

2006

Dec. 31	Sales revenue	521,700	
	Income summary..		521,700
Dec. 31	Income summary	443,325	
	Cost of goods sold		249,705
	Sales discounts		15,450
	Sales returns and allowances......................		12,300
	Salary expense...		126,075
	Rent expense		18,000
	Amortization expense.................................		3,975
	Utilities expense...		8,700
	Supplies expense		3,870
	Interest expense		5,250
Dec. 31	Income summary ($521,700 – $443,325)	78,375	
	Kathy Pittman, Capital		78,375
Dec. 31	Kathy Pittman, Capital	72,000	
	Kathy Pittman, Withdrawals		72,000

Income Summary

Clo.	443,325	Clo.	521,700
Clo.	78,375	Bal.	78,375

---

*Excess of inventory on hand over the balance in the Inventory account. This adjustment brings Inventory to its correct balance.

KATHY PITTMAN DISTRIBUTING COMPANY
Income Statement
For the Year Ended December 31, 2006

Sales revenue..		$521,700
Less: Sales discounts	$15,450	
Sales returns and allowances	12,300	27,750
Net sales revenue..		$493,950
Cost of goods sold..		249,705
Gross margin...		244,245
Operating expenses:		
Salaries expense	126,075	
Rent expense...	18,000	
Utilities expense..	8,700	
Amortization expense...	3,975	
Supplies expense	3,870	160,620
Income from operations		83,625
Other expense:		
Interest expense		5,250
Net income		$ 78,375

KATHY PITTMAN DISTRIBUTING COMPANY
Statement of Owner's Equity
For the Year Ended December 31, 2006

Kathy Pittman, capital, January 1, 2006...	$ 35,520
Add: Net income...	78,375
	113,895
Less: Withdrawals..	72,000
Kathy Pittman, capital, December 31, 2006...	$ 41,895

KATHY PITTMAN DISTRIBUTING COMPANY
Balance Sheet
December 31, 2006

Assets			Liabilities		
Current assets:			Current liabilities:		
Cash................................		$ 8,505	Accounts payable		$ 69,510
Accounts receivable.....		55,650	Salaries payable..................		1,950
Inventory........................		98,700	Interest payable		900
Supplies.........................		2,025	Unearned sales revenue		3,600
Prepaid Rent		1,500	Total current liabilities....		75,960
Total current assets....		166,380	Long-term liabilities		
Capital assets:			Notes payable		52,500
Furniture and			Total liabilities.................		128,460
fixtures.......................	$39,750				
Less: Accumulated			**Owner's Equity**		
amortization..............	35,775	3,975	Kathy Pittman, capital		41,895
Total assets.......................		$170,355	Total liabilities and owner's equity		$170,355

$$\text{Inventory turnover} = \frac{\text{Cost of goods sold}}{\text{Average inventory}} = \frac{\$249,705}{(\$89,250 + \$98,700)/2} = 2.7 \text{ times}$$

The increase in the rate of inventory turnover from 2.1 to 2.7 *suggests* higher profits in 2006 than in 2005. However, gross margin and expenses for both years must be checked to verify this suggestion.

Cyber Coach

Visit the Study Guide on the Media Companion CD-ROM and the Student Resources area of the *Accounting* Companion Website for extra practice with the new material in Chapter 5.

www.pearsoned.ca/horngren

Summary

1. **Use sales and gross margin to evaluate a company.** The major revenue of a merchandising business is *sales revenue*, or *net sales*. The major expense is *cost of goods sold*. Net sales minus cost of goods sold is called *gross margin*, or *gross profit*. This amount measures the business's success or failure in selling its products at a higher price than it paid for them.

2. **Account for the purchase and sale of inventory under the perpetual inventory system.** The merchandiser's major asset is *inventory*. In a merchandising entity the accounting cycle is from cash to inventory as the inventory is purchased for resale, and back to cash as the inventory is sold. The *invoice* is the business document generated by a purchase or sale transaction. Most merchandising entities offer *discounts* to their customers and allow them to *return* unsuitable merchandise. They also grant *allowances* for damaged goods that the buyer chooses to keep. Sales Discounts and Returns and Allowances are contra accounts to Sales Revenue.

3. **Adjust and close the accounts of a merchandising business under the perpetual inventory system.** The end-of-period adjusting and closing process of a merchandising business is similar to that of a service business. In addition, a merchandiser adjusts inventory for theft losses, damage, and accounting errors.

4. **Prepare a merchandiser's financial statements under the perpetual inventory system.** The income statement may appear in the *single-step format* or the *multi-step format*. A single-step income statement has only two sections—one for revenues and the other for expenses—and a single income amount for net income. A multi-step income statement has subtotals for gross margin and income from operations. The multi-step format is the most widely used format.

5. **Use the gross margin percentage and the inventory turnover ratio to evaluate a business.** Two key decision aids for a merchandiser are the *gross margin percentage* (gross margin/net sales revenue) and the *rate of inventory turnover* (cost of goods sold/average inventory). Increases in these measures usually signal an increase in profits.

6. **Compute the cost of goods sold under the periodic inventory system.** *Cost of goods sold* is the cost of the inventory that the business has sold. It is the largest single expense of most merchandising businesses. Cost of goods sold is the sum of the cost of goods sold amounts recorded during the period. In a periodic inventory system, Cost of goods sold = Beginning inventory + Purchases (net of any contra accounts) + Freight in – Ending inventory.

Self-Study Questions

Test your understanding of the chapter by marking the correct answer for each of the following questions:

1. The major expense of a merchandising business is (*p. 218*)
   a. Cost of goods sold   c. Rent
   b. Amortization   d. Interest

2. Sales total $880,000, cost of goods sold is $420,000, and operating expenses are $320,000. How much is gross margin? (*p. 218*)
   a. $880,000   c. $420,000
   b. $460,000   d. $140,000

3. A purchase discount results from (*p. 223*)
   a. Returning goods to the seller
   b. Receiving a purchase allowance from the seller

c. Buying a large enough quantity of merchandise to get the discount

d. Paying within the discount period

4. Which one of the following pairs includes items that are the most similar? (pp. 227–228)
   a. Purchase discounts and purchase returns
   b. Cost of goods sold and inventory
   c. Net sales and sales discounts
   d. Sales returns and sales allowances

5. Which of the following is *not* an account? (p. 218)
   a. Sales revenue   c. Inventory
   b. Net sales   d. Supplies expense

6. Cost of goods sold is computed by adding beginning inventory and net purchases and subtracting X. What is X? (p. 242)
   a. Net sales   c. Ending inventory
   b. Sales discounts   d. Net purchases

7. Which account causes the main difference between a merchandiser's adjusting and closing process and that of a service business? (pp. 237–238)
   a. Advertising expense   c. Cost of goods sold
   b. Interest revenue   d. Accounts receivable

8. The major item on a merchandiser's income statement that a service business does not have is (p. 218)
   a. Cost of goods sold   c. Salary expense
   b. Inventory   d. Total revenue

9. The closing entry for Sales Discounts includes (pp. 237–238)
   a. Sales Discounts
       Income Summary
   b. Sales Discounts
       Sales Revenue
   c. Income Summary
       Sales Discounts
   d. Not used: Sales Discounts is a permanent account, which is not closed.

10. Which income statement format reports income from operations? (p. 238)
    a. Account format   c. Single-step format
    b. Report format   d. Multi-step format

Answers to the Self-Study Questions follow the Similar Accounting Terms.

Accounting Vocabulary

Cost of goods sold (pp. 218, 274)
Cost of sales (pp. 218, 274)
Gross margin (p. 218)
Gross margin percentage (p. 239)
Gross profit (p. 218)
Income from operations (pp. 235, 280)
Inventory (p. 217)
Inventory turnover (p. 240)

Invoice (p. 221)
Multi-step income statement (p. 238)
Net purchases (pp. 242, 273)
Net sales (p. 218)
Operating expense (pp. 235, 278)
Operating income (pp. 235, 280)
Other expense (pp. 235, 280)
Other revenue (pp. 235, 280)

Periodic inventory system (p. 220)
Perpetual inventory system (p. 220)
Sales (p. 218)
Sales discounts (p. 227)
Sales returns and allowances (p. 227)
Sales revenue (p. 218)
Single-step income statement (p. 238)

Similar Accounting Terms

Freight	Freight in; Transportation costs; Shipping costs
Gross margin	Gross profit
Income from operations	Operating income
Invoice	Bill
List price	Full price; Price with no discounts deducted
Purchase discount	Cash discount; Discount given to reward prompt payment
Quantity discount	Trade discount; Discount given to reward purchase of more than one of a particular item
Sales revenue	Sales
Cost of goods sold	Cost of sales

Answers to Self-Study Questions

1. a
2. b ($880,000 − $420,000 = $460,000)
3. d
4. d
5. b
6. c
7. c
8. a
9. c
10. d

Assignment Material

Questions

1. Gross margin is often mentioned in the business press as an important measure of success. What does gross margin measure, and why is it important?

2. Describe the operating cycle for (a) the purchase and cash sale of inventory, and (b) the purchase and sale of inventory on account.

3. Identify ten items of information on an invoice.

4. Indicate which accounts are debited and credited under the perpetual inventory system for (a) a credit purchase of inventory and the subsequent cash payment, and (b) a credit sale of inventory and the subsequent cash collection. Assume no discounts, returns, allowances, or freight.

5. Inventory costing $2,000 is purchased and invoiced on July 28 under terms of 3/10 n/30. Compute the payment amount on August 6. How much would the payment be on August 9? What explains the difference? What is the latest acceptable payment date under the terms of sale?

6. Inventory listed at $70,000 is sold subject to a quantity discount of $6,000 and under payment terms of 2/15 n/45. What is the net sales revenue on this sale if the customer pays within 15 days?

7. Name the new contra accounts introduced in this chapter.

8. Briefly discuss the similarity in computing supplies expense and computing cost of goods sold by the method shown in Exhibit 5-12 on page 242.

9. Why is the title of Cost of Goods Sold especially descriptive? What type of account is Cost of Goods Sold?

10. Beginning inventory is $7,500, net purchases total $45,000, and freight in is $1,500. If ending inventory is $12,000, what is cost of goods sold?

11. You are evaluating two companies as possible investments. One entity sells its services; the other entity is a merchandiser. How can you identify the merchandiser by examining the two entities' balance sheets and income statements?

12. You are beginning the adjusting and closing process at the end of your company's fiscal year. Does the trial balance carry the final ending amount of inventory? Why or why not?

13. Give the adjusting entry for inventory if shrinkage is $10,200.

14. What is the identifying characteristic of the "other" category of revenues and expenses? Give an example of each.

15. Name and describe formats for the two income statements and identify the type of business to which each format best applies.

16. List eight different operating expenses.

17. Which financial statement reports sales discounts and sales returns and allowances? Show how they are reported, using any reasonable amounts in your illustration.

18. Does a merchandiser prefer a high or low rate of inventory turnover? Explain.

19. In general, what does a decreasing gross margin percentage, coupled with an increasing rate of inventory turnover, suggest about a business's pricing strategy?

Exercises

Exercise 5-1 *Evaluating a company's revenues, gross margin, operating income, and net income (Obj. 1)*

The Carpet Store reported the information shown on page 251:

Required

1. Is The Carpet Store a merchandising entity, a service business, or both? How can you tell? List the items in The Carpet Store financial statements that influence your answer.

2. Compute The Carpet Store's gross margin for fiscal years 2007 and 2006. Did the gross margin increase or decrease in 2007? Is this a good sign or a bad sign about the company?

3. Write a brief memo to the owner advising her of The Carpet Store's trend of sales, gross margin, and net income. Indicate whether the outlook for The Carpet Store is favourable or unfavourable, based on this trend. Use the following memo format:

Date: _____

To: The Owner

From: Student Name

Subject: Trend of sales, gross margin, and net income for The Carpet Store

THE CARPET STORE
Income Statement
(Dollars in thousands)

| | Fiscal Year Ended | |
	January 31, 2007	January 31, 2006
Net sales	$5,000	$4,750
Costs and expenses:		
Cost of sales	3,500	3,350
Selling, advertising, general, and administrative	1,015	950
Amortization	103	96
Other charges	30	198
Interest expense	50	52
Interest and other income	(9)	(9)
	4,689	4,637
Earnings before taxes on income	311	113
Taxes on income	125	45
Net earnings	$ 186	$ 68

THE CARPET STORE
Balance Sheet (partial)
(Dollars in thousands)

	January 31, 2007	January 31, 2006
Assets		
Current assets:		
Cash	$ 383	$ 103
Accounts and other receivables	72	115
Merchandise inventories	1,107	1,000
Prepaid expenses and other current assets	21	44
Total current assets	$1,583	$1,262

Exercise 5-2 *Recording purchase transactions under the perpetual inventory system (Obj. 2)*

Suppose Sears (www.sears.ca) purchases $100,000 of women's sportswear on account from Jones New York. Credit terms are 2/10 net 30. Sears pays electronically, and Jones New York receives the money on the tenth day.

Journalize Sears' (a) purchase and (b) cash payment transactions. What was Sears' net cost of this inventory?

Note: Exercise 5-3 covers this same situation for the seller.

Exercise 5-3 *Recording sales, cost of goods sold, and cash collections under the perpetual inventory system (Obj. 2)*

Jones New York sells $100,000 of women's sportswear to Sears under credit terms of 2/10 net 30. Jones New York's cost of the goods is $64,000, and it receives the appropriate amount of cash from Sears on the tenth day.

Journalize Jones New York's (a) sale, (b) cost of goods sold, and (c) cash receipt. How much gross margin did Jones New York earn on this sale?

Note: Exercise 5-2 covers the same situation for the buyer.

Exercise 5-4 *Journalizing purchase and sale transactions under the perpetual inventory system* **(Obj. 2)**

Journalize, without explanations, the following transactions of Current Fashions during the month of June 2007:

June 3 Purchased $2,100 of inventory under terms of 2/10 n/eom and FOB shipping point.
    7 Returned $900 of defective merchandise purchased on June 3.
    9 Paid freight bill of $330 on June 3 purchase.
   10 Sold inventory for $6,600, collecting cash of $1,200. Payment terms on the remainder were 2/15 n/30. The goods cost Current Fashions $3,900.
   12 Paid amount owed on credit purchase of June 3, less the discount and the return.
   16 Granted a sales allowance of $2,400 on the June 10 sale.
   23 Received cash from June 10 customer in full settlement of her debt, less the allowance and the discount.

Exercise 5-5 *Journalizing transactions from a purchase invoice under the perpetual inventory system* **(Obj. 2)**

As the proprietor of OK Auto Repair, you receive the invoice below from a supplier (GST has been disregarded).

Required

1. Record the May 14 purchase on account.

ABC AUTO PARTS WHOLESALE DISTRIBUTORS
2600 Victoria Avenue
Saskatoon, Saskatchewan S4P 1B3

Invoice date: May 14, 2006   **Payment terms:** 2/10 n/30

Sold to: OK Auto Repair
    4219 Cumberland Avenue
    Prince Albert, SK S7M 1X3

Quantity Ordered	Description	Quantity Shipped	Price	Amount
6	P135-X4 Radials.........	6	$83.56	$501.36
8	L912 Belted-bias........	8	92.97	743.76
14	R39 Truck tires........	10	112.54	1,125.40
	Total...$2,370.52			

Due date:		Amount:	
May 24, 2006		$2,323.11	
May 25 through June 13, 2006		$2,370.52	

Paid:

---

2. The R39 truck tires were ordered by mistake and therefore were returned to ABC. Journalize the return on May 19.

3. Record the May 22 payment of the amount owed.

Exercise 5-6 *Journalizing purchase transactions under the perpetual inventory system (Obj. 2)*

On April 30, Bocholo Jewellers purchased inventory of $15,000 on account from Forsyth Fine Gems Ltd., a jewellery importer. Terms were 3/15 n/45. On receiving the goods Bocholo checked the order and found $2,400 worth of items that were not ordered. Therefore, Bocholo returned this amount of merchandise to Forsyth on May 4.

To pay the remaining amount owing on the invoice, Bocholo had to borrow from the bank. On May 14 Bocholo signed a short-term note payable to the bank and immediately paid Forsyth Fine Gems Ltd. with the borrowed funds. On June 14, Bocholo paid the bank the net amount of the invoice, which Bocholo had borrowed, plus 1% interest monthly (round to the nearest dollar).

Required

Record the indicated transactions in the journal of Bocholo Jewellers. Explanations are not required.

Exercise 5-7 *Journalizing sale transactions under the perpetual inventory system (Obj. 2)*

Refer to the business situation in Exercise 5-6. Journalize the transactions of Forsyth Fine Gems Ltd. Forsyth's gross margin is 40 percent, so cost of goods sold is 60 percent of sales. Explanations are not required.

Exercise 5-8 *Making closing entries under a perpetual inventory system (Obj. 3)*

An independent hardware store's accounting records (partial) carried the following accounts at January 31, 2005:

Accounts receivable	$ 19,560	Selling expense	$167,040
Interest revenue	1,200	Sales revenue	928,200
Accounts payable	49,500	Interest expense	240
Other expense	30,960	Merchandise inventories	130,800
Cost of goods sold	671,100	General and administrative	
Withdrawals	40,800	expense	16,140

Required

Note: For simplicity, all operating expenses have been summarized in the accounts Selling Expense and General and Administrative Expenses.

1. Journalize all of this company's closing entries at January 31, 2005.

2. Set up T-accounts for the Income Summary account and the Capital account. Post to these accounts and calculate their ending balances. One year earlier, at January 31, 2004, the Capital balance was $20,652.

Exercise 5-9 *Using work sheet data to make the closing entries under the perpetual inventory system (Obj. 3)*

The trial balance and adjustments columns of the work sheet of Fox Decorating Centre include the accounts and balances at March 31, 2006 (on page 254).

Required

Journalize Fox Decorating Centre's closing entries at March 31, 2006.

Account Title	Trial Balance		Adjustments	
	Debit	Credit	Debit	Credit
Cash	$ 600			
Accounts receivable	5,100		(a) 1,860	
Inventory	22,260			(b) 702
Supplies	7,800			(c) 5,760
Store fixtures	25,482			
Accumulated amortization		$ 6,750		(d) 1,350
Accounts payable		4,980		
Salary payable		0		(e) 720
Note payable, long-term		4,500		
N. Fox, capital		20,352		
N. Fox, withdrawals	27,000			
Sales revenue		140,400		(a) 1,860
Sales discounts	1,200			
Cost of goods sold	66,960		(b) 702	
Selling expense	12,630		(c) 3,420	
			(e) 720	
General expense	6,300		(c) 2,340	
			(d) 1,350	
Interest expense	1,650			
Total	$176,982	$176,982	$10,392	$10,392

Exercise 5-10 *Preparing a multi-step income statement under the perpetual inventory system* ***(Obj. 4)***

Use the data in Exercise 5-9 to prepare the multi-step income statement of Fox Decorating Centre for the year ended March 31, 2006.

Exercise 5-11 *Using the gross margin percentage and the rate of inventory turnover to evaluate profitability* ***(Obj. 5)***

Refer to Exercise 5-10. After completing Fox Decorating Centre's income statement for the year ended March 31, 2006, compute these ratios to evaluate Fox Decorating Centre's performance:

- Gross margin percentage
- Inventory turnover (Ending inventory one year earlier, at March 31, 2005, was $18,300.)

Compare your figures with the 2005 gross margin percentage of 49 percent and the inventory turnover rate of 3.16 times for 2005. Does the two-year trend suggest that Fox Decorating Centre's profits are increasing or decreasing?

Media Companion CD-ROM

Exercise 5-12 *Preparing a merchandiser's multi-step income statement under the perpetual inventory system to evaluate the business* ***(Obj. 4, 5)***

Selected accounts of Hewitt Hardware Store are listed in alphabetical order, with their balances at December 31, 2007.

Accounts receivable	$16,200		J. Hewitt, capital	$126,070
Accumulated amortization	18,700		Sales discounts	9,000
Cost of goods sold	91,300		Sales returns	4,600
General expenses	23,500		Sales revenue	201,000
Interest revenue	1,500		Selling expense	37,800
Inventory, Dec. 31, 2006	21,000		Unearned sales revenue	6,500
Inventory, Dec. 31, 2007	19,400			

Required

1. Prepare the business's multi-step income statement for the year ended December 31, 2007.

2. Compute the rate of inventory turnover for the year. Last year the turnover was 3.8 times. Does this two-year trend suggest improvement or deterioration in profitability?

Exercise 5-13 *Preparing a single-step income statement for a merchandising business under the perpetual inventory system* **(Obj. 4, 5)**

Media Companion CD-ROM

Prepare Hewitt Hardware Store's single-step income statement for 2007, using the data from Exercise 5-12. Compute the gross margin percentage, and compare it with last year's value of 58 percent for Hewitt Hardware. Does this two-year trend suggest better or worse profitability during the current year?

Exercise 5-14 *Computing cost of goods sold in a periodic inventory system* **(Obj. 6)**

The periodic inventory records of Hewitt Hardware Store include these accounts at December 31, 2007:

Purchases of inventory	$90,600
Purchase discounts	3,000
Purchase returns and allowances	2,000
Freight in	4,100
Inventory	19,400

One year ago, at December 31, 2006, Hewitt Hardware's inventory balance stood at $21,000.

Required

Compute Hewitt Hardware's cost of goods sold for 2007. (Note: Your answer should be the same as the amount given in Exercise 5-12.)

Exercise 5-15 *Computing inventory and cost of goods sold under the periodic inventory system* **(Obj. 6)**

Supply the missing income statement amounts in each of the following situations:

Sales	Sales Discounts	Net Sales	Beginning Inventory	Net Purchases	Ending Inventory	Cost of Goods Sold	Gross Margin
$48,150	(a)	$46,750	$17,750	$33,350	$19,700	(b)	$15,350
41,200	$1,050	(c)	12,875	21,500	(d)	$22,050	(e)
46,750	900	45,850	(f)	22,450	11,300	29,700	(g)
(h)	1,500	(i)	20,350	(j)	24,115	36,250	19,300

Exercise 5-16 *Computing cost of goods sold under the periodic inventory system* **(Obj. 6)**

For the year ended December 31, 2006, Custom Fabrics, a retailer of home-related products, reported net sales of $507,000 and cost of goods sold of $231,000. The company's balance sheet at December 31, 2005 and 2006 reported inventories of $266,000 and $258,000, respectively. What were Custom Fabrics' net purchases during 2006?

Exercise 5-17 *Computing inventory purchases* **(Obj. 6)**

The Gap, Inc. (www.gap.com) reported Cost of Goods Sold totalling $3,285 million.

Ending inventory was $578 million, and beginning inventory was $483 million. How much inventory did The Gap purchase during the year?

Serial Exercise

This exercise completes the Melanie Clark Engineers situation begun in Exercise 2-15 of Chapter 2 and extended to Exercise 3-17 of Chapter 3 and Exercise 4-14 of Chapter 4.

Exercise 5-18   *Accounting for both merchandising and service transactions under the perpetual inventory system*   **(Obj. 2, 3, 4)**

The engineering practice of Melanie Clark now includes a great deal of systems consulting business. In conjunction with the consulting, the business has begun selling design software. During January 2006, the business completed these transactions:

Jan.	2	Completed a consulting engagement and received cash of $17,400.
	2	Prepaid three months' office rent, $4,500.
	7	Purchased design software on account for merchandise inventory, $12,000.
	16	Paid employee salary, $4,200.
	18	Sold design software on account, $3,300 (cost $2,100).
	19	Consulted with a client for a fee of $2,700 on account.
	21	Paid on account, $6,000.
	24	Paid utilities, $900.
	28	Sold design software for cash, $1,800 (cost $1,200).
	31	Recorded these adjusting entries:
		Accrued salary expense, $4,200.
		Accounted for expiration of prepaid rent.
		Amortization of office furniture, $600.

Required

1. Open the following T-accounts in the ledger: Cash, Accounts Receivable, Design Software Inventory, Prepaid Rent, Accumulated Amortization—Office Furniture, Accounts Payable, Salaries Payable, Melanie Clark, Capital, Income Summary, Service Revenue, Sales Revenue, Cost of Goods Sold, Salary Expense, Rent Expense, Utilities Expense, and Amortization Expense—Office Furniture.

2. Journalize and post the January transactions. Key all items by date. Compute each account balance, and denote the balance as *Bal.* Journalize and post the closing entries. Denote each closing amount as *Clo.* After posting, prove the equality of debits and credits in the ledger.

3. Prepare the January 2006 income statement of Melanie Clark Engineers. Use the single-step format.

Beyond the Numbers

Beyond the Numbers 5-1   *Evaluating a company's profitability*   **(Obj. 1, 5)**

Dodds Pharmaceuticals is a leading provider of pharmaceutical products. The company recently reported the figures on the following page.

Required

Evaluate Dodds Pharmaceuticals' operations during 2007 in comparison with 2006. Consider sales, gross margin, operating income, and net income. Track the gross margin percentage and inventory turnover in both years. Dodds Pharmaceuticals' inventories at December 31, 2007, 2006, and 2005 were $23,100, $36,480, and $30,540, in thousands, respectively. In the annual report Dodds Pharmaceuticals' management describes the restructuring charges in 2007, the costs of down-sizing the company, as a one-time event. How does this additional information affect your evaluation?

DODDS PHARMACEUTICALS Consolidated Statements of Operations (Adapted) For the Years Ended July 31, 2007 and 2006		
	Amounts in Thousands	
	2007	**2006**
Sales	$330,000	$246,000
Cost of sales	240,000	183,000
Gross margin	90,000	63,000
Cost and expenses:		
Selling, general, and administrative	66,000	51,000
Amortization	6,000	2,700
Restructuring charges	21,000	—
	93,000	53,700
Operating income (loss)	(3,000)	9,300
Other items (summarized)	(1,800)	(3,900)
Net income (loss)	$ (4,800)	$ 5,400

Ethical Issue

Gorries Bearing Company makes all sales of industrial bearings under terms of FOB shipping point. The company usually receives orders for sales approximately one week before shipping inventory to customers. For orders received late in December, Bob Gorries, the owner, decides when to ship the goods. If profits are already at an acceptable level, the company delays shipment until January. If profits are lagging behind expectations, the company ships the goods during December.

Required

1. Under Gorries Bearing Company's FOB policy, when should the company record a sale?

2. Do you approve or disapprove of Gorries Bearing Company's means of deciding when to ship goods to customers? If you approve, give your reason. If you disapprove, identify a better way to decide when to ship goods. (There is no accounting rule against Gorries Bearing Company's practice.)

Problems (Group A)

Problem 5-1A   *Explaining the perpetual inventory system*   *(Obj. 2)*

Keller Optical is a regional chain of optical shops in New Brunswick. The company offers a large selection of eyeglass frames, and Keller Optical stores provide while-you-wait service. Keller Optical has launched a vigorous advertising campaign promoting its two for the price of one frame sale.

Required

Keller Optical expects to grow rapidly and increase its level of inventory. As chief accountant of the company, you wish to install a perpetual inventory system. Write a memo to the company president to explain how the system would work.
   Use the following heading for your memo:

Date:	_____
To:	Company President
From:	Chief Accountant
Subject:	How a perpetual inventory system works

Problem 5-2A *Accounting for the purchase and sale of inventory under the perpetual inventory system* *(Obj. 2)*

The following transactions occurred between Procter & Gamble (www.pg.com) and Pharmasave Drug Stores (www.pharmasave.com) during June of the current year.

June 8 Procter & Gamble sold $29,400 worth of merchandise to Pharmasave on terms of 2/10 n/30, FOB shipping point. These goods cost Procter & Gamble $12,600. Procter & Gamble prepaid freight charges of $600 and included this amount in the invoice total. (Procter & Gamble's entry to record the freight payment debits Accounts Receivable and credits Cash.)

11 Pharmasave returned $3,600 of the merchandise purchased on June 8. Procter & Gamble issued a credit memo for this amount and returned the goods, in excellent condition, to inventory (cost $1,500).

17 Pharmasave paid $12,000 of the invoice amount owed to Johnson & Johnson for the June 8 purchase. This payment included none of the freight charge. Pharmasave took the purchase discount on the partial payment.

26 Pharmasave paid the remaining amount owed to Procter & Gamble for the June 8 purchase.

Required

Journalize these transactions, first on the books of Pharmasave, and second on the books of Procter & Gamble.

Problem 5-3A *Journalizing purchase and sale transactions under the perpetual inventory system* *(Obj. 2)*

Kustra Furniture Company engaged in the following transactions during July of the current year:

July 2 Purchased inventory for cash, $2,400, less a quantity discount of $450.

5 Purchased store supplies on credit terms of net eom, $1,350.

8 Purchased inventory of $9,000 less a quantity discount of 10%, plus freight charges of $460. Credit terms are 3/15 n/30.

9 Sold goods for cash, $3,600. Kustra's cost of these goods was $2,100.

11 Returned $600 (net amount after the quantity discount) of the inventory purchased on July 8. It was damaged in shipment.

12 Purchased inventory on credit terms of 3/10 n/30, $10,000.

14 Sold inventory on credit terms of 2/10 n/30, for $28,800, less a $1,800 quantity discount (cost, $15,000).

16 Received and paid the electricity and water bills, $800.

20 Received returned inventory from the July 14 sale, $1,200 (net amount after the quantity discount). Kustra shipped the wrong goods by mistake. Kustra's cost of the inventory received was $750.

21 Borrowed the amount owed on the July 8 purchase. Signed a note payable to the bank for $7,735, which takes into account the return of inventory on July 11.

21 Paid supplier for goods purchased on July 8 less the discount and the return.

23 Received $20,580 cash in partial settlement of the account from the customer who purchased inventory on July 14. Granted the customer a 2% discount and credited his account receivable for $21,000.

30 Paid for the store supplies purchased on July 5.

Required

1. Journalize the preceding transactions on the books of Kustra Furniture Company.

2. Compute the amount of the receivable at July 31 from the customer to whom Kustra sold inventory on July 14. What amount of cash discount applies to this receivable at July 31?

Problem 5-4A *Preparing a merchandiser's work sheet under the perpetual inventory system* *(Obj. 3)*

Media Companion CD-ROM

Sandford Produce Company's trial balance below pertains to December 31, 2006.

Additional data at December 31, 2006:

a. Insurance expense for the year should total $18,170.

b. Store fixtures have an estimated useful life of ten years and are expected to have no value when they are retired from service.

c. Accrued salaries at December 31, $3,780.

d. Accrued interest expense at December 31, $2,610.

e. Store supplies on hand at December 31, $2,280.

f. Inventory based on the inventory count on December 31, $298,950.

SANDFORD PRODUCE COMPANY Trial Balance December 31, 2006		
Cash	$ 8,730	
Accounts receivable	19,680	
Inventory	305,280	
Store supplies	5,970	
Prepaid insurance	9,600	
Store fixtures	191,700	
Accumulated amortization		$112,920
Accounts payable		89,310
Salaries payable		0
Interest payable		0
Notes payable, long-term		111,600
W. Sandford, capital		189,360
W. Sandford, withdrawals	108,900	
Sales revenue		859,110
Cost of goods sold	483,270	
Salary expense	139,740	
Rent expense	43,890	
Utilities expense	20,340	
Amortization expense	0	
Insurance expense	15,900	
Store supplies expense	0	
Interest expense	9,300	
Total	$1,362,300	$1,362,300

Required

Complete Sandford Produce Company's work sheet for the year ended December 31, 2006. Key adjustments by letter.

Problem 5-5A *Journalizing the adjusting and closing entries of a merchandising business under the perpetual inventory system* *(Obj. 4)*

Refer to the data in Problem 5-4A.

Required

1. Journalize the adjusting and closing entries of the Sandford Produce Company.
2. Determine the December 31, 2006 balance in the Capital account.

Media Companion CD-ROM

Problem 5-6A   *Preparing a multi-step income statement and a classified balance sheet under the perpetual inventory system   (Obj. 3, 4)*

Link Back to Chapter 4 (Classified Balance Sheet) For simplicity, all operating expenses are summarized in the accounts Selling Expenses and General Expenses. Selected accounts of Trumper Home Entertainment, at July 31, 2006, are listed in alphabetical order below.

Accounts payable	$190,950	Inventory: July 31, 2006	$280,950
Accounts receivable	46,800	Notes payable, long-term	240,000
Accumulated amortization		Salaries payable	9,150
—store equipment	24,600	Sales discounts	12,450
B. Trumper, capital	100,650	Sales returns and	
B. Trumper, withdrawals	16,950	allowances	26,850
Cash	18,450	Sales revenue	797,400
Cost of goods sold	541,350	Selling expenses	126,900
General expenses	113,700	Store equipment	189,000
Interest expense	1,800	Supplies	6,450
Interest payable	4,500	Unearned sales revenue	13,950
Interest revenue	450		

Required

1. Prepare the entity's multi-step income statement for the month ended July 31, 2006.

2. Prepare Trumper's classified balance sheet in *report format* at July 31, 2006. Show separately your computation of the July 31, 2006, balance of S. Trumper, Capital.

Problem 5-7A   *Preparing a single-step income statement and a classified balance sheet under the perpetual inventory system   (Obj. 4)*

Link Back to Chapter 4 (Classified Balance Sheet).

1. Use the data of Problem 5-6A to prepare Trumper Home Entertainment's *single-step* income statement for July 31, 2006.

2. Prepare Trumper 's classified balance sheet in *report format* at July 31, 2006. Show your computation of the July 31 balance of B. Trumper, Capital.

Problem 5-8A   *Using work sheet data to prepare financial statements and evaluate the business under the perpetual inventory system; multi-step income statement   (Obj. 4, 5, 6)*

The trial balance and adjustments columns of the work sheet of Vikman Trading Company include the accounts and balances at September 30, 2006, shown on the next page.

Required

1. Inventory on hand at September 30, 2005, was $5,500. Without completing a formal accounting work sheet, prepare the company's multi-step income statement for the year ended September 30, 2006.

2. Compute the gross margin percentage and the inventory turnover for 2006. For 2005, Vikman Trading Company's gross margin percentage was 60 percent and the inventory turnover rate was 9.8 times. Does the two-year trend in these ratios suggest improvement or deterioration in profitability?

Account Title	Trial Balance Debit	Trial Balance Credit	Adjustments Debit	Adjustments Credit
Cash...	$ 3,950			
Accounts receivable	2,180		(a) 1,000	
Inventory	4,815		(b) 1,050	
Supplies	6,500			(c) 4,800
Equipment.....................................	49,725			
Accumulated amortization..........		$ 14,900		(d) 4,950
Accounts payable		7,900		
Salaries payable		0		(f) 100
Unearned sales revenue		1,890	(e) 1,500	
Notes payable, long-term.............		5,000		
Carol Vikman, capital		21,530		
Carol Vikman, withdrawals.........	17,500			
Sales revenue		120,000		(a) 1,000
				(e) 1,500
Sales returns.................................	1,550			
Cost of goods sold........................	54,000			(b) 1,050
Selling expense	20,000		(c) 4,800	
			(f) 100	
General expense	10,500		(d) 4,950	
Interest expense...........................	500			
Total..	$171,220	$171,220	$13,400	$13,400

Problem 5-9A *Computing cost of goods sold and gross margin in a periodic system; evaluating the business* **(Obj. 5, 6)**

Selected accounts from the accounting records of TSE Imports at June 30, 2007, are shown below.

Cash..	$ 9,520
Purchases of inventory	68,670
Freight in..	3,010
Sales revenue...	125,370
Purchases returns and allowances....................................	980
Salaries payable	1,260
Jake Bradshaw, capital	25,200
Sales returns and allowances..	8,470
Inventory: June 30, 2003	16,660
June 30, 2004	19,950
Selling expenses...	20,860
Equipment...	31,290
Purchase discounts...	910
Accumulated amortization—equipment.............................	4,830
Sales discounts...	2,380
General expenses..	11,410
Accounts payable	16,660

Required

1. Show the computation of TSE Imports' net sales, cost of goods sold, and gross margin for the year ended June 30, 2007.

2. Jake Bradshaw, owner of TSE Imports, strives to earn a gross margin percentage of 40 percent. Did he achieve this goal?

3. Did the rate of inventory turnover reach the industry average of 3.4 times per year?

Problem 5-10A *Under the perpetual inventory system, accounting for the purchase and sale of inventory, computing cost of goods sold and gross margin, using the gross margin percentage to evaluate a business* **(Obj. 2, 5, 6)**

McCann Fitness Products uses the perpetual inventory method in tracking its inventory purchases and sales. All sales that result in a return, allowance, or discount are tracked in separate accounts in order to give management the proper information to control operations. The following information is available for the month of April 2007:

April   1   The balance of inventory on hand at the beginning of the month was $106,500.

         2   Purchased $12,000 of merchandise from Grier Corp., terms 2/10 n/30. The goods were expected to be resold for $27,000.

         4   Sold merchandise for $18,000 to Ladner Fitness Club Ltd., terms 2/10 n/60. The goods had a cost of $9,000 to McCann.

         6   McCann Fitness Products returned $3,000 of defective merchandise purchased from Grier Corp. on April 2.

         8   Sold merchandise for $27,000 cash; the goods had a cost of $18,000.

         9   Purchased $24,000 of merchandise from Keiser Corp., terms 2/10 n/30.

      10   McCann Fitness Products paid the balance owing to Grier Corp.

      12   McCann Fitness Products accepted the return of half of the merchandise sold on April 8 as it was not compatible with the customer's needs. The goods were returned to stock and a cash refund paid.

      18   Paid the balance owing to Keiser Corp. for the purchase of April 9.

      20   Sold merchandise for $15,000 to Clearbrook Health Clubs Ltd., terms 2/10 n/60. The goods had cost $10,500.

      22   Clearbrook Health Clubs Ltd. complained about the quality of goods it received, and McCann Fitness Products gave an allowance of $1,800.

      25   Purchased $21,000 of merchandise for cash and paid $1,200 for freight.

      29   McCann Fitness Products sold merchandise for $15,000 to England Fitness Ltd., terms 2/10 n/30. The goods had cost $9,000. The terms of the sale were FOB shipping point, but, as a convenience, McCann Fitness Products prepaid $900 of freight for England Fitness Ltd. and included the charge on its invoice.

      30   Collected the balance owing from Clearbrook Health Clubs Ltd.

Required

1. Record any journal entries required for the above transactions.

2. What is the inventory balance on April 30, 2007?

3. Prepare a multi-step income statement, to the point of gross margin, for the month of April 2007.

4. The average gross margin percentage for the industry is 48 percent; how does McCann Fitness Products compare to the industry?

Problem 5-11A *Under the perpetual inventory system, computing cost of goods sold and gross margin, adjusting and closing the accounts of a merchandising company, preparing a merchandiser's financial statements* **(Obj. 3, 4, 6)**

Donnon Sports Products has the following account balances (in alphabetical order) on August 31, 2007:

Accounts payable	$ 13,920
Accounts receivable	14,880
Accumulated amortization—equipment	41,280
Cash	4,800
C. Donnon, capital	151,200
C. Donnon, withdrawals	9,600
Cost of goods sold	265,440
Equipment	103,200
Interest earned	3,840
Inventory	89,760

Operating expenses	$188,160
Sales discounts	5,280
Sales returns and allowances	36,480
Sales revenues	516,000
Supplies	18,240
Unearned sales revenue	9,600

Note: For simplicity, all operating expenses have been summarized in the account Operating Expenses.

Additional data at August 31, 2007:

a. A physical count of items showed $312 of supplies were on hand.

b. An inventory count showed inventory on hand at August 31, 2007, $86,400.

c. The equipment is expected to last five years and have no value at the end of five years.

d. Unearned sales of $2,400 were earned by August 31, 2007.

Required

1. Record all adjustments and closing entries that would be required on August 31, 2007.

2. Prepare the financial statements of Donnon Sports Products for the year ended August 31, 2007.

Problems (Group B)

Problem 5-1B *Explaining the perpetual inventory system* **(Obj. 2)**

Zellers (www.hbc.com/zellers) is one of the largest retailers in Canada. The women's sportswear department of Zellers purchases clothing from many well-known manufacturers. Zellers uses a sophisticated perpetual inventory system.

Required

You are the manager of a Zellers store in Calgary. Write a memo to a new employee in the women's sportswear department that explains how the company accounts for the purchase and sale of merchandise inventory.

Use the following heading for your memo:

Date:	_____
To:	New Employee
From:	Store Manager
Subject:	Zellers's accounting system for inventories

Problem 5-2B *Accounting for the purchase and sale of inventory under the perpetual inventory system* **(Obj. 2)**

The following transactions occurred between Johnson & Johnson (J&J) (www.jnj.com) and Canadian Drug Trading Company (CDT) during February of the current year.

Feb.	6	J&J sold $25,200 worth of merchandise to CDT on terms of 2/10 n/30, FOB shipping point. J&J prepaid freight charges of $1,000 and included this amount in the invoice total. (J&J's entry to record the freight payment debits Accounts Receivable and credits Cash.) These goods cost J&J $16,400.
	10	CDT returned $3,600 of the merchandise purchased on February 6. J&J issued a credit memo for this amount and returned the goods to inventory (cost, $2,360).

Feb. 15 CDT paid $12,000 of the invoice amount owed to J&J for the February 6 purchase. This payment included none of the freight charge.

27 CDT paid the remaining amount owed to J&J for the February 6 purchase.

Required

Journalize these transactions, first on the books of Canadian Drug Trading Company, and second on the books of Johnson & Johnson.

Problem 5-3B *Journalizing purchase and sale transactions under the perpetual inventory system* *(Obj. 2)*

Yoon Distributing Company engaged in the following transactions during May of the current year:

May 3 Purchased office supplies for cash, $2,700.

7 Purchased inventory on credit terms of 3/10 net eom, $18,000.

8 Returned half the inventory purchased on May 7. It was not the inventory ordered.

10 Sold goods for cash, $4,050 (cost, $2,250).

13 Sold inventory on credit terms of 2/15 n/45, for $35,100, less $5,400 quantity discount offered to customers who purchased in large quantities (cost, $16,200).

16 Paid the amount owed on account from the purchase of May 7, less the discount and the return.

17 Received wrong-sized inventory as a sales return from May 13 sale, $8,100, which is the net amount after the quantity discount. Yoon's cost of the inventory received was $5,400.

18 Purchased inventory of $36,000 on account. Payment terms were 2/10 net 30.

26 Borrowed $35,280 from the bank to take advantage of the discount offered on the May 18 purchase. Signed a note payable to the bank for this amount.

26 Paid supplier for goods purchased on May 18, less the discount.

28 Received cash in full settlement of the account from the customer who purchased inventory on May 13, less the discount and the return.

29 Purchased inventory for cash, $18,000, less a quantity discount of $3,600, plus freight charges of $1,440.

Required

1. Journalize the preceding transactions on the books of Yoon Distributing Company.

2. The note payable signed on May 26 requires Yoon to pay $270 interest expense. Was the decision to borrow funds to take advantage of the cash discount wise or unwise? Support your answer by comparing the discount to the interest paid.

Media Companion CD-ROM

Problem 5-4B *Preparing a merchandiser's work sheet under the perpetual inventory system* *(Obj. 3)*

The trial balance of Stuart's Jewellery pertains to December 31, 2007 and is shown on the top of page 265.

Additional data at December 31, 2007:

a. Rent expense for the year, $36,720.

b. Jewellery-making equipment has an estimated useful life of ten years and is expected to have no value when it is retired from service.

c. Accrued salaries at December 31, $3,240.

d. Accrued interest expense at December 31, $1,296.

e. Inventory based on the inventory count on December 31, $263,520.

Required

Complete Stuart's Jewellery's work sheet for the year ended December 31, 2007.

STUART'S JEWELLERY
Trial Balance
December 31, 2007

Cash...	$ 4,572	
Accounts receivable...	15,948	
Inventory..	266,040	
Prepaid rent	15,840	
Jewellery-making equipment..........................	79,560	
Accumulated amortization..............................		$ 30,168
Accounts payable...		22,644
Salary payable		0
Interest payable		0
Note payable, long-term		64,800
J. Stuart, capital...		201,312
J. Stuart, withdrawals.....................................	142,380	
Sales revenue		612,540
Cost of goods sold...	244,332	
Salary expense...	88,920	
Rent expense	27,720	
Advertising expense...	16,236	
Utilities expense..	13,968	
Amortization expense	0	
Insurance expense...	9,972	
Interest expense..	5,976	
Total...	$931,464	$931,464

Problem 5-5B *Journalizing the adjusting and closing entries of a merchandising business under the perpetual inventory system* **(Obj. 3)**

Refer to the data in Problem 5-4B.

Required

1. Journalize the adjusting and closing entries.
2. Determine the December 31, 2007, balance of Capital for Stuart's Jewellery.

Problem 5-6B *Preparing a multi-step income statement and a classified balance sheet under the perpetual inventory system* **(Obj. 4)**

Media Companion CD-ROM

Link Back to Chapter 4 (Classified Balance Sheet). Items from the accounts of Okatooks Bakery at May 31, 2007, follow, listed in alphabetical order. The General Expenses account summarizes all operating expenses.

Accounts payable....................	$ 34,000	Interest revenue.....................	$ 340
Accounts receivable...............	85,000	Inventory: May 31, 2007......	111,350
Accumulated amortization		Notes payable, long-term	76,500
—equipment........................	64,600	Salaries payable....................	4,760
Carl Oka, capital	97,750	Sales discounts	17,680
Carl Oka, withdrawals...........	15,640	Sales returns and	
Cash...	13,260	allowances..........................	30,600
Cost of goods sold	657,900	Sales revenue	1,327,700
Equipment	248,200	Selling expenses	238,000
General expenses	204,000	Supplies..................................	8,670
Interest expense......................	680	Unearned sales revenue.......	23,460
Interest payable......................	1,870		

Required

1. Prepare the business's multi-step income statement for the month ended May 31, 2007.

2. Prepare Okatooks Bakery's classified balance sheet in *report format* at May 31, 2007. Show your computation of the May 31, 2007, balance of Capital.

Problem 5-7B *Preparing a single-step income statement and a balance sheet under the perpetual inventory system* **(Obj. 4)**

Link Back to Chapter 4 (Classified Balance Sheet).

1. Use the data of Problem 5-6B to prepare Okatooks Bakery's *single-step* income statement for the month ended May 31, 2007.

2. Prepare Okatooks Bakery's classified balance sheet in report format at May 31, 2007. Show your computation of the May 31 balance of Capital.

Problem 5-8B *Using work sheet data to prepare financial statements and evaluate the business under the perpetual inventory system; multi-step income statement* **(Obj. 4, 5)**

The trial balance and adjustments columns of the work sheet of Peace River Products include the accounts and balances at November 30, 2006, shown below.

Required

1. Inventory on hand at November 30, 2005, is $48,000. Without entering the preceding data on a formal work sheet, prepare the company's multi-step income statement for the year ended November 30, 2006.

2. Compute the gross margin percentage and the rate of inventory turnover for 2006. For 2005, Peace River Product's gross margin percentage was 58 percent, and inventory turnover was 1.8 times during the year. Does the two-year trend in these ratios suggest improvement or deterioration in profitability?

Account Title	Trial Balance Debit	Trial Balance Credit	Adjustments Debit	Adjustments Credit
Cash	$ 36,000			
Accounts receivable	21,750		(a) 9,000	
Inventory	52,500		(b) 1,500	
Supplies	4,200			(c) 3,000
Furniture	59,400			
Accumulated amortization		$ 7,350		(d) 3,675
Accounts payable		18,900		
Salary payable		0		(f) 1,500
Unearned sales revenue		20,355	(e) 10,500	
Note payable, long-term		22,500		
J. Curtis, capital		82,695		
J. Curtis, withdrawals	63,000			
Sales revenue		270,000		(a) 9,000
				(e) 10,500
Sales returns	10,200			
Cost of goods sold	109,500			(b) 1,500
Selling expense	43,500		(f) 1,500	
General expense	19,500		(c) 3,000	
			(d) 3,675	
Interest expense	2,250			
Total	$421,800	$421,800	$29,175	$29,175

Problem 5-9B *Computing cost of goods sold and gross margin in a periodic inventory system; evaluating the business* **(Obj. 5, 6)**

Selected accounts from the accounting records of Jagger Security had the balances shown below at November 30, 2006.

Purchases of inventory	$ 85,800
Selling expenses	5,720
Furniture and fixtures	24,180
Purchase returns and allowances	585
Salaries payable	195
K. Jagger, capital	34,320
Sales revenue	126,490
Sales returns and allowances	2,080
Inventory: November 30, 2005	27,105
November 30, 2006	26,975
Accounts payable	6,175
Cash	2,405
Freight in	1,040
Accumulated amortization—furniture and fixtures	8,840
Purchase discounts	390
Sales discounts	1,365
General expenses	12,545

Required

1. Show the computation of Jagger Security's net sales, cost of goods sold, and gross margin for the year ended November 30, 2006.

2. Kathy Jagger, the proprietor of Jagger Security, strives to earn a gross margin percentage of 25 percent. Did she achieve this goal?

3. Did the rate of inventory turnover reach the industry average of 3.4 times per year?

Problem 5-10B *Under the perpetual inventory system, accounting for the purchase and sale of inventory, computing cost of goods sold and gross margin, using the gross margin percentage to evaluate a business* **(Obj. 2, 5, 6)**

Book Warehouse uses the perpetual inventory method in tracking its inventory purchases and sales. All sales that result in a return, allowance, or discount are tracked in separate accounts in order to give management the proper information to control operations. The following information is available for the month of April 2007:

April 1   Inventory on hand at the beginning of the month was $55,200.

2   Purchased $20,000 of merchandise from Smith Publishing, terms 2/10 n/30. The goods were expected to be resold for $44,000.

4   Sold merchandise for $28,000 to Coast Bookstore, terms 2/10 n/60. The goods had a cost of $16,000 to Book Warehouse.

6   Book Warehouse returned $8,000 of defective merchandise purchased from Smith Publishing on April 2.

8   Sold merchandise for $32,000 cash; the goods had a cost of $24,000.

9   Purchased $36,000 of merchandise from Goodwin Publishing, terms 2/10 n/30.

10   Book Warehouse paid the balance owing to Smith Publishing.

12   Book Warehouse accepted the return of half of the merchandise sold on April 8 as it was not compatible with the customer's needs. The goods were returned to inventory and a cash refund paid.

18   Paid the balance owing to Goodwin Publishing from the purchase of April 9.

20   Sold merchandise for $16,000 to Prairie Bookstores, terms 2/10 n/60. The goods had cost $12,000.

22   Prairie Bookstores complained about the quality of goods it received, and Book Warehouse gave an allowance of $2,000.

25   Purchased $24,000 of merchandise for cash and paid $2,000 for freight.

April 29 Book Warehouse sold merchandise for $24,000 to Atlantic Bookstores, terms 2/10 n/30. The goods had cost $12,000. The terms of the sale were FOB shipping point, but, as a convenience, Book Warehouse prepaid $1,600 of freight for Atlantic Bookstores.

30 Collected the balance owing from Prairie Bookstores.

Required

1. Record any journal entries required for the above transactions.
2. What is the inventory balance on April 30, 2007?
3. Prepare a multi-step income statement, to the point of gross margin, for the month of April 2007.
4. The average gross margin percentage for the industry is 50 percent; how does Book Warehouse compare with the industry?

Problem 5-11B *Under the perpetual inventory system, computing cost of goods sold and gross margin, adjusting and closing the accounts of a merchandising company, preparing a merchandiser's financial statements* **(Obj. 3, 4, 6)**

Whitewater Adventures has the following account balances (in alphabetical order) on July 31, 2006:

Accounts payable	$ 4,350
Accounts receivable	4,650
Accumulated amortization—equipment	12,900
Cash	1,500
Cost of goods sold	136,950
David Whitehead, capital	72,750
David Whitehead, withdrawals	3,000
Equipment	36,000
Interest earned	1,200
Inventory	28,050
Operating expenses	72,300
Sales discounts	1,650
Sales returns and allowances	11,400
Sales revenues	207,000
Supplies	5,700
Unearned sales revenue	3,000

Note: For simplicity, all operating expenses have been summarized in the account Operating Expenses.

Additional data at July 31, 2006:

a. A physical count of items showed $600 of supplies on hand.

b. An inventory count showed inventory on hand at July 31, 2006, $29,550.

c. The equipment has an estimated useful life of eight years and is expected to have no value at the end of its life.

d. Unearned sales revenues of $1,050 were earned by July 31, 2006.

Required

1. Record all adjustments and closing entries that would be required on July 31, 2006.

2. Prepare the financial statements of Whitewater Adventures for the year ended July 31, 2006.

Challenge Problems

Problem 5-1C *Understanding purchasing and gross margin* **(Obj. 1, 2, 5)**

You have been recently hired as an accountant by Best Discount Stores, a small chain of discount stores. One of your first activities is to review the accounting system for Best Discount.

In your review, you discover that the company determines selling prices by adding a standard markup on cost of 10 percent (i.e., cost plus 10 percent of cost) to the cost of all products. The company uses a perpetual inventory system. You also discover that your predecessor, a bookkeeper, had set up the accounting system so that all purchase discounts and purchase returns and allowances were accumulated in an account that was treated as "other income" for financial statement purposes because he believed that they were financing items and not related to operations.

Camilla Cornell, owner of Best Discount, has an MBA and uses modern decision-making techniques in running Best Discount. Two ratios she particularly favours are the gross margin percentage and inventory turnover ratio.

Required

1. What is a possible effect of the accounting system described on the pricing of products and thus operations of Best Discount Stores?
2. What is the effect of the accounting system instituted by your predecessor on the two ratios Ms. Cornell favours?

Problem 5-2C *Using an inventory system for control* **(Obj. 1)**

David Dias is concerned about theft by shoplifters in his chain of three electronics stores and has come to your public accounting firm for advice. Specifically, he has several questions he would like you to answer.

a. He wonders if there is any inventory system he can use that will allow him to keep track of products that leave his stores as legitimate purchases and merchandise that is stolen?

b. He realizes that carrying inventory is expensive and wants to know if you have any suggestions as to how he can keep close tabs on his inventory at the three stores so he can be sure that the stores don't run out of product.

c. The space in the stores is limited. David also wants to install an inventory system that will tell him when a product is slow-moving or obsolete so he can clear it out and replace it with a potentially faster-moving product.

Required

Indicate whether a perpetual inventory system or a periodic inventory system will provide David with answers to the three questions he has asked. Explain how the inventory system indicated will provide the specific information he has requested.

Extending Your Knowledge

Decision Problems

1. Using financial statements to decide on a business expansion (Obj. 4, 5)

Link Back to Chapter 4 (Classified Balance Sheet, Current Ratio, Debt Ratio). Peter Jones owns the Sackville Drug Store, which has prospered during its second year of operation. To help Jones decide whether to open another pharmacy in the area, his bookkeeper has prepared the current financial statements of the business.

SACKVILLE DRUG STORE
Income Statement
For the Year Ended December 31, 2006

Sales revenue		$360,000
Interest revenue		49,200
Total revenue		409,200
Cost of goods sold		174,000
Gross margin		235,200
Operating expenses:		
Salary expense	40,000	
Rent expense	24,000	
Interest expense	12,000	
Amortization expense	9,800	
Utilities expense	4,660	
Supplies expense	3,000	
Total operating expenses		93,460
Income from operations		141,740
Other expense:		
Sales discounts ($7,200) and returns ($14,200)		21,400
Net income		$120,340

SACKVILLE DRUG STORE
Statement of Owner's Equity
For the Year Ended December 31, 2006

Peter Jones, capital, January 1, 2006	$ 60,000
Add: Net income	120,340
Peter Jones, capital, December 31, 2006	$180,340

SACKVILLE DRUG STORE
Balance Sheet
December 31, 2006

Assets

Current assets:	
Cash	$ 10,640
Accounts receivable	21,420
Inventory	60,200
Supplies	5,600
Store fixtures	126,000
Total current assets	223,860
Other asset:	
Withdrawals	90,000
Total assets	$313,860

Liabilities

Current liabilities:	
Accumulated amortization—store fixtures	$ 12,600
Accounts payable	19,120
Salaries payable	1,800
Total current liabilities	33,520
Other liability:	
Note payable due in 90 days	100,000
Total liabilities	133,520

Owner's Equity

Peter Jones, capital	180,340
Total liabilities and owner's equity	$313,860

Peter Jones recently read in an industry trade journal that a successful pharmacy meets all of these criteria:

a. Gross margin is at least 50%.

b. Current ratio is at least 2.0.

c. Debt ratio is no higher than 0.50.

d. Inventory turnover is at least 3.40 times per year. (Sackville Drug Store's inventory at December 31, 2005, was $38,400.)

Basing his opinion on the entity's financial statement data, Peter Jones believes the business meets all four criteria. He plans to go ahead with the expansion plan, and asks your advice on preparing the pharmacy's financial statements in accordance with generally accepted accounting principles. He assures you that all amounts are correct.

Required

1. Compute the four ratios based on the Sackville Drug Store financial statements prepared by Jones's bookkeeper. Does the business appear to be ready for expansion?

2. Prepare a correct multi-step income statement, a statement of owner's equity, and a classified balance sheet in report format.

3. On the basis of the corrected financial statements, compute correct measures of the four criteria listed in the trade journal.

4. Make a recommendation about whether to undertake the expansion at this time.

2. Understanding the operating cycle of a merchandiser   (Obj. 1, 3)

Frances Lau has come to you for advice. Earlier this year, she opened a record store in a plaza near the university she had attended. The store sells compact discs at very low prices and on special credit for students. Many of the students at the university are co-op students who alternate school and work terms. Frances allows co-op students to buy on credit while they are on a school term, with the understanding that they will pay their account shortly after starting a work term.

Business has been very good. Frances is sure it is because of her competitive prices and the unique credit terms she offers. Her problem is that she is short of cash, and her loan with the bank has grown significantly. The bank manager has indicated that he wishes to reduce Lau's line of credit because he is worried that she will get into financial difficulties.

Required

1. Explain to Lau why she, in your opinion, is short of cash.

2. Lau has asked you to explain her problem to the bank manager and to assist in asking for more credit. What might you say to the bank manager to assist Lau?

3. Correcting an inventory error (Obj. 6)

The employees of Oakville Furniture Company made an error when they performed the periodic inventory count at year end, October 31, 2006. Part of one warehouse was not counted and therefore was not included in inventory.

Required

1. Indicate the effect of the inventory error on cost of goods sold, gross margin, and net income for the year ended October 31, 2006.

2. Will the error affect cost of goods sold, gross margin, and net income in 2007? If so, what will be the effect?

Financial Statement Problem

Closing entries for a corporation that sells merchandise; evaluating ratio data (Obj. 3, 5)

This problem uses both the income statement (consolidated statement of operations) and the balance sheet of Intrawest Corporation in Appendix A. It will aid your understanding of the closing process of a business.

1. Journalize Intrawest's closing entries for the year ended June 30, 2003. You will be unfamiliar with certain revenues and expenses, but you should treat them all similarly. Make "General and administrative" the final expense you close. Instead of closing to a Capital account, close to the Retained Earnings account (since Intrawest is a corporation, not a proprietorship).

2. What amount was closed to Retained Earnings? What were dividends in 2003?

3. Intrawest is not a typical merchandiser but it does have two types of inventory: (1) Inventory related to ski operations (Note 8 in the financial statements); (2) Inventory of properties under development and held for sale (Note 6). The company develops resort properties for resale, some of which will be sold in the current year and are classified as current assets. The remainder of the properties will be sold in future years and are classified as long-term assets. What balances are reported as current assets on the *balance sheet* for the two types of inventory at June 30, 2003? At June 30, 2002?

Supplement to Chapter 5

Accounting for Merchandise in a Periodic Inventory System

Purchasing Merchandise in the Periodic Inventory System

Some businesses find it uneconomical to invest in a computerized (perpetual) inventory system that keeps up-to-the-minute records of merchandise on hand and cost of goods sold.

Recording Purchases of Inventory

OBJECTIVE S2
Account for the purchase and sale of inventory under the periodic inventory system

All inventory systems use the Inventory account. But in a periodic inventory system, purchases, purchase discounts, purchase returns and allowances, and transportation costs are recorded in separate expense accounts bearing these titles. Let's account for Austin Sound Centre's purchase of the JVC goods in Exhibit 5S-1. For the moment, disregard GST and use the invoice total of $707.00 when recording purchases and purchase discounts. GST is discussed on page 229. The following entries record the purchase and payment on account within the discount period:

May 27	Purchases	707.00	
	Accounts Payable		707.00
	Purchased inventory on account.		
June 10	Accounts Payable	707.00	
	Cash		685.79
	Purchase Discounts ($707.00 × 0.03)		21.21
	Paid for inventory on account within discount period.		
	The discount is $21.21.		

Recording Purchase Returns and Allowances

Suppose instead that prior to payment, Austin Sound returned to JVC goods costing $70 and also received from JVC a purchase allowance of $15. Austin Sound would record these transactions as follows:

June 3	Accounts Payable	70.00	
	Purchase Returns and Allowances		70.00
	Returned inventory to seller.		
June 4	Accounts Payable	15.00	
	Purchase Returns and Allowances		15.00
	Received a purchase allowance.		

KEY POINT

A contra account always has a companion account with the opposite balance. Thus, both Purchase Discounts and Purchase Returns and Allowances (credit balances) are reported with Purchases (debit balance) on the income statement.

During the period, the business records the cost of all inventory bought in the Purchases account. The balance of Purchases is a *gross* amount because it does not include subtractions for purchase discounts, returns, or allowances. **Net purchases** is the remainder computed by subtracting the contra accounts from Purchases:

> **Purchase (*debit* balance account)**
> **– Purchase Discounts (*credit* balance account)**
> **– Purchase Returns and Allowances (*credit* balance account)**
> **= Net purchases (a *debit* subtotal, not a separate account)**

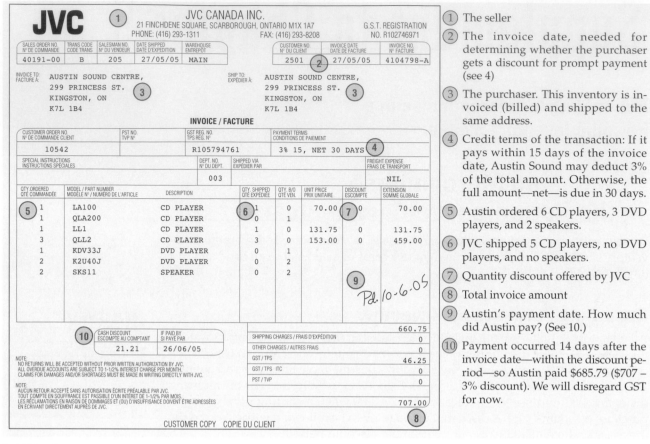

Exhibit 5S-1

An Invoice

Recording Transportation Costs

Under the periodic system, costs to transport purchased inventory from seller to buyer are debited to a separate expense account, as shown for payment of a $70 freight bill:

June 1	Freight In	70.00	
	Cash..		70.00
	Paid a freight bill.		

Recording the Sale of Inventory

Recording sales is streamlined in the periodic system. With no running record of inventory to maintain, we can record a $5,000 sale as follows:

June 5	Accounts Receivable	5,000	
	Sales Revenue		5,000
	Sale on account.		

No accompanying entry to Inventory and Cost of Goods Sold is required. Also, sales discounts and sales returns and allowances are recorded as shown for the perpetual system on page 228, but with no entry to Inventory and Cost of Goods Sold.

OBJECTIVE S3
Compute the cost of goods sold under the periodic inventory system

Cost of Goods Sold

Cost of goods sold (also called **cost of sales**) is the largest single expense of most businesses that sell merchandise, such as Danier Leather Inc. and Austin Sound. It is the cost of the inventory that the business has sold to customers. In a periodic system, cost of goods sold must be computed as in Exhibit 5S-2 and is *not* a ledger

Panel A

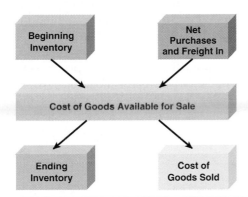

Beginning inventory
+ Net purchases ⟵──────
+ Freight in

= Cost of goods available for sale
– Ending inventory
= Cost of goods sold

{
Purchases of inventory
– Purchase discounts
– Purchase returns and allowances
= Net purchases
}

Panel B

```
Beginning          Net
Inventory          Purchases
                   and Freight In
        ↘         ↙
    Cost of Goods Available for Sale
        ↙         ↘
Ending              Cost of
Inventory           Goods Sold
```

account. It is the residual left when we subtract ending inventory from the cost of goods available for sale.

Exhibit 5S-3 summarizes the first half of this Supplement by showing Austin Sound's net sales revenue, cost of goods sold—including net purchases and freight in—and gross margin on the income statement for the periodic system. (All amounts are assumed.)

AUSTIN SOUND CENTRE
Income Statement
For the Year Ended December 31, 2007

PANEL A—Detailed Gross Margin Section—Often Required by Management

Sales revenue		$338,600
Less: Sales discounts		2,800
Sales returns and allowances		4,000
Net sales		$331,800
Cost of goods sold:		
Beginning inventory		77,200
Purchases	182,800	
Less: Purchase discounts	6,000	
Purchase returns and allowances	2,400	
Net purchases		174,400
Freight in		10,400
Cost of goods available for sale		262,000
Less: Ending inventory		80,400
Cost of goods sold		181,600
Gross margin		$150,200

PANEL B—Summary Gross Margin Section—Most Common in Annual Reports to Outsiders

Net sales	$331,800
Cost of goods sold	181,600
Gross margin	$150,200

OBJECTIVE S4
Adjust and close the accounts
of a merchandising business
under the periodic inventory
system

Adjusting and Closing the Accounts in a Periodic Inventory System

A merchandising business adjusts and closes the accounts much as a service entity does. The steps of this end-of-period process are the same: If a work sheet is used, the trial balance is entered and the work sheet completed to determine net income or net loss. The work sheet provides the data for journalizing the adjusting and closing entries and for preparing the financial statements.

At the end of the period, before any adjusting or closing entries, the Inventory account balance is still the cost of the inventory that was on hand at the end of the preceding period. It is necessary to remove this beginning balance and replace it with the cost of the inventory on hand at the end of the period. Various techniques may be used to bring the inventory records up to date.

To illustrate a merchandiser's adjusting and closing process under the periodic inventory system, let's use Austin Sound's December 31, 2007, trial balance in Exhibit 5S-4. All the new accounts—Inventory, Purchases, Freight In, and the contra accounts—are highlighted for emphasis. Inventory is the only account that is affected by the new closing procedures. The additional data item (h) gives the ending inventory figure $80,400.

Preparing and Using the Work Sheet in a Periodic Inventory System

The Exhibit 5S-5 work sheet on page 278 is similar to the work sheets we have seen so far, but a few differences appear. This work sheet is slightly different from the one you saw in Chapter 4; it does not include adjusted trial balance columns. In most accounting systems, a single operation combines trial balance amounts with the adjustments and extends the adjusted balances directly to the income statement and balance sheet columns. Therefore, to reduce clutter, the adjusted trial balance columns are omitted so that the work sheet contains four pairs of columns, not five.

Account Title Column The trial balance lists a number of accounts without balances. Ordinarily, these accounts are affected by the adjusting process. Examples include Interest Receivable, Interest Payable, and Amortization Expense. The accounts are listed in the order in which they appear in the ledger. If additional accounts are needed, they can be written in at the bottom, above net income.

Trial Balance Columns Examine the Inventory account, $77,200 in the trial balance. This $77,200 is the cost of the beginning inventory. The work sheet is designed to replace this outdated amount with the new ending balance, which in our example is $80,400 [additional data item (h) in Exhibit 5S-4]. As we shall see, this task is accomplished later in the columns for the income statement and the balance sheet.

Adjustments Columns The adjustments are similar to those discussed in Chapters 3 and 4. They may be entered in any order desired. The debit amount of each entry should equal the credit amount, and total debits should equal total credits. You should review the adjusting data in Exhibit 5S-5 to reassure yourself that the adjustments are correct.

Income Statement Columns The income statement columns contain adjusted amounts for the revenues and the expenses. Sales Revenue, for example, is $338,600, which includes the $2,600 adjustment.

You may be wondering why the two inventory amounts appear in the income statement columns. The reason is that both beginning inventory and ending inventory enter the computation of cost of goods sold. *Placement of beginning inventory ($77,200) in the work sheet's income statement debit column has the effect of adding*

AUSTIN SOUND CENTRE
Trial Balance
December 31, 2007

	Debit	Credit
Cash	$ 5,700	
Accounts receivable	9,200	
Note receivable, current	16,000	
Interest receivable	0	
Inventory	**77,200**	
Supplies	1,300	
Prepaid insurance	2,400	
Furniture and fixtures	66,400	
Accumulated amortization		$ 4,800
Accounts payable		94,000
Unearned sales revenue		4,000
Wages payable		0
Interest payable		0
Note payable, long-term		25,200
Steve Austin, capital		51,800
Steve Austin, withdrawals	108,200	
Sales revenue		336,000
Sales discounts	2,800	
Sales returns and allowances	4,000	
Interest revenue		1,200
Purchases	**182,800**	
Purchase discounts		**6,000**
Purchase returns and allowances		**2,400**
Freight in	**10,400**	
Wages expense	19,600	
Rent expense	16,800	
Amortization expense	0	
Insurance expense	0	
Supplies expense	0	
Interest expense	2,600	
Total	$525,400	$525,400

Additional data at December 31, 2007:

a. Interest revenue earned but not yet collected, $800.

b. Supplies on hand, $200.

c. Prepaid insurance expired during the year, $2,000.

d. Amortization for the year, $1,200.

e. Unearned sales revenue earned during the year, $2,600.

f. Accrued wage expense, $800.

g. Accrued interest expense, $400.

h. Inventory on hand based on inventory count, $80,400.

beginning inventory in computing cost of goods sold. Placing ending inventory ($80,400) in the credit column decreases cost of goods sold.

Purchases and Freight In appear in the debit column because they are added in computing cost of goods sold. Purchase Discounts and Purchase Returns and Allowances appear as credits because they are subtracted in computing cost of goods sold—$181,600 on the income statement in Exhibit 5S-6 on page 279.

The income statement column subtotals on the work sheet indicate whether the business earned net income or incurred a net loss. If total credits are greater, the result is net income, as shown in Exhibit 5S-5. If total debits are greater, a net loss has occurred.

AUSTIN SOUND CENTRE
Accounting Work Sheet
For the Year Ended December 31, 2007

Account Title	Trial Balance Debit	Trial Balance Credit	Adjustments Debit	Adjustments Credit	Income Statement Debit	Income Statement Credit	Balance Sheet Debit	Balance Sheet Credit
Cash	5,700						5,700	
Accounts receivable	9,200						9,200	
Note receivable, current	16,000						16,000	
Interest receivable	0		(a) 800				800	
Inventory	**77,200**				77,200	80,400	80,400	
Supplies	1,300			(b) 1,100			200	
Prepaid insurance	2,400			(c) 2,000			400	
Furniture and fixtures	66,400						66,400	
Accumulated amortization		4,800		(d) 1,200				6,000
Accounts payable		94,000						94,000
Unearned sales revenue		4,000	(e) 2,600					1,400
Wages payable		0		(f) 800				800
Interest payable		0		(g) 400				400
Note payable, long-term		25,200						25,200
Steve Austin, capital		51,800						51,800
Steve Austin, withdrawals	108,200						108,200	
Sales revenue		336,000		(e) 2,600		338,600		
Sales discounts	2,800				2,800			
Sales returns and allowances	4,000				4,000			
Interest revenue		1,200		(a) 800		2,000		
Purchases	**182,800**				182,800			
Purchase discounts		**6,000**				6,000		
Purchase returns and allowances		**2,400**				2,400		
Freight in	**10,400**				10,400			
Wages expense	19,600		(f) 800		20,400			
Rent expense	16,800				16,800			
Amortization expense	0		(d) 1,200		1,200			
Insurance expense	0		(c) 2,000		2,000			
Supplies expense	0		(b) 1,100		1,100			
Interest expense	2,600		(g) 400		3,000			
	525,400	525,400	8,900	8,900	321,700	429,400	287,300	179,600
Net income					107,700			107,700
					429,400	429,400	287,300	287,300

Balance Sheet Columns The only new item on the balance sheet is inventory. The balance listed is the ending amount of $80,400, which is determined by a physical count of inventory on hand at the end of the period.

Preparing the Financial Statements of a Merchandiser

Exhibit 5S-6 presents Austin Sound's financial statements. The *income statement* through gross margin repeats Exhibit 5S-3. This information is followed by the **operating expenses**, expenses other than cost of goods sold that are incurred in the entity's major line of business—merchandising. Wages expense is Austin Sound's cost of employing workers. Rent is the cost of obtaining store space. Insurance helps to protect the inventory. Store furniture and fixtures wear out; the expense is amortization. Supplies expense is the cost of stationery, mailing, and the like, used in operations.

AUSTIN SOUND CENTRE
Income Statement
For the Year Ended December 31, 2007

Sales revenue		$338,600
Less: Sales discounts		2,800
Sales returns and allowances		4,000
Net sales revenue		$331,800
Cost of goods sold:		
Beginning inventory		77,200
Purchases	182,800	
Less: Purchase discounts	6,000	
Purchase returns and allowances	2,400	
Net purchases		174,400
Freight in		10,400
Cost of goods available for sale		262,000
Less: Ending inventory		80,400
Cost of goods sold		181,600
Gross margin		150,200
Operating expenses:		
Wages expense		20,400
Rent expense		16,800
Insurance expense		2,000
Amortization expense		1,200
Supplies expense		1,100
		41,500
Income from operations		108,700
Other revenue and (expense):		
Interest revenue		2,000
Interest expense		(3,000)
		(1,000)
Net income		$107,700

AUSTIN SOUND CENTRE
Statement of Owner's Equity
For the Year Ended December 31, 2007

Steve Austin, capital, January 1, 2007	$ 51,800
Add: Net income	107,700
	159,500
Less: Withdrawals	108,200
Steve Austin, capital, December 31, 2007	$ 51,300

AUSTIN SOUND CENTRE
Balance Sheet
December 31, 2007

Assets

Current assets:		
Cash		$ 5,700
Accounts receivable		9,200
Note receivable		16,000
Interest receivable		800
Inventory		80,400
Prepaid insurance		400
Supplies		200
Total current assets		112,700
Capital assets:		
Furniture and fixtures	$66,400	
Less: Accumulated amortization	6,000	60,400
Total assets		$173,100

Liabilities

Current liabilities:		
Accounts payable		$ 94,000
Unearned sales revenue		1,400
Wages payable		800
Interest payable		400
Total current liabilities		96,600
Long-term liability:		
Note payable		25,200
Total liabilities		121,800

Owner's Equity

S. Austin, capital		51,300
Total liabilities and owner's equity		$173,100

Many companies report their operating expenses in two categories.

- *Selling expenses* are those expenses related to marketing the company's products—sales salaries; sales commissions; advertising; amortization, rent, utilities, and property taxes on store buildings; amortization on store furniture; delivery expense; and so on.
- *General expenses* include office expenses, such as the salaries of office employees; and amortization, rent, utilities, and property taxes on the home office building.

Gross margin minus operating expenses and plus any other operating revenues equals **operating income**, or **income from operations**. Many business people view operating income as the most reliable indicator of a business's success because it measures the entity's major ongoing activities.

The last section of Austin Sound's income statement is **other revenue and expenses**, which is handled the same way in both inventory systems. This category reports revenues and expenses that are outside the company's main line of business.

Journalizing the Adjusting and Closing Entries in the Periodic Inventory System

Exhibit 5S-7 on page 281 presents Austin Sound's adjusting entries. These entries follow the same pattern illustrated in Chapter 4 for a service entry.

The exhibit also gives Austin Sound's closing entries. The first closing entry closes the revenue accounts. Closing entries 2 and 3 are new. Entry 2 closes the beginning balance of the Inventory account ($77,200), along with Purchases and Freight In, into the temporary Cost of Goods Sold account. Entry 3 sets up the ending balance of Inventory ($80,400) with a debit and also closes the Purchases contra accounts to the temporary Cost of Goods Sold account.[1] Now Inventory and the temporary Cost of Goods Sold account have their correct ending balances as shown below.

Inventory			
Jan. 1	Bal. 77,200	Dec. 31	Clo. 77,200
Dec. 31	Clo. 80,400		
Dec. 31	Bal. 80,400		

Cost of Goods Sold (temporary)			
Beg. inv.	77,200	Pur. discts.	6,000
Purchases	182,800	Pur. ret. and	
Freight in	10,400	allowances	2,400
		End. inventory	80,400
Bal.	181,600		

The entries to the Inventory account deserve additional explanation. Recall that before the closing process Inventory still has the period's beginning balance. At the end of the period, this balance is one year old and must be replaced with the ending balance in order to prepare the financial statements at December 31, 2007. The closing entries give Inventory its correct ending balance of $80,400.

---

[1]Some accountants make the inventory entries as adjustments rather than as part of the closing process. The adjusting-entry approach adds these adjustments (shifted out of the closing entries):

Adjusting Entries

Dec. 31	Income Summary	77,200	
	Inventory (beginning balance)		77,200
Dec. 31	Inventory (ending balance)	80,400	
	Income Summary		80,400

When these entries are posted, the Inventory account will look exactly as shown above, except that the journal references will be "Adj." instead of "Clo." The financial statements are unaffected by the approach used for these inventory entries.

Journal

Adjusting Entries

a.	Dec. 31	Interest receivable	800	
		Interest revenue		800
b.	Dec. 31	Supplies expense ($1,300 – $200)	1,100	
		Supplies..		1,100
c.	Dec. 31	Insurance expense...	2,000	
		Prepaid insurance		2,000
d.	Dec. 31	Amortization expense	1,200	
		Accumulated amortization		1,200
e.	Dec. 31	Unearned sales revenue......................................	2,600	
		Sales revenue...		2,600
f.	Dec. 31	Wages expense..	800	
		Wages payable..		800
g.	Dec. 31	Interest expense..	400	
		Interest payable..		400

Closing Entries

1.	Dec. 31	Sales revenue	338,600	
		Interest revenue	2,000	
		Income summary		340,600
2.	Dec. 31	Cost of goods sold	270,400	
		Inventory (beginning balance)..................		77,200
		Purchases...		182,800
		Freight in		10,400
3.	Dec. 31	Inventory (ending balance)............................	80,400	
		Purchase discounts.......................................	6,000	
		Purchase returns and allowances..................	2,400	
		Cost of goods sold.......................................		88,800
4.	Dec. 31	Income summary..	232,900	
		Sales discounts..		2,800
		Sales returns and allowances........................		4,000
		Cost of goods sold ($270,400 – $88,800)		181,600
		Wages expense		20,400
		Rent expense		16,800
		Amortization expense....................................		1,200
		Insurance expense		2,000
		Supplies expense		1,100
		Interest expense		3,000
5.	Dec. 31	Income summary ($340,600 – $232,900)	107,700	
		Steve Austin, capital		107,700
6.	Dec. 31	Steve Austin, capital...	108,200	
		Steve Austin, withdrawals.........................		108,200

Closing entry 4 then closes the Sales contra accounts and the temporary Cost of Goods Sold account along with the other expense accounts into Income Summary. Closing entries 5 and 6 complete the closing process. All data for the closing entries are taken from the income statement columns of the work sheet. (Note that some companies close the accounts in closing entries 2 and 3 into the Income Summary account, instead of the temporary Cost of Goods Sold account. This has the same result overall. However, as mentioned above, Inventory and Cost of Goods Sold have their correct account balances before being closed to the Income summary account if they are closed to the temporary Cost of Goods Sold account first.)

Study Exhibits 5S-5, 5S-6, and 5S-7 carefully because they illustrate the entire end-of-period process that leads to the financial statements. As you progress through this book, you may want to refer to these exhibits to refresh your understanding of the adjusting and closing process for a merchandising business.

Net sales, cost of goods sold, operating income, and net income are unaffected by the choice of inventory system. You can prove this by comparing Austin Sound's financial statements given in Exhibit 5S-6 with the corresponding statements in Exhibit 5-7 on page 236. The only differences appear in the cost-of-goods-sold section of the income statement, and those differences are unimportant. In fact, virtually all companies report cost of goods sold in streamlined fashion, as shown for Danier Leather Inc. in Exhibit 5-1 and for Austin Sound in Exhibit 5-7.

Learning Tip   Here is an easy way to remember the closing process. First look at the work sheet. Then:
1. Debit all income statement accounts that have a credit balance. Credit Income Summary for the sum of all these debits.
2. Credit all income statement accounts that have a debit balance. Debit Income Summary for the sum of all these credits.
3. Credit the inventory account for the amount of opening inventory and debit inventory for the amount of ending inventory obtained from the year-end physical count.
4. Calculate the balance in the Income Summary account. If the account has a debit balance, there is a net loss; credit Income Summary for that amount, and debit Capital. If Income Summary has a credit balance, there is a net income for the period; debit Income Summary for that amount, and credit Capital.
5. Look at the debit balance of Withdrawals in the balance-sheet column. Credit Withdrawals for its balance, and debit Capital for the same amount.

Summary Problem
for Your Review

The following trial balance pertains to Kathy Pittman Distributing Company.

KATHY PITTMAN DISTRIBUTING COMPANY
Trial Balance
December 31, 2006

Cash	$ 8,505	
Accounts receivable	55,650	
Inventory	90,750	
Supplies	5,895	
Prepaid rent	9,000	
Furniture and fixtures	39,750	
Accumulated amortization		$ 31,800
Accounts payable		69,510
Salaries payable		0
Interest payable		0
Unearned sales revenue		5,250
Notes payable, long-term		52,500
Kathy Pittman, capital		35,520
Kathy Pittman, withdrawals	72,000	
Sales revenue		520,050
Sales discounts	15,450	
Sales returns and allowances	12,300	
Purchases	263,850	
Purchase discounts		9,000
Purchase returns and allowances		11,145
Freight in	13,950	
Salaries expense	124,125	
Rent expense	10,500	
Amortization expense	0	
Utilities expense	8,700	
Supplies expense	0	
Interest expense	4,350	
Total	$734,775	$734,775

Additional data at December 31, 2006:

a. Supplies used during the year, $3,870.

b. Prepaid rent remaining in force, $1,500.

c. Unearned sales revenue still not earned, $3,600. The company expects to earn this amount during the next few months.

d. Amortization. The furniture and fixtures' estimated useful life is ten years, and they are expected to have no value when they are retired from service.

e. Accrued salaries, $1,950.

f. Accrued interest expense, $900.

g. Inventory on hand based on an inventory count, $98,700.

Required

1. Enter the trial balance on a work sheet and complete the work sheet.

2. Journalize the adjusting and closing entries at December 31, 2006. Post to the Income Summary account as an accuracy check on the entries affecting that account. The credit balance closed out of Income Summary should equal net income computed on the work sheet.

3. Prepare the company's multi-step income statement, statement of owner's equity, and balance sheet in account format. Draw arrows connecting the statements, or state how the statements are linked.

4. Compute the inventory turnover for 2006. Turnover for 2005 was 2.1 times. Would you expect Kathy Pittman Distributing Company to be more or less profitable in 2006 than in 2005? Give your reason.

Solution

Requirement 1

KATHY PITTMAN DISTRIBUTING COMPANY
Work Sheet
For the Year Ended December 31, 2006

Account Title	Trial Balance Debit	Trial Balance Credit	Adjustments Debit	Adjustments Credit	Income Statement Debit	Income Statement Credit	Balance Sheet Debit	Balance Sheet Credit
Cash	8,505						8,505	
Accounts receivable	55,650						55,650	
Inventory	90,750				90,750	98,700	98,700	
Supplies	5,895			(a) 3,870			2,025	
Prepaid rent	9,000			(b) 7,500			1,500	
Furniture and fixtures	39,750						39,750	
Accumulated amortization		31,800		(d) 3,975				35,775
Accounts payable		69,510						69,510
Salaries payable		0		(e) 1,950				1,950
Interest payable		0		(f) 900				900
Unearned sales revenue		5,250	(c) 1,650					3,600
Notes payable, long-term		52,500						52,500
Kathy Pittman, capital		35,520						35,520
Kathy Pittman, withdrawals	72,000						72,000	
Sales revenue		520,050		(c) 1,650		521,700		
Sales discounts	15,450				15,450			
Sales returns and allowances	12,300				12,300			
Purchases	263,850				263,850			
Purchase discounts		9,000				9,000		
Purchase returns and allowances		11,145				11,145		
Freight in	13,950				13,950			
Salaries expense	124,125		(e) 1,950		126,075			
Rent expense	10,500		(b) 7,500		18,000			
Amortization expense	0		(d) 3,975		3,975			
Utilities expense	8,700				8,700			
Supplies expense	0		(a) 3,870		3,870			
Interest expense	4,350		(f) 900		5,250			
	734,775	734,775	19,845	19,845	562,170	640,545	278,130	199,755
Net income					78,375			78,375
					640,545	640,545	278,130	278,130

Adjusting Entries

2006

Dec. 31	Supplies expense...	3,870	
	Supplies...		3,870
Dec. 31	Rent expense...	7,500	
	Prepaid rent		7,500
Dec. 31	Unearned sales revenue ($5,250 – $3,600)	1,650	
	Sales revenue...		1,650
Dec. 31	Amortization expense ($39,750/10)...................	3,975	
	Accumulated amortization		3,975
Dec. 31	Salaries expense	1,950	
	Salaries payable		1,950
Dec. 31	Interest expense	900	
	Interest payable..		900

Closing Entries

2006

Dec. 31	Sales revenue	521,700	
	Income summary...		521,700
Dec. 31	Cost of goods sold	368,550	
	Inventory (beginning balance)		90,750
	Purchases..		263,850
	Freight in..		13,950
Dec. 31	Inventory (ending balance)	98,700	
	Purchase discounts	9,000	
	Purchase returns and allowances....................	11,145	
	Cost of goods sold		118,845
Dec. 31	Income summary	443,325	
	Sales discounts...		15,450
	Sales returns and allowances......................		12,300
	Cost of goods sold		
	($368,550 – $118,845)		249,705
	Salaries expense...		126,075
	Rent expense		18,000
	Amortization expense.................................		3,975
	Utilities expense..		8,700
	Supplies expense		3,870
	Interest expense		5,250
Dec. 31	Income summary ($521,700 – $443,325)	78,375	
	Kathy Pittman, capital		78,375
Dec. 31	Kathy Pittman, capital.......................................	72,000	
	Kathy Pittman, withdrawals........................		72,000

Income Summary

Clo.	443,325	Clo.	521,700
Clo.	78,375	Bal.	78,375

KATHY PITTMAN DISTRIBUTING COMPANY
Income Statement
For the Year Ended December 31, 2006

Sales revenue			$521,700
Less: Sales discounts			15,450
Sales returns and allowances			12,300
Net sales revenue			$493,950
Cost of goods sold:			
Beginning inventory		90,750	
Purchases	263,850		
Less: Purchase discounts	9,000		
Purchase returns and allowances	11,145		
Net purchases		243,705	
Freight in		13,950	
Cost of goods available for sale		348,405	
Less: Ending inventory		98,700	
Cost of goods sold			249,705
Gross margin			244,245
Operating expenses:			
Salary expense		126,075	
Rent expense		18,000	
Utilities expense		8,700	
Amortization expense		3,975	
Supplies expense		3,870	160,620
Income from operations			83,625
Other expense:			
Interest expense			5,250
Net income			$ 78,375

KATHY PITTMAN DISTRIBUTING COMPANY
Statement of Owner's Equity
For the Year Ended December 31, 2006

Kathy Pittman, capital, January 1, 2006	$35,520
Add: Net income	78,375
	113,895
Less: Withdrawals	72,000
Kathy Pittman, capital, December 31, 2006	$41,895

KATHY PITTMAN DISTRIBUTING COMPANY
Balance Sheet
December 31, 2006

Assets			Liabilities		
Current assets:			Current liabilities:		
Cash		$ 8,505	Accounts payable		$ 69,510
Accounts receivable		55,650	Salary payable		1,950
Inventory		98,700	Interest payable		900
Supplies		2,025	Unearned sales revenue		3,600
Prepaid rent		1,500	Total current liabilities		75,960
Total current assets		166,380	Long-term note payable		52,500
Capital assets:			Total liabilities		128,460
Furniture and					
fixtures	$39,750		**Owner's Equity**		
Less: Accumulated			Kathy Pittman, capital		41,895
amortization	35,775	3,975			
			Total liabilities and		
Total assets		$170,355	owner's equity		$170,355

$$\text{Inventory turnover} = \frac{\text{Cost of goods sold}}{\text{Average inventory}} = \frac{\$249,705}{(\$90,750 + \$98,700)/2} = 2.6 \text{ times per year}$$

The increase in the rate of inventory turnover from 2.1 to 2.6 times suggests higher profits in 2006 than in 2005.

Supplement Exercises

Exercise 5S-1 *Journalizing purchase and sale transactions under the periodic inventory system* **(Obj. OC)**

Journalize, without explanations, the following transactions of Current Fashions during the month of June 2007:

June   3   Purchased $2,800 of inventory under terms of 2/10 n/eom (end of month) and FOB shipping point.
           7   Returned $1,200 of defective merchandise purchased on June 3.
           9   Paid freight bill of $220 on June 3 purchase.
          10   Sold inventory for $8,800, collecting cash of $1,600. Payment terms on the remainder were 2/15 n/30.
          12   Paid amount owed on credit purchase of June 3, less the discount and the return.
          16   Granted a sales allowance of $3,200 on the June 10 sale.
          23   Received cash from June 10 customer in full settlement of her debt, less the allowance and the discount.

Exercise 5-S2 *Journalizing transactions from a purchase invoice under the periodic inventory system* **(Obj. S2)**

As the proprietor of OK Auto Repair, you receive the invoice on page 288 from a supplier (GST has been disregarded):

Required

1. Record the May 14 purchase on account.
2. The R39 truck tires were ordered by mistake and therefore were returned to ABC. Journalize the return on May 19.
3. Record the May 22 payment of the amount owed.

Exercise 5S-3 *Journalizing purchase transactions under the periodic inventory system* **(Obj. S2)**

On April 30, Bocholo Jewellers purchased inventory of $15,000 on account from Forsyth Fine Gems Ltd., a jewellery importer. Terms were 3/15 net 45. On receiving the goods, Bocholo checked the order and found $2,400 of unsuitable merchandise. Therefore, Bocholo returned $2,400 of merchandise to Forsyth on May 4.

To pay the remaining amount owed, Bocholo had to borrow from the bank. On May 14 Bocholo signed a short-term note payable to the bank in the amount owed to Forsyth and immediately paid the borrowed funds to Forsyth. On June 14, Bocholo paid the bank the net amount of the invoice, which Bocholo had borrowed, plus 1% interest monthly (round to the nearest dollar).

```
                ABC AUTO PARTS WHOLESALE DISTRIBUTORS
                          2600 Victoria Avenue
                       Saskatoon, Saskatchewan S4P 1B3

    Invoice date: May 14, 2006              Payment terms: 2/10 n/30


    Sold to: OK Auto Repair
             4219 Cumberland Avenue
             Prince Albert, SK S7M 1X3
```

Quantity Ordered	Description	Quantity Shipped	Price	Amount
6	P135-X4 Radials.........	6	$83.56	$501.36
8	L912 Belted-bias........	8	92.97	743.76
14	R39 Truck tires.........	10	112.54	1,125.40
	Total..			$2,370.52

```
    Due date:                                  Amount:
      May 24, 2006                               $2,323.11
      May 25 through June 13, 2006               $2,370.52

    Paid:
```

Required

Record the required transactions in the journal of Bocholo Jewellers. Explanations are not required.

Exercise 5S-4   *Journalizing sale transactions under the periodic inventory system*
                    (Obj. S2)

Refer to the business situation in Exercise 5S-3. Journalize the transactions of Forsyth Fine Gems Ltd. Explanations are not required.

Note: Exercise 5-14 (page 255), 5-15 (page 255), and 5-16 (page 255) also pertain to the periodic inventory system.

Supplement Problems

Problem 5S-1   *Accounting for the purchase and sale of inventory under the periodic system   (Obj. S2)*

The following transactions occurred between Johnson & Johnson (www.jnj.com) and Canadian Drug Trading Co. (CDT) during February of the current year.

Feb. 6   J&J sold $25,200 worth of merchandise to CDT on terms of 2/10 n/30, FOB shipping point. J&J prepaid freight charges of $1,000 and included this amount in the invoice total. (J&J's entry to record the freight payment debits Accounts Receivable and credits Cash.)

      10   CDT returned $3,600 of the merchandise purchased on February 6. J&J issued a credit memo for this amount.

      15   CDT paid $12,000 of the invoice amount owed to J&J for the February 6 purchase. This payment included none of the freight charge.

      27   CDT paid the remaining amount owed to J&J for the February 6 purchase.

288   Part One The Basic Structure of Accounting

Required

Journalize these transactions, first on the books of Canadian Drug Trading Co. and second on the books of Johnson & Johnson.

Problem 5S-2 *Journalizing purchase and sale transactions under the periodic inventory system* **(Obj. S2)**

Yoon Distributing Company engaged in the following transactions during May of the current year:

May	3	Purchased office supplies for cash, $2,700.
	7	Purchased inventory on credit terms of 3/10 net eom, $18,000.
	8	Returned half the inventory purchased on May 7. It was not the inventory ordered.
	10	Sold goods for cash, $4,050.
	13	Sold inventory on credit terms of 2/15 n/45 for $35,100, less $5,400 quantity discount offered to customers who purchased in large quantities.
	16	Paid the amount owed on account from the purchase of May 7, less the discount and the return.
	17	Received wrong-sized inventory returned from May 13 sale, $8,100, which is the net amount after the quantity discount.
	18	Purchased inventory of $36,000 on account. Payment terms were 2/10 net 30.
	26	Borrowed $35,280 from the bank to take advantage of the discount offered on the May 18 purchase. Signed a note payable to the bank for this amount.
	26	Paid supplier for goods purchased on May 18, less the discount.
	28	Received cash in full settlement of the account from the customer who purchased inventory on May 13, less the discount and the return.
	29	Purchased inventory for cash, $18,000, less a quantity discount of $3,600, plus freight charges of $1,440.

Required

1. Journalize the preceding transactions on the books of Yoon Distributing Company.

2. The note payable signed on May 26 requires Yoon to pay $270 interest expense. Was the decision to borrow funds to take advantage of the cash discount wise or unwise? Support your answer by comparing the discount to the interest paid.

Problem 5S-3 *Journalizing purchase and sale transactions under the periodic inventory system* **(Obj. S2)**

Kustra Furniture Company engaged in the following transactions during July of the current year:

July	2	Purchased inventory for cash, $2,400, less a quantity discount of $450.
	5	Purchased store supplies on credit terms of net eom, $1,350.
	8	Purchased inventory of $9,000, less a quantity discount of 10%, plus freight charges of $460. Credit terms are 3/15 n/30.
	9	Sold goods for cash, $3,600.
	11	Returned $600 (net amount after the quantity discount) of the inventory purchased on July 8. It was damaged in shipment.
	12	Purchased inventory on credit terms of 3/10 n/30, $10,000.
	14	Sold inventory on credit terms of 2/10 n/30, for $28,800, less a $1,800 quantity discount.
	16	Paid the electricity bill, $800.
	20	Received returned inventory from the July 14 sale, $1,200 (net amount after the quantity discount). Kustra shipped the wrong goods by mistake.
	21	Borrowed the amount owed on the July 8 purchase. Signed a note payable to the bank for $7,735, which takes into account the return of inventory on July 11.
	21	Paid supplier for goods purchased on July 8 less the discount and the return.

July 23 Received $20,580 cash in partial settlement of the account from the customer who purchased inventory on July 14. Granted the customer a 2% discount and credited his account receivable for $21,000.

30 Paid for the store supplies purchased on July 5.

Required

1. Journalize the preceding transactions on the books of Kustra Furniture Company.

2. Compute the amount of the receivable at July 31 from the customer to whom Kustra sold inventory on July 14. What amount of cash discount applies to this receivable at July 31?

Problem 5S-4 *Preparing a merchandiser's accounting work sheet, financial statements, and adjusting and closing entries under the periodic system* **(Obj. S3, S4, S5)**

The year-end trial balance of Bliss Sales Company on the following page pertains to March 31, 2007.

Additional data at March 31, 2007:

a. Accrued interest revenue, $2,060.
b. Insurance expense for the year, $6,000.
c. Furniture has an estimated useful life of six years. It is expected to have no value when it is retired from service.
d. Unearned sales revenue still not earned, $16,400.
e. Accrued salaries, $2,400.
f. Accrued sales commissions, $3,400.
g. Inventory on hand based on inventory count, $266,400.

Required

1. Enter the trial balance on an accounting work sheet, and complete the work sheet for the year ended March 31, 2007.

2. Prepare the company's multi-step income statement and statement of owner's equity for the year ended March 31, 2007. Also prepare its balance sheet at that date. Long-term notes receivable should be reported on the balance sheet between current assets and capital assets in a separate section labelled Investments.

3. Journalize the adjusting and closing entries at March 31, 2007.

4. Post to the W. Bliss, Capital account and to the Income Summary account as an accuracy check on the adjusting and closing process.

BLISS SALES COMPANY
Trial Balance
March 31, 2007

Cash..	$ 15,760	
Notes receivable, current	24,800	
Interest receivable	0	
Inventory...	260,100	
Prepaid insurance	7,200	
Notes receivable, long-term............................	124,000	
Furniture..	12,000	
Accumulated amortization...............................		$ 8,000
Accounts payable...		24,440
Sales commission payable		0
Salaries payable..		0
Unearned sales revenue...................................		19,220
W. Bliss, capital..		345,560
W. Bliss, withdrawals	132,080	
Sales revenue		880,000
Sales discounts	9,600	
Sales returns and allowances	22,600	
Interest revenue..		17,200
Purchases..	466,000	
Purchase discounts		6,200
Purchase returns and allowances		15,200
Freight in	20,000	
Sales commission expense...............................	156,600	
Salary expense...	49,400	
Rent expense..	12,000	
Utilities expense	3,680	
Amortization expense	0	
Insurance expense..	0	
Total...	$1,315,820	$1,315,820

Note: Problems 5-9A (p. 261) and 5-9B (p. 267) also pertain to the periodic inventory system.

CHAPTER

6

Accounting for Merchandise Inventory

CHAPTER OBJECTIVES

After studying this chapter, you should be able to

1 Compute perpetual inventory amounts under the FIFO, LIFO, and moving-weighted-average cost methods

2 Record perpetual inventory transactions

3 Compare the effects of the FIFO, LIFO, and moving-weighted-average cost methods

4 Compute the periodic inventory amounts under the FIFO, LIFO, and weighted-average cost methods

5 Apply the lower-of-cost-or-market rule to inventory

6 Determine the effects of inventory errors

7 Estimate ending inventory by the gross margin method and the retail method

 Media Companion CD-ROM

Visit the Media Companion CD-ROM that comes with this book for extra practice with the new material in Chapter 6.

The Forzani Group Ltd. (www.forzanigroup.com) is the largest sporting goods retailer in Canada. The company, headquartered in Calgary, started with one location in 1974. Since then, the corporation has expanded aggressively throughout Canada by acquiring various regional and national chains of stores. Forzani now operates a number of chains of stores, including SportChek, Sports Experts, and Coast Mountain Sports.

As a retailer, The Forzani Group Ltd. purchases products from various suppliers and resells them to its customers. The purchased products are included in the inventory account until they are sold, at which time they are transferred to cost of goods sold. As you can imagine, inventory is the largest single current asset for most retailers. A retailer must closely monitor its inventory. Too much inventory is costly; too little inventory may result in loss of customers.

The Forzani Group Ltd. understands the importance of inventory, as this excerpt from a recent news story shows:

"Fierce competition in clothing markets will force Canada's largest sporting goods retailer to back away from 'commodity-type' apparel lines and focus on exclusive labels …

'It's competitive as hell out there, there's no doubt about that,' Chief Executive Officer Bob Sartor told analysts.

Forzani said its strategy going forward will involve keeping inventories low and negotiating with its vendors for exclusive products."

Source : The Canadian Press via COMTEX, "Sporting Goods Retailer Forzani Backs Away from Competitive Clothing Market," August 26, 2003, as reported on the website Stockhouse.ca (accessed September 6, 2003).

THIS CHAPTER shows how one of The Forzani Group Ltd.'s chain of stores, SportChek (www.sportchek.ca), and other merchandisers apply various methods to account for their inventory. It picks up where Chapter 5 left off. That chapter shows how merchandisers track inventory. This chapter shows how merchandisers use various methods to compute inventory costs. To do this, they can use the perpetual system, which we introduced in Chapter 5, or the periodic system, which we cover in this chapter.

But first let's review the balance sheet and the income statement, because the financial statements show how merchandise inventory affects a company. Exhibit 6-1 gives the merchandising section of SportChek's parent company, The Forzani Group Ltd.'s balance sheet and income statement. Inventories, cost of goods sold, and gross margin are labelled A, B, and C, respectively, to indicate that, throughout the chapter, we will be computing them using various accounting methods.

The remainder of the chapter explores the various ways a company can determine the amount of

- Ending inventory (A) in Exhibit 6-1.

- Cost of goods sold (B) and gross margin (C) in Exhibit 6-1.

Inventory Costing Methods

As we saw in Chapter 5,

Ending inventory	=	number of units on hand × unit cost
Cost of goods sold	=	number of units sold × unit cost

THE FORZANI GROUP LTD.
Balance Sheet (partial; adapted)
February 2, 2003

Assets:	(thousands)
Current assets:	
Cash	$ 523
Accounts receivable	38,275
Inventories	**A**
Prepaid expenses	11,123

THE FORZANI GROUP LTD.
Income Statement (partial; adapted)
For the Year Ended February 2, 2003

	(thousands)
Net sales	$923,795
Cost of goods sold	**B**
Gross margin	**C**

Companies determine the number of units from perpetual inventory records that are verified by a physical count.

$$\text{Unit cost} = \text{Purchase price} - \text{Purchase discounts} - \text{Quantity discounts}$$
$$+ \text{ Any costs necessary to put the unit in a}$$
$$\text{saleable condition, such as freight in,}$$
$$\text{customs duties, and insurance}$$

Exhibit 6-2 gives assumed inventory data for a line of ski parkas carried by SportChek. In this illustration, SportChek began November with 1 parka on hand. After buying and selling, SportChek had 2 parkas at the end of the month.

Assume that SportChek's cost of each ski parka is $40. In this case,

Ending inventory	=	**Number of units on hand (Exhibit 6-2)**	×	**Unit cost**
	=	2	×	$40
	=	$80		

Cost of goods sold	=	**Number of units sold (Exhibit 6-2)**	×	**Unit cost**
	=	12	×	$40
	=	$480		

What would SportChek's ending inventory and cost of goods sold be if the cost of ski parkas increased from $40 to $45 or $50 during the period?

Companies face price increases like these during periods of inflation. To measure inventory amounts during such periods, the accounting profession has developed several costing methods.

Measuring the cost of inventory is easy when prices are constant. However, in reality, the unit cost often changes. A ski parka that cost SportChek $40 in January

EXHIBIT 6-2

Perpetual Inventory
Record—Quantities Only

Item: Ski Parkas

Date	Quantity Purchased	Quantity Sold	Quantity on Hand
Nov. 1			1
5	6		7
15		4	3
26	7		10
30		8	2
Totals	13	12	2

may cost $45 or $50 later in the year. Suppose SportChek sells 5,000 ski parkas in November. How many of the parkas cost $40? How many cost $45 or $50? To compute ending inventory and cost of goods sold, SportChek must assign a cost to each item. The four costing methods GAAP allow are

1. Specific-unit cost
2. Weighted-average cost
3. First-in, first-out (FIFO) cost
4. Last-in, first-out (LIFO) cost

A company can use any of these methods to account for its inventory.

The **specific-unit-cost method** is also called the **specific identification method**. This method uses the specific cost of each unit of inventory for items that have a distinctive identity. Some businesses deal in items that differ from unit to unit, such as automobiles, jewels, and real estate. For instance, a Chevrolet dealer may have two vehicles—a model with serial number 010 that costs $21,000 and a model with serial number 020 that costs $27,000. If the dealer sells the model with serial number 020, cost of goods sold is $27,000, the cost of the specific unit. Suppose the model with serial number 010 is the only unit left in inventory at the end of the period; ending inventory is $21,000, the dealer's cost of that particular car.

Amazon.ca uses the specific-unit-cost method to account for its inventory. But very few other companies use this method, and so we shift to the more popular inventory costing methods.

The other three methods are very different. First-in, first-out (FIFO) and last-in, first-out (LIFO) are exact opposites, and the weighted-average cost method falls between the extremes of FIFO and LIFO. Exhibit 6-3 illustrates how each method works.

- Under the first-in, first-out (FIFO) method, the cost of goods sold is based on the oldest purchases. This is illustrated by the cost of goods sold coming from the *bottom* of the container.

- Under the last-in, first-out (LIFO) method, the cost of goods sold is based on the most recent purchase. This is illustrated by the cost of goods sold coming from the *top* of the container.

- Under the weighted-average method, the cost of goods sold is based on an average cost for the period. This is illustrated by the cost of goods sold coming from the *middle* of the container.

Now let's see how to compute inventory amounts under the FIFO, LIFO, and weighted-average cost methods. The amounts we compute will complete The Forzani Group Ltd.'s financial statements in Exhibit 6-1. We use the following transaction data for all the illustrations:

Ski Parka		Number of Units	Unit Cost
Nov. 1	Beginning inventory	1	$40
5	Purchase	6	45
15	Sale	4	
26	Purchase	7	50
30	Sale	8	

We begin with inventory costing in a perpetual system.

Inventory Costing in a Perpetual System

First-in, First-out (FIFO) Method

Many companies use the **first-in, first-out (FIFO) method** to account for their inventory. FIFO costing is consistent with the physical movement of inventory for most companies. Under FIFO, the first costs incurred by SportChek each period

EXHIBIT 6-3

Cost Flows for the Three Most Popular Inventory Methods

Last–in, first-out (LIFO) costing

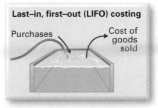

First–in, first-out (FIFO) costing

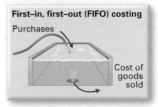

Weighted-average costing

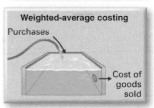

OBJECTIVE 1
Compute perpetual inventory amounts under the FIFO, LIFO, and moving-weighted-average cost methods

are the first costs to be assigned to cost of goods sold. FIFO leaves in ending inventory the last—the most recent—costs incurred during the period. This is illustrated in the FIFO perpetual inventory record in Exhibit 6-4. As we shall see, the various inventory costing methods produce different amounts for ending inventory and cost of goods sold. Let's begin with the first-in, first-out (FIFO) method.

OBJECTIVE 2
Record perpetual inventory transactions

SportChek began November with 1 ski parka that cost $40. After the November 5 purchase, the inventory on hand consists of 7 units (1 at $40 plus 6 at $45). On November 15, SportChek sold 4 units. Under FIFO, the first unit sold is costed at the oldest cost ($40 per unit). The next 3 units sold come from the group that cost $45 per unit. That leaves 3 units in inventory on hand, and those units cost $45 each.

The remainder of the inventory record follows that same pattern.

The FIFO monthly summary at November 30 is

- Cost of goods sold: 12 units that cost a total of $560

- Ending inventory: 2 units that cost a total of $100

If SportChek used the FIFO method, it would measure cost of goods sold and inventory in this manner to prepare its financial statements in Exhibit 6-1.

STOP & THINK

How does the perpetual inventory record in Exhibit 6-4 help SportChek manage its business? How will SportChek use the information in the perpetual inventory record? (To answer this question, consider how you would manage your inventory if you did *not* have any perpetual inventory records.) Explain your reasoning.

Answer:

SportChek uses perpetual inventory records to:
a. Meet customer demand for ski parkas. When a customer orders 10 parkas, SportChek can use the perpetual inventory records to determine whether the goods are available for sale.
b. Prepare financial statements. Each month SportChek gets inventory and cost of goods sold information from its inventory records, and uses these data to prepare monthly financial statements that managers use to operate the business.
c. Keep track of merchandise so that none is lost due to spoilage or theft.

EXHIBIT 6-4

Perpetual Inventory Record—FIFO Cost for SportChek

Ski Parka

Date	Purchases Qty.	Unit Cost	Total Cost	Cost of Goods Sold Qty.	Unit Cost	Total Cost	Inventory on Hand Qty.	Unit Cost	Total Cost
Nov. 1							1	$40	$ 40
5	6	$45	$270				1	40	40
							6	45	270
15				1	$40	$ 40			
				3	45	135	3	45	135
26	7	50	350				3	45	135
							7	50	350
30				3	45	135			
				5	50	250	2	50	100
30	13		$620	12		$560	2		$100

Last-in, First-out (LIFO) Method

Under the **last-in, first-out (LIFO) method**, cost of goods sold comes from the latest—the most recent—purchases. Ending inventory's cost comes from the oldest costs of the period. LIFO costing does not follow the physical movement of goods for most companies. Canada Customs and Revenue Agency does not allow the use of LIFO to determine taxable income because it often results in the highest cost of goods sold and the lowest net income. Although LIFO is acceptable for accounting purposes in Canada, most Canadian companies do not want to incur the cost of maintaining two sets of inventory records. Exhibit 6-5 gives a perpetual inventory record for the LIFO method.

Again, SportChek had 1 ski parka at the beginning of November. After the purchase on November 5, SportChek holds 7 units of inventory (1 at $40 plus 6 at $45). SportChek then sells 4 units on November 15. Under LIFO, the cost of goods sold always comes from the latest purchase. That leaves 3 ski parkas in inventory on November 15 (1 at $40 plus 2 at $45). The purchase of 7 units on November 26 adds $50 parkas to inventory. Then the sale of 8 units on November 30 reduces units in LIFO order. The LIFO monthly summary at November 30 is

- Cost of goods sold: 12 units that cost a total of $575

- Ending inventory: 2 units that cost a total of $85

If SportChek used the LIFO method, it would measure cost of goods sold and inventory in this manner to prepare its financial statements in Exhibit 6-1.

STOP & THINK

Examine Exhibit 6-4 (FIFO) and Exhibit 6-5 (LIFO). Focus on the sale of goods on November 15. Why is cost of goods sold different between first-in, first-out (FIFO) costing and last-in, first-out (LIFO) costing? Explain.

Answer: Cost of goods sold differs dramatically between FIFO costing and LIFO costing. The two methods make opposite assumptions about the timing of when costs leave inventory (an asset) and move into cost of goods sold (an expense).

- Under FIFO, the first costs into inventory are the first costs out to cost of goods sold. Under FIFO, the oldest costs are expensed first.

- Under LIFO, the last costs into inventory are the first costs out to cost of goods sold. The newest costs are expensed first.

FIFO and LIFO are opposites!

EXHIBIT 6-5

Perpetual Inventory Record—LIFO Cost for SportChek

Ski Parka

	Purchases			Cost of Goods Sold			Inventory on Hand		
Date	Qty.	Unit Cost	Total Cost	Qty.	Unit Cost	Total Cost	Qty.	Unit Cost	Total Cost
Nov. 1							1	$ 40	$ 40
5	6	$45	$270				1	40	40
							6	45	270
15				4	$45	$180	1	40	40
							2	45	90
26	7	50	350				1	40	40
							2	45	90
							7	50	350
30				7	50	350			
				1	45	45	1	40	40
							1	45	45
30	13		$620	12		$575	2		$85

Moving-Weighted-Average Method

Suppose SportChek uses the **moving-weighted-average cost method** to account for its inventory of ski parkas. With this method, the business computes a new weighted-average cost per unit after each purchase. Ending inventory and cost of goods sold are then based on the most recent weighted-average cost per unit.

Exhibit 6-6 shows a perpetual inventory record for the moving-weighted-average cost method. We round average unit cost to the nearest cent.

After the purchase on November 5, SportChek computes a new average cost per unit as follows:

	Total cost of inventory on hand		Number of units on hand		Average cost per unit
Nov. 5	$310	÷	7 units	=	$44.29

The goods sold on November 15 are then costed at $44.29 per unit. SportChek also computes a new average cost after the November 26 purchase, which is why it is called a "moving" weighted-average cost.

The moving-weighted-average cost summary at November 30 is

- Cost of goods sold: 12 units that cost a total of $563
- Ending inventory: 2 units that cost a total of $97

SportChek measures cost of goods sold and inventory in this manner to prepare its financial statements in Exhibit 6-1.

Comparing FIFO, LIFO, and Moving-Weighted-Average Cost

OBJECTIVE 3
Compare the effects of the FIFO, LIFO, and moving-weighted-average cost methods

What leads SportChek to select the moving-weighted-average cost method, and Celestica Inc. (www.celestica.com) to use FIFO? The different methods have different benefits.

Exhibit 6-7 summarizes the results for the three inventory methods for SportChek. It shows sales revenue, cost of goods sold, and gross margin for FIFO, LIFO, and moving-weighted-average cost. All data come from Exhibits 6-4, 6-5, and 6-6.

Exhibit 6-7 also shows that FIFO produces the lowest cost of goods sold and the highest gross margin. Net income is also the highest under FIFO when inventory costs are rising. Many companies wish to report high income to attract investors and borrow money on favourable terms. FIFO offers this benefit.

LIFO results in the highest cost of goods sold and the lowest gross margin. This leads to the lowest net income when inventory costs are rising. In Canada, this LIFO costing method is not allowed for income tax purposes, so very few companies use this method.

The moving-weighted-average cost method generates gross margin and net income amounts that fall between the extremes of FIFO and LIFO. Companies that seek a "middle-ground" solution, therefore, use the average cost method for inventory.

EXHIBIT 6-6

Perpetual Inventory Record—Weighted-Average Cost for SportChek

Ski Parka									
	Purchases			**Cost of Goods Sold**			**Inventory on Hand**		
Date	Qty.	Unit Cost	Total Cost	Qty.	Unit Cost	Total Cost	Qty.	Unit Cost	Total Cost
Nov. 1							1	$40.00	$40
5	6	$45	$270				7	44.29	310
15				4	$44.29	$177	3	44.29	133
26	7	50	350				10	48.30	483
30				8	48.30	386	2	48.30	97
30	13		$620	12		$563	2		$97

	FIFO	LIFO	Moving-Weighted-Average
Sales revenue (assumed)	$960	$960	$960
Cost of goods sold	560	575	563
Gross margin	$400	$385	$397

EXHIBIT 6-7

Comparative Results for FIFO, LIFO, and Moving-Weighted-Average Cost

Mid-Chapter Summary Problem
for Your Review

The Watch Shop carries only watches. Assume The Watch Shop began June with an inventory of 10 wristwatches that cost $50 each. The Watch Shop sells those watches for $90 each. During June, The Watch Shop bought and sold inventory as follows:

June	3	Sold 8 units for $90 each.
	16	Purchased 10 units at $55 each.
	23	Sold 8 units for $90 each.

Required

1. Prepare a perpetual inventory record for The Watch Shop under each method.
   - FIFO
   - LIFO
   - Moving-weighted-average cost

2. Journalize all of The Watch Shop's inventory transactions for June for each of these cost methods.

3. Show the computation of gross margin for each method.

4. Which method maximizes net income? Which method allowed in Canada (FIFO or moving-weighted-average) minimizes income taxes?

Solution

Requirement 1

Perpetual inventory records:

FIFO

Wristwatches

	Purchases			Cost of Goods Sold			Inventory on Hand		
Date	Qty.	Unit Cost	Total Cost	Qty.	Unit Cost	Total Cost	Qty.	Unit Cost	Total Cost
June 1							10	$50	$500
3				8	$50	$400	2	50	100
16	10	$55	$550				2	50	100
							10	55	550
23				2	50	100			
				6	55	330	4	55	220
30	10		$550	16		$830	4		$220

LIFO

Wristwatches									
	Purchases			Cost of Goods Sold			Inventory on Hand		
Date	Qty.	Unit Cost	Total Cost	Qty.	Unit Cost	Total Cost	Qty.	Unit Cost	Total Cost
June 1							10	$50	$500
3				8	$50	$400	2	50	100
16	10	$55	$550				2	50	100
							10	55	550
23				8	55	440	2	50	100
							2	55	110
30	10		$550	16		$840	4		$210

Moving-Weighted-Average

Wristwatches									
	Purchases			Cost of Goods Sold			Inventory on Hand		
Date	Qty.	Unit Cost	Total Cost	Qty.	Unit Cost	Total Cost	Qty.	Unit Cost	Total Cost
June 1							10	$50	$500
3				8	$50	$400	2	50	100
16	10	$55	$550				12	54.17	650
23				8	54.17	433	4	54.17	217
30	10		$550	16		$833	4		$217

Requirement 2

Journal Entries:

			FIFO		LIFO		Weighted-Average	
June 3	Accounts Receivable		720		720		720	
	Sales Revenue			720		720		720
3	Cost of Goods Sold		400		400		400	
	Inventory			400		400		400
16	Inventory		550		550		550	
	Accounts Payable			550		550		550
23	Accounts Receivable		720		720		720	
	Sales Revenue			720		720		720
23	Cost of Goods Sold		430*		440**		433***	
	Inventory			430		440		433

* (2 units × $50) + (6 units × $55) = $430
** 8 units × $55 = $440
*** (2 units × $50) + (10 units × $55) = $650; $650 ÷ 12 units = $54.17 per unit
   8 units × $54.17 = $433

Requirement 3

		FIFO	LIFO	Weighted-Average
Sales revenue	($720 + $720)	$1440	$1440	$1440
Cost of goods sold	($400 + $430)	830		
	($400 + $440)		840	
	($400 + $433)			833
Gross margin		$ 610	$ 600	$ 607

Requirement 4

FIFO maximizes net income.
Moving-weighted-average minimizes income taxes.

Inventory Costing in a Periodic System

We described the periodic inventory system briefly in Chapter 5. Accounting is simpler in a periodic system because the company keeps no daily running record of inventory on hand. The only way to determine the ending inventory and cost of goods sold in a periodic system is to count the goods—usually at the end of the year. The periodic system works well for a small business where the owner can control inventory by visual inspection. The Chapter 5 Appendix illustrates how the periodic system works.

Cost of goods sold in a periodic inventory system is computed by the following formula (using assumed amounts for this illustration):

Beginning inventory	
(the inventory on hand at the end of the preceding period)	$ 5,000
Net purchases (often abbreviated as Purchases)	20,000*
Cost of goods available for sale	25,000
Less: Ending inventory	
(the inventory on hand at the end of the current period)	(7,000)
Cost of goods sold	$18,000
*Net purchases is determined as follows (all amounts assumed):	
Purchases	$21,000
Less: Purchase discounts	(2,000)
Purchase returns and allowances	(5,000)
Add: Freight in	6,000
Net purchases	$20,000

The application of the various costing methods (FIFO, LIFO, and weighted-average) in a periodic inventory system follows the pattern illustrated earlier for the perpetual system. To show how the periodic inventory system works, we use the same SportChek data that we used for the perpetual system, as follows:

Ski Parka		Number of Units	Unit Cost
Nov. 1	Beginning inventory	1	$40
5	Purchase	6	$45
15	Sale	4	
26	Purchase	7	$50
30	Sale	8	

First-in, First-out (FIFO) Method

SportChek could use the FIFO costing method with a periodic inventory system. The FIFO computations follow:

Beginning inventory (1 unit at $40)	$ 40
Purchases (6 units at $45 + 7 units at $50)	620
Cost of goods available for sale (14 units)	660
Less: Ending inventory (2 units at $50)	(100)
Cost of goods sold (12 units)	$560

The cost of goods available is always the sum of beginning inventory plus purchases. Under FIFO, the ending inventory comes from the latest—the most recent—purchases, which cost $50 per unit. Ending inventory is therefore $100, and cost of goods sold is $560. These amounts are exactly the same as we saw for the perpetual system in Exhibit 6-4.

There are fewer journal entries in the periodic system because SportChek would record a sale with only a single entry. For example, SportChek's sale of four ski parkas for $80 each is recorded as follows:

Nov. 15 Accounts Receivable (4 × $80)	320	
Sales Revenue		320

There is no cost-of-goods-sold entry in the periodic system.

Last-in, First-out (LIFO) Method

The LIFO method fits well with a periodic inventory system. SportChek's LIFO computations follow:

Beginning inventory (1 unit at $40)	$ 40
Purchases (6 units at $45 + 7 units at $50)	620
Cost of goods available for sale (14 units)	660
Less: Ending inventory (1 unit at $40 + 1 unit at $45)	(85)
Cost of goods sold (12 units)	$575

Under LIFO, the ending inventory comes from the earliest units obtained—the single beginning unit that cost $40 plus one of the units purchased for $45. Ending inventory is therefore $85, and cost of goods sold is $575. These amounts are the same as we saw for the perpetual system in Exhibit 6-5. In some cases, the LIFO amounts can differ between the perpetual and the periodic systems.

Weighted-Average Cost Method

In the **weighted-average cost method**, we compute a single weighted-average cost per unit for the entire period as follows:

Cost of goods available for sale		Number of units available for sale		Average cost per unit for the entire period
$660	÷	14 units	=	$47.14

This average cost per unit is then used to compute the ending inventory and cost of goods sold as follows:

Beginning inventory (1 unit at $40)	$ 40
Purchases (6 units at $45 + 7 units at $50)	620
Cost of goods available for sale (14 units at weighted-average cost of $47.14)	660
Less: Ending inventory (2 units at $47.14)	(94)
Cost of goods sold (12 units at $47.14)	$566

Using the weighted-average cost method, ending inventory and cost of goods sold under the periodic system differ from the amounts in a perpetual system. Why? Because under the perpetual system, a new average cost is computed after each purchase (it is a "moving" weighted-average cost). But the periodic system uses a single average cost that is determined at the end of the period.

Accounting Principles and Inventories

Several accounting principles have special relevance to inventories. Among them are consistency, disclosure, materiality, and accounting conservatism.

Consistency Principle

The **consistency principle** states that businesses should use the same accounting methods and procedures from period to period. Consistency helps investors compare a company's financial statements from one period to the next.

Suppose you are analyzing a company's net income pattern over a two year period. The company switched from LIFO to FIFO during that time. Its net income increased dramatically, but only as a result of the change in inventory method. If you did not know of the change, you might believe that the company's income increased because of improved operations. Therefore, companies must report any changes in the accounting methods they use. Investors need this information in order to make wise decisions about the company.

Disclosure Principle

The **disclosure principle** holds that a company's financial statements should report enough information for outsiders to make knowledgeable decisions about the company. In short, the company should report *relevant*, *reliable*, and *comparable* information about its economic affairs. With respect to inventories, the disclosure principle means disclosing the method or methods used to value inventories. Suppose a banker is comparing two companies—one using LIFO and the other FIFO. The FIFO company reports higher net income, but only because it uses the FIFO inventory method. Without knowledge of the accounting methods the companies are using, the banker could loan money to the wrong business. In addition, different categories of inventory should be disclosed, such as raw materials, work-in-process, and finished goods categories.

Materiality Concept

The **materiality concept** states that a company must perform strictly proper accounting *only* for items that are significant to the business's financial statements. Information is significant—or, in accounting terminology, *material*—when its presentation in the financial statements would cause someone to change a decision. The materiality concept frees accountants from having to report every item in strict accordance with GAAP. For inventory, this means immaterial items can be expensed rather than included in inventory. For example, if freight for an inventory item is immaterial, then it could be expensed immediately, even if the inventory item is sold in a later period.

Accounting Conservatism

Conservatism in accounting means reporting items in the financial statements at amounts that lead to the most cautious immediate results. Conservatism appears in accounting guidelines such as

- "Anticipate no gains, but provide for all probable losses."
- "If in doubt, record an asset at the lowest reasonable amount and a liability at the highest reasonable amount."

- "When there's a question, record an expense rather than an asset."

The goal is for financial statements to report realistic figures. However, do not deliberately understate assets, revenues, and gains, nor deliberately understate liabilities, expenses, and losses.

OBJECTIVE 5
Apply the lower-of-cost-or-market rule to inventory

Lower-of-Cost-or-Market Rule

The **lower-of-cost-or-market rule** (abbreviated as **LCM**) shows accounting conservatism in action. LCM requires that inventory be reported in the financial statements at whichever is lower—the inventory's historical cost or its net realizable value. For inventories, *net realizable value* generally means the expected selling price (that is, the amount the business could get if it sold the inventory less the costs of selling it). If the net realizable value of inventory falls below its historical cost, the business must write down the value of its goods. The business reports ending inventory at its LCM value on the balance sheet.

LEARNING TIP

Note that the matching principle is applied to ending inventory with LCM. The reduction in the value of the inventory is shown in the year the inventory declines in value, *not* in the year the inventory is sold.

Suppose SportChek paid $6,000 for inventory on September 26. By December 31, the inventory can only be sold for $4,800, and the decline in value appears permanent. Net realizable value is below FIFO cost, and the entry to write down the inventory to LCM follows:

Costs of Goods Sold	1,200	
Inventory...		1,200

To write down inventory to net realizable value.
(cost, $6,000 – market, $4,800)

In this case, The Forzani Group Ltd.'s balance sheet would report this inventory as follows:

Balance Sheet

Current assets:
    Inventory, at market $4,800
        (which is lower than $6,000 cost)

Companies often disclose LCM in notes to their financial statements, as shown here for The Forzani Group Ltd., SportChek's parent company:

> NOTE 2: STATEMENT OF SIGNIFICANT ACCOUNTING POLICIES
> *Inventories*
> Inventories are carried at the lower of laid-down cost or net realizable value. Cost is determined using the average cost method.

OBJECTIVE 6
Determine the effects of inventory errors

Effects of Inventory Errors

Businesses count their inventories at the end of the period. As the Period 1 segment of Exhibit 6-8 shows, an error in the ending inventory amount creates errors in the cost of goods sold and gross margin. Compare Period 1's ending inventory, which is overstated, with Period 3's, which is correct. Period 1 *should* look exactly like Period 3.

Recall that one period's ending inventory is the next period's beginning inventory. Thus, the error in ending inventory carries over into the next period. Note the amounts highlighted in Exhibit 6-8.

Because ending inventory is *subtracted* in computing cost of goods sold in one period and the same amount is *added* as beginning inventory the next period, the error cancels out after two periods. The overstatement of cost of goods sold in Period 2 counterbalances the understatement for Period 1. Thus, the total gross margin for the two periods combined is correct. These effects are summarized in Exhibit 6-9.

KEY POINT

Recognize that a dollar change in ending inventory means a dollar change in income. This is one reason auditors examine the ending inventory so carefully. An income statement may be manipulated by altering the amount of ending inventory.

Ethical Issues

No area of accounting has a deeper ethical dimension than inventory. Owners and managers of companies whose profits do not meet expectations are sometimes tempted to "cook the books" to increase reported income. The increase in reported

EXHIBIT 6-8

Inventory Errors: An Example

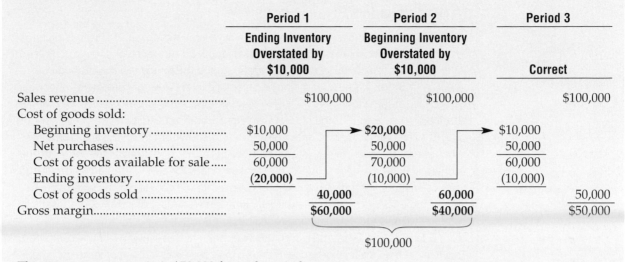

	Period 1	Period 2	Period 3
	Ending Inventory Overstated by $10,000	Beginning Inventory Overstated by $10,000	Correct
Sales revenue	$100,000	$100,000	$100,000
Cost of goods sold:			
Beginning inventory	$10,000	$20,000	$10,000
Net purchases	50,000	50,000	50,000
Cost of goods available for sale	60,000	70,000	60,000
Ending inventory	(20,000)	(10,000)	(10,000)
Cost of goods sold	40,000	60,000	50,000
Gross margin..	$60,000	$40,000	$50,000

$100,000

The correct gross margin is $50,000 for each period.

Source: The authors thank Carl High for this example.

income may lead investors and creditors into thinking the business is more successful than it really is.

There are two main schemes for using inventory to increase reported income. The easier, and the more obvious, is simply to overstate ending inventory. In Exhibit 6-9, we see how an error in ending inventory affects net income. A company can intentionally overstate its ending inventory. Such an error overstates assets and owner's equity, as shown in the accounting equation. The upward-pointing arrows indicate an overstatement—reporting more assets and equity than are actually present:

$$\begin{array}{ccccc} \text{Assets} & = & \text{Liabilities} & + & \text{Owner's Equity} \\ \hline \uparrow & = & 0 & + & \uparrow \end{array}$$

The second way of using inventory to increase reported income involves sales. Sales schemes are more complex than simple inventory overstatements. Datapoint Corporation and MiniScribe, both computer-related concerns, were charged with creating fictitious sales to boost reported profits.

Datapoint is alleged to have hired drivers to transport its inventory around San Antonio so that the goods could *not* be physically counted. Datapoint's plan seemed to be that excluding goods from ending inventory would mean they had been sold. This scheme broke down when the trucks returned the goods to the warehouse. What would you think of a company with $10 million in sales if $4 million worth of the goods were returned by consumers?

EXHIBIT 6-9

Effects of Inventory Errors

	Period 1		Period 2	
Inventory Error	**Cost of Goods Sold**	**Gross Margin and Net Income**	**Cost of Goods Sold**	**Gross Margin and Net Income**
Period 1 ending inventory *overstated*	Understated	Overstated	Overstated	Understated
Period 1 ending inventory *understated*	Overstated	Understated	Understated	Overstated

MiniScribe is alleged to have "cooked its books" by shipping boxes of bricks to its distributors right before year end. The distributors refused to accept the goods and returned them to MiniScribe—but in the next accounting period. The scheme affected MiniScribe's reported year-end assets and equity: sales and net income were overstated and inventories were understated by millions of dollars—but only temporarily. The offsetting effect of the scheme occurred in the next accounting period when MiniScribe had to record the sales returns. In virtually every area, accounting imposes a discipline that brings out the facts sooner or later.

OBJECTIVE 7
Estimate ending inventory by the gross margin method and the retail method

Estimating Inventory

Often a business must *estimate* the value of its inventory. Suppose the company suffers a fire loss and must estimate the value of the inventory destroyed.

The **gross margin method** (also known as the **gross profit method**) provides a way to estimate inventory using the cost of goods sold model (amounts are assumed for illustration):

Beginning inventory	$ 20
+ Purchases	100
= Cost of goods available for sale	120
– **Ending inventory**	(40)
= **Cost of goods sold**	$ 80

Beginning inventory		$14,000
Purchases		66,000
Cost of goods available for sale		80,000
Estimate cost of goods sold:		
Sales revenue	$100,000	
Less: Estimated gross margin of 40%	(40,000)	
Estimated cost of goods sold		(60,000)
Estimated cost of *ending inventory*		$20,000

Rearranging *ending inventory* and *cost of goods sold* makes the model useful for estimating ending inventory (amounts are assumed for illustration):

Beginning inventory	$ 20
+ Purchases	100
= Cost of goods available for sale	120
− **Cost of goods sold**	(80)
= **Ending inventory**	$ 40

Suppose a fire destroys your inventory. To collect insurance, you must estimate the cost of the ending inventory. Using your normal *gross margin percent* (that is, gross margin divided by net sales revenue), you can estimate cost of goods sold. Then subtract cost of goods sold from cost of goods available to estimate ending inventory. Exhibit 6-10 illustrates the gross margin method.

STOP & THINK

Beginning inventory is $70,000, net purchases total $298,000, and net sales are $480,000. With a normal gross margin of 40% of sales, how much is ending inventory?

Answer:

Beginning inventory		$ 70,000
Purchases		298,000
Cost of goods available for sale		368,000
Estimate of cost of goods sold:		
Sales revenue	$ 480,000	
Less: Estimated gross margin of 40%	(192,000)	
Estimated cost of goods sold		(288,000)
Estimated cost of *ending inventory*		$ 80,000

Retail Method The **retail method** of estimating the cost of ending inventory is often used by retail establishments that use the periodic system. This is because it is often easier for retail establishments to calculate the selling price, or retail price, of a wide range of items rather than to look at all the individual invoices to find the costs of each of those items.

Like the gross margin method, the retail method is based on the familiar cost of goods sold model, rearranged to calculate ending inventory:

Beginning inventory
+ Net purchases
= Cost of goods available for sale
− Cost of goods sold
= Ending inventory

EXHIBIT 6-11

Retail Method of Estimating Inventory (amounts assumed)

	Cost	Selling Price
Beginning inventory	$151,200	$216,000
Purchases	504,000	720,000
Goods available for sale	655,200	936,000
Net sales, at selling price (retail)		696,000
Ending inventory, at selling price (retail)		$240,000
Ending inventory, at cost ($240,000 × *70%)	$168,000	

*Retail ratio = ($655,200 ÷ 936,000) × 100 = 70%

REAL WORLD EXAMPLE

The gross margin and retail methods are also used to estimate inventory for interim periods when it is impractical to take a physical inventory.

However, to use the retail method, a business must know both the total cost and the total selling price of its opening inventory, as well as both the total cost and total selling price of its net purchases. Total selling price is determined by counting each item of inventory and multiplying it by the item's retail selling price (the price given on the price tag). By summing the costs and selling prices of beginning inventory and net purchases, the business knows the cost and retail selling price of the goods it has available for sale.

The business can calculate the selling price of its sales because this is the sum of the amounts recorded on the cash register when sales are made. The total of sales at retail is deducted from the total selling price of the goods available for sale to give the total selling price of ending inventory. To convert ending inventory at selling price to ending inventory at cost, the business multiplies the ending inventory at selling price by the *retail ratio*. The retail ratio is the ratio of cost of goods available for sale at *cost* to the cost of goods available for sale at *selling price*. It is usually expressed as a percent. Exhibit 6-11 illustrates the retail method.

The retail method can be used to estimate inventory at any point in time, and it is acceptable to use the retail method to calculate year-end inventory cost for financial statement and income tax purposes, although an inventory count must be done at least once per year.

The Decision Guidelines feature summarizes some basic decision guidelines that are helpful in managing a business's inventory operations.

DECISION GUIDELINES **Guidelines for Inventory Management**

Decision	Guidelines	System or Method
Which inventory system to use?	• Expensive merchandise • Cannot control inventory by visual inspection	→ Perpetual system
	• Can control inventory by visual inspection	→ Periodic system
Which costing method to use?	• Unique inventory items	→ Specific-unit cost
	• The most current cost of ending inventory • Maximizes reported income when costs are rising	→ FIFO
	• The most current measure of cost of goods sold and net income	→ LIFO
	• Middle-of-the-road approach for income tax and net income	→ Weighted-average
How to estimate the cost of ending inventory?	• The cost-of-goods-sold model provides the framework	Gross margin (gross profit) method
	• Standard mark-ups from cost price to selling price are used for all inventory items	→ Retail method

Suppose a division of Total Computer Sales that handles computer components has these inventory records for January 2006.

Date	Item	Quantity	Unit Cost	Sale Price
Jan. 1	Beginning inventory......................	100 units	$ 8	
6	Purchase	60 units	9	
13	Sale	70 units		$20
21	Purchase	150 units	9	
24	Sale	210 units		22
27	Purchase	90 units	10	
30	Sale	30 units		25

Company accounting records reveal that operating expenses for January were $1,900.

Required

Prepare the January income statement, showing amounts for FIFO, LIFO, and weighted-average cost. Label the bottom line "Operating income." (Round the average cost per unit to three decimal places and all other figures to whole-dollar amounts.) Show your computations, and use the periodic inventory model from page 301 to compute cost of goods sold.

Solution

TOTAL COMPUTER SALES
Income Statement for Computer Components
For the Month Ended January 31, 2006

	FIFO	LIFO	Weighted-Average
Sales revenue	$6,770	$6,770	$6,770
Cost of goods sold:			
Beginning inventory...	$ 800	$ 800	$ 800
Net purchases...	2,790	2,790	2,790
Cost of goods available for sale	3,590	3,590	3,590
Ending inventory...	(900)	(720)	(808)
Cost of goods sold	2,690	2,870	2,782
Gross margin	4,080	3,900	3,988
Operating expenses	1,900	1,900	1,900
Operating income	$2,180	$2,000	$2,088

Computations
Sales revenue: $(70 \times \$20) + (210 \times \$22) + (30 \times \$25) =$ $6,770
Beginning inventory: $100 \times \$8$ = $800
Purchases: $(60 \times \$9) + (150 \times \$9) + (90 \times \$10)$ = $2,790
Ending inventory
  FIFO $90^* \times \$10$ = $900
  LIFO $90 \times \$8$ = $720
  Average cost: $90 \times \$8.975^{**}$ = $808 (rounded from $807.75)

---

* Number of units in ending inventory = $100 + 60 - 70 + 150 - 210 + 90 - 30 = 90$.
** $3,590/400$ units[†] = $8.975 per unit.
† Number of units available = $100 + 60 + 150 + 90 = 400$.

Summary

1. **Compute perpetual inventory amounts under the FIFO, LIFO, and moving-weighted-average cost methods.** In a perpetual inventory system, the business keeps a continuous record for each inventory item to show the inventory on hand at all times. Businesses multiply the quantity of inventory items by their unit cost to determine inventory cost. To compute ending inventory and cost of goods sold, a cost is assigned to each inventory item. Three methods of assigning costs to similar items are: *first-in, first-out (FIFO), last-in, first-out (LIFO),* and *moving-weighted-average.* FIFO reports ending inventory at the most current cost. LIFO reports cost of goods sold at the most current cost. Moving-weighted-average falls in the middle.

2. **Record perpetual inventory transactions.** Since the perpetual inventory system keeps a continuous record for each inventory item, inventory is debited immediately at cost when an item is purchased and inventory is credited immediately at cost when an item is sold. A physical count of inventory at the end of the year or the accounting period is needed to ensure the accounting records are accurate.

3. **Compare the effects of the FIFO, LIFO, and moving-weighted-average cost methods.** FIFO reports ending inventory at the most current cost. LIFO reports cost of goods sold at the most current cost. Moving-weighted-average reports ending inventory and cost of goods sold at amounts between those of FIFO and LIFO. When prices are rising, LIFO produces the highest cost of goods sold and the lowest income; however, LIFO may not be used in Canada for income tax purposes. When prices are rising, FIFO produces the highest income. The moving-weighted-average method produces an income amount between the extremes of FIFO and LIFO.

4. **Compute the periodic inventory amounts under the FIFO, LIFO, and weighted-average cost methods.** In a periodic inventory system, the business does not keep an up-to-date balance for ending inventory. Instead, at the end of the period, the business counts the inventory on hand and updates its records. To compute ending inventory and cost of goods sold, a cost is assigned to each inventory item. Three methods of assigning costs to similar items are: *first-in, first-out (FIFO), last-in, first-out (LIFO),* and *weighted-average.* FIFO produces identical balances for ending inventory and cost of goods sold under the periodic and perpetual inventory systems, but LIFO and weighted-average produce different results under the periodic and perpetual systems.

5. **Apply the lower-of-cost-or-market rule to inventory.** The *lower-of-cost-or-market (LCM) rule*—an example of accounting *conservatism*—requires that businesses report inventory on the balance sheet at the lower of its cost or current replacement or net realizable value. Companies disclose their definition of "market" for purposes of applying LCM in notes to their financial statements.

6. **Determine the effects of inventory errors.** Although inventory overstatements in one period are counterbalanced by inventory understatements in the next period, effective decision making depends on accurate inventory information.

7. **Estimate ending inventory by the gross margin method and the retail method.** The *gross margin method* and the *retail method* are techniques for estimating the cost of ending inventory. They are useful for preparing interim financial statements and for estimating the cost of inventory destroyed by fire or other disasters.

Self-Study Questions

Test your understanding of the chapter by marking the correct answer to each of the following questions:

1. Suppose a Canadian chain store made sales of $9,363 million and ended the year with inventories totalling $966 million. Cost of goods sold was $6,110 million. Total operating expenses were $2,734 million. How much net income did the chain store earn for the year? (*p. 294*)
   a. $519 million   c. $5,663 million
   b. $3,253 million   d. $6,629 million

2. Which inventory costing method assigns to ending inventory the latest—the most recent—costs incurred during the period? (*p. 296*)
   a. Specific unit cost
   b. First-in, first-out (FIFO)
   c. Last-in, first-out (LIFO)
   d. Average cost

3. Assume Amazon.ca began June with 10 units of inventory that cost a total of $190. During June, Amazon purchased and sold goods as follows:

June 8 Purchase 30 units at $20
14 Sale 25 units at $40
22 Purchase 20 units at $22
27 Sale 30 units at $40

Assume Amazon uses the FIFO inventory method and the perpetual inventory system. How much is Amazon's cost of goods sold for the transaction on June 14? (*pp. 295–296*)

a. $790
b. $1,000
c. $500
d. $490

4. After the purchase on June 22 in question 3, what is Amazon's cost of the inventory on hand? (*p. 296*)

a. $300
b. $440
c. $740
d. $720

5. Amazon's journal entry (entries) on June 14 is (are) (*p. 296*)

a. Accounts Receivable 490
       Inventory 490
b. Accounts Receivable 1,000
       Sales Revenue 1,000
c. Cost of Goods Sold 490
       Inventory 490
d. Both b and c

6. Which inventory costing method results in the lowest net income during a period of rising inventory costs? (*p. 298*)

a. Specific unit cost
b. First-in, first out (FIFO)
c. Last-in, first-out (LIFO)
d. Average cost

7. Suppose Amazon.ca used the weighted-average cost method and the periodic inventory system. Use the Amazon data in question 3 to compute the cost of the company's inventory on hand at

June 30. Round unit cost to the nearest cent. (*p. 302*)

a. $102.50
b. $105.20
c. $205.00
d. $210.40

8. Which of the following is most closely tied to accounting conservatism? (*p. 304*)

a. Consistency principle
b. Disclosure principle
c. Materiality concept
d. Lower-of-cost-or-market rule.

9. At December 31, 2005, McAdam Company overstated ending inventory by $40,000. How does this error affect cost of goods sold and net income for 2005? (*p. 304*)

a. Overstates cost of goods sold, understates income
b. Understates cost of goods sold, overstates net income
c. Overstates both cost of goods sold and net income
d. Leaves both cost of goods sold and net income correct because the errors cancel each other

10. Suppose a SportChek location suffered a fire loss and needs to estimate the cost of the goods destroyed. Beginning inventory was $100,000, purchases totalled $600,000, and sales came to $1,000,000. SportChek's normal gross margin percentage is 45%. Use the gross margin method to estimate the cost of the inventory lost in the fire. (*p. 307*)

a. $150,000
b. $250,000
c. $300,000
d. $350,000

Answers to the Self-Study Questions follow the Similar Accounting Terms.

Accounting Vocabulary

Conservatism (*p. 303*)
Consistency principle (*p. 303*)
Disclosure principle (*p. 303*)
First-in, first-out (FIFO) inventory cost method (*p. 295*)
Gross margin method (*p. 306*)
Gross profit method (*p. 306*)
Last-in, first-out (LIFO) inventory cost method (*p. 297*)

Lower-of-cost-or-market (LCM) rule (*p. 304*)
Materiality concept (*p. 303*)
Moving-weighted-average cost method (*p. 298*)
Retail method (*p. 307*)
Specific identification method (*p. 295*)
Specific-unit-cost method (*p. 295*)
Weighted-average cost method (*p. 302*)

Similar Accounting Terms

Cost of goods sold	Cost of sales
Gross margin method	Gross profit method
Weighted-average cost method	Average-cost method

Assignment Material

Questions

1. Why is merchandise inventory so important to a retailer or wholesaler?

2. Suppose your business deals in expensive jewellery. Which inventory system should you use to achieve good internal control over the inventory? If your business is a hardware store that sells low-cost goods, which inventory system would you be likely to use? Why would you choose this system?

3. Identify the accounts debited and credited in the standard purchase and sale entries under (a) the perpetual inventory system, and (b) the periodic inventory system.

4. What is the role of the physical count of inventory in (a) the perpetual inventory system and (b) the periodic inventory system?

5. If beginning inventory is $10,000, purchases total $85,000, and ending inventory is $12,700, how much is cost of goods sold?

6. If beginning inventory is $32,000, purchases total $119,000, and cost of goods sold is $127,000, how much is ending inventory?

7. What two items determine the cost of ending inventory?

8. Briefly describe the four generally accepted inventory cost methods. During a period of rising prices, which method produces the highest reported income? Which produces the lowest reported income?

9. Which inventory costing method produces the ending inventory valued at the most current cost? Which method produces the cost-of-goods-sold amount valued at the most current cost?

10. Why is LIFO the most popular method in the United States? Why is it so little used in Canada? Do these reasons accord with the notion that the

inventory costing method should produce the most accurate data on the income statement?

11. Which inventory costing method produces the most accurate data on the balance sheet? Why?

12 How does the consistency principle affect accounting for inventory?

13. Briefly describe the influence that the concept of conservatism has on accounting for inventory.

14. Manley Company's inventory has a cost of $48,000 at the end of the year, and the net realizable value of the inventory is $51,000. At which amount should the company report the inventory on its balance sheet? Suppose the net relizable value of the inventory is $45,000 instead of $51,000. At which amount should Manley Company report the inventory? What rule governs your answers to these questions?

15. Gabriel Products accidentally overstated its ending inventory by $10,000 at the end of Period 1. Is gross margin of Period 1 overstated or understated? Is gross margin of Period 2 overstated, understated, or unaffected by the Period 1 error? Is total gross margin for the two periods overstated, understated, or correct? Give the reason for your answers.

16. Identify two important methods of estimating inventory amounts.

17. A fire destroyed the inventory of Olivera Supplies, but the accounting records were saved. The beginning inventory was $22,000, purchases for the period were $71,000, and sales were $140,000. Olivera's customary gross margin is 45 percent of sales. Use the gross margin method to estimate the cost of the inventory destroyed by the fire.

18. The retail method of estimating inventory seems simple but in reality can be difficult to apply. Why is this so?

Exercises

Exercise 6-1 *Measuring ending inventory and cost of goods sold in a perpetual system—FIFO (Obj. 1)*

Picker Paradise carries a large inventory of guitars and other musical instruments. Picker uses the FIFO method and a perpetual inventory system. Company records indicate the following for a particular line of Honeydew guitars:

Date	Item	Quantity	Unit Cost
May 1	Balance	5	$70
6	Sale...	3	
8	Purchase...	10	80
17	Sale...	4	
30	Sale...	5	

Required

Prepare a perpetual inventory record for the guitars. Then determine the amounts Picker should report for ending inventory and cost of goods sold by the FIFO method.

Exercise 6-2 *Recording perpetual inventory transactions (Obj. 2)*

After preparing the FIFO perpetual inventory record in Exercise 6-1, journalize Picker Paradise's May 8 purchase of inventory on account and cash sale on May 17 (sale price of each guitar was $140).

Exercise 6-3 *Measuring ending inventory and cost of goods sold in a perpetual system—LIFO (Obj. 1)*

Refer to the Picker Paradise inventory data in Exercise 6-1. Assume that Picker Paradise uses the LIFO cost method. Prepare Picker's perpetual inventory record for the guitars on the LIFO basis. Then identify the cost of ending inventory and cost of goods sold for the month.

Exercise 6-4 *Applying the average-cost method in a perpetual inventory system (Obj. 1)*

Refer to the Picker Paradise inventory data in Exercise 6-1. Assume that Picker uses the moving-weighted-average cost method. Prepare Picker's perpetual inventory record for the guitars on the moving-weighted-average cost basis. Round average cost per unit to the nearest cent and all other amounts to the nearest dollar.

Exercise 6-5 *Recording perpetual inventory transactions (Obj. 2)*

Cyclone's Sports Shop's accounting records yield the following data for the year ended December 31, 2005 (amounts in thousands):

Inventory, January 1, 2005......................................	$ 78
Purchases of inventory (on account)	630
Sales of inventory—80 percent on account;	
20 percent for cash (cost $564)...........................	880
Inventory at FIFO cost December 31, 2005..........	?

Required

1. Journalize Cyclone's Sports Shop's inventory transactions for the year in the perpetual system. Show all amounts in thousands.
2. Report ending inventory, sales, cost of goods sold, and gross margin on the appropriate financial statement (amounts in thousands). Show the computation of cost of goods sold in the periodic system.

Exercise 6-6 Applying the moving-weighted-average, FIFO, and LIFO methods in a perpetual inventory system *(Obj. 2)*

Beatty Office Products markets the ink used in laser printers. Beatty started the year with 100 containers of ink (weighted-average cost of $9.14 each; FIFO cost of $9 each; LIFO cost of $8 each). During the year, Beatty purchased 800 containers of ink at $12 and sold 700 units for $22 each, with all transactions on account. Beatty paid operating expenses throughout the year, a total of $4,700.

Journalize Beatty's purchases, sales, and operating expense transactions under the following format. Beatty uses the perpetual inventory system to account for laser-printer ink.

	DEBIT/CREDIT AMOUNTS		
Accounts	Moving-Weighted-Average*	FIFO	LIFO

*Round moving-weighted-average unit cost to the nearest cent.

Media Companion CD-ROM

Exercise 6-7 Computing ending inventory by applying four inventory costing methods in a periodic inventory system *(Obj. 4)*

Klein Electrical's inventory records for industrial switches indicate the following at November 30, 2006:

Nov.	1	Beginning inventory	7 units at	$80
	8	Purchase	4 units at	$80
	15	Purchase	11 units at	$85
	26	Purchase	5 units at	$88

The physical count of inventory at November 30, 2006 indicates that six units are on hand, and the company owns them.

Required

Compute ending inventory and cost of goods sold using each of the following methods, assuming the periodic inventory system:

1. Specific unit cost, assuming three $85 units and three $80 units are on hand
2. Weighted-average cost
3. First-in, first-out
4. Last-in, first-out

Exercise 6-8 Determining amounts for the income statement: periodic system *(Obj. 4)*

1. Supply the missing income statement amounts for each of the following companies for the year ended December 31, 2006:

Company	Net Sales	Beginning Inventory	Net Purchases	Ending Inventory	Cost of Goods Sold	Gross Margin
Arc Co.	$46,400	$ 6,250	$31,350	$ 9,700	(a)	$18,000
Bell Co.	(b)	13,725	46,500	(c)	$47,050	25,600
Court Co.	47,000	(d)	27,450	11,300	29,700	(e)
Dormer Co.	50,700	5,350	(f)	4,100	(g)	23,550

2. Prepare the income statement for Dormer Co., which uses the periodic inventory system. Dormer's operating expenses for the year were $16,050.

Exercise 6-9 Identifying income and other effects of the inventory methods *(Obj. 3)*

This exercise tests your understanding of the four inventory methods. In the space provided, write the name of the inventory method that best fits the description. Assume that the cost of inventory is rising.

_____ a. Enables a company to keep reported income from dropping lower by liquidating older layers of inventory.

_____ b. Matches the most current cost of goods sold against sales revenue.

_____ c. Results in an old measure of the cost of ending inventory.

_____ d. Results in a cost of ending inventory that is close to the current cost of replacing the inventory.

_____ e. Maximizes reported income.

_____ f. Enables a company to buy high-cost inventory at year end and thereby decrease reported income.

_____ g. Used to account for automobiles, jewellery, and art objects.

_____ h. Provides a middle-ground measure of ending inventory and cost of goods sold.

Exercise 6-10 *Applying the lower-of-cost-or-market rule to inventories: perpetual system (Obj. 1, 5)*

King Garden Supplies, which uses a perpetual inventory system, has these account balances at December 31, 2005, prior to releasing the financial statements for the year:

Inventory	Cost of Goods Sold	Sales Revenue
Beg. bal. 24,978		
End. bal. 42,080	Bal. 236,006	Bal. 450,000

A year ago, when King Garden Supplies prepared its 2004 financial statements, the net realizable value of ending inventory was $26,102. Jason King, the owner, has determined that the net realizable value of the December 31, 2005 ending inventory is $35,974.

Required

Prepare King Garden Supplies' 2005 income statement through gross margin to show how King would apply the lower-of-cost-or-market rule to its inventories. Include a complete heading for the statement.

Exercise 6-11 *Applying the lower-of-cost-or-market rule to inventories: periodic system (Obj. 4, 5)*

Media Companion CD-ROM

Bram Tool Company's income statement for the month ended August 31, 2006, reported the following data:

Income Statement

Sales revenue...		$133,500
Cost of goods sold		
Beginning inventory..	$ 25,800	
Net purchases...	101,550	
Cost of goods available for sale.....................................	127,350	
Ending inventory...	35,700	
Cost of goods sold		91,650
Gross margin..		$ 41,850

Before the financial statements were released, it was discovered that the current net realizable value of ending inventory was $26,700. Adjust the preceding income statement to apply the lower-of-cost-or-market rule to Bram Tool Company's inventory. Also, show the relevant portion of Bram Tool Company's balance sheet. The net realizable value of the beginning inventory was $27,900.

Exercise 6-12 *Correcting an inventory error* *(Obj. 6)*

Mackie Marine Supply reported the comparative income statement for the years ended September 30, 2005 and 2004 shown below.

MACKIE MARINE SUPPLY
Income Statements
For the Years Ended September 30, 2005 and 2004

	2005		2004	
Sales revenue		$219,680		$194,720
Cost of goods sold:				
Beginning inventory	$ 22,400		$ 20,480	
Net purchases	121,600		104,000	
Cost of goods available	144,000		124,480	
Ending inventory	31,360		22,400	
Cost of goods sold		112,640		102,080
Gross margin		107,040		92,640
Operating expenses		48,480		41,760
Net income before taxes............		$ 58,560		$ 50,880

During 2005, accountants for the company discovered that ending 2004 inventory was overstated by $4,800. Prepare the corrected comparative income statement for the two-year period, complete with a heading for the statement. What was the effect of the error on net income for the two years combined? Explain your answer.

Exercise 6-13 *Assessing the effect of an inventory error on two years' statements* *(Obj. 6)*

Janet Crawford, accountant of Future Electronics Ltd., learned that Future Electronics' $8 million cost of inventory at the end of last year was overstated by $2.4 million. She notified the company president of the accounting error and the need to alert the company's lenders that last year's reported net income was incorrect. Brad May, president of Future Electronics Ltd., explained to Crawford that there is no need to report the error to lenders because the error will counterbalance this year. This year's error will affect this year's net income in the opposite direction of last year's error. Even with no correction, May reasons, net income for both years combined will be the same whether or not Future Electronics Ltd. corrects its errors.

Required

1. Was last year's reported net income of $12.0 million overstated, understated, or correct? What was the correct amount of net income last year?

2. Is this year's net income of $13.6 million overstated, understated, or correct? What is the correct amount of net income for the current year?

3. Whose perspective is better, Crawford's or May's? Give your reason. Consider the trend of reported net income both without the correction and with the correction.

Exercise 6-14 *Ethical implications of inventory actions* *(Obj. 3, 5, 6)*

Determine whether each of the following actions in buying, selling, and accounting for inventories is ethical or unethical. Give your reason for each answer.

1. Buckeye Corporation consciously overstated purchases to produce a high figure for cost of goods sold (low amount of net income). The real reason was to decrease the company's income tax payments to the government.

2. In applying the lower-of-cost-or-market rule to inventories, Riverwind

Industries recorded an excessively low market value for ending inventory. This allowed the company to pay no income tax for the year.

3. Fast Photo Film purchased lots of inventory shortly before year end to increase the LIFO cost of goods sold and decrease reported income for the year.

4. Bonnis Electrical Products delayed the purchase of inventory until after December 31, 2005, in order to keep 2005's cost of goods sold from growing too large. The delay in purchasing inventory helped net income of 2005 to reach the level of profit demanded by the company's investors.

5. Highland Sales Company deliberately overstated ending inventory in order to report higher profits (net income).

Exercise 6-15   *Estimating inventory by the gross margin method*   *(Obj. 7)*

Bloor Bike Rack began April with inventory of $70,000. The business made net purchases of $75,200 and had net sales of $120,000 before a fire destroyed the company's inventory. For the past several years, Bloor Bike Rack's gross margin on sales has been 45 percent. Estimate the cost of the inventory destroyed by the fire. Identify another reason owners and managers use the gross margin method to estimate inventory on a regular basis.

Exercise 6-16   *Estimating inventory by the retail method*   *(Obj. 7)*

Stephie's Fine Clothes has three lines of women's sportswear: Teenage, Young Woman, and Mature. The selling price of each item is double its cost price. On May 18, 2006, Stephie's Fine Clothes had a fire that destroyed all the inventory. Sales for the period January 1 to May 18 were: Teenage, $220,000; Young Woman, $270,000; and Mature, $360,000. Inventory at January 1, 2006, was: Teenage, $45,000; Young Woman, $60,000; and Mature, $75,000. Purchases made from January 1 to May 18, at cost, were: Teenage, $100,000; Young Woman, $100,000; and Mature, $150,000.

Required

Use the retail method to calculate the cost of the inventory lost in the fire.

Challenge Exercises

Exercise 6-17   *Inventory policy decisions*   *(Obj. 3)*

For each of the following situations, identify the inventory method that you are using or would prefer to use, or, given the use of a particular method, state the strategy that you would follow to accomplish your goal.

a. Inventory costs are increasing. Your business uses LIFO and is having an unexpectedly good year. It is near year end, and you need to keep net income from increasing too much.

b. Inventory costs have been stable for several years, and you expect costs to remain stable for the indefinite future. (Give your reason for your choice of method.)

c. Suppliers of your inventory are threatening a labour strike, and it may be difficult for your business to obtain inventory.

d. Inventory costs are decreasing, and you want to maximize income.

e. Company management prefers a middle-of-the-road inventory policy that avoids extremes.

f. Your inventory turns over *very* rapidly, and the business uses a perpetual inventory system. Inventory costs are increasing, and the business prefers to report high income.

Exercise 6-18 *Evaluating a company's profitability* **(Obj. 3)**

Canada Glass Products Ltd. is a leading provider of bottles for the brewing industry. Suppose the company recently reported these figures.

CANADA GLASS PRODUCTS LTD.
Income Statement
For the Years Ended July 31, 2005 and 2004

	2005	2004
Sales...	$106,115,984	$81,685,715
Cost of sales	76,424,328	60,981,847
Gross Margin	29,691,656	20,703,868
Cost and expenses		
Selling, general and administrative	21,801,737	16,576,484
Amortization...	2,169,196	918,693
Restructuring charges.............................	7,096,774	—
	31,067,707	17,495,177
Operating income (loss)......................................	(1,376,051)	3,208,691
Other items (summarized)	(635,153)	(1,315,490)
Net income (loss)	$ (2,011,204)	$ 1,893,201

Required

Evaluate Canada Glass's operations during 2005 in comparison with 2004. Consider sales, gross margin, operating income, and net income. In the annual report, Canada Glass's management describes the restructuring charges in 2005 as a one-time event that is not expected to recur. How does this additional information affect your evaluation?

Beyond the Numbers

Assessing the impact of the inventory costing method on the financial statements **(Obj. 3, 5)**

The inventory costing method chosen by a company can affect the financial statements and thus the decisions of the users of those statements.

Required

1. A leading accounting researcher stated that one inventory costing method reports the most recent costs in the income statement, while another method reports the most recent costs in the balance sheet. In this person's opinion, this results in one or the other of the statements being "inaccurate" when prices are rising. What did the researcher mean?

2. Conservatism is an accepted accounting concept. Would you want management to be conservative in accounting for inventory if you were (a) a shareholder, and (b) a prospective shareholder? Give your reason.

3. Dunn's Cycle Shoppe follows conservative accounting and writes the value of its inventory of bicycles down to market, which has declined below cost. The following year, an unexpected cycling craze results in a demand for bicycles that far exceeds supply, and the market price increases well above the previous cost. What effect will conservatism have on the income of Dunn's Cycle Shoppe over the two years?

Ethical Issue

During 2005, Rooy Electronics changed to the LIFO method of accounting for inventory. Suppose that during 2006, Rooy Electronics changes back to the FIFO method, and in the following year switches back to LIFO again.

Required

1. What would you think of a company's ethics if it changed accounting methods every year?
2. What accounting principle would changing methods every year violate?
3. Who can be harmed when a company changes its accounting methods too often? How?

Problems (Group A)

Problem 6-1A *Accounting for inventory in a perpetual system—FIFO* **(Obj. 1, 2)**

Pier 1 Imports (www.pier1.com) operates almost 1,000 stores around the world. Assume you are dealing with a Pier 1 store in Vancouver. Assume the store began with an inventory of 50 chairs that cost a total of $1,500. The store purchased and sold merchandise on account as follows:

Purchase 1	60 chairs at $35
Sale 1	100 chairs at $60
Purchase 2	80 chairs at $40
Sale 2	70 chairs at $70

Assume that Pier 1 uses the FIFO cost method. Cash payments on account totalled $5,100. Operating expenses were $2,400; the store paid two-thirds in cash and accrued the rest as Accounts Payable.

Required

1. Prepare a perpetual inventory record, at FIFO cost, for this merchandise.
2. Make journal entries to record the store's transactions.

Problem 6-2A *Accounting for inventory in a perpetual system—moving-weighted-average cost* **(Obj. 1, 3)**

Refer to the Pier 1 Imports situation in Problem 6-1A. Keep all the data unchanged, except that Pier 1 actually uses the moving-weighted-average cost method.

Required

1. Prepare a perpetual inventory record at moving-weighted-average cost. Round average unit cost to the nearest cent and all other amounts to the nearest dollar.
2. Prepare a multistep income statement for the Pier 1 Imports store for the month of February.

Problem 6-3A *Using the perpetual inventory system—FIFO* **(Obj. 1, 3)**

Rambler Lawn Supply, which uses the FIFO method, began March with 50 units of inventory that cost $15 each. During March, Rambler completed these inventory transactions:

	Units	Unit Cost	Unit Sale Price
March 2 Purchase	12	$20	
8 Sale	40		$36
17 Purchase	24	$25	
22 Sale	31		$40

Required

1. Prepare a perpetual inventory record for the lawn supply merchandise.
2. Determine Rambler's cost of goods sold for March.
3. Compute gross margin for March.

Problem 6-4A *Accounting for inventory in a perpetual system—LIFO* *(Obj. 4)*

Home Depot purchases inventory in crates of merchandise, so each unit of inventory is a crate of tools or building supplies. Assume you are dealing with a single department in a Home Depot store in Brandon, Manitoba. The fiscal year of Home Depot ends each January 31.

Assume the department began fiscal year 2005 with an inventory of 40 units that cost a total of $2,400. During the year, the department purchased merchandise on account as follows:

April (60 units at $65)..	$ 3,900
August (100 units at $65)..	6,500
November (200 units at $70)	14,000
Total purchases...	$24,400

Cash payments on account during the year totalled $22,780.

During fiscal year 2005, the department sold 380 units of merchandise for $38,400, of which $6,600 was for cash and the balance was on account. Assume Home Depot uses the LIFO method for inventories. Department operating expenses for the year were $11,260. The department paid two-thirds of the operating expenses in cash and accrued the rest.

Required

1. Make summary journal entries to record the department transactions for the year ended January 31, 2005. Home Depot uses a perpetual inventory system.
2. Determine the LIFO cost of the store's ending inventory at January 31, 2005. Use a T-account.
3. Prepare the department's income statement for the year ended January 31, 2005. Include a complete heading, and show totals for the gross margin and net income.

Problem 6-5A *Computing inventory by three methods—periodic system* *(Obj. 3, 4)*

A Best Yet Electronic Centre began December with 140 units of inventory that cost $75 each. During December, the store made the following purchases:

Dec. 3	217 at $79
12	95 at $82
18	210 at $83
24	248 at $87

The store uses the periodic inventory system, and the physical count at December 31 indicates that 229 units of inventory are on hand.

Required

1. Determine the ending inventory and cost-of-goods-sold amounts for the December financial statements under the weighted-average cost, FIFO, and LIFO methods. Round average cost per unit to the nearest cent and all other amounts to the nearest dollar.
2. Sales revenue for December totalled $90,000. Compute Best Yet's gross margin for December under each method.
3. Which method will result in the lowest income taxes for Best Yet? Why? Which method will result in the highest net income for Best Yet? Why?

Problem 6-6A *Using the periodic inventory system—FIFO* *(Obj. 4)*

Mesa Hardware Company, which uses a periodic inventory system, began 2005 with 6,000 units of inventory that cost a total of $30,000. During 2005, Mesa purchased merchandise on account as follows:

Purchase 1 (10,000 units costing $60,000) .... $ 60,000
Purchase 2 (20,000 units costing $140,000) 140,000

At year end, the physical count indicated 5,000 units of inventory on hand.

Required

1. How many units did Mesa sell during the year? The sale price per unit was $10. Determine Mesa's sales revenue for the year.

2. Compute cost of goods sold by the FIFO method. Then determine gross margin for the year.

Problem 6-7A *Using the perpetual and periodic inventory systems* *(Obj. 1, 4)*

The Canvas Company (TCC) began May 2005 with 50 units of inventory that cost $50 each. The sale price of each of those units was $89. During May, TCC completed these inventory transactions:

			Units	Unit Cost	Unit Sales Price
May	3	Sale	16	$50	$89
	8	Purchase .	80	51	92
	11	Sale	34	50	89
	19	Sale	9	51	92
	24	Sale	35	51	92
	30	Purchase .	18	52	93
	31	Sale	6	51	92

Required

1. The above data are taken from TCC's perpetual inventory records. Which cost method does the company use?

2. Compute TCC's cost of goods sold for May under the
   a. Perpetual inventory system
   b. Periodic inventory system

3. Compute gross margin for May.

Problem 6-8A *Applying the lower-of-cost-or-market rule to inventories* *(Obj. 5)*

Ace Building Supplies has recently been plagued with declining sales. The rate of inventory turnover has dropped, and some of the company's merchandise is gathering dust. At the same time, competition has forced Ace Building Supplies to lower the selling prices of its inventory. It is now December 31, 2005, and the net realizable value of Ace Building Supplies' ending inventory is $910,000 below what the business actually paid for the goods, which was $6,370,000. Before any adjustments at the end of the period, Ace Building Supplies' Cost of Goods Sold account has a balance of $37,440,000.

What action should Ace Building Supplies take in this situation, if any? Give any journal entry required. At what amount should Ace Building Supplies report Inventory on the balance sheet? At what amount should the company report Cost of Goods Sold on the income statement? Discuss the accounting principle or concept that is most relevant to this situation.

Problem 6-9A *Correcting inventory errors over a three-year period* *(Obj. 6)*

The books of Kitchener Windows and Siding show these data (in thousands):

	2005		2004		2003
Net sales revenue	$720		$550		$480
Cost of goods sold:					
Beginning inventory	$130		$110		$140
Net purchases	390		270		260
Cost of goods available	520		380		400
Less ending inventory	140		130		110
Cost of goods sold		380		250		290
Gross margin		340		300		190
Operating expenses		238		218		144
Net income		$102		$ 82		$ 46

In early 2006, a team of Canada Customs and Revenue Agency auditors discovered that the ending inventory of 2003 had been overstated by $24 thousand. Also, the ending inventory for 2005 had been understated by $12 thousand. The ending inventory at December 31, 2004 was correct.

Required

1. Show corrected comparative income statements for the three years.

2. State whether each year's net income as reported here and the related owner's equity amounts are understated or overstated. For each incorrect figure, indicate the amount of the understatement or overstatement.

Media Companion CD-ROM

Problem 6-10A *Estimating ending inventory by the gross margin method; preparing the income statement* **(Obj. 7)**

Assume Sutherland Linen Stores estimates its inventory by the gross margin method when preparing monthly financial statements (it uses the periodic method otherwise). For the past two years, the gross margin has averaged 40 percent of net sales. Assume further that the company's inventory records for stores in Western Canada reveal the following data:

Inventory, June 1, 2005	$ 734,000
Transactions during June:	
Purchases	7,578,000
Sales	12,860,000

Required

1. Estimate the June 30, 2005 inventory using the gross margin method.

2. Prepare the June income statement through gross margin for the Sutherland Linen Stores stores in the Western Canada region.

Problem 6-11A *Accounting for inventory by the periodic system; estimating inventory by the gross margin method* **(Obj. 4, 7)**

Brar Company has a periodic inventory system and uses the gross margin method of estimating inventories for interim financial statements. The business had the following account balances for the fiscal year ended August 31, 2006:

Merchandise inventory—Sept. 1, 2005	$ 28,500
Purchases	245,250
Purchases returns and allowances	35,250
Freight in	1,800
Sales	331,500
Sales returns and allowances	6,000

Required

1. Use the gross margin method to estimate the cost of the business's ending inventory, assuming the business has an average gross margin rate of 40 percent.

2. The business has done a physical count of the inventory on hand on August 31, 2006. For convenience, this inventory was calculated using the retail

selling prices marked on the goods, which amounted to $60,975. Use the information from Requirement 1 to calculate the cost of the inventory counted.

3. What is the cost of the business's estimated inventory shortage?

4. Give the summary journal entries required at August 31, 2006 and the adjustment required for the shortage.

5. Of what other use would the information in Requirement 4 be to the business?

Problem 6-12A *Accounting for inventory by the perpetual inventory system, applying the LIFO and FIFO costing methods; estimating inventory by the gross margin method* **(Obj. 4, 7)**

Todd Sales uses the perpetual inventory system for the purchase and sale of inventory and had the following information available on August 31, 2005:

Purchases and Sales		Number of Units	Cost or Selling Price per Unit
Aug. 1	Balance of inventory	900	$12
7	Purchased	2,500	$11
8	Sold	2,000	$20
12	Purchased	1,750	$12
16	Sold	2,900	$21
21	Purchased	2,000	$13
25	Purchased	3,000	$15
29	Sold	4,000	$21

Required

1. Calculate the cost of goods sold and the cost of the ending inventory for August under each of the following inventory costing methods: (a) LIFO, (b) FIFO.

2. Prepare the journal entries required to record the August transactions using the perpetual inventory system with FIFO costing.

3. An internal audit has discovered that two new employees—an accounting clerk and an employee from the purchasing department—had been stealing merchandise and covering up the shortage by changing the inventory records. For example, if 130 units were purchased at $10 per unit, they would record it as 100 units purchased at $13 per unit and then steal the other 30 units.

   The external auditors examined the accounting records prior to the employment of the two individuals and noted that the company had an average gross margin rate of 48 percent. They estimate that 90 percent of the incorrectly costed units have been sold.

   Use the gross margin method to estimate the cost of the inventory shortage (under the FIFO costing method) and give the journal entry required to correct it.

4. What would be the effect on the net income for the year ending August 31, 2005, if the inventory shortage had not been discovered? For the year ending August 31, 2006?

Problems (Group B)

Problem 6-1B *Accounting for inventory using the perpetual system—LIFO* **(Obj. 1, 2)**

Assume Toys "R" Us Canada (www.toysrus.ca) purchases inventory in crates of merchandise, so each unit of inventory is a crate of toys. Assume you are dealing with a single department in the Toys "R" Us store in Whitby, Ontario

Assume the department began January with an inventory of 20 units that cost a total of $1,200. During the month, the department purchased and sold merchandise on account as follows:

Purchase 1	30 units at $65	Purchase 2	70 units at $70
Sale 1	40 units at $100	Sale 2	75 units at $110

Toys "R" Us uses the LIFO cost method.

Cash payments on account totalled $6,300. Department operating expenses for the month were $3,600. The department paid two-thirds in cash, with the rest accrued as Accounts Payable.

Required

1. Prepare a perpetual inventory record, at LIFO cost, for this merchandise.
2. Make journal entries to record the department's transactions.

Problem 6-2B *Accounting for inventory in a perpetual system—moving-weighted-average cost (Obj. 1, 3)*

Refer to the Toys "R" Us situation in Problem 6-1A. Keep all the data unchanged, except assume that Toys "R" Us uses the moving-weighted-average cost method.

Required

1. Prepared a perpetual inventory record at moving-weighted-average cost. Round average unit cost to the nearest cent and all other amounts to the nearest dollar.
2. Prepare a multistep income statement for the Toys "R" Us department for the month of January.

Problem 6-3B *Using the perpetual inventory system—FIFO (Obj. 1, 3)*

A Danier Leather Inc. (www.danier.com) outlet store, which uses the FIFO method, began August with 50 units of inventory that cost $40 each. During August, the store completed these inventory transactions:

	Units	Unit Cost	Unit Sale Price
Aug. 3 Sale...................................	40		$70
8 Purchase..........................	80	$44	
21 Sale...................................	70		$73
30 Purchase..........................	20	$48	

Required

1. Prepare a perpetual inventory record for this item.
2. Determine the store's cost of goods sold for August.
3. Compute gross margin for August.

Problem 6-4B *Accounting for inventory in a perpetual system—FIFO (Obj. 4)*

Wal-Mart operates department stores across Canada. Assume you are dealing with one department in a Wal-Mart store in Moncton, New Brunswick. Assume the company's fiscal year ends each January 31. Also assume the department began fiscal year 2006 with an inventory of 50 microwave ovens that cost $2,500. During the year, the department purchased merchandise on account as follows:

March (60 units at $53)...	$ 3,180
August (40 units at $57)..	2,280
October (180 units at $60).......................................	10,800
Total purchases..	$16,260

Cash payments on account during the year totalled $15,200.

During fiscal year 2006, the department sold 300 microwave ovens for $30,000, of which $2,100 was for cash and the balance was on account. Wal-Mart uses the FIFO method for inventories.

Operating expenses for the year were $5,000. The department paid 40 percent of the operating expenses in cash and accrued the rest.

Required

1. Make summary journal entries to record the department's transactions for the year ended January 31, 2006. The company uses a perpetual inventory system.

2. Determine the FIFO cost of the department's ending inventory at January 31, 2006. Use a T-account.

3. Prepare the department's income statement for the year ended January 31, 2006. Show totals for the gross margin and net income.

Problem 6-5B   *Computing inventory by three methods—periodic system*   *(Obj. 3, 4)*

Nelson Framing Co. began March with 73 units of inventory that cost $23 each. During the month, Nelson made the following purchases:

March	4	113 at $26
	12	81 at $30
	19	167 at $32
	25	44 at $35

The company uses the periodic inventory system, and the physical count at March 31 includes 51 units of inventory on hand.

Required

1. Determine the ending inventory and cost-of-goods-sold amounts for the March financial statements under (a) average cost, (b) FIFO cost, and (c) LIFO cost. Round average cost per unit to the nearest cent and all other amounts to the nearest dollar.

2. Sales revenue for March totalled $20,000. Compute Nelson's gross margin for March under each method.

3. Which method will result in the lowest income taxes for Nelson? Why?

4. Which method will result in the highest net income for Nelson? Why?

Problem 6-6B   *Using the periodic inventory system—LIFO*   *(Obj. 4)*

Century Soccer Balls, which uses a periodic inventory system, began 2005 with 6,000 units of inventory that cost a total of $30,000. During 2005, Century purchased merchandise on account as follows:

Purchase 1 (10,000 units costing $60,000)	$ 60,000
Purchase 2 (20,000 units costing $140,000)	140,000

At year end, the physical count indicated 15,000 units of inventory on hand.

Required

1. How many units did Century Soccer Balls sell during the year? The sale price per unit was $18. Determine Century's sales revenue for the year.

2. Compute cost of goods sold by the LIFO method. Then determine gross margin for the year.

Problem 6-7B   *Using the perpetual and periodic inventory systems*   *(Obj. 1, 4)*

Kimberly Performance Tire began June with 50 units of inventory that cost $98 each. The sale price of each was $132. During June, Kimberly Performance Tire completed these inventory transactions:

			Units	Unit Cost	Unit Selling Price
June	2	Purchase	12	$100	$134
	8	Sale	27	98	132
	13	Sale	23	98	132
		Sale	3	100	134
	17	Purchase	24	100	134
	22	Sale	31	100	134
	29	Purchase	24	102	138

Required

1. The above data are taken from Kimberly Performance Tire's perpetual inventory records. Which cost method does Kimberly Performance Tire use?

2. Compute Kimberly Performance Tire's cost of goods sold for June under the
   a. Perpetual inventory system
   b. Periodic inventory system

3. Compute gross margin for June.

Problem 6-8B   *Applying the lower-of-cost-or-market rule to inventories   (Obj. 5)*

Jillson's Home Furniture has recently been plagued with lacklustre sales. The rate of inventory turnover has dropped, and some of the business's merchandise is gathering dust. At the same time, competition has forced the business to lower the selling prices of its inventory. It is now December 31, 2006. Assume the net realizable value of a Jillson's Home Furniture store's ending inventory is $750,000 below what Jillson's Home Furniture paid for the goods, which was $6,150,000. Before any adjustments at the end of the period, assume the store's Cost of Goods Sold account has a balance of $34,095,000.

What action should Jillson's Home Furniture take in this situation, if any? Give any journal entry required. At what amount should Jillson's Home Furniture report Inventory on the balance sheet? At what amount should the business report Cost of Goods Sold on the income statement? Discuss the accounting principle or concept that is most relevant to this situation.

Problem 6-9B   *Correcting inventory errors over a three-year period   (Obj. 6)*

The accounting records of the Best Submarine restaurant chain show these data (in thousands):

	2005		2004		2003	
Net sales revenue...................		$228		$198		$204
Cost of goods sold						
Beginning inventory	$ 18		$ 30		$ 48	
Net purchases....................	138		120		108	
Cost of goods available....	156		150		156	
Less ending inventory	36		18		30	
Cost of goods sold............		120		132		126
Gross margin..........................		108		66		78
Operating expenses...............		74		46		55
Net income		$ 34		$ 20		$ 23

In early 2006, a team of auditors discovered that the ending inventory of 2003 had been understated by $4 thousand. Also, the ending inventory for 2005 had been overstated by $5 thousand. The ending inventory at December 31, 2004 was correct.

Required

1. Show corrected comparative income statements for the three years.

2. State whether each year's net income as reported here and the related owner's equity amounts are understated or overstated. For each incorrect figure, indicate the amount of the understatement or overstatement.

Media Companion CD-ROM

Problem 6-10B   *Estimating inventory by the gross margin method; preparing the income statement   (Obj. 7)*

Assume Franz Stores estimates its inventory by the gross margin method when preparing monthly financial statements (assume Franz Stores uses the periodic method otherwise). For the past two years, gross margin has averaged 30 percent of net sales. Assume further that the business's inventory records for stores in Nova Scotia and Prince Edward Island reveal the following data:

Inventory, July 1, 2005	$ 152,000
Transactions during July:	
Purchases	3,292,500
Purchases returns	16,000
Sales	4,687,500
Sales returns	8,500

Required

1. Estimate the July 31, 2005 inventory using the gross margin method.

2. Prepare the July 2005 income statement through gross margin for the Franz Stores in Nova Scotia and Prince Edward Island.

Problem 6-11B *Accounting for inventory by the periodic system; estimating inventory by the gross margin method* **(Obj. 4, 7)**

The Shuksan Shoe Company has a periodic inventory system and uses the gross margin method of estimating inventories for interim financial statements. The company had the following account balances for the fiscal year ended August 31, 2005:

Merchandise inventory—Sept. 1, 2004	$ 86,000
Purchases	492,000
Purchases returns and allowances	16,000
Freight in	3,200
Sales	802,000
Sales returns and allowances	26,000

Required

1. Use the gross margin method to estimate the cost of the business's ending inventory, assuming the business has an average gross margin rate of 35 percent.

2. The business has done a physical count of the inventory on hand on August 31, 2005. For convenience, this inventory was calculated using the retail selling prices marked on the goods, which amounted to $103,000. Use the information from Requirement 1 to calculate the cost of the inventory counted.

3. What is the cost of the business's estimated inventory overage?

4. Give the summary journal entries required at August 31, 2005. Also record any shortage or overage.

Problem 6-12B *Accounting for inventory by the perpetual inventory system; applying the LIFO and FIFO costing methods; estimating inventory by the gross margin method.* **(Obj. 7)**

Ed's Auto Parts uses the perpetual inventory system for the purchase and sale of inventory and had the following information available on May 31, 2006:

Purchases and Sales		Number of Units	Cost or Selling Price per Unit
May 1	Balance of inventory	3,900	$ 8
7	Purchased	6,000	$12
8	Sold	4,500	$17
12	Purchased	7,500	$11
16	Sold	9,000	$19
21	Purchased	4,500	$12
25	Purchased	10,500	$11
29	Sold	13,500	$19

Required

1. Calculate the cost of goods sold and the cost of the ending inventory for May under each of the following inventory costing methods: (a) LIFO, (b) FIFO.

2. Prepare the journal entries required to record the transactions using the perpetual inventory system with FIFO costing.

3. An internal audit has discovered that a new employee—an accounting clerk—had been stealing merchandise and covering up the shortage by changing the inventory records. For example, if 120 units were purchased at $10 per unit, he would record it as 100 units purchased at $12 per unit and then steal the other 20 units.

   The external auditors examined the accounting records prior to the employment of the individual and noted that the company has an average gross margin rate of 50 percent. They estimate that 95 percent of the incorrectly costed units have been sold.

   Use the gross margin method to estimate the cost of the inventory shortage (under the FIFO costing method) and give the journal entry required to correct it.

4. What would be the effect on the net income for the year ending May 31, 2006, if the inventory shortage had not been discovered? For the year ending May 31, 2007?

Challenge Problems

Problem 6-1C   *Inventory measurement and income*   *(Obj. 3)*

An anonymous source advised Canada Customs and Revenue Agency that Jim Hick, owner of Hick's Grocery Store, has been filing fraudulent tax returns for the past several years. You, a tax auditor with Canada Customs and Revenue Agency, are in the process of auditing Hick's Grocery Store for the year ended December 31, 2004. Hick's tax returns for the past five years show a decreasing value for ending inventory from 1999, when Hick bought the business, to 2003; the return for 2004 shows the same sort of decrease. You have performed a quick survey of the large store and the attached warehouse and observed that both seemed very well stocked.

Required

Does the information set forth above suggest anything to you that might confirm the anonymous tip? What would you do to confirm or deny your suspicions?

Problem 6-2C   *Estimating inventory from incomplete records*   *(Obj. 7)*

It is Monday morning. You heard on the morning news that a client of your public accounting firm, Eastern Stereo, had a fire the previous Friday night that destroyed its office and warehouse, and you concluded that inventory records as well as inventory probably perished in the fire. Since you had been at Eastern Stereo on the previous Friday preparing the monthly income statement for the previous month that ended on Thursday, you realize you probably have the only current financial information available for Eastern.

Upon arrival at your firm's office, you meet your partner who confirms your suspicions. Eastern Stereo lost all its inventory and its records. She tells you that the company wants your firm to prepare information for a fire loss claim for Eastern Stereo's insurance company for the inventory.

You know the audit file for the fiscal year that ended three months earlier contains a complete section dealing with inventory and the four product lines Eastern Stereo carried, including the most recent gross margin rate for each line. The file will show total inventory and how much inventory there was by product line at the year end. You also recall that the file contains an analysis of sales by product line for the past several years and that Eastern Stereo used a periodic inventory system.

Required

Explain how you would use the information available to you to calculate the fire loss by product line.

Extending Your Knowledge

Decision Problem

Assessing the impact of a year-end purchase of inventory—periodic system (Obj. 4)

BackCountry Camping Supplies is nearing the end of its first year of operations. The company uses the periodic inventory method and made inventory purchases of $111,750 during the year as follows:

January	150 units at $100.00 =	$ 15,000
July	600 units at 121.25 =	72,750
November	150 units at 160.00 =	24,000
Totals	900	$111,750

Sales for the year will be 750 units for $187,500 revenue. Expenses other than cost of goods sold will be $33,000. The owner of the company is undecided about whether to adopt FIFO or LIFO.

The company has storage capacity for 600 additional units of inventory. Inventory prices are expected to stay at $160 per unit for the next few months. The president is considering purchasing 150 additional units of inventory at $160 each before the end of the year. He wishes to know how the purchase would affect net income before taxes under both FIFO and LIFO.

Required

1. To help the owner make the decision, prepare income statements under FIFO and under LIFO, both without and with the year-end purchase of 150 units of inventory at $160 per unit.

2. Compare net income before taxes under FIFO without and with the year-end purchase. Make the same comparison under LIFO. Under which method does the year-end purchase have the greater effect on net income before taxes?

3. Under which method can a year-end purchase be made in order to manipulate net income before taxes? Can this method be used for income-tax purposes in Canada?

Financial Statement Problem

Inventories   (Obj. 2, 3)

The notes are an important part of a company's financial statements, giving valuable details that would clutter the tabular data presented in the statements. This problem will help you learn to use a company's inventory notes. Refer to the Intrawest Corporation statements and the related notes in Appendix A. Answer the following questions:

1. How much were Intrawest Corporation's ski and resort operations inventories at June 30, 2003? June 30, 2002?

2. How does Intrawest Corporation value its inventories?

3. Identify Intrawest Corporation's inventory other than that for ski and resort operations. (Hint: See Note 6.) What is the value of the other inventory?

4. What do the notes suggest the cost of the other inventory includes?

Appendix

Comparing the Perpetual and Periodic Inventory Systems

Exhibit 6A-1 provides a side-by-side comparison of the two inventory accounting systems. It gives the journal entries, the T-accounts, and all financial-statement effects of both inventory systems.

In the periodic system, the purchase of inventory is *not* recorded in the Inventory account. Instead, purchases are recorded in the Purchases account, which is an expense (see transaction 1 in the exhibit, right column). A sale transaction includes *no* cost of goods sold entry (transaction 2). How, then, does the business record inventory and cost of goods sold?

Transactions 3a and 3b give the end-of-period entries to update the Inventory account and record Cost of Goods Sold. Transaction 3c closes the Purchases account into Cost of Goods Sold to complete the periodic process.

Panel B of the exhibit shows the financial statements under both systems.

Exhibit 6A-1 Comparing the Perpetual and Periodic Inventory systems (amounts assumed)

Panel A—Recording in the Journal and Posting to the Accounts

Perpetual System	Periodic System
1. Credit purchases of $560,000: Inventory .... 560,000 　　Accounts Payable 560,000	**1. Credit purchases of $560,000:** Purchases.............................. 560,000 　　Accounts Payable........ 560,000
2. Credit sales of $900,000 (cost $540,000): Accounts Receivable .... 900,000 　　Sales Revenue .... 900,000 Cost of Goods Sold................... 540,000 　　Inventory 540,000	**2. Credit sales of $900,000:** Accounts Receivable........... 900,000 　　Sales Revenue .... 900,000 **3. End-of-period entries to update Inventory and record Cost of Goods Sold:** **a. Transfer the cost of beginning inventory ($100,000) to Cost of Goods Sold:** Cost of Goods sold.............. 100,000 　　Inventory (beginning balance) 100,000 **b. Record the cost of ending inventory ($120,000) based on a physical count:** Inventory (ending balance) 120,000 　　Cost of Goods Sold ..... 120,000 **c. Transfer the cost of purchases to Cost of Goods Sold:** Cost of Goods Sold .... 560,000 　　Purchases...................... 560,000
3. End-of-period entries: No entries required. Both Inventory and Cost of Goods Sold are up-to-date.	

INVENTORY AND COST OF GOODS SOLD ACCOUNTS

Inventory		Cost of Goods Sold	
100,000*	540,000	540,000	
560,000			
120,000			

*Beginning inventory was $100,000.

INVENTORY AND COST OF GOODS SOLD ACCOUNTS

Inventory		Cost of Goods Sold	
100,000**	100,000	100,000	120,000
120,000		560,000	
120,000		540,000	

**Beginning inventory was $100,000.

Panel B-Reporting in the Financial Statements

Perpetual System	Periodic System
Income Statement (partial) Sales revenue .... $900,000 Cost of goods sold .... 540,000 Gross margin............................... $360,000	**Income Statement** Sales revenue............................. $900,000 Cost of goods sold: 　Beginning inventory .... $100,000 　Purchases............................. 560,000 　Cost of goods available for sale 660,000 　Less: Ending inventory ...... (120,000) 　Cost of goods sold .... 540,000 Gross margin............................. $360,000
Balance Sheet (partial) Current assets:................................. 　Cash... $　XXX 　Accounts receivable .... XXX 　Inventories............................... 120,000	**Balance Sheet** Current assets: 　Cash.. $　XXX 　Accounts receivable .... XXX 　Inventories 120,000

Accounting Information Systems

CHAPTER OBJECTIVES

After studying this chapter, you should be able to

1 Describe an effective accounting information system

2 Understand computerized and manual accounting systems

3 Understand how spreadsheets are used in accounting

4 Use the sales journal, the cash receipts journal, and the accounts receivable subsidiary ledger

5 Use the purchases journal, the cash payments journal, and the accounts payable subsidiary ledger

 Media Companion CD-ROM

Visit the Media Companion CD-ROM that comes with this book for extra practice with the new material in Chapter 7.

ruce Dunn is a chartered accountant in Vancouver. Bruce has been a sole practitioner for several years and his business has slowly evolved into one that specializes in accounting for small- and medium-size businesses. Bruce's company provides services such as bookkeeping, financial statement preparation, and income tax planning. As well, Bruce files income tax returns with the Canada Customs and Revenue Agency for his clients. Bruce has always relied on a computerized accounting package, such as Simply Accounting®, to manage his clients' (and his own) business affairs.

"The computerized accounting packages have become very sophisticated," Bruce observed recently. "Most of my clients can use these packages without extensive training in the fundamentals of accounting. The program will help them manage accounts receivable and accounts payable, and will provide the company with preliminary financial statements. I can then review the statements and make the adjustments necessary to finalize them. It is a real value-added approach. It allows the clients to do their own data entry, and they only pay me for my accounting knowledge, rather than my bookkeeping skills. I can concentrate on analyzing their businesses, and advising them on significant accounting and tax issues. It's a win-win situation for both the client and me. I am so happy with the computerized accounting package I use that I will often buy a copy for a client and install it on their computer for them. It makes my job so much simpler and more rewarding."

EVERY organization needs an accounting system. An **accounting information system** is the combination of personnel, records, and procedures that a business uses to meet its needs for financial data. We have already been using an accounting information system in this text. It consists of two basic components:

- A general journal
- A general ledger

Every accounting system has these components, but this simple system can efficiently handle only a few transactions per accounting period. Businesses cope with heavy transaction loads in two ways: computerization and specialization. We *computerize* to do the accounting faster and more reliably. *Specialization* combines similar transactions to speed the process. A key feature of specialization is the set of special journals that we cover in the second half of this chapter.

Effective Accounting Information Systems

OBJECTIVE 1
Describe an effective accounting information system

Good personnel are critical to success. Employees must be both competent and honest. Design features also make accounting systems run efficiently. A good system—whether computerized or manual—includes four features: control, compatibility, flexibility, and a favourable cost/benefit relationship.

Features

Control Managers must *control* operations. *Internal controls* are the methods and procedures used to authorize transactions, to ensure adherence to management policy, to safeguard assets and records, to prevent and detect error and fraud, and to ensure that information produced is accurate and timely.

For example, in companies such as Intrawest (www.intrawest.com) and Nortel

Networks Corp. (www.nortelnetworks.com), managers control cash payments to avoid theft through unauthorized payments. VISA (www.visa.com), MasterCard (www.mastercard.com/canada), American Express (www.americanexpress.com/canada), and other credit-card companies keep accurate records of their accounts receivable to ensure that customers are billed and collections are received on time.

Compatibility A *compatible* system is one that works smoothly with the business's operations, personnel, and organizational structure. An example is The Bank of Nova Scotia (www.scotiabank.com), which is organized as a network of branch offices. The bank's top managers want to know how much revenue was generated in each region where the bank does business. They also want to analyze the bank's loans in different geographic regions. If revenues and loans in Alberta or Nova Scotia are lagging, the managers can concentrate their collection efforts in that region. They may relocate some branch offices, open new branches, or hire new personnel to increase their revenues and net income. A compatible accounting *information* system conforms to the particular needs of the business.

Flexibility Organizations evolve. They develop new products, sell off unprofitable operations and acquire new ones, and adjust employee pay scales. Changes in the business often call for changes in the accounting system. A well-designed system is *flexible* if it accommodates changes without needing a complete overhaul. Consider Bombardier's acquisition of Canadair, the aircraft manufacturer. Bombardier's accounting system had the flexibility to fold Canadair's financial statements into those of Bombardier Inc. (www.bombardier.com), the parent company.

Favourable Cost/Benefit Relationship Achieving control, compatibility, and flexibility costs money. Managers strive for a system that offers maximum benefits at a minimum cost—that is, a favourable *cost/benefit relationship.* Most small companies, such as Steveston Hardware, an independent hardware store near Vancouver, use off-the-shelf computerized accounting packages. Such packages include ACCPAC® (www.accpac.com), Simply Accounting® (www.accpac.com), MYOB® (www.myob.com),and Peachtree® (www.peachtree.com). The very smallest businesses might not computerize at all. But large companies, such as the brokerage firm ScotiaMcLeod (www.scotiamcleod.com), have specialized needs for information. For them, customized programming is a must because the benefits—in terms of information tailored to the company's needs—far outweigh the cost of the system. The result? Better decisions.

Components of a Computerized Accounting System

THINKING IT OVER

How might a business, such as Zellers, save money with a computerized information system?

A: Personnel time saved from collecting sales data manually and stocking excess inventories; revenue saved from avoiding deep discounts on slow-moving goods; costs saved by avoiding errors.

Three components form the heart of a computerized accounting system: hardware, software, and company personnel. Each component is critical to the system's success.

Hardware is the electronic equipment that includes computers, disk drives, monitors, printers, and the network that connects them. Most systems require a **network** to link different computers sharing the same information. In a networked system, a **server** stores the program and the data. With its network, a KPMG auditor in Calgary can access the data of a client located in Tokyo, Japan. The result is a speedier audit for the client, often at lower cost than if the auditor had to perform all the work on site in Tokyo.

Software is the set of programs that drive the computer. Accounting software reacts, edits (alters), and stores transaction data. It also generates the reports managers use to run the business. Many software packages operate independently. For example, a company that is only partly computerized may use software programs to account for employee payrolls, and sales and accounts receivable. The other parts of the accounting system may not be fully computerized.

For large enterprises, such as Molson Canada (www.molson.com) and the Royal Bank of Canada (www.royalbank.ca), the accounting software is integrated into the company **database**, or computerized storehouse of information. Many business databases, or *management information systems*, include both accounting and nonaccounting data. For example, VIA Rail (www.viarail.ca), in negotiating a union contract, often needs to examine the relationship between the employment history and salary levels of company employees. VIA's database provides the data that managers need to negotiate effectively with their labour unions. During negotiations, both parties carry laptops so that they can access the database and analyze data on the spot.

Personnel who operate the system must be properly trained. Properly trained staff are critical to the success of any accounting information system. Modern accounting systems give nonaccounting personnel access to parts (but not all) of the system. For example, a Frito-Lay Canada (www.pepsico.com) marketing manager (a nonaccountant) may use a computer and regional sales data (accounting information) to identify the territory that needs a promotional campaign. Management of a computerized accounting system requires careful consideration of data security and screening of the people in the organization who will have access to the data. Security is usually achieved with *passwords,* codes that restrict access to computerized records.

How Computerized and Manual Accounting Systems Work

Computerized accounting systems have replaced manual systems in many organizations—even small businesses such as Steveston Hardware. As we discuss the stages of data processing, observe the differences between a computerized system and a manual system. The relationship among the three stages of data processing (inputs, processing, outputs) is shown in Exhibit 7-1.

Inputs represents data from source documents, such as fax orders received from customers, sales receipts, and bank deposit slips. Inputs are usually grouped by type. For example, a firm would enter cash sale transactions separately from credit sales and purchase transactions.

In a manual system, *processing* includes journalizing transactions, posting to the accounts, and preparing the financial statements. A computerized system also processes transactions, but without the intermediate steps (journal, ledger, and trial balance).

Outputs are the reports used for decision making, including the financial statements (income statement, balance sheet, and so on). Business owners can make better decisions with the reports produced by the company's accounting system. In a computerized accounting system, a trial balance is a report (an output). But a manual system would treat the trial balance as a *processing* step leading to the preparation of financial statements. Exhibit 7-2 is an overview of a computerized accounting system.

Designing an Accounting System: The Chart of Accounts

An accounting system begins with the chart of accounts. Recall from Chapter 2, page 70, that the chart of accounts lists all accounts and their account numbers in the general ledger. In the accounting system of a company such as CanWest Global

EXHIBIT 7-1

The Three Stages of Data Processing

Inputs (Data) → Processing (Accounting) → Outputs (Reports)

EXHIBIT 7-2

Overview of a Computerized
Accounting System

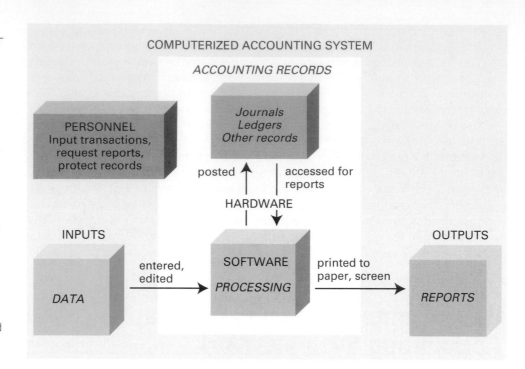

COMPUTERIZED ACCOUNTING SYSTEM

Businesses use account numbers
to input transactions. The account
numbers can be chosen to provide
additional data. For example,
account numbers for the
housewares department might end
with the digit 2. Thus, a
departmental income statement
could easily be prepared for the
housewares department by
selecting all revenue and expense
accounts that end in "2".

Communications Corp. (www.canwestglobal.com), the account numbers take on
added importance. It is efficient to represent a complex account title, such as
Accumulated Amortization—Photographic Equipment, with a concise account
number (for example, 16570).

Recall the asset accounts generally begin with the digit 1, liabilities with the digit 2,
owner's equity accounts with the digit 3, revenues with 4, and expenses with 5.
Exhibit 7-3 diagrams one structure for computerized accounts. Assets are divided
into current assets, capital assets (property, plant, and equipment), and other as-

EXHIBIT 7-3

Structure for Computerized
Accounts

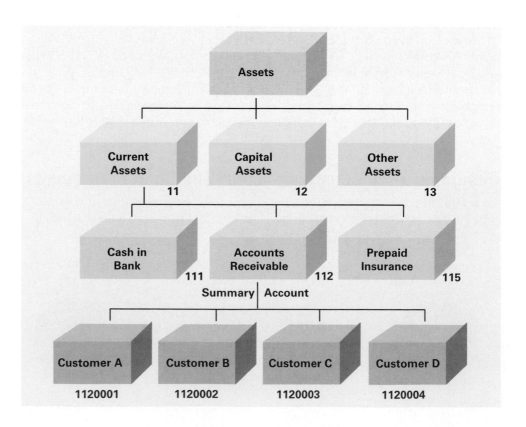

sets. Among the current assets we illustrate only three general ledger accounts: Cash in Bank (Account No. 111), Accounts Receivable (No. 112), and Prepaid Insurance (No. 115). Accounts Receivable holds the *total* dollar amount receivable from all customers.

The account numbers in Exhibit 7-3 get more detailed as you move from top to bottom. For example, Customer A's account number is 1120001, in which 112 represents Accounts Receivable and 0001 refers to Customer A.

The importance of a well-structured chart of accounts cannot be over-emphasized. This is because the reporting component of a computerized accounting system relies on *account number ranges* to translate accounts and their balances into properly organized financial statements and other reports. For example, the accounts numbered 101–399 (assets, liabilities, and owner's equity) are sorted to the balance sheet, and the accounts numbered 401–599 (revenues and expenses) go to the income statement.

Processing Transactions: Manual and Menu-Driven Accounting Systems

Recording transactions in an actual accounting system requires an additional step that we have skipped thus far. A business of any size *classifies* transactions by type for efficient handling. In a manual system, credit sales, purchases on account, cash receipts, and cash payments are treated as four separate categories. Each has its own special journal. (We discuss these journals in detail later in this chapter.) For example:

- Credit sales of merchandise are recorded in a *sales journal*.
- Cash receipts are entered in a *cash receipts journal*.
- Credit purchases of inventory and other assets are recorded in a *purchases journal*.
- Cash payments are entered in a *cash payments journal*.
- Payroll payments are recorded in the *payroll journal*.
- Transactions that do not fit any of the special journals, such as the adjusting and closing entries at the end of the period, are recorded in the *general journal*, which serves as the "journal of last resort."

> **KEY POINT**
>
> The general journal will have the fewest entries. Most transactions fall into one of these four categories: credit sales, cash receipts, credit purchases, or cash payments.

Computerized systems are organized by function, or task. Access to functions is arranged in terms of menus. A **menu** is a list of options for choosing computer functions. In such a *menu-driven* system, you first access the *main menu*. You then choose from one or more submenus until you finally reach the function you want.

Exhibit 7-4 illustrates one type of menu structure. The menu bar at the top gives the main menu. The computer operator (or accountant) had chosen the General option (short for General Ledger), as shown by the highlighting. This action opened a submenu of four items—Transactions, Posting, Account Maintenance, and Closing. The Transactions option was then chosen (highlighted).

Posting in a computerized system can be performed continuously (**online** or

EXHIBIT 7-4

Main Menu of a
Computerized Accounting
System

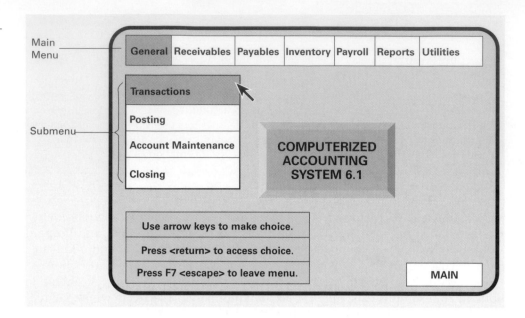

The computer reduces both time and personnel costs. Because of the efficient handling of large numbers of transactions, a computer requires fewer employees to perform the same tasks previously performed manually. The computer frees employees from repetitive bookkeeping, provides time for decision making, and reduces the number of errors.

real-time processing) or later for a group of similar transactions (batch processing). In either case, posting is automatic. In effect, the transaction data are "parked" or stored in the computer to await posting. The posting then updates the account balances. Outputs—accounting reports—are the final stage of data processing. In a computerized system, the financial statements can be printed automatically. For example, the Reports option in the main menu gives the operator various report choices, which are expanded in the Reports submenu of Exhibit 7-5. In the exhibit, the operator is working with the financial statements, specifically the balance sheet, as shown by the highlighting.

Exhibit 7-6 summarizes the accounting cycle in a computerized system and in a manual system. As you study the exhibit, compare and contrast the two types of systems.

Enterprise Resource Planning (ERP) Systems

Many small businesses use QuickBooks® (www.intuit.com/canada) or Simply Accounting®. But larger companies like Nova Scotia Power (www.nspower.ca) and

EXHIBIT 7-5

Reports Submenu of a
Computerized Accounting
System

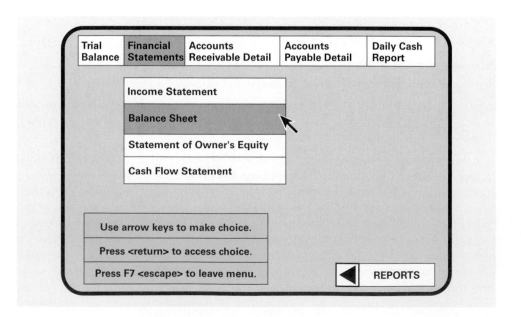

Computerized System	Manual System
1. Start with the account balances in the ledger at the beginning of the period.	1. Same.
2. Analyze and classify business transactions by type. Access appropriate menus for data entry.	2. Analyze and journalize transactions as they occur.
3. Computer automatically posts transactions as a batch or when entered on-line.	3. Post journal entries to the ledger accounts.
4. The unadjusted balances are available immediately after each posting.	4. Compute the unadjusted balance in each account at the end of the period.
5. The trial balance, if needed, can be accessed as a report.	5. Enter the trial balance on the work sheet, and complete the work sheet (optional).
6. Enter and post adjusting entries. Print the financial statements. Run automatic closing procedures after backing up the period's accounting records.	6. Prepare the financial statements. Journalize and post the adjusting entries. Journalize and post the closing entries.
7. The next period's opening balances are created automatically as a result of closing.	7. Prepare the postclosing trial balance. This trial balance becomes step 1 for the next period.

EXHIBIT 7-6

Comparison of the Accounting Cycle in a Computerized and a Manual System

◖ KEY POINT ◗

You may think a computer skips steps when data are entered because the computer performs some of the steps internally. However, a computerized system performs all the steps a manual system does, except for the work sheet. Even if you never keep a manual set of books, you still need to understand the entire accounting system.

Eastlink Telephone (www.eastlink.ca/telephone/) are using **enterprise resource planning (ERP)** systems to manage their data. ERP systems such as SAP® (www.sap.com), Oracle® (www.oracle.com), and PeopleSoft® (www.peoplesoft.com) can integrate all company data into a single data warehouse. The ERP system feeds the data into software for all company activities—from purchasing to production and customer service.

Advantages of ERP systems include:

- A centralized ERP system can save lots of money.

- ERP helps companies adjust to changes. A change in sales ripples through the purchasing, shipping, and accounting systems.

- An ERP system can replace hundreds of separate software systems, such as different payroll and production software.

ERP is expensive. Major installations can cost millions of dollars. Implementation also requires a large commitment of time and people. For example, Hershey Foods Corporation (www.hersheys.com) tried to shrink a four-year ERP project into two-and-a-half years. The result? The software did not map into Hershey's operations, and the resulting disrupted deliveries decreased profits in the critical Halloween candy-buying season.

Integrated Accounting Software: Spreadsheets

OBJECTIVE 3
Understand how spreadsheets are used in accounting

Computerized accounting packages are organized by **modules**, which are integrated units that are compatible and that function together. Changes affecting one module will affect others. For example, entering and posting a credit-sales transaction will update two modules: Accounts Receivable/Sales and Inventory/Cost of Goods Sold. Accounting packages, such as ACCPAC Plus Accounting®, Simply Accounting®, Great Plains™, and QuickBooks®, come as a complete set of accounting modules to form an integrated system.

Spreadsheets are computer programs that link data by means of formulas and functions. Spreadsheets are organized by *cells*, each defined by a column number and

EXHIBIT 7-7

A Spreadsheet Screen

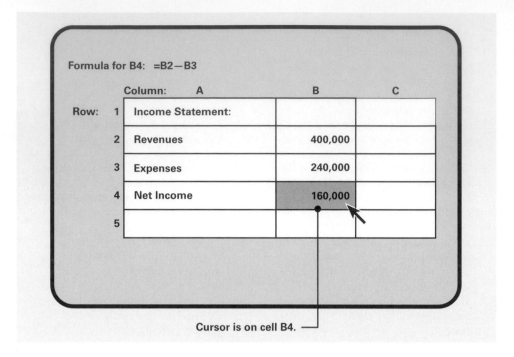

Cursor is on cell B4.

a row number. A cell can contain words (called labels), numbers, or formulas (relationships among cells). The *cursor,* or electronic highlighter, indicates which cell is active, and it can be moved around the spreadsheet. When the cursor is placed over any cell, information can be entered there for processing.

Exhibit 7-7 shows an income statement on a spreadsheet screen. The labels were entered in cells A1 through A4. The dollar amount of revenues was entered in cell B2 and expenses in cell B3. A formula was placed in B4 as follows: =B2–B3. This formula subtracts expenses from revenues to compute net income in cell B4. If revenues in cell B2 increase to $440,000, net income in B4 automatically increases to $200,000. No other cells will change.

Spreadsheets are ideally suited to preparing a budget, which summarizes the financial goals of a business. Consider Canada's Molson Breweries, whose annual advertising budget is in millions of dollars. Suppose Molson allocates $4–5 million for its Canadian brand and $500,000 for a new product. Molson's advertising expenses will increase in both cases. The company will also forecast an increase in sales revenue, cost of goods sold, and other expenses. A spreadsheet computes all these changes automatically in response to the change in advertising. The spreadsheet lets Molson's managers track relative profitability of each product. Armed with current data, the managers can make informed decisions. The result is higher profits.

We can add or delete whole rows and columns of data and move blocks of numbers and words on a spreadsheet. The power and versatility of spreadsheets are

EXHIBIT 7-8

Basic Arithmetic Operations
in Excel Spreadsheets

Operation	Symbol
Addition	+
Subtraction	–
Multiplication	*
Division	/
Addition of a range of cells	=SUM(beginning cell:ending cell)
Examples:	
Add the contents of cells A2 through A9	=SUM(A2:A9)
Divide the contents of cell C2 by the	
contents of cell D1	=C2/D1

apparent when enormous amounts of data are entered on the spreadsheet with formula relationships. Change only one number, and you can save hours of manual recalculation. Exhibit 7-8 shows the basic arithmetic operations in Excel spreadsheets.

Accounting and the *e*-World

Accounting Pioneers on the Virtual Frontier

Computer and Internet technology are remaking the bookkeeping and tax aspects of accounting. There are "virtual" software consultants, and now there are "virtual" or "online" accountants who serve clients via the Internet. Companies with slogans like "Real Accounting in a Virtual World" and "Outsourced Accounting Services for a Wired World" are advertising services like basic bookkeeping, full-service outsourcing, real-time accounting, and 24-hour access to accounting data.

TADOnline (TAD), a business founded by Lance and Deanna Gildea in San Diego, is one such service currently operating in the United States. TAD has clients scan their invoices, bank statements, and other documents into the computer; TAD even provides the scanner free-of-charge to some clients. The scanned documents are then transmitted to TAD, and within minutes, TAD updates the client's accounts. Clients then use a Web browser to sign in to their home page (prepared by TAD), where clients can view, print, and download reports, cheques, and other information. Soon clients will be able to get real-time access to their accounting data through a new Web-based service.

For clients—typically small- to mid-sized businesses—the key benefits of TADOnline are price and reliability. In some cases, TAD's monthly fees are half of what it would cost to hire a bookkeeper—and TAD never calls in sick or takes vacations. In Canada, companies in remote areas can gain access to accounting expertise that might be unavailable to them otherwise. A big plus for the "virtual accountants" is being able to live wherever they please, regardless of where clients are located.

Adapted from Antoinette Alexander, "Pioneers on the Virtual Frontier," *Accounting Technology*, Jan/Feb 2000, pp. 18–24.

Special Journals

Exhibit 7-9 diagrams a typical accounting system for a merchandising business. The remainder of this chapter describes this system.

Special Accounting Journals

The journal entries illustrated so far in this book have been made in the **general journal**. The general journal is used to record all transactions that do not fit one of the special journals. In a manual system, it is not efficient to record all transactions in the general journal, so we use special journals. A **special journal** is an accounting journal designed to record one specific type of transaction.

Most transactions fall into one of five categories, so accountants use five different journals. This system reduces the time and cost otherwise spent journalizing, as we will see. The five categories of transactions, the special journal, and the posting abbreviations are as follows:

KEY POINT

Transactions are recorded in either the general journal or a special journal, but not in both.

Transaction	Special Journal	Posting Abbreviation
1. Sale of merchandise on account	Sales journal	S
2. Cash receipt	Cash receipts journal	CR
3. Purchase on account	Purchases journal	P
4. Cash payment*	Cash payments journal	CP
5. All others	General journal	J

*Some companies also use a Payroll Journal for payroll transactions, which is a part of the companies' *payroll system*. Payroll systems are covered in Chapter 11.

Adjusting and closing entries are entered in the general journal. Transactions are recorded in either the general journal or a special journal, but not in both.

You may be wondering why we cover manual accounting systems, since many businesses have computerized accounting systems. There are three main reasons:

1. Learning a manual system will help you master accounting. One of the authors of this book has a friend who uses QuickBooks for his proprietorship. This man knows little beyond which keys to punch. If he knew the accounting, he could better manage his business and have more confidence that his records are accurate.

2. Learning a manual system will equip you to work with both manual and electronic systems. The accounting is the same regardless of the system.

3. Few small businesses have computerized all their accounting. Even companies that use QuickBooks or Simply Accounting keep some manual accounting records. Also, many small businesses use manual systems, and they follow the principles and procedures that we illustrate in this chapter.

EXHIBIT 7-9

Overview of an Accounting System with Special Journals for a Merchandising Business

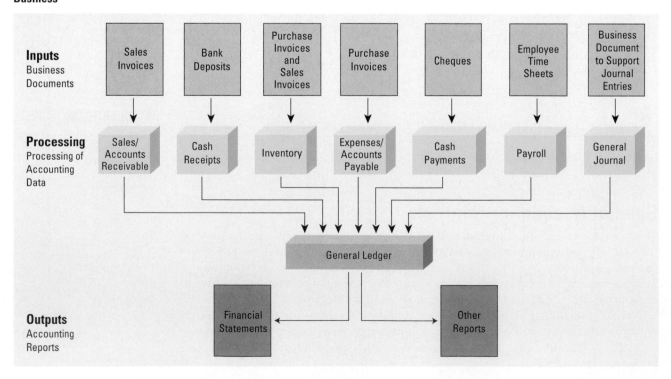

Using the Sales Journal

OBJECTIVE 4
Use the sales journal, the cash receipts journal, and the accounts receivable subsidiary ledger

Most merchandisers sell inventory on account. These *credit sales* are recorded in the **sales journal**. Credit sales of assets other than inventory—for example, buildings—occur infrequently and may be recorded in the general journal.

Exhibit 7-10 illustrates a sales journal (Panel A) and the related posting to the ledgers (Panel B) of Austin Sound Centre, the stereo shop we introduced in Chapter 5. Each entry in the Accounts Receivable/Sales Revenue column of the sales journal in

EXHIBIT 7-10

Sales Journal (Panel A) and Posting to Ledgers (Panel B) under the Perpetual Inventory System

Panel A: Sales Journal

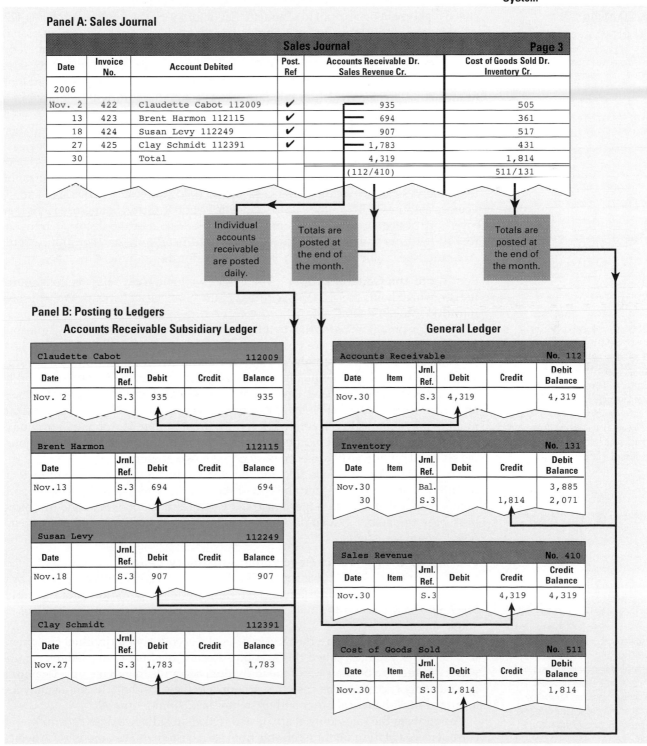

Panel B: Posting to Ledgers

KEY POINT

Only credit sales of merchandise are recorded in the sales journal.

KEY POINT

The purpose of a subsidiary ledger account is to provide detail of a customer's account to facilitate billing and collection. The subsidiary ledger should show all sales to, and collections from, the customer—the customer's credit history.

KEY POINT

The accounts debited and credited are the same whether or not the accounting system uses special journals. However, the debits and credits are arranged differently in a special journal system.

KEY POINT

You may think that posting to the subsidiary ledger and to the general ledger is double posting. However, the subsidiary ledger is *not* part of the general ledger and the subsidiary accounts will *not* appear on the trial balance. Posting to both the subsidiary ledger and the general ledger is necessary to keep the two in balance.

Exhibit 7-10 is a debit (Dr.) to Accounts Receivable and a credit (Cr.) to Sales Revenue, as the heading above this column indicates. For each transaction, the accountant enters the date, invoice number, customer account, and transaction amount. This streamlined way of recording sales on account saves a vast amount of time that, in a manual system, would be spent entering account titles and dollar amounts in the general journal.

In recording credit sales in the previous chapter, we did not keep a record of the names of credit-sale customers. In practice the business must know the amount receivable from each customer. How else can the company identify who owes it money, when payment is due, and how much?

Consider the first transaction in Panel A. On November 2, Austin Sound sold stereo equipment on account to Claudette Cabot for $935. The invoice number is 422. All this information appears on a single line in the sales journal. No explanation is necessary. The transaction's presence in the sales journal means that it is a credit sale, debited to Accounts Receivable—Claudette Cabot and credited to Sales Revenue. To gain any additional information about the transaction, we would look at the actual invoice (which in this case shows a $35 discount will be granted for prompt payment).

Recall from Chapter 5 that Austin Sound uses a *perpetual* inventory system. When recording the sale, Austin Sound also records the cost of goods sold and the decrease in inventory. Many computerized accounting systems are programmed to read both the sales amount and the cost of goods sold from the bar code on the package of the item sold. A separate column of the sales journal holds the cost of goods sold and inventory amount—$505 for the sale to Claudette Cabot. If Austin Sound used a *periodic* inventory system, it would not record cost of goods sold or the decrease in inventory at the time of sale. The sales journal would need only one column to debit Accounts Receivable and to credit Sales Revenue for the amount of the sale.

Posting to the General Ledger The ledger we have used so far is the **general ledger**, which holds the accounts reported in the financial statements. We will soon introduce other ledgers.

Posting from the sales journal to the general ledger can be done at any time, but for efficiency, most companies post only once each month. In Exhibit 7-10 (Panel A), November's credit sales total $4,319. This column has two headings, Accounts Receivable and Sales Revenue. In a manual system, when the $4,319 is posted to Accounts Receivable and Sales Revenue in the general ledger, their account numbers are written beneath the total in the sales journal. In Panel B of Exhibit 7-10, the account number for Accounts Receivable is 112 and the account number for Sales Revenue is 410. Printing these account numbers beneath the credit sales total in the sales journal shows that the $4,319 has been posted to the two accounts.

The debit to Cost of Goods Sold and the credit to Inventory for the monthly total of $1,814 is normally posted at the end of the month. After posting, these account numbers are entered beneath the total to show that Cost of Goods Sold and Inventory have been updated. No such posting would be made if Austin Sound used a periodic inventory system.

Posting to the Accounts Receivable Subsidiary Ledger The $4,319 debit to Accounts Receivable does not identify the amount receivable from any specific customer. A business may have thousands of customers. For example, *MacLean's Magazine* (www.macleans.com) has a customer account for each of its subscribers.

To streamline operations, businesses place the accounts of individual customers in a subsidiary ledger, called the Accounts Receivable Subsidiary ledger. A **subsidiary ledger** is a book or file of the individual accounts that make up a total for a general ledger account. The customer accounts in the subsidiary ledger usually are arranged in alphabetical order and often have a customer number.

Amounts in the sales journal are posted to the subsidiary ledger *daily* to keep a current record of the amount receivable from each customer. The amounts are debits.

Daily posting allows the business to answer customer inquiries promptly. Suppose Claudette Cabot telephones Austin Sound on November 11 to ask how much money she owes. The subsidiary ledger readily provides that information, $935 in Exhibit 7-10, Panel B.

When each transaction amount is posted to the subsidiary ledger in a manual system, a check mark or some other notation is entered in the posting reference column of the sales journal (see Exhibit 7-10, Panel A). This is because subsidiary ledger accounts are not part of the general ledger, and, thus, have no general ledger account numbers.

Journal References in the Ledgers   When amounts are posted to the ledgers, the journal page number is written in the account to identify the source of the data. All transaction data in Exhibit 7-10 originated on page 3 of the sales journal so all posting references in the ledger accounts are S.3. The "S." indicates sales journal.

Trace all the postings in Exhibit 7-10. The most effective way to learn about accounting systems and special journals is to study the flow of data. The arrows indicate the direction of the information. The arrows show the links between the individual customer accounts in the subsidiary ledger and the Accounts Receivable account. (The arrows are for illustration only—they do not appear in the accounting records.) The Accounts Receivable debit balance in the general ledger should equal the sum of the individual customer balances in the subsidiary ledger, as follows:

KEY POINT

In a manual system, the dates recorded in the subsidiary ledger and the general ledger must reflect the date of the transaction, not the date on which the transaction was posted. In a computerized system, the computer will automatically record the date entered by the computer operator.

General Ledger

Accounts Receivable debit balance.........................	$4,319

Subsidiary Ledger: Customer Accounts Receivable

Customer	Balance
Claudette Cabot 112009	$ 935
Brent Harmon 112115..	694
Susan Levy 112249...	907
Clay Schmidt 112391	1,783
Total accounts receivable...	$4,319

KEY POINT

After *all* postings, the control account should equal the sum of all its subsidiary accounts.

Accounts Receivable in the general ledger is an example of a **control account**. A control account's balance equals the sum of the balances of a group of related accounts in a subsidiary ledger. The individual customer accounts are subsidiary accounts. They are said to be "controlled" by the Accounts Receivable account in the general ledger.

Additional data can be recorded in the sales journal. For example, a company may add a column to record sale terms, such as 2/10 n/30. The design of the journal depends on the managers' needs for information. Special journals are flexible—they can be tailored to meet any special needs of a business.

STOP & THINK

Suppose Austin Sound had 400 credit sales for the month. How many postings to the general ledger would be made from the sales journal? (Ignore Cost of Goods Sold and Inventory.) How many postings would there be if all sales transactions were routed through the general journal?

Answer: There are only two postings from the sales journal to the general ledger: one to Accounts Receivable and one to Sales Revenue. There would be 800 postings from the general journal: 400 to Accounts Receivable and 400 to Sales Revenue. This difference clearly shows the benefit of a sales journal.

Using Documents as Journals in a Manual Accounting System

Many small businesses streamline their accounting by using business documents as the journals. This practice avoids the need to keep special journals and thereby saves money. For example, Austin Sound could keep sales invoices in a looseleaf binder and let the invoices themselves serve as the sales journal. At the end of the period, the accountant simply totals the sales on account and posts the total as a debit to Accounts Receivable and a credit to Sales Revenue. Also, the accountant can post directly from invoices to customer accounts in the accounts receivable subsidiary ledger.

Using the Cash Receipts Journal

Cash transactions are common in most businesses because cash receipts from customers are the lifeblood of business. To record a large number of cash receipt transactions, accountants use the **cash receipts journal**.

Exhibit 7-11, Panel A, illustrates the cash receipts journal. The related posting to the ledgers is shown in Panel B. The exhibit illustrates November transactions for Austin Sound Centre.

Every transaction recorded in this journal is a cash receipt, so the first column is for debits to the Cash account. The next column is for debits to Sales Discounts on collections from customers. In a typical merchandising business, the main sources of cash are collections on account, and cash sales.

The cash receipts journal has credit columns for Accounts Receivable and Sales Revenue. The journal also has a credit column for Other Accounts, which lists sources of cash other than cash sales and collections on account. This Other Accounts column is also used to record the names of customers from whom cash is received on account.

In Exhibit 7-11, cash sales occurred on November 6, 19, and 28. Observe the debits to Cash and the credits to Sales Revenue ($517, $853, and $1,802). Each sale entry is accompanied by an entry that debits Cost of Goods Sold and credits Inventory for the cost of the merchandise sold, since the perpetual inventory system is being used. The column for this entry is at the far right side of the cash receipts journal. No such entry would be made if Austin Sound used a periodic inventory system.

On November 12, Austin Sound borrowed $1,000 from Scotiabank. Cash is debited, and Note Payable to Scotiabank is credited in the Other Accounts column because it is a rare transaction and no specific credit column is set up to account for borrowings. For this transaction, we enter the account title, Note Payable to Scotiabank, in the Other Accounts/Account Title column. This entry records the source of cash.

On November 25, Austin Sound collected $762 of interest revenue. The account credited, Interest Revenue, must be written in the Other Accounts column. The November 12 and 25 transactions illustrate a key fact about business. Different entities have different types of transactions, and they design their special journals to meet their particular needs for information. In this case, the Other Accounts Credit column is the catch-all that is used to record all nonroutine cash receipt transactions.

On November 14, Austin Sound collected $900 from Claudette Cabot. Referring back to Exhibit 7-10, we see that on November 2 Austin Sound sold merchandise for $935 to Claudette Cabot. The terms of sale allowed a $35 discount for prompt payment and she paid within the discount period. Austin's cash receipt is recorded by debiting Cash for $900 and Sales Discounts for $35 and by crediting Accounts Receivable for $935. The customer's name appears in the Other Accounts/Account Title column.

Total debits must equal total credits in the cash receipts journal. This equality holds for each transaction and for the monthly totals. For the month, total debits ($6,134 + $35 = $6,169) equal total credits ($1,235 + $3,172 + $1,762 = $6,169). The debit to Cost of Goods Sold and the credit to Inventory are separate, and only apply to the perpetual inventory system.

EXHIBIT 7-11

Cash Receipts Journal (Panel A) and Posting to the Ledgers (Panel B) under the Perpetual Inventory System

Panel A: Cash Receipts Journal

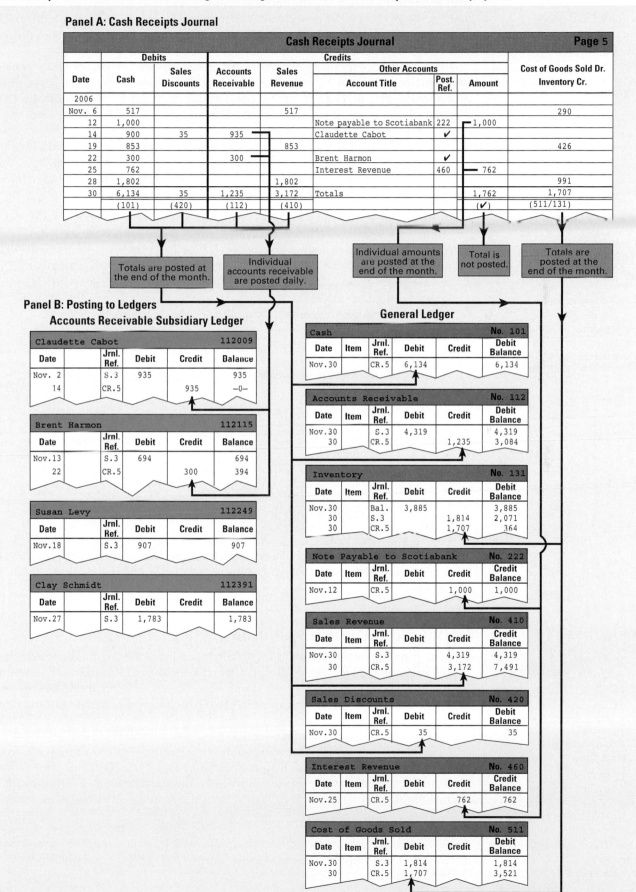

	Debits		Credits					Cost of Goods Sold Dr.
Cash Receipts Journal							**Page 5**	
					Other Accounts			
Date	Cash	Sales Discounts	Accounts Receivable	Sales Revenue	Account Title	Post. Ref.	Amount	Inventory Cr.
2006								
Nov. 6	517			517				290
12	1,000				Note payable to Scotiabank	222	1,000	
14	900	35	935		Claudette Cabot	✔		
19	853			853				426
22	300		300		Brent Harmon	✔		
25	762				Interest Revenue	460	762	
28	1,802			1,802				991
30	6,134	35	1,235	3,172	Totals		1,762	1,707
	(101)	(420)	(112)	(410)			(✔)	(511/131)

Totals are posted at the end of the month.

Individual accounts receivable are posted daily.

Individual amounts are posted at the end of the month.

Total is not posted.

Totals are posted at the end of the month.

Panel B: Posting to Ledgers
Accounts Receivable Subsidiary Ledger

Claudette Cabot   112009

Date		Jrnl. Ref.	Debit	Credit	Balance
Nov. 2		S.3	935		935
14		CR.5		935	–0–

Brent Harmon   112115

Date		Jrnl. Ref.	Debit	Credit	Balance
Nov.13		S.3	694		694
22		CR.5		300	394

Susan Levy   112249

Date		Jrnl. Ref.	Debit	Credit	Balance
Nov.18		S.3	907		907

Clay Schmidt   112391

Date		Jrnl. Ref.	Debit	Credit	Balance
Nov.27		S.3	1,783		1,783

General Ledger

Cash   No. 101

Date	Item	Jrnl. Ref.	Debit	Credit	Debit Balance
Nov.30		CR.5	6,134		6,134

Accounts Receivable   No. 112

Date	Item	Jrnl. Ref.	Debit	Credit	Debit Balance
Nov.30		S.3	4,319		4,319
30		CR.5		1,235	3,084

Inventory   No. 131

Date	Item	Jrnl. Ref.	Debit	Credit	Debit Balance
Nov.30		Bal.	3,885		3,885
30		S.3		1,814	2,071
30		CR.5		1,707	364

Note Payable to Scotiabank   No. 222

Date	Item	Jrnl. Ref.	Debit	Credit	Credit Balance
Nov.12		CR.5		1,000	1,000

Sales Revenue   No. 410

Date	Item	Jrnl. Ref.	Debit	Credit	Credit Balance
Nov.30		S.3		4,319	4,319
30		CR.5		3,172	7,491

Sales Discounts   No. 420

Date	Item	Jrnl. Ref.	Debit	Credit	Debit Balance
Nov.30		CR.5	35		35

Interest Revenue   No. 460

Date	Item	Jrnl. Ref.	Debit	Credit	Credit Balance
Nov.25		CR.5		762	762

Cost of Goods Sold   No. 511

Date	Item	Jrnl. Ref.	Debit	Credit	Debit Balance
Nov.30		S.3	1,814		1,814
30		CR.5	1,707		3,521

Posting to the General Ledger   The column totals are usually posted monthly. To indicate their posting, the account number is written below the column total in the cash receipts journal. Note the account number for Cash (101) below the column total $6,134, and trace the posting to Cash in the general ledger. Likewise, the Sales Discounts, Accounts Receivable, and Sales Revenue column totals also are posted to the general ledger.

The column total for *Other Accounts* is *not* posted. Instead, these credits are posted individually. In Exhibit 7-11, the November 12 transaction reads "Note Payable to Scotiabank." This account's number (222) in the Post. Ref. column indicates that the transaction amount was posted individually. The check mark, instead of an account number, below the column total indicates that the column total was not posted. The November 25 collection of interest revenue is also posted individually. These amounts can be posted to the general ledger at the end of the month. But their date in the ledger accounts should be their actual date in the journal to make it easy to trace each amount back to the cash receipts journal.

Posting to the Subsidiary Ledger   Amounts from the cash receipts journal are posted to the subsidiary accounts receivable ledger daily to keep the individual balances up to date. The postings to the accounts receivable ledger are credits. Trace the $935 posting to Claudette Cabot's account. It reduces the balance in her account to zero. The $300 receipt from Brent Harmon reduces his accounts receivable balance to $394.

After posting, the sum of the individual balances that remain in the accounts receivable ledger equals the general ledger balance in Accounts Receivable.

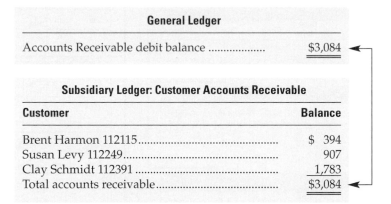

Austin Sound's list of account balances from the subsidiary ledger helps it follow up on slow-paying customers. Good accounts receivable records help a business manage its cash.

······· **THINKING IT OVER** ·······

If Austin Sound did not use an accounts receivable subsidiary ledger and Claudette Cabot asked you for her account balance, could you answer her?

A: It would be difficult! A subsidiary ledger is needed for ready access to the data for each customer. The alternative is to look through all transactions in the general journal for the ones involving Claudette Cabot. (This would be a very inefficient and error-prone alternative.)

Using the Purchases Journal

OBJECTIVE 5
Use the purchases journal, the cash payments journal, and the accounts payable subsidiary ledger

KEY POINT
The source document for entries in the purchases journal is the supplier's (creditor's) invoice.

A merchandising business purchases inventory and supplies frequently. Such purchases are usually made on account. The **purchases journal** is designed to account for all purchases of inventory, supplies, and other assets *on account*. It can also be used to record expenses incurred *on account*. Cash purchases are recorded in the cash payments journal.

Exhibit 7-12 illustrates Austin Sound's purchases journal (Panel A) and posting to the ledgers (Panel B).[1] The purchases journal in Exhibit 7-12 has amount columns for credits to Accounts Payable and debits to Inventory, Supplies, and Other Accounts. A periodic inventory system would replace the Inventory column with a column entitled "Purchases." The Other Accounts columns accommodate purchases

---

[1]This is the only special journal that we illustrate with the credit column usually placed to the left and the debit columns to the right. This arrangement of columns focuses on Accounts Payable, which is credited for each entry to this journal, and on the individual supplier to be paid.

EXHIBIT 7-12

Purchases Journal (Panel A)
and Posting to the Ledgers
(Panel B) under the Perpetual
Inventory System

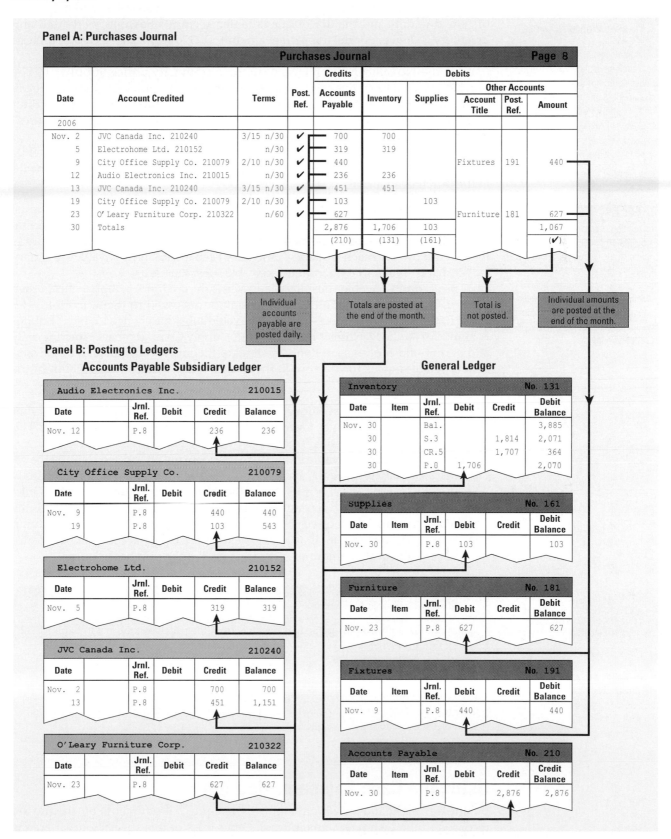

Panel A: Purchases Journal

				Credits	Debits		Other Accounts		
Date	Account Credited	Terms	Post. Ref.	Accounts Payable	Inventory	Supplies	Account Title	Post. Ref.	Amount
2006									
Nov. 2	JVC Canada Inc. 210240	3/15 n/30	✔	700	700				
5	Electrohome Ltd. 210152	n/30	✔	319	319				
9	City Office Supply Co. 210079	2/10 n/30	✔	440			Fixtures	191	440
12	Audio Electronics Inc. 210015	n/30	✔	236	236				
13	JVC Canada Inc. 210240	3/15 n/30	✔	451	451				
19	City Office Supply Co. 210079	2/10 n/30	✔	103		103			
23	O'Leary Furniture Corp. 210322	n/60	✔	627			Furniture	181	627
30	Totals			2,876	1,706	103			1,067
				(210)	(131)	(161)			(✔)

Purchases Journal — Page 8

Individual accounts payable are posted daily.

Totals are posted at the end of the month.

Total is not posted.

Individual amounts are posted at the end of the month.

Panel B: Posting to Ledgers

Accounts Payable Subsidiary Ledger

Audio Electronics Inc.   210015

Date		Jrnl. Ref.	Debit	Credit	Balance
Nov. 12		P.8		236	236

City Office Supply Co.   210079

Date		Jrnl. Ref.	Debit	Credit	Balance
Nov. 9		P.8		440	440
19		P.8		103	543

Electrohome Ltd.   210152

Date		Jrnl. Ref.	Debit	Credit	Balance
Nov. 5		P.8		319	319

JVC Canada Inc.   210240

Date		Jrnl. Ref.	Debit	Credit	Balance
Nov. 2		P.8		700	700
13		P.8		451	1,151

O'Leary Furniture Corp.   210322

Date		Jrnl. Ref.	Debit	Credit	Balance
Nov. 23		P.8		627	627

General Ledger

Inventory   No. 131

Date	Item	Jrnl. Ref.	Debit	Credit	Debit Balance
Nov. 30		Bal.			3,885
30		S.3		1,814	2,071
30		CR.5		1,707	364
30		P.0	1,706		2,070

Supplies   No. 161

Date	Item	Jrnl. Ref.	Debit	Credit	Debit Balance
Nov. 30		P.8	103		103

Furniture   No. 181

Date	Item	Jrnl. Ref.	Debit	Credit	Debit Balance
Nov. 23		P.8	627		627

Fixtures   No. 191

Date	Item	Jrnl. Ref.	Debit	Credit	Debit Balance
Nov. 9		P.8	440		440

Accounts Payable   No. 210

Date	Item	Jrnl. Ref.	Debit	Credit	Credit Balance
Nov. 30		P.8		2,876	2,876

of assets other than inventory and supplies. Each business designs its purchases journal to meet its own needs for information and efficiency. Accounts Payable is credited for all transactions recorded in the purchases journal.

On November 2, Austin Sound purchased stereo inventory costing $700 from JVC Canada Inc. The creditor's name (JVC Canada Inc.) is entered in the Account Credited column. The purchase terms of 3/15 n/30 are also entered to help identify the due date and the discount available. Accounts Payable is credited and Inventory is debited for the transaction amount. On November 19, a credit purchase of supplies is entered as a debit to Supplies and a credit to Accounts Payable.

Note the November 9 purchase of fixtures from City Office Supply Co. The purchases journal contains no column for fixtures, so the Other Accounts debit column is used. Because this was a credit purchase, the accountant enters the creditor name (City Office Supply Co.) in the Account Credited column and writes "Fixtures" in the Other Accounts/Account Title column.

The total credits in the purchases journal ($2,876) must equal the total debits ($1,706 + $103 + $1,067 = $2,876). This equality proves the accuracy of the entries in the purchases journal.

Accounts Payable Subsidiary Ledger   To pay debts on time, a company must know how much it owes each creditor. The Accounts Payable account in the general ledger shows only a single total for the amount owed on account. It does not indicate the amount owed to each creditor. Companies keep an accounts payable subsidiary ledger that is similar to the accounts receivable subsidiary ledger.

The accounts payable subsidiary ledger lists the creditors in alphabetical order, often by account number, along with the amounts owed to them. Exhibit 7-12, Panel B, shows Austin Sound's accounts payable subsidiary ledger, which includes accounts for Audio Electronics Inc., City Office Supply Co., and others. After the daily and period-end postings are done, the total of the individual balances in the subsidiary ledger equals the balance in the Accounts Payable control account in the general ledger.

Posting from the Purchases Journal   Posting from the purchases journal is similar to posting from the sales journal and the cash receipts journal. Exhibit 7-12, Panel B, illustrates the posting process.

Individual accounts payable in the purchases journal are posted daily to the *accounts payable subsidiary ledger*, and column totals and other amounts are usually posted to the *general ledger* at the end of the month. The column total for *Other Accounts* is not posted. Each account's number in the Post. Ref. column indicates the transaction amount was posted individually. The check mark below the column total indicates the column total was *not* posted. In the ledger accounts, P.8 indicates the source of the posted amounts—that is, page 8 of the purchases journal.

> ### STOP & THINK
>
> Contrast the number of general ledger postings from the purchases journal in Exhibit 7-12 with the number that would be required if the general journal were used to record the same seven transactions.
>
> **Answer:** Use of the purchases journal requires only five general ledger postings— $2,876 to Accounts Payable, $1,706 to Inventory, $103 to Supplies, $440 to Fixtures, and $627 to Furniture. Without the purchases journal, there would have been 14 postings, two for each of the seven transactions.

Using the Cash Payments Journal

Businesses make most cash payments by cheque. All payments by cheque are recorded in the **cash payments journal**. Other titles of this special journal are the *cheque register* and the *cash disbursements journal*. Like the other special journals, it has multiple columns for recording cash payments that occur frequently.

Exhibit 7-13, Panel A, illustrates the cash payments journal, and Panel B shows the postings to the ledgers of Austin Sound. This cash payments journal has two debit columns—for Other Accounts and Accounts Payable. It has two credit columns—one for purchase discounts, which are credited to the Inventory account in a perpetual inventory system, and one for Cash. This special journal also has columns for the date, cheque number, and payee of each cash payment.

The cash payments journal for a company using a periodic inventory system would have the same two debit columns as those shown in Exhibit 7-13, Panel A—Other Accounts and Accounts Payable—and two credit columns—for Purchase Discounts and Cash.

Suppose a business makes numerous cash purchases of inventory and uses the perpetual inventory system. What additional column would its cash payments journal need to be most useful? A Debit column for Inventory would be added.

All entries in the cash payments journal include a credit to Cash. Payments on account are debits to Accounts Payable. On November 15, Austin Sound paid JVC Canada Inc. on account, with credit terms of 3/15 n/30 (for details, see the first transaction in Exhibit 7-12). Therefore, Austin took the 3 percent discount and paid $679 ($700 less the $21 discount). The discount is credited to the Inventory account.

The Other Accounts column is used to record debits to accounts for which no special column exists. For example, on November 3, Austin Sound paid rent expense of $1,200.

As with all other journals, the total debits ($3,461 + $819 = $4,280) must equal the total credits ($21 + $4,259 = $4,280).

Posting from the Cash Payments Journal

Posting from the cash payments journal is similar to posting from the cash receipts journal. Individual creditor amounts are posted daily. Column totals and Other Accounts are usually posted at the end of the month. Exhibit 7-13, Panel B, illustrates the posting process.

Observe the effect of posting to the Accounts Payable account in the general ledger. The first posted amount in the Accounts Payable account (credit $2,876) originated in the purchases journal, page 8 (P.8). The second posted amount (debit $819) came from the cash payments journal, page 6 (CP.6). The resulting credit balance in Accounts Payable is $2,057. Also, see the Cash account. After posting, its debit balance is $1,875.

Amounts in the Other Accounts column are posted individually (for example, Rent Expense—debit $1,200). When each Other Accounts amount is posted to the general ledger, the account number is written in the Post. Ref. column of the journal. The check mark below the column total signifies that the total is *not* posted.

To review their accounts payable, companies list the individual creditor balances in the accounts payable subsidiary ledger:

General Ledger	
Accounts Payable credit balance	$2,057

Subsidiary Ledger: Accounts Payable	
Creditor	**Balance**
Audio Electronics Inc. 210015.............................	$ 236
City Office Supply Co. 210079............................	543
Electrohome Ltd. 210152	200
JVC Canada Inc. 210240..	451
O'Leary Furniture Co. 210322	627
Total accounts payable..	$2,057

THINKING IT OVER

(1) How many postings would normally be in the general ledger Cash account in one month?
(2) How many postings would normally be in the Sales Revenue Account in one month?
A: (1) Two—one from cash receipts and one from cash payments.
(2) Two—one from the sales journal and one from cash receipts. (In addition, there may also be adjustments.)

THINKING IT OVER

In which journal would you record each transaction?
(1) Cash dividend paid
(2) Sale of land
(3) Bank loans business cash
(4) Business purchases a personal computer for cash
(5) Purchase of supplies on credit
(6) Accrue salary payable.

A: (1) Cash payments
(2) Cash receipts
(3) Cash receipts
(4) Cash payments
(5) Purchases
(6) General.

This total agrees with the Accounts Payable balance in Exhibit 7-13. Agreement of the two amounts indicates that the resulting account balances are correct.

The payroll register is a special form of cash payments journal and is discussed in Chapter 11.

EXHIBIT 7-13

Cash Payments Journal (Panel A) and Posting to the Ledgers (Panel B) under the Perpetual Inventory System

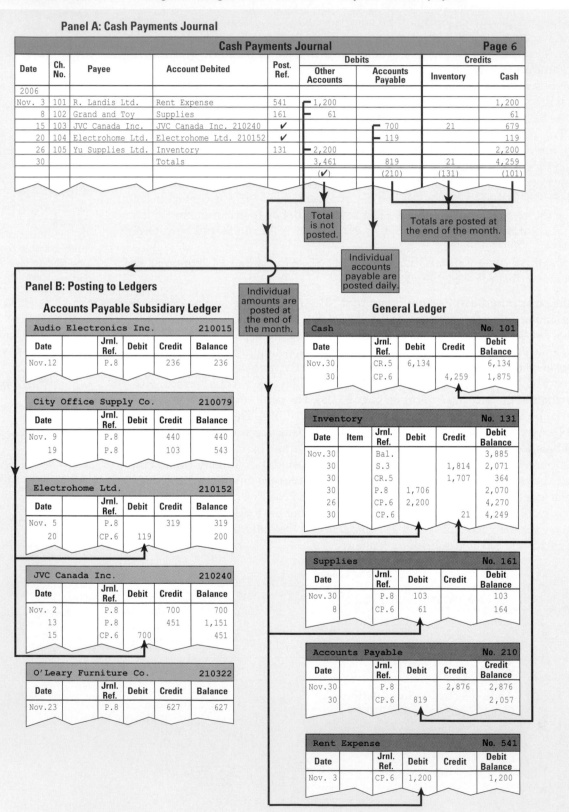

The Role of the General Journal

Special journals save much time in recording repetitive transactions and posting to the ledgers. But some transactions do not fit into any of the special journals. Examples include the amortization of buildings and equipment, the expiration of prepaid insurance, and the accrual of salary payable at the end of the period. Therefore, *even the most sophisticated accounting system needs a general journal. The adjusting entries and the closing entries that we illustrated in Chapters 3 through 5 are recorded in the general journal, along with other non-routine transactions.*

Many companies record their sales returns and allowances and their purchase returns in the general journal. Let's turn now to sales returns and allowances, and the related business document, the *credit memorandum*.

The Credit Memorandum—The Document for Recording Sales Returns and Allowances

As we saw in Chapter 5, customers sometimes return merchandise to the seller, and sellers grant sales allowances to customers because of product defects and for other reasons. The effect of sales returns and sales allowances is the same—both decrease net sales in the same way a sales discount does. The document issued by the seller for a credit to the customer's Account Receivable is called a **credit memorandum**, or **credit memo**, because the company gives the customer credit for the returned merchandise. When a company issues a credit memo, it debits Sales Returns and Allowances and credits Accounts Receivable.

On November 27, Austin Sound sold four stereo speakers for $1,783 on account to Clay Schmidt. Later, Schmidt discovered a defect and returned the speakers. Austin Sound then issued to Schmidt a credit memo like the one in Exhibit 7-14.

To record the *sale return* and receipt of the defective speakers from the customer, Clay Schmidt, Austin Sound would make the following entries in the general journal:

	General Journal			Page 9
Date	**Accounts**	**Post Ref.**	**Debit**	**Credit**
Dec. 1	Sales Returns and Allowances..	430	1,783	
	Accounts Receivable—Clay Schmidt 112391	112/✓		1,783
	Credit memo no. 27.			
Dec. 1	Inventory	131	431	
	Cost of Goods Sold..	511		431
	Received defective goods from customer.			

Focus on the first entry. The debit side of the entry is posted to Sales Returns and Allowances. Its account number (430) is written in the posting reference column when $1,783 is posted. The credit side of the entry requires two $1,783 postings, one to Accounts Receivable, the *control account* in the general ledger (account number 112), and the other to Clay Schmidt's *individual account* in the accounts receivable subsidiary ledger, account number 112391. These credit postings explain why the document is called a *credit memo*.

Observe that the posting reference of the credit includes two notations. The account number (112) denotes the posting to Accounts Receivable in the general ledger. The check mark (✓) denotes the posting to Schmidt's account in the subsidiary ledger. Why are two postings needed? Because this is the general journal. Without specially designed columns, it is necessary to write both posting references on the same line.

A business with a high volume of sales returns, such as a department store chain, may use a special journal for sales returns and allowances.

The second entry records Austin Sound's receipt of the defective inventory from the customer. The speakers cost Austin Sound $431, and Austin Sound, like all other

EXHIBIT 7-14

Credit Memorandum

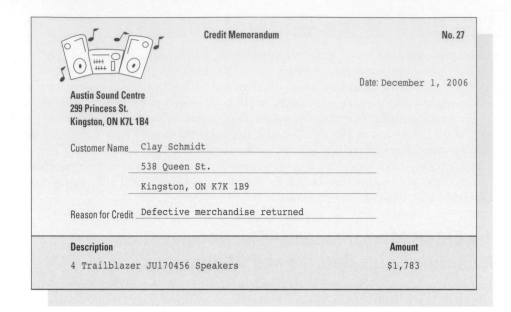

| Credit Memorandum | | No. 27 |

Austin Sound Centre
299 Princess St.
Kingston, ON K7L 1B4

Date: December 1, 2006

Customer Name ___Clay Schmidt___

___538 Queen St.___

___Kingston, ON K7K 1B9___

Reason for Credit ___Defective merchandise returned___

Description	Amount
4 Trailblazer JU170456 Speakers	$1,783

merchandisers, records its inventory at cost. Now let's see how Austin Sound records the return of the defective speakers to JVC, from which Austin Sound purchased them.

The Debit Memorandum—The Business Document for Recording Purchase Returns and Allowances

Purchase returns occur when a business returns goods to the seller. The procedures for handling purchase returns are similar to those dealing with sales returns. The purchaser gives the merchandise back to the seller and receives either a cash refund or replacement goods.

When a business returns merchandise to the seller, it may also send a business document known as a **debit memorandum**, or **debit memo**. This document states that the buyer no longer owes the seller for the amount of the returned purchases. The buyer debits the Accounts Payable to the seller and credits Inventory for the cost of the goods returned to the seller.

Many businesses record their purchase returns in the general journal. Austin Sound would record its return of defective speakers to JVC as follows:

General Journal					Page 9
Date	Accounts	Post Ref.	Debit	Credit
Dec. 2	Accounts Payable—JVC Corp. 210240	210/✓	431	
	Inventory	131		431
	Debit memo no. 16.			

Balancing the Ledgers

At the end of the period, after all postings have been made, equality should exist as follows:

1. *General ledger:*

$$\text{Total debits} = \text{Total credits}$$

2. *General ledger and Accounts receivable subsidiary ledger:*

$$\begin{array}{ccc} \text{Balance of the} & & \text{Sum of all the customer balances} \\ \text{Accounts Receivable} & = & \text{in the Accounts Receivable} \\ \text{control account} & & \text{Subsidiary Ledger} \end{array}$$

....
...... **THINKING IT OVER**

Suppose Brown Sales Co. returned $700 of goods to the vendor from whom the goods were originally purchased. What account is credited and why?
A: When using a perpetual inventory system, Inventory must be kept up to date for all such transactions. Therefore, Inventory is credited, because the items are no longer on hand. When using a periodic inventory system, the Purchase Returns and Allowances account would be credited so that cost of goods sold can be calculated properly.

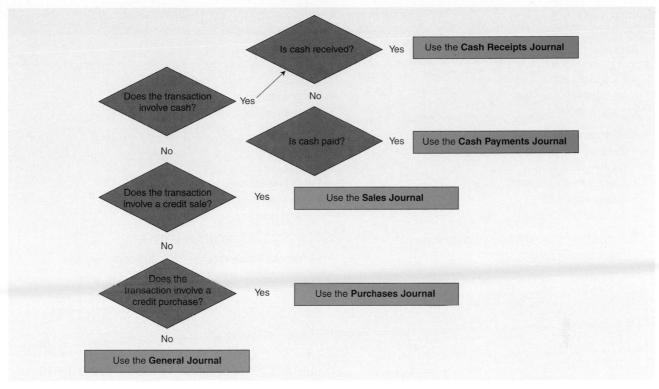

3. *General ledger and Accounts payable subsidiary ledger:*

$$\begin{array}{c}\text{Balance of the}\\\text{Accounts Payable}\\\text{control account}\end{array} = \begin{array}{c}\text{Sum of all the creditor}\\\text{balances in the Accounts Payable}\\\text{Subsidiary Ledger}\end{array}$$

This process of ensuring that these equalities exist is called *balancing the ledgers, reconciling the ledgers,* or *proving the ledgers*. It is an important control procedure because it helps ensure the accuracy of the accounting records.

Blending Computers and Special Journals in an Accounting Information System

Computerizing special journals to create accounting modules requires no drastic change in the accounting system's design. Systems designers create a special screen for each accounting application (module)—credit sales, cash receipts, credit purchases, payroll, and cash payments. The special screen for credit sales would prompt the operator entering the data, for example, on a terminal or a cash register, to type in the following information: date, customer number, customer name, invoice number, and the dollar amount of the sale. These data can generate debits to the subsidiary accounts receivable and can generate monthly statements for customers that show activity and ending balances.

Exhibit 7-15 summarizes a process you can follow to choose the special journal to use for a transaction.

The Decision Guidelines feature on the next page provides guidelines for some of the major decisions that accountants must make as they use an information system.

Sales Tax

In Chapter 5, the federal Goods and Services Tax (GST) was discussed; recall that the GST is collected at each level of transaction right down to the consumer, the final level. The discussion that follows relates to consumption or sales taxes levied by

EXHIBIT 7-15

A Method of Choosing the Special Journal to Use for a Transaction

The authors would like to thank Sharon Hatten for suggesting this flowchart.

 **REAL WORLD EXAMPLE**

Periodically, a list (print-out) is prepared that shows each customer's name and account balance. The total of the individual balances must equal Accounts Receivable (control) in the general ledger. This process is called *balancing*, or proving, the ledgers. Likewise, the total of the creditor balances from the accounts payable subsidiary ledger must equal the balance of Accounts Payable (control) in the general ledger.

Decision	Guidelines
What are the main components of an accounting system?	**Journals** • General journal • Special journals **Ledgers** • General ledger • Subsidiary ledgers
Where to record • Sales of merchandise on account? • Cash receipts? • Purchases on account? • Cash payments? • All other transactions?	Journals: Sales journal Cash receipts journal Purchases journal Cash payments journal General journal

How does the general ledger relate to the subsidiary ledgers?

GENERAL LEDGER

Accounts Receivable	Accounts Payable
X,XXX	XX

SUBSIDIARY LEDGERS

ACCOUNTS RECEIVABLE FROM:

Arnold	Barnes
XX	XX

ACCOUNTS PAYABLE TO:

Agnew	Black
X	X

When to post from the journals to
- General ledger?
- Subsidiary ledgers?

—Monthly (or more often, if needed)
—Daily

How to achieve control over
- Accounts receivable?
- Accounts payable?

Balance the ledgers, as follows:

General Ledger		Subsidiary Ledger
Accounts receivable	=	Sum of individual *customer* accounts receivable
Accounts payable	=	Sum of individual *creditor* accounts payable

all the provinces except Alberta. The Yukon, the Northwest Territories, and Nunavut also do not have a sales tax. Sellers must add the tax to the sale amount, then pay or remit the tax to the provincial government. In most jurisdictions, sales tax is levied only on final consumers, so retail businesses usually do not pay sales tax on the goods they purchase for resale. For example, Gunz Stereo Company would not pay sales tax on a purchase of equipment from JVC Canada Inc., a wholesaler. However, when retailers like Gunz Stereo make sales, they must collect sales tax from the consumer. In effect, retailers serve as collecting agents for the taxing authorities. The amount of tax depends on the total sales and the provincial tax rate.

Retailers set up procedures to collect the sales tax, account for it, and pay it on time. Invoices may be preprinted with a place for entering the sales tax amount, and the general ledger has a liability account entitled Sales Tax Payable. The sales journal may include a special column for sales tax, such as the one illustrated in Exhibit 7-16. The sales tax rate in the exhibit is 7 percent, the rate of sales tax in Manitoba.

Note that the amount debited to Accounts Receivable ($3,783.66) is the sum of the

Sales Journal							**Page 4**
Date	Inv. No.	Account Debited	Post. Ref.	Accounts Receivable Dr.	Sales Tax Payable Cr.	GST Payable Cr.	Sales Revenue Cr.
2006							
Nov. 2	422	Anne Fortin	✔	1,065.90	65.45	65.45	935.00
13	423	Brent Mooney	✔	791.16	48.58	48.58	694.00
18	424	Debby Levy	✔	1,033.98	63.49	63.49	907.00
27	425	Dan Girardi	✔	892.62	54.81	54.81	783.00
30		Totals		3,783.66	232.33	232.33	3,319.00

EXHIBIT 7-16

Sales Journal Designed to Account for Sales Tax

credits to Sales Tax Payable ($232.33), GST Payable ($232.33), and Sales Revenue ($3,319.00). This is so because the customers' payments, the Accounts Receivable figures, are partly for the purchase of merchandise (Sales Revenue) and partly for taxes charged on the sale. The check marks in the Posting Reference column show that individual amounts have been posted to the customer accounts. The absence of account numbers under the column totals shows that the total amounts have not yet been posted.

Most companies that use point-of-sale cash registers have them programmed to calculate separate totals, as sales are being rung in, of taxable items and nontaxable items; the register then calculates the relevant taxes—sales tax, if applicable, and GST—and computes the total owing. Provincial sales tax and the federal GST are not applicable to all items. (For example, food and prescription medicines are excluded from both; reading material is excluded from most sales taxes but not from the GST.) Most businesses calculate sales tax and GST at the time of sale.

Sales tax and GST are discussed more fully in Chapter 11.

Summary Problem
for Your Review

Taylor Company completed the following selected transactions during March:

Mar. 4 Received $1,000 from a cash sale to a customer (cost $638).

6 Received $120 on account from Jim Bryant. The full invoice amount was $130, but Bryant paid within the discount period to earn the $10 discount.

9 Received $2,160 on a note receivable from Lesley Cliff. This amount includes the $2,000 note receivable plus $160 of interest revenue.

15 Received $1,600 from a cash sale to a customer (cost $1,044).

24 Borrowed $4,400 by signing a note payable to the Bank of Nova Scotia.

27 Received $2,400 on account from Lance Au. Payment was received after the discount period lapsed.

The general ledger showed the following balances at February 28: Cash, $2,234; Accounts Receivable, $5,580; Note Receivable—Lesley Cliff, $2,000; Inventory, $3,638. The accounts receivable subsidiary ledger at February 28 contained debit balances as follows: Lance Au, $3,680; Melinda Fultz, $1,770; Jim Bryant, $130.

Required

1. Record the transactions in the cash receipts journal, page 7. Taylor Company uses a perpetual inventory system.

2. Compute column totals at March 31. Show that total debits equal total credits in the cash receipts journal.

3. Post to the general ledger and the accounts receivable subsidiary ledger. Use complete posting references, including the following account numbers: Cash, 11; Accounts Receivable, 12; Note Receivable—Lesley Cliff, 13; Inventory, 14; Note Payable—Bank of Nova Scotia, 22; Sales Revenue, 41; Sales Discounts, 42; Interest Revenue, 46; and Cost of Goods Sold, 51. Insert Bal. in the posting reference column (Jrnl. Ref.) for each February 28 account balance.

4. Show that the total of the balances in the subsidiary ledger equals the general ledger balance in Accounts Receivable.

Solution

Requirements 1 and 2

Cash Receipts Journal   Page 7

	Debits		Credits					
	Cash	Sales Discounts	Accounts Receivable	Sales Revenue	Other Accounts			Cost of Goods Sold Dr. Inventory Cr.
Date					Account Title	Post. Ref.	Amount	
Mar. 4	1,000			1,000				638
6	120	10	130		Jim Bryant	✔		
9	2,160				Note Receivable — Lesley Cliff	13	2,000	
					Interest Revenue	46	160	
15	1,600			1,600				1,044
24	4,400				Note Payable— Bank of Nova Scotia	22	4,400	
27	2,400		2,400		Lance Au	✔		
31	11,680	10	2,530	2,600	Total		6,560	1,682
	(11)	(42)	(12)	(41)			(✔)	(51/14)

Total Dr. = 11,690   Total Cr. = 11,690

Requirement 3

Accounts Receivable Subsidiary Ledger
Lance Au

Date	Item	Jrnl. Ref.	Debit	Credit	Balance
Feb. 28		Bal.			3,680
Mar. 27		CR. 7		2,400	1,280

Melinda Fultz

Date	Item	Jrnl. Ref.	Debit	Credit	Balance
Feb. 28		Bal.			1,770

Jim Bryant

Date	Item	Jrnl. Ref.	Debit	Credit	Balance
Feb. 28		Bal.			130
Mar. 6		CR. 7		130	—

General Ledger
Cash — No. 11

Date	Item	Jrnl. Ref.	Debit	Credit	Debit Balance
Feb. 28		Bal.			2,234
Mar. 31		CR. 7	11,680		13,914

Accounts Receivable — No. 12

Date	Item	Jrnl. Ref.	Debit	Credit	Debit Balance
Feb. 28		Bal.			5,580
Mar. 31		CR. 7		2,530	3,050

Note Receivable—Lesley Cliff — No. 13

Date	Item	Jrnl. Ref.	Debit	Credit	Debit Balance
Feb. 28		Bal.			2,000
Mar. 9		CR. 7		2,000	—

Inventory — No. 14

Date	Item	Jrnl. Ref.	Debit	Credit	Balance
Feb. 28		Bal.			3,638
Mar. 31		CR.7		1,682	1,956

Note Payable—Bank of Nova Scotia — No. 22

Date	Item	Jrnl. Ref.	Debit	Credit	Credit Balance
Mar. 24		CR. 7		4,400	4,400

Sales Revenue — No. 41

Date	Item	Jrnl. Ref.	Debit	Credit	Credit Balance
Mar. 31		CR. 7		2,600	2,600

Sales Discounts — No. 42

Date	Item	Jrnl. Ref.	Debit	Credit	Debit Balance
Mar. 31		CR. 7	10		10

Interest Revenue — No. 46

Date	Item	Jrnl. Ref.	Debit	Credit	Credit Balance
Mar. 9		CR. 7		160	160

Cost of Goods Sold — No. 51

Date	Item	Jrnl. Ref.	Debit	Credit	Debit Balance
Mar. 31		CR. 7	1,682		1,682

General Ledger

Accounts Receivable debit balance.................................... $3,050

Accounts Receivable Subsidiary Ledger: Customer Accounts Receivable

Customer	Balance
Lance Au...	$1,280
Melinda Fultz...	1,770
Total accounts receivable..	$3,050

Note: If Taylor Company had used the periodic inventory system, account No. 51, Cost of Goods Sold, would not exist, so there would be no Cost of Goods Sold column in the cash receipts journal. As well, there would be no $1,682 credit posting to Inventory.

Cyber Coach

Visit the Study Guide on the Media Companion CD-ROM and the Student Resources area of the *Accounting* Companion Website for extra practice with the new material in Chapter 7.

www.pearsoned.ca/horngren

Summary

1. **Describe an effective accounting information system.** An effective *accounting information system* captures and summarizes transactions quickly, accurately, and usefully. The four major aspects of a good accounting system are (1) control over operations, (2) compatibility with the particular features of the business, (3) flexibility in response to changes in the business, (4) a favourable cost/benefit relationship, with benefits outweighing costs.

2. **Understand computerized and manual accounting systems.** Computerized accounting systems process inputs faster than do manual systems and can generate more types of reports. The key components of a computerized accounting system are *hardware*, *software*, and *company personnel*. Account numbers play a bigger role in the operation of computerized systems than they do in manual systems, because computers classify accounts by account numbers. Both computerized and manual accounting systems require transactions to be classified by type.

   Computerized systems use a *menu* structure to organize accounting functions. Posting, trial balances, financial statements, and closing procedures are usually carried out automatically in a computerized accounting system. Computerized accounting systems are integrated so that the different *modules* of the system are updated together.

3. **Understand how spreadsheets are used in accounting.** *Spreadsheets* are electronic work sheets whose grid points, or cells, are linked by means of formulas. The numerical relationships in the spreadsheet are maintained whenever changes are made to the spreadsheet. Spreadsheets are ideally suited to detailed computations, as in budgeting.

4. **Use the sales journal, the cash receipts journal, and the accounts receivable subsidiary ledger.** Many accounting systems use *special journals* to record transactions by category. Credit sales are recorded in a *sales journal*, and cash receipts in a *cash receipts journal*. Posting from these journals is to the *general ledger* and from the sales journal to the *accounts receivable subsidiary ledger*, which lists each customer and the amount receivable from that customer. The accounts receivable subsidiary ledger is the main device for ensuring that the company collects from customers.

5. **Use the purchases journal, the cash payments journal, and the accounts payable subsidiary ledger.** Credit purchases are recorded in a *purchases journal*, and cash payments in a *cash payments journal*. Posting from these journals is to the *general ledger* and to the *accounts payable subsidiary ledger*. The accounts payable subsidiary ledger helps the company stay current in payments to suppliers and take advantage of purchase discounts.

Self-Study Questions

Test your understanding of the chapter by marking the correct answer for each of the following questions:

1. Why does a jewellery store need an accounting system different from that which a physician uses? (*p. 334*)
   a. They have different kinds of employees.
   b. They have different kinds of journals and ledgers.
   c. They have different kinds of business transactions.
   d. They work different hours.

2. Which feature of an effective information system is most concerned with safeguarding assets? (*p. 333*)
   a. Control
   b. Compatibility
   c. Flexibility
   d. Favourable cost/benefit relationship

3. The account number 211031 most likely refers to (*pp. 336–337*)
   a. Liabilities
   b. Current liabilities
   c. Accounts payable
   d. An individual vendor

4. If the amount of total revenues is in cell E7 of a spreadsheet and the amount for total expenses is in cell E20, then net income would be computed by the formula (*p. 340*)
   a. =E7+E20
   b. =E7–E20
   c. =E20–E7
   d. None of the above formulas will work

5. Special journals help most by (*p. 341*)
   a. Limiting the number of transactions that have to be recorded
   b. Reducing the cost of operating the accounting system
   c. Improving accuracy in posting to subsidiary ledgers
   d. Easing the preparation of the financial statements

6. Galvan Company recorded 785 credit sale transactions in the sales journal. Ignoring Cost of Goods Sold and Inventory, how many postings would be required if these transactions were recorded in the general journal? (*p. 345*)
   a. 785
   b. 1,570
   c. 2,355
   d. 3,140

7. Which two dollar-amount columns in the cash receipts journal will be used the most by a department store that makes half of its sales for cash and half on credit? (*pp. 346–347*)
   a. Cash Debit and Sales Discounts Debit
   b. Cash Debit and Accounts Receivable Credit
   c. Cash Debit and Other Accounts Credit
   d. Accounts Receivable Debit and Sales Revenue Credit

8. Entries in the purchases journal are posted to the (*pp. 348–350*)
   a. General ledger only
   b. General ledger and the accounts payable subsidiary ledger
   c. General ledger and the accounts receivable subsidiary ledger
   d. Accounts receivable subsidiary ledger and the accounts payable subsidiary ledger

9. Every entry in the cash payments journal includes a (*pp. 350–352*)
   a. Debit to Accounts Payable
   b. Debit to an Other Account
   c. Credit to Inventory
   d. Credit to Cash

10. Balancing the ledgers at the end of the period is most closely related to (*pp. 354–355*)
    a. Control
    b. Compatibility
    c. Flexibility
    d. Favourable cost/benefit relationship

Answers to the Self-Study Questions follow the Similar Accounting Terms.

Accounting Vocabulary

Accounting information system (*p. 333*)
Batch processing (*p. 338*)
Cash payments journal (*p. 350*)
Cash receipts journal (*p. 346*)
Control account (*p. 345*)
Credit memorandum or credit memo (*p. 353*)
Database (*p. 334*)
Debit memorandum or debit memo (*p. 354*)
Enterprise resource planning (ERP) system (*p. 339*)
General journal (*p. 341*)
General ledger (*p. 344*)
Hardware (*p. 334*)

Menu (*p. 337*)
Module (*p. 339*)
Network (*p. 334*)
Online processing (*p. 337*)
Purchases journal (*p. 348*)
Real-time processing (*p. 338*)
Sales journal (*p. 343*)
Server (*p. 334*)
Software (*p. 334*)
Special journal (*p. 341*)
Spreadsheet (*p. 339*)
Subsidiary ledger (*p. 344*)

Similar Accounting Terms

Accounts payable subsidiary ledger	Accounts payable ledger
Accounts receivable subsidiary ledger	Accounts receivable ledger
Balancing the ledgers	Proving the ledgers, reconciling the ledgers
Cash payments journal	Cash disbursements journal, cheque register
Credit memorandum	Credit memo
Database	Management information system
Debit memorandum	Debit memo
Online processing	Real-time processing

Assignment Material

Questions

1. Describe the four criteria of an effective accounting system.

2. Distinguish batch computer processing from online computer processing.

3. What accounting categories correspond to the account numbers 1, 2, 3, 4, and 5 in the chart of accounts in a typical computerized accounting system?

4. Why might the number 112 be assigned to Accounts Receivable and the number 1120708 to Carl Erickson, a customer?

5. Describe the function of menus in a computerized accounting system.

6. How do formulas in spreadsheets speed the process of budget preparation and revision?

7. Name four special journals used in accounting systems. For what type of transaction is each designed?

8. Describe the two advantages that special journals have over recording all transactions in the general journal.

9. What is a control account, and how is it related to a subsidiary ledger? Name two common control accounts.

10. Graff Company's sales journal has one amount column headed Accounts Receivable Dr. and Sales Revenue Cr. In this journal, 86 transactions are recorded. How many posting references appear in the journal? State what each posting reference represents.

11. The accountant for Bannister Co. posted all amounts correctly from the cash receipts journal to the general ledger. However, she failed to post three credits to customer accounts in the accounts receivable subsidiary ledger. How would this error be detected?

12. At what two times is posting done from a special journal? What items are posted at each time?

13. Describe two ways to account for sales tax collected from customers.

14. What is the purpose of balancing the ledgers?

15. Posting from the journals of McKedrick Realty is complete. But the total of the individual balances in the accounts payable subsidiary ledger does not equal the balance in the Accounts Payable control account in the general ledger. Does this necessarily indicate that the trial balance is out of balance? Explain.

16. Assume that posting is completed. The trial balance shows no errors, but the sum of the individual accounts payable does not equal the Accounts Payable control balance in the general ledger. What two errors could cause this problem?

Exercises

Exercise 7-1   *Features of an effective accounting information system* *(Obj. 1)*

Suppose you have just invested your life savings in a company that prints rubberized logos on T-shirts. The business is growing fast, and you need a better accounting information system. Consider the features of an effective system, as discussed on pages 333–334. Which features do you regard as most important? Why? Which feature must you consider if your financial resources are limited?

Exercise 7-2   *Assigning account numbers* *(Obj. 2)*

Assign account numbers (from the list that follows) to the accounts of LP Gas Co. Identify the headings, which are *not* accounts and would not be assigned an account number.

Assets	Capital
Current Assets	Withdrawals
Capital Assets	Revenues
Accounts Payable	Selling Expenses

Numbers from which to choose:

1	12	32
2	16	33
3	17	53
4	21	121
5	28	131
11	31	411

Exercise 7-3   *Setting up a chart of accounts* *(Obj. 2)*

Use account numbers 11 through 16, 21, 22, 31, 32, 41, 51, and 52 to correspond to the following selected accounts from the general ledger of Mountainview Gift Shop. List the accounts and their account numbers in proper order, starting with the most liquid current asset.

Capital	Amortization expense
Cost of goods sold	Cash
Accounts payable	Withdrawals
Inventory	Prepaid insurance
Sales revenue	Accumulated amortization
Store fixtures	Accounts receivable
Note payable, long-term	

Exercise 7-4   *Using a trial balance* *(Obj. 2)*

The following accounts and sums of accounts in the computerized accounting system of Drayton Supplies show some of the company's adjusted balances before closing:

Total assets	?
Current assets	16,800
Capital assets	40,200
Total liabilities	?
Current liabilities	3,300
Long-term liabilities	?
Capital	40,800
Withdrawals	15,000
Total revenues	54,000
Total expenses	33,000

Compute the missing amounts.

Exercise 7-5   Using a spreadsheet to compute amortization *(Obj. 3)*

A capital asset listed on a spreadsheet has a cost of $180,000; this amount is located in cell E7. The number of years of the asset's useful life is found in cell E9. Write the spreadsheet formula to express annual amortization expense for this asset. Assume the value at the end of the useful life will be zero.

Exercise 7-6   Using a spreadsheet *(Obj. 3)*

Refer to the spreadsheet screen in Exhibit 7-7, page 340. Suppose cells B1 through B4 are your business's actual income statement for the current year. You wish to develop your financial plan for the coming year. Assume that you expect revenues to increase by 10 percent and expenses to increase by 8 percent. Write the formulas in cells C2 through C4 to compute the amounts of expected revenues, expenses, and net income for the coming year.

Exercise 7-7   Computing financial statement amounts with a spreadsheet *(Obj. 3)*

Suppose the values of the following items are stored in the cells of Joe's Photos Co.'s spreadsheet:

Item	Cell
Total assets	E7
Current assets	E8
Capital assets	E9
Total liabilities	E10
Current liabilities	E11
Long-term liabilities	E12

Write the spreadsheet formula to calculate the store's:

a. Current ratio
b. Total owner's equity
c. Debt ratio

Exercise 7-8   Using the sales and cash receipts journals (perpetual inventory system) *(Obj. 4)*

The sales and cash receipts journals of Northern Electronics include the following entries:

Sales Journal

Date	Invoice No.	Account Debited	Post. Ref.	Accounts Receivable Dr. Sales Revenue Cr.	Cost of Goods Sold Dr. Inventory Cr.
Oct. 7	671	I. Woods	✔	2,232	1,320
10	672	W. Singh	✔	9,120	4,728
10	673	F. Weir	✔	1,656	984
12	674	J. Leggatt	✔	13,128	8,016
31		Total		26,136	15,048

Cash Receipts Journal

	Debits				Credits			
						Other Accounts		
Date	Cash	Sales Discounts	Accounts Receivable	Sales Revenue	Account Title	Post. Ref.	Amount	Cost of Goods Sold Dr. Inventory Cr.
Oct. 16					I. Woods	✔		
19					F. Weir	✔		
24	720			720				432
30					W. Singh	✔		

Northern Electronics makes all sales on credit terms of 2/10 n/30. Complete the cash receipts journal for those transactions indicated. Also, total the journal and show that total debits equal total credits. Each cash receipt was for the full amount of the receivable.

Exercise 7-9 *Classifying postings from the cash receipts journal* **(Obj. 4)**

The cash receipts journal of Campbell Sports follows:

Cash Receipts Journal   Page 7

	Debits				Credits		
					Other Accounts		
Date	Cash	Sales Discounts	Accounts Receivable	Sales Revenue	Account Title	Post. Ref.	Amount
Dec. 2	2,382	48	2,430		Magna Corp.	(a)	
9	737		737		Kamm, Inc.	(b)	
14	5,856			5,856			
19	9,720				Note Receivable	(c)	9,000
					Interest Revenue	(d)	720
30	471	10	481		J. T. Kazarian	(e)	
31	6,352			6,352			
31	25,518	58	3,648	12,208	Totals		9,720
	(f)	(g)	(h)	(i)			(j)

Campbell Sports' chart of accounts (general ledger) includes the following selected accounts, along with their account numbers:

Number	Account	Number	Account
111	Cash	511	Sales revenue
112	Accounts receivable	512	Sales discounts
113	Note receivable	513	Sales returns
119	Land	521	Interest revenue

Required

Indicate whether each posting reference (a) through (j) should be a

- Check mark (✔) for a posting to a customer account in the accounts receivable subsidiary ledger.
- Account number for a posting to an account in the general ledger. If so, give the account number.
- Letter (x) for an amount not posted.

Exercise 7-10 *Identifying transactions from postings to the accounts receivable ledger (Obj. 4)*

An account in the accounts receivable subsidiary ledger of Kettle Valley Office Supplies follows:

Beaver Valley Lumber Inc.   112590

Date		Jrnl. Ref.	Dr.	Cr.	Debit Balance
May 1	....				1,209
6	....	S.5	3,540		4,749
19	....	J.8		573	4,176
21	....	CR.9		2,109	2,067

Required

Describe the three posted transactions.

Exercise 7-11 *Recording purchase transactions in the general journal and purchases journal (Obj. 5)*

During June, Durant Dairy completed the following credit purchase transactions:

June	4	Purchased inventory, $1,904, from McDonald Ltd. Durant Dairy uses a perpetual inventory system.
	7	Purchased supplies, $107, from Central Co.
	19	Purchased equipment, $1,750, from Baker Corp.
	27	Purchased inventory, $2,210, from Khalil Inc.

Record these transactions first in the general journal—with explanations—and then in the purchases journal. Omit credit terms and posting references. Which procedure for recording transactions is quicker? Why?

Exercise 7-12 *Posting from the purchases journal; balancing the ledgers (Obj. 5)*

The purchases journal of Lightning Snowboards follows:

Purchases Journal   Page 7

Date	Account Credited	Terms	Post. Ref.	Accounts Payable Cr.	Inventory Dr.	Supplies Dr.	Other Accounts Dr. Acct. Title	Other Accounts Dr. Post. Ref.	Other Accounts Dr. Amt. Dr.
Sept. 2	Brotherton Inc.	n/30		4,160	4,160				
5	Rolf Office Supply	n/30		560		560			
13	Brotherton Inc.	2/10 n/30		2,710	2,710				
26	Marks Equipment Company	n/30		2,931			Equipment		2,931
30	Totals			10,361	6,870	560			2,931

Required

1. Open general ledger accounts for Inventory, Supplies, Equipment, and Accounts Payable. Post to these accounts from the purchases journal. Use dates and posting references in the ledger accounts.

2. Open accounts in the accounts payable subsidiary ledger for Brotherton Inc., Rolf Office Supply, and Marks Equipment Company. Post from the purchases journal. Use dates and journal references in the ledger accounts.

3. Balance the Accounts Payable control account in the general ledger with the total of the balances in the accounts payable subsidiary ledger.

4. Does Lightning Snowboards use a perpetual or a periodic inventory system?

Exercise 7-13   Using the cash payments journal (Obj. 5)

During February, Dean Products had the following transactions:

Feb. 3   Paid $2,700 on account to Marquis Corp. net of a $24 discount for an earlier purchase of inventory.
   6   Purchased inventory for cash, $3,800.
   11   Paid $1,150 for supplies.
   15   Purchased inventory on credit from Monroe Corporation, $1,548.
   16   Paid $24,186 on account to LaGrange Ltd.; there was no discount.
   21   Purchased furniture for cash, $2,880.
   26   Paid $11,460 on account to Graff Software Ltd. for an earlier $11,730 purchase of inventory. The purchase discount was $270.
   28   Made a semiannual interest payment of $2,400 on a long-term note payable. The entire payment was for interest. (Assume none of the interest had been accrued previously.)

Required

1. Draw a cash payments journal similar to the one illustrated in this chapter. Omit the payee column.

2. Record the transactions in the journal. Which transaction should not be recorded in the cash payments journal? In what journal does it belong?

3. Total the amount columns of the journal. Determine that the total debits equal the total credits.

Exercise 7-14   Using business documents to record transactions (Obj. 5)

Link Back to Chapter 5 (Recording Purchases, Sales, and Returns). The following documents describe two business transactions:

Invoice	
Date:	March 14, 2006
Sold to:	Eddie's Bicycle Shop
Sold by:	Schwinn Company
Terms:	2/10 n/30

Items Purchased   Bicycles

Quantity	Price	Total
8	$152	$1,216
2	112	224
10	96	960
Total...................		$2,400

Debit Memo	
Date:	March 20, 2006
Issued to:	Schwinn Company
Issued by:	Eddie's Bicycle Shop

Items Returneed   Bicycles

Quantity	Price	Total
2	$152	$304
2	112	224
Total...................		$528

Reason: Damaged in shipment

Use the general journal to record these transactions and Eddie's Bicycle Shop's cash payment on March 21. Record the transactions first on the books of Eddie's

Bicycle Shop and, second, on the books of Schwinn Company, which makes and sells bicycles. Both Eddie's Bicycle Shop and Schwinn Company use a perpetual inventory system as illustrated in Chapter 5. Schwinn Company's cost of the bicycles sold to Eddie's Bicycle Shop was $1,280. Schwinn Company's cost of the returned merchandise was $256. Round to the nearest dollar. Explanations are not required. Using the perpetual system of inventory, set up your answer in the following format:

Date	Eddie's Bicycle Shop Journal Entries	Schwinn Journal Entries

Challenge Exercise

Exercise 7-15   *Using the special journals (Obj. 4, 5)*

Link Back to Chapter 5 (Cost of goods sold, gross margin).

1. Austin Sound Centre's special journals in Exhibits 7-10 through 7-13 (pages 343–352) provide the manager with much of the data needed for preparation of the financial statements. Austin Sound uses the *perpetual* inventory system, so the amount of cost of goods sold is simply the ending balance in that account. The manager needs to know the business's gross margin for November. Compute the gross margin.

2. Suppose Austin Sound used the *periodic* inventory system. In that case, the business must compute cost of goods sold by the formula:

    Cost of goods sold:
    Beginning inventory... $ X*
    + Net purchases...   XXX
    = Cost of goods available for sale.....................   X,XXX
    − Ending inventory...   (XX)
    = Cost of goods sold .... $ XX

    Perform this calculation of cost of goods sold for Austin Sound. Does this computation of cost of goods sold agree with your answer to requirement 1?

Beyond the Numbers

Beyond the Numbers 7-1   *Designing a special journal (Obj. 4, 5)*

King Technology Associates creates and sells cutting-edge network software. King's quality control officer estimates that 20 percent of the company's sales and purchases of inventory are returned for additional debugging. King needs special journals for

- Sales returns and allowances
- Purchase returns and allowances

Required

1. Design the two special journals. For each journal, include a column for the appropriate business document.

2. Enter one transaction in each journal, using the Austin Sound transaction data illustrated on pages 353 and 354. Show all posting references, including those for column totals. In the purchase returns and allowances journal, assume debit memo number 14.

Ethical Issue

On a recent trip to Brazil, Carlo Degas, sales manager of Cyber Systems, took his wife along for a vacation and included her airfare and meals on his expense report, which he submitted for reimbursement. Chelsea Brindley, vice-president of sales and Degas' boss, thought his total travel and entertainment expenses seemed excessive. However, Brindley approved the reimbursement because she owed Degas a favour. Brindley, well aware that the company president routinely reviewed all expenses recorded in the cash payments journal, had the accountant record the expenses of Degas' wife in the general journal as follows:

Sales Promotion Expense	7,500	
Cash		7,500

Required

1. Does recording the transaction in the general journal rather than in the cash payments journal affect the amounts of cash and total expenses reported in the financial statements?

2. Why did Ms. Brindley want this transaction recorded in the general journal?

3. What is the ethical issue in this situation? What role does accounting play in the ethical issue?

Problems (Group A)

Problem 7-1A *Using a spreadsheet to prepare a partial balance sheet and evaluate financial positions* **(Obj. 3)**

Media Companion CD-ROM

The spreadsheet below shows the assets section of the TCP Products balance sheet:

	A	B
5	Assets:	
6	Current assets:	
7	Cash	
8	Receivables	
9	Inventory	
10		
11	Total current assets	
12		
13	Equipment	
14	Accumulated amortization	
15		
16	Equipment, net	
17		
18	Total assets	
19		

Required

1. Write the word *number* in the cells (indicated by colour) where numbers will be entered.

2. Write the appropriate formula in each cell that will need a formula. Symbols from which to choose are:

+	add	/	divide
–	subtract		=SUM(beginning cell:ending cell)
*	multiply		

3. Last year TCP Products used this spreadsheet to prepare the company's balance sheet for the current year. The budgeted balance sheet shows the company's goal for total current assets at the end of the year. It is now one year later, and TCP Products has prepared its actual year-end balance sheet. State how the company can use this balance sheet in decision making.

Problem 7-2A *Using the sales, cash receipts, and general journals (with the perpetual inventory system)* **(Obj. 4)**

The general ledger of Corgan Systems Supply includes the following accounts:

Cash	111	Sales Revenue	411
Accounts Receivable	112	Sales Discounts	412
Notes Receivable	115	Sales Returns and Allowances	413
Inventory	131	Interest Revenue	417
Equipment	141	Gain on Sale of Land	418
Land	142	Cost of Goods Sold	511

All credit sales are on the company's standard terms of 2/10 n/30. Transactions in February that affected sales and cash receipts were as follows:

Feb. 1   Sold inventory on credit to Ijiri Ltd., $4,000. Corgan Systems Supply's cost of these goods was $2,228.

5   As a favour to another company, sold new equipment for its cost of $3,080, receiving cash in this amount.

6   Cash sales of merchandise for the week totalled $8,428 (cost, $5,448).

8   Sold merchandise on account to McNair Ltd., $11,320 (cost, $7,156).

9   Sold land that cost $44,000 for cash of $80,000.

11   Sold goods on account to Nickerson Builders Inc., $12,198 (cost, $7,706).

11   Received cash from Ijiri Ltd. in full settlement of its account receivable from February 1.

13   Cash sales of merchandise for the week were $7,980 (cost, $5,144).

15   Sold inventory on credit to Montez and Montez, a partnership, $3,200 (cost, $2,068).

18   Received inventory sold on February 8 to McNair Ltd. for $480. The goods shipped were the wrong colour. These goods cost Corgan Systems Supply $292.

19   Sold merchandise on account to Nickerson Builders, $10,400 (cost, $7,854).

20   Cash sales of merchandise for the week were $9,320 (cost, $6,296).

21   Received $4,800 cash from McNair Ltd. in partial settlement of its account receivable.

22   Received payment in full from Montez and Montez for its account receivable from February 15.

22   Sold goods on account to Diamond Inc., $8,088 (cost, $5,300).

25   Collected $8,400 on a note receivable, of which $400 was interest.

27   Cash sales of merchandise for the week totalled $8,910 (cost, $5,808).

27   Sold inventory on account to Littleton Corporation, $4,580 (cost, $2,868).

28   Received goods sold on February 22 to Diamond Inc. for $2,720. The goods were shipped in error, so were returned to inventory. The cost of these goods was $1,920.

28   Received $6,040 cash on account from McNair Ltd.

Required

1. Use the appropriate journal to record the above transactions in a sales journal (omit the Invoice No. column), a cash receipts journal, and a general journal. Corgan Systems Supply records sales returns and allowances in the general journal.

2. Total each column of the cash receipts journal. Determine that the total debits equal the total credits.

3. Show how postings would be made from the journals by writing the account numbers and check marks in the appropriate places in the journals.

Problem 7-3A *Correcting errors in the cash receipts journal (perpetual inventory system)*
(Obj. 4)

The Cash Receipts Journal (A) below contains five entries. All five entries are for legitimate cash receipt transactions, but the journal contains some errors in recording the transactions. In fact, only one entry is correct, and each of the other four entries contains one error.

Required

1. Identify the correct entry in Cash Receipts Journal (A).
2. Identify the error in each of the other four entries in Cash Receipts Journal (A).
3. Using the Cash Receipts Journal (B) format, prepare a corrected cash receipts journal.

(A)   Cash Receipts Journal   Page 16

| | Debits | | | | Credits | | | |
| | | | | | Other Accounts | | | |
Date	Cash	Sales Discounts	Accounts Receivable	Sales Revenue	Account Title	Post. Ref.	Amount	Cost of Goods Sold Dr. Inventory Cr.
Sept.								
3	711	34	745		Alcon Labs Ltd.	✔		
9			346	346	Carl Ryther	✔		
10	11,000			11,000	Land	19		
19	73							44
30	1,060			1,133				631
	12,844	34	1,091	12,479	Totals			675
	(11)	(42)	(12)	(41)			(✔)	51/13

Total Dr. = $12,878   Total Cr. = $13,570

(B)   Cash Receipts Journal   Page 16

| | Debits | | | | Credits | | | |
| | | | | | Other Accounts | | | |
Date	Cash	Sales Discounts	Accounts Receivable	Sales Revenue	Account Title	Post. Ref.	Amount	Cost of Goods Sold Dr. Inventory Cr.
Sept.								
3					Alcon Labs Ltd.	✔		
9					Carl Ryther	✔		
10					Land	19		
19								
30								
	13,190	34	1,091	1,133	Totals		11,000	675
	(11)	(42)	(12)	(41)			(✔)	51/13

Total Dr. = $13,224   Total Cr. = $13,244

Problem 7-4A *Using the purchases, cash payments, and general journals* **(Obj. 5)**

The general ledger of Hackman Luggage Company includes the following accounts:

Cash	111	Equipment	189
Inventory	131	Accounts Payable	211
Prepaid Insurance	161	Rent Expense	562
Supplies	171	Utilities Expense	565

Transactions in November that affected purchases and cash payments were as follows:

Nov. 1   Paid monthly rent, debiting Rent Expense for $1,350.
   3   Purchased inventory on credit from Sylvania Ltd., $2,000. Terms were 2/15 n/45.
   4   Purchased supplies on credit terms of 2/10 n/30 from Harmon Sales Ltd., $800.
   7   Paid gas and water bills, $406.
  10   Purchased equipment on account from Lancer Corp., $1,100. Payment terms were 2/10 n/30.
  11   Returned the equipment to Lancer Corp. It was defective.
  12   Paid Sylvania Ltd. the amount owed on the purchase of November 3.
  12   Purchased inventory on account from Lancer Corp., $1,100. Terms were 2/10 n/30.
  14   Purchased inventory for cash, $1,600.
  15   Paid an insurance premium, debiting Prepaid Insurance, $2,416.
  16   Paid the account payable to Harmon Sales Ltd. from November 4.
  17   Paid electricity bill, $200.
  20   Paid the November 12 account payable to Lancer Corp., less the purchase discount.
  21   Purchased supplies on account from Master Supply Ltd., $754, terms net 30.
  22   Purchased inventory on credit terms of 1/10 n/30 from Linz Brothers Inc., $3,400.
  26   Returned $500 of inventory purchased on November 22 to Linz Brothers Inc.
  30   Paid Linz Brothers Inc. the net amount owed.

Required

1. Use the appropriate journal to record the above transactions in a purchases journal, a cash payments journal (do not use the Cheque No. column), and a general journal. Hackman Luggage Company records purchase returns in the general journal.

2. Total each column of the special journals. Show that the total debits equal the total credits in each special journal.

3. Show how postings would be made from the journals by writing the account numbers and check marks in the appropriate places in the journals.

Problem 7-5A *Understanding how manual accounting systems are used; using the cash payments journal (perpetual inventory system)* **(Obj. 2, 4)**

Carey Distributing had the following transactions for the month of June 2006:

June 1   Sold $6,000 of merchandise to Thoms Supply Ltd., terms 2/10 n/30. Inventory had a cost of $4,125.
   3   Purchased $4,500 of merchandise from STU Suppliers Inc., terms net 30.
   6   Paid for the purchase of June 3 (STU Suppliers Inc.), cheque #12.
   7   Paid $8,250 wages to employee, cheque #13.
   9   Owner withdrew $11,250 for personal use, cheque #14.
  11   Collected $1,470 from Thoms Supply Ltd. (June 1) with the discount allowed and issued a credit memo for $750 allowance for damaged merchandise.
  13   Purchased equipment from DE Machinery Inc., $7,500, terms 2/10 n/30.
  14   Issued a debit memo to DE Machinery Inc. (June 13) for $1,500 of equipment returned as defective.
  15   Sold $3,750 of merchandise to DePloy Construction Ltd., receiving $1,500 and a promise to pay the balance in 30 days. Inventory had a cost of $2,250.
  16   Paid the account owing to DE Machinery Inc. (June 13, 14), cheque #15.
  17   Purchased $22,500 of equipment from Alfreds Equipment Inc., terms net 60.

June 22 Paid a $7,500 note due to the Commercial Bank, plus interest of $750, cheque #16.
24 Sold $2,625 of merchandise for cash; inventory cost was $1,500.
25 Paid $1,125 to Canada Customs and Revenue Agency for income taxes owing for the year 2006, cheque #17.
26 Returned $750 of the merchandise purchased from STU Suppliers Inc.
28 Purchased inventory for $4,500 from Damon Ltd., paying $1,500 down (cheque #18) and promising to pay the balance in 30 days.
30 Recorded the adjusting journal entries for the month of June.

Required

1. Indicate which journal would be used to record each of the transactions assuming Carey Distributing uses a general journal, a sales journal, a cash receipts journal, a purchases journal, and a cash payments journal.
2. Record the appropriate transactions in the cash payments journal, using the cash payments journal format shown in this chapter.
3. Show how postings would be made from the cash payments journal by writing the account numbers and check marks in the appropriate place in the cash payments journal. Select your own three-digit account numbers.

Problem 7-6A   *Using all the journals, posting, and balancing the ledgers*   *(Obj. 4, 5)*

Whitehead Sales Company, which uses the perpetual inventory system and makes all credit sales with terms 2/10 n/30, had these transactions during January:

Jan. 2 Issued invoice no. 191 for sale on account to Wooten Design Ltd., $9,400. Whitehead's cost of this inventory was $5,560.
3 Purchased inventory on credit terms of 3/10 n/60 from Delwood Co., $23,600.
4 Sold inventory for cash, $3,232 (cost, $2,040).
5 Issued cheque no. 473 to purchase furniture for cash, $4,348.
8 Collected interest revenue of $9,760.
9 Issued invoice no. 192 for sale on account to Vachon Inc., $25,000 (cost, $13,200).
10 Purchased inventory for cash, $3,104, issuing cheque no. 474.
12 Received $9,212 cash from Wooten Design Ltd. in full settlement of its account receivable.
13 Issued cheque no. 475 to pay Delwood Co. net amount owed from January 3.
13 Purchased supplies on account from Havrilla Corp., $2,756. Terms were net end of month.
15 Sold inventory on account to Wakeland Ltd., issuing invoice no. 193 for $2,972 (cost, $1,640).
17 Issued credit memo to Wakeland Ltd. for $2,972 for merchandise sent in error and returned to Whitehead by Wakeland. Also accounted for receipt of the inventory.
18 Issued invoice no. 194 for credit sale to Wooten Design Ltd., $7,300 (cost, $3,880).
19 Received $24,500 from Vachon Inc. in full settlement of its account receivable from January 9.
20 Purchased inventory on credit terms of net 30 from Jasper Sales Ltd., $8,600.
22 Purchased furniture on credit terms of 3/10 n/60 from Delwood Co., $3,100.
22 Issued cheque no. 476 to pay for insurance coverage, debiting Prepaid Insurance for $5,380.
24 Sold supplies to an employee for cash of $344, which was the cost of the supplies.
25 Issued cheque no. 477 to pay utilities, $1,552.
28 Purchased inventory on credit terms of 2/10 n/30 from Havrilla Corp., $1,684.
29 Returned damaged inventory to Havrilla Corp., issuing a debit memo for $1,684.
29 Sold goods on account to Vachon Inc., issuing invoice no. 195 for $2,268 (cost, $1,256).
30 Issued cheque no. 478 to pay Havrilla Corp. on account from January 13.
31 Received cash in full on account from Wooten Design Ltd. for credit sale of January 18. There was no discount.
31 Issued cheque no. 479 to pay monthly salaries of $10,400.

Required

1. For Whitehead Sales Company, open the following general ledger accounts using the account numbers given:

Cash	111	Sales Discounts	412
Accounts Receivable	112	Sales Returns and	
Supplies	116	Allowances	413
Prepaid Insurance	117	Interest Revenue	419
Inventory	118	Cost of Goods Sold	511
Furniture	151	Salary Expense	531
Accounts Payable	211	Utilities Expense	541
Sales Revenue	411		

2. Open these accounts in the subsidiary ledgers: Accounts receivable subsidiary ledger—Vachon Inc., Wakeland Ltd., and Wooten Design Ltd.; accounts payable subsidiary ledger—Delwood Co., Havrilla Corp., and Jasper Sales Ltd.

3. Enter the transactions in a sales journal (page 8), a cash receipts journal (page 3), a purchases journal (page 6), a cash payments journal (page 9), and a general journal (page 4), as appropriate.

4. Post daily to the accounts receivable subsidiary ledger and to the accounts payable subsidiary ledger. On January 31, post to the general ledger.

5. Total each column of the special journals. Show that the total debits equal the total credits in each special journal.

6. Balance the total of the customer account balances in the accounts receivable subsidiary ledger against Accounts Receivable in the general ledger. Do the same for the accounts payable subsidiary ledger and Accounts Payable in the general ledger.

Problems (Group B)

Media Companion CD-ROM

Problem 7-1B *Using a spreadsheet to prepare an income statement and evaluate operations (Obj. 3)*

The following spreadsheet shows the income statement of McBride Wholesalers.

	A	B
5	Revenues:	
6	Service revenue	
7	Rent revenue	
8		
9	Total revenue	
10		
11	Expenses	
12	Salary expense	
13	Supplies expense	
14	Rent expense	
15	Amortization expense	
16		
17	Total expenses	
18		
19	Net income	
20		

Required

1. Write the word *number* in the cells (indicated by colour) where numbers will be entered.

2. Write the appropriate formula in each cell that will need a formula. Symbols from which to choose are:

+	add
–	subtract
*	multiply
/	divide

=SUM(beginning cell:ending cell)

3. Last year McBride Wholesalers used this spreadsheet to prepare the company's budgeted income statement—which shows the company's net income goal—for the current year. It is now one year later, and McBride has prepared its actual income statement for the year. State how the owner of the company can use this income statement in decision making.

Problem 7-2B *Using the sales, cash receipts, and general journals (with the perpetual inventory system)* *(Obj. 4)*

The general ledger of Jarvis Distributors includes the following accounts, among others:

Cash	11	Sales Revenue	41
Accounts Receivable	12	Sales Discounts	42
Inventory	13	Sales Returns and Allowances	43
Notes Receivable	15	Interest Revenue	47
Supplies	16	Cost of Goods Sold	51
Land	18		

All credit sales are on the company's standard terms of 2/10 n/30. Transactions in May that affected sales and cash receipts were as follows:

May 2 Sold inventory on credit to Fortin Inc., $2,800. Jarvis's cost of these goods was $1,600.

4 As a favour to a competitor, sold supplies at cost, $340, receiving cash.

7 Cash sales of merchandise for the week totalled $7,560 (cost, $6,560).

9 Sold merchandise on account to A. L. Price, $29,280 (cost, $20,440).

10 Sold land that cost $40,000 for cash of $40,000.

11 Sold goods on account to Sloan Forge Ltd., $20,416 (cost, $14,080).

12 Received cash from Fortin Inc. in full settlement of its account receivable from May 2.

14 Cash sales of merchandise for the week were $8,424 (cost, $6,120).

15 Sold inventory on credit to the partnership of Wilkie & Blinn, $14,600 (cost, $9,040).

18 Received inventory sold on May 9 to A. L. Price for $2,400. The goods shipped were the wrong size. These goods cost Jarvis $1,760.

20 Sold merchandise on account to Sloan Forge Ltd., $2,516 (cost, $1,800).

21 Cash sales of merchandise for the week were $3,960 (cost, $2,760).

22 Received $16,000 cash from A. L. Price in partial settlement of his account receivable.

25 Received cash from Wilkie & Blinn for its account receivable from May 15.

25 Sold goods on account to Olsen Inc., $6,080 (cost, $4,200).

27 Collected $20,500 on a note receivable, of which $500 was interest.

28 Cash sales of merchandise for the week were $15,096 (cost, $9,840).

29 Sold inventory on account to R. O. Bankston Inc., $968 (cost, $680).

30 Received goods sold on May 25 to Olsen Inc. for $160. The wrong items were shipped. The cost of the goods was $100.

31 Received $10,880 cash on account from A. L. Price.

Required

1. Jarvis Distributors records sales returns and allowances in the general journal. Use the appropriate journal to record the above transactions in a sales journal (omit the Invoice No. column), a cash receipts journal, and a general journal.

2. Total each column of the cash receipts journal. Show that the total debits equal the total credits.

3. Show how postings would be made from the journals by writing the account numbers and check marks in the appropriate places in the journals.

Problem 7-3B *Correcting errors in the cash receipts journal (perpetual inventory system)* **(Obj. 4)**

The cash receipts journal below contains five entries. All five entries are for legitimate cash receipt transactions, but the journal contains some errors in recording the transactions. In fact, only one entry is correct, and each of the other four entries contains one error.

Cash Receipts Journal Page 22

| | Debits | | Credits | | | | | |
| | | | | | Other Accounts | | | |
Date	Cash	Sales Discounts	Accounts Receivable	Sales Revenue	Account Title	Post. Ref.	Amount	Cost of Goods Sold Dr. Inventory Cr.
May 6		420		420				203
7	600	22			Marc Fortin	✔	622	
14	5,740				Note Receivable	13	5,390	
					Interest Revenue	45	350	
18				462				210
24	1,540		1,078					
	7,880	442	1,078	882	Totals		6,362	413
	(11)	(42)	(12)	(41)			(✔)	51/13

Total Dr. = $8,322   Total Cr. = $8,322

Required

1. Identify the correct entry.
2. Identify the error in each of the other four entries.
3. Using the following format, prepare a corrected cash receipts journal.

Cash Receipts Journal Page 22

| | Debits | | Credits | | | | | |
| | | | | | Other Accounts | | | |
Date	Cash	Sales Discounts	Accounts Receivable	Sales Revenue	Account Title	Post. Ref.	Amount	Cost of Goods Sold Dr. Inventory Cr.
May 6								
7					Marc Fortin	✔		
14					Note Receivable	13		
					Interest Revenue	45		
18								
24								
	8,300	22	1,700	882	Totals		5,740	
	(11)	(42)	(12)	(41)			(✔)	

Total Dr. = $8,322   Total Cr. = $8,322

Problem 7-4B *Using the purchases, cash payments, and general journals* *(Obj. 5)*

The general ledger of Nell Supplies includes the following accounts:

Cash	111	Furniture	187
Inventory	131	Accounts Payable	211
Prepaid Insurance	161	Rent Expense	564
Supplies	171	Utilities Expense	583

Transactions in August that affected purchases and cash payments were as follows:

Aug. 1   Purchased inventory on credit from Worth Corp., $1,900. Terms were 2/10 n/30.
     1   Paid monthly rent, debiting Rent Expense for $2,000.
     5   Purchased supplies on credit terms of 2/10 n/30 from Ross Supply Ltd., $450.
     8   Paid electricity bill, $300.
     9   Purchased furniture on account from Rite Office Supply, $4,100. Payment terms were net 30.
    10   Returned the furniture to Rite Office Supply. It was the wrong colour.
    11   Paid Worth Corp. the amount owed on the purchase of August 1.
    12   Purchased inventory on account from Wynne Inc., $4,400. Terms were 3/10 n/30.
    13   Purchased inventory for cash, $655.
    14   Paid a semiannual insurance premium, debiting Prepaid Insurance, $600.
    15   Paid the account payable to Ross Supply Ltd., from August 5.
    18   Paid gas and water bills, $100.
    21   Purchased inventory on credit terms of 1/10 n/45 from Cyber Software Ltd., $5,200.
    21   Paid account payable to Wynne Inc., from August 12.
    22   Purchased supplies on account from Favron Sales, $274. Terms were net 30.
    25   Returned $1,200 of the inventory purchased on August 21 to Cyber Software Ltd.
    31   Paid Cyber Software Ltd. the net amount owed from August 21.

Required

1. Nell Supplies records purchase returns in the general journal. Use the appropriate journal to record the above transactions in a purchases journal, a cash payments journal (omit the Cheque No. column), and a general journal.

2. Total each column of the special journals. Show that the total debits equal the total credits in each special journal.

3. Show how postings would be made from the journals by writing the account numbers and check marks in the appropriate places in the journals.

Problem 7-5B *Understanding how manual accounting systems are used; using the cash payments journal (perpetual inventory system)* *(Obj. 2, 4)*

Quail Distributors had the following transactions for the month of April 2007:

April 1   Sold $1,500 of merchandise to James Inc., terms 2/10 n/30. Inventory had a cost of $670.
     3   Purchased $14,250 of merchandise from MNO Suppliers Ltd., terms net 30.
     6   Paid for the purchase of April 3 (MNO Suppliers Ltd.), cheque #12.
     7   Paid $5,250 wages to employee, cheque #13.
     9   Owner withdrew $7,500 for personal use, cheque #14.
    11   Collected $735 from James Inc. (April 1) with the discount allowed and issued a credit memo for $375 allowance for damaged merchandise.
    13   Purchased equipment from MB Machinery Ltd., $11,250, terms 2/10 n/30.
    14   Issued a debit memo to MB Machinery Ltd. (April 13) for $750 of equipment returned as defective.
    15   Sold $6,000 of merchandise to St. Boniface Supply Corp., receiving $750 and a promise to pay the balance in 30 days. Inventory cost, $3,750.

April 16   Paid the account owing to MB Machinery Ltd., cheque #15.

17   Purchased $18,750 of equipment from Dearing Equipment Inc., terms net 60.

22   Paid a $4,500 note due to the Commercial Bank, plus interest of $450, cheque #16.

24   Sold $1,125 of merchandise for cash; inventory cost was $750.

25   Paid $750 to Canada Customs and Revenue Agency for income taxes owing from December 31, 2006, cheque #17.

26   Returned $2,250 of the merchandise purchased from MNO Suppliers Ltd.

28   Purchased inventory for $3,000 from Artois Ltd., paying $750 now (cheque #18) and promising to pay the balance in 30 days.

30   Recorded the adjusting journal entries for the month of April.

Required

1. Indicate which journal would be used to record each of the transactions assuming Quail Distributors uses a general journal, a sales journal, a cash receipts journal, a purchases journal, and a cash payments journal.

2. Record the appropriate transactions in the cash payments journal, using the cash payments journal format shown in this chapter.

3. Show how postings would be made from the cash payments journal by writing the account numbers and check marks in the appropriate place in the cash payments journal. Select your own three-digit account numbers.

Problem 7-6B   *Using all the journals, posting, and balancing the ledgers*   *(Obj. 4, 5)*

McCabe Distributors, which uses the perpetual inventory system and makes all credit sales on terms of 2/10 n/30, completed the following transactions during July:

July   2   Issued invoice no. 913 for sale on account to N. J. Seiko Inc., $12,300. McCabe's cost of this inventory was $5,400.

3   Purchased inventory on credit terms of 3/10 n/60 from Chicosky Corp., $7,401.

5   Sold inventory for cash, $3,231 (cost, $1,440).

5   Issued cheque no. 532 to purchase furniture for cash, $6,555.

8   Collected interest revenue of $5,325.

9   Issued invoice no. 914 for sale on account to Bell Ltd., $16,650 (cost, $6,930).

10   Purchased inventory for cash, $3,429, issuing cheque no. 533.

12   Received cash from N. J. Seiko Inc. in full settlement of its account receivable from the sale on July 2.

13   Issued cheque no. 534 to pay Chicosky Corp. the net amount owed from July 3. (Round to the nearest dollar.)

13   Purchased supplies on account from Manley Inc., $1,323. Terms were net end of month.

15   Sold inventory on account to M. O. Brown, issuing invoice no. 915 for $1,995 (cost, $720).

17   Issued credit memo to M. O. Brown for $1,995 for merchandise sent in error and returned by Brown. Also accounted for receipt of the inventory.

18   Issued invoice no. 916 for credit sale to N. J. Seiko Inc., $1,071 (cost, $381).

19   Received $16,317 from Bell Ltd. in full settlement of its account receivable from July 9.

20   Purchased inventory on credit terms of net 30 from Sims Distributing Ltd., $6,141.

22   Purchased furniture on credit terms of 3/10 n/60 from Chicosky Corp., $1,935.

22   Issued cheque no. 535 to pay for insurance coverage, debiting Prepaid Insurance for $3,000.

24   Sold supplies to an employee for cash of $162, which was the cost of the supplies.

25   Issued cheque no. 536 to pay utilities, $1,359.

28   Purchased inventory on credit terms of 2/10 n/30 from Manley Inc., $2,025.

29   Returned damaged inventory to Manley Inc., issuing a debit memo for $2,025.

July 29 Sold goods on account to Bell Ltd., issuing invoice no. 917 for $1,488 (cost, $660).
30 Issued cheque no. 537 to pay Manley Inc. in full on account from July 13.
31 Received cash in full on account from N. J. Seiko Inc.
31 Issued cheque no. 538 to pay monthly salaries of $7,041.

Required

1. For McCabe Distributors, open the following general ledger accounts using the account numbers given:

Cash	111	Sales Revenue	411
Accounts Receivable	112	Sales Discounts	412
Supplies	116	Sales Returns and Allowances	413
Prepaid Insurance	117	Interest Revenue	419
Inventory	118	Cost of Goods Sold	511
Furniture	151	Salary Expense	531
Accounts Payable	211	Utilities Expense	541

2. Open these accounts in the subsidiary ledgers: Accounts receivable subsidiary ledger—Bell Ltd., M. O. Brown, and N. J. Seiko Inc.; accounts payable subsidiary ledger—Chicosky Corp., Manley Inc., and Sims Distributing Ltd.

3. Enter the transactions in a sales journal (page 7), a cash receipts journal (page 5), a purchases journal (page 10), a cash payments journal (page 8), and a general journal (page 6), as appropriate.

4. Post daily to the accounts receivable subsidiary ledger and to the accounts payable subsidiary ledger. On July 31, post to the general ledger.

5. Total each column of the special journals. Show that the total debits equal the total credits in each special journal.

6. Balance the total of the customer account balances in the accounts receivable subsidiary ledger against Accounts Receivable in the general ledger. Do the same for the accounts payable subsidiary ledger and Accounts Payable in the general ledger.

Challenge Problems

Problem 7-1C *Advantage of an effective accounting system* *(Obj. 1)*

An accounting information system that provides timely, accurate information to management is an important asset of any organization. This is especially true as organizations become larger and move into different parts of the world. The integration of computers into many organizations' information systems has enhanced their usefulness to the organization.

Required

Assume your older sister is a pharmacist. She regards an information system as simply an accounting system that keeps track of her company's revenues and expenses. Explain to her how an effective accounting information system can make her a more effective pharmacist.

Problem 7-2C *Providing advice about a computerized accounting system* *(Obj. 2)*

Information technology is increasingly sophisticated and everyone wants the latest technology. Your brother has asked you about installing this "wonderful" computer system in his car dealership and auto repair business. The salesperson has promised your brother that the system "will do everything you want and then some." Your brother has come to you for advice about acquiring this new computerized accounting information system. At present he uses a manual accounting system.

Required

Provide the advice your brother wants, focusing on the costs of the new computerized accounting information system; your brother has been told all the positive aspects of purchasing the system.

Extending Your Knowledge

Decision Problems

1. Reconstructing transactions from amounts posted to the accounts receivable subsidiary ledger   (Obj. 4)

A fire destroyed some accounting records of Red River Company. The owner, Jennifer Chu, asks for your help in reconstructing the records. *She needs to know the beginning and ending balances of Accounts Receivable and the credit sales and cash receipts on account from customers during March.* All Red River Company sales are on credit, with payment terms of 2/10 n/30. All cash receipts on account reached Red River Company within the 10-day discount period, except as noted. The only accounting record preserved from the fire is the accounts receivable subsidiary ledger, which follows:

Adam Chi

Date		Jrnl. Ref.	Debit	Credit	Balance
Mar. 8		S.6	7,500		7,500
16		S.6	1,500		9,000
18		CR.8		7,500	1,500
19		J.5		300	1,200
27		CR.8		1,200	-0-

Anna Fowler

Date		Jrnl. Ref.	Debit	Credit	Balance
Mar. 1	Balance				1,650
5		CR.8		1,650	-0-
11		S.6	600		600
21		CR.8		600	-0-
24		S.6	6,000		6,000

Norris Associates Ltd.

Date		Jrnl. Ref.	Debit	Credit	Balance
Mar. 1	Balance				4,500
15		S.6	4,500		9,000
29		CR.8		4,350*	4,650

Robertson Inc.

Date		Jrnl. Ref.	Debit	Credit	Balance
Mar. 1	Balance				750
3		CR.8		750	-0-
25		S.6	6,000		6,000
29		S.6	1,800		7,800

*Cash receipt did not occur within the discount period.

2. Understanding an accounting system   (Obj. 4, 5)

The external auditor must ensure that the amounts shown on the balance sheet for Accounts Receivable represent actual amounts that customers owe the company. Each customer account in the accounts receivable subsidiary ledger must represent an actual credit sale to the person or company indicated, and the customer's balance must not have been collected. This auditing concept is called *validity,* or *validating* the accounts receivable.

The auditor must also ensure that all amounts that the company owes are included in Accounts Payable and other liability accounts. For example, all credit purchases of inventory made by the company (and not yet paid) should be included in the balance of the Accounts Payable account. This auditing concept is called *completeness.*

Required

Suggest how an auditor might test a customer's account receivable balance for validity. Indicate how the auditor might test the balance of the Accounts Payable account for completeness.

Comprehensive Problem
for Part One

1. Completing a Merchandiser's Accounting Cycle

The end-of-month trial balance of Lakehead Building Materials at January 31, 2006, is shown on the next page.

Additional data at January 31, 2006:

a. Supplies consumed during the month, $3,000. One-half is selling expense, and the other half is general expense.

b. Amortization for the month: building, $8,000; fixtures, $9,600. One-fourth of amortization is selling expense, and three-fourths is general expense.

c. Unearned sales revenue still unearned, $2,400.

d. Accrued salaries, a general expense, $2,300.

e. Accrued interest expense, $1,560.

f. Inventory on hand, $127,440. Lakehead Building Materials uses the perpetual inventory system.

LAKEHEAD BUILDING MATERIALS
Trial Balance
January 31, 2006

Account Number	Account	Balance Debit	Balance Credit
110	Cash...	$ 32,860	
120	Accounts receivable	38,180	
130	Inventory	130,800	
140	Supplies	5,400	
150	Building	376,340	
151	Accumulated amortization—building..................		$ 72,000
160	Fixtures	91,200	
161	Accumulated amortization—fixtures....................		11,600
200	Accounts payable..		56,600
205	Salary payable...		0
210	Interest payable		0
240	Unearned sales revenue		13,120
250	Note payable, long-term		174,000
300	G. Wells, capital...		289,960
311	G. Wells, withdrawals...	18,400	
400	Sales revenue		375,940
402	Sales discounts...	14,600	
430	Sales returns and allowances...............................	16,280	
500	Cost of goods sold...	206,000	
600	Selling expense	43,040	
700	General expense	20,120	
705	Interest expense...	0	
	Total..	$993,220	$993,220

Required

1. Using three-column accounts, open the accounts listed on the trial balance, inserting their unadjusted balances. Date the balances of the following accounts January 1: Supplies; Building; Accumulated Amortization—Building; Fixtures; Accumulated Amortization—Fixtures; Unearned Sales Revenue; and G. Wells, Capital. Date the balance of G. Wells, Withdrawals, January 31.

2. Enter the trial balance on an accounting work sheet, and complete the work sheet for the month ended January 31, 2006. Lakehead Building Materials groups all operating expenses under two accounts, Selling Expense and General Expense. Leave two blank lines under Selling Expense and three blank lines under General Expense.

3. Prepare the company's multi-step income statement and statement of owner's equity for the month ended January 31, 2006. Also prepare the balance sheet at that date in report form.

4. Journalize the adjusting and closing entries at January 31, 2006, using page 3 of the general journal.

5. Post the adjusting and closing entries, using dates and posting references.

6. Compute Lakehead Building Materials' current ratio and debt ratio at January 31, 2006, and compare these values with the industry averages of 1.9 for the current ratio and 0.57 for the debt ratio. Compute the gross margin percentage and the rate of inventory turnover for the month (the inventory balance at the end of December 2005, was $133,000) and compare these ratio values with the industry averages of 0.36 for the gross margin ratio and 1.7 times for inventory turnover. Does Lakehead Building Materials appear to be stronger or weaker than the average company in the building materials industry?

2. Completing the Accounting Cycle for a Merchandising Entity

Note: This problem can be solved with or without special journals. See Requirement 2.
Yellowknife Distributors closes its books and prepares financial statements at the end of each month. Yellowknife uses the perpetual inventory system. The company completed the following transactions during August 2007.

Aug. 1   Issued cheque no. 682 for August office rent $1,000. (Debit Rent Expense.)

2   Issued cheque no. 683 to pay salaries of $620, which includes salary payable of $465 from July 31. Yellowknife does *not* use reversing entries.

2   Issued invoice no. 503 for sale on account to R. T. Loeb, $300. Yellowknife's cost of this merchandise was $95.*

3   Purchased inventory on credit terms of 1/15 n/60 from Grant Ltd., $700.

4   Received net amount of cash on account from Fullam Corp., $1,078, within the discount period.

4   Sold inventory for cash, $165 (cost, $52).

5   Received from Park-Hee Inc. merchandise that had been sold earlier for $275 (cost, $87). The wrong merchandise had been sent.

5   Issued cheque no. 684 to purchase supplies for cash, $390.

6   Collected interest revenue of $550.

7   Issued invoice no. 504 for sale on account to K. D. Skipper Inc., $1,200 (cost, $380).

8   Issued cheque no. 685 to pay Fayda Corp. $1,300 of the amount owed at July 31. This payment occurred after the end of the discount period.

11   Issued cheque no. 686 to pay Grant Ltd. the net amount owed from August 3.

12   Received cash from R. T. Loeb in full settlement of her account receivable from August 2.

16   Issued cheque no. 687 to pay salary expense of $620.

19   Purchased inventory for cash, $425, issuing cheque no. 688.

22   Purchased furniture on credit terms of 3/15 n/60 from Beaver Corporation, $255.

23   Sold inventory on account to Fullam Corp., issuing invoice no. 505 for $4,983 (cost, $1,576).

24   Received half the July 31 amount receivable from K. D. Skipper Inc.—after the end of the discount period.

25   Issued cheque no. 689 to pay utilities, $216.

26   Purchased supplies on credit terms of 2/10 n/30 from Fayda Corp., $90.

30   Returned damaged inventory to company from whom Yellowknife made the cash purchase on August 19, receiving cash of $425.

30   Granted a sales allowance of $88 to K. D. Skipper Inc.

31   Purchased inventory on credit terms of 1/10 n/30 from Suncrest Supply Ltd., $4,165.

31   Issued cheque no. 690 to Jack West, owner of Yellowknife, for $850.

---

* On August 2, Yellowknife Distributors sold inventory to R. T. Loeb and collected in full on August 12. Upon learning that the shipment to Loeb was incomplete, Yellowknife plans to ship the goods to her during September. At August 31, $225 of unearned sales revenue needs to be recorded and the cost of this merchandise ($71) needs to be removed from Cost of Goods Sold and returned to Inventory.

Required

1. Open the following accounts with their account numbers and July 31 balances in the ledgers indicated.

General Ledger:

101	Cash	$ 2,245
102	Accounts Receivable	11,280
104	Interest Receivable	0
105	Inventory	20,900
109	Supplies	670
117	Prepaid Insurance	1,100
140	Note Receivable, Long-term	5,500

160	Furniture	18,635
161	Accumulated Amortization—Furniture	5,275
201	Accounts Payable	6,300
204	Salary Payable	465
207	Interest Payable	160
208	Unearned Sales Revenue	0
220	Note Payable, Long-term	21,000
301	Jack West, Capital	27,130
303	Jack West, Withdrawals	0
400	Income Summary	0
401	Sales Revenue	0
402	Sales Discounts	0
403	Sales Returns and Allowances	0
410	Interest Revenue	0
501	Cost of Goods Sold	0
510	Salary Expense	0
513	Rent Expense	0
514	Amortization Expense—Furniture	0
516	Insurance Expense	0
517	Utilities Expense	0
519	Supplies Expense	0
523	Interest Expense	0

Accounts Receivable Subsidiary Ledger: Fullam Corp., $1,100; R. T. Loeb; Park-Hee Inc., $5,795; K. D. Skipper Inc., $4,385.

Accounts Payable Subsidiary Ledger: Beaver Corporation; Fayda Corp., $6,300; Grant Ltd.; Suncrest Supply Ltd.

2. Ask your professor for directions. Journalize the August transactions either in the general journal (page 9; explanations not required) or, as illustrated in Chapter 7, in a series of special journals: a sales journal (page 4), a cash receipts journal (page 11), a purchases journal (page 8), a cash payments journal (page 5), and a general journal (page 9). Yellowknife makes all credit sales on terms of 2/10 n/30.

3. Post daily to the accounts receivable subsidiary ledger and the accounts payable subsidiary ledger. On August 31, 2007, post to the general ledger.

4. Prepare a trial balance in the Trial Balance columns of a work sheet, and use the following information to complete the work sheet for the month ended August 31, 2007.

   a. Accrued interest revenue, $50.
   b. Supplies on hand, $495.
   c. Prepaid insurance expired, $275.
   d. Amortization expense, $115.
   e. Accrued salary expense, $515.
   f. Accrued interest expense, $160.
   g. Unearned sales revenue, $225.*
   h. Inventory on hand, $23,350.

5. Prepare Yellowknife's multi-step income statement and statement of owner's equity for August. Prepare the balance sheet at August 31, 2007.

6. Journalize and post the adjusting and closing entries.

7. Prepare a postclosing trial balance at August 31, 2007. Also, balance the total of the customer accounts in the accounts receivable subsidiary ledger against the Accounts Receivable balance in the general ledger. Do the same for the accounts payable subsidiary ledger and Accounts Payable in the general ledger.

Earth Buddy to Spin Master and Beyond: The Role of Accounting in a New Business

Many young people dream of owning their own business. Four entrepreneurs started their own business after graduating from university in 1993. The product they produced and sold was a head-shaped object that sprouted hair (grass) when watered. The concept was very simple: a nylon stocking was filled with sawdust and some grass seed; the head was shaped and a face was painted on it; then, the head was placed in a printed box ready for shipping.

The company was successful with orders from Canadian Tire and Zellers. It then landed an order from KMart U.S. for 500,000 Earth Buddies.

The partners were good at marketing and production. They were able to get the large order and produce the needed Earth Buddies. But successful companies need more than a product, marketing, and production skills. They also need accounting skills.

The four partners learned early on that to be successful they needed to be as concerned about accounting as they were about marketing. It was this attention to all of the details—marketing, purchasing, production, and accounting—that enabled Spin Master to be as successful.

Epilogue

When we first met the partners, they were enthusiastic but inexperienced, but over the 10 years since they began producing Earth Buddy, the partners have become business professionals.

From 1993 to 2003, Earth Buddy morphed into Spin Master with an increasing range of products such as Air Hogs, Shrinky Dinks, Catch-A-Bubble, McDonald's McFlurry ice cream maker, and the newest hit product, Mighty Beanz. Each product raised the company to new heights. Customers include Wal-Mart, Toys Я Us, and McDonald's. Sales were in the $50 million range in 2000.

Since then, the company has become North America's ninth-largest toy company with more than 100 employees and annual sales between $200 to $300 million.

CASE QUESTIONS

1. Initially, the four partners were able to make and sell the Earth Buddy but lacked the accounting skills to be successful. "Accounting skills" are important to any organization, but especially important to a new company. Why are "accounting skills" so important to a company such as Earth Buddy?

2. In Earth Buddy's early days the partners were vitally concerned with sales and production and not so concerned with records and record-keeping. The company's accountant stated that the partners "were too busy making money to keep track of it." What do you think the accountant meant? Was he right?

3. Why do you think customers such as Wal-Mart might be interested in Spin Master Ltd.'s financial statements?

4. What have you learned about accounting from these video cases?

Sources: CBC *Venture*, "Earthbuddies" (1994), Earthbuddies—The Sequel (2000); Won, Shirley, "Toy maker plays a different game," *The Globe and Mail Report on Business*, January 5, 2004, pp. B1 and B4; Horowitz, Bruce, "McDonald's ventures beyond burgers to duds, toys," *USA Today*, November 14–16, 2003; Pereira, Joseph, "Sales of Mighty Beanz are jumping ahead of the holidays," *The Wall Street Journal*, October 6, 2003, page B1; Strauss, Marina, "Mighty Beanz set to be this year's hot toy, " *The Globe and Mail*, September 19, 2003.

Internal Control and Cash

CHAPTER OBJECTIVES

After studying this chapter, you should be able to

1 Define internal control

2 Tell how to achieve good internal control

3 Prepare a bank reconciliation and the related journal entries

4 Apply internal controls to cash receipts

5 Apply internal controls to cash payments

6 Make ethical business judgments

 Media Companion CD-ROM

Visit the Media Companion CD-ROM that comes with this book for extra practice with the new material in Chapter 8.

Bob Madden worked as a cashier for the investment firm Grand Investments Ltd. Cashiers handle cash, so they are highly trusted employees. Madden was so dedicated to the company that he never took a vacation and never missed a day of work. It took an auto accident to reveal that he was embezzling money.

Madden stole $600,000 by using a well-known scheme. Here is how he did it. Grand Investments customers made deposits to their accounts through cashier Madden, or so they thought. Madden was quietly transferring customer deposits into his own account—and manipulating the Grand Investments customer records. When a customer called to ask Madden why a deposit had not appeared on the customer's statement, he would explain that the missing amount would show up on next month's statement. And it did, as long as Madden could apply Customer B's deposit to cover money stolen from Customer A. He kept the scheme going for five years.

While Madden was in the hospital, a co-worker took over as cashier. The new cashier couldn't explain the missing amounts. All the evidence pointed toward the absent employee. The Grand Investments office manager figured out why Madden never missed a day of work: he had to be present to cover his tracks. After his stay in the hospital, he also did time in prison. All of this could have been avoided if Grand Investments had used some basic internal controls.

To avoid situations like this, good corporate governance dictates that companies maintain a system of internal control. As a result of the recent financial debacles such as Enron, WorldCom, and Tyco, the United States Congress passed the Sarbanes–Oxley Act of 2002. The act will have an impact on Canadian companies in two ways:

1. Canadian companies, such as the Bank of Montreal and EnCana Corporation, are listed on the New York Stock Exchange and, therefore, must abide by Sarbanes–Oxley.

2. Canadian regulators, such as the Ontario Securities Commission, are considering implementing some of the requirements of Sarbanes–Oxley.

Of particular concern at this point is the Sarbanes–Oxley requirement that managers give careful attention to internal control in their companies.

This chapter discusses *internal control*—the organizational plan that organizations use to protect their assets and records. The chapter applies internal control techniques mainly to cash, because cash is the most liquid asset. The chapter also provides a framework for making ethical judgments in business. The material covered in this chapter is some of the most important in all of business. Unfortunately, it is often overlooked, as in the actual case of the cashier in the Grand Investments office.

Cash

Cash—including cash on hand in funds such as *petty cash funds*, cash on deposit in banks and trust companies, and cash equivalents, such as Treasury Bills—is the most liquid asset an organization has. Accordingly, it is usually the first item under the heading "Current Assets" on the balance sheet.

Cash's liquidity is a virtue because it is easily exchangeable for other assets. However, cash's liquidity is also a fault because it is the most easily stolen asset. The next section will explain how organizations strive to protect their cash by using internal controls.

Internal Control

One of a manager's key responsibilities is to control operations. The owners set goals, managers lead the way, and employees carry out the plan.

Both in Canada, in the *CICA Handbook,* and internationally, **internal control** consists of the policies and procedures that management establishes and maintains to govern an organization and minimize risks. The *Handbook* indicates that management's internal control objectives are:

1. Optimizing the use of resources by providing reliable information for decision making, and monitoring the implementation and compliance with management's business policies.
2. Preventing and detecting error and fraud.
3. Safeguarding assets and records.
4. Maintaining reliable control systems to provide reliable information for decision making.

Everyone in an organization needs to work toward the same goals. The international accounting firm of Arthur Andersen collapsed soon after a few members of the firm refused to follow its professional standards. They went against company policy, approved financial statements that held large misstatements, and Andersen collapsed.

Companies cannot afford to waste resources. WorldCom, a leading telephone-service provider, lent $366 million to its Chief Executive Officer. Is that an efficient use of WorldCom resources? Not to the company's enraged owners. WorldCom should have spent the money on new technology and better service for customers.

A company must safeguard its assets and prevent error and fraud; otherwise it's wasting resources. Grand Investments failed to safeguard customer cash, and Bob Madden spent the money he stole. In the end, Grand Investments had to replace the missing $600,000—a total waste of company resources.

Accurate, reliable records are essential. Without reliable records, a manager cannot tell what investments to make or how much to charge for products, and banks cannot determine whether to make a loan.

Internal control is the organizational plan and all related measures adopted by an entity to meet management's internal control objectives. When determining internal control, top management should ask these questions:

1. Is our organization likely to achieve its objectives?
2. Is our organization resilient enough to learn and adapt amidst change?
3. Are we appropriately managing the risks facing the organization?
4. Are we appropriately recognizing opportunities and acting on them?[1]

A company's internal control consists of two elements: (1) the control environment, which in essence consists of the actions, policies, and procedures that reflect the attitudes of the owners and top management of a company about control and its importance to the entity; and (2) the control systems, which can be divided into two components—the accounting system and the control procedures. The accounting system refers to the policies and procedures that pertain to the collection, recording, and processing of data and reporting information, while the control procedures pertain to enhancing the reliability of the data and information.

Internal control is a management priority, not merely a part of the accounting system. Thus it is a responsibility of not only accountants but also of managers in all the functional areas throughout the organization. Internal controls are most

REAL WORLD EXAMPLE

One of the auditor's first steps in auditing a business is to understand and evaluate its internal controls. If a company has good controls, then misstatements are minimized and are usually corrected before the financial statements are prepared. If the control system is weak, then misstatements can go undetected. The auditor determines the extent of testing of the accounting records on the basis of the strength of the company's internal control system.

---

[1] Criteria of Control Board, *Guidance on Assessing Control.* (Toronto: Canadian Institute of Chartered Accountants, 1995), p. 1.

Management's Responsibility for Financial Statements

The accompanying financial statements and other financial information contained in [Danier Leather Inc.'s] annual report are the responsibility of management. The financial statements have been prepared in conformity with Canadian generally accepted accounting principles using management's best estimates and judgements based on currently available information, where appropriate . . .

Management is also responsible for a system of internal controls which is designed to provide reasonable assurance that assets are safeguarded, liabilities are recognized, and that financial records are properly maintained to provide timely and accurate financial reports. The Board of Directors is responsible for ensuring that management fulfills its responsibility in respect of financial reporting and internal control. The Audit Committee of the Board . . . meets regularly to review significant accounting and auditing matters with management and the independent auditors and to review the interim and annual financial statements.

Jeffrey Wortsman
President and CEO

Bryan Tatoff, C.A.
Senior Vice-President, CFO and Secretary

effective when employees at all levels and in all areas adopt the organization's goals and ethical standards. Top managers need to set the standard ("tone at the top") and communicate these goals and standards to workers.

Exhibit 8-1 presents an excerpt from the 2003 Annual Report of Danier Leather Inc. (www.danier.com), the fashion retailer. Danier's top managers take responsibility for the financial statements and the related system of internal control. Another example of a statement of management's responsibility is that of Intrawest Corporation in Appendix A. Note that the management of Intrawest states "[Intrawest] maintains appropriate systems of internal control, policies, and procedures that provide management with reasonable assurance that assets are safeguarded and that financial records are reliable and form a proper basis for the preparation of the financial statements."

Let's examine in detail how businesses create the goals of an effective system of internal control.

An Effective System of Internal Control

OBJECTIVE 2
Tell how to achieve good internal control

 **REAL WORLD EXAMPLE**

Whether the business is Grand Investments or a local department store, its system of internal controls, if effective, has the characteristics discussed below.

Competent, Reliable, and Ethical Personnel   Employees should be *competent*, *reliable*, and *ethical*. Paying good salaries to attract high-quality employees, training them to do the job, and supervising their work all help build a competent staff.

Assignment of Responsibilities   In a business with good internal controls, no important duty is overlooked. Each employee has certain responsibilities. A model of such *assignment of responsibilities* appears in Exhibit 8-2. This company has a vice-president of finance and accounting. Two other officers, the treasurer and

In a small business (or a small office of a large company), the owner/manager can ensure that assets are protected. In a larger business, internal controls can help protect assets by ensuring that policies are in place and are followed.

the controller, report to that vice-president. The treasurer is responsible for cash management. The **controller** is the chief accounting officer.

Within this organization, the controller approves invoices (bills) for payment and the treasurer signs the cheques. Notice that each officer has duties assigned so that all duties are carried out.

Proper Authorization   An organization generally has written rules that outline approved procedures. Any deviation from policy requires *proper authorization*. For example, managers or assistant managers of retail stores must approve customer cheques for amounts above the store's usual limit. Likewise, deans or heads of departments of colleges and universities must give the authorization for a first- or second-year student to enroll in courses that are restricted to upper-year students.

Separation of Duties   Smart management divides the responsibilities for transactions between two or more people or departments. *Separation of duties* (also called segregation of duties) limits the chances for fraud and promotes the accuracy of accounting records by dividing up the three tasks of authorization, recording, and custody. Separation of duties, which can be divided into three parts, is illustrated in Exhibit 8-2.

1. *Separation of operations from accounting.* Accounting should be completely separate from operating departments, such as production and marketing. What would happen if sales personnel had access to the company's revenue records? Sales figures could be inflated, and top managers wouldn't know how much the company actually sold. This is why accounting and marketing (sales) are separate in Exhibit 8-2.

2. *Separation of the custody of assets from accounting.* Accountants must not handle cash, and cashiers must not have access to the accounting records. If one

EXHIBIT 8-2

Organization Chart of a Corporation

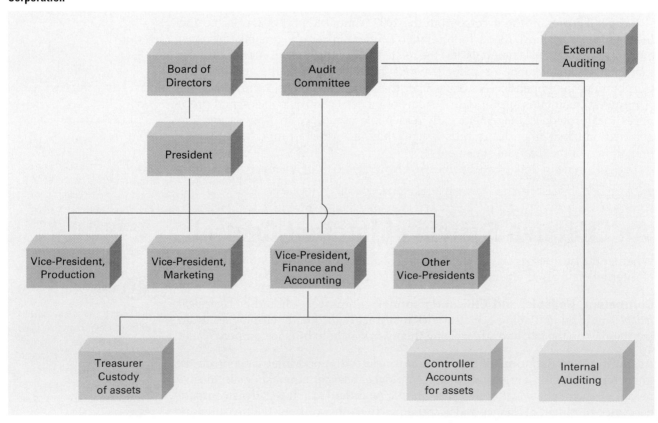

employee had both cash-handling and accounting duties, that person could steal cash and conceal the theft by making a fictitious entry on the books. We see this separation of duties in Exhibit 8-2. The treasurer handles cash and the controller accounts for cash. Neither person has both responsibilities. At Grand Investments, Bob Madden had access to cash and the company's accounting records (recording and custody). With both duties, he was able to apply one customer's cash deposit to another's account. The result was a $600,000 loss to the company.

Warehouse employees with no accounting duties should have custody of inventory. If they were allowed to account for the inventory, they could steal it and write it off as obsolete. A *write-off* is an entry that credits an asset account. This write-off could be recorded by debiting Loss on Inventory Obsolescence and crediting Inventory.

3. *Separation of the authorization of transactions from the custody of related assets.* Persons who authorize transactions should not handle the related asset. For example, the same individual should not authorize the payment of a supplier's invoice and also sign the cheque to pay the invoice.

Even small businesses should have internal controls and some separation of duties. For example, if the bookkeeper writes all cheques and keeps the general ledger records, the owner should sign all cheques and reconcile the monthly bank statement.

Internal and External Audits   To demonstrate to users and to satisfy management that the financial statements fairly present the financial position of an organization and the results of its operations, most companies have a periodic audit. An **audit** is an examination of the organization's financial statements and the accounting systems, controls, and records that produced them. To evaluate the company's accounting system, auditors examine the system of internal controls.

Audits can be internal or external. *Internal auditors* are employees of the organization. They ensure that employees are following company policies and that operations are running efficiently.

External auditors are completely independent of the organization. They are hired to determine that the organization's financial statements are prepared in accordance with generally accepted accounting principles. Both internal and external auditors should be independent of the operations they examine, and both should suggest improvements that can help the business run efficiently.

Documents and Records   Business *documents and records* provide the details of business transactions. Such documents include sales invoices and purchase orders and records include journals and ledgers. Documents should be pre-numbered because a gap in the numbered sequence draws attention to a possible missing document.

In a bowling alley, for example, a key document is the score sheet. The manager can check on cashiers by comparing the number of games scored with the amount of cash received. By multiplying the number of games by the price per game to estimate the revenue and comparing this amount with each day's cash receipts, the manager can see whether the business is collecting all its revenues.

Electronic Devices and Computer Controls   Accounting systems are relying less on documents and more on digital storage devices. Computers shift the internal controls to the people who write the programs. Programmers then become the focus of internal controls because they can write programs that transfer assets to themselves.

Businesses use electronic devices to protect assets. For example, retailers such as Winners control their inventories by attaching an *electronic sensor* to merchandise. The cashier removes the sensor at checkout. If a customer tries to remove from the store an item with the sensor attached, an alarm sounds. According to Checkpoint Systems, which manufactures electronic sensors, these devices reduce loss due to theft by as much as 50 percent.

....
THINKING IT OVER

What problems can result when a sales clerk can also grant credit approval and record the sales in addition to handling the cash?

A: The clerk could grant credit approval to friends and others who do not meet the credit standards, steal merchandise and hide the theft in the accounting records, fail to do all three jobs well and make mistakes, or forget to perform a task when the sales floor is busy.

REAL WORLD EXAMPLE

In some audits of financial institutions, the first day of the audit may occur as a surprise to the employees so that they cannot cover up fraud and/or weaknesses in the system.

REAL WORLD EXAMPLE

If a clerk in a retail store makes a mistake on the sales receipt, the receipt is not destroyed but is marked VOID. Most businesses use pre-numbered sales receipts, so a missing receipt would be noted.

WorldCom Inc.: Internal Auditor's Heroism Is Silver Lining in Cloud of Scandal

WorldCom Inc.'s internal auditor, Cynthia Cooper, met with controller David Myers on June 17, 2002. This was no ordinary coffee break. Cooper asked some questions that would later cost Myers his job and uncover a huge scandal.

Cooper wondered why WorldCom was counting everyday expenses as long-term assets. A company can boost reported profits by doing this, because expenses of one quarter can be spread out over several years. When Cooper finished her audit, she revealed that WorldCom had inflated its income by $3.9 billion. When all the facts came out, this figure grew to a whopping $9 billion.

The internal audit forced WorldCom into the largest corporate bankruptcy in U.S. history, leaving creditors holding nearly $30 billion in bad receivables. It also turned Cooper into a national heroine. In December 2002, *Time* magazine named Cynthia Cooper, along with two other corporate whistle-blowers, a "person of the year" for "doing right by just doing the job rightly."

Documents show how WorldCom's senior management overrode internal controls to hide the company's true financial condition. It turned out that Myers had promised to "do whatever necessary" to improve the company's profit margins. Fortunately, while Myers and other top WorldCom executives were doing what they deemed *necessary*, internal auditor Cynthia Cooper was doing what was *right*.

The Decision Guidelines at the end of this chapter outline the sad story of another auditor who did whatever was necessary to keep his client happy.

Based on: Yochi J. Dreazen and Deborah Solomon, "Leading the News: WorldCom Aide Conceded Flaws—Controller Said Company Was Forced to Disguise Expenses, Ignore Warnings," *Wall Street Journal*, July 16, 2002, p. A3. Karen Kaplan and James S. Granelli, "The Nation; WorldCom Says It Inflated Books by $3.9 Billion; Telecom: an internal audit by MCI's parent uncovers accounting irregularities. The disclosure may force the firm to file for bankruptcy," *The Los Angeles Times*, June 26, 2002, p. A1. Associated Press, "The Nation; 3 Whistle-Blowers Get Time Magazine Honors; It names women its 'persons of the year' for doing 'right just by doing their jobs rightly.'" *The Los Angeles Times*, December 23, 2002, p. A14. Peter Elstrom, "How to Hide $3.8 Billion in Expenses," *Business Week*, July 8, 2002, p. 41.

Other Controls   Businesses of all types keep cash and important documents in *fireproof vaults. Burglar alarms* protect buildings and other property.

Retailers receive most of their cash from customers on the spot. To safeguard cash, they use *point-of-sale terminals* that serve as a cash register and also record each transaction. Several times each day a supervisor removes the cash for deposit in the bank.

Employees who handle cash are in a tempting position. Many businesses purchase *fidelity bonds* on cashiers. The bond is an insurance policy that reimburses the company for any losses due to the employee's theft. Before issuing a fidelity bond, the insurance company investigates the employee's record.

Mandatory vacations and *job rotation* require that employees be trained to do a variety of jobs. Some companies, such as General Electric Canada, move employees from job to job. This improves morale by giving employees a broad view of the business. Also, knowing that someone else will be doing that job next month keeps an employee honest. Had Grand Investments required Bob Madden to take a vacation, his embezzlement would have been detected much earlier.

Internal Controls for E-Commerce

E-commerce creates its own risks. Hackers may gain access to confidential information that is unavailable in face-to-face transactions. Confidentiality is a significant challenge for "dot.com" companies. Pitfalls include stolen credit-card numbers, computer viruses and Trojan horses, and impersonation of companies. To convince people to buy online, companies must ensure security of customer data.

Pitfalls E-commerce pitfalls include:

- Stolen credit-card numbers
- Computer viruses and Trojan horses
- Impersonation of companies

Stolen credit-card numbers. Suppose you buy several CDs from Futureshop.ca. To make the purchase, your credit-card number must travel through cyberspace. In the U.S., amateur hacker Carlos Salgado Jr. used his home computer to steal 100,000 credit-card numbers from an internet service provider. The cards represented a combined credit limit exceeding $1 billion. Salgado was caught when he tried to sell the credit-card numbers to an undercover FBI agent.

Computer viruses and Trojan horses. A **computer virus** is a malicious program that (a) reproduces itself, (b) enters program code without consent, and (c) performs destructive actions. A **Trojan horse** works like a virus, but it does not reproduce. Viruses can destroy or alter data, make bogus calculations, and infect files. The International Computer Security Association reports that virtually all the firms it surveyed found a virus somewhere in their organization.

Impersonation of companies. Hackers sometimes create bogus websites, such as AOL4Free.com. This neat-sounding website attracts lots of visitors. Via such a website, hackers can solicit confidential data from unsuspecting visitors, then use the data for illicit purposes.

Firewalls and Encryption Internet information can be secure, but the server holding the information may not be. Two standard techniques for securing e-commerce data are encryption and firewalls.

Encryption rearranges messages by a mathematical process. The encrypted message cannot be read by anyone who does not know the process. An accounting example uses check-sum digits for account numbers. Each account number has its last digit equal to the sum of the previous digits, for example, for Customer Number 2237, where 2 + 2 + 3 = 7. Any account number that fails this test triggers an error message.

Firewalls limit access to a local network. They enable members of the local network to access the internet but keep non-members out of the network. Usually several firewalls are built into the network. Think of a fortress with multiple walls protecting the queen's chamber at the centre. At the point of entry, passwords, personal identification numbers (PINs), and signatures are used to restrict entry. More sophisticated firewalls are used deeper in the network.

The Limitations of Internal Control

Unfortunately, most internal controls can be circumvented or overcome. Collusion—where two or more employees work as a team—can beat internal controls and defraud the firm. Consider the Classic Theatre. Geoff and a fellow employee could put together a scheme in which the ticket seller pockets the cash from 10 customers and the ticket taker admits 10 customers without tickets. To prevent this situation, the manager must take additional steps, such as counting the people in the theatre and matching that figure against the number of ticket stubs retained. But that takes time away from other duties.

The stricter the internal control system, the more it costs. A system of internal control that is too complex may strangle the business with red tape. How tight should controls be? Internal controls must be judged in the light of the costs and benefits.

The Bank Account as a Control Device

Cash is the most liquid asset because it is a medium of exchange. Increasingly, cash consists of electronic impulses in a bank's accounting system with no paper cheques or deposit slips. Cash is easy to conceal, easy to move, and relatively easy to steal. As a result, most businesses create specific controls for cash.

Keeping cash in a *bank account* helps because banks have established practices for safeguarding customers' money. Banks also provide customers with detailed records of their transactions. To take full advantage of these control features, the business should deposit all cash receipts in the bank and make all cash payments through the bank. An exception is a petty cash transaction, which we look at later.

The documents used to control a bank account include the

- signature card
- bank statement
- deposit ticket
- bank reconciliation
- cheque

Signature Card Banks require each person authorized to transact business through an account to sign a *signature card*. The bank issues a signature card to protect against forgery.

Deposit Ticket Banks supply standard forms such as *deposit tickets* or *deposit slips*. The customer fills in the dollar amount of each deposit. As proof of the transaction, the customer keeps a deposit receipt.

Cheque To draw money from an account, the depositor writes a **cheque**, which is the document that tells the bank to pay the designated party a specified amount of money. There are three parties to a cheque: the *maker*, who signs the cheque; the *payee*, to whom the cheque is paid; and the *bank* on which the cheque is drawn.

Exhibit 8-3 shows a cheque drawn on the bank account of Business Research Inc., the maker. The cheque has two parts: the cheque itself and the *remittance advice,* an optional attachment that tells the payee the reason for payment. Business Research retains a duplicate copy of the cheque for its cash payments journal.

Bank Statement   Banks send monthly statements to their customers. A **bank statement** is the document on which the bank reports what it did with the customer's cash. The statement shows the account's beginning and ending balances for the period and lists cash receipts and payments transacted through the bank. Included with the statement are the maker's *cancelled cheques.* The statement also lists deposits and other changes in the account. Deposits appear in chronological order, and cheques are listed by cheque number. Exhibit 8-4 is the bank statement of Business Research Inc. for the month ended January 31, 2005. The summary in the boxes above the Chequing Account Transactions shows the beginning balance, total deposits, total withdrawals, service charges, and the ending balance. Details of the transactions follow.

Electronic funds transfer (EFT) is a system that moves cash by electronic communications. It is much cheaper for a company to pay employees by EFT (direct deposit) than by issuing hundreds of payroll cheques. Also, many people make mortgage, rent, insurance, credit-card, and other payments either by prior arrangement with their bank or by means of electronic banking; they never write cheques for those payments. The bank statement lists EFT deposits and payments.

One method of transferring funds electronically is through the use of a *debit card.* When you make a purchase from a store and pay with a debit card, you authorize your bank to immediately withdraw the money for the purchase from your bank account and deposit it into the store's bank account. You will see the amount of the withdrawal on your monthly bank statement or passbook, and the store will see the amount of the deposit on its monthly bank statement. Debit cards, or bank cards, will be discussed more fully in Chapter 9.

EXHIBIT 8-3

Cheque with Remittance Advice

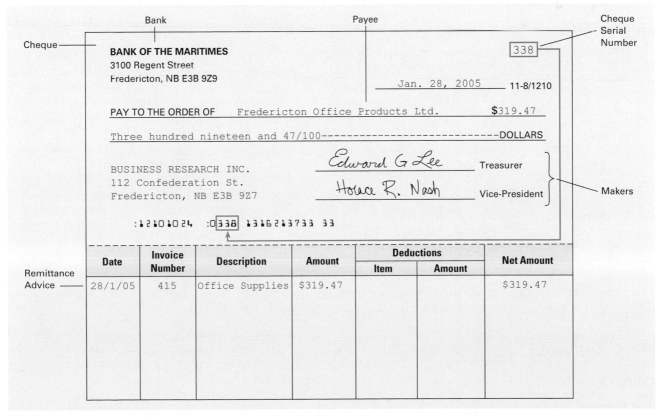

Bank of the Maritimes
3100 REGENT STREET
FREDERICTON, NEW BRUNSWICK
E3B 9Z9

```
                      1024/   0/   5
        BUSINESS RESEARCH INC.
        112 CONFEDERATION ST.
        FREDERICTON, NB

        E3B 9Z7
```

For Current Interest Rates:	Statement of Account		Statement From – To	
CALL OUR INFOLINE 1-800-386-2093 QUEBEC 1-800-386-1600 TORONTO 416-987-7735	**Branch No.**	**Account No.**	JAN 01/05 JAN 31/05	
	1024	1316213733	**Page** 1 **of** 1	

BEGINNING BALANCE	TOTAL DEPOSITS	TOTAL WITHDRAWALS	SERVICE CHARGES	ENDING BALANCE
6556.12	4352.64	4963.00	39.25	5906.51

CHEQUING ACCOUNT TRANSACTIONS

```
DEPOSITS

DEPOSIT                                        JAN 04      1000.00
DEPOSIT                                        JAN 04       112.00
DEPOSIT                                        JAN 08       194.60
EFT    COLLECTION OF RENT                      JAN 17       904.03
BANK COLLECTION                               JAN 26      2114.00
INTEREST                                       JAN 31        28.01


CHARGES

SERVICE CHARGES (INCLUDES NSF CHARGE, $25.00)  JAN 31        39.25
```

CHEQUES			CHEQUES			BALANCE	
NUMBER	DATE	AMOUNT	NUMBER	DATE	AMOUNT	DATE	BALANCE
256	JAN 06	100.00	335	JAN 10	100.00	DEC 31	6556.12
332	JAN 12	3000.00	334	JAN 06	100.00	JAN 04	7616.12
333	JAN 12	150.00	336	JAN 31	1100.00	JAN 06	7416.12
						JAN 08	7610.72
						JAN 10	7510.72
						JAN 12	4360.72
						JAN 17	5264.75
						JAN 20	4903.75
						JAN 26	7017.75
						JAN 31	5906.51

OTHER CHARGES	DATE	AMOUNT
NSF	JAN 04	52.00
EFT INSURANCE	JAN 20	361.00

```
                        MONTHLY SUMMARY

9 WITHDRAWALS          4360.72 MINIMUM BALANCE       6091.00 AVERAGE BALANCE
```

EXHIBIT 8-4

Bank Statement

Debits and Credits in Accounting and Banking

In this introductory accounting course, you have learned that
• Debit means the **left** side of an account
• Credit means the **right** side of an account
In banking
• Debits are bad (for you)
• Credits are good (for you)

Both perspectives are correct. To illustrate, let's consider two transactions: (1) your receipt of $1,000 cash, which you deposit in the bank, and (2) your payment of cash by writing a $600 cheque. Record these transactions, first on your own books, and then on the bank's books. You will understand debits and credits much better.

On *your* books, journalize (1) receipt of $1,000 cash for service revenue (you immediately deposit the cash in your bank account), and (2) payment of $600 cash to purchase supplies (you write a cheque to an office supply store).

Answer:
Journal Entries on Your Books:

Cash	1,000	
Service Revenue		1,000
Received cash for revenue earned.		
Supplies	600	
Cash		600
Purchased supplies.		

In these journal entries you correctly debit the Cash account for a receipt, and you credit Cash for a payment. Now let's see how the bank accounts for your cash.

When you deposit cash in your account, the amount of cash in the bank increases. Then, when you write a cheque, the bank pays cash from your account. As a result, the amount of cash in the bank decreases. The critical thing to remember is this: *The bank owes your money to you because you can withdraw it or write cheques on it at any time. The bank thus has a Deposit Payable, a liability, for your cash on deposit.*

On the bank's books, journalize the same two transactions: (1) receipt of $1,000 cash from you (when you deposit cash in your account), and (2) payment of $600 cash for you.

Answer:
Journal Entries on the Bank's Books:

Cash	1,000	
Deposit Payable		1,000
Received cash from deposit customer.		
Deposit Payable	600	
Cash		600
Paid cash for deposit customer.		

In the first entry the bank debits Cash when it receives your deposit. The bank also credits Deposit Payable, a liability, to indicate that it owes you $1,000 whenever you wish to withdraw the money or write a cheque. This explains why a credit is "good" for you in a banking relationship. The bank has a liability for the amount of your money it has on deposit.

Now let's examine the bank's journal entry for the cash payment. The bank credits Cash when it pays your cheque. The bank debits Deposit Payable (to you) because the bank paid the $600 cheque that you wrote. As a result, the bank no longer owes you the $600. This explains why a debit is "bad" for you in a banking relationship: The bank has less liability to you.

The confusion about debits and credits in banking arises because many people view their own cash from the perspective of the bank. This is backwards, because:
• To the bank, your deposit account is a liability (a credit-balance account).
• To you, your cash is an asset (a debit-balance account).

The Bank Reconciliation   There are two records of the business's cash: (1) the Cash account in its own general ledger (Exhibit 8-5), and (2) the bank statement, which shows the cash receipts and payments transacted through the bank.

The books and the bank statement usually show different amounts. Differences arise because of a time lag in recording transactions. When you write a cheque, you immediately deduct the amount of the cheque from the balance in your cheque book. But the bank does not subtract this amount from your account until the bank pays it. That may take days, even weeks, if the payee waits to cash the cheque. Likewise, you immediately add the amount of the cash receipt for each deposit you make to your account. But it may take a day or more for the bank to add this amount to your balance.

To ensure accurate cash records, you need to update your cheque book often—either online or after you receive your bank statement. All businesses do the same. The result of this updating process is a document called the **bank reconciliation**, which is prepared by the company (not the bank). Properly done, the bank reconciliation explains the differences between the company's cash records and the bank statement figures. It ensures that all cash transactions have been accounted for. It also establishes that bank and book records of cash are correct.

Here are some common reconciling items. They all cause differences between the bank balance and the book balance. (We refer to the company's cash records as the "Book" records.)

1. Items to show on the Bank side of the bank reconciliation:

   a. **Deposits in transit** (outstanding deposits). The company has recorded these deposits, but the bank has not.

   b. **Outstanding cheques**. These cheques have been issued by the company and recorded on its books but the bank has not yet paid them.

   c. **Bank errors**. Correct all bank errors on the Bank side of the reconciliation.

EXHIBIT 8-5

Cash Records of Business Research Inc.

General Ledger:

ACCOUNT Cash   **No. 1100**

Date	Item	Jrn. Ref.	Debit	Credit	Balance
2005					
Jan. 1	Balance	✔			6,556.12 Dr
2	Cash receipt	CR. 9	1,112.00		7,668.12 Dr
7	Cash receipt	CR. 9	194.60		7,862.72 Dr
31	Cash payments	CP. 17		6,160.14	1,702.58 Dr
31	Cash receipt	CR. 10	1,591.63		3,294.21 Dr

Cash Payments:

Cheque No.	Amount
332	$3,000.00
333	510.00
334	100.00
335	100.00
336	1,100.00
337	286.00
338	319.47
339	83.00
340	203.14
341	458.53
Total	$6,160.14

2. Items recorded on the Book side of the bank reconciliation:

a. **Bank collections.** Banks sometimes collect money on behalf of depositors. Many businesses have their customers pay directly to the company bank account. This practice, called a *lock-box system*, reduces theft and circulates cash faster than if the cash had to be collected and deposited by company personnel. An example is a bank's collecting cash on a note receivable for the depositor. Bank collections are cash receipts.

b. **Electronic funds transfers.** The bank may receive or pay cash on behalf of the depositor. An EFT may be a cash receipt or a cash payment.

c. **Service charge.** This is the bank's fee for processing the depositor's transactions. It is a cash payment.

d. **Interest revenue on chequing account.** Depositors earn interest if they keep a specified amount of cash in their accounts. This is sometimes true of business chequing accounts. The bank notifies the depositor of this interest on the bank statement. It is a cash receipt.

e. **Nonsufficient funds cheques (NSF).** These are cash receipts that turn out to be worthless. NSF cheques (sometimes called *bounced cheques* or *hot cheques*) should be subtracted on the Book side of the bank reconciliation.

f. **The cost of printed cheques.** This cash payment is handled like a service charge.

g. **Book errors.** Correct all book errors on the Book side of the reconciliation.

Preparing the Bank Reconciliation

The steps in preparing the bank reconciliation are as follows:

1. Start with two figures, the balance in the business's Cash account in the general ledger (*balance per books*) and the balance shown on the bank statement (*balance per bank*). These two amounts will probably disagree because of the timing differences discussed earlier.

2. Add to, or subtract from, the *bank* balance those items that appear correctly on the books but not on the bank statement.

a. Add *deposits in transit* to the bank balance. Deposits in transit are identified by comparing the deposits listed on the bank statement to the business's list of cash receipts. They appear as cash receipts on the books but not as deposits on the bank statement.

b. Subtract *outstanding cheques* from the bank balance. Outstanding cheques are identified by comparing the cancelled cheques returned with the bank statement to the business's list of cheques written for cash payment. Outstanding cheques appear as cash payments on the books but not as paid cheques on the bank statement. If cheques were outstanding on the bank reconciliation for the preceding month and have still not been cashed, add them to the list of outstanding cheques on this month's bank reconciliation. Outstanding cheques are usually the most numerous item on a bank reconciliation.

3. Add to, or subtract from, the *book* balance those items that appear on the bank statement but not on the company books.

a. Add to the book balance (1) *bank collections,* (2) *EFT cash receipts,* and (3) *interest revenue* earned on the money in the bank. These items are identified by comparing the deposits listed on the bank statement with the business's list of cash receipts. They show up as cash receipts on the bank statement but not on the books.

b. Subtract from the book balance (1) *EFT cash payments,* (2) *service charges,* (3) *cost of printed cheques,* and (4) *other bank charges* (for example, charges for NSF or stale-date cheques). These items are identified by comparing the other charges listed on the bank statement to the cash payments recorded on the business's books. They appear as subtractions on the bank statement but not as cash payments on the books.

4. Compute the *adjusted bank balance* and *adjusted book balance*. The two adjusted balances should be equal.

5. Journalize each item in step 3, that is, each item listed on the book portion of the bank reconciliation. These items must be recorded on the business's books because they affect cash.

6. Correct all book errors, and notify the bank of any errors it has made.

Bank Reconciliation Illustrated   The bank statement in Exhibit 8-4 (page 396) indicates that the January 31, 2005, bank balance of Business Research Inc. is $5,906.51. However, the company's Cash account has a balance of $3,294.21, as shown in Exhibit 8-5. This situation calls for a bank reconciliation. Exhibit 8-6, Panel A, lists the reconciling items, and Panel B shows the completed reconciliation.

STOP & THINK

Why does the company *not* need to record the reconciling items on the bank side of the reconciliation?

Answer: Those items have already been recorded on the company books.

Journalizing Transactions from the Reconciliation   The bank reconciliation is an accountant's tool that is separate from the company's books. It explains the effects of all cash receipts and all cash payments through the bank. But it does *not* account for transactions in the journals. To get the transactions into the accounts, we must make journal entries and post to the general ledger. Each item on the Book side of the bank reconciliation requires a journal entry. The bank reconciliation in Exhibit 8-6 requires Business Research Inc. to make the following journal entries. They are dated January 31 to bring the Cash account to the correct balance on that date. The numbers in parentheses correspond to the reconciling items listed in Exhibit 8-6, Panel A.

(4)	Jan. 31	Cash..	904.03	
		Rent revenue		904.03
		Receipt of monthly rent.		
(5)	Jan. 31	Cash..	2,114.00	
		Notes receivable		2,000.00
		Interest revenue		114.00
		Note receivable collected by bank.		
(6)	Jan. 31	Cash..	28.01	
		Interest revenue		28.01
		Interest earned on bank balance.		
(7)	Jan. 31	Cash..	360.00	
		Accounts payable—Brown Corp.		360.00
		Correction of cheque no. 333.		
(8)	Jan. 31	Bank charges expense	39.25	
		Cash..		39.25
		Bank service charges.		
(9)	Jan. 31	Accounts receivable—L. Ross...............................	52.00	
		Cash..		52.00
		NSF cheque returned by bank.		
(10)	Jan. 31	Insurance expense	361.00	
		Cash..		361.00
		Payment of monthly insurance.		

These entries update the company's books.

The entry for the NSF cheque (entry 9) needs explanation. Upon learning that L. Ross's $52 cheque was not good, Business Research Inc. credits Cash to update the Cash account. Since Business Research Inc. still has a receivable from L. Ross, it debits Accounts Receivable—L. Ross and pursues collection from him.

EXHIBIT 8-6

Bank Reconciliation

Panel A: Reconciling Items

1. Deposit in transit, $1,591.63.
2. Bank error: The bank deducted $100 for a cheque written by another company. Add $100 to bank balance.
3. Outstanding cheques: no. 337, $286.00; no. 338, $319.47; no. 339, $83.00; no. 340, $203.14; no. 341, $458.53.
4. EFT receipt of rent revenue, $904.03.
5. Bank collection of note receivable, $2,114, including interest revenue of $114.00.
6. Interest earned on bank balance, $28.01.
7. Book error: cheque no. 333 for $150.00 paid to Brown Corp. on account was recorded as $510.00.
8. Bank service charges, $39.25.
9. NSF cheque from L. Ross, $52.00.
10. EFT payment of insurance expense, $361.00.

Panel B: Bank Reconciliation

BUSINESS RESEARCH INC.
Bank Reconciliation
January 31, 2005

Bank			Books		
Balance, January 31, 2005		$5,906.51	Balance, January 31, 2005		$3,294.21
Add:			Add:		
1. Deposit of January 31 in transit		1,591.63	4. EFT receipt of rent revenue		904.03
2. Correction of bank error —Business Research Associates cheque erroneously charged against company account		100.00	5. Bank collection of note receivable, including interest revenue of $114		2,114.00
		$7,598.14	6. Interest revenue earned on bank balance		28.01
3. Less: outstanding cheques			7. Correction of book error—Overstated amount of cheque no. 333		360.00
No. 337	$286.00				6,700.25
338	319.47		Less:		
339	83.00		8. Service charges	$39.25	
340	203.14		9. NSF cheque	52.00	
341	458.53	(1,350.14)	10. EFT payment of insurance expense	361.00	(452.25)
Adjusted bank balance		$6,248.00	Adjusted book balance		$6,248.00

Amounts should agree

Each reconciling item is treated in the same way in every situation. Here is a summary of how to treat the various reconciling items:

BANK BALANCE—ALWAYS
- *Add* deposits in transit.
- *Subtract* outstanding cheques.
- *Add* or *subtract* corrections of bank errors.

BOOK BALANCE—ALWAYS
- *Add* bank collections, interest revenue, and EFT receipts.
- *Subtract* service charges, NSF cheques, and EFT payments.
- *Add* or *subtract* corrections of book errors.

Online and Telephone Banking   Canadian banks now permit online and telephone banking, where customers use their computers or telephones to effect transactions such as paying bills, transferring money from one account to another, and arranging a loan. With telephone banking, the bank gives the customer a transaction number over the telephone when the transaction is completed; the transaction is confirmed by its appearance in the passbook or on a subsequent bank statement. There is no other "paper trail" as evidence of the transaction. Similarly, with online banking, customers use a computer and a modem or an internet connection to effect transactions. The bank supplies a confirmation number on the customer's computer screen to show the transaction has occurred, and the transaction is confirmed by its appearance in the passbook or on a subsequent bank statement. Again, there is no other paper trail as evidence of the transaction.

Since bank statements are usually received monthly, a bank reconciliation is often performed only once a month. However, with online access to bank account information, you are able to print your bank account transaction data at any time. Thus, companies and individuals could prepare bank reconciliations more frequently than once a month.

How Owners and Managers Use the Bank Reconciliation

The bank reconciliation can be a powerful control device as the following example illustrates.

Randy Vaughn is a CA in Regina, Saskatchewan. Vaughn owns several apartment complexes that are managed by his cousin Alexis Vaughn. His accounting practice keeps him busy, so he has little time to devote to the properties. Vaughn's cousin approves tenants, collects the monthly rent cheques, arranges custodial and maintenance work, hires and fires employees, writes the cheques, and performs the bank reconciliation. This concentration of duties in one person is terrible from an internal control standpoint. Vaughn's cousin could be stealing from him. As a CA, he is aware of this possibility.

Vaughn exercises some internal controls over his cousin's activities. Periodically he drops by his properties to see whether the apartments are in good condition.

To control cash, Vaughn uses a bank reconciliation. On an irregular basis, he examines the bank reconciliations as prepared by his cousin. He matches every cheque that cleared the bank to the journal entry on the books. Vaughn would know immediately if his cousin were writing cheques to herself. Vaughn sometimes prepares his own bank reconciliation to see whether it agrees with his cousin's work. To keep his cousin on her toes, Vaughn lets her know that he periodically checks her work.

Vaughn has a simple method for controlling cash receipts. He knows the occupancy level of his apartments. He also knows the monthly rent he charges. He multiplies the number of apartments—say 100—by the monthly rent (which averages $500 per unit) to arrive at expected monthly rent revenue of $50,000. By tracing the $50,000 revenue to the bank statement, Vaughn can tell that his rent money went into his bank account.

Control activities such as these (often referred to as "executive controls") are critical in small businesses. With only a few employees, a separation of duties may not be feasible. The owner must oversee the operations of the business, or the assets will disappear, as they did for Grand Investments in the chapter-opening story on page 387.

Mid-Chapter Summary Problem
for Your Review

The cash account of Lethbridge Dental Associates at February 28, 2006, follows:

Cash

Feb.	1	Balance	3,995	Feb.	3		400
	6		800		12		3,100
	15		1,800		19		1,100
	23		1,100		25		500
	28		2,400		27		900
	28	Balance	4,095				

Lethbridge Dental Associates receives this bank statement in the first week of March 2006 (as always, negative amounts appear in parentheses):

Bank Statement for February 2006

Beginning balance		$3,995
Deposits:		
Feb. 7..	$ 800	
15..	1,800	
24..	1,100	3,700
Cheques (total per day):		
Feb. 8..	$ 400	
16..	3,100	
23..	1,100	(4,600)
Other items:		
Service charge		(10)
NSF cheque from M. E. Crown		(700)
Bank collection of note receivable for the company		1,000*
EFT—monthly rent expense		(330)
Interest on account balance...		15
Ending balance...		$3,070

*Includes principal of $881 plus interest of $119.

Additional data: Lethbridge Dental Associates deposits all cash receipts in the bank and makes all cash payments by cheque.

Required

1. Prepare the bank reconciliation of Lethbridge Dental Associates at February 28, 2006.

2. Journalize the entries based on the bank reconciliation.

Solution

LETHBRIDGE DENTAL ASSOCIATES
Bank Reconciliation
February 28, 2006

Bank

Balance, February 28, 2006	$3,070
Add: Deposit of February 28 in transit.....................................	2,400
	5,470
Less: Outstanding cheques issued on Feb. 25 ($500)	
and Feb. 27 ($900)	(1,400)
Adjusted bank balance, February 28, 2006	$4,070

Books

Balance, February 28, 2006		$4,095
Add: Bank collection of note receivable,		
including interest of $119		1,000
Add: Interest earned on bank balance		15
		5,110
Less: Service charge	$ 10	
NSF cheque	700	
EFT—Rent expense	330	(1,040)
Adjusted book balance, February 28, 2006		$4,070

Requirement 2

Feb.	28	Cash..	1,000	
		Note Receivable		881
		Interest Revenue		119
		Note receivable collected by bank ($1,000 – $119).		
Feb.	28	Cash..	15	
		Interest Revenue		15
		Interest earned on bank balance.		
Feb.	28	Bank Charges Expense.....................................	10	
		Cash..		10
		Bank service charge.		
Feb.	28	Accounts Receivable—M. E. Crown...............	700	
		Cash..		700
		NSF cheque returned by bank.		
Feb.	28	Rent Expense..	330	
		Cash..		330
		Monthly rent expense.		

Cyber Coach

Visit the Study Guide on the Media Companion CD-ROM and the Student Resources area of the *Accounting* Companion Website for extra practice with the new material in Chapter 8.

www.pearsoned.ca/horngren

Internal Control over Cash Receipts

OBJECTIVE 4
Apply internal controls to cash receipts

Internal control over cash receipts (the term includes cash, cheques, credit card charges, and debit card payments) ensures that all cash receipts are deposited for safekeeping in the bank. Companies receive cash over the counter and through the mail. Each source of cash calls for its own security measures.

Cash Receipts over the Counter Exhibit 8-7 illustrates a cash receipt made over the counter in a department store. The point-of-sale terminal (cash register) provides control over cash receipts. Consider a Canadian Tire store. The terminal is positioned so that customers can see the amounts the cashier enters into the terminal. No person willingly pays more than the marked price for an item, so the customer helps prevent the sales clerk from overcharging. Company policy requires issuance of a receipt to ensure that each sale is recorded correctly.

The cash drawer opens only when the clerk enters an amount on the keypad, and the machine records each transaction. At the end of the day, a manager proves the cash by comparing the total amount in the cash drawer against the machine's record of sales. This step helps prevent outright theft by the clerk.

At the end of the day, the cashier or other employee with cash-handling duties deposits the cash in the bank. The machine tape then goes to the accounting department as the basis for the journal entry to record sales revenue. These security measures, coupled with oversight by a manager, discourage theft.

Cash Receipts by Mail Many companies receive payments (cheques and credit card authorizations) by mail. Exhibit 8-8 shows how companies control payments received by mail. All incoming mail is opened by a mailroom employee.

The mailroom then sends all customer payments to the treasurer, who deposits the money in the bank. The remittance advices go to the accounting department for the journal entries to Cash and customers' accounts. As a final step, the controller compares the records of the day's cash receipts:

1. Bank deposit amount from the treasurer

2. Debit to Cash from the accounting department.

This comparison ensures that the debit to cash is for the amount actually deposited in the bank.

EXHIBIT 8-7

Cash Receipts over the Counter

REAL WORLD EXAMPLE

It is important to deposit all cash receipts *intact* daily. Neither managers nor employees should use cash received to make purchases or other cash payments. The deposit then can be an additional record of business transactions. In some rare circumstances where records are destroyed or missing, the bank statement can be used to reconstruct transactions.

STOP & THINK

What keeps the mailroom employee from pocketing a customer cheque and destroying the remittance advice?

Answer: If a customer gets billed a second time, the customer can show the paid cheque to prove he/she already paid. That would point to the dishonest mailroom employee.

EXHIBIT 8-8

Cash Receipts by Mail

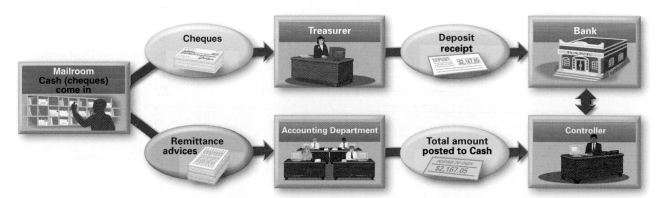

Many companies use a lock-box system to separate cash duties and establish control over cash receipts. Customers send their cheques directly to the company's bank account. Internal control is tight because company personnel never touch incoming cash. The lock-box system improves efficiency because cash is added to the bank account and can be used by the company immediately.

Cash Short and Over   A difference may exist between actual cash receipts and the day's record of cash received. Usually the difference is small and results from honest errors. When the recorded cash balance exceeds cash on hand, we have a *cash short* situation. When the actual cash exceeds the recorded cash balance, we have a *cash over* situation. Suppose the tapes from a cash register at Little Short Stop convenience store indicated sales revenue of $15,000, but the cash received was $14,980. To record the day's sales for that register, the store would make this entry:

Cash	14,980	
Cash Short and Over	20	
Sales Revenue		15,000
Daily cash sales.		

As the entry shows, Cash Short and Over, an expense account, is debited when sales revenue exceeds cash receipts. This account is credited when cash receipts exceed sales. A debit balance in Cash Short and Over appears on the income statement as Miscellaneous Expense; a credit balance may be shown as Other Revenue.

The Cash Short and Over account's balance should be small. The debits and credits for cash shorts and overs collected over an accounting period tend to cancel each other out. A large balance signals the accountant to investigate. For example, too large a debit balance may mean an employee is stealing. Cash Short and Over, then, acts as an internal control device.

Exhibit 8-9 summarizes the internal controls over cash receipts.

EXHIBIT 8-9

Internal Controls over Cash Receipts

Element of Internal Control	Internal Controls over Cash Receipts
Competent, reliable, ethical personnel	Companies carefully screen employees for undesirable personality traits. They commit time and effort to training programs.
Assignment of responsibilities	Specific employees are designated as cashiers, supervisors of cashiers, or accountants for cash receipts.
Proper authorization	Only designated employees, such as department managers, can grant exceptions for customers, approve cheque receipts above a certain amount, allow customers to purchase on credit, and void sales.
Separation of duties	Cashiers and mailroom employees who handle cash do not have access to the accounting records. Accountants who record cash receipts have no opportunity to handle cash.
Internal and external audits	Internal auditors examine company transactions for agreement with management policies. External auditors examine the internal controls over cash receipts to determine whether the accounting system produces accurate amounts for revenues, receivables, and other items related to cash receipts.
Documents and records	Customers receive receipts as transaction records. Bank statement lists cash receipts for deposit. Customers who pay by mail include a remittance advice showing the amount of cash they sent to the company.
Electronic devices and computer control	Cash registers serve as transaction records. Each day's receipts are matched with customer remittance advices and with the day's deposit ticket with the bank.
Other controls	Cashiers are bonded. Cash is stored in vaults and banks. Employees are rotated among jobs and are required to take vacations.

Internal Control over Cash Payments

OBJECTIVE 5
Apply internal controls to cash payments

Cash payments are as important as cash receipts. It is therefore critical to control cash payments. Companies make most payments by cheque. They also pay small amounts from a petty cash fund. Let's begin with cash payments by cheque.

Controls over Payment by Cheque

Payment by cheque is an important internal control. First, the cheque provides a record of payment. Second, to be valid the cheque must be signed by an authorized official. Before signing the cheque, the manager should study the evidence supporting the payment. To illustrate the internal control over cash payments, let's suppose the business is paying for merchandise inventory.

Controls over Purchase and Payment The purchasing and payment process—outlined in Exhibit 8-10—starts when the company sends a *purchase order* to the supplier. When the supplier ships the merchandise, the supplier also mails the *invoice*, or bill. (We introduced the invoice in Chapter 5.) The goods arrive and the receiving department checks the goods for damage and prepares a list of the goods received on a *receiving report*. The accounting department combines all the foregoing documents and forwards this *payment packet* with a completed cheque to officers for approval. Exhibit 8-11 shows the documents that make up the payment packet.

Before signing the cheque for payment, the controller or the treasurer should examine the packet to prove that all the documents agree. Only then does the company know that:

1. It received the goods ordered.
2. It is paying only for the goods received.

These two proofs are needed for good internal control over cash payments by cheque.

After payment, the cheque signer should punch a hole through the payment packet or otherwise mark the packet and its contents. These actions alert the company that it has paid the bill. Dishonest employees have been known to present a bill for cash payment two or more times.

Streamlined Procedures Technology is streamlining payment procedures. Evaluated Receipts Settlement (ERS) compresses the approval process into a single step: comparing the receiving report with the purchase order. If the two

········ **THINKING IT OVER**

Two officers' signatures are required for cheques over $1,000. One officer is going on vacation and pre-signs several cheques so that the cheques will be available if needed while she is gone. The cheques are locked in the vault. What is the internal control feature in this scenario?

A: Proper authorization. Two signatures are required to ensure that no unauthorized expenditures are made. Pre-signing the cheques defeats the control and should be discouraged.

EXHIBIT 8-10

Cash Payments by Cheque

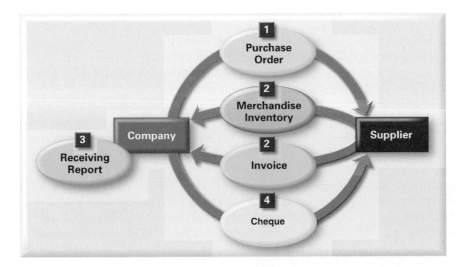

EXHIBIT 8-11

Payment Packet

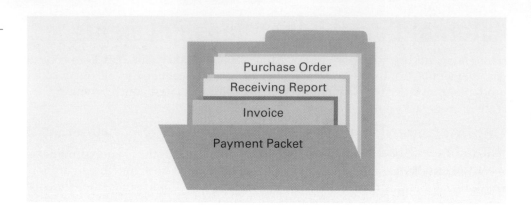

documents match, that proves, for example, that Kinko's received the paper it ordered. Then Kinko's pays Hammermill Paper, the supplier.

An even more streamlined process bypasses people and documents altogether. In Electronic Data Interchange (EDI), Canadian Tire's (www.canadiantire.ca) computers can communicate directly with the computers of suppliers like General Tire, Rubbermaid, and Procter & Gamble. When Canadian Tire's automobile tires reach a certain (low) level, the computer sends a purchase order to General Tire. General Tire ships the tires and invoices Canadian Tire electronically. Then an electronic fund transfer (EFT) sends the payment from Canadian Tire to General Tire.

Exhibit 8-12 summarizes the internal controls over cash payments.

EXHIBIT 8-12

Internal Controls over Cash Payments

Element of Internal Control	Internal Controls over Cash Payments
Competent, reliable, ethical personnel	Cash payments are entrusted to high-level employees, with larger amounts paid by the treasurer or assistant treasurer.
Assignment of responsibility	Specific employees approve purchase documents for payment. Executives examine approvals, then sign cheques.
Proper authorization	Large expenditures must be authorized by the company owner or board of directors to ensure agreement with organizational goals.
Separation of duties	Computer operators and other employees who handle cheques have no access to the accounting records. Accountants who record cash payments have no opportunity to handle cash.
Internal and external audits	Internal auditors examine company transactions for agreement with management policies. External auditors examine the internal controls over cash payments to determine whether the accounting system produces accurate amounts for expenses, assets, and other items related to cash payments.
Documents and records	Suppliers issue invoices that document the need to pay cash. Bank statements list cash payments (cheques and EFT payments) for reconciliation with company records. Cheques are prenumbered and used in sequence to account for payments.
Electronic devices, computer controls and other controls	Blank cheques are stored in a vault and controlled by a responsible official with no accounting duties. Machines stamp the amount on a cheque in indelible ink. Paid invoices are punched or otherwise mutilated to avoid duplicate payment.

Controlling Petty Cash Payments

It is wasteful to get approval and write a cheque for an executive's taxi fare, or the delivery of a package across town. To meet these needs, companies keep cash on hand to pay small amounts. This fund is called **petty cash**.

Even though petty cash payments are small, the business needs to set up internal controls, such as the following:

1. Designate an employee to serve as custodian of the petty cash fund.

2. Keep a specific amount of cash on hand.

3. Support all fund payments with a petty cash ticket.

The petty cash fund is opened when a cheque for the designated amount is issued to Petty Cash. Assume that on February 28 the business creates a petty cash fund of $200. The custodian cashes a $200 cheque and places the money in the fund. Starting the fund is recorded as follows:

Feb. 28	Petty Cash	200	
	Cash		200
	To open the petty cash fund.		

For each petty cash payment, the custodian prepares a *petty cash ticket* like the one illustrated in Exhibit 8-13.

Signatures (or initials) identify the recipient of the cash (Lewis Wright) and the fund custodian (MAR). Requiring both signatures reduces fraudulent payments. The custodian keeps all the pre-numbered petty cash tickets in the fund. The sum of the cash plus the total of the ticket amounts should equal the opening balance ($200) at all times. Also, the Petty Cash account keeps its $200 balance at all times.

Maintaining the Petty Cash account at its designated balance is the nature of an **imprest system**. This system clearly identifies the amount of cash for which the fund custodian is responsible and is the system's main internal control feature.

Payments reduce the cash in the fund, so periodically the fund must be replenished. On March 31 this fund has $115 in cash and $82 in tickets. A cheque for $85, made payable to Petty Cash, is issued to replenish the fund. The fund custodian cashes this cheque for currency and coins, and puts the $85 in the fund to return its actual cash to $200.

The petty cash tickets identify the accounts to be debited, as shown in the entry to replenish the fund:

Mar. 31	Office Supplies	23	
	Delivery Expense	17	
	Cash Short and Over	3	
	Selling Expense	42	
	Cash		85
	To replenish the petty cash fund.		

KEY POINT

No journal entries are made for petty cash payments until the fund is replenished. At that time, all petty cash payments will be recorded in a summary entry. This procedure avoids the need to journalize many payments for small amounts.

KEY POINT

Attached to the petty cash ticket is a cash register receipt, invoice, or other documentation to support the payment.

EXHIBIT 8-13

Petty Cash Ticket

PETTY CASH TICKET

Date ___Mar. 25, 2006___   No. _45_

Amount ___$17.00___

For ___Payment for delivery of contract.___

Debit ___Delivery Expense, Acct. No. 545___

Received by ___Lewis Wright___   Fund Custodian ___MAR___

The cash payments appear to have exceeded the sum of the tickets, since the fund was short $3, so Cash Short and Over was debited for the missing amount ($3). If the sum of the tickets exceeds the payment, Cash Short and Over would be credited. Replenishing the fund does *not* affect the Petty Cash account. Petty Cash keeps its $200 balance at all times.

The petty cash fund *must* be replenished on the balance sheet date. Otherwise, the income statement will understate the expenses listed on the tickets.

The Petty Cash account in the General Ledger is debited only when the fund is started (see the February 28 entry) or when its amount is changed. In our illustration, suppose the business decides to raise the fund amount from $200 to $250 because of increased demand for petty cash. This step would require a $50 debit to the Petty Cash account.

Reporting Cash on the Balance Sheet

Cash is the first asset listed on the balance sheet because it is the most liquid asset. Businesses often have several bank accounts and several petty cash funds, but they combine all cash amounts into a single total called "Cash and Cash Equivalents."

Cash equivalents include liquid assets such as time deposits and certificates of deposit. These interest-bearing accounts can be withdrawn with no penalty after a short period of time. These assets are sufficiently similar to be reported along with cash. For example, the balance sheet of Nortel Networks Corporation (www.nortelnetworks.com) reported the following current assets:

NORTEL NETWORKS CORPORATION
Balance Sheet (Adapted)
December 31, 2002

(In millions of U.S. dollars)

Assets
Current assets:

Cash and equivalents	$3,864
Restricted cash and equivalents	249
Accounts receivable	1,911
Inventories—net	889
Future income taxes	799
Other current assets	777
Total current assets	$8,489

Nortel's cash balance means that $3,864 million is available for use as needed. Cash that is restricted and unavailable for immediate use should not be reported as a current asset if the company does not expect to spend the cash within a year or within the company's operating cycle, if longer than a year. For example, some banks require their depositors to maintain a *compensating balance* on deposit in the bank in order to borrow from the bank. Nortel reports restricted cash and equivalents of $249 million as a current asset.

OBJECTIVE 6
Make ethical business judgments

Ethics and Accounting

A *Wall Street Journal* (services.wsj.com) article described a young Russian entrepreneur who claimed that he was getting ahead in business by breaking laws. He stated that "Older people have an ethics problem. By that I mean they *have* ethics."

Conversely, Robert Schad, President and CEO of Husky Injection Molding Systems Ltd. (www.husky.ca), in Bolton, Ontario, said, "Ethical practice is, quite simply, good business." Schad has been in business long enough to see the danger in unethical behaviour. Sooner or later unethical conduct comes to light, as was true in our chapter-opening story on page 387. Moreover, ethical behaviour wins out in the end because it is the right thing to do.

Corporate and Professional Codes of Ethics

Most large companies have a code of ethics to encourage employees to behave ethically. But codes of ethics are not enough by themselves. Senior management must set a high ethical tone. They must make it clear that the company will not tolerate unethical conduct.

Accountants have additional incentives to behave ethically. As professionals, they are expected to maintain higher standards than society in general. Their ability to attract business depends entirely on their reputation.

As you learned in Chapter 1, there are three bodies of professional accountants in Canada: the CAs, the CGAs, and the CMAs. Members of each of the bodies must adhere to the rules of professional conduct of their respective organizations. These documents set minimum standards of conduct for members. Unacceptable actions can result in expulsion from the organization, which makes it impossible for the person to remain a professional accountant.

REAL WORLD EXAMPLE

In a survey, 81 percent of companies had a corporate code of conduct. Another 7 percent planned to establish such a code.

Ethical Issues in Accounting

In many situations the ethical choice is easy. For example, stealing cash, as in the chapter-opening story, is illegal and unethical. The cashier's actions led to a jail sentence. In other cases, the choices are more difficult. But, in every instance, ethical judgments are a personal decision. What should I do in a given situation? Let's consider two ethical issues in accounting.

Situation 1 Sonja Kleberg is preparing the income tax return of a client who earned more income than expected. On January 2, the client pays for advertising to run in late January and asks Sonja to backdate the expense to the preceding year. The tax deduction would help the client more in the year just ended than in the current year. Backdating would decrease taxable income of the earlier year and postpone a few dollars in tax payments. After all, there is a difference of only two days between January 2 and December 31. This client is important to Kleberg. What should she do?

> **She should refuse the request because the transaction took place in January of the new year.**

What internal control device could prove that Kleberg behaved unethically if she backdated the transaction in the accounting records? A Canada Customs and Revenue Agency audit could prove that the expense occurred in January rather than in December. Falsifying tax returns is both illegal and unethical.

Situation 2 David Duncan, the lead auditor for Enron Corporation, thinks Enron may be understating the liabilities on its balance sheet. Enron's transactions are very complex, and no one may ever figure this out. Duncan asks his firm's (Arthur Andersen) Standards Committee how he should handle the situation. They reply, "Require Enron to report all its liabilities." Enron is Duncan's most important client, and Enron is pressuring Duncan to certify the liabilities. Duncan can rationalize that Enron's reported amounts are okay. What should Duncan do?

To make his decision, Duncan could follow the framework outlined in the Decision Guidelines feature that follows.

DECISION GUIDELINES   *Framework for Making Ethical Judgments*

Weighing tough ethical judgments requires a decision framework. Consider these six questions as general guidelines; they will guide you through answering tough ethical questions.

Let's apply these guidelines to David Duncan.

Decision	Guidelines
1. What are the facts?	1. *Determine the facts.*
2. What is the ethical issue, if any?	2. *Identify the ethical issues.* The root word of ethical is *ethics,* which Webster's dictionary defines as "the discipline dealing with what is good and bad and with moral duty and obligation." Duncan's ethical dilemma is to decide what he should do with the information he has uncovered.
3. What are the alternatives?	3. *Specify the alternatives.* For David Duncan, the alternatives include: (a) go along with Enron's liabilities as reported (i.e., do nothing) or (b) force Enron's management to report liabilities at more correct amounts.
4. Who is involved in the situation?	4. *Identify the stakeholders, the people involved.* Individuals who could be affected inlude Duncan, the partners and staff of Arthur Andersen, the management and employees of Enron, Enron's investors, Enron's creditors, the U.S. federal and various state governments.
5. What are the possible consequences of each alternative in question 3?	5. *Assess the possible outcomes of each alternative.* (a) If Duncan certifies Enron's present level of liabilities—and if no one ever objects—Duncan will keep this valuable client. But if Enron's actual liabilities turn out to be higher than reported, Enron's investors and creditors may lose money and take Duncan to court. That would damage his reputation as an auditor and hurt his firm. (b) If Duncan follows the policy suggestion of his company, he must force Enron to increase its reported liabilities. That will anger Enron, and Enron may fire Duncan and Arthur Anderson as its auditor. In this case Duncan will save his reputation, but it will cost him and his firm business in the short run.
6. What should Duncan do?	6. *Make a decision.* In the end Duncan went along with Enron and certified Enron's liabilities. He went directly against his firm's policies. Enron later admitted understating its liabilities, Duncan had to retract his audit opinion, and Duncan's firm, Arthur Andersen, collapsed soon after. Duncan should have followed company policy. Rarely is one person smarter than a team of experts. Not following company policy cost him and many others dearly.

STOP & THINK

Can you identify the external control in the chapter-opening story on page 387? How did it impose discipline on the cashier?

Answer: The external control was the monthly statement that Grand Investments Ltd. sends each client. When customers saw their account balances underreported on the monthly statements, they called in to ask why. Bob Madden must have spent half his time explaining the out-of-balance conditions of clients' accounts. Sooner or later he was bound to get caught. That's how external controls work.

Summary Problem
for Your Review

Kimber Design Studios established a $300 petty cash fund. James C. Brown (JCB) is the fund custodian. At the end of the first week, the petty cash fund contains the following:

1. Cash: $171

2. Petty cash tickets

No.	Amount	Issued to	Signed by	Account Debited
44	$14	B. Jarvis	B. Jarvis and JCB	Office Supplies
45	39	S. Bell	S. Bell	Delivery Expense
47	43	R. Tate	R. Tate and JCB	—
48	33	G. Blair	G. Blair and JCB	Travel Expense

Required

1. Identify three internal control weaknesses revealed in the given data.

2. Prepare the general journal entries to record
   a. Establishment of the petty cash fund.
   b. Replenishment of the fund. Assume petty cash ticket no. 47 was issued for the purchase of office supplies.

3. What is the balance in the Petty Cash account immediately before replenishment? Immediately after replenishment?

Solution

Requirement 1

The three internal control weaknesses are

1. Petty cash ticket no. 46 is missing. There is no indication of what happened to this ticket. The company should investigate.

2. The petty cash custodian (JCB) did not sign petty cash ticket no. 45. This omission may have been an oversight on his part. However, it raises the question of whether he authorized the payment. Both the fund custodian and recipient of cash should sign the ticket.

3. Petty cash ticket no. 47 does not indicate which account to debit. What did Tate do with the money, and what account should be debited? At worst, the funds have been stolen. At best, asking the custodian to reconstruct the transaction from memory is haphazard. Since we are instructed to assume petty cash ticket no. 47 was issued for the purchase of office supplies, debit Office Supplies.

Requirement 2

Petty cash journal entries

a. Entry to establish the petty cash fund

Petty Cash...	300	
Cash...		300
To open the petty cash fund.		

b. Entry to replenish the fund

Office Supplies ($14 + $43)	57	
Delivery Expense	39	
Travel Expense	33	
Cash		129

To replenish the petty cash fund.

Requirement 3

The balance in Petty Cash is *always* its specified balance, in this case $300, as shown by posting the above entries to the account.

Petty Cash

(a) 300	

Cyber Coach

Visit the Study Guide on the Media Companion CD-ROM and the Student Resources area of the *Accounting* Companion Website for extra practice with the new material in Chapter 8.

www.pearsoned.ca/horngren

Summary

1. **Define internal control.** *Internal control* is the organizational plan and all related measures adopted by an entity to meet management's objectives of discharging statutory responsibilities, profitability, prevention and detection of fraud and error, safeguarding of assets, reliability of accounting records, and timely preparation of reliable financial information.

2. **Tell how to achieve good internal control.** An effective internal control system includes these features: *competent, reliable and ethical personnel; clear assignment of responsibilities; proper authorization; separation of duties; internal and external audits; documents and records;* and *electronic devices and computer controls.* Many companies also make use of fireproof vaults, point-of-sale terminals, fidelity bonds, mandatory vacations, and job rotation. Effective computerized internal control systems must meet the same basic standards that good manual systems do.

3. **Prepare a bank reconciliation and the related journal entries.** The *bank account* helps to control and safeguard cash. Businesses use the *bank statement* and the *bank reconciliation* to account for banking transactions.

4. **Apply internal controls to cash receipts.** To control cash receipts over the counter, companies use point-of-sale terminals that customers can see, and require that cashiers provide customers with receipts. A duplicate tape inside the machine or a link to a central computer records each sale and cash transaction. Pricing with uneven amounts means that cashiers must open the drawer to make change, which requires the transaction to be recorded on tape.

To control cash receipts by mail, a mailroom employee should be assigned the responsibility for opening the mail, comparing the enclosed amount with the remittance advice, and preparing a control tape. This is an essential separation of duties—the accounting department should not open the mail. At the end of the day, the controller compares the three records of the day's cash receipts: the control tape total from the mailroom, the bank deposit amount from the cashier, and the debit to Cash from the accounting department.

5. **Apply internal controls to cash payments.** To control payments by cheque, cheques should be issued and signed only when a *payment packet* including the purchase order, invoice (bill), and receiving report (all with appropriate signatures) has been prepared. To control petty cash payments, the custodian of the fund should require a completed petty cash ticket for all payments.

6. **Make ethical business judgments.** To make ethical decisions, people should proceed in six steps: (1) Determine the facts. (2) Identify the ethical issues. (3) Specify the alternatives. (4) Identify the stakeholders, the people involved. (5) Assess the possible outcomes of each alternative. (6) Make the decision.

Self-Study Questions

Test your understanding of the chapter by marking the correct answer for each of the following questions:

1. Which of the following is an objective of internal control? (*p. 388*)
   a. Safeguarding assets
   b. Maintaining reliable control systems
   c. Optimizing the use of resources
   d. Preventing and detecting fraud and error
   e. All the above are objectives of internal control.

2. Which of the characteristics of an effective system of internal control is violated by allowing the employee who handles inventory to also account for inventory? (*pp. 389–392*)
   a. Competent and reliable personnel
   b. Assignment of responsibilities
   c. Proper authorization
   d. Separation of duties

3. What control function is performed by auditors? (*p. 391*)
   a. Objective opinion on the fair presentation of the financial statements
   b. Assurance that all transactions are accounted for correctly
   c. Communication of the results of the audit to regulatory agencies
   d. Guarantee that a proper separation of duties exists within the business

4. The bank account serves as a control device over (*pp. 394–397*)
   a. Cash receipts   c. Both of the above
   b. Cash payments   d. None of the above

5. Which of the following items appears on the Bank side of a bank reconciliation? (*p. 398*)
   a. Book error
   b. Outstanding cheque
   c. NSF cheque
   d. Interest revenue earned on bank balance

6. Which of the following reconciling items requires a journal entry on the books of the company? (*p. 399*)
   a. Book error
   b. Outstanding cheque
   c. NSF cheque
   d. Interest revenue earned on bank balance
   e. All of the above, except (b)
   f. None of the above

7. What is the major internal control measure over the cash receipts of a SAAN store? (*pp. 405–406*)
   a. Reporting the day's cash receipts to the controller
   b. Preparing a petty cash ticket for all payments from the fund
   c. Pricing merchandise at uneven amounts, coupled with use of a cash register
   d. Channelling all cash receipts through the mailroom, whose employees have no cash-accounting responsibilities

8. Before signing a cheque to pay for goods purchased, the company should determine that the (*pp. 407–408*)
   a. Invoice is for the goods ordered
   b. Merchandise was received
   c. Amount of the invoice is correct
   d. All of the above are correct.

9. The internal control feature that is specific to petty cash is (*p. 409*)
   a. Separation of duties
   b. Assignment of responsibility
   c. Proper authorization
   d. The imprest system

10. Ethical judgments in accounting and business (*p. 411*)
    a. Require employees to break laws to get ahead
    b. Force decision makers to think about what is good and bad
    c. Always hurt someone
    d. Are affected by internal controls but not by external controls

Answers to the Self-Study Questions follow the Similar Accounting Terms.

Accounting Vocabulary

Audit (*p. 391*)
Bank collection (*p. 399*)
Bank reconciliation (*p. 398*)
Bank statement (*p. 395*)
Cheque (*p. 394*)
Computer virus (*p. 393*)
Controller (*p. 390*)
Deposit in transit (*p. 398*)
Electronic funds transfer (EFT) (*p. 395*)

Encryption (*p. 394*)
Firewall (*p. 394*)
Imprest system (*p. 409*)
Internal control (*p. 388*)
Nonsufficient funds (NSF) cheque (*p. 399*)
Outstanding cheque (*p. 398*)
Petty cash (*p. 409*)
Trojan horse (*p. 393*)

Similar Accounting Terms

Cash receipts	Cash, cheques, and other negotiable instruments received
Separation of duties	Segregation of duties, division of duties
Invoice	Bill

Answers to Self-Study Questions

1. e	3. a	5. b	7. c	9. d
2. d	4. c	6. e	8. d	10. b

Assignment Material

Questions

1. Which of the features of effective internal control is the most fundamental? Why?

2. Which company employees bear primary responsibility for a company's financial statements and for maintaining the company's system of internal control? How do these persons carry out this responsibility?

3. Identify at least seven features of an effective system of internal control.

4. Separation of duties may be divided into three parts. What are they?

5. What is an audit? Identify the two types of audit and the differences between them.

6. Why are documents and records a feature of internal control systems?

7. How has an accounting system's reliance on electronic devices altered internal control?

8. Why should the same employee not write the computer programs for cash payments, sign cheques, and mail the cheques to payees?

9. Briefly state how each of the following serves as an internal control measure over cash: bank account, signature card, deposit ticket, and bank statement.

10. Are internal control systems designed to be fool-proof and perfect? What is a fundamental constraint in planning and maintaining systems?

11. How can internal control systems be circumvented?

12. Each of the items in the following list must be accounted for in the bank reconciliation. Next to each item, enter the appropriate letter from the following possible treatments: (a) bank side of reconciliation—add the item; (b) bank side of reconciliation—subtract the item; (c) book side of reconciliation—add the item; and (d) book side of reconciliation—subtract the item.

_____	Outstanding cheque
_____	NSF cheque
_____	Bank service charge
_____	Cost of printed cheques
_____	EFT receipt
_____	Bank error that decreased bank balance
_____	Deposit in transit
_____	Bank collection
_____	EFT payment
_____	Customer's cheque returned because of unauthorized signature
_____	Book error that increased balance of Cash account

13. What purpose does a bank reconciliation serve?

14. What role does a cash register play in an internal control system?

15. Describe internal control procedures for cash received by mail.

16. What documents make up the payment packet? Describe three procedures that use the payment packet to ensure that each payment is appropriate.

17. What balance does the Petty Cash account have at all times? Does this balance always equal the amount of cash in the fund? When are the two amounts equal? When are they unequal?

18. Suppose a company has six bank accounts, two petty cash funds, and three certificates of deposit that can be withdrawn on demand. How many cash amounts would this company likely report separately on its balance sheet?

19. Why should accountants adhere to a higher standard of ethical conduct than many other members of society do?

20. "Our managers know that they are expected to meet budgeted profit figures. We don't want excuses. We want results." Discuss the ethical implications of this policy.

Exercises

Exercise 8-1 *Definition of internal control* **(Obj. 1)**

Internal controls are designed to safeguard assets and records, encourage employees to follow company policies, promote operational efficiency, and ensure accurate records. Which of these four goals of internal control is most important? Stated differently, which goal must the internal controls accomplish for the business to survive? Give your reason.

Exercise 8-2 *Achieving good internal control* **(Obj. 2)**

Explain why separation of duties is often described as the cornerstone of internal control for safeguarding assets. Describe what could happen if the same person has custody of an asset and also accounts for the asset.

Exercise 8-3 *Achieving good internal control* **(Obj. 2)**

Review the characteristics of an effective system of internal control, the discussion of which begins on page 389. Then identify two things that Grand Investments Ltd. in the chapter-opening story could have done to make it harder for Bob Madden to steal from the company and hide the theft. Explain how each new measure taken by Grand Investments would have accomplished its goal.

Exercise 8-4 *Correcting an internal control weakness* **(Obj. 2)**

Trader Nick Leeson worked for Baring Securities (Singapore) Limited (BSS) as the general manager and head trader. Due to his experience in operations, he also acted as head of the "back office" that does the record keeping and tracks who owes what to whom. Leeson appeared to be making huge profits by speculating on Japan's Nikkei stock market—until he fled Singapore, leaving behind a £827,000,000 loss hidden in an unused error account on the Barings balance sheet. As a result of this situation, Britain's Barings Bank collapsed.

What internal control weaknesses at BSS allowed this loss to grow so large? How could Barings have avoided and/or limited the size of the loss?

Exercise 8-5 *Identifying internal control strengths and weaknesses* **(Obj. 2)**

The following situations suggest either a strength or weakness in internal control. Identify each as *strength* or *weakness* and give the reason for each answer.

a. Top managers delegate all internal control measures to the accounting department.

b. The accounting department orders merchandise and approves vouchers for payment.

c. Cash received by mail goes straight to the accountant, who debits Cash and credits Accounts Receivable from the customer.

d. The vice-president who signs cheques assumes the accounting department has matched the invoice with other supporting documents and therefore does not examine the payment packet.

e. The operator of the computer has no other accounting or cash-handling duties.

f. Cash received over the counter is controlled by the clerk, who rings up the sale and places the cash in the register. The clerk has access to the control tape stored in the register.

Exercise 8-6 *Identifying internal controls* *(Obj. 2)*

Identify the missing internal control characteristic in the following situations:

a. Business is slow at the Paramount Theatre on Tuesday, Wednesday, and Thursday nights. To reduce expenses, the owner decides not to use a ticket taker on those nights. The ticket seller (cashier) is told to keep the tickets as a record of the number sold.

b. When business is brisk, Stop Seven and many other retail stores deposit cash in the bank several times during the day. The manager at another convenience store wants to reduce the time spent by employees delivering cash to the bank, so he starts a new policy. Cash will build up over Saturdays and Sundays, and the total two-day amount will be deposited on Sunday evening.

c. In the course of auditing the records of a company, you find that the same employee orders merchandise and approves invoices for payment.

d. The manager of a discount store wants to speed the flow of customers through checkout. She decides to reduce the time spent by cashiers making change, so she prices merchandise at round dollar amounts—such as $8.00 and $15.00—instead of the customary amounts—$7.95 and $14.95.

e. Grocery stores such as No-Frills and Big Box Groceries purchase large quantities of their merchandise from a few suppliers. At one grocery store, the manager decides to reduce paperwork. He eliminates the requirement that a receiving department employee prepare a receiving report, which lists the quantities of items received from the supplier.

Exercise 8-7 *Explaining the role of internal control* *(Obj. 2)*

The following questions pertain to internal control. Consider each situation separately.

1. Wong Company requires that all documents supporting a cheque be cancelled (stamped Paid) by the person who signs the cheque. Why do you think this practice is required? What might happen if it were not?

2. Separation of duties is an important consideration if a system of internal control is to be effective. Why is this so?

3. Cash may be a relatively small item on the financial statements. Nevertheless, internal control over cash is very important. Why is this true?

4. Many managers think that safeguarding assets is the most important objective of internal control systems, while auditors emphasize internal control's role in ensuring reliable accounting data. Explain why managers are more concerned about safeguarding assets and auditors are more concerned about the quality of the accounting records.

Exercise 8-8 *Classifying bank reconciliation items* *(Obj. 3)*

The following seven items may appear on a bank reconciliation:

1. Bank collection of a note receivable on our behalf
2. Book error: We debited Cash for $200. The correct debit was $2,000
3. NSF cheque
4. Service charge
5. Deposits in transit
6. Bank error: The bank charged our account for a cheque written by another customer
7. Outstanding cheques

Classify each item as (a) an addition to the bank balance, (b) a subtraction from the bank balance, (c) an addition to the book balance, or (d) a subtraction from the book balance.

Exercise 8-9   *Preparing a bank reconciliation*   *(Obj. 3)*

Judi Carter's cheque book lists the entries shown below.

Required

Prepare Judi Carter's bank reconciliation at July 31, 2004.

Date	Cheque No.	Item	Cheque	Deposit	Balance
July					
1					$ 725
4	622	Hobby Store	$ 39		686
9		Dividends received		$ 75	761
13	623	TELUS	57		704
14	624	Esso	52		652
18	625	Cash	50		602
26	626	Canadian Cancer Society	25		577
28	627	Park Lane Apartments	550		27
31		Paycheque		3,250	3,277

Carter's July bank statement shows:

Balance..		$725
Add: Deposits..		75
Deduct cheques: No.	Amount	
622	$39	
623	57	
624	58*	
625	50	(204)
Other charges		
Printed cheques..	$10	
Service charge	7	(17)
Balance		$579

* This is the correct amount of cheque number 624.

Exercise 8-10   *Preparing a bank reconciliation*   *(Obj. 3)*

François Ouimet operates two Shell stations. He has just received the monthly bank statement at May 31 from the Royal Bank, and the statement shows an ending balance of $5,860. Listed on the statement are an EFT rent collection of $400, a service charge of $15, two NSF cheques totalling $95, and a $25 charge for printed cheques. In reviewing his cash records, Ouimet identifies outstanding cheques totalling $429 and a May 31 deposit in transit of $2,265. During May, he recorded a $360 cheque for the salary of a part-time employee by debiting Salary Expense and crediting Cash for $36. Ouimet's cash account shows a May 31 cash balance of $7,755. Prepare the bank reconciliation at May 31, 2005.

Exercise 8-11   *Making journal entries from a bank reconciliation*   *(Obj. 3)*

Using the data from Exercise 8-10, record the entries that Ouimet should make in the general journal on May 31. Include an explanation for each of the entries.

Exercise 8-12 *Applying internal controls to the bank reconciliation* **(Obj. 2, 3)**

A jury convicted the treasurer of Call Us Taxi Company of stealing cash from the company. Over a three-year period, the treasurer allegedly took almost $65,000 and attempted to cover the theft by manipulating the bank reconciliation.

Required

What is a likely way that a person would manipulate a bank reconciliation to cover a theft? Be specific. What internal control arrangement could have avoided this theft?

Exercise 8-13 *Evaluating internal control over cash receipts* **(Obj. 4)**

A cash register is located in each department of Mario's Discount Store. The register shows the amount of each sale, the cash received from the customer, and any change returned to the customer. The machine also produces a customer receipt but keeps no record of sales transactions. At the end of the day, the clerk counts the cash in the register and gives it to the cashier for deposit in the company bank account.

Required

Write a memo to convince Mario Da Silva, the owner, that there is an internal control weakness over cash receipts. Identify the weakness that gives an employee the best opportunity to steal cash, and state how to prevent such a theft.

Exercise 8-14 *Petty cash, cash short and over* **(Obj. 5)**

Record the following selected transactions of Kelly's Fine Foods in general journal format (explanations are not required):

2004
June 1 Established a petty cash fund with a $500 balance.
      2 Journalized the day's cash sales. Cash register tapes show a $3,250 total, but the cash in the register is $3,260.
     10 The petty cash fund has $175 in cash and $312 in petty cash tickets issued to pay for Office Supplies ($161), Delivery Expense ($93) and Entertainment Expense ($58). Replenished the fund.

Exercise 8-15 *Accounting for petty cash* **(Obj. 5)**

The Canadian Cancer Society's Winnipeg, Manitoba branch, created a $1,000 imprest petty cash fund. During the first month of use, the fund custodian authorized and signed petty cash tickets as shown below.

Ticket No.	Item	Account Debited	Amount
1	Delivery of pledge cards to donors	Delivery Expense	$ 80.50
2	Stamp purchase	Postage Expense	66.24
3	Newsletter	Supplies Expense	212.75
4	Key to closet	Miscellaneous Expense	5.95
5	Wastebasket	Miscellaneous Expense	28.74
6	Staples	Supplies Expense	9.20

Required

1. Make general journal entries for creation of the petty cash fund and its replenishment. Include explanations.
2. Describe the items in the fund immediately prior to replenishment.
3. Describe the items in the fund immediately after replenishment.

Exercise 8-16 *Evaluating the ethics of conduct by a manager* *(Obj. 6)*

You have a part-time job in a local delicatessen, which is part of a chain of delicatessens. You received the job through your parent's friendship with Margo Watt, the deli manager. The job is going well, but you are puzzled by the actions of Margo and her husband, Joe. Each day, one or both of them fills takeout orders and takes them to Margo's office. Later you notice Joe and Margo enjoying the takeout orders, sometimes with friends. You know the orders were not rung through the checkout counter. When you ask a co-worker about the practice, you are told that Margo is the boss and can do as she wishes, and besides, many employees help themselves to meals.

Required

You have been given the assignment in a business ethics course to comment on the issue. Apply the decision guidelines for ethical judgments outlined in the Decision Guidelines feature on page 412 to decide whether a manager of a deli should help herself or himself to meals on a regular basis and not pay for what she or he takes.

Beyond the Numbers

Beyond the Numbers 8-1 *Correcting an internal control weakness* *(Obj. 1, 5)*

This case is based on a situation experienced by one of the authors. Alpha Construction Company, headquartered in Chattanooga, Tennessee, built a Roadway Inn Motel in Cleveland, 35 kilometres east of Chattanooga. The construction foreman, whose name was Slim, moved into Cleveland in March to hire the 40 workers needed to complete the project. Slim hired the construction workers, had them fill out the necessary tax forms, and sent the employment documents to the home office, which opened a payroll file for each employee.

Work on the motel began on April 1 and ended September 1. Each Thursday evening, Slim filled out a time card that listed the hours worked by each employee during the five-day workweek ended at 5 p.m. on Thursday. Slim faxed the time sheets to the home office, which prepared the payroll cheques on Friday morning. Slim drove to the home office after lunch on Friday, picked up the payroll cheques, and returned to the construction site. At 5 p.m. on Friday, Slim distributed the payroll cheques to the workers.

a. Describe in detail the internal control weakness in this situation. Specify what negative result(s) could occur because of the internal control weakness.

b. Describe what you would do to correct the internal control weakness.

Ethical Issue

John Sullivan owns apartment buildings in Nova Scotia, New Brunswick, and Quebec. Each property has a manager who collects rent, arranges for repairs, and runs advertisements in the local newspaper. The property managers transfer cash to Sullivan monthly and prepare their own bank reconciliations.

The manager in New Brunswick has been stealing large sums of money. To cover the theft, she understates the amount of outstanding cheques on the monthly bank reconciliation. As a result, each monthly bank reconciliation appears to balance. However, the balance sheet reports more cash than Sullivan actually has in the bank. In negotiating the sale of the New Brunswick property, Sullivan is showing the balance sheet to prospective investors.

Required

1. Identify two parties other than Sullivan who can be harmed by this theft. In what ways can they be harmed?
2. Discuss the role accounting plays in this situation.

Problems (Group A)

Problem 8-1A *Identifying the characteristics of an effective internal control system (Obj. 1, 2)*

Okanogan Communications prospered during the lengthy economic expansion of the 1980s and 1990s. Business was so good that the company bothered with few internal controls. The recent decline in the local real estate market, however, has caused Okanogan to experience a shortage of cash. Mary Messenger, the company owner, is looking for ways to save money.

Required

As controller of the company, write a memorandum to convince Mary Messenger of the company's need for a system of internal control. Be specific in telling her how an internal control system could possibly lead to saving money. Include the definition of internal control, and briefly discuss each characteristic beginning with competent, reliable, and ethical personnel.

Problem 8-2A *Identifying internal control weaknesses (Obj. 2, 4, 5)*

Each of the following situations has an internal control weakness:

a. In evaluating the internal control over cash payments, an auditor learns that the purchasing agent is responsible for purchasing uranium for use in the company's manufacturing process, approving the invoices for payment, and signing the cheques. No supervisor reviews the purchasing agent's work.

b. Sally Southward owns a firm that performs decorating services. Her staff consists of twelve professional designers, and she manages the office. Often her work requires her to travel to meet with clients. During the past six months, she has observed that when she returns from a business trip, the design jobs in the office have not progressed satisfactorily. She learns that when she is away several of her senior employees take over office management and neglect their design duties. One employee could manage the office.

c. Alice de Boeuf has been an employee of Your Kitchen Store for many years. Because the business is relatively small, Alice performs all accounting duties, including opening the mail, preparing the bank deposit, and preparing the bank reconciliation.

d. Most large companies have internal audit staffs that continuously evaluate the business's internal control. Part of the internal auditor's job is to evaluate how efficiently the company is running. For example, is the company purchasing inventory from the least expensive wholesaler? After a particularly bad year, Lamay Software eliminates its internal audit department to reduce expenses.

e. Public accounting firms, law firms, and other professional organizations use paraprofessional employees to do some of their routine tasks. For example, an accounting paraprofessional might examine documents to assist a public accountant in conducting an audit. In the public accounting firm of Bradshaw and Bos, Nancy Bos, the senior partner, turns over a significant portion of her high-level audit work to her paraprofessional staff.

Required

1. Identify the missing internal control characteristic in each situation.
2. Identify the problem that could be caused by each missing control.
3. Propose a solution to each possible internal control problem.

Media Companion CD-ROM

Problem 8-3A *Preparing and using the bank reconciliation as a control device (Obj. 3)*

The cash receipts and the cash payments of Stanton Hardware for January 2005 are as follows:

Cash Receipts (Posting reference is CR)			Cash Payments (Posting reference is CP)	
Date	**Cash Debit**		**Cheque No.**	**Cash Credit**
Jan. 3	$ 5,247		311	$ 918
8	370		312	417
10	495		313	3,190
16	1,872		314	646
22	5,184		315	2,147
29	601		316	900
31	432		317	326
Total	$14,201		318	1,567
			319	200
			320	3,241
			Total	$13,552

Assume that the Cash account of Stanton Hardware shows the following information at January 31, 2005:

Cash

Date	Item	Jrnl. Ref.	Debit	Credit	Balance
Jan. 1	Balance				9,171 Dr
31		CR. 6	14,201		23,372 Dr
31		CP. 11		13,552	9,820 Dr

Stanton Hardware received the bank statement shown below on January 31, 2005.

Bank Statement for January 2005

Beginning balance		$ 9,171
Deposits and other Credits:		
Jan. 1	$ 263 EFT	
4	5,247	
9	370	
12	495	
17	1,872	
22	3,186 BC	
23	5,184	16,617
Cheques and other Debits:		
Jan. 7	$ 918	
13	3,109	
14	839 US	
15	417	
18	646	
21	329 EFT	
26	2,147	
30	900	
31	35 SC	(9,340)
Ending balance		$16,448

Explanations: EFT—electronic funds transfer, BC—bank collection, US—unauthorized signature, SC—service charge.

Additional data for the bank reconciliation:

a. The EFT deposit was a receipt of monthly rent. The EFT debit was payment of monthly insurance.

b. The unauthorized-signature cheque was received from A. N. Garner.

c. The $3,186 bank collection of a note receivable on January 22 included $125 interest revenue.

d. The correct amount of cheque number 313, a payment on account, is $3,109. (Stanton Hardware's accountant mistakenly recorded the cheque for $3,190.)

Required

1. Prepare the Stanton Hardware bank reconciliation at January 31, 2005.
2. Describe how a bank account and the bank reconciliation help the Stanton Hardware's owner control the business's cash.

Media Companion CD-ROM

Problem 8-4A *Preparing a bank reconciliation and the related journal entries* *(Obj. 3)*

The July 31, 2005, bank statement of Lamarr Shoes has just arrived from the Royal Bank. To prepare the Lamarr Shoes bank reconciliation, you gather the following data:

a. The Lamarr Shoes Cash account shows a balance of $6,586.42 on July 31.
b. The bank statement includes two charges for returned cheques from customers. One is a $593 cheque received from St. Mary's Collegiate and deposited on July 20, returned by St. Mary's bank with the imprint "Unauthorized Signature." The other is an NSF cheque in the amount of $164.59 received from Mavis Jones. This cheque had been deposited on July 17.
c. Lamarr Shoes pays rent ($975) and insurance ($320) each month by EFT.
d. The following Lamarr Shoes cheques are outstanding at July 31:

Cheque No.	Amount
291	$ 51.10
322	179.00
327	785.50
329	13.91
330	516.09
331	5.55
332	310.16

e. The bank statement includes a deposit of $1,911.23, collected by the bank on behalf of Lamarr Shoes. Of the total, $1,834.78 is collection of a note receivable, and the remainder is interest revenue.
f. The bank statement shows that Lamarr Shoes earned $4.36 in interest on its bank balance during July. This amount was added to the Lamarr Shoes account by the bank.
g. The bank statement lists a $25.00 subtraction for the bank service charge.
h. On July 31, the Lamarr Shoes accountant deposited $563.19, but this deposit does not appear on the bank statement.
i. The bank statement includes a $700.00 deposit that Lamarr Shoes did not make. The bank had erroneously credited the Lamarr Shoes account for another bank customer's deposit.
j. The July 31 bank balance is $8,422.54.

Required

1. Prepare the bank reconciliation for Lamarr Shoes at July 31, 2005.
2. Record in general journal form the entries necessary to bring the book balance of Cash into agreement with the adjusted book balance on the reconciliation. Include an explanation for each entry.

Problem 8-5A *Identifying internal control weaknesses in cash receipts* *(Obj. 4)*

Fresh Today Bakery makes all sales of its bread to retailers on credit. Cash receipts arrive by mail, usually within 30 days of the sale. Joan Sharp opens envelopes and separates the cheques from the accompanying remittance advices. Sharp forwards the cheques to another employee, who makes the daily bank deposit but has no access to the accounting records. Sharp sends the remittance advices, which show the amount of cash received, to the accounting department for entry in the accounts. Sharp's only other duty is to grant sales allowances to customers. (Recall that a *sales allowance* decreases the amount that the customer must pay.) When she receives a customer cheque for less than the full amount of the invoice, she records the sales allowance and forwards the document to the accounting department.

Required

You are a new management employee of Fresh Today Bakery. Write a memo to the company president, John Fresh, identifying the internal control weakness in this situation. State how to correct the weakness.

Problem 8-6A *Applying internal controls to cash payments, including petty cash transactions* **(Obj. 5)**

P.E.I. Potatoes is located in Charlottetown, P.E.I., with a sales territory covering the Maritime provinces and Newfoundland. Employees live in P.E.I. and all report to work at the company's offices in Charlottetown.

The company has established a large petty cash fund to handle cash payments and cash advances to its salespeople to cover trips to and from P.E.I. on sales calls.

The controller, Dan Martin, has decided that two people (Sarah Wong and Martha Davis) should be in charge of the petty cash fund, as money is often needed when one person is out of the office. Martin also feels this will increase internal control, as the work of one person will serve as a check on that of the other.

Regular small cash payments are handled by either Wong or Davis, who make the payment and have the person receiving the money sign a sheet of paper giving the date and reason for the payment. Whenever a salesperson requires an advance for a sales trip, that person simply signs a receipt for the money received. The salespeople later submit receipts for their costs to either Wong or Davis to offset the cash advance.

Martin, a family friend as well as the controller, doesn't think the system is working and, knowing you are studying accounting, has asked for your advice.

Required

Write a memo to Dan Martin commenting on the internal control procedures of P.E.I. Potatoes. Suggest changes that you think would improve the system.

Problem 8-7A *Accounting for petty cash transactions* **(Obj. 5)**

Suppose that on September 1, Docherty Motors opens a new showroom in Kamloops, B.C., and creates a petty cash fund with an imprest balance of $600. During September, Barbara Reitzel, the fund custodian, signs the petty cash tickets shown below.

On September 30, prior to replenishment, the fund contains these tickets plus $193.61. The accounts affected by petty cash payments are Office Supplies Expense, Entertainment Expense, and Delivery Expense.

Ticket Number	Item	Amount
1	Courier for package received	$ 23.60
2	Refreshments for showroom opening	169.20
3	Computer disks	33.69
4	Office supplies	45.00
5	Dinner money for sales manager entertaining a customer	105.00

Required

1. Explain the characteristics and the internal control features of an imprest fund.

2. Make the general journal entries to create the fund and to replenish it. Include explanations. Also, briefly describe what the custodian does on these dates.

3. Make the entry on October 1 to increase the fund balance to $750. Include an explanation and briefly describe what the custodian does.

Problem 8-8A *Preparing a bank reconciliation and related journal entries (Obj. 3)*

Marv's Communications had a computer failure on February 1, 2004, which resulted in the loss of data, including the balance of its cash account and its bank reconciliation from January 31, 2004. The accountant, Sasha Barker, has been able to obtain the following information from the records of the company and its bank:

a. An examination showed that two cheques (#461 for $230 and #492 for $350) had not been cashed as of February 1. Barker recalled that there was only one deposit in transit on the January 31 bank reconciliation, but was unable to recall the amount.

b. The cash receipts and cash payments journal contained the following entries for February 2004:

Cash Receipts: Amounts	Cash Payments: Cheque #	Amount
$ 584	499	$ 452
820	500	434
830	501	1,519
608	502	564
1,640	503	218
$4,482	504	547
	505	void
	506	209
	507	562
		$4,505

c. The bank provided the following statement as of February 29, 2004:

Date	Cheques and Other Debits		Deposits and Other Credits		Balance
Feb. 1	#500	434.00		880.00	2,386.00
3	#492	350.00			2,036.00
5	#501	1,519.00			517.00
8				584.00	1,101.00
16	#499	452.00		390.00	1,039.00
17	EFT	295.00			744.00
19			EFT	480.00	1,224.00
21	#503	218.00		820.00	1,826.00
22	#504	574.00	EFT	225.00	1,477.00
24			EFT	314.00	1,791.00
26	NSF	995.00		830.00	1,626.00
27	SC	25.00			1,601.00
27	#507	562.00		608.00	1,647.00

d. The deposit made on February 16 was for the collection of a note receivable ($375) plus interest.

e. The electronic funds transfers (EFTs) had not yet been recorded by Marv's Communications as the bank statement was the first notification of them.

- The February 17 EFT was for the monthly payment on an insurance policy for Marv's Communications.

- The February 19 and 24 EFTs were collections on accounts receivable.

- The February 22 EFT was in error—the transfer should have been to Marvin Motors.

f. The NSF cheque on February 26 was received from a customer as payment of $995 for installation of a satellite purchased from Marv's for $995.

g. Cheque #504 was correctly written for $574 for the purchase of office supplies, but incorrectly recorded by the cash payments clerk.

Required

1. Prepare a bank reconciliation as of February 29, 2004, including the calculation of the book balance of January 31, 2004.

2. Prepare all journal entries that would be required by the bank reconciliation.

Problem 8-9A *Making an ethical judgment* *(Obj. 5, 6)*

Hans Skinner is a vice-president of the Laurentian Bank in Markham, Ontario. Active in community affairs, Skinner serves on the board of directors of Orson Tool & Dye. Orson is expanding rapidly and is considering relocating its plant. At a recent meeting, board members decided to try to buy 20 hectares of land on the edge of town. The owner of the property is Sherri Alkiore, a customer of the Laurentian Bank. Alkiore is a recent widow. Skinner knows that Alkiore is eager to sell her local property. In view of Alkiore's anguished condition, Skinner believes she would accept almost any offer for the land. Realtors have appraised the property at $4 million.

Required

Apply the ethical judgment framework outlined in the Decision Guidelines feature on page 412 to help Skinner decide what his role should be in Orson's attempt to buy the land from Sherri Alkiore.

Problems (Group B)

Problem 8-1B *Identifying the characteristics of an effective internal control system* *(Obj. 1,2)*

An employee of Marchant Marketing recently stole thousands of dollars of the company's cash. The company has decided to install a new system of internal controls.

Required

As controller of Marchant Marketing, write a memo to the president, Elizabeth Bean, explaining how a separation of duties helps to safeguard assets.

Problem 8-2B *Identifying internal control weaknesses* *(Obj. 2, 4, 5)*

Each of the following situations has an internal control weakness:

a. Maura Lucenti employs three professional interior designers in her design studio. She is located in an area with a lot of new construction, and her business is booming. Ordinarily, Lucenti does all the purchasing of furniture, draperies, carpets, fabrics, sewing services, and other materials and labour needed to complete jobs. During the summer she takes a long vacation, and in her absence she allows each designer to purchase materials and labour. At her return, Lucenti reviews operations and notes that expenses are much higher and net income much lower than in the past.

b. Waterloo Software Associates is a software company that specializes in computer programs with accounting applications. The company's most popular program prepares the general journal, cash receipts journal, voucher register, cheque register, accounts receivable subsidiary ledger, and general ledger. In the company's early days, the owner and eight employees wrote the computer programs, lined up manufacturers to produce the diskettes, sold the products to stores such as Office Depot, and performed the general management and accounting of the company. As the company has grown, the number of employees has increased dramatically. Recently, the development of a new software program stopped while the programmers redesigned Waterloo Software Associates' accounting system. Waterloo Software Associates' own accountants could have performed this task.

c. Judy Sloan, a widow with no known sources of outside income, has been a trusted employee of Gateway Designs for 15 years. She performs all cash handling and accounting duties, including opening the mail, preparing the bank deposit, accounting for all aspects of cash and accounts receivable, and preparing the bank reconciliation. She has just purchased a new BMW and a new home in an expensive suburb. Mac Brown, the owner of the company, wonders how she can afford these luxuries on her salary.

d. Discount stores such as Wal-Mart receive a large portion of their sales revenue in cash, with the remainder in debit card and credit card sales. To reduce expenses, a store manager ceases purchasing fidelity bonds on the cashiers.

e. The office supply company from which The Family Shoe Store purchases cash receipt forms recently notified Family that the last shipped receipts were not prenumbered. Louise Bourseault, the owner, replied that she did not use the receipt numbers, so the omission is not important.

Required

1. Identify the missing internal control characteristic in each situation.
2. Identify the business's possible problem.
3. Propose a solution to the problem.

Media Companion CD-ROM

Problem 8-3B *Using the bank reconciliation as a control device* *(Obj. 3)*

The cash receipts and the cash payments of Red Deer Development for November 2004 are as follows:

Cash Receipts (Posting reference is CR)		Cash Payments (Posting reference is CP)	
Date	**Cash Debit**	**Cheque No.**	**Cash Credit**
Nov. 5	$3,124	1221	$ 1,654
7	427	1222	1,040
13	1,566	1223	390
15	968	1224	101
19	401	1225	742
24	795	1226	99
30	2,362	1227	4,062
Total	$9,643	1228	907
		1229	300
		1230	2,476
		Total	$11,771

The Cash account of Red Deer Development shows the following information on November 30, 2004:

Cash

Date	Item	Jrnl. Ref.	Debit	Credit	Balance
Nov. 1	Balance				16,566 Dr
30		CR. 10	9,643		26,209 Dr
30		CP. 16		11,771	14,438 Dr

On December 3, 2004, Red Deer Development received this bank statement:

Bank Statement for November 2004

Balance, November 1, 2004...		$16,566
Deposits and other Credits:		
Nov. 1	$ 800 EFT	
6	3,124	
10	427	
14	1,566	
15	968	
20	401	
25	795	
30	1,300 BC	9,381
Cheques and other Debits:		
Nov. 8	$ 394 NSF	
9	1,654	
13	1,040	
14	390	
15	101	
19	250 EFT	
22	742	
29	99	
30	4,602	
30	25 SC	(9,297)
Balance, November 30, 2004...		$16,650

Explanations: BC—bank collection, EFT—electronic funds transfer, NSF—nonsufficient funds cheque, SC—service charge.

Additional data for the bank reconciliation:

a. The EFT deposit was a receipt of monthly rent. The EFT debit was payment of monthly insurance.

b. The NSF cheque was received late in October from Rod Jenkins.

c. The $1,300 bank collection of a note receivable on November 30 included $100 interest revenue.

d. The correct amount of cheque number 1227, a payment on account, is $4,602. (The Red Deer Development accountant mistakenly recorded the cheque for $4,062.)

Required

1. Prepare the bank reconciliation of Red Deer Development at November 30, 2004.

2. Describe how a bank account and the bank reconciliation help Red Deer managers control the business's cash.

Problem 8-4B   *Preparing a bank reconciliation and related journal entries*   *(Obj. 3)*

The October 31, 2005, bank statement of St. John's Academy has just arrived from Scotiabank. To prepare the St. John's Academy's bank reconciliation, you gather the following data:

Media Companion CD-ROM

a. The October 31 bank balance is $21,462.75.

b. The bank statement includes two charges for returned cheques from students. One is an NSF cheque in the amount of $75.75 received from Charles Ham, recorded on the books by a debit to Cash and deposited on October 19. The other is a $203.07 cheque received from Carlotta Guam and deposited on October 21. It was returned by Guam's bank with the imprint "Unauthorized Signature."

c. The following St. John's Academy cheques are outstanding at October 31:

Cheque No.	Amount
712	$604.00
922	47.52
934	63.06
939	611.83
940	229.50
941	492.00

d. A few students pay monthly fees by EFT. The October bank statement lists a $7,000 deposit for student fees.

e. The bank statement includes two special deposits: $987.41, which is the amount of dividend revenue the bank collected from TCL on behalf of St. John's Academy; and $17.54, the interest revenue St. John's Academy earned on its bank balance during October.

f. The bank statement lists a $34.50 subtraction for the bank service charge.

g. On October 31, the St. John's Academy treasurer deposited $512.41, but this deposit does not appear on the bank statement.

h. The bank statement includes a $4.50 deduction for a cheque drawn by St. John's Auto Ltd. St. John's Academy promptly notified the bank of its error.

i. St. John's Academy's Cash account shows a balance of $12,240.12 on October 31.

Required

1. Prepare the bank reconciliation for St. John's Academy at October 31, 2004.

2. Record in general journal form the entries necessary to bring the book balance of Cash into agreement with the adjusted book balance on the reconciliation. Include an explanation for each entry.

Problem 8-5B   *Identifying internal control weakness in cash receipts*   *(Obj. 4)*

Office Designs makes all sales on credit. Cash receipts arrive by mail, usually within 30 days of sale. Sarah Romano opens envelopes and separates the cheques from the accompanying remittance advices. Romano forwards the cheques to another employee, who makes the daily bank deposit but has no access to the accounting records. Romano sends the remittance advices, which show the amount of cash received, to the accounting department for entry in the accounts. Her only other duty is to grant sales allowances to customers. (Recall that a *sales allowance* decreases the amount that the customer must pay.) When she receives a customer cheque for less than the full amount of the invoice, she records the sales allowance and forwards the document to the accounting department.

Required

You are a new management employee of Office Designs. Write a memo to the company president, William Kennedy, identifying the internal control weakness in this situation. State how to correct the weakness.

Problem 8-6B *Applying internal controls to cash payments, including petty cash transactions* *(Obj. 5)*

Mid-West Machines is located in Saskatoon, Saskatchewan, with a sales territory covering the province.

The company has established a large petty cash fund to handle small cash payments and cash advances to the salespeople to cover frequent sales trips.

The controller, Tara Goldsmith, has decided that two people (Anne Bloom and Tom Hurry) should be in charge of the fund as money is often needed when one person may be out for coffee or lunch. Goldsmith also feels this will increase internal control, as the work of one person will serve as a check on that of the other.

Regular small cash payments are handled by either Bloom or Hurry, who make the payment and have the person receiving the money sign a sheet of paper listing the date and reason for the payment. Whenever a salesperson requires an advance for a trip, he or she simply signs a receipt for the money received. The salespeople later submit receipts for the cost of the trip to either Bloom or Hurry to offset the cash advance.

Goldsmith is puzzled that the fund is almost always out of balance and either over or short.

Required

Comment on the internal control procedures of Mid-West Machines. Suggest changes that you think would improve the system.

Problem 8-7B *Accounting for petty cash transactions* *(Obj. 5)*

Suppose that, on June 1, Hydro-Québec opens a regional office in Rivière-du-Loup and creates a petty cash fund with an imprest balance of $600. During June, Lucie Ducharme, the fund custodian, signs the following petty cash tickets:

Ticket Number	Item	Amount
101	Office supplies	$ 94.98
102	Cab fare for executive	45.00
103	Delivery of package across town	22.00
104	Dinner money for sales manager entertaining a customer	100.00
105	Office supplies	95.40
106	Water for cooler	45.00
107	Six boxes of computer disks	45.75

On June 30, prior to replenishment, the fund contains these tickets plus $160.04. The accounts affected by petty cash payments are Office Supplies Expense, Travel Expense, Delivery Expense, Entertainment Expense, and Water Cooler Expense.

Required

1. Explain the characteristics and internal control features of an imprest fund.
2. Make general journal entries to create the fund and to replenish it. Include explanations. Also, briefly describe what the custodian does on these dates.

Problem 8-8B *Preparing a bank reconciliation and related journal entries* *(Obj. 3)*

Moncton Electronics had a computer failure on March 1, 2004, which resulted in the loss of data, including the balance of its cash account and its bank reconciliation from February 29, 2004. The accountant, Manny Palmo, has been able to obtain the following information from the records of the company and its bank:

a. An examination showed that two cheques (#244 for $150 and #266 for $275) had not been cashed as of March 1. Palmo recalled that there was only one deposit in transit on the February 29 bank reconciliation, but was unable to recall the amount.

b. The cash receipts and cash payments journal contained the following entries for March 2004:

Cash Receipts: Amounts		Cash Payments: Cheque #	Amount
$ 395		275	$ 135
760		276	195
1,620		277	203
850		278	353
320		279	251
$3,945		280	1,703
		281	void
		282	195
		283	460
			$3,495

c. The company's bank provided the following statement as of March 31, 2004:

Date	Cheques and Other Debits		Deposits and Other Credits		Balance
Mar. 1	#276	195.00		1,020.00	2,835.00
2	#266	275.00			2,560.00
5	#277	203.00			2,357.00
8				395.00	2,752.00
14	#275	135.00		520.00	3,137.00
17	EFT	230.00			2,907.00
19			EFT	180.00	3,087.00
22	#279	251.00		760.00	3,596.00
22	#280	1,730.00	EFT	520.00	2,386.00
24			EFT	205.00	2,591.00
27	NSF	350.00		1,620.00	3,861.00
28	SC	25.00			3,836.00
31	#283	460.00		850.00	4,226.00

d. The deposit made on March 14 was for the collection of a note receivable ($500) plus interest.

e. The electronic funds transfers (EFTs) had not yet been recorded by Moncton Electronics as the bank statement was the first notification of them.

 • The March 17 EFT was for the monthly payment on an insurance policy for Moncton Electronics.

 • The March 19 and 24 EFTs were collections on accounts receivable.

 • The second March 22 EFT was in error—the transfer should have been to Moncton Auto Parts.

f. The NSF cheque on March 27 was received from a customer as payment for a player purchased for $350.

g. Cheque #280 was correctly written for $1,730 for the purchase of office supplies, but incorrectly recorded by the cash payments clerk.

Required

1. Prepare a bank reconciliation as of March 31, 2004, including the calculation of the book balance of February 29, 2004.

2. Prepare all journal entries that would be required by the bank reconciliation.

Problem 8-9B *Making an ethical judgement* *(Obj. 6)*

North Venture Capital in Sudbury, Ontario, has received a request for investment funds from Different View Products. The funds are for the production of a new product that will dramatically enhance communications on mining sites. Stewart Donolo, an account manager at North Venture, is assigned to research the application.

With unlimited access to Different View's records, Donolo learns that one of the potential major customers for this product is Goldore, a local mining company. North Venture Capital has invested in Goldore. Donolo has access to confidential information about Goldore—operations will be on hold pending further investigation of identified deposits. The future of Goldore will be strong, but in the short term, Goldore will not be making large operational purchases.

Donolo believes there will be a market for the Different Views product. He has a strong motivation to have Different Views succeed and North Venture Capital to share in this success.

Required

Apply the ethical judgment framework outlined in the Decision Guidelines feature on page 412 to help Stewart Donolo plan his next action.

Challenge Problems

Problem 8-1C *Management's role in internal control* *(Obj. 1)*

"Effective internal control must begin with top management." "The 'tone at the top' is a necessary condition if an organization is to have an effective system of internal control."

These statements are becoming a more important part of internal control literature and thought.

The chapter lists a number of characteristics that are important for an effective system of internal control. Many of these characteristics have been part of the internal control literature for years.

Required

Explain why you think a commitment to good internal control by top management is fundamental to an effective system of internal control.

Problem 8-2C *Applying internal controls to cash transactions* *(Obj. 4, 5)*

Many companies require some person other than the person preparing the bank reconciliation to review the reconciliation. Organizations routinely require cheques over a certain amount to be signed by two signing officers. The purchasing department orders goods but the receiving department receives the goods.

Required

All of the above situations have a common thread. What is that common thread and why is it important?

Extending Your Knowledge

Decision Problem

Using the bank reconciliation to detect a theft   (Obj. 3)

Surrey Tech Solutions has poor internal control over its cash transactions. Recently Shikha Ghandi, the owner, has suspected the cashier of stealing. Details of the business's cash position at April 30, 2004 follow:

1. The Cash account shows a balance of $21,522. This amount includes an April 30 deposit of $4,974 that does not appear on the April 30 bank statement.

2. The April 30 bank statement shows a balance of $18,404. The bank statement lists an $800 credit for a bank collection, an $18 debit for the service charge, and a $76 debit for an NSF cheque. C. J. Ellis, the Surrey Tech Solutions accountant, has not recorded any of these items on the books.

3. At April 30 the following cheques are outstanding:

Cheque No.	Amount
402	$ 132
527	134
531	293
561	150
562	296
563	1,145

4. Arlo Bing, the cashier, handles all incoming cash and makes bank deposits. He also reconciles the monthly bank statement. His April 30 reconciliation follows:

Balance per books, April 30...............................		$21,522
Add: Outstanding cheques................................		1,150
Bank collection		800
		23,472
Less: Deposits in transit.....................................	$4,974	
Service charge..	18	
NSF cheque..	76	5,068
Balance per bank, April 30................................		$18,404

Ghandi has requested that you determine whether Bing has stolen cash from the business and, if so, how much. Ghandi also asks you to identify how Bing has attempted to conceal the theft. To make this determination, you perform your own bank reconciliation, using the format illustrated on page 401. There are no bank or book errors. Ghandi also asks you to evaluate the internal controls and recommend any changes needed to improve them.

Financial Statement Problem

Audit opinion, management responsibility, internal controls and cash   (Obj. 1)

Study the management report (titled "Management's Responsibility") and the auditors' report on Intrawest Corporation's financial statements, given in Appendix A. Answer the following questions about Intrawest's internal controls and cash position:

1. What is the name of Intrawest's outside auditing firm? What office of this firm signed the auditor's report? How long after Intrawest's year end did the auditors issue their opinion?

2. Who bears primary responsibility for the financial statements? How can you tell?

3. Which of the two reports indicates who bears primary responsibility for internal controls?

4. What standard of auditing did the outside auditors use in examining Intrawest's financial statements? By what accounting standards were the statements evaluated?

5. By how much did Intrawest's cash position change during 2003? The cash flow statement (discussed in detail in Chapter 17) tells why this change occurred. Which type of activity—operating, financing, or investing—contributed most to this change?

CHAPTER

9

Receivables

CHAPTER OBJECTIVES

After studying this chapter, you should be able to

1 Design internal controls for receivables

2 Use the allowance method to account for uncollectibles and estimate uncollectibles by the percent-of-sales and the aging-of-accounts methods

3 Use the direct write-off method to account for uncollectibles

4 Account for credit-card and debit-card sales

5 Account for notes receivable

6 Report receivables on the balance sheet

7 Use the acid-test ratio and days' sales in receivables to evaluate a company

 Media Companion CD-ROM

Visit the Media Companion CD-ROM that comes with this book for extra practice with the new material in Chapter 9.

Research In Motion (RIM) (www.rim.com) is a leading designer, manufacturer, and marketer of innovative wireless solutions for the worldwide mobile communications market. Its most widely known product is the BlackBerry® wireless solution, used by thousands of companies and organizations around the world.

One example of the growing success of BlackBerry is the recent announcement that Royal Caribbean International (www.royalcaribbean.com) and Celebrity Cruises Inc. (www.celebrity.com) have selected BlackBerry to help increase productivity throughout the organization and enhance customer services.

As a result of RIM's leading and innovative products, alliances have been formed with industry leaders such as IBM, Sony Ericsson, Nokia, HP, Verizon Wireless, Rogers Wireless, Bell Mobility, and TELUS Mobility.

RIM's financial statements reflect the success of the company and BlackBerry. Revenue has climbed from $33,159,000 in 1998 to $306,732,000 in 2003 (all amounts in US dollars). At the same time, accounts receivable has grown from $14,954,426 in 1998 to $40,803,000 in 2003.

Companies like RIM that grow very quickly have to monitor their cash flow. They have to translate production into inventory, inventory into sales and receivables, and receivables into cash. A challenge is that a company can be sales rich and cash poor. Well-managed companies like RIM monitor their increased accounts receivables. As an illustration, RIM's cash and cash equivalents amounted to $340,681,000 at March 1, 2003. It is this attention to all aspects of business that makes a company such as RIM highly successful.

Sources: 2003 and 1999 Research In Motion Annual Reports; Research In Motion press release, October 29, 2003.

As Research In Motion Ltd. (RIM) grows, so do its revenues and receivables. Accounts receivable are RIM's second-largest current asset. This chapter shows how to predict how much of its receivables RIM will collect in cash. The chapter also covers notes receivable, a more formal type of receivable that includes a written promise to pay and a stated interest rate.

A *receivable* arises when a business (or person) sells goods or services to another party on credit. The receivable is the seller's claim for the amount of the transaction. Each credit transaction involves two parties:

- The **creditor** who sells something and obtains a receivable, which is an asset.

- The **debtor** who makes the purchase and has a payable, which is a liability.

A receivable also arises when one person lends money to another. Here's an example you can identify with: Suppose your best friend runs out of cash and needs $100 to make it to the end of the month. You lend $100 to your friend, and he promises to pay you back on May 31. You gave up your cash and got a $100 receivable from your friend. The receivable is an asset to you, just as the cash was. But the receivable is a slightly different asset. It's very close to cash, but it's not cash yet. In this situation you are the creditor, and your friend is the debtor.

This chapter focuses on accounting for receivables by the seller (the creditor).

Receivables: An Introduction

Types of Receivables

Receivables are monetary claims against businesses and individuals. The two major types of receivables are accounts receivable and notes receivable. A business's *accounts receivable* are amounts to be collected from customers. Accounts receivable, which are *current assets*, are also called *trade receivables*.

The Accounts Receivable account in the general ledger serves as a *control account* because it summarizes the total of the receivables from all customers. As we saw in Chapter 7, companies also keep a *subsidiary ledger* of the receivable from each customer. This is illustrated as follows:

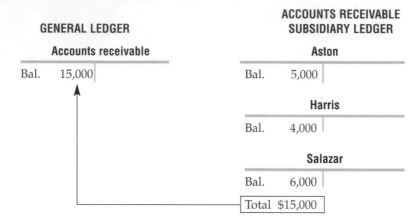

Notes receivable are more formal than accounts receivable. The debtor promises in writing to pay the creditor a definite sum at a definite future date—the *maturity* date. A written document known as a *promissory note* serves as the evidence of the receivable. Notes receivable due within one year, or one operating cycle if longer than one year, are current assets. Notes due beyond one year are *long-term*. Some notes receivable are collected in periodic instalments. The portion due within one year is a current asset, and the remaining amount a long-term asset. The Bank of Nova Scotia (www.scotiabank.com) may hold a $6,000 note receivable from you, but only the $1,500 you owe on it this year is a current asset to the Bank of Nova Scotia. The remaining $4,500 is a long-term asset.

Other receivables is a miscellaneous category that may include loans to employees. Usually these are long-term receivables, but they are current assets if receivable within one year or less. Long-term receivables are often reported as assets on the balance sheet after current assets, as shown in Exhibit 9-1. Receivables are highlighted for emphasis.

Establishing Internal Control over the Collection of Receivables

REAL WORLD EXAMPLE

Credit-card companies conduct extensive research on credit risks. They research an applicant's job history, credit history, salary, home rental or ownership, length of time at current address, and other credit transactions.

Businesses that sell on credit receive most cash receipts by mail. Internal control over collections is very important. A critical element of internal control (introduced in Chapter 8) is the separation of cash-handling and cash-accounting duties. Consider the following case:

> Butler Supply Co. is family-owned and takes pride in the loyalty of its workers. Most company employees have been with Butler for at least five years. The company makes 90 percent of its sales on account.
>
> The office staff consists of a bookkeeper and a supervisor. The bookkeeper maintains the general ledger and the accounts receivable subsidiary ledger. He also makes the daily bank deposit. The supervisor prepares monthly financial statements and special reports.

Can you identify the internal control weakness here? The bookkeeper has access to the general ledger and the accounts receivable subsidiary ledger, and also has custody of the cash. The bookkeeper could steal a customer's cheque and

EXHIBIT 9-1

Assets with Receivables
Highlighted

EXAMPLE COMPANY
Assets
Date

Assets
Current assets:

Cash		$X,XXX
Accounts receivable............	**X,XXX**	
Less: Allowance for uncollectible accounts ...	(XXX)	X,XXX
Notes receivable, short-term................		**X,XXX**
Inventories		X,XXX
Prepaid expenses..................................		X,XXX
Total current assets.........................		X,XXX

Investments and long-term receivables:

Investments in other companies........		X,XXX
Notes receivable, long-term..............		**X,XXX**
Other receivables		**X,XXX**
Total non-current assets..................		X,XXX

Capital assets:

Property, plant, and equipment (net of amortization)........................		X,XXX
Total assets		$X,XXX

write off the customer's account as uncollectible.[1] Unless someone reviews the bookkeeper's work regularly, the theft may go undetected.

How can Butler Supply correct this control weakness? *The bookkeeper should not be allowed to handle cash.* Only the remittance advices should be forwarded to the bookkeeper to indicate which customer accounts to credit.

Using a bank lock box can achieve the same result. Customers send their payments directly to Butler Supply Co.'s bank, which deposits the customer's payment into the company's bank account. We examined the lock-box system in detail in Chapter 8, page 399.

Managing the Collection of Receivables:
The Credit Department

Most companies have a credit department to evaluate customers. The extension of credit requires a balancing act. The company does not want to lose sales to good customers, but it also wants to avoid uncollectible receivables.

For good internal control over cash collections of receivables, the credit department should have no access to cash. For example, if a credit employee handles cash, he or she could pocket the money received from a customer. He or she could also

---

[1]The bookkeeper would need to forge the endorsements of the cheques and deposit them in a bank account he controls.

then label the customer's account as uncollectible, and the company would write off the account receivable as discussed in the next section. Since the company stops billing that customer, the employee has covered up the embezzlement. For this reason, a sharp separation of duties is important.

The Decision Guidelines feature below identifies the main issues in controlling and managing receivables. These guidelines serve as a framework for the remainder of the chapter.

DECISION GUIDELINES — *Controlling, Managing, and Accounting for Receivables*

Butler Supply, RIM, and all other companies that sell on credit face the same accounting challenges. The main issues in *controlling* and *managing* the collection of receivables, plus a plan of action, are as follows:

Issue	Action
Extend credit only to customers most likely to pay.	Run a credit check on prospective customers.
Separate cash-handling (custody), credit (authorization), and accounting duties (recording) to keep employees from stealing cash collected from customers.	Design the internal control system to separate the duties of custody, authorization, and recording.
Pursue collection from customers to maximize cash flow.	Keep a close eye on collections from customers.

The main issues in *accounting* for receivables, and the related plans of action, are as follows:

Issue	Action
Report receivables at their *net realizable value,* the amount we expect to collect.	Estimate the amount of uncollectible receivables. Report receivables at net realizable value (accounts receivable – allowance for uncollectible accounts).
Report the expense associated with failure to collect receivables. This expense is called *uncollectible-account expense.*	Report the expense of failing to collect from our customers.

Accounting for Uncollectible Accounts (Bad Debts)

Selling on credit creates both a benefit and a cost.

- *The benefit:* The business increases sales revenues and profits by making sales to a wide range of customers.
- *The cost:* The company will be unable to collect from some customers, and that creates an expense. The expense is called **uncollectible-account expense, doubtful-account expense,** or **bad-debt expense.**

Uncollectible-account expense varies from company to company. The older the receivable, the less valuable it is because of the decreasing likelihood of collection. At Albany Ladder Ltd., a $23 million construction-equipment and supply firm, 85 percent of company sales are on account. Each $1.00 of accounts receivable is worth $0.98 because of bad debts. Uncollectible-account expense is an operating expense, in the same way as salary expense and amortization expense are. To account for uncollectible receivables, accountants use the allowance method or, in certain limited cases, the direct write-off method.

The Allowance Method Most companies use the **allowance method** to measure bad debts. This method attempts to record bad-debt expense in the same period as it makes sales on account. The business doesn't wait to see which customers will not pay. Instead, it records bad-debt expense on the basis of estimates developed from past experience.

The business records Uncollectible-Account Expense for the estimated amount, and sets up **Allowance for Uncollectible Accounts** (or **Allowance for Doubtful Accounts**), a contra account to Accounts Receivable. This allowance account shows the amount of receivables that the business expects *not* to collect.

Subtracting the allowance from Accounts Receivable yields the net amount that the company does expect to collect, as shown here (using assumed numbers):

Balance sheet (partial):

Accounts receivable $10,000
Less Allowance for uncollectible accounts.................... (900)
Accounts receivable, net.. $ 9,100

Customers owe this company $10,000, of which the business expects to collect $9,100. The company estimates that it will not collect $900 of its accounts receivable.

Many Canadian companies do not provide information on their gross receivables and allowance for doubtful accounts, but rather simply report the net receivable. For example, Research In Motion, in its annual report for the year ended March 31, 2003, reported as follows (amounts in U.S. dollars):

Accounts receivable.. $40,803,000

The income statement reports Uncollectible-Account Expense, included in operating expenses, as follows (using assumed figures):

Income statement (partial):

Expenses:
Uncollectible-account expense.. $2,000

Estimating Uncollectibles

How are bad debts estimated? Companies base estimates on their past experience. There are two ways to estimate uncollectibles:

- *Percent-of-sales method*
- *Aging-of-accounts method*

Both approaches work under the allowance method.

Percent-of-Sales Method The **percent-of-sales method** computes uncollectible-account expense as a percent of net credit sales. This method is also called the **income-statement approach** because it focuses on the amount of expense. Uncollectible-account expense is recorded by an adjusting entry at the end of the period. Assume it is December 31, 2005, and the accounts have these balances *before the year-end adjustments*:

Accounts Receivable	Allowance for Uncollectible Accounts
120,000	500

Prior to any adjustments, net receivables total $119,500 ($120,000 − $500). That is more than the business expects to collect from customers. Based on prior experience, the credit department estimates that uncollectible-account expense is

2 percent of net credit sales, which were $500,000 in 2005. The adjusting entry to record uncollectible-account expense for 2005 and to update the allowance is:

```
2005
Dec. 31    Uncollectible-Account Expense.............................   10,000
               Allowance for Uncollectible Accounts..............              10,000
           To record expense for the year ($500,000 × 0.02).
```

KEY POINT

The percent-of-sales approach is often referred to as the income-statement approach to estimating bad-debt expense because the entry is based on credit sales for the period (an income statement figure).

The accounting equation shows that the transaction to record the expense decreases the business's assets by the amount of the expense:

Assets	=	Liabilities	+	Owner's Equity	−	Expenses
−10,000	=	0			−	10,000

Now the accounts are ready for reporting in the 2005 financial statements.

Accounts Receivable		Allowance for Uncollectible Accounts	
120,000			500
		Adj.	10,000
			10,500

Customers owe the business $120,000, and now the allowance for uncollectible accounts is realistic. The balance sheet will report accounts receivable at the net amount of $109,500 ($120,000 − $10,500). The income statement will report 2005's uncollectible-account expense of $10,000, along with other operating expenses for the period.

Aging-of-Accounts Method   The second popular method for estimating uncollectible accounts is the **aging-of-accounts method.** This method is also called the **balance-sheet approach** because it focuses on accounts receivable. In the aging approach, individual accounts receivable are grouped according to how long they have been receivable from the customer. The computer sorts customer accounts by their age. For example, Schmidt Builders Supply groups its accounts receivable into 30-day periods, as Exhibit 9-2 shows.

Schmidt's total balance of accounts receivable is $143,000. Of this amount, the aging schedule indicates that the company will *not* collect $3,800. Prior to the year-end adjustment, Schmidt's customers owed the company $143,000. The allowance for uncollectible accounts is not up-to-date. Schmidt Builders Supply's accounts appear as follows *before the year-end adjustment*:

Accounts Receivable		Allowance for Uncollectible Accounts	
143,000			1,100

KEY POINT

The aging-of-accounts method is often referred to as the balance-sheet approach to estimating bad debts because the computation focuses on Accounts Receivable (a balance sheet figure).

The aging method brings the balance of the allowance account to the needed amount ($3,800) determined by the aging schedule in Exhibit 9-2 (see the lower right corner for the final result—a needed credit balance of $3,800.)

To update the allowance, Schmidt makes this adjusting entry at the end of the period:

```
2005
Dec. 31    Uncollectible-Account Expense.............................   2,700
               Allowance for Uncollectible Accounts..............               2,700
           To record expense for the year ($3,800 − $1,100).
```

		Age of Account			
Customer Name	1–30 Days	31–60 Days	61–90 Days	Over 90 Days	Total Balance
Baring Tools Co..............	$ 20,000				$ 20,000
Calgary Pneumatic Parts Ltd.	10,000				10,000
Red Deer Pipe Corp.		$13,000	$10,000		23,000
Seal Coatings, Inc.			3,000	$1,000	4,000
Other accounts*..............	70,000	12,000	2,000	2,000	86,000
Totals...............................	$100,000	$25,000	$15,000	$3,000	$143,000
Estimated percent uncollectible.................	× 0.1%	× 1%	× 5%	× 90%	
Allowance for Uncollectible Accounts.........................	$100	$250	$750	$2,700	$3,800

* Each of the "Other accounts" would appear individually.

The expense decreases the total assets and owner's equity. The accounting equation of the expense is

Assets	=	Liabilities	+	Owner's Equity	−	Expenses
−2,700	=	0			−	2,700

Now the balance sheet can report the amount that Schmidt Builders Supply expects to collect from customers, $139,200 ($143,000 − $3,800), as follows:

Accounts Receivable		Allowance for Uncollectible Accounts	
143,000			1,100
		Adj.	2,700
			3,800

Net accounts receivable, $139,200

KEY POINT
It is a common mistake to forget to include the unadjusted balance in the Allowance account when computing uncollectible-account expense under the aging approach. The unadjusted balance of the Allowance account represents current accounts receivable that have already been expensed as uncollectible accounts but have not yet been written off. These doubtful accounts should *not* be included in the uncollectible-account expense again.

As with the percent-of-sales method, the income statement reports the uncollectible-account expense.

The *net* amount of accounts receivable—$139,200—is called net realizable value because it is the amount Schmidt expects to realize (collect in cash).

Using the Percent-of-Sales and the Aging-of-Accounts Methods Together In practice, many companies use the percent-of-sales and the aging-of-accounts methods together.

- For *interim statements* (monthly or quarterly), companies use the percent-of-sales method because it is easier to apply. The percent-of-sales method focuses on the amount of uncollectible-account *expense*.

- At the end of the year, these companies use the aging-of-accounts method to ensure that Accounts Receivable is reported at *expected realizable value*. The aging method focuses on the amount of the receivables—the *asset*—that is uncollectible.

EXHIBIT 9-3

Comparing the Percent-of-
Sales and the Aging-of-
Accounts Methods for
Estimating Uncollectibles

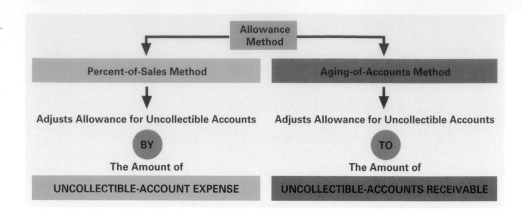

- Using the two methods together provides good measures of both the expense and the asset. Exhibit 9-3 summarizes and compares the two methods.

STOP & THINK

(1) What problems are encountered if a company records a sale in 2006 to a customer whose account will eventually be uncollectible, but does not record the doubtful-account expense until 2007?
(2) Is recording the expense in 2007 incorrect?

Answers: (1) Accounts Receivable for 2006 will be overstated and the matching principle is violated.
(2) Yes. The question could be rephrased: When did the account become uncollectible? The account was uncollectible at the time of sale and should therefore be deducted from revenue in the period of sale (2006).

Writing Off Uncollectible Accounts

During 2006 Schmidt Builders Supply collects on most of its $143,000 accounts receivable and records the cash receipts as follows:

2006			
Jan–Mar.	Cash..	123,000	
	Accounts Receivable......................................		123,000
	To record collections on account.		

Suppose that, after repeated attempts to collect, Schmidt's credit department determines that Schmidt Builders Supply cannot collect a total of $1,200 from customers Auger ($900) and Kirsh ($300). Schmidt then writes off the receivables of these delinquent customers:

2006			
Mar. 31	Allowance for Uncollectible Accounts	1,200	
	Accounts Receivable—Auger......................		900
	Accounts Receivable—Kirsh		300
	To write off uncollectible accounts.		

The write-off of uncollectible accounts has no effect on total assets, liabilities, or equity.

Assets	=	Liabilities	+	Owner's Equity
+1,200 −1,200	=	0	+	0

The Direct Write-Off Method

OBJECTIVE 3
Use the direct write-off method to account for uncollectibles

There is an alternative way to account for uncollectible receivables that is not appropriate for most companies. Under the **direct write-off method**, Schmidt Builders would wait until it decides that a customer's account receivable is uncollectible. Then Schmidt would write off the customer's account receivable by debiting Uncollectible-Account Expense and crediting the customer's Account Receivable, as follows (using assumed data):

```
2006
Jan. 2    Uncollectible-Account Expense......................    2,000
              Accounts Receivable—Kwan......................               2,000
          Wrote off an uncollectible account.
```

The direct write-off method is defective for two reasons:

1. It does not set up an allowance for uncollectible accounts. As a result, the direct write-off method always reports the receivables at their full amount. Assets are then overstated on the balance sheet, since the business does not expect to collect the full amount of accounts receivable.

2. It does not match the uncollectible-account expense against revenue very well. In this example, Schmidt made the sale to Kwan in 2005 and should have recorded the uncollectible-account expense during 2005. That is the only way to measure net income properly. By recording the uncollectible account expense in 2006, Schmidt overstates net income in 2005 and understates net income in 2006.

Do not confuse the direct write-off method with the allowance method. The two methods of accounting for uncollectible receivables are opposite. A company uses one method or the other. The direct write-off method is acceptable only when the amount of uncollectible receivables is very low. It works well for retailers, such as Roots (www.roots.com) and Wal-Mart (www.walmart.com), which carry almost no receivables.

KEY POINT

The direct write-off method is easier to use, but it fails to match expenses and revenues properly. It is acceptable only if uncollectibles are immaterial in amount or if the difference between using an allowance method and the direct write-off method is immaterial.

Recovery of Accounts Previously Written Off

When an account receivable is written off as uncollectible, the customer still owes the money. However, the company may stop pursuing collection and write off the account as uncollectible.

Some companies turn delinquent receivables over to a lawyer or collection agency to help recover some of the cash. This is called *recovery of a bad account*. Let's see how to record the recovery of an account that we wrote off earlier. Recall that on March 31, 2006, Schmidt Builders Supply wrote off the $900 receivable from customer Auger (see page 444). Suppose it is now October 4, 2006, and the company unexpectedly receives $900 from Auger. To account for this recovery,

KEY POINT

Follow through the entries to Auger's subsidiary ledger account: first the credit sale, then the write-off, then the reversal of the write-off, and finally the credit to the account when Auger pays in full. The customer's subsidiary account shows the complete credit history—an important feature of the subsidiary ledger system.

Accounts Receivable—Auger

Sale	900	900	Write-off
Recovery	900	900	Collection

Schmidt makes two journal entries to (1) reverse the earlier write-off and (2) record the cash collection, as follows:

2006			
Oct. 4	(1) Accounts Receivable—Auger	900	
	Allowance for Uncollectible Accounts		900
	Reinstated Auger's account receivable.		

2006			
Oct. 4	(2) Cash	900	
	Accounts Receivable—Auger		900
	Collected on account.		

OBJECTIVE 4
Account for credit-card and debit-card sales

REAL WORLD EXAMPLE

Retailers offer credit-card sales to increase revenue. Not only are credit cards more convenient for the customer, but research shows that customers purchase more with credit cards than with cash only. After a credit-card sale is made, the retailer receives the amount of a sale less a fee, usually within a few days. This transaction is essentially a sale of the receivable to the credit-card company. The credit-card company usually assumes the risk of uncollectible accounts.

Credit-Card and Debit-Card Sales

Credit-Card Sales

Credit-card sales are common in both traditional and online retailing. American Express (www.americanexpress.com/canada), Diners Club enRoute (www.diners clubnorthamerica.com), VISA[2] (www.visa.com), and MasterCard[2] (www. mastercard.com/canada) are popular. The customer presents the credit card to pay for purchases. The credit-card company then pays the seller and bills the customer, who pays the credit-card company.

Credit cards offer consumers the convenience of buying without having to pay the cash immediately. A VISA customer receives a monthly statement from VISA, detailing each of the customer's credit-card transactions. The customer can write a single cheque to cover the entire month's credit-card purchases.

Retailers also benefit from credit-card sales. They do not have to check a customer's credit rating. The credit-card company has already done so. Retailers do not have to keep accounts receivable records, and they do not have to collect cash from customers.

These benefits to the seller do not come free. The seller receives less than 100 percent of the face value of the sale. The credit-card company takes a fee of 1 to 5 percent[3] on the sale. Suppose you and your family have lunch at Hy's Steak

---

[2]VISA and MasterCard are also known as *bank cards*.
[3]The rate varies among companies and over time.

House. You pay the bill—$100—with a Diners Club enRoute card. Hy's entry to record the $100 Diners Club enRoute card sale, subject to the credit-card company's (assumed) 2-percent discount, is

2005			
Mar. 2	Accounts Receivable—Diners Club enRoute.............	98	
	Credit-Card Discount Expense....................................	2	
	Sales Revenue		100
	Recorded credit-card sales.		

On collection of the cash, Hy's Steak House records the following:

2005			
Mar. 15	Cash...	98	
	Accounts Receivable—Diners Club enRoute........		98
	Collected from Diners Club enRoute.		

In this example, the customer pays $100, Hy's Steak House receives $98, and Diners Club enRoute receives $2.

Debit-Card Sales

Debit cards are fundamentally different from credit cards. Using a *debit card* to buy groceries is like paying with cash, except that you don't have to carry cash or write a cheque. Most banks issue debit cards. The Toronto-Dominion Bank's (www.tdcanadatrust.com) Personal Access Green Card is an example. When a business makes a sale, the customer "swipes" her debit card through an Interac card reader and enters her personal identification number (PIN). The bank deducts the cost of the purchase from the customer's account and transfers the purchase amount, less a fee, into the business's account. For example, suppose you buy groceries at a Loblaws store for a total cost of $56.35. You swipe your debit card, enter your PIN, and Loblaws records the sale as follows:

Cash	55.85	
Debit Card Service Fee	0.50	
Sales Revenue		56.35
To record a debit-card sale.		

Credit-Card and Debit-Card Risk Both credit cards and debit cards bear a risk for the card holder, the issuer, and the business accepting the card. The cards can be lost, and stolen cards can be used to make purchases for which the card-issuer will not receive payment. All parties should recognize this risk when they use, issue, and accept credit and debit cards.

Credit Balances in Accounts Receivable

Occasionally, customers overpay their accounts or return merchandise for which they have already paid. The result is a credit balance in the customer's accounts receivable. For example, Leather and Stuff's subsidiary ledger contains 213 accounts, with balances as shown:

210	accounts with *debit* balances totalling	$185,000
3	accounts with *credit* balances totalling	2,800
	Net total of all balances	$182,200

Leather and Stuff should *not* report the asset Accounts Receivable at the net amount—$182,200. Why not? The credit balance—$2,800—is a liability, even though most customers will apply an overpayment to their next purchase. Like any other liability, customer credit balances are debts of the business. A balance sheet that did not indicate this liability would be misleading. Therefore, Leather and Stuff would report on its balance sheet:

Assets		Liabilities	
Current:		Current:	
Accounts receivable.....	$185,000	Credit balances in	
		customer accounts........	$2,800

Many companies would include this $2,800 with Other Accounts Payable.

Mid-Chapter Summary Problem
for Your Review

Antigonish Building Supplies is a chain of hardware and building supply stores concentrated in the Maritimes. The company's year-end balance sheet for 2005 reported:

Accounts receivable	$8,102,942
Allowance for uncollectible accounts	(345,000)

Required

1. How much of the December 31, 2005, balance of accounts receivable did Antigonish Building Supplies expect to collect? Stated differently, what was the expected realizable value of these receivables?

2. Journalize, without explanations, year 2006 entries for Antigonish Building Supplies, assuming:
   a. Estimated Uncollectible-Account Expense of $275,000, based on the percent-of-sales method.
   b. Write-offs of accounts receivable totalled $315,000.
   c. December 31, 2006, aging of receivables, which indicates that $387,000 of the total receivables of $8,310,492 is uncollectible. Post all three entries to Allowance for Uncollectible Accounts.

3. Show how Antigonish Building Supplies' receivables and related allowance will appear on the December 31, 2006, balance sheet.

4. What is the expected realizable value of receivables at December 31, 2006? How much is uncollectible-account expense for 2006?

Solution

Requirements

1. Antigonish Building Supplies expected to collect $7,757,942 (i.e., $8,102,942 – $345,000).

2. a. Uncollectible-Account Expense 275,000
      Allowance for Uncollectible Accounts 275,000

   b. Allowance for Uncollectible Accounts 315,000
      Accounts Receivable 315,000

   c. Uncollectible-Account Expense ($387,000 – $305,000) ... 82,000
      Allowance for Uncollectible Accounts 82,000

Allowance for Uncollectible Accounts

2006 Write-offs	315,000	Dec. 31, 2005, Bal.	345,000
		2006 Expense	275,000
		Bal. before Adj.	305,000
		Dec. 31, 2006, Adj.	82,000
		Dec. 31, 2006, Bal.	387,000

3. Accounts receivable... $8,310,492
   Less: Allowance for uncollectible accounts 387,000

4. Expected realizable value of receivables at
   December 31, 2006 ($8,310,492 – $387,000) $7,923,492

   Uncollectible-account expense for 2006
   ($275,000 + $82,000)... 357,000

Notes Receivable: An Overview

Notes receivable are more formal than accounts receivable. The debtor signs a promissory note as evidence of the debt. Before launching into the accounting, let's define the special terms used for notes receivable:

Promissory note. A written promise to pay a specified sum of money at a particular future date.

Maker of the note (**debtor**). The entity that signs the note and promises to pay the required amount; the maker of the note is the *debtor*.

Payee of the note (**creditor**). The entity to whom the maker promises future payment; the payee of the note is the *creditor*.

Principal amount or **principal**. The amount lent by the payee and borrowed by the maker of the note.

Interest. The revenue to the payee for lending money; the expense to the debtor.

Interest period. The period of time during which interest is to be computed. It extends from the original date of the note to the maturity date. Also called the **note term**, or simply **time**.

Interest rate. The percentage rate of interest specified by the note. Interest rates are almost always stated for a period of one year. Therefore, a 9-percent note means that the amount of interest for *one year* is 9 percent of the note's principal amount.

Maturity date (also called **due date**). The date on which final payment of the note is due.

Maturity value. The sum of principal and interest due at maturity.

Exhibit 9-4 illustrates a promissory note. Study it carefully.

Identifying the Maturity Date of a Note

Some notes specify the maturity date of a note, as shown in Exhibit 9-4. Other notes state the period of the note, in days or months. When the period is given in months, the note matures on the same day of the month as the date the note was issued. A 6-month note dated February 16 matures on August 16.

When the period is given in days, the maturity date is determined by counting the days from date of issue. A 120-day note dated September 14, 2005, matures on January 12, 2006, as shown below:

Month		Number of Days	Cumulative Total
Sept.	2005	16*	16
Oct.	2005	31	47
Nov.	2005	30	77
Dec.	2005	31	108
Jan.	2006	12	120

*30 − 14 = 16

The note would have to be *repaid* by January 12, 2006. In counting the days remaining for a note, remember to count the maturity date and to omit the date the note was issued.

Computing Interest on a Note

The formula for computing interest is:

Amount of Interest = Principal × Interest Rate × Time

Using the data in Exhibit 9-4, Foothills Trust Company computes its interest revenue for one year on its note receivable as:

Amount of Interest		Principal		Interest Rate		Time
$90	=	$1,000	×	0.09	×	1 (yr.)

The maturity value of the note is $1,090 ($1,000 principal + $90 interest). The time element is one (1) because the note's term is one year.

When the term of a note is stated in months, we compute the interest based on the 12-month year. Interest on a $2,000 note at 15 percent for three months is computed as:

Amount of Interest		Principal		Interest Rate		Time
$75	=	$2,000	×	0.15	×	$3/12$

When the interest period of a note is stated in days, we usually compute interest based on a 365-day year. The interest on a $5,000 note at 12 percent for 60 days is computed as:

Amount of Interest		Principal		Interest Rate		Time
$98.63	=	$5,000	×	0.12	×	$60/365$

Keep in mind that interest rates are stated as an annual rate. Therefore, the time in the interest formula should also be expressed in terms of a year.

Accounting for Notes Receivable

OBJECTIVE 5
Account for notes receivable

Recording Notes Receivable

Consider the loan agreement shown in Exhibit 9-4. After Lauren Holland signs the note and presents it to the trust company, Foothills Trust Company gives her $1,000 cash. At maturity date, Holland pays the trust company $1,090 ($1,000 principal + $90 interest). The trust company's entries (assuming it has a September 30 year end) are

Sept. 30, 2005	Note Receivable—L. Holland	1,000	
	Cash		1,000
	Lent money.		

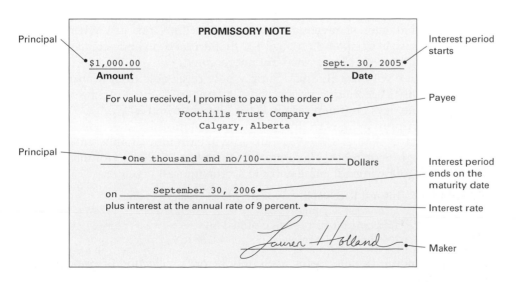

EXHIBIT 9-4

A Promissory Note

```
Sept. 30, 2006    Cash................................................................  1,090
                        Note Receivable—L. Holland..............                    1,000
                        Interest Revenue ..................................                        90
                   Collected note at maturity.
                   (Interest revenue = $1,000 × 0.09 × 1)
```

Some companies sell merchandise in exchange for notes receivable. This arrangement occurs often when the payment term extends beyond the customary accounts receivable period, which generally ranges from 30 to 60 days.

Suppose that on October 20, 2006, EMCO Ltd. (www.emco.ca) sells plumbing supplies for $15,000 to Dorman Builders. Dorman signs a 90-day promissory note at 10 percent interest. EMCO's entries to record the sale and collection from Dorman (EMCO's year end is June 30) are

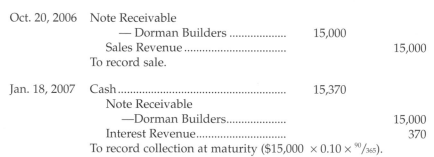

```
Oct. 20, 2006   Note Receivable
                     — Dorman Builders ...................   15,000
                     Sales Revenue .................................                15,000
                To record sale.

Jan. 18, 2007   Cash.......................................................   15,370
                     Note Receivable
                     —Dorman Builders....................             15,000
                     Interest Revenue...............................                370
                To record collection at maturity ($15,000  × 0.10 × ⁹⁰/₃₆₅).
```

A company may accept a note receivable from a trade customer who fails to pay an account receivable. The customer signs a promissory note—that is, becomes the maker of the note—and gives it to the creditor, who becomes the payee.

Suppose Maison Caron sees that it will not be able to pay off its account payable to Hoffman Supply, which is due in 15 days. Hoffman Supply may accept a 12-month, $3,400 note receivable, with 9 percent interest, from Maison Caron on October 1, 2006. Hoffman Supply's entry is

```
Oct. 1, 2006   Note Receivable—Maison Caron........................   3,400
                    Accounts Receivable—
                        Maison Caron ..............................................                3,400
                  Received a note on account from a customer.
```

Accruing Interest Revenue

A note receivable may be outstanding at the end of the accounting period. The interest revenue earned on the note up to the year end is part of that year's earnings. Recall that interest revenue is earned over time, not just when cash is received. We saw in Chapter 3 on page 120 that accrued revenue creates an asset for the amount that has been earned but not received.

Let's continue with the Hoffman Supply note receivable from Maison Caron. Hoffman Supply's accounting period ends December 31. How much of the total interest revenue does Hoffman earn in 2006? How much in 2007?

Hoffman Supply will earn three months' interest in 2006—for October, November, and December. In 2007, Hoffman will earn nine months' interest—for January through September. Therefore, at December 31, 2006, Hoffman Supply will make the following adjusting entry to accrue interest revenue:

```
Dec. 31, 2006   Interest Receivable............................................   76.50
                     Interest Revenue .........................................                76.50
                 To accrue interest revenue earned in
                 2006 but not yet received ($3,400 × 0.09 × ³/₁₂).
```

Then, on the maturity date Hoffman Supply records collection of principal and interest as follows:

Sept. 30, 2007	Cash	3,706.00	
	Note Receivable—Maison Caron		3,400.00
	Interest Receivable		76.50
	Interest Revenue		229.50

To collect note receivable on which interest has been accrued previously. Interest receivable is $76.50 ($3,400 × 0.09 × 3/12) and interest revenue is $229.50 ($3,400 × 0.09 × 9/12).

The entries for accrued interest at December 31, 2006 and for collection in 2007 assign the correct amount of interest to each year.

Dishonoured Notes Receivable

If the maker of a note does not pay a note receivable at maturity, the maker **dishonours** or **defaults** on the note. Because the term of the note has expired, the note agreement is no longer in force. But the payee still has a claim against the debtor. In this case, the payee will transfer the note receivable amount to Accounts Receivable.

Suppose Whitehorse Hardware has a six-month, 10-percent note receivable for $1,200 from Dora Hatachi. On the February 3 maturity date, Hatachi defaults. Whitehorse Hardware would record the default as follows:

Feb. 3	Accounts Receivable—Dora Hatachi	1,260	
	Note Receivable—Dora Hatachi		1,200
	Interest Revenue		60

To record dishonour of note receivable.
Accounts receivable is $1,260
[$1,200 + ($1,200 × 0.10 × 3/12)] and interest
revenue is $60 ($1,200 × 0.10 × 6/12).

Whitehorse Hardware would pursue collection from Dora Hatachi as an account receivable and would account for the receivable in the normal way.

Reporting Receivables on the Balance Sheet: Actual Company Reports

OBJECTIVE 6
Report receivables on the balance sheet

Let's look at how some companies report their receivables on the balance sheet. Terminology and set-up vary.

Paragraph 3020.01 in the *CICA Handbook* indicates that it is not necessary to present the allowance for doubtful accounts in the financial statements because it is assumed that an adequate allowance for doubtful accounts has been made. The 2002 edition of *Financial Reporting in Canada,* published by the CICA, indicates that only 22 percent of the 200 companies surveyed made reference, on the balance sheet or in the notes, to the allowance in 2001.[4]

One Canadian company that did provide information was Canadian National Railway Company (CN) (www.cn.ca). In its 2002 annual report, CN reported the following (amounts in millions):

| | December 31 | |
	2002	2001
Current assets		
Accounts receivable (note 4)	$722	$645
Notes to the Consolidated Financial Statements		
4. Accounts receivable	$781	726
Provision for doubtful accounts	(59)	(81)
	$722	$645

[4]Byrd, C., I. Chen, and H. Chapman, *Financial Reporting in Canada 2002.* Twenty-seventh edition (Toronto: Canadian Institute of Chartered Accountants, 2002), p. 226.

While some companies, like CN, provide information about the allowance for doubtful accounts, as was suggested above, many companies in Canada, such as Enbridge Inc. (www.enbridge.com), the Calgary-based energy company, and Sobey's (www.sobeys.com), the food retailer, tend to show only net accounts receivable. They do not show the allowance.

Bombardier Inc. (www.bombardier.com), the transportation, aerospace, consumer products, and financial services giant, lists trade accounts receivable of $2,349.2 million and asset-based financing items of $7,013.3 million at January 31, 2003. The latter account includes commercial loans, leases receivable, finance receivables, and others. The notes to the financial statements provide more complete information about the various receivables, including the allowances for credit losses of the asset-based financing items.

Some companies factor or sell their accounts and notes receivable to raise immediate cash. This subject is discussed in the appendix to this chapter, beginning on page 480.

Computers and Accounts Receivable

Accounting for receivables for a company like McCain Foods Ltd. (www.mccain.com) requires thousands of postings to customer accounts each month for credit sales and cash collections. Manual accounting methods cannot keep up.

As we saw in Chapter 7, Accounts Receivable can be computerized. The order entry, shipping, and billing departments at McCain Foods work together to meet customer demand and ensure that McCain collects on its receivables.

Using Accounting Information for Decision Making

The balance sheet lists assets in their order of relative liquidity (closeness to cash):

- Cash comes first because it *is* the most liquid asset.
- Short-term investments (covered in a later chapter) come next because they are almost as liquid as cash. They can be sold for cash whenever the owner wishes.
- Current receivables are less liquid than short-term investments because the company must collect the receivables.
- Merchandise inventory is less liquid than receivables because the goods must first be sold.

A partial balance sheet of Winpak Ltd. (www.winpak.com), the packaging company whose head office is in Winnipeg, provides an example in Exhibit 9-5.

EXHIBIT 9-5

Winpak Ltd.'s Partial
Balance Sheet

WINPAK LTD.
Consolidated Balance Sheet (adapted)
As at December 31, 2002

(thousands of dollars)	2002	2001
CURRENT ASSETS		
Cash and cash equivalents	$ 2,585	$ 15,161
Accounts receivable..	61,879	57,981
Inventories	69,654	66,911
Future income taxes..	4,087	2,913
Prepaid expenses...	2,819	2,221
	$141,024	$145,187
CURRENT LIABILITIES		
Accounts payable and accrued liabilities..............	45,831	41,681
Current portion of long-term debt.........................	—	1,590
	$ 45,831	$ 43,271

Acid-Test (or Quick) Ratio

OBJECTIVE 7
Use the acid-test ratio and
days' sales in receivables to
evaluate a company

Owners and managers use ratios for decision making. In Chapter 4, for example, we discussed the current ratio, which indicates the ability to pay current liabilities with current assets. A more stringent measure of the ability to pay current liabilities is the **acid-test** (or **quick**) **ratio**. The acid-test ratio tells whether the entity could pay all its current liabilities if they came due immediately.

REAL WORLD EXAMPLE

The average acid-test ratio in the computer industry is 1.20. For auto dealers, the average is 0.20, and for restaurants, 0.40.

$$\text{Acid-test ratio} = \frac{\text{Cash + Short-term investments}}{\text{Total current liabilities}}$$

For Winpak Ltd. (Exhibit 9-5)
(Dollar amounts in thousands)

$$\frac{\$2,585 + \$0 + \$61,879}{\$45,831} = 1.41$$

The higher the acid-test ratio, the better able the business is to pay its current liabilities. Winpak's ratio was 1.41, showing good liquidity.

What is an acceptable acid-test ratio value? The answer depends on the industry. Automobile dealers can operate smoothly with an acid-test ratio of 0.20. Several things make this possible: Car dealers have almost no current receivables. The acid-test ratio for most department stores clusters about 0.80, while travel agencies average 1.10. In general, an acid-test ratio of 1.00 is considered safe.

STOP & THINK

Use the data in Exhibit 9-5 to compute Winpak Ltd.'s current ratio at December 31, 2002. Then compare Winpak Ltd.'s current ratio and acid-test ratio. Why is the current ratio higher?

Answers: Current ratio = $\dfrac{\text{Total current assets}}{\text{Total current liabilities}}$

$$= \frac{\$141,024}{\$45,831}$$

$$= 3.08$$

Acid-test ratio = 1.41

The current ratio is higher because assets in the numerator include inventory, prepayments, and other current assets, which are excluded from the acid-test ratio.

Days' Sales in Receivables

After a business makes a credit sale, the next critical event in the business cycle is collection of the receivable. Several financial ratios centre on receivables. **Days' sales in receivables**, also called the **collection period**, indicates how many days it takes to collect the average level of receivables. The shorter the collection period, the more quickly the organization has cash to use for operations. The longer the collection period, the less cash is available to pay bills and expand. Days' sales in receivables can be computed in two steps, as follows:

1. One day's sales $= \dfrac{\text{Net sales}}{\text{365 days}}$

2. $\begin{array}{l}\text{Days' sales in} \\ \text{average accounts} \\ \text{receivable}\end{array} = \dfrac{\begin{array}{c}\text{Average net} \\ \text{accounts receivable}\end{array}}{\text{One day's sales}} = \dfrac{\text{(Beginning net receivables} + \text{Ending net receivables})/2}{\text{One day's sales}}$

For Winpak Ltd. (Exhibit 9-5) (Dollar amounts in thousands):

1. One day's sales $= \dfrac{\$491,067^*}{365} = \$1,345 \text{ per day}$

2. $\begin{array}{l}\text{Days' sales in} \\ \text{average accounts} \\ \text{receivable}\end{array} = \dfrac{(\$57,981 + \$61,879)/2}{\$1,345} = 45 \text{ days}$

*Taken from Winpak's 2002 income statement, not reproduced here.

The length of the collection period depends on the credit terms of the sale. For example, sales on net 30 terms should be collected within approximately 30 days. When there is a discount, such as 2/10 net 30, the collection period may be shorter. Terms of net 45 result in a longer collection period.

A company should watch its collection period closely. Whenever the collection period lengthens, the business must find other sources of financing, such as borrowing. During recessions, customers pay more slowly, and a longer collection period may be unavoidable.

STOP & THINK

Can days' sales in receivables be computed in one step instead of two?

Answer: Yes. It can be calculated as:

$$\dfrac{\begin{array}{c}\text{Average net} \\ \text{accounts receivable}\end{array}}{\text{Net sales}} \times 365$$

Investors and creditors do not evaluate a company on the basis of one or two ratios. Instead they analyze all the information available. They then stand back and ask, "What is our overall impression of this company?"

Accounting for receivables is the same for your own start-up business as it is for a company like Research In Motion Inc. Suppose you open a business to maintain websites for local companies and you bill your clients monthly for your services. How should you account for your receivables? These guidelines show the way.

Decision	Guidelines
Accounts Receivable	
How much of our receivables will we collect?	Less than the full amount of the receivables because we cannot collect from some customers.
How to report receivables at their net realizable value?	1. Use the *allowance method* to account for uncollectible receivables. Set up the Allowance for Uncollectible Accounts.
	2. Estimate uncollectibles by the
	a. *Percent-of-sales method* (income-statement approach) (page 441)
	b. *Aging-of-account method* (balance-sheet approach) (page 442)
	3. Write off uncollectible receivables as they prove uncollectible.
	4. $\text{Net accounts receivable} = \text{Accounts Receivable} - \text{Allowance for Uncollectible Accounts}$
Is there another way to account for uncollectible receivables?	The *direct write-off method* uses no Allowance for Uncollectible Accounts and thus reports receivables at their full amount. Under this method, simply debit Uncollectible-Account Expense and credit the customer's account. This method is acceptable only when uncollectibles are insignificant.
Notes Receivable	
What two other accounts are related to notes receivable?	Notes receivable are related to:
	• *Interest Revenue*
	• *Interest Receivable* (interest revenue earned but not collected)
How to compute the interest on a note receivable?	$\text{Amount of Interest} = \text{Principal} \times \text{Interest Rate} \times \text{Time}$
Receivables in General	
What are the two key decision aids that use receivables to evaluate a company's financial position?	• $\text{Acid-test ratio} = \dfrac{\text{Cash} + \text{Short-term investments} + \text{Net current receivables}}{\text{Total current liabilities}}$
	• $\dfrac{\text{Days' sales in average accounts receivable}}{} = \dfrac{\text{Average net accounts receivable}}{\text{One day's sales}}$
How to report receivables on the balance sheet?	Accounts (or Notes) receivable $XXX Less: Allowance for uncollectible accounts (X) Net accounts (or notes) receivable $ XX

Suppose Petro-Canada engaged in the following transactions:

2006
Apr. 1   Lent $10,000 to Arnie Gerber, a service station operator. Received a six-month, 10-percent note.
Oct. 1   Collected the Gerber note at maturity.
Nov. 30 Lent $6,000 to Réjean Fortino, a regional distributor of Petro-Canada products, on a three-month, 12-percent note.
Dec. 31 Accrued interest revenue on the Fortino note.

2007
Feb. 28 Collected the Fortino note at maturity.

Petro-Canada's accounting period ends on December 31.

Required

Explanations are not needed.

1. Record the 2006 transactions on April 1, October 1, and November 30 on Petro-Canada's books.
2. Make the adjusting entry needed on December 31, 2006.
3. Record the February 28, 2007, collection of the Fortino note.

Solution

Requirement 1

2006			
Apr. 1	Note Receivable—Arnie Gerber.....................	10,000	
	Cash..		10,000
Oct. 1	Cash...	10,500	
	Note Receivable—Arnie Gerber.............		10,000
	Interest Revenue ($10,000 × 0.10 × 6/12)...		500
Nov. 30	Note Receivable—Réjean Fortino..................	6,000	
	Cash...		6,000

Requirement 2

Adjusting Entry

2006			
Dec. 31	Interest Receivable	60	
	Interest Revenue......................................		60
	Interest receivable is $60 ($6,000 × 0.12 × 1/12).		

Requirement 3

2007			
Feb. 28	Cash	6,180	
	Note Receivable—Réjean Fortino...........		6,000
	Interest Receivable....................................		60
	Interest Revenue		120
	Interest revenue is $120 ($6,000 × 0.12 × 2/12).		
	Cash is $6,180 [$6,000 + ($6,000 × 0.12 × 3/12)].		

Summary

1. **Design internal controls for receivables.** Companies that sell on credit receive most customer collections in the mail. Good *internal control* over mailed-in cash receipts means separating cash-handling duties from cash-accounting duties.

2. **Use the allowance method to account for uncollectibles, and estimate uncollectibles by the percent-of-sales and the aging-of-account methods.** Uncollectible receivables are accounted for by the allowance method or the direct write-off method. The *allowance method* matches expenses to sales revenue and also results in a more realistic measure of net accounts receivable. The *percent-of-sales method* and the *aging-of-accounts method* are the two main approaches to estimating bad debts under the allowance method.

3. **Use the direct write-off method to account for uncollectibles.** The *direct write-off method* is easy to apply, but it fails to match the uncollectible-account expense to the corresponding sales revenue. Also, Accounts Receivable are reported at their full amount, which is misleading because it suggests that the company expects to collect all its accounts receivable.

4. **Account for credit-card and debit-card sales.** When customers pay for their purchases using a *credit card* such as MasterCard, the credit-card company pays the vendor and collects from the customer. When a customer pays with a *debit card*, the issuer (usually a financial institution) removes the amount of the purchase from the customer's bank account and puts it into the vendor's account.

5. **Account for notes receivable.** *Notes receivable* are formal credit agreements. Interest earned by the creditor is computed by multiplying the note's principal amount by the interest rate times the length of the interest period.

6. **Report receivables on the balance sheet.** All accounts receivable, notes receivable, and allowance accounts appear in the balance sheet. However, companies use various formats and terms to report these assets.

7. **Use the acid-test ratio and days' sales in receivables to evaluate a company.** The *acid-test ratio* measures ability to pay current liabilities from the most liquid current assets. *Days' sales in receivables* indicates how long it takes to collect the average level of receivables.

Self-Study Questions

Test your understanding of the chapter by marking the correct answer for each of the following questions:

1. The party that holds a receivable is called the (*p. 437*)
   a. Creditor   c. Maker
   b. Debtor   d. Security holder

2. The function of the credit department is to (*pp. 439–440*)
   a. Collect accounts receivable from customers
   b. Report bad credit risks to other companies
   c. Evaluate customers who apply for credit
   d. Write off uncollectible accounts receivable

3. Keady Marina made the following entry related to uncollectibles:

   Uncollectible-Account Expense ..   700
      Allowance for Uncollectible
         Accounts   700

   The purpose of this entry is to (*pp. 440–444*)
   a. Write off uncollectibles
   b. Close the expense account
   c. Age the accounts receivable
   d. Record uncollectible-account expense

4. Keady Marina also made this entry:

   Allowance for Uncollectible
      Accounts   1,800
         Accounts Receivable (detailed)   1,800

   The purpose of this entry is to (*p. 444*)
   a. Write off uncollectibles
   b. Close the expense account
   c. Age the accounts receivable
   d. Record uncollectible-account expense

5. Keady Marina also made this entry:

   Accounts Receivable (detailed) ...   640
      Allowance for Uncollectible
         Accounts   640

   The purpose of this entry is to (*p. 445*)
   a. Write off uncollectibles
   b. Close the expense account
   c. Reverse the write-off of receivables
   d. Record uncollectible-account expense

6. The credit balance in Allowance for Uncollectibles is $12,600 prior to the adjusting entries at the end of the period. The aging of the accounts indicates that an allowance of $81,200 is needed. The amount of expense to record is (*pp. 441–442*)

a. $12,600   c. $81,200
b. $68,600   d. $93,800

7. A critical element of internal control over cash receipts is (p. 438)
   a. Assigning an honest employee the responsibility for handling cash
   b. Separating the cash-handling and cash-accounting duties
   c. Ensuring that cash is deposited in the bank daily
   d. Centralizing the opening of incoming mail in a single location

8. A six-month, $40,000 note specifies interest of 8 percent. The full amount of interest on this note will be (pp. 450–451)

a. $400   c. $1,600
b. $800   d. $3,200

9. The note in Self-Study Question 8 was issued on August 31, and the company's accounting year ends on December 31. The year-end balance sheet will report interest receivable of (pp. 451–452)
   a. $533   c. $1,600
   b. $1,067   d. $3,200

10. The best acid-test ratio among the following is (pp. 454–455)
    a. 0.10   c. 1.0
    b. 0.80   d. 1.2

Answers to the Self-Study Questions follow the Similar Accounting Terms.

Accounting Vocabulary

Acid-test ratio (p. 455)
Aging-of-accounts method (p. 442)
Allowance for Doubtful Accounts (p. 441)
Allowance for Uncollectible Accounts (p. 441)
Allowance method (p. 441)
Bad-debt expense (p. 440)
Balance-sheet approach (p. 442)
Collection period (p. 456)
Creditor (pp. 437, 450)
Days' sales in receivables (p. 456)

Debtor (pp. 437, 450)
Default on a note (p. 453)
Direct write-off method (p. 445)
Discounting a note receivable (p. 480)
Dishonour of a note (p. 453)
Doubtful-account expense (p. 440)
Due date (p. 450)
Income-statement approach (p. 441)
Interest (p. 450)
Interest period (p. 450)
Interest rate (p. 450)

Maker of a note (p. 450)
Maturity date (p. 450)
Maturity value (p. 450)
Note term (p. 450)
Payee of a note (p. 450)
Percent-of-sales method (p. 441)
Principal (p. 450)
Principal amount (p. 450)
Promissory note (p. 450)
Quick ratio (p. 455)
Receivable (p. 437)
Time (p. 450)
Uncollectible-account expense (p. 440)

Similar Accounting Terms

Acid-test ratio	Quick ratio
Aging-of-accounts method (of estimating uncollectibles)	Balance-sheet approach (of estimating uncollectibles)
Allowance for Uncollectible Accounts	Allowance for Doubtful Accounts; Allowance for Bad Debts
Days' sales in receivables	Collection period
Dishonour a note	Default on a note
Interest period	Note period; Note term; Time
Maturity date	Due date
Percent-of-Sales Method (of estimating uncollectibles)	Income-statement approach (of estimating uncollectibles)
Uncollectible-account expense	Bad-debt expense; Doubtful-account expense

Answers to Self-Study Questions
1. a   6. b ($81,200 – $12,600 = $68,600)
2. c   7. b
3. d   8. c ($40,000 × 0.08 × $\frac{6}{12}$ = $1,600)
4. a   9. b ($40,000 × 0.08 × $\frac{4}{12}$ = $1,067)
5. c   10. d

Assignment Material

Questions

1. Name the two parties to a receivable/payable transaction. Which party has the receivable? Which has the payable? The asset? The liability?

2. List three categories of receivables. State how each category is classified for reporting on the balance sheet.

3. Many businesses receive most of their cash on credit sales through the mail. Suppose you own a business so large that you must hire employees to handle cash receipts and perform the related accounting duties. What internal control feature should you use to ensure that cash received from customers is not taken by a dishonest employee?

4. What duty must be withheld from a company's credit department in order to safeguard cash? If the credit department does this job, what can a dishonest credit department employee do?

5. Name the two methods of accounting for uncollectible receivables. Which method is easier to apply? Which method is consistent with generally accepted accounting principles?

6. Which of the two methods of accounting for uncollectible accounts—the allowance method or the direct write-off method—is preferable? Why?

7. Identify the accounts debited and credited to account for uncollectibles under (a) the allowance method, and (b) the direct write-off method.

8. What is another term for Allowance for Uncollectible Accounts? What are two other terms for Uncollectible-Account Expense?

9. Which entry decreases net income under the allowance method of accounting for uncollectibles: the entry to record uncollectible-account expense, or the entry to write off an uncollectible account receivable?

10. Identify and briefly describe the two ways to estimate uncollectible-account expense and uncollectible accounts.

11. Briefly describe how a company may use both the percent-of-sales method and aging-of-accounts method to account for uncollectibles.

12. How does a credit balance arise in a customer's account receivable? How does the company report this credit balance on its balance sheet?

13. Show three ways to report Accounts Receivable of $100,000 and Allowance for Uncollectible Accounts of $2,800 on the balance sheet or in the related notes.

14. What are the benefits of credit-card sales to a retailer? What is the cost to the retailer? How is the cost of a credit-card sale recorded?

15. Use the terms *maker, payee, principal amount, maturity date, promissory note,* and *interest* in an appropriate sentence or two describing a note receivable.

16. Name three situations in which a company might receive a note receivable. For each situation, show the account debited and the account credited to record receipt of the note.

17. For each of the following notes receivable, compute the amount of interest revenue earned during 2004:

	Principal	Interest Rate	Interest Period	Maturity Date
a. Note 1	$ 10,000	3%	60 days	Nov. 30, 2004
b. Note 2	50,000	7%	3 months	Sept. 30, 2004
c. Note 3	100,000	5%	1 ½ years	Dec. 31, 2005
d. Note 4	15,000	9%	90 days	Jan. 15, 2005

18. When the maker of a note dishonours the note at maturity, what accounts does the payee debit and credit?

19. Why does the payee of a note receivable usually need to make adjusting entries for interest at the end of the accounting period?

20. Why is the acid-test ratio a more stringent measure of the ability to pay current liabilities than is the current ratio?

21. Which measure of days' sales in receivables is preferable, 30 or 40? Give your reason.

Exercises

Exercise 9-1   *Identifying and correcting an internal control weakness (Obj. 1)*

Suppose the Campbell Soup Company (www.campbellsoup.ca), the U.S. food products company, is opening a district office in Sackville, New Brunswick. Sylvester Heath, the office manager, is designing the internal control system for the office.

Heath proposes the following procedures for credit checks on new customers, sales on account, cash collections, and write-offs of uncollectible receivables:

- The credit department will run a credit check on all customers who apply for credit.

- Sales on account are the responsibility of the Campbell Soup Company salespersons. Credit sales above $50,000 (which is a reasonable limit) require the approval of the sales manager.

- Cash receipts come into the credit department, which separates the cash received from the customer remittance slips. The credit department lists all cash receipts by name of customer and the amount of cash received. The cash goes to the treasurer for deposit in the bank. The remittance slips go to the accounting department for posting to individual customer accounts in the accounts receivable subsidiary ledger. Each day's listing of cash receipts goes to the controller for her end-of-day comparison with the daily deposit slip and the day's listing of the total dollar amount posted to customer accounts from the accounting department. The three amounts must agree.

- The credit department reviews customer accounts receivable monthly. Late-paying customers are notified that their accounts are past due. After 90 days, the credit department turns over past-due accounts to a lawyer or collection agency for collection. After 180 days, the credit department writes off a customer account as uncollectible.

Identify the internal control weakness in this situation, and propose a way to strengthen the controls.

Exercise 9-2 *Using the allowance method (percent of sales) for bad debts and reporting receivables on the balance sheet (Obj. 2, 6)*

On February 28, Snow Mountain Ski Equipment had a $46,000 debit balance in Accounts Receivable. During March, the company had sales of $119,000, which included $105,000 in credit sales. March collections were $96,000, and write-offs of uncollectible receivables totalled $2,160. Other data include:

a. February 28 credit balance in Allowance for Uncollectible Accounts, $2,300.

b. Uncollectible account expense, estimated as 2 percent of credit sales.

Required

1. Prepare journal entries to record sales, collections, uncollectible-account expense by the allowance method (using the percent-of-sales method), and write-offs of uncollectibles during February.

2. Show the ending balances in Accounts Receivable, Allowance for Uncollectible Accounts, and *net* accounts receivable at February 28. Does Snow Mountain expect to collect the net amount of the receivable?

3. Show how Snow Mountain will report Accounts Receivable on its February 28 balance sheet.

Media Companion CD-ROM

Exercise 9-3 *Using the aging approach to estimate bad debts and reporting receivables on the balance sheet (Obj. 2, 6)*

At November 30, 2004, the accounts receivable balance of Black Jack's Electronics is $626,000. The allowance for doubtful accounts has a $9,095 credit balance. Accountants for Black Jack's Electronics prepare the following aging schedule for its accounts receivable:

Total Balance	Age of Accounts			
	1–30 Days	31–60 Days	61–90 Days	Over 90 Days
$626,000	$275,440	$179,700	$139,560	$31,300
Estimated percent uncollectible	0.2%	1.8%	5.0%	50.0%

Required

1. Journalize the adjusting entry for doubtful accounts based on the aging schedule. Show the T-account for the allowance.
2. Show how Black Jack's Electronics will report Accounts Receivable on its November 30, 2004, balance sheet.

Exercise 9-4 *Using the allowance method to account for uncollectibles* **(Obj. 2)**

Quick Landscaping Services started the year 2005 with an accounts receivable balance of $17,500 and an allowance for uncollectible accounts balance of $1,050. During the year, $1,950 of accounts receivable were identified as uncollectible. Sales revenue for 2005 was $195,000, including credit sales of $192,000. Cash collections on account were $188,000 during the year.

The aging of accounts receivable yields these data:

	Age of Accounts				
	0–30 Days	31–60 Days	61–90 Days	Over 90 Days	Total Receivables
Amount receivable	$12,000	$3,000	$2,500	$2,050	$19,550
Percent uncollectible	× 1%	× 1%	× 3%	× 50%	

You're the accountant preparing the year-end entries.

Required

1. Journalize Quick's (a) credit sales, (b) cash collections on account, (c) the write-off of the accounts receivable identified as uncollectible, and (d) the uncollectible-account expense based on 1 percent of credit sales.
2. Prepare a T-account for the Accounts Receivable and Allowance for Uncollectible Accounts accounts.
3. Calculate the balance in the Allowance for Uncollectible Accounts based on the aging-of-accounts methods.
4. Make any adjustment required to the Allowance for Uncollectible Accounts based on your calculation in Requirement 3.
5. Show how Quick Landscaping Services should report accounts receivable on the balance sheet.

Exercise 9-5 *Using the direct write-off method for bad debts* **(Obj. 3)**

Refer to the situation of Exercise 9-2.

Required

1. Record uncollectible-account expense for February by the direct write-off method.
2. What amount of net accounts receivable would Snow Mountain Ski Equipment

report on its February 28 balance sheet under the direct write-off method? Does Snow Mountain Ski Equipment expect to collect this much of the receivable? Give your reason.

Exercise 9-6 *Contrasting the allowance method and the direct write-off method to account for uncollectibles* *(Obj. 2, 3)*

Return to the Schmidt Builders Supply example of accounting for uncollectibles that begins under the heading "Writing Off Uncollectible Accounts" on page 444. Suppose Schmidt Builders Supply's past experience indicates that the company will fail to collect 2 percent of net credit sales, which totalled $125,000 during the three-month period January through March of 2006.

Record Schmidt Builders Supply's uncollectible-account expense for the three-month period January through March under

a. The allowance method

b. The direct write-off method (You need not identify individual customer accounts. Use the data given for Auger and Kirsh on page 444.)

Which method of accounting for uncollectibles is better? What makes this preferred method better? Mention accounting principles in your answer.

Exercise 9-7 *Recording notes receivable and accruing interest revenue* *(Obj. 5)*

Record the following transactions in the journal of Golfview Properties:

Oct.   1   Lent $80,000 cash to Joe Lazarus on a one-year, 2-percent note.
Nov.   3   Sold goods to Highwater Inc., receiving a 100-day, 4-percent note for $5,750.
      16   Received a $4,000, six-month, 4-percent note on account from STM Inc.
      30   Accrued interest revenue on all notes receivable.

Exercise 9-8 *Accounting for debit-card sales and notes receivables* *(Obj. 4, 5)*

Record the following transactions in the general journal of Bob's Hardware Store:

2004
Mar. 31   Recorded Scotiabank debit-card sales of $10,000.
      31   Recorded VISA credit-card sales of $15,000.
Apr. 1   Lent $5,000 to Sam Brown on a one-year, 4-percent note.
Dec. 31   Accrued interest revenue on the Brown note.

2005
Apr. 1   Received the maturity value of the note from Brown.

Assume Scotiabank charges merchants 2 percent and VISA charges 3 percent of sales as service fees.

Exercise 9-9 *Evaluating ratio data* *(Obj. 7)*

Marshall's Ltd., a gift store, reported the amounts on the next page in its 2004 financial statements. The 2003 figures are given for comparison.

Required

1. Determine whether Marshall's Ltd.'s acid-test ratio improved or deteriorated from 2003 to 2004. How does Marshall's Ltd.'s acid-test ratio compare with the industry average of 0.90?

2. Compare the days' sales in receivables measure for 2004 with the company's credit terms of net 30. What action, if any, should Marshall's Ltd. take?

		2004		2003
Current assets:				
Cash...		$ 8,100		$ 14,800
Short-term investments.............		31,050		0
Accounts receivable...................	$116,100		$103,900	
Less: Allowance for uncollectibles.................	9,500	106,600	6,700	97,200
Inventory......................................		259,200		255,100
Prepaid insurance		2,700		2,700
Total current assets		407,650		369,800
Total current liabilities....................		170,100		144,400
Net sales...		951,750		988,200

Exercise 9-10   *Analyzing a real company's financial statements*   *(Obj. 6)*

The Hudson's Bay Company (www.hbc.com/bay) is Canada's largest department-store retailer and oldest corporation. Hudson's Bay Company's annual report for the year ended January 31, 2003, included these figures in millions of dollars:

	January 31	
	2003	2002
Sales and revenues	$7,383	$7,446
Credit-card receivables	559	487

The Bay's financial statements report credit-card receivables net of uncollectible-account expense. Credit card receivables at January 31, 2001, were $500.

Required

1. Compute The Bay's days' sales in average credit-card receivables for 2002 and 2001.

2. Comment on the number of days in credit-card receivables, indicating whether you think the number is high or low, and explaining your evaluation. Suggest how The Bay might manage the average collection period, providing reasons for your recommendations.

Challenge Exercise

Exercise 9-11   *Evaluating debit-card sales for profitability* *(Obj. 4)*

Media Companion CD-ROM

Murray's Shoe Store has sold on store credit and managed its own receivables. Average experience for the past three years has been:

	Cash	Credit	Total
Sales	$260,000	$175,000	$435,000
Cost of goods sold	156,000	105,000	261,000
Uncollectible-account expense	—	7,000	7,000
Other expenses	36,400	31,500	67,900

Walter Murray, the owner, is considering whether to accept debit cards (using the Interac system). Typically, the availability of debit cards increases sales by 15 percent. But the Interac system charges approximately 2 percent of sales. If Murray switches to debit cards, he can save $5,000 on accounting and other expenses. He figures that cash customers will continue buying in the same volume regardless of the type of credit the store offers.

Required

Should Murray's Shoe Store start offering debit-card service using the Interac system? Show the computations of net income under the present plan and under the debit-card plan.

Beyond the Numbers

Beyond the Numbers 9-1   *Reporting receivables on the balance sheet* (*Obj. 6*)

Portage Communications' cash flow statement reported the following *cash* receipts and *cash* payments (the amounts in brackets) for the year ended August 31, 2004:

PORTAGE COMMUNICATIONS
Cash Flow Statement
For the Year Ended August 31, 2004

Cash flows from operating activities:	
Cash receipts from customers	$3,010,000
Interest received...	3,750
Cash flows from investing activities:	
Loans made on notes receivable	(50,000)
Collection of loans on notes receivable.............................	100,000

Portage's balance sheet one year earlier—at August 31, 2003—reported Accounts Receivable of $340,000 and Notes Receivable of $75,000. Credit sales for the year ended August 31, 2004, totalled $3,125,000, and the company collects all of its accounts receivable because uncollectibles rarely occur.

Portage Communications needs a loan and the manager is preparing the company's balance sheet at August 31, 2004. To complete the balance sheet, the owner needs to know the balances of Accounts Receivable and Notes Receivable at August 31, 2004. Supply the needed information; T-accounts are helpful.

Ethical Issue

Big M's auto showroom sells cars. Big M's bank requires Big M to submit quarterly financial statements in order to keep its line of credit. Notes Receivable and Accounts Receivable are 50 percent of current assets. Therefore, Uncollectible-Account Expense and Allowance for Uncollectible Accounts are important accounts.

Big M's president, Marc LeMoyne, likes net income to increase in a smooth pattern rather than to increase in some periods and decrease in other periods. To report smoothly increasing net income, LeMoyne underestimates Uncollectible-Account Expense in some accounting periods. In other accounting periods, LeMoyne overestimates the expense. He reasons that the income overstatements roughly offset the income understatements over time.

Required

Is Big M's practice of smoothing income ethical? Give your reasons, mentioning any accounting principles that might be violated.

Problems (Group A)

Problem 9-1A Controlling accounts receivable (Obj. 1)

North Toronto Laboratories provides laboratory testing for samples that veterinarians send in. All work is performed on account, with regular monthly billing to participating veterinarians. Pete Wilson, accountant for North Toronto Laboratories, receives and opens the mail. Company procedure requires him to separate customer cheques from the remittance slips, which list the amounts he posts as credits to customer accounts receivable in the subsidiary ledger. Wilson deposits the cheques in the bank. He computes each day's total amount posted to customer accounts and makes sure that this total agrees with the bank deposit slip. This is intended to ensure that all receipts are deposited in the bank. Wilson does all customer credit checks, authorizes customer credit limits, and deals with all customer inquiries.

Required

As the auditor of North Toronto Laboratories, write a memo to the owners evaluating the company's internal controls over accounts receivable. If the system is effective, identify its strong features. If the system has flaws, propose a way to strengthen the controls.

Problem 9-2A Accounting for uncollectibles by the direct write-off and allowance methods (Obj. 2, 3, 6)

On June 30, 2005, B.C. Wireless had a $921,000 debit balance in Accounts Receivable. During July, the company had sales revenue of $1,300,000, which included $1,287,000 in credit sales. Other data for July include:

a. Collections of accounts receivable, $999,950.

b. Write-offs of uncollectible receivables, $21,650.

Required

1. Record uncollectible account expense for July by the direct write-off method. Show all July activity in Accounts Receivable and Uncollectible-Account Expense.

2. Record uncollectible-account expense and write-offs of customer accounts for July by the allowance method. Show all July activity in Accounts Receivable, Allowance for Uncollectible Accounts, and Uncollectible-Account Expense. The June 30 unadjusted balance in Allowance for Uncollectible Accounts was $14,500 (credit). Uncollectible-Account Expense was estimated at 1 percent of credit sales.

3. What amount of uncollectible-account expense would B.C. Wireless report on its July income statement under the two methods? Which amount better matches expense with revenue? Give your reason.

4. What amount of net accounts receivable would B.C. Wireless report on its July 31 balance sheet under the two methods? Which amount is more realistic? Give your reason.

Problem 9-3A Using the percent-of-sales and aging-of-accounts methods for uncollectibles (Obj. 2, 6)

The November 30, 2005, balance sheet of e.FindIt reports the following:

Accounts Receivable... $341,000
Allowance for Uncollectible Accounts (credit balance).................... 7,300

At the end of each quarter, e.FindIt estimates uncollectible-account expense to be 2 percent of credit sales. At the end of the year, the company ages its accounts receivable and adjusts the balance in Allowance for Uncollectible Accounts to correspond to the aging schedule. During the last month of 2005, e.FindIt completes the following selected transactions:

Dec. 9 Made a compound entry to write off the following uncollectible accounts: M. Yang, $675; Tory Ltd., $299; and S. Roberts, $995.

18 Wrote off as uncollectible the $1,293 account receivable from Acme Ltd. and the $750 account receivable from Data Services.

31 Recorded uncollectible-account expense based on credit sales of $400,000.

31 Recorded uncollectible-account expense based on the following summary of the aging of accounts receivable.

Total Balance	Age of Accounts			
	1–30 Days	31–60 Days	61–90 Days	Over 90 Days
$325,600	$179,400	$74,700	$38,600	$32,900
Estimated percent uncollectible	0.15%	0.5%	6.0%	35.0%

Required

1. Record the transactions in the journal.

2. Open the Allowance for Uncollectible Accounts, and post entries affecting that account. Keep a running balance.

3. Most companies report two-year comparative financial statements. If e.FindIt's Accounts Receivable balance was $285,000 and the Allowance for Uncollectible Accounts stood at $9,500 on December 31, 2004, show how the company will report its accounts receivable on a comparative balance sheet for 2005 and 2004.

Problem 9-4A *Using the percent-of-sales and aging-of-accounts methods for uncollectibles (Obj. 2, 6)*

Link Back to Chapter 4 (Closing Entries). Best Buy Clothing completed the following selected transactions during 2004 and 2005:

2004
Dec. 31 Estimated that uncollectible-account expense for the year was 1 percent of credit sales of $650,000 and recorded that amount as expense.

31 Made the closing entry for uncollectible-accounts expense.

2005
Feb. 17 Sold inventory to Bruce Jones, $1,402, on credit terms of 2/10 n/30. Ignore the cost of goods sold.

July 29 Wrote off Bruce Jones' account as uncollectible after repeated efforts to collect from the customer.

Sep. 6 Received $1,000 from Bruce Jones, along with a letter stating his intention to pay his debt in full within 45 days. Reinstated the account in full.

Oct. 21 Received the balance due from Bruce Jones.

Dec. 31 Made a compound entry to write off the following accounts as uncollectible: Sean Rooney, $1,400; Sargent Ltd., $2,675; and Linda Lod, $1,375.

31 Estimated that uncollectible account expense for the year was 1 percent of credit sales of $750,000 and recorded the expense.

31 Made the closing entry for uncollectible-account expense.

Required

1. Open general ledger accounts for Allowance for Uncollectible Accounts and Uncollectible-Account Expense. Keep running balances.

2. Record the transactions in the general journal and post to the two ledger accounts.

3. The December 31, 2005, balance of Accounts Receivable is $435,500. Show how Accounts Receivable would be reported at that date.

4. Assume that Best Buy Clothing begins aging its accounts on December 31, 2005. The balance in Accounts Receivable is $435,500; the credit balance in Allowance for Uncollectible Accounts is $8,550; and the company estimates that $16,100 of its accounts receivable will prove uncollectible.

   a. Make the adjusting entry for uncollectibles.

   b. Show how Accounts Receivable will be reported on the December 31, 2005, balance sheet.

Problem 9-5A   *Accounting for notes receivable, including accruing interest revenue* *(Obj. 5)*

Loans For You issued the following notes during 2004.

Note	Date	Principal Amount	Interest Rate	Term
(a)	October 31	$22,000	6%	6 months
(b)	November 10	8,000	4%	60 days
(c)	December 5	20,000	7%	1 year

Required

Identify each note by letter, compute interest using a 365-day year for all notes, round all interest amounts to the nearest cent, and present entries in general journal form. Explanations are not required.

1. Determine the due date and maturity value of each note.

2. Journalize a single adjusting entry at December 31, 2004, to record accrued interest revenue on all three notes.

3. Journalize the collection of principal and interest on note (b).

4. Show how these notes will be reported on December 31, 2004.

Problem 9-6A   *Accounting for credit-card sales, notes receivable, dishonoured notes, and accrued interest revenue* *(Obj. 4, 5)*

Record the following selected transactions in the general journal of Consumer Research Ltd. Explanations are not required.

2005
Dec. 12 Received a $5,250, 90-day, 8 percent note from Jacques Alard to settle his $5,250 account receivable balance.
      31 Made an adjusting entry to accrue interest on the Alard note.
      31 Made an adjusting entry to record uncollectible-account expense in the amount of 2.5 percent of credit sales of $262,000.
      31 Recorded $80,000 of debit-card sales. The Royal Bank debit-card fee is 1.75 percent.
      31 Made a compound closing entry for interest revenue, uncollectible-account expense, and debit-card discount expense.

2006
Mar. 12 Collected the maturity value of the Alard note.
June   1 Lent $15,000 cash to Mercury Inc., receiving a six-month, 7 percent note.
Oct. 31 Received a $2,750, 60-day, 8 percent note from Jim Keller on his past-due account receivable.
Dec.   1 Collected the maturity value of the Mercury Inc. note.
      30 Jim Keller dishonoured (failed to pay) his note at maturity; wrote off the receivable as uncollectible, debiting Allowance for Uncollectible Accounts.
      31 Wrote off as uncollectible the account receivable of Art Pierce, $775 and John Grey, $567.

Problem 9-7A Journalizing credit-card sales, uncollectibles, notes receivable, and accrued interest revenue (Obj. 4, 5)

Assume that Maple Leaf Foods Inc. (www.mapleleaf.com), a leading Canadian food processor, completed the following selected transactions:

2004
Nov. 1   Sold goods to Loblaws, receiving a $250,000, six-month, 5 percent note. Ignore cost of goods sold.
Dec. 5   Recorded VISA credit-card sale of $25,000. VISA charges a 2.5 percent fee.
31   Made an adjusting entry to accrue interest on the Loblaws note.
31   Made an adjusting entry to record uncollectible-account expense based on an aging of accounts receivable. The aging analysis indicates that $145,000 of accounts receivable will not be collected. Prior to this adjustment, the credit balance in Allowance for Uncollectible Accounts is $125,000.

2005
May 1   Collected the maturity value of the Loblaws note.
15   Received a 60-day, 8 percent, $6,000 note from Sherwood Market on account.
June 23   Sold merchandise to Matt's Foods, receiving a 30-day, 7 percent note for $15,000. Ignore cost of goods sold.
July 14   Collected the maturity value of the Sherwood Market note.
23   Matt's Foods dishonoured (failed to pay) its note at maturity; converted the maturity value of the note to an account receivable.
Nov. 16   Lent $13,000 cash to Urban Provisions, receiving a 120-day, 9 percent note.
Dec. 5   Collected in full from Matt's Foods.
31   Accrued the interest on the Urban Provisions note.

Required

Record the transactions in the journal. Explanations are not required.

Media Companion CD-ROM

Problem 9-8A Using ratio data to evaluate a company's financial position (Obj. 7)

The comparative financial statements of West Heights for 2006, 2005, and 2004 included the selected data shown below.

Required

1. Compute these ratios for 2006 and 2005:
   a. Current ratio
   b. Acid-test ratio
   c. Days' sales in receivables
2. Write a memo explaining to Jack Dodds, owner of West Heights, which ratio values showed improvement from 2005 to 2006, and which ratio values showed deterioration. Which item in the financial statements caused some ratio values to improve and others to deteriorate? Discuss whether this factor conveys a favourable or an unfavourable impression about the company.

	2006	2005	2004
	(In millions)		
Balance Sheet			
Current assets:			
Cash	$ 78	$ 82	$ 61
Short-term investments	144	177	124
Receivables, net of allowance for uncollectible accounts of $7, $7, and $6	293	270	222
Inventories	442	348	308
Prepaid expenses	22	28	47
Total current assets	979	905	762
Total current liabilities	535	530	421
Income statement			
Sales revenue	$5,660	$5,110	$4,791
Cost of sales	2,816	2,689	2,466

Problem 9-9A
Using the allowance method of accounting for uncollectibles, estimating uncollectibles using the aging-of-accounts method, and reporting receivables on the balance sheet **(Obj. 2, 5, 6)**

Penticton Services Inc. started business on March 1, 2005. The company produces monthly financial statements and had total sales of $500,000 (of which $475,000 were on credit) during the first four months.

On June 30, the Accounts Receivable account had a balance of $175,000 (no accounts have been written off to date), which was made up of the following accounts aged according to the date of the provision of services:

| | Month of Service: | | | |
Customer	March	April	May	June
Torrance Trucks.............................	$ 2,100	$ 1,000	$ 1,500	$ 1,200
Milloy Ltd.	1,250	950	1,360	3,620
Marsha Wayne	5,730	3,720	7,640	6,590
Mort Black	5,340	2,890	10,520	13,260
Other Accounts Receivable.........	12,300	19,930	26,150	47,950
	$26,720	$28,490	$47,170	$72,620

The following accounts receivable transactions took place in July 2005:

July 12   Determined the account of Milloy Ltd. was uncollectible and wrote it off.

    15   Collected $3,500 from Torrance Trucks for services in the first three months.

    21   Decided the account of Marsha Wayne was uncollectible and wrote it off.

    24   Collected $5,340 from Mort Black for services in the month of March.

    26   Received a cheque from Marsha Wayne for $8,000 plus two cheques, of $7,840 each, post-dated to September 10 and November 10.

    31   Total sales of service in the month were $135,000; 90 percent of these were on credit and 60 percent of the credit sales were collected in the month.

Required

1. Penticton Services Inc. has heard that other companies in the industry use the allowance method of accounting for uncollectibles, with many of these estimating the uncollectibles through an aging of accounts. Journalize the adjustments that would have to be made on June 30 (for the months of March through June), as well as the transactions of July 2005, and the month-end adjustment, assuming the following estimates of uncollectibles:

Age of Accounts Receivable	Estimated Percent to Be Uncollectible
From current month's sales of service...	1%
From prior month's sales of service..	3%
From two months prior	7%
From three months prior	20%
From four months prior...	35%

(Round your total estimate to the nearest whole dollar.)

2. For the method of accounting for the uncollectibles used above, show
   a. the balance sheet presentation of the accounts receivable.
   b. the overall effect of the credit sales and uncollectibles on the income statement for July 2005.

Problem 9-10A
Using the allowance method of accounting for uncollectibles, estimating uncollectibles by the percent-of-sales and the aging-of-accounts methods, and accounting for notes receivable **(Obj. 2, 5)**

Yukon Mines Inc. uses the allowance method in accounting for uncollectible accounts with the estimate based on an aging of accounts receivable. The company had the following account balances on September 30, 2004:

Accounts Receivable	$453,000
Allowance for Doubtful Accounts (credit balance).................	51,000

The following transactions took place during the month of October 2004:

Oct. 2   Albert Morrison, who owes $46,000, is unable to pay on time and has given a 20-day, 8 percent note in settlement of the account.

6   Determined the account receivable for Donald Timble ($15,000) was uncollectible and wrote it off.

9   Received notice that a customer (Will Wong) has filed for bankruptcy. Wong owes $32,000 to Yukon Mines Inc.

11   Determined the account receivable for Susan Knight ($6,490) was uncollectible and wrote it off.

15   Donald Timble, whose account was written off on October 6, paid $10,000 on his account and promises to pay the balance in 60 days.

18   Received a cheque from the courts in the amount of $21,000 as final settlement of Will Wong's account.

22   Albert Morrison paid the note received on October 2.

25   Determined the account receivable for Donald Purcell ($7,400) was uncollectible and wrote it off.

31   Sales for the month totalled $675,000 (of which 95 percent were on credit) and collections on account totalled $473,000.

31   Yukon Mines Inc. did an aging of accounts receivable that indicated that $54,260 is expected to be uncollectible. The company recorded the appropriate adjustment.

Required

1. Record the above transactions in the general journal.

2. What would be the adjusting entry required on October 31 if the company used the percent-of-sales method with an estimate of uncollectibles equal to 2 percent of credit sales?

3. Which of the two methods of estimating uncollectible accounts would normally be more accurate? Why?

Problems (Group B)

Problem 9-1B   *Designing internal controls for receivables* **(Obj. 1)**

Lougheed Golf Gear distributes merchandise to sporting goods stores and golf club pro shops. All sales are on credit, so virtually all cash receipts arrive in the mail. Business has tripled in the last year, and the owner, Stu Lougheed, has hired an accountant to manage the financial aspect of the business. Lougheed has requested that strong internal controls over cash receipts and receivables be the first priority.

Required

Assume you are Paul Bean, the new accountant. Write a memo to Stu Lougheed outlining the internal controls you intend to establish for Lougheed Golf Gear. Assume also that you have two employees in the accounting department and a receptionist who report to you. Use this format for your memo:

Date:	_____
To:	Stu Lougheed
From:	Paul Bean, Accountant
RE:	Proposed internal controls over cash receipts and receivables

Problem 9-2B   *Accounting for uncollectibles by the direct write-off and allowance methods* **(Obj. 2, 3, 6)**

On March 31, 2005, MoPac had a $250,000 debit balance in Accounts Receivable. During April, the business had sales revenue of $905,000, which included $860,000 in credit sales. Other data for April include

a. Collections on accounts receivable, $790,000.

b. Write-offs of uncollectible receivables, $3,500.

Required

1. Record uncollectible-account expense for April by the direct write-off method. Show all April activity in Accounts Receivable and Uncollectible-Account Expense.

2. Record uncollectible-account expense and write-offs of customer accounts for April by the allowance method. Show all April activity in Accounts Receivable, Allowance for Uncollectible Accounts, and Uncollectible-Account Expense. The March 31 unadjusted balance in Allowance for Uncollectible Accounts was $1,000 (debit). Uncollectible-Account Expense was estimated at 1 percent of credit sales.

3. What amount of uncollectible account expense would MoPac report on its April income statement under the two methods? Which amount better matches expense with revenue? Give your reason.

4. What amount of *net* accounts receivable would MoPac report on its April 30 balance sheet under the two methods? Which amount is more realistic? Give your reason.

Problem 9-3B *Use the percent-of-sales and aging-of-accounts methods for uncollectibles* **(Obj. 2, 6)**

The June 30, 2004, balance sheet of Bernard Rubber Products reports the following:

Accounts Receivable.. $562,000

Allowance for Uncollectible Accounts (credit balance)...................... 15,000

At the end of each quarter, Bernard Rubber Products estimates uncollectible-account expense to be 1.5 percent of credit sales. At the end of the year, the company ages its accounts receivable and adjusts the balance in Allowance for Uncollectible Accounts to correspond to the aging schedule. During the second half of 2004, Bernard Rubber Products completes the following selected transactions:

July 14 Made a compound entry to write off the following uncollectible accounts: C.D. Minor, $6,000; Plumbers Inc., $1,500; and Barb Hale, $500.

Sept. 30 Recorded uncollectible-account expense based on credit sales of $1,000,000.

Nov. 22 Wrote off the following accounts receivable as uncollectible: Bert Almond, $4,500; Blocked, Inc., $3,900; and Small Mall, $2,000.

Dec. 31 Recorded uncollectible-account expense based on the following summary of the aging of accounts receivable.

| Total Balance | Age of Accounts | | | |
	1–30 Days	31–60 Days	61–90 Days	Over 90 Days
$597,000	$325,000	$173,100	$68,400	$30,500
Estimated percent uncollectible	0.1%	0.3%	5.0%	50.0%

Required

1. Record the transactions in the journal.

2. Open the Allowance for Uncollectible Accounts, and post entries affecting that account. Keep a running balance.

3. Most companies report two-year comparative financial statements. If Bernard Rubber Products' Accounts Receivable balance was $565,000 and the

Allowance for Uncollectible Accounts stood at $18,000 at December 31, 2003, show how the company will report its accounts receivable in a comparative balance sheet for 2004 and 2003.

Problem 9-4B *Using the percent-of-sales and aging-of-accounts approaches for uncollectibles (Obj. 2, 6)*

Link Back to Chapter 4 (Closing Entries). Baton Co. completed the following transactions during 2004 and 2005:

2004
Dec. 31 Estimated that uncollectible-account expense for the year was 2 percent of credit sales of $700,000 and recorded that amount as expense.
31 Made the closing entry for uncollectible-account expense.

2005
Mar. 26 Sold inventory to Mabel Arnold, $11,250, on credit terms of 2/10 n/30. Ignore cost of goods sold.
Sept. 15 Wrote off Mabel Arnold's account as uncollectible after repeated efforts to collect from her.
Nov. 10 Received $3,000 from Mabel Arnold, along with a letter stating her intention to pay her debt in full within 30 days. Reinstated her account in full.
Dec. 5 Received the balance due from Mabel Arnold.
31 Made a compound entry to write off the following accounts as uncollectible: Curt Major, $4,000; Bernadette Lalonde, $1,750; Ellen Smart, $2,670.
31 Estimated that uncollectible-account expense for the year was 1 percent on credit sales of $890,000 and recorded the expense.
31 Made the closing entry for uncollectible-account expense.

Required

1. Open general ledger accounts for Allowance for Uncollectible Accounts and Uncollectible-Account Expense. Keep running balances.

2. Record the transactions in the general journal and post to the two ledger accounts.

3. The December 31, 2004, balance of Accounts Receivable is $265,000. Show how Accounts Receivable would be reported at that date.

4. Assume that Baton Co. begins aging accounts receivable on December 31, 2005. The balance in Accounts Receivable is $265,000, the credit balance in Allowance for Uncollectible Accounts is $14,480 (use your calculations from Requirement #3), and the company estimates that $18,000 of its accounts receivable will prove uncollectible.
   a. Make the adjusting entry for uncollectibles.
   b. Show how Accounts Receivable will be reported on the December 31, 2005, balance sheet after this adjusting entry.

Problem 9-5B *Accounting for notes receivable, including accruing interest revenue (Obj. 5)*

A company received the following notes during 2004:

Note	Date	Principal Amount	Interest Rate	Term
(a)	September 30	$ 9,000	4%	3 months
(b)	November 19	12,000	3%	60 days
(c)	December 1	15,000	5%	1 year
(d)	December 15	20,000	6%	2 years

Required

Identify each note by letter, compute interest using a 365-day year for all notes, round all interest amounts to the nearest cent, and present entries in general journal form. Explanations are not required.

1. Determine the due date and maturity value of each note.
2. Journalize a single adjusting entry at December 31, 2004, to record accrued interest revenue on the notes.
3. Journalize the collection of principal and interest on note (b).
4. Show how these notes will be reported on December 31, 2004.

Problem 9-6B *Accounting for credit-card sales, notes receivable, dishonoured notes, and accrued interest revenue* **(Obj. 4, 5)**

Record the following selected transactions in the general ledger of Thompson Paper Products. Explanations are not required.

2004
Nov. 21 Received a $7,000, 60-day, 4 percent note from Mary Fisher on account.
      30 Recorded VISA credit card sales of $10,000. VISA charges 2.5 percent of sales.
Dec. 31 Made an adjusting entry to accrue interest on the Mary Fisher note.
      31 Made an adjusting entry to record uncollectible-account expense based on 2 percent of credit sales of $750,000.
      31 Made a compound closing entry for interest revenue and uncollectible-account expense (ignore credit-card sales and charges).

2005
Jan. 20 Collected the maturity value of the Mary Fisher note.
Mar. 14 Lent $4,000 cash to Morgan Supplies, receiving a six-month, 5 percent note.
      30 Received a $2,135, 30-day, 10 percent note from Marv Leech on his past-due account receivable.
May 29 Marv Leech dishonoured (failed to pay) his note at maturity; wrote off the account as uncollectible.
Sept. 14 Collected the maturity value of the Morgan Supplies note.
      30 Wrote off as uncollectible the accounts receivable of Sue Parsons, $1,250 and Mac Gally, $1,995.

Problem 9-7B *Journalizing uncollectible notes receivable and accrued interest revenue* **(Obj. 4, 5)**

Assume that MacMillan Tire, a large tire distributor, completed the following selected transactions:

2005
Dec. 1 Sold tires to Select Movers Inc., receiving a $25,000, six-month, 5 percent note. Ignore cost of goods sold.
      31 Made an adjusting entry to accrue interest on the Select Movers note.
      31 Made an adjusting entry to record uncollectible-account expense based on an aging of accounts receivable. The aging analysis indicates that $35,100 of accounts receivable will not be collected. Prior to this adjustment, the credit balance in Allowance for Uncollectible Accounts is $29,570.

2006
June 1 Collected the maturity value of the Select Movers note.
      30 Sold tires for $10,000 on MasterCard. MasterCard charges 1.75 percent.
July 21 Sold merchandise to Marco Donolo, receiving a 45-day, 3 percent note for $7,000. Ignore cost of goods sold.
Sept. 4 Marco Donolo dishonoured (failed to pay) its note at maturity; converted the maturity value of the note to an account receivable.
Nov. 11 Sold merchandise to Solomon Tractor for $6,000, receiving a 120-day, 5 percent note. Ignore cost of goods sold.
Dec. 2 Collected in full from Marco Donolo.
      31 Accrued the interest on the Solomon Tractor note.

Required

Record the transactions in the journal. Explanations are not required. Round interest amounts to the nearest cent.

**Media Companion
CD-ROM**

Problem 9-8B   *Using ratio data to evaluate a company's financial position* **(Obj. 7)**

Link Back to Chapter 4 (Current Ratio). The comparative financial statements of Albania Company for 2005, 2004, and 2003 included the following selected data:

	2005	2004	2003
	(In millions)		
Balance Sheet			
Current assets:			
Cash	$ 91	$ 27	$ 23
Short-term investments	77	106	72
Receivables, net of allowance for uncollectible accounts of $8, $7, and $5	153	172	133
Inventories	428	402	358
Prepaid expenses	34	33	26
Total current assets	783	740	612
Total current liabilities	494	506	435
Income Statement			
Sales revenue	$2,805	$2,630	$2,041
Cost of sales	1,449	1,428	1,011

Required

1. Compute these ratios for 2005 and 2004:
   a. Current ratio
   b. Acid-test ratio
   c. Days' sales in receivables

2. Write a memo explaining to Tony Albania, owner of Albania Company, which ratio values showed improvement from 2004 to 2005 and which ratio values deteriorated. Which item in the financial statements caused some ratio values to improve and others to deteriorate? Discuss whether this factor conveys a favourable or unfavourable sign about the company.

Problem 9-9B   *Using the allowance method of accounting for uncollectibles, estimating uncollectibles using the aging-of-accounts method, and reporting receivables on the balance sheet* **(Obj. 2, 6)**

Sally's Secretarial Services started business on January 1, 2004. The company produced monthly financial statements and had total sales of $125,000 (of which $100,000 was on credit) during the first four months.

On April 30, the Accounts Receivable account had a balance of $59,100 (no accounts have been written off to date), which was made up of the following accounts aged as to the date of the sale:

Customer:	January	February	March	April
		Month of Sale:		
Arthur Mason	$ 900	$ 250	$ 500	$ 450
Kelly Radisson	250	300	850	600
Parsons Personnel	1,250	3,500	2,000	1,000
Nixon & Nixon	500	1,850	2,030	7,100
Other Accounts Receivable	5,940	4,090	13,370	12,370
	$8,840	$9,990	$18,750	$21,520

The following accounts receivable transactions took place in May 2004:

May 12 Decided the Kelly Radisson account was uncollectible and wrote it off.
   15 Collected $1,650 from Arthur Mason for sales made in the first three months.
   21 Decided the Parsons Personnel account was uncollectible and wrote it off.
   24 Collected $500 from Nixon & Nixon for sales made in the month of January.
   26 Received a cheque from Parsons Personnel for $4,550 plus four cheques of $800 each, post-dated to June 26, July 26, August 26, and September 26.
   31 Total sales in the month were $95,000; 90 percent of these were on credit, and 75 percent of the credit sales were collected in the month.

Required

1. Sally's Secretarial Services has heard that other companies in the industry use the allowance method of accounting for uncollectibles, with many of these estimating the uncollectibles through an aging of accounts receivable. Journalize the adjustments that would have to be made on April 30 (for the months of January through April) as well as the transactions of May 2004, and the month-end adjustment, assuming the following estimates of uncollectibles:

Age of Accounts Receivable:	Percent Estimated to be Uncollectible:
From current month's sales	3%
From prior month's sales	5%
From two months prior	7%
From three months prior	20%
From four months prior	45%

(Round your total estimate to the nearest whole dollar.)

2. For the method of accounting for the uncollectibles used above, show
   a. The balance sheet presentation of the accounts receivable.
   b. The overall effect of the credit sales and uncollectibles on the income statement for the month of May 2004.

Problem 9-10B *Using the allowance method of accounting for uncollectibles, estimating uncollectibles by the percent-of-sales and the aging-of-accounts methods, and accounting for notes receivable* **(Obj. 2, 5)**

Maritime Ltd. uses the allowance method in accounting for uncollectible accounts with the estimate based on the aging-of-accounts method. The company had the following account balances on August 31, 2005:

Accounts Receivable	$572,500
Allowance for Uncollectible Accounts (credit balance)	60,500

The following transactions took place during September 2005:

Sept. 2 Elbow Inc., which owes $40,000, is unable to pay on time and has given a 25-day, 8 percent note in settlement of the account.
   6 Determined the account receivable from Irma Good ($10,500) was uncollectible and wrote it off.
   9 Received notice that a customer (Tony Goad) has filed for bankruptcy. Goad owes $16,000 to Maritime Ltd.
   11 Determined the account receivable from Kay Walsh ($7,600) was uncollectible and wrote it off.
   15 Irma Good, whose account was written off on September 6, has paid $7,500 on the account and promises to pay the balance in 30 days.
   18 Received a cheque from the courts in the amount of $12,500 as final settlement of Tony Goad's account.
   27 Elbow Inc. paid the note received on September 2.
   27 Determined the account receivable for Dave Campbell ($4,200) was uncollectible and wrote it off.
   30 Sales for the month totalled $600,000 (of which 85 percent were on credit) and collections on account totalled $501,000.

Sept. 30   Maritime Ltd. did an aging of accounts receivable that indicated that $62,500 is expected to be uncollectible. The company recorded the appropriate adjustment.

Required

1. Record the above transactions in the general journal.

2. What would be the adjusting entry required on September 30 if the company used the percent-of-sales method with an estimate of uncollectibles equal to 8 percent of credit sales?

3. Which of the two methods of estimating uncollectible accounts would normally be more accurate? Why?

Challenge Problems

Problem 9-1C   *Understanding accounts receivable management*   *(Obj. 1, 2)*

DIY Builders Supply is a six-store chain of retail stores selling home renovation materials and supplies mainly on credit; the company has its own credit card and does not accept other cards. DIY Builders Supply had a tendency to institute policies that conflicted with each other. Management rarely became aware of these conflicts until they became serious.

Recently, the owner, Angela Kim, who has been reading all the latest management texts, has instituted a new bonus plan. All managers are to be paid bonuses based on the success of their department. For example, for George Tatulis, the sales manager, his bonus is based on how much he can increase sales. For Sonia Petrov, the credit manager, her bonus is based on reducing the uncollectible-account expense.

Required

Describe the conflict that the bonus plan has created for the sales manager and the credit manager. How might the conflict be resolved?

Problem 9-2C   *Explaining days' sales in accounts receivable*   *(Obj. 2)*

Days' sales in receivables is a good measure of a company's ability to collect the amounts owing to it. You have owned shares in Locking Office Equipment Ltd. for some years and follow the company's progress by reading the annual report. You noticed the most recent report indicated that the days' sales in receivables had increased over the previous year, and you are concerned.

Required

Suggest reasons that may have resulted in the increase in the number of days' sales in receivables.

Extending Your Knowledge

Decision Problems

1   ***Comparing allowance and direct write-off methods for uncollectibles***
   (Obj. 2, 3)

Otto Jacina Advertising has always used the direct write-off method to account for uncollectibles. The company's revenues, bad-debt write-offs, and year-end receivables for the most recent year follow.

Year	Revenues	Write-Offs	Receivables at Year End
2006	$170,000	$3,000	$40,000

Otto Jacina is applying for a bank loan, and the loan officer requires figures based on the allowance method of accounting for bad debts. Jacina estimates that bad debts run about 4 percent of revenues each year.

Required

Otto Jacina must give the banker the following information:

1. How much more or less would net income be for 2006 if Jacina were to use the allowance method for bad debts?
2. How much of the receivables balance at the end of 2006 does Jacina expect to collect?

Compute these amounts, and then explain for Otto Jacina why net income is more or less for 2006 using the allowance method versus the direct write-off method for uncollectibles.

2 Uncollectible accounts and evaluating a business (Obj. 2, 3)

Garneau Camping Products sells its products either for cash or on notes receivable that earn interest. The business uses the direct write-off method to account for uncollectible accounts. Rae Garneau, the owner, has prepared Garneau Camping Products' financial statements. The most recent comparative income statements, for 2006 and 2005, are as follows:

	2006	2005
Total revenue	$440,000	$390,000
Total expenses	235,500	210,000
Net income	$204,500	$180,000

Based on the increase in net income, Garneau seeks to expand her operations. She asks you to invest $50,000 in the business. You and Garneau have several meetings, at which you learn that notes receivable from customers were $100,000 at the end of 2004, and $450,000 at the end of 2005. Also, total revenues for 2006 and 2005 include interest at 12 percent on the year's beginning notes receivable balance. Total expenses include doubtful-account expense of $6,000 each year, based on the direct write-off basis. Garneau estimates that doubtful-account expense would be 4 percent of sales revenue if the allowance method were used.

Required

1. Prepare for Garneau Camping Products a comparative single-step income statement that identifies sales revenue, interest revenue, uncollectible-account expense, and other expenses, all computed in accordance with generally accepted accounting principles.
2. Is Garneau Camping Products' future as promising as Garneau's income statement makes it appear? Give the reason for your answer.

Financial Statement Problem

Accounts receivable and related uncollectibles (Obj. 2, 7)

Answer the following questions using the financial statements for Intrawest Corporation in Appendix A.

1. Analyze the Amounts Receivable account at June 30, 2003. What is the total receivable? How much of Intrawest Corporation's Amounts Receivable are due in the year ended June 30, 2004? In the year 2005?

2. How many days' sales are in Amounts Receivable from Ski and Resort Operations at June 30, 2003? How many days' sales are in Amounts Receivable from Sales of Real Estate at June 30, 2003? Why do you think the two numbers are different?

3. Certain amounts receivable have been pledged as security for borrowings. What was the average interest rate Intrawest paid on those borrowings?

4. Have either of the two categories of receivables discussed in question 2 increased from 2002 to 2003? Has either decreased from 2002 to 2003?

5. Compute Intrawest Corporation's acid-test ratio at June 30, 2003 and June 30, 2002. Has it improved or worsened?

Appendix

Discounting (Selling) a Note Receivable

A payee of a note receivable may need cash before the maturity date of the note. When this occurs, the payee may sell the note, a practice called **discounting a note receivable**. The price to be received for the note is determined by present-value concepts. We discuss these concepts in detail in Chapter 15. But the transaction between the seller and the buyer of the note can take any form agreeable to the two parties. Here we illustrate one procedure used for discounting short-term notes receivable. To receive cash immediately, the seller is willing to accept a lower price than the note's maturity value.

To illustrate discounting a note receivable, suppose EMCO Ltd. lent $15,000 to Dartmouth Builders on October 20, 2005. The maturity date of the 90-day, 10 percent Dartmouth note is January 18, 2006. Suppose EMCO discounts the Dartmouth Builders note at the National Bank on December 9, 2005, when the note is 50 days old. The bank applies a 12 percent annual interest rate in computing the discounted value of the note. The bank will use a discount rate that is higher than the interest rate on the note in order to earn some interest on the transaction. EMCO may be willing to accept this higher rate in order to get cash quickly. The discounted value, called the *proceeds*, is the amount EMCO receives from the bank. The proceeds can be computed in five steps, as shown in Exhibit 9-1A. At maturity the bank collects $15,370 from the maker of the note and earns $202 interest revenue from holding the note.

EMCO Ltd.'s entry to record discounting (selling) the note on December 9, 2005, is

Dec. 9, 2005	Cash	15,168	
	Note Receivable		
	— Dartmouth Builders.........................		15,000
	Interest Revenue		168
	To record discounting a note receivable.		

When the proceeds from discounting a note receivable are less than the principal amount of the note, the payee records a debit to Interest Expense for the amount of the difference. For example, EMCO could discount the note receivable for cash proceeds of $14,980. The entry to record this transaction is

Dec. 9, 2005	Cash...	14,980	
	Interest Expense...	20	
	Note Receivable—Dartmouth Builders ..		15,000

Step	Computation	
1. Compute the original amount of interest of the note receivable.	$15,000 x 0.10 x 90/365	= $ 370
2. Maturity value of note = principal + interest	$15,000 + $370	= $15,370
3. Determine the period (number of days, months, or years) the bank will hold the note (the discount period).	Dec. 9, 2005, to Jan. 18, 2006	= 40 days
4. Compute the bank's discount on the note. This is the bank's interest revenue from holding the note.	$15,370 x 0.12 x 40/365	= $ 202
5. Seller's proceeds from discounting the note receivable* = maturity value of note – bank's discount on the note	$15,370 – $202	= $15,168

*(Buyer's cost of purchasing)

The authors thank Doug Hamilton for suggesting this exhibit.

In the discounting of the note receivable just described, interest revenue accrued from the original date of the note (October 20, 2005) to the date of discounting (December 9, 2005). Since the amount is not material, we will recognize this fact but disregard the interest revenue in the rest of this Appendix.

STOP & THINK

If a 60-day note dated April 16 is discounted on May 2, what is the discount period?

Answer: 44 days. Method: Compute the number of days the note was held prior to discounting (April 16 to May 2 is 16 days). Subtract the days held from the length of the note (60 − 16 − 44). This method eliminates the necessity of determining the maturity date and then having to count from the discount date to the maturity date.

Appendix Exercises

Exercise 9-1A   Nortel Networks Corporation (www.nortelnetworks.com) installs switching systems and receives its pay in the form of notes receivable. Nortel installed a system for the city of Brandon, Manitoba, receiving a nine-month, 10 percent, $800,000 note receivable on May 31, 2006. To obtain cash quickly, Nortel discounted the note with HSBC on June 30, 2006. The bank charged a discount rate of 11 percent.

Compute Nortel Networks' cash proceeds from discounting the note. Follow the five-step procedure outlined in Exhibit 9-1A, above. Round to the nearest dollar.

Exercise 9-2A   *Link Back to Chapter 5 (Recording a Sale).* Use your answers to Exercise 9-1A to journalize Nortel Networks' transactions as follows:

May	31	Sold a telecommunications system, receiving a 9-month, 10 percent, $800,000 note from the city of Brandon. Nortel Networks' cost of the system was $525,000.
June	30	Received cash for interest revenue for one month.
	30	Discounted the note to HSBC at a discount rate of 11 percent.

Exercise 9-3A   Gander Outdoors Store sells on account. When a customer account becomes three months old, Gander Outdoors Store converts the account to a note receivable and immediately discounts the note to a bank. During 2006, Gander Outdoors Store completed these transactions:

May   29   Sold goods on account to Raj Sivakumar, $2,400.
Sept.   1   Received a $2,000, 60-day, 8 percent note and cash of $400 from Raj Sivakumar in satisfaction of his past-due account receivable.
      1   Sold the Sivakumar note by discounting it to a bank for proceeds of $1,860.

Required

Record the transactions in Gander Outdoors Store's journal.

Appendix Problems

Problem 9-1A   A company received the following notes during 2006. The notes were discounted on the dates and at the rates indicated.

Note	Date	Principal Amount	Interest Rate	Term	Date Discounted	Discount Rate
(a)	June 15	$20,000	8%	3 months	July 15	12%
(b)	Aug. 1	9,000	10%	90 days	Aug. 27	12%
(c)	Nov. 21	12,000	15%	90 days	Dec. 4	15%

Required

Identify each note by letter, compute interest using a 365-day year for all notes, round all interest amounts to the nearest cent, and present entries in general journal form. Explanations are not required.

1. Determine the due date and maturity value of each note.
2. Determine the discount and proceeds from the sale (discounting) of each note.
3. Journalize the discounting of notes (a) and (b).

Problem 9-2A   A company received the following notes during 2005. The notes were discounted on the dates and at the rates indicated.

Note	Date	Principal Amount	Interest Rate	Term	Date Discounted	Discount Rate
(a)	Aug. 18	$10,000	11%	6 months	Nov. 18	13%
(b)	July 15	9,000	10%	90 days	July 26	12%
(c)	Sept. 1	8,000	10%	180 days	Nov. 2	13%

Required

Identify each note by letter, compute interest using a 365-day year for each note, round all interest amounts to the nearest cent, and present entries in general journal form. Explanations are not required.

1. Determine the due date and maturity value of each note.
2. Determine the discount and proceeds from the sale (discounting) of each note.
3. Journalize the discounting of notes (a) and (b).

CHAPTER

10

Capital Assets and Intangibles

CHAPTER OBJECTIVES

After studying this chapter, you should be able to

1   Measure the cost of a capital asset

2   Account for amortization

3   Explain capital cost allowance and amortization for income tax purposes

4   Account for the disposal of a capital asset

5   Account for wasting assets

6   Account for intangible assets

 Media Companion CD-ROM

Visit the Media Companion CD-ROM that comes with this book for extra practice with the new material in Chapter 10.

Have you ever taken a flight on a commercial airline—Air Canada, WestJet, or CanJet? These companies have some of the most interesting assets in the world—airplanes.

How long can a commercial airplane keep flying safely and efficiently? Air Canada uses each of its planes for around 20 years. The airlines like to use a Boeing 737 for a long time because that delays spending cash to buy new planes. Top managers of the airlines try to strike a balance between getting the most use from a plane and using one that consumes less fuel.

How do the airlines account for the use of an airplane? They record amortization over the plane's useful life. Managers also have to consider how much they can sell a plane for when it's taken out of service. The airlines don't amortize this residual value because they get it back when they sell a plane.

This chapter covers these and other matters about capital assets. **Capital assets** are the long-term tangible assets that a business uses to operate, such as airplanes for WestJet, copy equipment for Kinko's and automobiles for Discount Car Rental. The chapter also shows how to account for natural resources such as oil and timber, and **intangibles**, those assets with no physical form, such as trademarks and copyrights.

CHAPTER 10 concludes our coverage of assets, except for long-term investments. After completing this chapter, you should understand the various assets of a business and how to account for them. Let's begin with an example that is familiar to you.

You may have an automobile—a Chevy or a Honda. Your car is a capital asset if you use it for day-to-day operations. But if you bought the car to resell it, it would be part of your inventory. If your car was bought for regular use, as it wears out, it declines in usefulness. You should record amortization on all the capital assets used in a business, except for land.

Capital assets have their own terminology. Exhibit 10-1 shows which expense account applies to each category of capital asset.

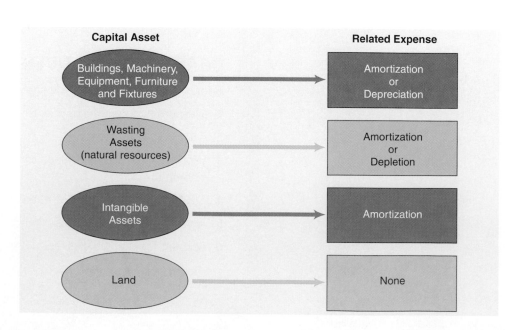

Measuring the Cost of Capital Assets (Property, Plant, and Equipment)

OBJECTIVE 1
Measure the cost of a capital asset

The *cost principle* directs a business to carry an asset on the balance sheet at its cost—the amount paid for the asset. The general rule for measuring cost (repeated from Chapter 6) is

The cost of an asset	=	The sum of all the costs incurred to bring the asset to its intended purpose, net of all discounts

The *cost of a capital asset,* such as *property, plant, and equipment,* is the purchase price, taxes, purchase commissions, and all other costs incurred to acquire the asset and to ready it for its intended use. In Chapter 6, we applied this principle to determine the cost of inventory. The types of cost differ for the various capital assets, so we discuss each asset individually.

KEY POINT

Long-lived assets are classified as capital assets. They are often called long-term assets; property, plant, and equipment; or fixed assets.

KEY POINT

Land is not amortized because it does not wear out as do buildings and equipment.

LEARNING TIP

The cost of an asset includes all costs necessary to ready the asset for its intended use; "cost" will even include amounts not yet paid in cash, such as a note payable on the asset.

Land and Land Improvements

The cost of land includes its purchase price, brokerage commission, survey and legal fees, and any property taxes in arrears. Land cost also includes the cost for grading and clearing the land, and for demolishing or removing any unwanted buildings. The cost of land is not amortized.

The cost of land does *not* include the cost of fencing, paving, sprinkler systems, and lighting. These separate capital assets—called *land improvements*—are subject to amortization.

Suppose the Potash Corporation of Saskatchewan Inc. (PotashCorp) (www.potashcorp.com) signs a $300,000 note payable to purchase 100 hectares of land. The company also pays $10,000 in brokerage commission, $8,000 in transfer taxes, $5,000 for removal of an old building, and a $1,000 survey fee. What is the cost of this land? Exhibit 10-2 shows that all the costs incurred to bring the land to its intended use are part of the land's cost.

PotashCorp's entry to record the purchase of the land follows:

Land	324,000	
Note Payable		300,000
Cash		24,000

We would say that PotashCorp *capitalized* the cost of the land at $324,000. This means that the company debited an asset account (Land) for $324,000.

Suppose PotashCorp also spent $26,000 for the construction of fences around the land. The entry to record the expenditure follows:

Land Improvements	26,000	
Cash		26,000

Note that the cost for the construction of fences, $26,000, is *not* included in the Land account. The fences are a land improvement and their cost will be amortized over the useful life of the fences.

Purchase price of land		$300,000
Add related costs:		
Brokerage commission	$10,000	
Transfer taxes	8,000	
Removal of building	5,000	
Survey fee	1,000	
Total incidental costs		24,000
Total cost of land		$324,000

EXHIBIT 10-2

Measuring the Cost of a Capital Asset

Land and Land Improvements are two entirely separate asset accounts. Land improvements include lighting, signs, fences, paving, sprinkler systems, and landscaping. These costs are debited to the Land Improvements account and then amortized over their useful lives.

Buildings

The cost of constructing a building includes architectural fees, building permits, contractors' charges, and payments for materials, labour, and overhead. The time to complete a new building can be many months, even years, and the number of separate expenditures can be numerous. If the company constructs its own assets, the cost of the building may include the cost of interest on money borrowed to finance the construction. When an existing building is purchased, its cost includes all the usual items (but not GST), plus all the costs to repair and renovate the building for its intended use.

····················

······ **THINKING IT OVER**

Which of the following would you include in the cost of machinery: (1) installation charges; (2) testing of the machine; (3) repair to machinery necessitated by installer's error; (4) first-year maintenance cost?

A: Include 1 and 2, but not 3 or 4.

Machinery and Equipment

The cost of machinery and equipment includes its purchase price (less any discounts), plus transportation charges, insurance while in transit, provincial sales tax (PST), purchase commission, installation costs, and the cost of testing the asset before it is used. After the asset is set up, we cease capitalizing these costs to the Machinery and Equipment account. Thereafter, insurance, taxes, and maintenance costs are recorded as expenses. WestJet has an account for baggage-handling equipment, Kinko's for copy equipment, and Purolator for delivery trucks.

The goods and services tax (GST) paid on the purchase of an asset is recoverable if the acquired asset is used to earn income. Therefore, it would not be part of the capitalized cost of the asset. For example, a computer purchased for $2,000 in Ontario would incur PST of 8 percent ($160.00) and GST of 7% ($140.00) for a total cost of $2,300.00. Assuming the computer was to be used to earn revenue, the cost of the asset would be $2,160.00, not $2,300.00, since the GST would be recovered from Canada Customs and Revenue Agency (CCRA).

Furniture and Fixtures

Furniture and fixtures include desks, chairs, filing cabinets, and display racks. The cost of furniture and fixtures includes the basic cost of the asset (less any discounts), plus all other costs to get the asset ready for use. As was indicated above for machinery and equipment, GST is recoverable from CCRA. All companies have furniture and fixtures, but they are most important to service organizations and retail businesses.

Leasehold Improvements

Leasehold improvements are similar to land improvements. *Leasehold improvements* are alterations to assets the company is leasing. For example, IPSCO Inc., the Saskatchewan steel producer (www.ipsco.com), leases some of its vehicles. The company also customizes some of these assets to meet its special needs. For example, IPSCO Inc. may paint its logo on a rental truck and install a special lift on the truck. These improvements are assets of IPSCO Inc. even though the company does not own the truck. The cost of improvements to leased assets appears on the company's balance sheet as *leasehold improvements*. The cost of leasehold improvements should be amortized over the term of the lease or the useful life of the leased asset, whichever is shorter.

Construction in Progress and Capital Leases

If you were to look at IPSCO Inc.'s financial statements, you would notice two additional categories of capital assets: Construction in progress and Capital leases.

Construction in Progress *Construction in progress* is an asset, such as a warehouse, that the company is constructing for its own use. On the balance sheet date, December 31, 2002, the construction is incomplete and the building is not ready for use. However, the construction costs are assets because IPSCO Inc. expects the building, when completed, to render future benefits for the company.

Capital Leases A *capital lease* is an arrangement where a capital asset is acquired by making regular periodic payments that are required by the lease contract. Companies report assets leased through capital leases on the balance sheet the same way as purchased assets. Why? Because their lease payments secure the use of the asset over the term of the lease. For example, WestJet has long-term capital leases running until 2006.

A capital lease is different from an *operating lease*, which is an ordinary rental agreement, such as an apartment lease or the rental of a Budget automobile or a photocopier. The lessee (the renter) records operating lease payments as Rent expense.

Capitalizing the Cost of Interest

IPSCO Inc. constructs some of its capital assets itself and contracts with others to construct other capital assets. Often the construction is financed with borrowed money, on which IPSCO Inc. must pay interest. The *CICA Handbook* Section 3060, "Capital Assets," permits a company to include interest costs up to the date the asset goes into service as part of the cost of the asset. The practice of including interest as part of an asset's cost is called *capitalizing interest*. To **capitalize a cost** means to debit an asset (versus an expense) account.

Capitalizing interest cost is an exception to the normal practice of recording interest as an expense. Ordinarily, a company that borrows money records interest expense. But on assets that the business builds for its own use, or has built, the company should, if it chooses, capitalize some of its interest cost. The reason is this: Suppose IPSCO Inc. contracts Argo Construction Co. to build a building for it. The price of the building will include Argo's interest cost that was incurred to finance the construction. Since self-constructed assets and assets that are paid for during construction should be treated as equivalent assets, it makes sense to capitalize any interest incurred to finance the construction.

The amount of interest to capitalize is based on the average accumulated construction expenditures for the asset. The interest capitalized should not exceed the company's actual interest cost.

A Lump-Sum (or Basket) Purchase of Assets

A company may purchase several assets as a group—in a "basket purchase"—for a single price. For example, Halifax–Dartmouth Bridge Commission may pay one price for land and an office building. But for accounting purposes, Halifax–Dartmouth Bridge Commission must identify the cost of each asset as shown in the diagram at right. The total cost (100%) is divided among the assets according to their relative sales values. This allocation technique is called the *relative-sales-value method*.

Suppose High Liner Foods Incorporated (www.highlinerfoods.com), the seafood and pasta company located in Nova Scotia, purchases land and a building in Lunenberg for administrative purposes. The combined purchase price of

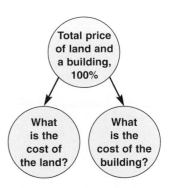

the land and building is $280,000. An appraisal indicates that the land's market (sales) value is $30,000 and the building's market (sales) value is $270,000.

First, calculate the ratio of each asset's market value to the total market value of both assets combined. Total appraised value is $30,000 + $270,000 = $300,000. Thus, the land, valued at $30,000, is 10 percent of the total market value. The building's appraised value is 90 percent of the total. The cost of each asset is determined as follows:

Asset	Market (Sales) Value	Percentage of Total Value		Total Purchase Price		Cost of Each Asset
Land	$ 30,000	$ 30,000 ÷ $300,000 = 10%	×	$280,000	=	$ 28,000
Building	$270,000	$270,000 ÷ $300,000 = 90%	×	$280,000	=	$252,000
Total	$300,000					$280,000

Suppose High Liner pays cash. The entry to record the purchase of the land and building is

Land	28,000	
Building	252,000	
Cash		280,000

STOP & THINK

How would Tim Hortons divide a $120,000 lump-sum purchase price for land, building, and equipment with estimated market values of $40,000, $95,000, and $15,000, respectively? Round decimals to three places.

Answer:

Asset	Market (Sales) Value	Percentage of Total Value		Total Purchase Price		Cost of Each Asset
Land.....................	$ 40,000	$40,000/$150,000 =	26.7% ×	$120,000	=	$ 32,040
Building..............	95,000	$95,000/$150,000 =	63.3% ×	120,000	=	75,960
Equipment	15,000	$15,000/$150,000 =	10.0% ×	120,000	=	12,000
Total	$150,000		100.0%			$120,000

Betterments versus Repairs

When a company spends money on a capital asset it already owns, it must decide whether to debit an asset account or an expense account. Examples of these expenditures range from replacing the windshield on an Airways Limo Co. automobile in Toronto to adding a wing to a building at Big Rock Brewery in Alberta.

Expenditures that increase the capacity or efficiency of the asset or extend its useful life are called **betterments**. For example, the cost of a major overhaul that extends an Airways Limo automobile's useful life is a betterment. The amount of the expenditure, said to be *capitalized*, for a betterment is a debit to an asset account. For the cost of a betterment on the automobile, we would debit the asset account Automobile.

Other expenditures do not extend the asset's capacity or efficiency but merely maintain the asset in working order. These costs are called **repairs** and are matched against revenue. Examples include the following costs incurred after a period of use: repainting a Big Rock Brewery truck, repairing a dented fender, and replacing tires. These costs are debited to Repair Expense.

The distinction between betterments and repairs requires judgement. Does the

EXHIBIT 10-3

Delivery Truck
Expenditures—Betterment or
Repair?

Betterment: Debit an Asset Account	Repair: Debit Repair and Maintenance Expense

Betterments
     Major engine overhaul
     Modification of truck for new use
     Addition to storage capacity of
       truck
	Repairs
	     Repair of transmission or other
	       mechanism
	     Oil change, lubrication, and so on
	     Replacement tires or windshield
	     Paint job

cost extend the life of the asset (a betterment), or does it only maintain the asset in good order (a repair)?

Exhibit 10-3 illustrates the distinction between betterments (capital expenditures) and repairs (expenses) for several delivery truck expenditures.

Treating a betterment as a repair, or vice versa, creates an accounting error. Suppose a company incurs the cost of a betterment to enhance the service potential of equipment and expenses this cost. This is an accounting error because the cost should have been debited to an asset account. This error overstates expenses and understates net income. On the balance sheet, the equipment account is understated. Capitalizing an expense creates the opposite error. Expenses are understated and net income is overstated. And the balance sheet overstates assets.

Measuring Capital Asset Amortization

As we have seen previously, **amortization** is the allocation of a capital asset's cost to expense over its useful life. The term is defined in Section 3060 of the *CICA Handbook*. Another term used to describe the allocation of the cost when referring to capital assets such as property, plant, and equipment is *depreciation*. Amortization matches the asset's cost (expense) against the revenue earned by the asset (see Chapter 3, page 111, for a discussion of the matching principle). Exhibit 10-4 shows this process for the purchase of a Boeing 757 jet by Air Canada. The primary purpose of amortization accounting is to measure income. Of less importance is the need to account for the asset's decline in usefulness.

Suppose Winpak Ltd. (www.winpak.com), the Winnipeg-based packaging company, buys a computer to use in its accounting system. Winpak believes it will get four years of service from the computer, which will then be worthless. Using straight-line amortization, Winpak expenses one-quarter of the asset's cost in each of its four years of use.

Let's contrast what amortization *is* with what it *is not*.

1. *Amortization is not a process of valuation.* Businesses do not record amortization based on the market (sales) value of their capital assets.

EXHIBIT 10-4

Amortization and the
Matching of Expense to
Revenue

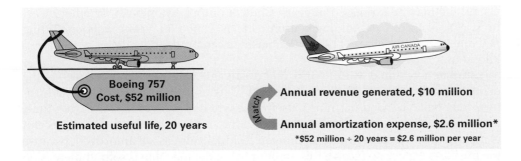

Boeing 757
Cost, $52 million

Estimated useful life, 20 years

Match

Annual revenue generated, $10 million

Annual amortization expense, $2.6 million*

*$52 million ÷ 20 years = $2.6 million per year

2. *Amortization does not mean that the business sets aside cash to replace assets as they become fully amortized.* Amortization has nothing to do with establishing a cash fund for the replacement of assets.

STOP & THINK

On January 1, 2004, Armstrong Marketing Co. purchased, for $15,000, equipment that had an expected 4-year life and $3,000 residual value. Through an accounting error, Armstrong expensed the entire cost of the equipment at the time of purchase. What is the effect (overstated, understated, or correctly stated) on (1) total assets, and (2) net income in 2004 to 2007?

Answer:

Total assets will be understated each year. Net income will be understated in 2004 by $15,000 and net income will be overstated each year by the amount of the amortization that should have been recorded [($15,000 − $3,000) ÷ 4] = $3,000.

	Total Assets	Net Income
2004	$12,000 U	$12,000 U
2005	$ 9,000 U	$ 3,000 O
2006	$ 6,000 U	$ 3,000 O
2007	$ 3,000 U	$ 3,000 O

Causes of Amortization

All assets except land wear out. For some capital assets, physical *wear and tear* creates the need to amortize their value. For example, physical deterioration wears out Intrawest's Bombardier snow-grooming machines and the golf carts on its golf courses. The same is true of Zellers' store fixtures.

Assets such as computers, software, and other electronic equipment, and airplanes may become *obsolete* before they wear out. An asset is obsolete when another asset can do the job more efficiently. Thus an asset's useful life may be shorter than its physical life. Accountants usually amortize computers over a short period of time—perhaps two to four years—even though they know the computers will remain in working condition much longer. In all cases, the asset's cost is amortized over its expected useful life.

Measuring Amortization

Amortization for a capital asset is based on three factors about the asset:

1. Cost
2. Estimated useful life
3. Estimated residual value

The asset's cost is known. The other two factors must be estimated.

Estimated useful life is the length of the service period expected from the asset. Useful life may be expressed in years, units of output, kilometres, or other measures. For example, a building's useful life is stated in years, a bookbinding machine's in the number of books the machine can bind, and a delivery truck's in kilometres.

Estimated residual value—also called **salvage value** or **scrap value**—is the expected cash value of the asset at the end of its useful life. For example, a business may believe that a machine's useful life will be seven years. After that time, the company expects to sell the machine as scrap metal. The expected cash receipt is the machine's residual value. Estimated residual value is *not* amortized, because the business expects to receive this amount when the machine is sold. If there is no residual value, then the company amortizes the full cost of the asset. Cost minus residual value is called **amortizable cost**.

Of the factors entering the computation of amortization, only one factor is known—cost. The other two factors—useful life and residual value—must be estimated. Amortization, then, is an estimated amount.

Amortization Methods

Three methods exist for computing amortization:

- straight-line
- units-of-production
- declining-balance

The declining-balance method is one of two *accelerated* amortization methods, so-called because they expense greater amounts of amortization near the start of a capital asset's life and lesser amounts towards the end. The other accelerated method is sum-of-the-year's digits; it is little used in Canada and will not be discussed in this text. The three methods listed allocate different amounts of amortization expense to each period, but they all result in the same total amortization over the life of the asset. Exhibit 10-5 presents the data we will use to illustrate amortization for a Canadian Tire delivery truck. We cover the three most widely used methods.

Straight-Line Method   The **straight-line method** allocates an equal amount of amortization to each year of asset use. Amortizable cost is divided by useful life in years to determine annual amortization. The equation for straight-line amortization, applied to the Canadian Tire delivery truck data from Exhibit 10-5, is

$$\text{Straight-line amortization} = \frac{\text{Cost} - \text{Residual value}}{\text{Useful life in years}}$$

$$= \frac{\$55,000 - \$5,000}{5}$$

$$= \$10,000 \text{ per year}$$

The entry to record each year's amortization is

Amortization Expense.............................. 10,000
    Accumulated Amortization.................   10,000

Assume that this truck was purchased on January 1, 2004, and the business's fiscal year ends on December 31. A *straight-line amortization schedule* is presented in Exhibit 10-6. The final column of Exhibit 10-6 shows the asset's *book value*, which is cost less accumulated amortization. We introduced book value in Chapter 3.

As an asset is used, accumulated amortization increases and the asset's book value decreases. See the Accumulated Amortization and the Asset Book Value columns in Exhibit 10-6. An asset's final book value is its *residual value* ($5,000 in Exhibit 10-6). At the end of its useful life, the asset is said to be *fully amortized*.

Data Item	Amount
Cost of truck	$55,000
Estimated residual value	5,000
Amortizable cost..	$50,000
Estimated useful life	
Years	5 years
Units of production.......................................	400,000 units (kilometres)

KEY POINT

The total amount of amortization recorded for an asset cannot exceed its amortizable cost. An asset can be used after it is fully amortized.

OBJECTIVE 2
Account for amortization

KEY POINT

It is impossible to quantify the exact amount of the useful life of an asset that has been used up during the period, but there is no doubt that a portion of the asset has been consumed. An estimate of the amount must be made using one of the amortization methods. Without this expense, there would be no *matching* of the cost of the asset with the revenues generated during the time the asset is used.

LEARNING TIP

The formula for the straight-line rate is: 1/useful life. If an asset has a 5-year useful life, then 1/5 of the asset is amortized each year. The straight-line rate is 1/5, or 20%.

EXHIBIT 10-5

Data for Recording Amortization for a Truck

Date	Asset Cost	Amortization Rate		Amortizable Cost		Amortization Amount	Accumulated Amortization	Asset Book Value
				Amortization for the Year				
1-1-2004	$55,000							$55,000
31-12-2004		0.20	×	$50,000	=	$10,000	$ 10,000	45,000
31-12-2005		0.20	×	50,000	=	10,000	20,000	35,000
31-12-2006		0.20	×	50,000	=	10,000	30,000	25,000
31-12-2007		0.20	×	50,000	=	10,000	40,000	15,000
31-12-2008		0.20	×	50,000	=	10,000	50,000	5,000

EXHIBIT 10-6

Straight-Line Amortization for a Truck

STOP & THINK

1. An asset that cost $10,000 and has a useful life of five years and a residual value of $2,000 was purchased on January 1. What was the straight-line amortization for the first year? For the second year? For the fifth year?

2. What are some advantages of using the straight-line method?

Answers:

1.

$$\text{Amortization} = \frac{\text{Cost} - \text{Residual value}}{\text{Useful life, in years}} = \frac{\$10,000 - \$2,000}{5 \text{ years}} = \frac{\$1,600 \text{ per year}}{\textit{every year}}$$

2. It is easy to calculate, and it smoothes net income over the life of the asset because amortization is constant from year to year.

Units-of-Production (UOP) Method The **units-of-production method** allocates a fixed amount of amortization to each unit of output produced by the asset. The equation for the units-of-production method, applied to the Exhibit 10-5 data, is

$$\begin{aligned}
\text{Units-of-production amortization per unit of output} &= \frac{\text{Cost} - \text{Residual Value}}{\text{Useful life, in units of production}} \\
&= \frac{\$55,000 - \$5,000}{400,000 \text{ kilometres}} \\
&= \$0.125 \text{ per kilometre}
\end{aligned}$$

Assume that this truck is likely driven 90,000 kilometres the first year, 120,000 the second, 100,000 the third, 60,000 the fourth, and 30,000 the fifth. The amount of units-of-production (UOP) amortization per period varies with the number of units the asset produces. Exhibit 10-7 shows the UOP schedule for this asset.

Double-Declining-Balance (DDB) Method The **double-declining-balance (DDB) method** involves computing annual amortization by multiplying the asset's book value by a constant percentage, which is two times the straight-line amortization rate. DDB rates are computed as follows:

1. Compute the straight-line amortization rate per year. For example, for a computer with an expected life of 5 years, the straight-line amortization rate is 100 percent divided by 5, or 20 percent per year. For an asset with an expected life of 10 years, such as a desk, the straight-line amortization rate is 100 percent divided by 10, or 10 percent per year, and so on.

2. Multiply the straight-line rate by 2. The DDB rate for a ten-year asset is 20 percent per year ([100% ÷ 10] × 2 = 20%). For a five-year asset like the truck in Exhibit 10-5, the double-declining-balance rate is 40 percent ([100% ÷ 5] × 2 = 40%).

Date	Asset Cost	Amortization for the Year				Accumulated Amortization	Asset Book Value
		Amortization Per Unit	Number of Units		Amortization Amount		
1-1-2004	$55,000						$55,000
31-12-2004		$0.125	×	90,000	= $11,250	$11,250	43,750
31-12-2005		0.125	×	120,000	= 15,000	26,250	28,750
31-12-2006		0.125	×	100,000	= 12,500	38,750	16,250
31-12-2007		0.125	×	60,000	= 7,500	46,250	8,750
31-12-2008		0.125	×	30,000	= 3,750	50,000	5,000

EXHIBIT 10-7

Units-of-Production Amortization for a Truck

3. Compute the year's DDB amortization. Multiply the asset's book value (cost less accumulated amortization) at the beginning of the year by the DDB rate. Ignore residual value except for the last year. The first year's amortization for the truck in Exhibit 10-5 is

Double-declining-balance amortization for the first year	=	Asset book value at the beginning of the period	×	Double-declining-balance rate
	=	$55,000	×	0.40
	=	$22,000		

The same approach is used to compute DDB amortization for all later years, except for the final year.

The final year's amortization is the amount needed to reduce the asset's book value to its residual value. In the DDB amortization schedule in Exhibit 10-8, the fifth and final year's amortization is $2,128—the $7,128 book value less the $5,000 residual value.

The DDB method differs from the other methods in two ways:

KEY POINT

With declining-balance amortization, the asset's book value will rarely equal its residual value in the final year. Amortization expense in the final year is a "plug" figure, the amount that will reduce the asset's book value to the residual value.

Date	Asset Cost	Double-Declining-Balance Rate		Asset Book Value		Amortization Amount	Accumulated Amortization	Asset Book Value
					Amortization for the Year			
1-1-2004	$55,000							$55,000
31-12-2004		0.40	×	$55,000	=	$22,000	$22,000	33,000
31-12-2005		0.40	×	33,000	=	13,200	35,200	19,800
31-12-2006		0.40	×	19,800	=	7,920	43,120	11,880
31-12-2007		0.40	×	11,880	=	4,752	47,872	7,128
31-12-2008						2,128*	50,000	5,000

* Amortization in year 2008 is the amount needed to reduce asset book value to the residual value ($7,128 – $5,000 = $2,128).

EXHIBIT 10-8

Double-Declining-Balance Amortization for a Truck

1. Residual value is ignored initially. In the first year, amortization is calculated on the asset's full cost.

2. Final-year amortization is the amount needed to bring the asset's book value to the residual value. It is a "plug" figure.

STOP & THINK

What is the DDB amortization for each year for the asset in the Stop & Think on page 492?

Answer:

DDB rate = $\frac{100}{5} \times 2 = 40\%$

Yr. 1: $4,000 ($10,000 × 40%)
Yr. 2: $2,400 [($10,000 – $4,000 = $6,000) × 40%]
Yr. 3: $1,440 [($6,000 – $2,400 = $3,600) × 40%]
Yr. 4: $160 ($3,600 – $1,440 – $2,000*)

*Asset cost is not amortized below residual value.

Comparing Amortization Methods

Let's compare the three methods we've just discussed. Annual amounts vary by method but the total is the same for all methods—$50,000.

Which method is best? That depends on the asset and the company's situation. A business should match an asset's expense against the revenue that asset generates.

Year	Straight-Line	Units-of-Production	Double-Declining-Balance
	Amount of Amortization per Year		
2004	$10,000	$11,250	$22,000
2005	10,000	15,000	13,200
2006	10,000	12,500	7,920
2007	10,000	7,500	4,752
2008	10,000	3,750	2,128
Total	$50,000	$50,000	$50,000

Exhibit 10-9

Amortization Patterns for the Various Methods

Straight-Line	Units-of-Production	Double-Declining-Balance
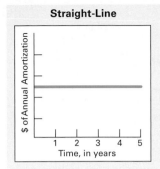	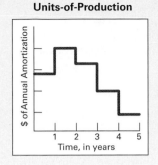	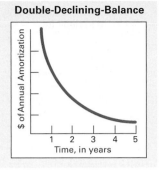

Straight-line method   For a capital asset that generates revenue fairly evenly over time, the straight-line method follows the matching principle. During each period the asset is used, an equal amount of amortization is recorded.

Units-of-production method   The units-of-production method best fits an asset that wears out because of physical use, rather than obsolescence. Amortization is recorded only when the asset is used, and more use leads to greater amortization.

Double-declining-balance method   The double-declining-balance or accelerated method works best for assets that produce more revenue in their early years. The greater expense recorded in the early periods matches best against those periods' greater revenue.

Comparisons   Exhibit 10-9 graphs the relationship between annual amortization amounts for the three methods.

- The graph of straight-line amortization is flat because annual amortization is the same amount in each period.

- Units-of-production amortization follows no particular pattern because annual amortization varies depending on the use of the asset.

- DDB amortization is greatest in the first year and less in the later years.

A recent survey indicated that over 93 percent of companies use the straight-line method, approximately 28 percent use an accelerated method, and approximately 21 percent use the units-of-production method. (Some companies use more than one method for different kinds of capital assets, so the total may exceed 100 percent.)[1] For example, ATCO Ltd., the conglomerate based in Calgary, uses straight-line, while WestJet uses straight-line for most capital assets and units of production for its aircraft.

WORKING IT OUT

Give the amortization method that is described by the following statements:

a. Amortization expense declines over the life of the asset
A: double-declining-balance

b. Book value declines over the life of the asset.
A: all methods

c. Amortization expense fluctuates with use.
A: units-of-production

d. Amortization expense is the same each period.
A: straight-line

e. This method best fits an asset that amortizes because of physical use.
A: units-of-production

f. This method best fits an asset that generates revenue evenly each period.
A: straight-line

g. This method is the most common.
A: straight-line

h. This method records the most amortization over the life of the asset.
A: all methods record the same amount of amortization

Mid-Chapter Summary Problem for Your Review

Cardozo Plastics purchased equipment on January 2, 2005, for $44,000. The expected life of the equipment is ten years or 100,000 units of production, and its residual value is $4,000. Under three amortization methods, the annual amortization expense and total accumulated amortization at the end of 2005 and 2006 are:

---

[1] Byrd, C., I. Chen, and H. Chapman, *Financial Reporting in Canada, 2002,* Twenty-seventh edition. (Toronto: Canadian Institute of Chartered Accountants, 2002), p. 275.

	Method A		Method B		Method C	
	Annual		*Annual*		*Annual*	
	Amortization	*Accumulated*	*Amortization*	*Accumulated*	*Amortization*	*Accumulated*
Year	*Expense*	*Amortization*	*Expense*	*Amortization*	*Expense*	*Amortization*
2005	$4,000	$4,000	$8,800	$ 8,800	$1,200	$1,200
2006	4,000	8,000	7,040	15,840	5,600	6,800

Required

1. Identify the amortization method used in each instance, and show the equation and computation for each. (Round off to the nearest dollar.)

2. Assume continued use of the same method through the year 2007. Determine the annual amortization expense, accumulated amortization, and book value of the equipment for 2005 through 2007 under each method, assuming 12,000 units of production in 2007.

Solution

Requirement 1

Method A: Straight-line method

Amortizable cost = $40,000 ($44,000 − $4,000)

Each year: $40,000 ÷ 10 years = $4,000

Method B: Double-declining-balance method

$$\text{Rate} = \frac{100\%}{10 \text{ years}} \times 2 = 10\% \times 2 = 20\%$$

2005: 0.20 × $44,000 = $8,800

2006: 0.20 × ($44,000 − $8,800) = $7,040

Method C: Units-of-production method

$$\text{Amortization per unit} = \frac{\$44,000 - \$4,000}{100,000 \text{ units}} = \$0.40$$

2005: $0.40 × 3,000 units = $1,200
(since $1,200 ÷ $0.40 = 3,000 units)

2006: $0.40 × 14,000 units = $5,600
(since $5,600 ÷ $0.40 = 14,000 units)

Requirement 2

	Method A Straight-Line			Method B Double-Declining-Balance			Method C Units-of-Production		
	Annual			*Annual*			*Annual*		
	Amortization	*Accumulated*	*Book*	*Amortization*	*Accumulated*	*Book*	*Amortization*	*Accumulated*	*Book*
Year	*Expense*	*Amortization*	*Value*	*Expense*	*Amortization*	*Value*	*Expense*	*Amortization*	*Value*
Start			$44,000			$44,000			$44,000
2005	$4,000	$ 4,000	40,000	$8,800	$ 8,800	35,200	$1,200	$ 1,200	42,800
2006	4,000	8,000	36,000	7,040	15,840	28,160	5,600	6,800	37,200
2007	4,000	12,000	32,000	5,632	21,472	22,528	4,800	11,600	32,400

Computations for 2007

Straight-line:	$40,000 ÷ 10 years = $4,000
Double-declining-balance:	0.20 × $28,160 = $5,632
Units-of-production:	$0.40 × 12,000 units = $4,800

Other Issues in Accounting for Capital Assets

OBJECTIVE 3
Explain capital cost allowance and amortization for income tax purposes

Amortization affects income taxes through the claiming of capital cost allowance (discussed below). Also, companies have gains and losses when they sell capital assets, such as property, plant, and equipment. This section covers these topics.

The Relationship between Amortization and Income Taxes

Most companies use the straight-line method for reporting capital asset values and amortization expense to their owners and creditors on their financial statements. But businesses must often keep a separate set of records for calculating the amortization expense they claim on their tax returns. This is because, whatever amortization method a business uses, amortization expense on the income statement is often different from amortization deducted for income tax purposes. Canada Customs and Revenue Agency (CCRA) allows corporations, as well as individuals earning business or professional income, to deduct from income **capital cost allowance (CCA)**, the term Canada Customs and Revenue Agency uses to describe amortization for tax purposes. CCRA specifies the *maximum* CCA rate a taxpayer may use. Different classes of assets have different CCA rates. The CCA rates published by CCRA are maximums. A taxpayer may claim from zero to the maximum capital cost allowance allowed in a year. Most taxpayers claim the maximum CCA since this provides the largest deduction from taxable income as quickly as possible, thus decreasing the immediate tax payment. Claiming the maximum CCA reduces taxable income and thus tax payable, leaving more cash available for investment or other business uses.

Capital cost allowance is discussed in more detail in the Appendix at the end of this chapter.

Amortization for Partial Years

Companies purchase capital assets whenever they need them. They do not wait until the beginning of a year or a month. Therefore, companies develop policies to compute amortization for partial years. Suppose Falconbridge Limited (www.falconbridge.com), the mining company, purchases a building in Timmins, Ontario, as a maintenance shop on April 1, 2005, for $500,000. The building's estimated life is 20 years and its estimated residual value is $80,000. Falconbridge Limited's fiscal year ends on December 31. How does the company compute amortization for the year ended December 31?

Many companies compute partial-year amortization by first calculating a full year's amortization. They then multiply full-year amortization by the fraction of the year during which they used the asset. Assuming the straight-line method, the 2005 amortization for the maintenance shop is $15,750, computed as follows:

Full-year amortization: $\frac{\$500,000 - \$80,000}{20 \text{ years}} = \$21,000$

Partial-year amortization: $\$21,000 \times 9/12 = \$15,750$

What if the company bought the asset on April 18? One policy suggests businesses record no amortization on assets purchased after the 15th of the month and record a full month's amortization on an asset bought on or before the 15th. Thus the company would record no amortization for April for an April 18 purchase. In this case, the year's amortization for eight months would be $14,000 ($21,000 × 8/12).

Partial-year amortization is computed under the other amortization methods in the same way—by applying the appropriate percentage of the year during which the asset is used.

Most companies use computerized systems to account for capital assets. The system will automatically calculate the amortization expense for each period.

Change in the Useful Life of an Amortizable Asset

Estimating the useful life of each capital asset poses an accounting challenge. As previously discussed, a business must estimate the useful life of a capital asset to compute amortization on that asset. This prediction is the most difficult part of accounting for amortization. As the asset is used, the business may change the asset's estimated useful life, based on experience and new information. Such a change is called a change in accounting estimate. Empire Company Limited (www.empireco.ca), the parent company of Sobeys Inc., IGA Stores, and Price Chopper, included the following note in its April 30, 2001, annual report:

> **Note 1. Accounting Policies**
> **Depreciation**
> ". . . During the year the Company changed the estimated useful lives of its rental properties based on a review of its properties. This change in accounting estimate has been applied prospectively [applied to the current and future periods]. Prior to 2001, estimated lives ranged from 20 to 50 years from the date of acquisition.

The April 30, 2003, annual report indicates that rental properties were amortized over 20 to 40 years.

Accounting changes like these are very rare despite the fact that no business has perfect foresight. To *record* a change in accounting estimate, the remaining book value of the asset is spread over its adjusted, or new, remaining useful life, that is, it is accounted for prospectively.

Assume that a Big Rock Brewery Income Trust machine cost $40,000, and the company originally believed the asset had a 16-year useful life with no residual value. Using the straight-line method, the company would record $2,500 amortization each year ($40,000 ÷ 16 years = $2,500). Suppose Big Rock Brewery used the asset for four years. Accumulated amortization reached $10,000, leaving a book value of $30,000 ($40,000 − $10,000). From its experience with the asset during the first four years, management believes the asset will remain useful for the next 20 years. The company would compute a revised annual amortization amount and record it as follows:

Asset's Remaining Amortizable Book Value	÷	(New) Estimated Useful Life Remaining	=	(New) Annual Amortization Amount
$30,000	÷	20 years	=	$1,500

The yearly amortization entry based on new estimated useful life is

Amortization Expense—Machine..	1,500	
Accumulated Amortization—Machine.................................		1,500

WORKING IT OUT

In 1985, ABC Co. purchased for $600,000 a building that had an estimated residual value of $100,000 and a life of 40 years. In 2005, a $200,000 addition to the building increased its residual value by $50,000. The accumulated amortization on the building is $250,000. Calculate straight-line amortization expense for 2005.

A: Calculate book value:

Cost (new)	$800,000*
Acc. Amort.	250,000
Revised book value	$550,000

Revised straight-line amortization:

$$= \frac{\$550,000 - \$150,000}{20}$$

= $20,000 per year

*$600,000 + $200,000

The equation for revised straight-line amortization is

$$\text{Revised Straight-line Amortization} = \frac{\text{Cost} - \text{Accumulated Amortization} - \text{New Residual Value}}{\text{Estimated remaining useful life in years}}$$

STOP & THINK

1. Suppose Hi Value Stores was having a bad year—net income below expectations and lower than last year's income. For amortization purposes Hi Value Stores decided to extend the estimated useful lives of its amortizable assets. This decision was *not* based on any belief that the actual useful life was longer than originally thought. How would this accounting change affect Hi Value Stores' (a) amortization expense, (b) net income, and (c) owner's equity?

Answer: An accounting change that lengthens the estimated useful lives of amortizable assets (a) decreases amortization expense, and (b) and (c) increases net income and owner's equity.

2. Suppose that the Hi Value Stores' change in accounting estimate turned a loss year into a profitable year. Without the change, the company would have reported a net loss for the year. But the change enabled the company to report positive net income. Under GAAP, Hi Value Stores' annual report must disclose the change in accounting estimate. Would users of the financial statements, such as the bank, evaluate Hi Value Stores as better or worse in response to this disclosure?

Answer: Users' reactions are not always predictable. There is evidence, however, that businesses cannot fool users. If users have enough information—such as the knowledge of a change in accounting estimate disclosed in the annual report—they can process the information correctly. In this case, analysts would *probably* subtract from Hi Value Stores' reported net income the amount caused by the change in accounting estimate. Users could then use the resulting net *loss* figure to evaluate Hi Value Stores' lack of progress during the year. Users would probably view Hi Value Stores less favourably for having made this change in accounting estimate. For this reason, and because the ethics behind such a change are questionable, many owners and managers would not engage in this type of income manipulation.

Using Fully Amortized Assets

A *fully amortized asset* is one that has reached the end of its *estimated* useful life. No more amortization is recorded for the asset. If the asset is no longer useful, it is disposed of. But the asset may still be useful, and the company may continue using this fully amortized asset. The asset account and its accumulated amortization remain on the books, but no additional amortization is recorded.

STOP & THINK

A fully amortized asset has a cost of $80,000 and zero residual value. What is the asset's accumulated amortization?

Answer: $80,000 (same as the asset's cost)

Now suppose the asset's residual value is $10,000. How much is its accumulated amortization?

Answer: $70,000 ($80,000 − $10,000).

Disposing of a Capital Asset (Property, Plant, and Equipment)

Eventually, a capital asset no longer serves its purpose. The asset may be worn out, obsolete, or for some other reason, no longer useful to the business. The owner may sell the asset or exchange it. If the asset cannot be sold or exchanged, then it is junked. Whatever the method of disposal, the business should bring amortization up to date to measure the asset's final book value properly.

To record the disposal of a capital asset, credit the asset account and debit its accumulated amortization, that is, remove the asset from the books. Suppose the final year's amortization expense has just been recorded for a machine. The cost was $6,000, and there is no residual value. The machine's accumulated amortization thus totals $6,000. Assume this asset cannot be sold or exchanged, so it is junked. The entry to record its disposal is

Accumulated Amortization—Machinery 6,000
    Machinery..   6,000
To dispose of a fully amortized machine.

Now both accounts have a zero balance, as shown in the T-accounts below:

Machinery		Accumulated Amortization—Machinery	
6,000	6,000	6,000	6,000

If assets are junked before being fully amortized, the company records a loss equal to the asset's book value. Suppose Zellers' store fixtures that cost $4,000 are junked at a loss. Accumulated amortization is $3,000 and book value is therefore $1,000. Disposal of these store fixtures generates a loss, as follows:

Accumulated Amortization—Store Fixtures............................ 3,000
Loss on Disposal of Capital Assets... 1,000
    Store Fixtures   4,000
To dispose of store fixtures.

All losses, including this Loss on Disposal of Capital Assets, decrease net income. Along with expenses, losses are reported on the income statement.

Selling a Capital Asset

Suppose Placer Dome Inc. (www.placerdome.com), the gold-mining company, sells surplus office furniture on September 30, 2005, for $5,000 cash. The furniture cost $10,000 when purchased on January 1, 2002, and has been amortized on a straight-line basis. Managers estimated a ten-year useful life and no residual value. Prior to recording the sale of the furniture, Placer Dome accountants must update its amortization. Since Placer Dome uses the calendar year as its accounting period, partial amortization must be recorded for nine months from January 1, 2005, to the sale date of September 30. The straight-line amortization entry at September 30, 2005, is

Sept. 30   Amortization Expense—Furniture 750
               Accumulated Amortization—Furniture.....................   750
             To update amortization ($10,000/10 years × $\frac{9}{12}$).

Now, after this entry is posted, the Furniture and the Accumulated Amortization—Furniture accounts appear as follows:

Furniture		Accumulated Amortization—Furniture	
Jan. 1, 2002 10,000		Dec. 31, 2002 1,000	
		Dec. 31, 2003 1,000	
		Dec. 31, 2004 1,000	
		Sept. 30, 2005 750	
		Balance 3,750	

Book value = $6,250

Suppose Placer Dome sells the office furniture for $5,000 cash. The loss on the sale is $1,250, computed as follows:

Cash received from selling the asset		$5,000
Book value of asset sold:		
Cost...	$10,000	
Accumulated amortization		
up to date of sale	3,750	6,250
Gain (loss) on sale of the asset..		($1,250)

Placer Dome's entry to record the sale of the furniture for $5,000 cash is

Sept. 30	Cash	5,000	
	Loss on Disposal of Capital Assets......................	1,250	
	Accumulated Amortization—Furniture.............	3,750	
	Furniture...		10,000
	To dispose of furniture.		

When recording the sale of a capital asset, Placer Dome must

- Remove the balances in the asset account (Furniture, in this case) and its related accumulated amortization account

- Record a gain or a loss if the cash received differs from the asset's book value.

In our example, cash of $5,000 is less than the book value of $6,250. The result is a loss of $1,250.

If the sale price had been $7,000, Placer Dome would have had a gain of $750 (Cash, $7,000 – asset book value, $6,250). The entry to record this gain would be

Sept. 30	Cash	7,000	
	Accumulated Amortization—Furniture.............	3,750	
	Furniture...		10,000
	Gain on Disposal of Capital Assets		750
	To dispose of furniture.		

A gain is recorded when an asset is sold for more than book value. A loss is recorded when the sale price is less than book value. Gains increase net income and losses decrease net income. All gains and losses are reported on the income statement.

Exchanging Capital Assets

Businesses often exchange old capital assets for newer, more efficient assets. The most common exchange transaction is a trade-in. When a business exchanges a capital asset it owns, it may sell the asset for cash, or it may trade in the asset for a *similar* asset (an old truck for a newer truck) or for a *dissimilar* asset (an old tractor for a new truck). The accounting treatment differs, depending on whether the assets are similar or dissimilar, and depending on the amount of cash involved in the exchange.

Suppose Tim Hortons owns a 1998 Ford Econoline van that it purchased for $32,000 on January 2, 1999. The van was expected to last eight years and was amortized on a straight-line basis.

Exchange of an Asset for a Dissimilar Asset If an asset is exchanged for a dissimilar asset, the accounting treatment is similar to that for the sale of an asset for cash. Any gain or loss on the transaction must be recorded.

Assume that, on January 2, 2004, Tim Hortons exchanged the van described above for a light-duty truck that had a list price of $43,000. Tim Hortons was allowed a trade-in of $8,000 for the van and paid the seller $35,000 cash. The entry to record the exchange of dissimilar assets would be:

THINKING IT OVER

Why is the trade-in allowance usually different from the book value?

A: The book value depends on the asset's historical cost and on the amortization method used. The trade-in allowance is based on the market value of the asset being traded in (or may be an adjustment to the selling price).

Truck	43,000	
Loss on exchange of assets	4,000	
Accumulated Amortization—Van (5 × $4,000)	20,000	
Cash		35,000
Van		32,000

To record exchange of the van and cash for a new light-duty truck.

If the van was exchanged for the truck but the trade-in allowed was $14,000 and cash payment was $29,000, the entry to record the exchange would be:

Truck	43,000	
Accumulated Amortization—Van	20,000	
Cash		29,000
Van		32,000
Gain on exchange of assets		2,000

To record exchange of the van and cash for a new light-duty truck.

Exchanges of Similar Assets

The *CICA Handbook* indicates that in an exchange transaction where the cash paid is less than 10 percent of the value of the asset acquired, the exchange is *nonmonetary*. To illustrate, if a company exchanged its truck and $3,000 cash for another truck that had a market value of $48,000, the transaction would be nonmonetary, since the $3,000 cash is less than 10 percent of $48,000 ($48,000 × 10% = $4,800).

The reason that the classification of the transaction as *monetary* or *nonmonetary* is important is that gains (or losses) are recognized on monetary transactions (as was shown above) but they are not recognized on nonmonetary transactions. Instead, for nonmonetary exchanges of similar assets, the cost of the asset received is recorded as the book value of the asset traded in plus any cash paid or less any cash received. However, the recorded cost of the asset received can be no higher than its market value.

To illustrate, assume Inco Limited (www.inco.com) owns a bulldozer that has an original cost of $200,000 and accumulated amortization of $110,000. Inco exchanges this old bulldozer for a new one with a market value of $150,000. The company is allowed a trade-in of $140,000 and pays $10,000 cash. This is a nonmonetary transaction because the cash paid, $10,000, is less than 10 percent of the market value of the new bulldozer, $15,000 ($150,000 × 10% = $15,000).

The entry to record this nonmonetary exchange of similar assets would be:

Bulldozer (new)	100,000	
Accumulated Amortization—Bulldozer (old)	110,000	
Cash		10,000
Bulldozer (old)		200,000

To record the nonmonetary exchange of an old bulldozer for a new bulldozer.

Notice that the gain that would have been recognized in a monetary exchange of assets [market value of new asset − (book value of old asset + cash)] is deducted from the cost of the new bulldozer, since no gain is recognized on a nonmonetary exchange of assets. Therefore, the new bulldozer's cost is $100,000 (calculated as $150,000 − [$200,000 − $110,000 + $10,000] = $50,000; $150,000 − $50,000 = $100,000).

The nonmonetary exchange of similar assets shown above would be recorded differently if the old asset's book value and cash given were greater than the market value of the new asset. Suppose all the details of the exchange of assets above were the same except that the accumulated amortization of the old bulldozer is only $50,000, not $110,000. The entry to record this nonmonetary exchange of similar assets would now be:

Bulldozer (new)	150,000	
Accumulated Amortization—Bulldozer (old)	50,000	
Loss on the exchange of assets	10,000	
Cash		10,000
Bulldozer (old)		200,000

To record the nonmonetary exchange of an old bulldozer for a new bulldozer.

As was mentioned above, although the rule is that a gain or loss is not recognized on nonmonetary transactions, the cost of the new bulldozer must not be recorded at more than its market value of $150,000. Since the book value of the old bulldozer ($150,000) and the cash given ($10,000) is greater than the market value of the new bulldozer ($150,000), a loss of $10,000 must be recorded.[2]

STOP & THINK

Suppose Quik Trip Stores' comparative income statement for two years included these items:

	2005	2004
	($ thousands)	
Net sales	$7,200	$6,800
Income from operations	$ 49	$ 65
Gain on sale of store facilities	28	—
Income before income taxes	$ 67	$ 65

Which was a better year for Quik Trip—2005 or 2004?

Answer: From a *sales* standpoint, 2005 was better because sales were higher. But from an *income* standpoint, 2004 was the better year. In 2004, merchandising operations— Quik Trip's main business—generated $65 thousand of income before taxes. In 2005, merchandising produced only $49 thousand of income before taxes. Part of the company's income in 2005 came from selling store facilities. A business cannot hope to continue on this path very long. This example illustrates why investors and creditors are interested in the sources of a company's profits, not just the final amount of net income.

Internal Control of Capital Assets (Property, Plant, and Equipment)

Internal control of capital assets (property, plant, and equipment) includes safeguarding them and having an adequate accounting system. Recall from Chapter 8 the importance of a strong system of internal controls within a business. To see the need for controlling capital assets, consider the following situation. The home office and top managers of Petrol Mfg. Ltd. are in Calgary. The company manufactures gas pumps in Michigan, then sells them in Europe. Top managers and owners of the company rarely see the manufacturing plant and therefore cannot control their capital assets by on-the-spot management. What features does their internal control system need?

Safeguarding capital assets (property, plant, and equipment) includes:

1. Assigning responsibility for custody of the assets.
2. Separating custody of assets from accounting for the assets. (This separation of duties is a cornerstone of internal control in almost every area.)
3. Setting up security measures—for instance, guards and restricted access to property, plant, and equipment—to prevent theft.
4. Protecting capital assets from the elements (rain, snow, and so on).
5. Having adequate insurance against fire, storm, and other casualty losses.
6. Training operating personnel in the proper use of the assets.
7. Checking capital assets regularly for existence and condition.
8. Keeping a regular maintenance schedule.

---

[2] GAAP rules for exchanges may differ from income tax rules. In this discussion, we are concerned with the accounting rules.

Accounting for Wasting Assets (Natural Resources)

Wasting assets are so-called because they are used up in the process of production. Wasting assets or *natural resources* are capital assets. Examples include iron ore, coal, oil, gas, and timber. Natural resources are like inventories in the ground (coal) or on top of the ground (timber). Natural resources are expensed through amortization. Some companies use the word **depletion** to describe amortization of wasting assets. **Amortization expense**, or *depletion*, is that portion of the cost of natural resources that is used up in a particular period. Amortization expense for wasting assets is computed by the *units-of-production* formula:

$$\text{Amortization expense} = \frac{\text{Cost} - \text{Residual value}}{\text{Estimated total units of natural resource}} \times \text{Number of units removed}$$

An oil well may cost $100,000 and contain an estimated 10,000 barrels of oil. (Natural resources usually have no residual value.) The amortization rate would be $10 per barrel ($100,000/10,000 barrels). If 3,000 barrels are extracted during the first year, amortization expense is $30,000 (3,000 barrels × $10 per barrel). The amortization entry for the year is

Amortization Expense	30,000	
Accumulated Amortization—Oil		30,000

If 4,500 barrels are removed the next year, amortization is $45,000 (4,500 barrels × $10 per barrel).

Accumulated Amortization for wasting assets is a contra account similar to Accumulated Amortization for property, plant, and equipment. Natural resource assets can be reported on the balance sheet shown for oil in the following example.

Capital Assets:		
Property, plant, and equipment		
Land		$120,000
Buildings	$800,000	
Equipment..	160,000	
	960,000	
Less: Accumulated amortization.................................	410,000	
Net property, plant, and equipment		550,000
Oil and gas properties		
Oil..	$340,000	
Less: Accumulated amortization................................	**90,000**	
Net oil and gas properties...		250,000
Total capital assets		$920,000

Stop & Think

Suppose West Fraser Timber Co. Ltd. purchases, for $500,000, land that contains an estimated 500,000 fbm (foot-board measure) of timber. The land can be sold for $100,000 after the timber has been cut. If West Fraser harvests 200,000 fbm in the year of purchase, how much amortization should be recorded?

Answer:

$$= \frac{\text{Cost} - \text{Residual value}}{\text{Estimated total units}} \times \text{Number of units produced}$$

$$= \frac{(\$500,000 - \$100,000)}{500,000 \text{ fbm}} \times 200,000 \text{ fbm}$$

$$= \$0.80/\text{fbm} \times 200,000 \text{ fbm}$$

$$= \$160,000$$

Future Removal and Site Restoration Costs

There is increasing concern by individuals and governments about the environment. Often, in the past, a company exploiting natural resources, such as a mining company, would simply abandon the site once the ore body was mined completely. Now, there is legislation in most jurisdictions requiring a natural resource company to remove buildings, equipment, and waste, and to restore the site once a location is to be dismantled and abandoned.

The costs of future removal and site restoration at a property are a charge against all revenues earned from that property; the matching principle suggests that such costs should be accumulated over the economic life of the location. The *CICA Handbook* requires a natural resource company to accrue future removal and site restoration costs net of expected recoveries by charging income on a reasonable basis. The accrual should be shown as a liability on the balance sheet. When the costs cannot be reasonably determined, a contingent liability (a potential liability) should be disclosed in the notes to the financial statements.

Accounting for Intangible Assets

OBJECTIVE 6
Account for intangible assets

As we saw earlier in this chapter, **intangible assets** have no physical form. Instead, these assets convey special rights from patents, copyrights, trademarks, franchises, leaseholds, and goodwill.

In our technology-driven economy, intangibles rival tangible assets in value. Customer loyalty is all-important. Consider online auctioneer eBay. The company has no physical products or equipment, but it helps people buy and sell everything from toys to bathroom tiles. Each month eBay serves millions of customers. In a sense, eBay is a company of intangibles.

The intellectual capital of eBay, Research In Motion or Open Text is difficult to measure, but when one company buys another, we get a glimpse of the value of the acquired intellectual capital. Intangibles can account for most of a company's market value, so companies are finding ways to evaluate their intangibles just as they do their physical and financial assets.

A patent is an intangible asset that protects a process or formula. The acquisition cost of a patent is debited to Patents, an asset account. The intangible is expensed as it expires through amortization. Amortization applies to intangibles in the same way as it applies to property, plant, and equipment, and wasting assets.

Amortization is computed over the lesser of the asset's legal life or estimated useful life. Obsolescence often shortens an intangible asset's useful life. Amortization expense for intangibles can be written off directly against the intangible asset account with no accumulated amortization account. The residual value of most intangibles is zero.

Some intangibles have indefinite lives. For these intangibles, the company records no systematic amortization in each period. Instead, it accounts for any decrease in the value of the intangible, as we shall see for goodwill.

 **REAL WORLD EXAMPLE**

Companies protect their exclusive rights to an invention. In the U.S., Polaroid Corporation filed suit against Eastman Kodak Company, charging an infringement of certain Polaroid patents for instant cameras and instant film. Polaroid sought an injunction and damages. An injunction prohibited Kodak from manufacturing and selling such products in the U.S. Eastman Kodak appealed the injunction, but the appeal was denied.

Specific Intangibles

Patents Patents are federal government grants conveying an exclusive right for 20 years to produce and sell an invention. The invention may be a product or a process. Patented products include Bombardier Ski-doos and the Research In Motion BlackBerry. Like any other asset, a patent may be purchased. Suppose Nortel pays $200,000 to acquire a patent, and Nortel believes the expected useful life of the patent is five years. Amortization expense is $40,000 per year ($200,000 ÷ 5 years). The company's acquisition and amortization entries for this patent are:

Jan.	1	Patent	200,000	
		Cash		200,000
		To acquire a patent.		
Dec.	31	Amortization Expense—Patent.............................	40,000	
		Patent..		40,000
		To amortize the cost of a patent ($200,000 ÷ 5).		

At the end of the first year, Nortel would report the patent at $160,000 ($200,000 minus the first year's amortization of $40,000).

Copyrights Copyrights are exclusive rights to reproduce and sell software, a book, musical composition, film, or other work of art. Issued by the federal government, copyrights extend 50 years beyond the author's life. A company may pay a large sum to purchase an existing copyright from the owner. For example, the publisher McClelland & Stewart Ltd. may pay the author of a popular novel tens of thousands of dollars or more for the book's copyright. The useful life of a copyright for a popular book may be two or three years; on the other hand, some copyrights, especially of musical compositions, such as works by the Beatles, seem to be popular over several decades.

Trademarks and Brand Names Trademarks and **brand names** (or **trade names**) are distinctive identifications of products or services. For example, The Sports Network has its distinctive logo of the yellow letters TSN on a black background shaped like a television screen; Apple Computer has the multi-colored apple with a bite out of it; and the Edmonton Oilers and Toronto Blue Jays have insignia that identify their respective teams. Molson Canadian, Swiss Chalet chicken, WestJet, and Roots are everyday trade names. Advertising slogans such as Speedy Muffler's "At Speedy you're a somebody," or Shoppers Drug Mart's "Everything you want in a drugstore" are also legally protected. The cost of a trademark or trade name is amortized over its useful life.

Franchises and Licences Franchises and **licences** are privileges granted by a private business or a government to sell a product or service in accordance with specified conditions. The Vancouver Canucks hockey organization is a franchise granted to its owners by the National Hockey League. Tim Hortons and Re/Max Ltd. are well-known franchises. The acquisition cost of a franchise or licence is amortized over its useful life.

······· **THINKING IT OVER**

Why might a business have goodwill? Why could a business earn more than a normal rate of return on its assets? Why might an acquiring company pay an amount greater than the market value of net assets acquired when purchasing a going business?

A: Good customer relations, good location of the business, efficient operations, monopoly in the marketplace, strong sources of financing, and so on. A business could earn more than a normal rate of return on its assets because of these factors. Thus, a purchaser will pay more than the market value of net assets for a business that has these factors.

Leaseholds A **leasehold** is a prepayment that a lessee (renter) makes to secure the use of an asset from a lessor (landlord). For example, most malls lease the space to the mall stores and shops that you visit. Often, leases require the lessee to make this prepayment in addition to monthly rental payments. The prepayment is a debit to an intangible asset account entitled Leaseholds. This amount is amortized over the life of the lease by debiting Rent Expense and crediting Leaseholds.

Sometimes lessees modify or improve the leased asset. For example, a lessee may construct a fence on leased land. The lessee debits the cost of the fence to a separate intangible asset account, Leasehold Improvements, and amortizes its cost over the lesser of the term of the lease and of its useful life.

Goodwill Goodwill in accounting is a more limited term than in everyday use, as in "goodwill among men." In accounting, **goodwill** is the excess of the cost to purchase a company over the market value of its net assets (assets minus liabilities). Suppose James Richardson International acquires Manitoba Express Ltd. at a cost of $10 million. The market value of Manitoba Express's assets is $9 million, and its liabilities total $1 million. In this case, James Richardson International paid $2 million for goodwill, computed as follows:

Purchase price paid for Manitoba Express Ltd.		$10 million
Sum of the market value of Manitoba Express's assets...	$9 million	
Less: Manitoba Express's liabilities	1 million	
Market value of Manitoba Express's net assets..............		8 million
Excess is called *goodwill*		$ 2 million

James Richardson International's entry to record the acquisition of Manitoba Express Ltd., including its goodwill, would be

Assets (Cash, Receivables, Inventories, Capital Assets, all at market value)..............................	9,000,000	
Goodwill	2,000,000	
Liabilities		1,000,000
Cash..		10,000,000
Purchased Manitoba Express Ltd.		

Accounting and the *e*-World

How Do You Value Human Assets, the Drivers of the e-Economy?

The rules for valuing "hard" capital assets, such as computers, desks, trucks, buildings, mines, and copyrights, for financial reporting purposes are clear. The assets are valued at historical cost less accumulated amortization.

How do you value the programmers and systems designers at high-tech companies like Research in Motion (RIM) (www.rim.com), JDS Uniphase (www.jdsu.com), and Nortel Networks (www.nortelnetworks.com)? These companies are as dependent on their "human capital" as Bombardier and Air Canada are on their physical, non-human assets, yet RIM's and Nortel's financial statements show no value for these human assets.

This inability to capitalize the value of human assets and include them on the balance sheet can cause problems for high-tech companies. They tend not to have significant amounts of capital assets as would a manufacturing company like IPSCO, the steel producer, or Magna International, the auto parts manufacturer. Borrowing money can be a problem because high-tech companies do not have the hard assets that old-line companies, like Bombardier, IPSCO, and Magna, possess to secure a loan. Unsophisticated lenders and investors have difficulty valuing the human capital of high-tech companies.

Assigning a value to a programmer is very difficult. Should the future income of the programmer be calculated and discounted, then recorded as an intangible asset and amortized? Should the revenue the programmer will generate in the future for the company be calculated, discounted, and capitalized? Should a value be assigned to the cost of the programmer's education and experience? Should a programmer's hiring cost (for example, the fee paid to a search company who found the programmer for the company) be recorded and amortized?

If there was a method of assigning a cost to a programmer that was then amortized, should the cost of courses taken by the programmer be treated as "repairs" or "betterments"?

As you can see, there are many difficult and, so far, unanswered questions about valuing the employees of high-tech companies. Yet, until such employees are valued, high-tech companies' financial statements will not reflect the full value of their assets.

Goodwill has the following special features:

1. Goodwill is recorded, at its cost, only when it is purchased in the acquisition of another company. A company's favourable location, superior product, or outstanding reputation may create goodwill for a company, but it is never recorded by that entity. Instead, goodwill is recorded *only* by the acquiring entity when it buys another company. A purchase transaction provides objective evidence of the value of the goodwill.

2. Goodwill has an indefinite life, so it is not amortized like other intangibles. Instead, the purchaser must assess the goodwill every year and, if its value is impaired, the goodwill must be written down to reflect the impairment. The write-down amount is accounted for as an expense in the year of the write-down.

International Accounting for Research and Development Costs Accounting for research and development (R&D) costs is one of the most difficult issues the accounting profession has faced. R&D is the lifeblood of companies such as Bombardier, Research in Motion, Open Text, and Nortel Networks because it is vital to the development of new products and processes. The cost of R&D activities is one of these companies' most valuable (intangible) assets.

Canada requires *development costs* meeting certain criteria to be capitalized, while other countries require such costs to be expensed in the year incurred. Canada and most other countries require *research costs* to be expensed as incurred.

Some critics argue that R&D costs represent future benefits and should be capitalized; others agree with the present accounting standards, and still others think all R&D costs should be expensed.

STOP & THINK

How could companies around the world be placed on the same accounting basis?

Answer: If all companies worldwide followed the same accounting rules, they would be reporting income and other amounts computed similarly. But this is not the case. A company must follow the accounting rules of its own nation, and there are differences, as the goodwill situation illustrates. This is why international investors keep abreast of accounting methods used in different nations—much the same as a Canadian investor cares whether a company uses FIFO or average cost for inventories. An international body, the International Accounting Standards Board (IASB) (www.iasb.org.uk) sets accounting standards, called *International Accounting Standards* or IAS. The Canadian Institute of Chartered Accountants, through its Liaison, Patricia O'Malley, FCA, is a strong supporter of international accounting standards, and the CICA's Accounting Standards Board (ACSB) is working to harmonize Canadian standards with the IAS. It is working with those bodies and other accounting bodies around the world to harmonize accounting standards worldwide.

Ethical Issues: Capital Assets and Intangibles

The main ethical issue in accounting for capital assets and intangibles is whether to capitalize or expense a particular cost. In this area, companies have split personalities. On the one hand, they all want to save on taxes. This motivates companies to expense all costs in order to decrease taxable income. But they also want their financial statements to look as good as possible, with high net income and high reported amounts for assets.

In most cases, a cost that is capitalized or expensed for tax purposes must be treated the same way in the financial statements. What, then, is the ethical path? Accountants should follow the general guidelines for capitalizing a cost: Capitalize all costs that provide a future benefit for the business, and expense all other costs, as outlined in the Decision Guidelines below.

Many companies have gotten into trouble by capitalizing costs that really should have been expensed. They made their financial statements look better than the facts warranted. But there are few cases of companies getting into trouble by following the general guidelines, or even by erring on the side of expensing questionable costs. This is another example of accounting conservatism. We discussed accounting conservatism in Chapter 6, page 303.

DECISION GUIDELINES   Accounting for Capital Assets and Related Expenses

Suppose you buy a GoodLife Fitness Club franchise and invest in Life Cycle and other fitness equipment. You have some decisions to make about how to account for the franchise and the equipment. The Decision Guidelines will help you maximize your cash flow and do the accounting properly.

Decision	Guidelines
Capitalize or expense a cost?	General rule: Capitalize all costs that provide *future benefit*. Expense all costs that provide *no future benefit*.
Capitalize or expense:	
• Cost associated with a new asset?	Capitalize all costs that bring the asset to its intended use.
• Cost associated with an existing asset?	Capitalize only those costs that add to the asset's usefulness or its useful life.
	Expense all other costs as maintenance or repairs.
• Interest cost incurred to finance an asset's construction?	Capitalize interest cost only on assets constructed by the business for its own use.
	Expense all other interest costs.
Which amortization method to use:	
• For financial reporting?	Use the method that best matches amortization expense against the revenues produced by the asset.
• For income tax?	Use the maximum capital cost allowance rates allowed by Canada Customs and Revenue Agency to produce the greatest deductions from taxable income. A company can use different amortization methods for financial reporting and for income tax purposes. In Canada, this practice is considered both legal and ethical.

Summary Problem
for Your Review

Problem 1

The figures that follow on page 510 appear in Requirement 2, Solution, on page 496.

Cardozo Plastics purchased the equipment on January 2, 2005. Management has amortized the equipment by using the double-declining-balance method. On July 2, 2007, Cardozo sold the equipment for $27,000 cash.

	Method A Straight-Line			Method B Double-Declining-Balance		
Year	Annual Amortization Expense	Accumulated Amortization	Book Value	Annual Amortization Expense	Accumulated Amortization	Book Value
Start			$44,000			$44,000
2005	$4,000	$ 4,000	40,000	$8,800	$ 8,800	35,200
2006	4,000	8,000	36,000	7,040	15,840	28,160
2007	4,000	12,000	32,000	5,632	21,472	22,528

Required

1. Both methods could be used for income tax purposes, since neither exceeds the allowable capital cost allowance if the half-year rule is ignored. The half-year rule is explained in this chapter's Appendix.) Which amortization method would you select for income tax purposes? Why?

2. Record Cardozo Plastics amortization for 2007, and the sale of the equipment on July 2, 2007.

Problem 2

Meben Logistics purchased a building at a cost of $500,000 on January 2, 2001. Meben has amortized the building by using the straight-line method, a 35-year life, and a residual value of $150,000. On July 2, 2005, the business sold the building for $575,000 cash. The fiscal year of Meben Logistics ends on December 31.

Required

Record amortization for 2005 and record the sale of the building on July 2, 2005.

Solution

Problem 1

1. Canada Customs and Revenue Agency will allow a company to use any amortization method it chooses as long as the amount of capital cost allowance claimed for tax purposes does not exceed the maximum amount allowed by CCRA. For tax purposes, most companies select the maximum amount allowed by CCRA, which results in accelerated amortization of the equipment. Accelerated amortization minimizes taxable income and income tax payments in the early years of the asset's life, thereby maximizing the business's cash at the earliest possible time. Straight-line amortization spreads amortization evenly over the life of the asset, which would *not* minimize income tax in the same way.

2. 2007

July 2	Amortization Expense—Equipment		
	($28,160 × 0.20 × ½)...	2,816	
	Accumulated Amortization—Equipment.............		2,816
	To record amortization expense for the period		
	January 1, 2007, to June 30, 2007		
July 2	Cash	27,000	
	Accumulated Amortization—Equipment*	18,656	
	Equipment		44,000
	Gain on sale		1,656
	To record sale of equipment		

*$8,800 + $7,040 + $2,816 = $18,656

2005
July 2   Amortization Expense—Building   5,000

       Accumulated Amortization—Building   5,000

       To update amortization—$5,000 expense

       [(($500,000 – $150,000) ÷ 35 years) × ½ year]

July 2   Cash   575,000

       Accumulated Amortization—Building   45,000

         Building..   500,000

         Gain on sale of building   120,000

       To record sale of building.

       Accumulated amortization is $45,000.

       [(($500,000 – $150,000) ÷ 35 years) × 4½ years]

Cyber Coach

Visit the Study Guide on the Media Companion CD-ROM and the Student Resources area of the *Accounting* Companion Website for extra practice with the new material in Chapter 10.

www.pearsoned.ca/horngren

Summary

1. **Measure the cost of a capital asset.** *Capital assets*, of which property, plant, and equipment are a category, are long-lived assets that the business uses in its operations. The cost of a capital asset is the purchase price plus applicable taxes (but not GST), purchase commissions, and all other amounts incurred to acquire the asset and to prepare it for its intended use.

2. **Account for amortization.** The process of allocating a capital asset's cost to expense over the period the asset is used is called *amortization*. Businesses may account for the amortization of property, plant, and equipment by three methods: *straight-line*, *units-of-production*, and *declining-balance*. All these methods require accountants to estimate the asset's useful life and residual value.

3. **Explain capital cost allowance and amortization for income tax purposes.** Canada Customs and Revenue Agency allows companies and individuals to claim capital cost allowance (amortization) against taxable income but sets maximum rates that may be claimed for each class of capital assets. Many companies use the maximum rates allowed for tax purposes but lower rates (for example, straight-line) for income statement purposes.

4. **Account for the disposal of a capital asset.** Before disposing of, selling, or trading in a capital asset, the business updates the asset's amortization. Disposal is then recorded by removing the book balances from both the asset account and its related accumulated amortization account. Sales often result in a gain or a loss, which is reported on the income statement. Disposal may or may not result in a reported gain or loss, depending on the circumstances.

5. **Account for wasting assets (natural resources).** The cost of natural resources, a special category of long-lived assets, is expensed through *amortization*. Amortization of natural resources is computed on a units-of-production basis.

6. **Account for intangible assets.** *Intangible assets* are assets that have no physical form. They give their owners a special right to current and expected future benefits. The major types of intangible assets are patents, copyrights, trademarks, franchises and licences, leaseholds, and goodwill. Amortization of most intangibles (except goodwill) is computed on a straight-line basis over the lesser of the legal life and useful life.

Self-Study Questions

Test your understanding of the chapter by marking the correct answer for each of the following questions:

1. Which of the following payments is not included in the cost of land? (*p. 485*)
   a. Removal of old building
   b. Legal fees
   c. Property taxes in arrears paid at acquisition
   d. Cost of fencing and lighting

2. Roche Products paid $120,000 for two machines valued at $90,000 and $60,000. Roche will record these machines at (*p. 488*)
   a. $90,000 and $60,000   c. $72,000 and $48,000
   b. $60,000 each   d. $70,000 and $50,000

3. Which of the following items is a repair? (*pp. 488–489*)
   a. New brakes for delivery truck
   b. Paving of a company parking lot
   c. Cost of a new engine for a truck
   d. Building permit paid to construct an addition to an existing building

4. Which of the following definitions fits amortization? (*p. 489*)
   a. Allocation of the asset's market value to expense over its useful life
   b. Allocation of the asset's cost to expense over its useful life
   c. Decreases in the asset's market value over its useful life
   d. Increases in the fund set aside to replace the asset when it is worn out

5. Which amortization method's amounts are not computed based on time? (*pp. 491–494*)
   a. Straight-line
   b. Units-of-production
   c. Double-declining balance
   d. All are based on time

6. Which amortization method gives the largest amount of expense in the early years of using the asset and therefore is best for income tax purposes, assuming the amount does not exceed the allowed capital cost allowance? (*pp. 492–493*)
   a. Straight-line
   b. Units-of-production
   c. Double-declining balance
   d. All are equal

7. A company paid $450,000 for a building and was amortizing it by the straight-line method over a 40-year life with estimated residual value of $50,000. After ten years, it became evident that the building's remaining useful life would be 40 years. Amortization for the eleventh year is (*pp. 498–499*)
   a. $7,500   c. $10,000
   b. $8,750   d. $12,500

8. Labrador Stores scrapped an automobile that cost $14,000 and had a book value of $1,100. The entry to record this disposal is (*pp. 500–503*)
   a. Loss on Disposal of Automobile 1,100
         Automobile   1,100
   b. Accumulated Amortization 14,000
         Automobile   14,000
   c. Accumulated Amortization 12,900
         Automobile   12,900
   d. Accumulated Amortization 12,900
      Loss on Disposal of Automobile 1,100
         Automobile   14,000

9. Amortization of a wasting asset is computed in the same manner as which amortization method? (*p. 504*)
   a. Straight-line
   b. Units-of-production
   c. Declining-balance

10. Lacy Company paid $550,000 to acquire Gentech Systems. Gentech's assets had a market value of $900,000 and its liabilities were $400,000. In recording the acquisition, Lacy will record goodwill of (*pp. 506–508*)
   a. $50,000   c. $550,000
   b. $100,000   d. $0

Answers to the Self-Study Questions follow the Similar Accounting Terms.

Accounting Vocabulary

Amortizable cost (*p. 491*)
Amortization (*p. 489*)
Amortization expense (*p. 504*)
Betterment (*p. 488*)
Brand name (*p. 506*)
Capital asset (*p. 484*)
Capital cost allowance (CCA) (*p. 497*)
Capitalize (a cost) (*p. 487*)
Copyright (*p. 506*)
Depletion (*p. 504*)
Double-declining-balance (DDB) method (*p. 492*)
Estimated residual value (*p. 490*)
Estimated useful life (*p. 490*)
Franchise (*p. 506*)

Goodwill (*p. 506*)
Intangible asset (*pp. 484, 505*)
Leasehold (*p. 506*)
Licence (*p. 506*)
Patent (*p. 505*)
Repair (*p. 488*)
Salvage value (*p. 490*)
Scrap value (*p. 490*)
Straight-line method (*p. 491*)
Trademark (*p. 506*)
Trade name (*p. 506*)
Units-of-production method (*p. 492*)
Wasting asset (*p. 504*)

Similar Accounting Terms

Amortization   Depreciation (for assets such as property, plant, and equipment); Depletion (for wasting assets)

Capital assets   Property, plant, and equipment; Fixed assets; Long-lived assets; Long-term assets

Wasting assets   Natural resources

Trade name   Brand name

Residual value   Salvage value; Scrap value

Answers to Self-Study Questions

1. d
2. c [($90,000/($90,000 + $60,000)) × $120,000 = $72,000;
   ($60,000/($90,000 + $60,000)) × $120,000 = $48,000]
3. a   4. b   5. b   6. c
7. a Amortizable cost = $450,000 − $50,000 = $400,000
   $400,000/40 years = $10,000 per year
   $400,000 − ($10,000 × 10 years) = $300,000
   $300,000/40 years = $7,500 per year
8. d   9. b
10. a [$550,000 − ($900,000 − $400,000) = $50,000]

Assignment Material

Questions

1. Describe how to measure the cost of a capital asset. Would an ordinary cost of repairing the asset after it is placed in service be included in the asset's cost?

2. Suppose land with a building on it is purchased for $525,000. How do you account for the $55,000 cost of removing this unwanted building?

3. When assets are purchased as a group for a single price and no individual asset cost is given, how is each asset's cost determined?

4. Distinguish a betterment from a repair. Why are they treated differently for accounting purposes?

5. Define amortization. What are common misconceptions about amortization?

6. To what types of long-lived assets does amortization expense apply?

7. Which amortization method does each of the graphs at the bottom of the page characterize: straight-line, units-of-production, or double-declining-balance?

8. When is it appropriate to capitalize interest? Prepare the journal entry for $25,000 interest cost during construction of a building.

9. Explain the concept of accelerated amortization. Which of the three amortization methods results in the most amortization in the first year of the asset's life?

10. The level of business activity fluctuates widely for Milton Schoolbus Co., reaching its slowest time in June through August each year. At other times, business is brisk. What amortization method is most appropriate for the company's fleet of school buses?

11. Felix Data Centre uses the most advanced computers available to keep a competitive edge over other

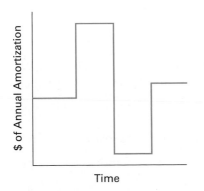

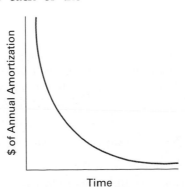

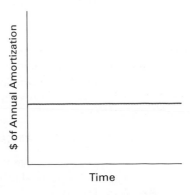

service centres. To maintain this advantage, the company usually replaces its computers before they are worn out. Describe the major factors affecting the useful life of a capital asset, and indicate which seems more relevant to this company's computers.

12. Which amortization method does not consider estimated residual value in computing amortization during the early years of the asset's life?

13. What is capital cost allowance?

14. Does amortization affect income taxes? How does amortization affect cash provided by operations?

15. Describe how to compute amortization for less than a full year, and how to account for amortization for less than a full month.

16. Hudson Company paid $12,000 for office furniture. The company expected it to remain in service for six years and to have a $1,500 residual value. After two years' use, company accountants believe the furniture will last for the next seven years. How much amortization will Hudson record for each of these last seven years, assuming straight-line amortization and no change in the estimated residual value?

17. When a company sells a capital asset before the year's end, what must it record before accounting for the sale?

18. Describe how to determine whether a company experiences a gain or a loss when an old capital asset is exchanged for a similar new capital asset. Does GAAP favour the recognition of gains or losses? Which accounting concept underlies your answer?

19. What expense applies to wasting assets? By which amortization method is this expense computed?

20. How do intangible assets differ from most other assets? Why are they assets at all? What expense applies to intangible assets?

21. Why is the cost of patents and other intangible assets often expensed over a shorter period than the legal life of the asset?

22. Your company has just purchased another company for $500,000. The market value of the other company's net assets is $350,000. What is the $150,000 excess called? What type of asset is it? How is goodwill amortized under GAAP?

23. Nortel Networks is recognized as a world leader in the manufacture and sale of communications equipment. The company's success has created vast amounts of business goodwill. Would you expect to see this goodwill reported on Nortel's financial statements? Why, or why not?

Exercises

Exercise 10-1 *Determining the cost of property, plant, and equipment* *(Obj. 1)*

The law firm of Marshall & Wilson purchased land, paying $95,000 cash as a down payment and signing a $155,000 note payable for the balance. In addition, the company paid delinquent property tax of $2,750, a legal fee of $1,500, and a $19,500 charge for levelling the land and removing an unwanted building. The company constructed an office building on the land at a cost of $750,000. It also paid $20,000 for a fence around the boundary of the property, $8,500 for the company sign near the entrance to the property, and $11,800 for special lighting of the grounds. Determine the cost of the company's land, land improvements, and building.

Exercise 10-2 *Measuring the cost of a capital asset* *(Obj. 1)*

Pages 485–486 of this chapter list the costs included for the acquisition of land. First is the purchase price of the land, which is obviously included in the cost of the land. The reasons for including the related costs are not so obvious. For example, property tax is ordinarily an expense, not part of the cost of an asset. State why the related costs listed on pages 485–486 are included as part of the cost of the land. After the land is ready for use, will these related costs be capitalized or expensed?

Exercise 10-3 *Allocating cost to assets acquired in a lump-sum purchase* *(Obj. 1)*

Lalonde Trucking bought three used trucks for $48,000. An independent appraisal of the trucks produced the following figures:

Truck No.	Appraised Value
1	$18,500
2	19,000
3	16,500

Lalonde Trucking paid 25 percent in cash and signed a note for the remainder. Record the purchase in the journal, identifying each truck's individual cost in a separate Truck account. Round costs to two decimal places.

Exercise 10-4 *Measuring the cost of an asset; distinguishing betterments from repairs (Obj. 1)*

Classify each of the following expenditures as a cost/betterment or a repair (expense) related to a machine used to earn revenue: (a) purchase price; (b) sales tax paid on the purchase price; (c) transportation and insurance while the machine is in transport from seller to buyer; (d) installation; (e) training of personnel for initial operation of the machine; (f) special reinforcement to the machine platform; (g) income tax paid on income earned from the sale of products manufactured by the machine; (h) major overhaul to extend useful life by three years; (i) ordinary recurring repairs to keep the machine in good working order; (j) lubrication of the machine before it is placed in service; (k) periodic lubrication after the machine is placed in service; and (l) goods and services tax on the purchase price.

Exercise 10-5 *Explaining the concept of amortization (Obj. 2)*

Sal Marino has just slept through the class in which Professor Larston explained the concept of amortization. Because the next test is scheduled for Wednesday, Marino telephones Nancy Wu to get her notes from the lecture. Wu's notes are concise: "Amortization—Sounds like Greek to me." Marino next tries Sally Nadeau, who says she thinks amortization is what happens when an asset wears out. Barry Orwell is confident that amortization is the process of building up a cash fund to replace an asset at the end of its useful life. Explain the concept of amortization for Marino. Evaluate the explanations of Nadeau and Orwell. Be specific.

Exercise 10-6 *Determining amortization amounts by three methods (Obj. 3)*

Tarot Machine & Dye bought a machine on January 2, 2003, for $50,000. The machine was expected to remain in service for three years and produce 2,000,000 parts. At the end of its useful life, company officials estimated that the machine's residual value would be $2,000. The machine produced 700,000 parts in the first year, 660,000 in the second year, and 650,000 in the third year.

Media Companion CD-ROM

Required

1. Prepare a schedule of *amortization expense* per year for the machine using the straight-line, units-of-production, and double-declining-balance amortization methods.
2. Which method tracks the wear and tear on the machine most closely? Why?
3. After one year under the double-declining-balance method, the company switched to the straight-line method. Prepare a schedule of amortization expense for this situation, showing all calculations.

Exercise 10-7 *Selecting the amortization method for income tax purposes (Obj. 3)*

In 2004, Maxwell Inc. paid $125,000 for equipment that is expected to have a five-year life. In this industry, the residual value is estimated to be five percent of the asset's cost. Maxwell Inc. plans to use straight-line amortization for accounting purposes. Discuss which amortization method Maxwell Inc. should use for income tax purposes? Should the same method be used for reporting on the financial statements?

Exercise 10-8 *Changing a capital asset's useful life* *(Obj. 2)*

Vachon Marketing Services purchased a building for $850,000 and amortized it on a straight-line basis over a 50-year period. The estimated residual value was $75,000. After using the building for 20 years, the company realized that wear and tear on the building would force the company to replace it before 50 years. Starting with the 21st year, the company began amortizing the building over a revised *total* life of 35 years, increasing the estimated residual value to $135,000. Record amortization expense on the building for years 20 and 21.

Exercise 10-9 *Analyzing the effect of a sale of a capital asset; double-declining-balance amortization* *(Obj. 4)*

On January 2, 2004, Baldwin Gifts purchased store fixtures for $21,500 cash, expecting the fixtures to remain in service for seven years. Baldwin Gifts has amortized the fixtures on a double-declining-balance basis with an estimated residual value of $1,000. On October 31, 2005, Baldwin Gifts sold the fixtures for $15,000 cash. Record both the amortization expense on the fixtures for 2004 and 2005, and the sale of the fixtures on October 31, 2005. Baldwin Gifts' year end is December 31. Round all calculations to the nearest dollar.

Exercise 10-10 *Measuring a capital asset's cost, using units-of-production amortization, and trading in a used asset* *(Obj. 1, 2, 4)*

Robertson Distribution, based in Brampton, Ontario, is a large warehousing and distribution company that operates throughout Eastern Canada. Robertson Distribution uses the units-of-production method to amortize its trucks because its managers believe units-of-production amortization best measures the wear and tear on the trucks. Robertson Distribution trades in used trucks often to keep driver morale high and to maximize fuel efficiency. Consider these facts about one Mack truck in the company's fleet:

When acquired in 2001, the tractor/trailer rig cost $385,000 and was expected to remain in service for eight years, or 1,500,000 kilometres. Estimated residual value was $75,000. The truck was driven 150,000 kilometres in 2001, 195,000 kilometres in 2002, and 235,000 kilometres in 2003. After 100,000 kilometres in 2004, the company traded in the Mack truck for a less expensive Freightliner rig. Robertson Distribution paid cash of $100,000. Determine Robertson Distribution's cost of the new truck. Journal entries are not required.

Exercise 10-11 *Recording wasting assets and depletion* *(Obj. 5)*

Lakefield Mining Ltd. paid $435,000 for the right to extract ore from a 300,000-tonne mineral deposit. In addition to the purchase price, the company also paid a $1,000 filing fee, a $2,500 licence fee to the province of Quebec, and $55,000 for a geological survey. Because Lakefield Mining Ltd. purchased the rights to the minerals only, the company expected the asset to have zero residual value when fully depleted. During the first year of production, the company removed 59,000 tonnes of ore. Make general journal entries to record (1) purchase of the mineral rights (debit Mineral Asset), (2) payment of fees and other costs, and (3) amortization for first-year production.

Exercise 10-12 *Recording intangibles, amortization, and a change in the asset's useful life* *(Obj. 6)*

Part 1 Curzon Company manufactures flat screen monitors for the graphics industry and has recently purchased for $350,000 a patent for the design of a new monitor. Although it gives legal protection for 20 years, the patent is expected to provide Curzon Company with a competitive advantage for only four years. Assuming the straight-line method of amortization, use general journal entries to record (1) the purchase of the patent, and (2) amortization for year 1.

Part 2   After using the patent for two years, Curzon Company learns at an industry trade show that another company is designing a more effective monitor. Based on this new information, Curzon Company decides to amortize the remaining cost of the patent over the current year, giving the patent a total useful life of three years. Record amortization for year 3.

Exercise 10-13   *Measuring goodwill*   *(Obj. 6)*

Thomson Corporation's (www.thomson.com) annual report for the year ended December 31, 2002, indicated that Thomson acquired companies with assets with a market value of $145 million and liabilities of $50 million. Thompson paid $277 million for these acquisitions.

Required

1. How would a value be assigned to the net assets acquired?
2. What value would be assigned to goodwill?
3. Will the goodwill be amortized? If so, by how much?

Exercise 10-14   *Accounting for goodwill*   *(Obj. 6)*

The financial statements of Mullen Transportation Inc. (www.mullen-trans.com) for the year ended December 31, 2002, reported the following details of acquisitions (adapted):

Assets:	In thousands
Cash	$ 1,775
Current assets.................................	4,207
Fixed assets.....................................	35,988
Intangibles	350
	$42,320

Liabilities:	
Long-term debt	$ 6,177
Future income taxes	2,209
	$ 8,386

Mullen Transportation Inc. paid $58,544 cash and $1,418 in common shares for the acquisitions.

Required

1. How much goodwill did Mullen Transportation Inc. purchase as part of the 2002 acquisitions?
2. Prepare the Mullen Transportation Inc. summary journal entry to record the acquisition for 2002.
3. Write the company's note to the financial statements for the accounting policy for goodwill.
4. Assume that, in 2003, the annual review of goodwill identified a 15-percent impairment of the goodwill accquired in 2002. Prepare the journal entry required to record this impairment.

Exercise 10-15   *Computing and recording goodwill*   *(Obj. 6)*

In 2002, Caledon Electronics Company purchased Ratheon Radio Ltd., paying $1.5 million in a note payable. The market value of Ratheon Radio Ltd.'s assets was $2.6 million, and Ratheon Radio Ltd. had liabilities of $1.5 million.

Required

1. Compute the cost of the goodwill purchased by Caledon Electronics Company.

2. Record the purchase by Caledon Electronics Company.

3. At 2003 year end, the annual review of goodwill value indicated no impairment of goodwill. Record the entry Caledon will make for goodwill expense for 2003.

4. At 2005 year end, the annual review of goodwill value indicated a 10-percent impairment of Ratheon Radio Ltd.'s goodwill. Record the entry for goodwill expense for 2005.

Challenge Exercises

Exercise 10-16   *Capitalizing versus expensing; measuring the effect of an error*   *(Obj. 1)*

Braeside Shoes is a family-owned retail shoe operation with stores in Owen Sound and Thornbury. The company's assets consist of inventory, store fixtures, and office equipment. Assume that early in year 1, Braeside Shoes purchased computerized point-of-sale and operating systems costing $100,000 to integrate inventory control and accounting for both stores. Bob Braeside expects this equipment will support the inventory and accounting requirements for four years. Because of technology obsolescence, no residual value is anticipated. Through error, Braeside Shoes accidentally expensed the entire cost of the equipment at the time of the purchase. Braeside Shoes' accounting policy for equipment is the straight-line amortization method. The company is operated as a sole proprietorship, so it pays no corporate income tax.

Required

Prepare a schedule to show the overstatement or understatement in the following items at the end of each year over the four-year life of the equipment.

1. Total current assets
2. Equipment, net
3. Net income
4. Total owner's equity
5. Debt ratio

Exercise 10-17   *Reconstructing transactions from the financial statements*   *(Obj. 2, 4)*

Leon's Furniture Limited's (www.leons.ca) 2002 financial statements reported these amounts (in thousands of dollars):

| | December 31 | | | |
| | 2002 | | 2001 | |
Properties	Cost	Accumulated Amortization	Cost	Accumulated Amortization
Land	$ 41,378	—	$ 35,073	—
Buildings	116,832	$ 51,566	105,325	$ 46,981
Equipment	17,940	11,712	16,575	10,678
Vehicles	13,994	11,533	13,513	10,680
Computer hardware and software	6,869	4,335	5,885	3,614
Leasehold improvements	26,178	7,461	21,081	6,220
	$223,191	$ 86,607	$197,452	$ 78,173
Net book value		$136,584		$119,279

In the 2002 annual report, Leon's Furniture Limited reported amortization expense in 2002 of $8,552,000. In addition, the company reported it had disposed of certain capital assets and acquired others. The gain on disposal of capital assets was $56,000.

Required

1. What was the accumulated amortization of the assets disposed of during 2002?
2. Assume that Leon's Furniture Limited acquired assets costing $24,681,000 during 2002. What was the cost price of the assets sold during the year?
3. Write the journal entry to record the disposal of the assets during the year.

Beyond the Numbers

Beyond the Numbers 10-1

The following questions are unrelated except that they apply to capital assets:

1. Charlotte Quick, the owner of Quick Secreterial Services, regularly debits the cost of repairs and maintenance of capital assets to Plant and Equipment. Why would she do that, since she knows she is violating GAAP?
2. It has been suggested that, since many intangible assets have no value except to the company that owns them, they should be valued at $1.00 or zero on the balance sheet. Many accountants disagree with this view. Which view do you support? Why?
3. Marv Brown, the owner of Lakeshore Motors, regularly buys capital assets (property, plant, and equipment) and debits the cost to Repairs and Maintenance Expense. Why would he do that, since he knows this action violates GAAP?

Ethical Issue

City Centre Condos purchased land and a building for a lump sum of $3.5 million. To get the maximum tax deduction, City Centre Condos' owner allocated 85 percent of the purchase price to the building and only 15 percent to the land. A more realistic allocation would have been 75 percent to the building and 25 percent to the land.

Required

1. Explain the tax advantage of allocating too much to the building and too little to the land.
2. Was City Centre Condos' allocation ethical? If so, state why. If not, why not? Identify who was harmed.

Problems (Group A)

Problem 10-1A   *Identifying the elements of a capital asset's cost*   **(Obj. 1, 2)**

Murray Young, the owner of Young Movers, incurred the following costs in acquiring land, making land improvements, and constructing and furnishing his company's office building in the year ended December 31, 2005.

a. Purchase price of four hectares of land, including an old building that will be used for a garage (land appraised market value is $350,000; building appraised market value is $45,000)	$325,000
b. Additional dirt and earth moving	6,500
c. Fence around the boundary of the land	12,500
d. Legal fee for title search on the land	500
e. Real estate taxes in arrears on the land to be paid by Young Movers	4,800
f. Company signs at front of the company property.................................	3,000
g. Building permit for the office building...	500

h. Architect fee for the design of the office building................................. $ 29,750

i. Masonry, carpentry, roofing, and other labour to construct
   office building 811,000

j. Concrete, wood, steel girders, and other materials used in the
   construction of the office building.. 295,000

k. Renovation of the garage 31,000

l. Flowers and plants.. 7,500

m. Parking lot and concrete walks on the property 23,450

n. Lights for the parking lot, walkways, and company signs.................... 8,700

o. Supervisory salary of construction supervisor (95 percent to
   office building and 5 percent to garage renovation)............................. 50,000

p. Office furniture for the office building.. 85,000

q. Transportation and installation of office furniture................................. 1,950

Young Movers amortizes buildings over 35 years, land improvements over 15 years, and furniture over five years, all on a straight-line basis with zero residual value.

Required

1. Set up columns for Land, Land Improvements, Office Building, Garage Building, and Furniture. Show how to account for each of Young Movers' costs by listing the cost under the correct account. Determine the total cost of each asset.

2. Assuming that all construction was complete and the assets were placed in service on June 10, record amortization for the year ending December 31, 2005. Round off figures to the nearest dollar.

Problem 10-2A   *Recording capital asset transactions; exchanges; changes in useful life   (Obj. 1, 2, 4)*

Punjab Freight provides general freight service in Canada. The business's balance sheet includes the following assets under Capital Assets: Land, Buildings, and Motor Carrier Equipment. Punjab Freight has a separate accumulated amortization account for each of these assets except land.

Assume that Punjab Freight completed the following transactions:

Feb.   6   Traded in motor-carrier equipment with a book value of $43,000 (cost of $140,000) for similar new equipment with a cash cost of $165,000. Punjab Freight received a trade-in allowance of $60,000 on the old equipment and paid the remainder in cash.

June   3   Sold a building that had cost $625,000 and had accumulated amortization of $295,350 through December 31 of the preceding year. Amortization is computed on a straight-line basis. The building has a 35-year useful life and a residual value of $75,000. Punjab Freight received $250,000 cash and a $500,000 note receivable.

Sept.   25   Purchased land and a building for a single price of $395,000. An independent appraisal valued the land at $130,000, and the building at $285,000.

Dec.   31   Recorded amortization as follows:
   Motor-carrier equipment has an expected useful life of four years and an estimated residual value of 6 percent of cost. Amortization is computed using the double-declining-balance method.
   Amortization on buildings is computed by the straight-line method. The company had assigned to its older buildings, which cost $3,900,000, an estimated useful life of 25 years with a residual value equal to 15 percent of the asset cost. However, the owner of Punjab Freight has come to believe that the buildings will remain useful for a total of 30 years. Residual value remains unchanged. The company has used all its buildings, except for the one purchased on September 25, for ten years. The

new building carries a 30-year useful life and a residual value equal to 15 percent of its cost. Make separate entries for amortization on the building acquired on September 25 and the other buildings purchased in earlier years.

Required

Record the transactions in Punjab Freight's general journal.

Problem 10-3A *Explaining the concept of amortization* **(Obj. 2)**

The board of directors of Raglan Properties Ltd. is reviewing the 2005 annual report. A new board member, a dermatologist with little business experience, questions the company accountant about the amortization amounts. The dermatologist wonders why amortization expense has decreased from $250,000 in 2003, to $230,000 in 2004, and to $215,000 in 2005. He states that he could understand the decreasing annual amounts if the company had been disposing of properties each year, but that has not occurred. Further, he notes that growth in the city is increasing the values of company properties. Why is the company recording amortization when the property values are increasing?

Required

Write a paragraph or two to explain the concept of amortization to the dermatologist and to answer his questions.

Problem 10-4A *Computing amortization by three methods* **(Obj. 2, 3)**

Media Companion CD-ROM

On January 5, 2005, Technology Wizards paid $219,000 for equipment used in manufacturing computer equipment. In addition to the basic purchase price, the business paid $1,100 transportation charges, $150 insurance for the goods in transit, $17,520 provincial sales tax, and $5,000 for a special platform on which to place the equipment in the plant. Technology Wizards' owner estimates that the equipment will remain in service for four years and have a residual value of $15,000. The equipment will produce 75,000 units in the first year, with annual production decreasing by 10,000 units during each of the next three years (that is, 65,000 units in year 2, 55,000 units in year 3, and so on). In trying to decide which amortization method to use, owner Deborah Balfour has requested an amortization schedule for each of the three generally accepted amortization methods: straight-line, units-of-production, and double-declining-balance.

Required

1. For each of the generally accepted amortization methods, prepare an amortization schedule showing asset cost, amortization expense, accumulated amortization, and asset book value. Assume a December 31 year end.

2. Technology Wizards prepares financial statements for its creditors , using the amortization method that maximizes reported income in the early years of asset use. For income tax purposes, however, the business uses the amortization method that minimizes income tax payments in those early years. Identify the amortization methods that meet each of the business's objectives.

Problem 10-5A *Journalizing capital asset transactions; betterments versus repairs*
           (Obj. 1, 2, 4)

Assume that Airport Limousines completed the following transactions:

2005
Jan.   5   Paid $35,000 cash for a used limousine.
       8   Paid $1,200 to have the engine overhauled.
       9   Paid $2,500 to have the company logo put on the limousine.
June 15   Paid $150 for a minor tune-up after limousine was put into use.

Dec.	31	Recorded amortization on the limousine by the double-declining-balance method. (Assume a four-year life.)

2006

Mar.	9	Traded in the limousine for a new limousine costing $50,000. The dealer granted a $15,000 allowance on the old limousine, and the company paid the balance in cash. Recorded year 2006 amortization for the year to date and then recorded the exchange of the limousines.
Aug.	9	Repaired the new limousine's damaged fender for $3,500 cash.
Dec.	31	Recorded amortization on the new limousine by the double-declining-balance method. (Assume a four-year life and a residual value of $10,000.)

Required

Record the transactions in the general journal, indicating whether each transaction amount should be capitalized as an asset or expensed. Round all calculations to the nearest dollar.

Problem 10-6A   *Analyzing capital asset transactions from information taken from a company's financial statements   (Obj. 2, 4)*

Bombardier Inc. (www.bombardier.com) is one of Canada's more successful companies, exporting its products all over the world and growing in size to assets of $29 billion in 2003. The following excerpts come from Bombardier Inc.'s 2003 financial statements:

BOMBARDIER INC.
Notes to the Financial Statements
For the Years Ended January 31, 2003, and 2002 (adapted)
(millions of dollars)

	2003		
	Cost	**Accumulated amortization**	**Net book value**
Land	$ 250.3	$ —	$ 250.3
Buildings	2,548.6	833.2	1,715.4
Equipment	2,486.2	1,273.4	1,212.8
Other	308.3	79.5	228.8
	$5,593.4	$2,186.1	$3,407.3

	2002		
	Cost	**Accumulated amortization**	**Net book value**
Land	$ 213.8	$ —	$ 213.8
Buildings	2,062.2	417.1	1,645.1
Equipment	2,295.3	1,162.7	1,132.6
Other	367.5	113.7	253.8
	$4,938.8	$1,693.5	$3,245.3

Required

1. At January 31, 2003, what was the cost of Bombardier Inc.'s capital assets? What was the amount of accumulated amortization?

2. Bombardier Inc.'s amortization expense was $863.8 million in 2003 and $791.6 million in 2002. Why did accumulated amortization increase from 2002 to 2003 by less than the 2003 amortization expense?

3. Bombardier Inc. paid $683.1 million for capital assets in 2003. Prepare a

T-account for capital assets at cost to determine whether Bombardier Inc. bought or sold more capital assets during the year.

Problem 10-7A *Accounting for wasting assets, intangibles, and the related expenses*
(Obj. 5, 6)

Part 1 Alcan Inc. is a global producer and marketer of rolled aluminum products.
Suppose Alcan Inc. paid $2.2 million cash for a lease giving the firm the right to work a mine that contained an estimated 200,000 tonnes of bauxite. Assume that the company paid $15,000 to remove unwanted buildings from the land and $65,000 to prepare the surface for mining. Further assume that Alcan Inc. signed a $70,000 note payable to a landscaping company to return the land surface to its original condition after the lease ends. During the first year, Alcan Inc. removed 37,000 tonnes of bauxite, which it sold on account for $40 per tonne.

Required

Make general journal entries to record all transactions related to the bauxite, including amortization and sale of the first-year production.

Part 2 The Second Cup Ltd., a division of Cara Operations Limited (www.cara.com), operates the franchised coffee shops. Assume that The Second Cup Ltd. purchased another company, which carried these figures:

Book value of assets	$1.2 million
Market value of assets	1.8 million
Liabilities	0.9 million

Required

1. Make the general journal entry to record Second Cup's purchase of the other company for $1.1 million cash.
2. How should The Second Cup Ltd. account for goodwill at year end and in the future? Explain in detail.

Part 3 Suppose Sarah Belyea purchased a Second Cup franchise licence for $425,000. In addition to the basic purchase price, Belyea also paid a lawyer $7,500 for assistance with the negotiations. Belyea believes the appropriate amortization period for the cost of the franchise licence is 10 years.

Required

Make general journal entries to record the franchise transactions, including straight-line amortization for one year.

Problem 10-8A *Identifying the elements of property, plant, and equipment's cost; accounting for amortization by two methods; accounting for disposal of property, plant, and equipment; distinguishing betterments from repairs*
(Obj. 1, 2, 4)

CJYX TV Station's year end is June 30. The company completed the following capital asset transactions:

2005
Apr.   1   Paid $375,000 plus $37,500 in legal fees (pertaining to all assets purchased) to purchase the following assets from a competitor who was going out of business:

Asset	Appraised Value	Estimated Useful Life	Estimated Residual Value
Land	$170,000	—	—
Buildings	148,000	30 years	$30,000
Equipment	106,000	5 years	10,000

CJYX TV Station plans to use the straight-line amortization method for the building and for the equipment.

May	1	Purchased a mobile broadcast unit with a list price of $75,000 for $65,000 cash. The truck is expected to be used for four years and driven a total of 300,000 kilometres; it is then expected to be sold for $15,000. It will be amortized using the units-of-production method.
	3	Paid $5,500 to paint the truck with the station's colours and logo.
June	30	Recorded amortization on the assets. The mobile unit had been driven 12,500 kilometres since it was purchased.
Dec.	30	CJYX TV Station paid $10,550 to Maxwell Auto for work done on the equipment. The job consisted of annual maintenance ($550) and the addition of automatic controls ($10,000), which will increase the expected useful life of the equipment by one year (making a total of six years) and increase its expected residual value by $5,000.

2006

June	1	Sold the mobile unit for $25,000. The unit had an odometer reading of 82,000 kilometres.
	30	Recorded amortization on the assets.

Required

1. Record the above transactions of CJYX TV Station. Round all amounts to the nearest dollar.

2. Show the balance sheet presentation of the assets at June 30, 2006.

Problem 10-9A *Accounting for property, plant and equipment, and amortization; accounting for wasting assets and amortization; accounting for intangible assets and amortization* **(Obj. 2, 5, 6)**

On January 4, 2005, Ginko Mines Ltd. acquired Lost Mines Inc. for $3,750,000. At the time of the acquisition, Lost Mines Inc.'s balance sheet contained the following items, which were transferred to Ginko Mines Ltd.:

- Mining Equipment: original cost of $1,500,000 and a present market value of $1,000,000. The equipment is expected to last another eight years and have a residual value of $45,000 at that time.

- Mineral Rights: the rights to mine property by Long Lac. The mineral rights originally cost Lost Mines Inc. $2,500,000 but now have an appraised market value of $3,250,000. The mine is expected to produce 60,000,000 tonnes of ore over the next 12 years.

- Leasehold: the rights to rent office space in a nearby town for $4,750 per month for the next eight years. The leasehold has a market value today of $25,000 because of high rental rates in the area.

- Mortgage Payable: a $750,000 mortgage is outstanding on the mining equipment with interest at current rates.

Required

1. Journalize the purchase of Lost Mines Inc. by Ginko Mines Ltd.

2. Journalize the adjusting entries required for the year ending December 31, 2005, to amortize the cost of the assets—assuming 5,500,000 tonnes of ore were taken out of the mine. Use the most appropriate methods and time frames from the data given.

3. Show how the assets would appear in the capital assets section of Ginko Mines Ltd.'s balance sheet as of December 31, 2005.

Problems (Group B)

Problem 10-1B *Identifying the elements of a capital asset's cost* **(Obj. 1, 2)**

Garneau Landscaping incurred the following costs in acquiring land and a building, making land improvements, and constructing and furnishing an office building for its own use.

a. Purchase price of 2 hectares of land, including an old building
   that will be used as a shed for storage of landscaping and
   maintenance equipment (land appraised market value is
   $650,000; building appraised market value is $75,000) $575,000

b. Real estate taxes in arrears on the land to be paid by
   Garneau Landscaping.. 3,000

c. Additional dirt and earth moving... 2,995

d. Legal fees on the land acquisition 2,225

e. Fence around the boundary of the land 35,000

f. Building permit for the office building.. 500

g. Architect fee for the design of the office building 40,000

h. Company signs near front and rear approaches to the
   company property.. 9,500

i. Renovation of the storage building.. 40,000

j. Concrete, wood, steel girders, and other materials used in the
   construction of the office building.. 335,000

k. Masonry, carpentry, roofing, and other labour to construct the
   office building... 275,000

l. Parking lots and concrete walks on the property 15,775

m. Lights for the parking lot, walkways, and company signs 10,350

n. Supervisory salary of construction supervisor (90 percent to
   office building and 10 percent to shed renovation)..................................... 50,000

o. Office furniture for the office building 67,500

p. Transportation of furniture from seller to the office
   building.. 1,000

q. Flowers and plants... 1,750

Garneau Landscaping amortizes buildings over 40 years, land improvements over 20 years, and furniture over eight years, all on a straight-line basis with zero residual value.

Required

1. Set up columns for Land, Land Improvements, Office Building, Maintenance Shed, and Furniture. Show how to account for each of Garneau's costs by listing the cost under the correct account. Determine the total cost of each asset.

2. Assuming that all construction was complete and the assets were placed in service on February 25, record amortization for the year ended December 31. Round figures to the nearest dollar.

Problem 10-2B *Recording capital asset transactions; exchanges; changes in useful life* **(Obj. 1, 2, 4)**

Decima Research (www.decima.ca) surveys Canadian opinions. The company's balance sheet reports the following assets under Property and Equipment: Land, Buildings, Office Furniture, Communication Equipment, and Televideo

Equipment. The company has a separate accumulated amortization account for each of these assets except land. Assume that the company completed the following transactions:

Feb. 2 Traded in communication equipment with a book value of $13,000 (cost of $101,000) for similar new equipment with a cost of $98,000. The seller gave Decima a trade-in allowance of $18,000 on the old equipment, and the company paid the remainder in cash.

July 19 Sold a building that had cost $525,000 and had accumulated amortization of $370,666 through December 31 of the preceding year. Amortization is computed on a straight-line basis. The building has a 30-year useful life and a residual value of $45,000. Decima received $175,000 cash and a $650,000 note receivable.

Oct. 21 Purchased used communication and televideo equipment from the A.C. Neilsen Company of Canada Ltd. Total cost was $100,000 paid in cash. An independent appraisal valued the communication equipment at $85,000 and the televideo equipment at $40,000.

Dec. 31 Recorded amortization as follows:
Equipment is amortized by the double-declining-balance method over a five-year life. Record amortization on the equipment purchased on February 2 and on October 21 separately.
Amortization on buildings is computed by the straight-line method. The company had assigned buildings an estimated useful life of 25 years and a residual value that is 15 percent of cost. After using the buildings for 15 years, the company has come to believe that their *total* useful life will be 35 years. Residual value remains unchanged. The buildings cost $15,000,000.

Required

Record the transactions in the journal of Decima Research.

Problem 10-3B *Explaining the concept of amortization* *(Obj. 2)*

The board of directors of Little People Nursery School is having its regular quarterly meeting. Accounting policies are on the agenda, and amortization is being discussed. A new board member, a personal trainer, has some strong opinions about two aspects of amortization policy. Marcia Goldblatt argues that amortization must be coupled with a fund to replace company assets. Otherwise, she argues, there is no substance to amortization. She also challenges the five-year estimated life over which Little People Nursery School is amortizing the centre's computers. She notes that the computers will last much longer and should be amortized over at least 10 years.

Required

Write a paragraph or two to explain the concept of amortization to Ms. Goldblatt and to answer her arguments.

Media Companion CD-ROM

Problem 10-4B *Computing amortization by three methods* *(Obj. 2, 3)*

On January 5, 2004, Bassegio Construction purchased a used crane at a total cost of $250,000. Before placing the crane in service, the company spent $10,500 painting it, $4,000 replacing tires, and $9,500 overhauling the engine. Carlo Bassegio, the owner, estimates that the crane will remain in service for four years and have a residual value of $35,000. The crane's annual usage is expected to be 2,400 hours in each of the first three years and 2,200 hours in the fourth year. In trying to decide which amortization method to use, Mary Sharp, the accountant, requests an amortization schedule for each of the following generally accepted amortization methods: straight-line, units-of-production, and double-declining-balance.

Required

1. Assuming Bassegio Construction amortizes this crane individually, prepare an amortization schedule for each of the three generally accepted amortization methods, showing asset cost, amortization expense, accumulated amortization, and asset book value. Assume a December 31 year end.

2. Bassegio Construction prepares for its bankers financial statements using the amortization method that maximizes reported income in the early years of asset use. For income tax purposes, however, the company uses the amortization method that minimizes income tax payments in those early years. Identify the amortization methods that meet each of the company's objectives.

Problem 10-5B *Journalizing capital asset transactions; betterments versus repairs (Obj. 1, 2, 4)*

Assume that Rooney Warehousing completed the following transactions:

2004
Mar.	3	Paid $5,000 cash for a used forklift.
	5	Paid $1,500 to have the forklift engine overhauled.
	7	Paid $650 to have the forklift modified for specialized moving of auto parts.
Nov.	3	Paid $794 for transmission repair and oil change after the forklift was put into use.
Dec.	31	Used the double-declining-balance method to record amortization on the forklift. (Assume a three-year life.)

2005
Feb.	13	Replaced the forklift's broken fork for $200 cash, the deductible on Rooney Warehousing's insurance.
July	20	Traded in the forklift for a new forklift costing $15,000. The dealer granted a $3,000 allowance on the old forklift, and Rooney Warehousing paid the balance in cash. Recorded 2005 amortization for the year to date and then recorded the exchange of forklifts.
Dec.	31	Used the double-declining-balance method to record amortization on the new forklift. (Assume a five-year life.)

Required

Record the transactions in the general journal, indicating whether each transaction amount should be capitalized as an asset or expensed. Round all calculations to the nearest dollar.

Problem 10-6B *Analyzing capital asset transactions from a company's financial statements (Obj. 2, 4)*

Alberta Treasury Branches (ATB) (www.atb.com) is a regional bank based in Alberta. See the next page for an excerpt from ATB's 2003 financial statements.

Required

1. At March 31, 2003, what was Alberta Treasury Branches' cost of its capital assets? What was the amount of accumulated amortization? What was the book value of the capital assets? Does book value measure how much the company could sell the assets for? Why or why not?

2. ATB's amortization expense for 2003 was $20,107,000. Why is the amount of amortization expense so different from accumulated amortization at March 31, 2003?

3. ATB paid $26,768,000 for capital assets during 2003. Prepare a T-account for Capital Assets at cost to determine whether the company bought more or sold more capital assets during the year.

ALBERTA TREASURY BRANCHES
Consolidated Balance Sheet (adapted)

(Amounts in thousands)	March 31, 2003	2002
Assets		
Current assets:		
Cash resources	$ 670,102	$ 872,330
Securities	578,850	807,793
Loans (net of allowances)	11,691,482	10,400,563
Total current assets	12,940,434	12,080,686
Property, plant, and equipment, at cost:		
Land	7,531	7,649
Buildings	63,453	62,879
Equipment and software	98,127	100,164
Leasehold improvements	67,313	55,349
	236,424	226,041
Accumulated amortization	155,102	151,380
Property, plant, and equipment, net	81,322	74,661
Other assets	179,984	198,463
Total assets	$13,201,740	$12,353,810

Problem 10-7B   *Recording intangibles and the related expenses (Obj. 5, 6)*

Part 1   Shell Canada Limited (www.shell.ca) sells refined petroleum products. The company's balance sheet includes reserves of oil assets.

Suppose Shell paid $10 million cash for an oil lease that contained an estimated reserve of 995,000 barrels of oil. Assume that the company paid $375,000 for additional geological tests of the property and $115,000 to prepare the surface for drilling. Prior to production, the company signed an $80,000 note payable to have a building constructed on the property. Because the building provides on-site headquarters for the drilling effort and will be abandoned when the oil is depleted, its cost is debited to the Oil Properties account and included in amortization charges. During the first year of production, Shell removed 125,000 barrels of oil, which it sold on credit for $23 per barrel.

Required

Make general journal entries to record all transactions related to the oil and gas property, including amortization and sale of the first-year production.

Part 2   Bell Canada (www.bell.ca) provides telephone service to most of Canada. Assume that Bell Canada purchased another company, which carried these figures:

Book value of assets	$1,280,000
Market value of assets	1,500,000
Liabilities	450,000

Required

1. Make the general journal entry to record Bell Canada's purchase of the other company for $1,350,000 cash.

2. How should Bell Canada account for goodwill at year end and in the future? Explain in detail.

Part 3   Suppose Research in Motion Limited (RIM) purchased a patent for $1,000,000. Before using the patent, RIM incurred an additional cost of $125,000 for a lawsuit to defend the company's right to purchase it. Even though the patent gives RIM legal protection for 20 years, company management has decided to amortize its cost over a five-year period because of the industry's fast-changing technologies.

Required

Make general journal entries to record the patent transactions, including straight-line amortization for one year.

Problem 10-8B *Identifying the elements of property, plant, and equipment's cost; accounting for amortization by two methods; accounting for disposal of property, plant, and equipment; distinguishing betterments from repairs (Obj. 1, 2, 4)*

Radisson Toy Co. has a fiscal year ending August 31. The company completed the following capital asset transactions:

2004

Feb. 2 Paid $350,000 plus $20,000 in legal fees (pertaining to all assets purchased) to purchase the following assets from a competitor who was going out of business:

Asset	Appraised Value	Estimated Useful Life	Estimated Residual Value
Land......................	$150,000	—	—
Buildings...............	100,000	8 years	$10,000
Equipment.............	50,000	3 years	4,000

Radisson Toy Co. plans to use the straight-line amortization method for the building and for the equipment.

June 2 Purchased a delivery truck with a list price of $30,000 for $27,000 cash. The truck is expected to be used for three years and driven a total of 300,000 kilometres; it is then expected to be sold for $2,500. It will be amortized using the units-of-production method.

3 Paid $3,000 to paint the truck with the company's colours and logo.

Aug. 31 Recorded amortization on the assets. The truck had been driven 20,000 kilometres since it was purchased.

2005

Jan. 4 Radisson Toy Co. paid $9,000 to Lawson Services Ltd. for work done on the equipment. The job consisted of annual maintenance ($1,000) and the addition of automatic controls ($8,000), which will increase the expected useful life of the equipment to a total of five years and increase its expected residual value by $1,000.

Aug. 25 Sold the truck for $18,000. The truck had an odometer reading of 140,000 kilometres.

Aug. 31 Recorded amortization on the assets.

Required

1. Record the above transactions of Radisson Toy Co. Round all amounts to the nearest dollar.
2. Show the balance sheet presentation of the assets at August 31, 2005.

Problem 10-9B *Accounting for wasting assets, intangible assets, and related expenses (Obj. 2, 5, 6)*

On October 2, 2005, Nunavut Mines Inc. acquired Resolute Exploration Ltd. for $6,500,000. At the time of the acquisition, Resolute's balance sheet contained the following items, which were transferred to Nunavut Mines Inc.:

- Mining Equipment: original cost of $11,000,000 and a present market value of $750,000. The equipment is expected to last another 10 years and have a residual value of $15,000 at that time.
- Mineral Rights: the rights to mine property by Grise Fiord. The mineral rights originally cost Resolute $1,500,000 but now have an appraised market value of $5,200,000. The mine is expected to produce 75,000,000 tonnes of ore over the next 10 years.
- Leasehold: the rights to rent office space in a nearby town for $5,500 per month for the next 10 years. The leasehold has a market value today of $60,000 because of high rental rates in the area.
- Mortgage Payable: a $700,000 mortgage is outstanding on the mining equipment with interest at current rates.

Required

1. Journalize the purchase of Resolute Exploration Ltd. by Nunavut Mines Inc.
2. Journalize the adjusting entries required for the year ending September 30, 2006, to amortize the cost of the assets, assuming 3,500,000 tonnes of ore were taken out of the mine. Use the most appropriate methods and time frames from the data given.
3. Show how the assets would appear in the capital assets section of Nunavut Mines Inc.'s balance sheet as of September 30, 2006.

Challenge Problems

Problem 10-1C   *Understanding amortization and betterments and repairs*   *(Obj. 1, 2)*

The owner of newly formed Georgian Bay Air Taxi, a friend of your family, knows you are taking an accounting course and asks for some advice. Mr. Lind tells you that he is pretty good at running the company but doesn't understand accounting. Specifically, he has two concerns:

1. The company has just paid $1,000,000 for two used float planes. His accountants tell him that he should use accelerated amortization for his financial statements but he understands that straight-line amortization will result in lower charges to expense in the early years. He wants to use straight-line amortization.
2. A friend told him that Georgian Bay Air Taxi should capitalize all repairs to the planes and "spread the cost out over the life of the planes." He wonders if there is anything wrong with this advice.

Required

Respond to Mr. Lind's questions using your understanding of amortization and betterments and repairs.

Problem 10-2C   *Accounting for wasting assets (Obj. 5)*

Zadok Mining Corp. is a new company that has been formed to mine for nickel in Northern Ontario. The ore body is estimated to contain 100,000,000 kilograms of pure nickel for which the world price is $14,400 per tonne. The costs of mine development are estimated to be $80,000,000.

Required

Calculate the costs that would be charged against the nickel production in the form of amortization on a per-1,000-kilogram basis. Estimate any costs you think should also be included. Do not include the costs to mine and refine the ore, or shipping and selling costs.

Extending Your Knowledge

Decision Problem

Measuring profitability based on different inventory and amortization methods (Obj. 2)

Link Back to Chapter 6 (Inventory Methods). Suppose you are considering investing in two businesses, Krug Associates and Tsui Co. The two companies are virtually identical, and both began operations at the beginning of 2005. During the year, each company purchased inventory as follows:

Jan.	10	12,000	units at $ 7	=	$ 84,000
Mar.	11	5,000	units at 9	=	45,000
July	9	10,000	units at 10	=	100,000
Oct.	12	12,000	units at 11	=	132,000
Totals		39,000			$361,000

During 2005, both companies sold 30,000 units of inventory.

In early January 2005, both companies purchased equipment costing $200,000 that had a five-year estimated useful life and a $20,000 residual value. Krug Associates uses the first-in, first-out (FIFO) method for its inventory and straight-line amortization for its equipment. Tsui Co. uses last-in, first-out (LIFO) and double-declining-balance amortization. Both companies' trial balances at December 31, 2005 included the following:

Sales revenue	$560,000
Operating expenses	110,000

Required

1. Prepare both companies' income statements.

2. Write an investment newsletter to address the following questions for your clients: Which company appears to be more profitable? Which company will have more cash to invest in promising projects? If prices continue rising in both companies' industries over the long term, which company would you prefer to invest in? Why?

Financial Statement Problem

Property, plant, and equipment, and intangible assets   (Obj. 2, 4, 6)

Refer to Intrawest Corporation's financial statements in Appendix A and answer the following questions.

1. With respect to ski and resort operations, which amortization method does Intrawest Corporation use for the purpose of reporting to shareholders and creditors in the financial statements? Where did you find your answer?

2. What was the total amount of amortization expense for 2003?

3. Intrawest Corporation indicates one amount for amortization on the income statement, yet the change in accumulated amortization from 2002 to 2003 in Note 5 is a lesser amount. Why do you think this is the case?

4. Intrawest Corporation classifies one type of asset as both a current asset and as long-term. Why do you think this differentiation is done?

5. Does Intrawest Corporation capitalize interest costs? If so, how much was capitalized in 2003?

Appendix

Capital Cost Allowance

Canada Customs and Revenue Agency (CCRA) allows corporations as well as individuals with business or professional income to compute deductions from income to recognize the consumption or using up of capital assets. The deductions are called **capital cost allowance (CCA)**. CCRA specifies the *maximum* rates allowed for each asset class, called *capital cost allowance rates*. Some typical CCRA rates and classes are:

	Rate	Class
Automobiles	30%	10
Brick, concrete, or stone buildings bought after 1987	4%	1
Computer software	100%	12
Office furniture and fixtures	20%	8
Computers	30%	10

CCRA allows the taxpayer to claim only 50 percent of the normal CCA rate in the year of acquisition. However, there are some exceptions and Class 12 is one of them. Class 12 assets have a full 100 percent capital cost allowance rate in the year of acquisition.

The CCA rate is applied to the balance in the asset class at the end of the year (cost minus accumulated CCA claimed to date) in the same manner as with the double-declining-balance method discussed on pages 492 to 494.

To illustrate, during the year beginning January 2, 2004, Brad Taylor, the entrepreneur from Chapter 1, bought a computer and an accounting software package to help him account for his business income. The computer cost $2,200 and the software cost $300. Brad decided to amortize the computer and the software on a straight-line basis over five years, and expects the computer and software to have no value at the end of five years. These assumptions lead to an amortization expense of $440 per year ($2,200 ÷ 5 years) for the computer and an amortization expense of $60 per year ($300 ÷ 5 years) for the software.

For income tax purposes, the computer is considered to be a Class 10 asset. The capital cost allowance rate for Class 10 assets is 30 percent. The software is considered to be a Class 12 asset. The CCA rate for Class 12 assets is 100 percent. Remember that for most asset classes, a taxpayer can claim only 50 percent of normal CCA in the year of acquisition, which in Brad's case is the year 2004. In 2004, Brad could claim up to the maximum capital cost allowance of $330 ([$2,200 × 30%] × 50%) for the computer. However, he can claim up to the maximum capital cost allowance of $300 for the software in 2004. These are the only capital assets in these classes.

In 2005, Brad would apply the Class 10 rate of 30 percent to the cost of the computer remaining after the 2004 CCA is deducted. In 2005, he could claim up to the maximum CCA of $561 ([$2,200 − $330] × 30%) for the computer. Following the same process in 2006, Brad could claim up to the maximum capital cost allowance of $393 ([$2,200 − $330 − $561] × 30%) for the computer. The table below shows the maximum CCA Brad could deduct from his business income for the first six years:

	2004	2005	2006	2007	2008	2009
Computer	$330	$561	$393	$275	$192	$135
Software	$300	0	0	0	0	0

Notice that in 2009, the sixth year that Brad owned the computer, he is able to deduct CCA for income tax purposes. However, for accounting purposes, the computer would be fully amortized at the end of 2008, the fifth year, since Brad decided to amortize the computer on a straight-line basis over five years. This example shows that amortization expense deducted from income on the income statement often differs from the capital cost allowance claimed by a taxpayer on the tax return.

Capital cost allowance and amortization issues are quite complicated. These issues are studied more fully in advanced accounting courses and tax courses.

Current Liabilities and Payroll

CHAPTER OBJECTIVES

After studying this chapter, you should be able to

1 Account for current liabilities of known amount

2 Account for current liabilities that must be estimated

3 Compute payroll amounts

4 Record basic payroll transactions

5 Use a payroll system

6 Report current liabilities on the balance sheet

 Media Companion CD-ROM

Visit the Media Companion CD-ROM that comes with this book for extra practice with the new material in Chapter 11.

Most products are guaranteed against defects. Computers, video equipment, and automobiles are prime examples. When you buy a digital camera, a computer, or a new car, the manufacturer agrees to repair it if something goes wrong. Do you ever consider this guarantee when you buy a product? That may be what motivates you to select a Honda over a Chevrolet. If not, you should consider the product guarantee because it can vary from company to company and repairs can be expensive.

Product guarantees are called warranties, and warranties are a major liability of companies such as Bombardier Recreational Products Inc., General Motors, and Nortel Networks. Warranties pose an accounting chal lenge because companies such as Bombardier Recreational Products don't know which vehicle might have to be recalled or repaired. If this type of information could be known in advance, companies such as Bombardier might question whether or not to sell these products. But it's almost certain that companies will have unforeseen problems with some of their new products, so companies like Bombardier and General Motors record a warranty liability based on estimates.

In this chapter we will see how Bombardier, General Motors, Nortel Networks and other companies account for their product warranties. We will also learn about the other current liabilities, such as accounts payable and payroll liabilities.

CURRENT liabilities are obligations due within one year or within the company's operating cycle if it is longer than one year. Obligations due beyond that period of time are classified as *long-term liabilities*. We discussed current liabilities and long-term liabilities in Chapter 4, pages 175 and 176.

Current Liabilities of Known Amount

OBJECTIVE 1
Account for current liabilities of known amount

The amounts of most current liabilities are known. A few current liabilities must be estimated. Let's begin with current liabilities of known amount.

Accounts Payable

Amounts owed for products or services that are purchased on account are *accounts payable*. We have seen many accounts payable examples in previous chapters. For example, most businesses purchase inventories and office supplies on account. Collicutt Energy Services Ltd. (www.collicutt.com), a Red Deer, Alberta-based company engaged in natural-gas service and the fabrication of compression and power-generation equipment, reported accounts payable and accrued liabilities of $16 million at March 1, 2003 (see Exhibit 11-1).

Let's see how Collicutt Energy Services Ltd.'s accounts payable get onto the company's balance sheet. One of Collicutt's common transactions is the credit purchase of its inventory. Collicutt's accounts payable and perpetual inventory systems are integrated. When certain inventory dips below a predetermined level, the system automatically places an order to buy the goods. After the order is placed and the goods are received, clerks enter inventory and accounts payable data into the system. Collicutt Energy Services Ltd. records the purchase of inventory on account as follows (amount assumed):

Nov. 22
Inventory	600	
Accounts Payable		600
Purchase on account.		

COLLICUTT ENERGY SERVICES LTD.
Balance Sheet (partial, adapted)
March 1, 2003

Liabilities	(In thousands)
Current	
Operating loan	$14,457
Accounts payable and accrued liabilities	16,060
Deferred revenue	3,969
Current portion of long-term debt	3,709
Other	19,376
	$57,571

The purchase increases both Inventory and Accounts Payable. Then, to pay the liability, the accounting system debits Accounts Payable and credits Cash, as follows:

Dec. 5		
Accounts Payable	600	
Cash		600
Paid on account.		

Short-Term Notes Payable

Short-term notes payable are a common form of financing. For example, the Hudson's Bay Company discloses in its January 31, 2003, annual report that it owes $24,744,000 in short-term borrowings. Short-term notes payable are promissory notes that must be paid within one year. The following entries are typical for a short-term note payable that the Hudson's Bay Company might issue to purchase inventory:

2005		
Oct. 31	Inventory	16,000	
	Note Payable, Short-Term		16,000
	Purchase of inventory by issuing a one-year 10 percent note payable.		
2006		
Jan. 31	Interest Expense	403	
	Interest Payable		403
	Accrued interest expense at year end ($16,000 $\times$ 0.10 $\times$ $^{92}/_{365}$).		

The balance sheet at January 31, 2006, will report the Note Payable of $16,000 and the related Interest Payable of $403 as current liabilities. The income statement for fiscal 2006 will report interest expense of $403. Both the balance sheet and income statement are as follows:

KEY POINT

The interest on a note is separate from the principal. The accrued interest should be credited to Interest Payable—*not* to Note Payable.

HUDSON'S BAY COMPANY
Balance Sheet
January 31, 2006

Assets		Liabilities	
		Current liabilities:	
Various	$XXX	Note payable, short-term	$16,000
		Interest payable	403

HUDSON'S BAY COMPANY
Income Statement
For the Year Ended January 31, 2006

Revenues:....................	$XXX
Expenses:	
Interest expense	$403

The following entry records payment of the note at maturity:

2006				
Oct. 31	Note Payable, Short-Term	16,000		
	Interest Payable..	403		
	Interest Expense	1,197		
	Cash		17,600	

Paid a note payable and interest at
maturity. Interest expense is $1,196.71 ($16,000 \times 0.10 \times {}^{273}\!/_{365}$).
Cash paid is $17,600 [$16,000 + ($16,000 \times 0.10)].

> **LEARNING TIP**
>
> Interest Payable must have a zero balance after the October 31, 2006, note payment is recorded. After interest is paid, it is no longer a liability; the amount previously accrued must be reduced with a debit to Interest Payable.

Interest expense of $403 was correctly allocated to the year ended January 31, 2006. The Hudson's Bay Company's interest expense will be $1,197 for 2007. At maturity, the Hudson's Bay Company will pay a full year's interest, allocated as shown in this diagram.

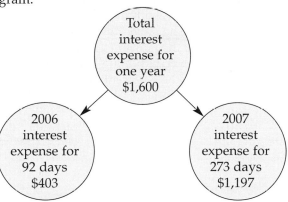

Goods and Services Tax and Sales Tax Payable

There are two basic consumption taxes levied on purchases in Canada that are visible to the consumer: the goods and services tax (GST) levied by the federal government and the provincial sales taxes (PST) levied by all the provinces except Alberta; there are, at present, no sales taxes in the Yukon, Nunavut, or the Northwest Territories. The goods and services tax was introduced in Chapter 5, page 229. There are also excise or luxury taxes, which are a form of sales tax levied by the federal and provincial governments on products such as cigarettes, jewellery, and alcoholic beverages; these taxes are hidden in that they are collected by the manufacturer. The focus of discussion in this section will be on the consumption or visible taxes; the goods and services tax and provincial sales taxes will be discussed in turn below. In order to simplify the discussion, the material concerning calculation and payment of the GST will exclude the PST and the material concerning calculation and payment of the PST will generally exclude the GST. Nova Scotia, New Brunswick, and Newfoundland and Labrador have harmonized the GST with their PST. Quebec has partially harmonized its sales tax (QST), and Prince Edward Island has also partly harmonized its sales tax (PST) with the GST. The Harmonized Sales Tax (HST) will be described below.

Goods and Services Tax   In 1991, the federal government passed legislation eliminating existing taxes imposed on manufactured and imported goods. At the same time, it implemented a goods and services tax (GST) that is collected from the ultimate consumer and includes most goods and services consumed in Canada. The tax and its application may be covered in an introductory tax course and is beyond the scope of this text; the ensuing discussion deals primarily with basic facts about the tax and how to account for it.

There are three categories of goods and services with respect to the GST:

1. Zero-rated supplies such as basic groceries, prescription drugs, and medical devices;

2. Exempt supplies such as educational services, health care services, and financial services; and

3. Taxable supplies, which basically includes everything that is not zero-rated or exempt.

The GST rate is 7 percent. The tax is collected by the individual or entity (called the *registrant*) supplying the taxable good or service (called *taxable supplies*) to the final consumer. The GST is remitted to the Receiver General. Suppliers of taxable goods and services have to pay tax on their purchases. However, they are able to deduct the amount of GST paid (called an *input tax credit*) from the GST they have collected from their sales of goods and services in calculating the amount due to the federal government. The GST Return and the net tax must be remitted to the Receiver General quarterly for most registrants and monthly for larger registrants.

For example, Mary Janicek, who lives in Whitehorse in the Yukon, purchased a power lawn mower on July 2, 2005, with the intention of earning money by cutting grass during the summer.[1] The lawn mower cost $250; the GST was $17.50. Because Mary is planning to use the mower exclusively to cut grass for a fee, she could recover the $17.50. However, assuming she were a registrant, she would have to charge all her customers the 7 percent GST on sales of her lawn-mowing services and remit it to the government. During the three-month first quarter, Mary earned revenue of $2,000.00, related GST of $140.00, and thus collected $2,140.00. She spent $107.00—$100.00 plus GST of $7.00—on gasoline for the mower. Her input tax credit of $24.50 included the $17.50 GST on the lawn mower and $7.00 GST on gasoline for the mower. The entries to record these transactions would be

2005

July 2	Equipment	250.00	
	GST Receivable	17.50	
	Cash..		267.50
	To record purchase of power mower.		
July–Sept.	Supplies Expense..	100.00	
	GST Receivable	7.00	
	Cash..		107.00
	To record purchase of gasoline for power mower.		
July–Sept.	Cash	2,140.00	
	Lawn-mowing Revenue...		2,000.00
	GST Payable		140.00
	To record revenue from mowing lawns.		

Mary would be required to remit $115.50 ($140.00 − $17.50 − $7.00) as her first quarterly payment. Since Mary would be recovering the GST paid on the purchase of the mower and gasoline of $24.50 ($17.50 + $7.00), she would credit the recovery to the GST Receivable account, to bring its balance to zero. The entry would be as follows:

_____

[1] If your business earns less than $30,000 per year, it does not have to be registered for GST purposes. In reality, Mary Janicek's business would be below the minimum threshold of $30,000, so Mary is unlikely to be a registrant. The scenario is illustrative. A business is only required to become a GST registrant if taxable supplies exceed $30,000 per year.

Oct. 31
GST Payable... 140.00
    Cash... 115.50
    GST Receivable... 24.50
To record payment of GST payable net of input tax credits to Receiver General.

In the Mary Janicek example, we used two accounts—GST Receivable and GST Payable—to illustrate input tax credits and GST collections to be remitted to the Receiver General. Some registrants use only one account—GST Payable—to record input tax credits *and* GST collections. When the GST Return is sent to the Receiver General, the final account balance in the GST Payable account is remitted if the balance is a credit, or a refund is requested if the balance is a debit. However, in the remainder of this chapter, we will continue to use the two-account approach to illustrate input tax credits and GST collections.

Because they collect the GST for the federal government, the registrants owe the Receiver General the net tax collected; the account Goods and Services Tax Payable is a current liability. Most companies include GST owing with Accounts Payable and Accrued Liabilities, and GST receivable as a current asset on their balance sheets.

Provincial Sales Tax   As was mentioned above, all the provinces except Alberta (as well as the Yukon, Nunavut, and the Northwest Territories) levy a sales tax on sales to the final consumers of products; sales tax is not levied on sales to wholesalers or retailers. The final sellers charge their customers the sales tax in addition to the price of the item sold. The following provincial sales tax rates were in effect at the time of writing:

British Columbia	7.5%	
Saskatchewan	6%	
Manitoba	7%	
Ontario	8%	
Quebec	7.5%	(PST based on price including GST)
Prince Edward Island	10%	(PST based on price including GST)
New Brunswick	15%	(blended with GST)
Nova Scotia	15%	(blended with GST)
Newfoundland and Labrador	15%	(blended with GST)

As this list shows, four provinces charge PST and GST separately on the purchase price of a taxable good or service. Two provinces charge PST on the sum of the purchase price and the GST. Three provinces charge a combined GST and PST rate of 15 percent on the purchase price. This 15 percent rate is known as *Harmonized Sales Tax (HST)*. By harmonizing their PST with the GST, New Brunswick, Nova Scotia, and Newfoundland and Labrador have reduced the cost of collecting and administering consumption taxes.

Consider a taxable item that costs $100 before tax. Ontario charges PST and GST separately; a taxable sale of $100.00 would have GST of $7.00 (0.07 × $100.00) and PST of $8.00 (0.08 × $100.00). Prince Edward Island charges PST on GST; a taxable sale of $100.00 would have GST of $7.00 (0.07 × $100.00) and PST of $10.70 [0.10 × ($100.00 + $7.00)]. Nova Scotia has harmonized the PST and the GST; a taxable sale of $100.00 would have PST and GST of $15.00 (0.15 × $100.00).

Consider Super Stereo Products, an electronics superstore located in Ottawa. Super Stereo does not pay provincial sales tax on its purchase of a TV set from Panasonic because it is inventory for resale, but you, as a consumer, would have to pay the province of Ontario's 8 percent provincial sales tax to Super Stereo when you buy a Panasonic TV from the store. Super Stereo pays the sales tax it collected from you to the provincial government. Panasonic, the manufacturer, would not have a sales tax liability at its year end, but Super Stereo probably would. (For purposes of the discussion of sales tax, we will ignore the GST.)

E-commerce continues to grow in popularity. It provides consumers with a convenient method for shopping and may help them save money in the process.

Suppose you decided to buy a friend a book as a birthday gift. The book sells for $26.59 at a local bookstore. In addition you will pay the Goods and Services Tax (GST) and provincial sales tax (PST)—unless you live in Alberta, Ontario, the Northwest Territories, and Nunavut—on the purchase price. If we assume that both GST and PST are 7 percent, you will pay $1.86 in GST and $1.86 in PST, for a total cost of $30.31 for the book.

How can buying a book online help you save money? If you buy a book or any other item online from Indigo.ca or another e-commerce bookseller, you will not have to pay PST. Why not? It appears that provincial-sales-tax legislation has not yet been changed to reflect this new form of retailing. If companies do not have a physical presence in a province, such as an office or a warehouse, they do not have to charge PST and so will not have a sales tax liability to the provincial government. While no dollar figures are available for Canada, in the United States, where similar state-sales-tax legislation exists, it is believed that sales tax revenue lost because of internet sales will amount to $20 billion by 2005.

Consumers can voluntarily pay sales tax on products they purchase over the internet, but most are not aware that they can and most do not want to pay more for a product than they have to. This issue of lost sales-tax revenue will become a growing concern to provincial governments because provincial sales tax is one of the provinces' largest sources of revenue. Expect to hear more on this issue, especially as e-commerce sales continue to increase.

Suppose one Saturday's sales at the Super Stereo store totalled $20,000. The business would have collected an additional 8 percent in sales tax, which would equal $1,600 ($20,000 × 0.08). The business would record that day's sales as follows:

Cash	21,600	
Sales Revenue		20,000
Sales Tax Payable		1,600

To record cash sales of $20,000 and the related sales tax of 8 percent.

Because the retailers owe to the province the sales tax collected, the account Sales Tax Payable is a current liability. Most companies include sales tax payable with Accounts Payable and Accrued Liabilities on their balance sheets.

Companies forward the collected sales tax to the taxing authority at regular intervals, at which time they debit Sales Tax Payable and credit Cash. Observe that Sales Tax Payable does not correspond to any sales tax expense that the business is incurring. Nor does this liability arise from the purchase of any asset. Rather, it is the cash that the business is collecting on behalf of the government.

Many companies consider it inefficient to credit Sales Tax Payable when recording each sale. Instead, they record sales revenue and sales tax together. Then, prior to paying tax to the province, they make a single entry for the entire period's transactions to bring Sales Revenue and Sales Tax Payable to their correct balances.

Suppose a company located in Vancouver had sales in July of $100,000, subject to the BC retail sales tax of 7.5 percent. Its summary entry to record the month's sales revenue and sales tax collected would be

July 31	Cash	107,500	
	Sales Revenue		100,000
	Sales Tax Payable		7,500
	To record sales for the month and the related sales tax of 7.5 percent.		

Current Portion of Long-Term Debt

Some long-term notes payable and bonds payable are paid in instalments, which means that equal portions of the principal are repaid at specific time intervals. The **current portion of long-term debt** is the amount of the principal that is payable within one year—a current liability. The remaining portion of the long-term debt is a long-term liability. At the end of the year, the company may make an adjusting entry to shift the current instalment of the long-term debt to a current liability amount as follows (amounts assumed):

(LEARNING TIP sidebar:) A current liability is due within one year, or within the company's operating cycle if it is longer than one year. The portion of a long-term debt payable within the year is classified as a current liability. The interest payable is classified separately from the principal.

2005

Dec. 31	Long-Term Debt	10,000	
	Current Portion of Long-Term Debt		10,000
	To transfer the portion of long-term debt due in 2006 to the current liability account.		

Collicutt Energy Services Ltd.'s balance sheet (Exhibit 11-1, page 536) reports Current Portion of Long-Term Debt as a current liability. On its full balance sheet, Collicutt reports long-term debt immediately after total current liabilities. *Long-term debt* refers to the notes and bonds payable that are payable later than one year beyond the balance sheet date.

The liabilities for the current portion of long-term debt do *not* include any accrued interest payable. The account, Current Portion of Long-Term Debt, represents only the appropriate portion of the *principal amount owed*. Interest Payable is a separate account for a different liability—the interest that must be paid. Collicutt Energy Services Ltd. includes interest payable under the current liability caption Accounts Payable and Accrued Liabilities.

STOP & THINK

Suppose that Collicutt Energy Services Ltd. reported its full liability as long-term. Identify two ratios that would have been distorted by this accounting error. State whether the ratio values would be overstated or understated and whether they would report an overly positive or negative view of the company.

Answer: Reporting a liability as long-term could mislead external users because it understates current liabilities and has these effects:

Ratio	Overstated or Understated	View of the Company
Current ratio	Overstated	Overly positive
Acid-test ratio	Overstated	Overly positive

This example shows that accounting includes both *recording* transactions and *reporting* the information. Reporting is every bit as important as recording.

Accrued Expenses (Accrued Liabilities)

An **accrued expense** is an expense that has not yet been paid. An accrued expense creates a liability. This explains why accrued expenses are also called **accrued liabilities**. Accrued expenses typically occur with the passage of time, such as interest payable on long-term debt. We introduced accrued expenses in Chapter 3, page 119.

(LEARNING TIP sidebar:) Every accrued expense (liability) involves a debit to an *expense* and a credit to a *liability*.

Like most other companies, Collicutt Energy Services Ltd. has salaries payable, other payroll liabilities, interest payable, and property taxes payable. We illustrated the accounting for interest payable on pages 536 and 537. The next section, plus the second half of this chapter, covers accounting for payroll liabilities.

Payroll Liabilities

Payroll, also called **employee compensation**, is a major expense of many businesses. For service organizations—such as public accounting firms and real-estate brokers—payroll is *the* major expense. Payroll expense for salaries and wages usually causes an accrued liability at year end. We show how to account for payroll expense in the second half of this chapter.

Unearned Revenues

Unearned revenues are also called *deferred revenues* and *revenues collected in advance*. As we saw in Chapter 3, page 121, an unearned revenue is a liability because it represents an obligation to provide a good or service. Each account title indicates that the business has received cash from its customers before it has earned the revenue. The company has an obligation to provide goods or services to the customer. Exhibit 11-1 shows Collicutt Energy Services Ltd. has received cash from customers for future services of $3,969,000 at March 1, 2003. Let's consider another example.

Canadian Business (www.canadianbusiness.com) may be purchased every two weeks or by means of a subscription. When subscribers pay in advance to have *Canadian Business* delivered to their home or business, Rogers Publishing incurs a liability to provide future service. The liability account is called Unearned Subscription Revenue (which could also be titled Unearned Subscription Income or Deferred Subscription Income).

Assume that Rogers Publishing charges $39.95 for Bob Bish's one-year subscription to *Canadian Business*. Rogers Publishing's entries would be

```
2005
July 2    Cash...................................................................................    39.95
               Unearned Subscription Revenue.........................................         39.95
          To record receipt of cash at the start of a one-year subscription.
```

After receiving the cash on July 2, 2005, Rogers Publishing owes its customer magazines that Rogers Publishing will provide over the next 12 months. Rogers Publishing's liability is:

Unearned Subscription Revenue

	39.95

During 2005, Rogers Publishing delivers one-half of the magazines and earns $19.98 ($39.95 × ½) of the subscription revenue. At December 31, 2005, Rogers Publishing makes the following adjusting entry to decrease (debit) the liability Unearned Subscription Revenue and increase (credit) Subscription Revenue:

```
2005
Dec. 31    Unearned Subscription Revenue ..............................................    19.98
                Subscription Revenue.........................................................         19.98
           Earned revenue that was collected in advance  ($39.95 × ½).
```

After posting, Rogers Publishing still owes the subscriber $19.97 for unearned revenue. Rogers Publishing has earned $19.98 of the revenue, as follows:

Unearned Subscription Revenue				Subscription Revenue	
Dec. 31	19.98	July 2	39.95	Dec. 31	19.98
		Bal.	19.97		

Customer Deposits Payable

Some companies require cash deposits from customers as security on borrowed assets. These amounts are called Customer Deposits Payable because the company must refund the cash to the customer under certain conditions. For example, telephone companies may demand a cash deposit from a customer before installing a telephone. Utility companies and businesses that lend tools and appliances commonly demand a deposit as protection against damage and theft. Certain manufacturers of products sold through individual dealers, such as Avon (www.avon.com) or Mary Kay (www.marykay.com), require deposits from the dealers who sell their products; the deposit is usually equal to the cost of the sample kit provided to the merchandiser. Companies whose products are sold in returnable containers collect deposits on those containers. Because the deposit is returned to the customer, the amount collected represents a liability.

Current Liabilities That Must Be Estimated

OBJECTIVE 2
Account for current liabilities that must be estimated

A business may know that a liability exists but not know the exact amount. It cannot simply ignore the liability. This liability must be reported on the balance sheet.

Estimated current liabilities vary among companies. A prime example is Estimated Warranty Payable, which is common for companies such as Bombardier Recreational Products Inc. and Nortel Networks.

Estimated Warranty Payable

Many companies guarantee their products against defects under *warranty* agreements. Ninety-day warranties and one-year warranties are common.

The matching principle leads us to record the *warranty expense* in the same period we record the revenue. The expense occurs when you make a sale, not when you pay the warranty claim. For a review of the matching principle, see Chapter 3, page 111. At the time of the sale, the company does not know the exact amount of warranty expense, but the business must estimate its warranty expense and the related liability.

Assume that Collicutt Energy Services Ltd. made sales in 2003 of $80 million that are subject to warranty. In Note 2, "Significant Accounting Policies," Collicutt indicates that the company provides warranty coverage for its products for one year from date of sale. Assume that, in the past, the warranty provision and actual warranty cost was 1 percent of fabricating sales. Further, assume the company believes that 0.9 percent of products sold in 2003 will require warranty work during the one-year period. The company would record the sales of $80 million and the warranty expense of $720,000 ($80,000,000 × 0.009) in the same period as follows:

2003		
Various dates		
Accounts Receivable	80,000,000	
Sales Revenue (fabricating)		80,000,000
Sales on account.		
Dec. 31		
Warranty Expense	720,000	
Estimated Warranty Payable		720,000
To accrue warranty expense.		

Assume that the value of defective merchandise totals $700,000. If Collicutt repairs the defective products, Collicutt makes this journal entry:

2003–2004

Various dates

Estimated Warranty Payable..	700,000	
Various Expenses...		700,000

To *repair* defective products sold under warranty.

Collicutt Energy Services Ltd.'s expense on the income statement is the estimated amount of $720,000, not the $700,000 actually paid. After paying these warranty claims, Collicutt Energy Services Ltd.'s liability account would have a credit balance of $20,000.

Estimated Warranty Payable

700,000		720,000
	Bal.	20,000

STOP & THINK

Maxim Limited, a new company, made sales of $400,000. The company estimated warranty repairs at 5 percent of the sales. Maxim's actual warranty payments were $19,000. Record sales, warranty expense, and warranty payments. How much is Maxim's estimated warranty payable at the end of the period?

Answer:

Accounts Receivable	400,000	
Sales Revenue		400,000
Warranty Expense ($400,000 × 0.05)	20,000	
Estimated Warranty Payable		20,000
Estimated Warranty Payable	19,000	
Cash..		19,000

Estimated Warranty Payable

19,000		20,000
	Bal.	1,000

Estimated Vacation Pay Liability

Most companies grant paid vacations to their employees. The employees receive this benefit when they take their vacation, but they earn the compensation by working the other days of the year. The law requires most employers to provide a minimum number of weeks holiday per year (usually two, but sometimes more, based on the number of years worked). To match expense with revenue properly, the company accrues the vacation pay expense and liability for each of the 50 work weeks of the year. Then, the company records payment during the two-week vacation period. Employee turnover, terminations, and ineligibility (for example, no vacation allowed until one full year has been worked) force companies to estimate the vacation pay liability.

Suppose a company's January payroll is $100,000 and vacation pay adds 4 percent, or $4,000 (with the 4 percent calculated as two weeks of annual vacation divided by 50 work weeks each year). Experience indicates that only 90 percent of the available vacations will be taken. Therefore, the January vacation pay estimate is $3,600 ($4,000 × 0.90). In January, the company records the vacation pay accrual as follows:

Jan. 31	Vacation Pay Expense	3,600	
	Estimated Vacation Pay Liability....................................		3,600

Each month thereafter, the company makes a similar entry.

If an employee takes a two-week vacation in August, his or her $2,000 monthly salary is recorded as follows:

Aug. 31	Estimated Vacation Pay Liability	2,000	
	Various Withholding Accounts and		
	Wages Payable[2]		2,000

Income Tax Payable (for a Corporation)

Corporations pay income tax in the same way as individual taxpayers do. Corporations file their income tax returns with Canada Customs and Revenue Agency (CCRA) and their provincial governments after the end of the fiscal year, so they must estimate their income tax payable for reporting on the balance sheet. During the year, corporations make monthly tax payments to the governments, based on their estimated tax for the year. A corporation with a December 31 year end would record the payment of $100,000 of income tax expense for September as follows:

Sept. 30	Income Tax Expense	100,000	
	Cash		100,000
	To pay monthly income tax instalment.		

At December 31, the corporation calculates actual tax expense for the year to be $1,240,000. Accordingly, the corporation pays the monthly instalment of $100,000 on December 30, and accrues the additional $40,000 at December 31. The entries are

Dec. 30	Income Tax Expense	100,000	
	Cash		100,000
	To pay monthly income tax.		

Dec. 31	Income Tax Expense	40,000	
	Income Tax Payable		40,000
	To accrue income tax at year end.		

The corporation will pay off this tax liability during the next year, when it files its tax returns with Canada Customs and Revenue Agency and its provincial government, so Income Tax Payable is a current liability.

Contingent Liabilities

A *contingent liability* is not an actual liability. Instead, it is a potential liability that depends on a *future* event arising out of past events. For example, Packenham town council may sue North Ontario Electric Supply Ltd., the company that installed new street lights in Packenham, claiming that the electrical wiring is faulty. The past transaction is the street-light installation. The future event is the court case that will decide the suit. North Ontario Electric Supply Ltd. thus faces a contingent liability, which may or may not become an actual obligation.

It would be misleading for North Ontario Electric Supply Ltd. to withhold knowledge of the lawsuit from its creditors or from anyone considering investing in the business. The *disclosure principle* of accounting (see Chapter 6, page 303) requires a company to report any information deemed relevant to outsiders to the business. The goal is to give people relevant, reliable information for decision making.

The *CICA Handbook* requires *contingent losses* generally to be accrued or disclosed in the financial statements but bars *contingent gains* from being recognized *until* they are realized. This approach follows the principle of conservatism. The accounting profession divides contingent liabilities into three categories. Each category indicates a likelihood that a contingency will cause a loss and become an

---

[2] The various payroll accounts are discussed later in the chapter.

actual liability. The three categories of contingent liabilities, along with how to report them, are shown in Exhibit 11-2.

Sometimes the contingent liability has a definite amount. Sometimes the amount that will have to be paid, if the contingent liability becomes an actual liability, is not known at the balance sheet date. For example, companies face lawsuits, which may cause possible future obligations of amounts to be determined by the courts. In another case, Canada Customs and Revenue Agency (CCRA) may have indicated to the entity that a reassessment of its income and taxes has been made or is forthcoming but the company may not know the amount of its liability at the financial statement date.

Enbridge Inc. (www.enbridge.com), the Calgary-based pipeline and natural gas distribution company, reported the following in Note 18 in the Notes to the Consolidated Financial Statements for the year ended December 31, 2002:

18. COMMITMENTS AND CONTINGENCIES
Enbridge Gas

The remediation of discontinued manufactured gas plant sites may result in future costs. The probable overall cost of remediation cannot be determined at this time due to uncertainty about the existence or extent of environmental risks, the complexity of laws and regulations, particularly with respect to sites decommissioned years ago and no longer owned by Enbridge Gas, and the selection of alternative remediation approaches. Although there are no known regulatory precedents in Canada, there are precedents in the United States for recovery in rates of costs of a similar nature. If Enbridge Gas must contribute to any remediation costs, it would be generally allowed to recover in rates those costs not recovered through insurance or by other means and believes that the ultimate outcome of these matters would not have a significant impact on its financial position.

In October 2002, the Supreme Court of Canada granted an Application for Leave to Appeal to a customer who commenced an action against Enbridge Gas claiming that the OEB-approved late payment penalties charged to customers were contrary to Canadian federal law. The Court will hear the plaintiff's appeal of the Ontario Court of Appeal's decision, released in December 2001, to dismiss a Notice of Appeal filed by the plaintiff in April 2000. The Company believes it has sound defences to the plaintiff's claim and it intends to vigorously defend the action.

CAPLA Claim

The Canadian Alliance of Pipeline Landowner's Associations and two individual landowners have commenced an action, which they will be applying for certification as a class action, against the Company and TransCanada PipeLines Limited. The claim relates to restrictions in the National Energy Board Act on the landowners' use of land within a 30-metre control zone on either side of the pipeline easements. The Company believes it has a sound defence and intends to vigorously defend the claim. Since the outcome is indeterminable, the Company has made no provision for any potential liability.

Enbridge Energy Partners

Enbridge Energy Company, Inc. (EEC), which holds a portion of the Company's equity interest in EEP, has agreed to indemnify EEP from and against substantially

EXHIBIT 11-2

Contingent Liabilities: Three Categories

Level of Uncertainty*	How to Report the Contingency
Likely	Amount can be estimated: Accrue an expense (loss) and report an actual liability
	Amount cannot be estimated: Disclose in the notes.
Unlikely	If loss would be significant, note disclosure is suggested.
Not determinable	Note disclosure is required.

*Determined by management. Management also determines the appropriate disclosure.

all liabilities, including liabilities relating to environmental matters, arising from operations prior to the transfer of its pipeline operations to EEP in 1991. This indemnification does not apply to amounts that EEP would be able to recover in its tariff rates if not recovered through insurance, or to any liabilities relating to a change in laws after December 27, 1991. In addition, in the event of default, EEC, as the General Partner, is subject to recourse with respect to a portion of EEP's long-term debt which amounts to US$279 million at December 31, 2002.

Ethical Issues in Accounting for Current and Contingent Liabilities

Accounting for current liabilities poses an ethical challenge. Businesses want to look as successful as possible. A company likes to report a high level of net income on the income statement because that makes the company look successful. High asset values and low liabilities make the company look safe to lenders and help the company borrow at lower interest rates.

Owners and managers may be tempted to overlook some expenses and liabilities at the end of the period. For example, a company can fail to accrue warranty expense or employee vacation pay. This will cause total expenses to be understated and net income to be overstated on the income statement.

Contingent liabilities also pose an ethical challenge. Because contingencies are not real liabilities, they are easy to overlook. But a contingent liability can be very important. A business with a contingent liability walks a tightrope between (1) disclosing enough information to enable outsiders to evaluate the company realistically, and (2) not giving away too much information. Ethical business owners and managers do not play games with their accounting. Falsifying financial statements can ruin one's reputation. It can also lead to a prison term.

At this half-way point of the chapter, review what you have learned by studying the following Decision Guidelines.

DECISION GUIDELINES | *Accounting for Current and Contingent Liabilities*

Decision	Guidelines
What are the two main issues in accounting for current liabilities?	• *Recording* the liability and the asset acquired or the expense incurred • *Reporting* the liability on the balance sheet

What are the two basic categories of current liabilities?	• Current liabilities of *known amount*:
	  Accounts payable Accrued expenses (accrued liabilities)
	  Short-term notes payable Payroll liabilities
	  Sales tax payable Salary, wages, commission,
	  GST payable and bonus payable
	  Current portion of long-term debt Unearned revenues
	
	• Current liabilities that *must be estimated*:
	  Estimated warranty payable
	  Estimated vacation pay liability
	  Income tax payable (for a corporation)

How to account for contingent (potential) liabilities?	• Report contingent liabilities with an explanatory note
What is the ethical and legal challenge in accounting for current and contingent liabilities?	• Ensure that the balance sheet (and the related notes) reports the *full amount* of *all* the business's current and contingent liabilities

Answer each question separately:

1. Suppose a Harvey's hamburger restaurant in Charlottetown, Prince Edward Island, made cash sales of $4,000 subject to the 7 percent GST and 10 percent provincial sales tax. Record the sales and the related consumption taxes (P.E.I. charges PST on GST). Also record payment of the sales tax to the provincial government and the GST to the Receiver General (assume input tax credits amount to $109.00).

2. WestJet Airlines Ltd. (www.westjet.ca) reported a 9.03 percent long-term debt at December 31, 2002, as follows:

Current Liabilities (in part)	millions
Portion of long-term debt due within one year..............	$ 1.296
Interest payable*..	0.787
Long-Term Debt (in part)	
Long-term debt..	$10.324

*Calculated as $11.620 \times 0.0903 \times \frac{9}{12}$

Show how WestJet would report its liabilities on the year-end balance sheet at December 31, 2003. Assume the debt is repayable in monthly installments of the principal of $108,000 plus interest; the final payment is due April 1, 2011; and that interest is payable on April 1 each year.

3. How does a contingent liability differ from an actual liability?

Solution

1.

Cash..	4,708	
Sales Revenue...		4,000
GST Payable..		280
Sales Tax Payable		428

To record cash sales and related GST and provincial sales tax. Cash is $4,708 [($4,000 \times 1.07) \times 1.10]. GST Payable is $280 ($4,000 \times 0.07). Sales Tax Payable is $428 ($4,280 \times 0.10).

GST Payable	280	
Cash...		171
GST Receivable...		109

To pay GST to the Receiver General, net of the input tax credit.

Sales Tax Payable..	428	
Cash...		428

To pay sales tax to the provincial government.

2. WestJet Airlines Ltd.'s balance sheet at December 31, 2003, would be as follows:

Current Liabilities (in part)	millions
Portion of long-term debt due within one year	$1.296
Interest payable*	0.699

Long-Term Debt (in part)	
Long-term debt ($10.324 – $1.296)....................................	$9.028

*Calculated as 10.324 × 0.0903 × ⁹⁄₁₂

3. A contingent liability is a potential liability, which may or may not become an actual liability. It arises out of a past transaction and depends on a future event to determine if it will become an actual liability.

Visit the Study Guide on the Media Companion CD-ROM and the Student Resources area of the *Accounting* Companion Website for extra practice with the new material in Chapter 11.

www.pearsoned.ca/horngren

Accounting for Payroll

OBJECTIVE 3
Compute payroll amounts

Payroll costs are so important that most businesses develop a special payroll system. This section covers the basics of accounting for payroll.

Businesses pay employees at a base rate for a set number of hours—called *straight time*. For additional hours—called *overtime*—the employee may get a higher rate of pay.

Lucy Childres is an accountant for MicroAge Electronics Inc. Lucy earns $700 per week for straight time (35 hours), so her hourly pay rate is $20 ($700 ÷ 35). The company pays *time and a half* for overtime. That rate is 150 percent (1.5 times) the straight-time rate. Thus Lucy earns $30.00 for each hour of overtime ($20.00 × 1.5 = $30.00). For working 37 hours during a week, she earns $760, computed as follows:

Straight-time pay for 35 hours	$700
Overtime pay for 2 overtime hours (2 × $30.00)	60
Total pay	$760

Gross Pay and Net Pay

The federal government and most provincial governments demand that employers act as collection agents for employee's income taxes, which are deducted from employee paycheques. Insurance companies, labour unions, charitable organizations such as the United Way, and other organizations may also take portions of employees' pay. Amounts withheld from an employee's cheque are called *deductions*.

Gross pay is the total amount of salary, wages, commissions, or any other employee compensation before taxes and other deductions are subtracted. **Net pay**—or "take-home pay"—equals gross pay minus all deductions. Exhibit 11-3 illustrates gross and net pay.

In addition to employee income taxes, Canada (or Quebec) Pension Plan contributions, and Employment Insurance premiums that employers must withhold from pay, employers themselves must pay some payroll expenses, such as the employer's share of Canada (or Quebec) Pension Plan and Employment Insurance. Many companies also pay employee *fringe benefits*, such as medical and life insurance premiums and pension plan payments.

Payroll Deductions

Payroll deductions that are *withheld* from employees' pay fall into two categories: (1) *required* (or *statutory) deductions*, which include employee income tax, Employment Insurance, and Canada Pension Plan or Quebec Pension Plan deductions; and (2) *optional deductions*, which include union dues (which may be automatic deductions for all unionized employees), insurance premiums, charitable contributions, and other amounts that are withheld at the employee's request. After they are withheld, payroll deductions become the liability of the employer, who assumes responsibility for paying the outside party. For example, the employer pays the government the employee income tax withheld and pays the union the employee union dues withheld.

Required Payroll Deductions

Employee's Withheld Income Tax Payable   The law requires most employers to withhold income tax from their employees' salaries and wages. The amount of income tax deducted from gross pay is called **withheld income tax**. For many employees, this deduction is the largest. The amount withheld depends on the employee's gross pay and on the number of non-refundable tax credits the employee claims. Each employee files a Personal Tax Credits Return (Form TD1), which is used by employers to determine how much income tax to withhold from an employee's gross pay.

The employer sends its employees' withheld income tax to the government. The amount of the income tax withheld determines how often the employer submits tax payments. Most employers must remit the taxes to the government at least monthly; larger employers must remit two or four times a month, depending on the total amounts withheld. Every business must account for payroll taxes on a calendar-year basis regardless of its fiscal year.

The employer accumulates taxes withheld in the Employees' Withheld Income Tax Payable account. The word *payable* indicates that the account is a liability of the employer, even though the employees are the people taxed.

Employee's Withheld Canada (or Quebec) Pension Plan Contributions Payable   The **Canada** (or **Quebec**) **Pension Plan** (CPP or QPP) provides retirement, disability, and death benefits to employees who are covered by it. Employers are required to deduct premiums from each employee required to make a contribution (basically all employees between 18 and 70 years of age). The federal government, through the CCRA, determines annually the maximum pensionable earnings level, the basic annual exemption, and the contribution rate. The contribution rate changes each year and has been steadily increasing. At the time of writing, the following information was applicable:

EXHIBIT 11-3

Gross Pay and Net Pay

Gross Pay   −   (Taxes + Other Deductions)   =   Net Pay

Maximum pensionable earnings	$39,900
Basic annual exemption	3,500
Maximum contributory earnings	36,400
Contribution rate	4.95%
Maximum employee contribution ($36,400 × 4.95 percent)	$1,801.80

CCRA provides tables that the employer uses to calculate the amount to deduct from each employee's pay each pay period; the tables take into account the basic exemption of $3,500 of income but also assume that the employee will be working for twelve months. For example, if your total employment income was earned when you worked for two months during the summer and earned $2,500 per month, the withholding would be $109.31 each month, the normal deduction for an employee earning $2,500 per month. However, based on your total income of $5,000 (2 × $2,500) and the basic exemption of $3,500, CPP is $74.25 [($5,000 − $3,500) × 0.0495] and your overpayment of $144.37 will be recovered when you file your income tax return.

Once the employee reaches the maximum contribution of $1,801.80, the employer stops deducting for that year. Some employees may have had more than one employer in a year; for example, you may have had a job for the summer and now have a part-time job while you are back at school. CCRA requires each employer to deduct Canada Pension Plan contributions; however, you recover the overpayment when you file your income tax return for the year. The employers do not recover any overpayment.

The employer must remit the Canada Pension Plan contributions withheld and the employer's share, discussed below, every month to CCRA. Larger employers must remit two or four times a month, depending on the amounts withheld.

Employee's Withheld Employment Insurance (EI) Premiums Payable   The Employment Insurance Act requires employers to deduct **Employment Insurance** premiums from each employee each time that employee is paid. The purpose of the Employment Insurance Fund is to provide assistance to contributors to the fund who cannot work for a variety of reasons. The most common reason is that the employee has been laid off; another reason is maternity leave.

The federal government, through CCRA, establishes annually the maximum annual insurable earnings level and the Employment Insurance premium rate. The rate has been decreasing in recent years. At the time of writing, the following information was applicable:

Maximum insurable earnings	$39,000
Premium rate	2.1%
Maximum employee contribution ($39,000 × 2.1 percent)	$819.00

CCRA provides tables that the employer uses to calculate the amount to deduct from each employee's gross pay each pay period. For example, if you earned $2,000 per month, $42.00 ($2,000 × 2.1 percent) per month would be deducted for Employment Insurance.

As with the Canada Pension Plan, CCRA requires every employer to deduct Employment Insurance premiums from every eligible employee. Overpayments may be recovered when the employee files his or her income tax return.

The employer must remit the Employment Insurance premiums withheld and the employer's share, discussed below, to CCRA every month. Larger employers must remit two or four times a month depending on the amounts withheld.

Optional Payroll Deductions

As a convenience to their employees, many companies make payroll deductions and disburse cash according to employee instructions. Union dues (which may not be optional), insurance payments, registered pension plan payments, payroll savings plans, and donations to charities such as the United Way are examples. The account Employees' Union Dues Payable holds employee deductions for union membership.

Employer Payroll Costs

Employers bear expenses for at least three payroll costs: (1) Canada Pension Plan contributions, (2) Employment Insurance Plan premiums, and (3) Workers' Compensation Plan premiums. In addition, Manitoba and Newfoundland levy a health and post-secondary education tax on employers, while Ontario and Quebec levy a health tax on employers in those provinces. As mentioned above, most employers must remit both employee and employer shares monthly. Larger employers must remit twice or four times monthly depending on the size of their payroll. Workers' Compensation payments are remitted quarterly.

Employer Canada Pension Plan Contributions In addition to being responsible for deducting and remitting the employee contribution to the Canada Pension Plan, the employer must also pay into the program. The employer must match exactly the employee's contribution. Every employer must do so whether or not the employee also contributes elsewhere. Unlike the employee, the employer may not obtain a refund for overpayment.

Employer Employment Insurance Premiums The employer calculates the employee's premium and remits it together with the employer's share, which is generally 1.4 times the employee's premium, to CCRA. The maximum dollar amount of the employer's contribution would be 1.4 times the maximum employee's contribution of $819.00, which amounts to $1,146.60. Almost all employers and employees are covered by this program, unless self-employed.

Workers' Compensation Premiums Unlike the previous two programs, which are administered by the federal government, the **Workers' Compensation** plan is administered provincially. The purpose of the program is to provide financial support for workers injured on the job. The cost of the coverage is borne by the employer; the employee does not pay a premium to the fund.

In Manitoba, almost all employees are covered by the program. There are over 70 different categories that the Workers' Compensation Board uses to determine the cost of coverage. The category a group of workers is assigned to is based on the risk of injury to workers in that group, which is based on that group's and like groups' experience. The employer pays a premium equal to the rate assessed times the employer's gross payroll. Thus, in February 2005, the employer estimates gross payroll for 2005 and sends that information plus any premium owing from 2004 to the provincial government. Premiums, based on that estimated payroll, are remitted quarterly in most cases. In February 2006, the employer estimates gross payroll for 2006, calculates any premium owing for 2005 based on the excess of actual wages over estimated wages for 2005, and sends the estimate and premium owing to the provincial government.

Provincial Payroll Taxes As was mentioned earlier, certain provinces levy taxes on employers to pay for provincial health care while others levy a combined health care and post-secondary education tax to pay for provincial health care and post-secondary education. Quebec and Newfoundland have fixed rates of tax while Ontario and Manitoba vary the rate employers are taxed. In Ontario, the rate of tax increases with the annual payroll amount, while in Manitoba, there is no tax on the first $1 million of payroll, and thereafter it decreases as the annual payroll exceeds $2 million.

Payroll Withholding Tables

We have discussed the tables that employers use in calculating the withholdings that must be made from employees' wages for income taxes, Canada (or Quebec) Pension

Plan contributions, and Employment Insurance premiums. Exhibit 11-4 provides illustrations of all four tables for a resident of Saskatchewan for 2003. Suppose an employee, Roberta Dean, is paid a salary of $2,000 twice a month (semi-monthly).

EXHIBIT 11-4

Payroll Withholding Tables

Panel A

Saskatchewan
Federal Tax Deductions
Effective January 1, 2003
Semi-Monthly: 24 Pay Periods Per Year

Pay		Federal claim codes										
From	Less than	0	1	2	3	4	5	6	7	8	9	10
		Deduct from each pay										
1987 –	2013	342.05	290.35	284.65	273.15	261.70	250.20	238.75	227.25	215.80	204.30	192.85
2013 –	2039	347.80	296.10	290.35	278.85	267.40	255.95	244.45	233.00	221.50	210.05	198.55
2039 –	2065	353.50	301.80	296.05	284.60	273.10	261.65	250.15	238.70	227.25	215.75	204.30
2065 –	2091	359.25	307.50	301.80	290.30	278.85	267.35	255.90	244.40	232.95	221.45	210.00
2091 –	2117	364.95	313.25	307.50	296.05	284.55	273.10	261.60	250.15	238.65	227.20	215.70

Panel B

Saskatchewan
Provincial Tax Deductions
Effective January 1, 2003
Semi-Monthly: 24 Pay Periods Per Year

Pay		Federal claim codes										
From	Less than	0	1	2	3	4	5	6	7	8	9	10
		Deduct from each pay										
1998 –	2024	220.25	183.60	179.90	172.60	165.25	157.90	150.60	143.25	135.90	128.60	121.25
2024 –	2050	223.65	186.95	183.30	175.95	168.65	161.30	153.95	146.65	139.30	131.95	124.65
2050 –	2076	227.00	190.35	186.70	179.35	172.00	164.70	157.35	150.00	142.70	135.35	128.00
2076 –	2102	230.40	193.70	190.05	182.70	175.40	168.05	160.70	153.40	146.05	138.70	131.40
2102 –	2128	233.75	197.10	193.45	186.10	178.75	171.45	164.10	156.75	149.45	142.10	134.75

Panel C
Canada Pension Plan Contributions
Semi-Monthly (24 pay periods per year)

Pay		CPP
From	To	
1992.70 –	2002.69	91.67
2002.70 –	2012.69	92.16
2012.70 –	2022.69	92.66
2022.70 –	2032.69	93.15
2032.70 –	2042.69	93.65
2042.70 –	2052.69	94.14
2052.70 –	2062.69	94.64
2062.70 –	2072.69	95.13
2072.70 –	2082.69	95.63

Panel D
Employment Insurance Premiums
Semi-Monthly (24 pay periods per year)

Insurable Earnings		EI
From	To	Premium
1997.39 –	1997.85	41.95
1997.86 –	1998.33	41.96
1998.34 –	1998.80	41.97
1998.81 –	1999.28	41.98
1999.29 –	1999.76	41.99
1999.77 –	2000.23	42.00
2000.24 –	2000.71	42.01
2000.72 –	2001.19	42.02
2001.20 –	2001.66	42.03

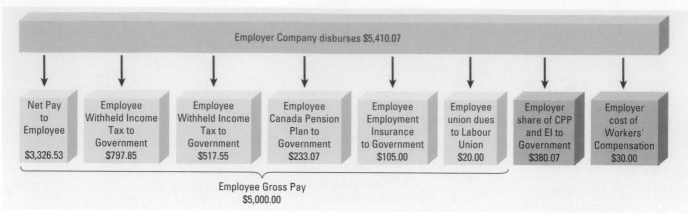

Net Pay to Employee	Employee Withheld Income Tax to Government	Employee Withheld Income Tax to Government	Employee Canada Pension Plan to Government	Employee Employment Insurance to Government	Employee union dues to Labour Union	Employer share of CPP and EI to Government	Employer cost of Workers' Compensation
$3,326.53	$797.85	$517.55	$233.07	$105.00	$20.00	$380.07	$30.00

Employee Gross Pay
$5,000.00

EXHIBIT 11-5

Typical Disbursement of Payroll Costs by an Employer Company (Saskatchewan)

Roberta is single and so her TD1 form for both federal and provincial taxes indicates a claim code of 1. From Panel A of Exhibit 11-4, you can see that Roberta will have $290.35 deducted for federal income taxes, and from Panel B, you can see that she will have $183.60 deducted for Saskatchewan income taxes. Panel C indicates that Roberta would have $91.67 deducted from each pay for Canada Pension Plan (CPP), and Panel D shows that $42.00 would be deducted for Employment Insurance (EI). Roberta Dean's employer would keep track, as we will demonstrate later in the chapter, of Dean's Canada Pension Plan and Employment Insurance deductions and, when they reached the maximums of $1,801.80 and $819.00 respectively, would stop deducting premiums from Dean's pay. The employer's share would be $91.67 for Canada Pension Plan (matches employee's share), while the employer's share for Employment Insurance would be $58.80 (1.4 times employee share).

Exhibit 11-5 shows a typical disbursement of payroll costs by a Saskatchewan employer company for a single employee (claim code 1) who is paid $5,000 monthly.

OBJECTIVE 4
Record basic payroll transactions

Payroll Entries

Exhibit 11-6 summarizes an employer's entries to record a monthly payroll of $60,000 (all amounts are assumed for illustration only).

Entry A in Exhibit 11-6 records the employer's salary expense, which is the gross salary of all employees ($60,000) for a month. From this amount the employer collects the employees' federal and provincial income taxes, CPP (QPP in Quebec), and EI, all of which are remitted to the federal government. Union dues are also collected from gross salary by the employer on behalf of the union that represents the employees. The remaining amount is the employees' net (take-home) pay of $46,278. In this payroll transaction the employer acts as a collection agent for CCRA (income tax and Canada Pension), the provincial government (income tax), the Employment Insurance Commission, and the union, withholding the employees' contributions from their gross pay.

Entry B represents the employer's share of Canada Pension Plan and Employment Insurance. Remember, the employer's share is 1.0 times and 1.4 times the employee's share respectively for these two deductions.

Entry C records employee benefits paid by the employer. This company has a dental benefits plan for its employees for which it pays the premiums.

In the exhibit, the total payroll expense for the month is made up of base salary ($60,000) plus the employer's share of Canada Pension Plan and Employment Insurance ($4,478) plus fringe benefits ($1,092) for a total of $65,570. There would also be Workers' Compensation, which, you will recall, is paid completely by the employer.

EXHIBIT 11-6

Payroll Accounting by the
Employer

A.	Salary Expense (or Wages or Commission Expense)..................	60,000	
	Employee (federal and provincial) Withheld Income Tax		
	Payable...		8,100
	Canada Pension Plan Payable..		2,770
	Employment Insurance Payable...		1,220
	Employee Union Dues Payable		1,632
	Salaries Payable to Employees (net pay)..............................		46,278
	To record salary expense and employee withholdings.		

B.	Canada Pension Plan and Employment Insurance Expense.....	4,478	
	Canada Pension Plan Payable..		2,770
	Employment Insurance Payable...		1,708
	To record employer's share of Canada Pension Plan ($1.0 \times \$2,770$) and Employment Insurance ($1.4 \times \$1,220$).		

C.	Employee Dental Benefits Expense...	1,092	
	Employee Benefits Payable...		1,092
	To record employee benefits payable by employer.		

A company's payments to people who are not employees—outsiders called independent contractors—are *not* company payroll expenses. Consider two Chartered Accountants, Fermi and Scott. Fermi is the corporation's chief financial officer. Scott is the corporation's outside auditor. Fermi is an employee of the corporation, and his compensation is a debit to Salary Expense. Scott, however, performs auditing services for many clients, and the corporation debits Auditing Expense when it pays her. Any payment for services performed by a person outside the company is a debit to an expense account other than payroll.

STOP & THINK

Record the payroll, payroll deductions, and employer payroll costs, given the following information about an Ontario company:

Gross pay	$190,000	
Employee withheld income tax	22,800	
Employee withheld Canada Pension Plan	4,900	
Employee withheld employment insurance	4,560	
Union dues	2,945	
Employer cost for Canada Pension Plan	1.0	× employee amount
Employer cost for employment insurance	1.4	× employee amount
Pension plan paid by employer only	1.0%	of gross pay

Answer:

Payroll entry:

Salary expense...	190,000	
Employee withheld Income Tax Payable		22,800
Canada Pension Plan (CPP) Payable		4,900
Employment Insurance (EI) Payable		4,560
Union Dues Payable		2,945
Salaries Payable...		154,795

Employer payroll cost entry:

Canada Pension Plan and Employment		
Insurance Expense	$11,284	
Canada Pension Plan (CPP) Payable		4,900
Employment Insurance (EI) Payable		6,384

Fringe benefits:

Pension Expense	1,900	
Employment Benefits Payable		1,900

The Payroll System

Good business means paying employees accurately and on time. A payroll system accomplishes these goals. The components of the payroll system are:

- A payroll register
- Payroll cheques
- Employee earnings records

Payroll Register

Each pay period, the company organizes payroll data in a special journal called the *payroll register*. The payroll register resembles the cash payments journal and serves as a cheque register. We introduced the cash payments journal in Chapter 7, page 350.

Exhibit 11-7 is a payroll register for Red Deer Provisioners. The payroll register has columns for each employee's gross pay, deductions, and net pay. This record gives the employer the information needed to record salary expense for the pay period as follows:

2003			
Dec. 31	Office Salaries Expense	4,464.00	
	Sales Salaries Expense	9,190.00	
	Employee Withheld Income Tax Payable		2,588.00
	Employee Withheld Canada Pension		
	Plan Payable..		402.70
	Employee Withheld Employment		
	Insurance Payable		302.12
	Employee Gifts to United Way Payable...........		155.00
	Salaries Payable to Employees		10,206.18
	To record payroll expenses for the week		
	ended December 31, 2003.		
2003			
Dec. 31	Canada Pension Plan Expense................................	402.70	
	Employment Insurance Expense	422.97	
	Employer Canada Pension Plan Payable.........		402.70
	Employer Employment Insurance Payable		422.97
	To record the cost of employer's portion of		
	payroll expenses for the week ended December 31, 2003.		

Payroll Cheques

Most companies pay employees by cheque or by electronic funds transfer (EFT). A *payroll cheque* has an attachment that details the employee's gross pay, payroll deductions, and net pay. These amounts come from the payroll register, like that in Exhibit 11-7. Exhibit 11-8 (on page 559) shows payroll cheque number 1622, issued to C.L. Drumm for net pay of $400.99 earned during the week ended December 31, 2003. To enhance your ability to use payroll data, trace all amounts on the cheque attachment to the payroll register in Exhibit 11-7.

Increasingly, companies are paying employees by electronic funds transfer. The employee can authorize the company to make all deposits directly to her or his bank. With no cheque to write and deliver to the employee, the company saves time and money. As evidence of the deposit, most companies issue to employees either a paper or an electronic pay summary slip showing the data for that pay period plus year-to-date data.

EXHIBIT 11-7

Payroll Register for Red Deer Provisioners

Week ended December 31, 2003

	a		b	c	d	e	f	g	h	i	j	k	l	m
		Gross Pay			**Deductions**						**Net Pay**		**Account Debited**	
Employee Name	Hours	Straight time	Overtime	Total	Federal Income Tax	Prov. Inc. Tax (Alberta)	Canada Pension Plan	Employ-ment Insurance	Red Deer United Way	Total	(c–h) Amount	Cheque No.	Office Salaries Expense	Sales Salaries Expense
Chen, W.L.*	40	500.00		500.00	48.10	18.80	21.42	10.50	2.00	100.82	399.18	1621	500.00	
Drumm, C.L.	46	400.00	90.00	490.00	41.60	14.20	20.92	10.29	2.00	89.01	400.99	1622		490.00
Elias, M.	41	560.00	21.00	581.00	54.70	22.75	25.43	12.20		115.08	465.92	1623	581.00	
Vokovich, E.A.**	40	1,360.00		1,360.00	222.80	95.65			15.00	333.45	1,026.55	1641		1,360.00
Total		12,940.00	714.00	13,654.00	1,810.35	777.65	402.70	302.12	155.00	3,447.82	10,206.18		4,464.00	9,190.00

*W.L. Chen earned gross pay of $500. His net pay was $399.18, paid with cheque number 1621. Chen is an office worker, so his salary is debited to Office Salaries Expense.

**E.A. Vokovich has exceeded maximum pensionable earnings of $39,900 and so has had the Canada Pension Plan maximum, $1,801.80, already deducted. Vokovich has also exceeded the max-imum insurable Employment Insurance earnings of $39,000 and so has already had the maximum, $819.00, deducted.

Recording Cash Payments for Payroll

Most employers must record at least three cash payments: for payments of net pay to employees, for payments of payroll withholdings to the government, and for payments to third parties for employee fringe benefits.

Net Pay to Employees When the employer pays employees, the company debits Salaries Payable to Employees and credits Cash. Using the data in Exhibit 11-7, the company would make the following entry to record the cash payment (column (j)) for the December 31 weekly payroll:

2003
Dec. 31   Salaries Payable to Employees 10,206.18
                    Cash 10,206.18

Payroll Withholdings to the Government and Other Organizations The employer must send income taxes withheld from employees' pay and the employee deductions and employer's share of Canada (or Quebec) Pension Plan contributions and Employment Insurance premiums to Canada Customs and Revenue Agency (CCRA). The payment for a given month is due on or before the 15th day of the following month. In addition, the employer has to remit any withholdings for union dues, charitable donations, etc.; the payment would probably be made in the following month. Assume federal income tax of $5,972.80, Province of Alberta income tax of $2,217.40, Canada Pension Plan contributions of $1,225.02, Employment Insurance premiums of $897.02, and United Way contributions of $465.00 were deducted in calculating the net pay for the employees of Red Deer Provisioners for the three weeks ended December 10, 17, and 24, 2003. Based on those amounts and columns (d) through (j) in Exhibit 11-7, the business would record payments to CCRA and Red Deer United Way for the month of December 2003 as follows:

2004
Jan. 3   Employee Withheld Federal and Provincial Income Tax
                 Payable ($5,972.80 + $1,810.35 + $2,217.40 + $777.65)....... 10,778.20
              Employee Withheld Canada Pension
                 Plan Payable ($1,225.02 + $402.70).. 1,627.72
              Employee Withheld Employment
                 Insurance Payable ($897.02 + $302.12) 1,199.14
              Canada Pension Plan Expense (1 × $1,627.72) 1,627.72
              Employment Insurance Expense
                 (1.4 × $1,199.14)... 1,678.80
                    Cash...   16,911.58
              To record payment to CCRA for
              December 2003 withholdings.

2004
Jan. 3   Employee Donations to United Way Payable 620.00
                    Cash...   620.00
              To record payment to United Way for December
              2003 withholdings ($465.00 + $155.00).

STOP & THINK

According to this journal entry, what is the total amount that the business will pay to the government on January 3, 2004, for taxes, Canada Pension Plan, and Employment Insurance withheld for the month of December 2003?

Answer: $10,778.20 + $1,627.72 + $1,199.14 = $13,605.06

EXHIBIT 11-8

Payroll Cheque

Red Deer Provisioners										1622
Payroll Account										
Red Deer, Alberta							January 2, 2004			

Pay to the Order of ___ C.L. Drumm ___ $ 400.99

Four hundred --- 99/100 Dollars

The Bank of Nova Scotia
Red Deer
Alberta T4P 3L9

Anna Figaro
Treasurer

⑈1119000311⑈ 0787⑈500004541⑈

Pay			Deductions							Net Pay	Cheque No.
Straight-time	Over-time	Gross	Federal Income Tax	Prov. Income Tax	C.P.P.	Employ-ment Ins.	United Way	Total			
400.00	90.00	490.00	41.60	14.20	20.92	10.29	2.00	89.01		400.99	1622

Payments to Third Parties for Fringe Benefits The employer sometimes pays for employees' dental benefits coverage and for a company pension plan. Assuming the total cash payment for these benefits is $1,927.14 and the payment is made to one company, this entry would be

2004			
Jan. 10	Employee Benefits Payable—Dental Plan	600.14	
	Employee Benefits Payable—Pension Plan	1,327.00	
	Cash		1,927.14
	To record payment for employee dental benefits coverage and company pension plan.		

Earnings Record

The employer must file Summary of Remuneration Paid returns with Canada Customs and Revenue Agency (CCRA) and must provide the employee with a Statement of Remuneration Paid, Form T4, at the end of the year. Therefore, employers maintain an earnings record for each employee. (These earnings records are also used for Employment Insurance claims.) Exhibit 11-9 is a five-week excerpt from the earnings record of employee J.C. Jenkins.

The employee earnings record is not a journal or a ledger, and it is not required by law. It is an accounting tool—like the work sheet—that the employer uses to prepare payroll withholdings reports. The information provided on the earnings record with respect to year-to-date earnings also indicates when an employee has earned $39,900, the point at which the employer can stop withholding Canada Pension Plan contributions. The same is true for Employment Insurance deductions: the employer stops withholding Employment Insurance contributions after the employee has earned $39,000. There is no maximum income tax deduction.

Exhibit 11-10 is the Statement of Remuneration Paid, Form T4, for employee J.C. Jenkins. The employer prepares this form for each employee and a form called a T4 Summary, which summarizes the information on all the T4s issued by the employer for that year. The employer sends the T4 Summary and one copy of each T4 to CCRA by February 28 each year. CCRA uses the documents to ensure that the employer has correctly paid to the government all amounts withheld on its behalf from employees, together with the employer's share. The employee gets two copies of the T4; one copy must be filed with the employee's income tax

EXHIBIT 11-9

Employee Earnings Record for 2003

Employee Name and Address:

Jenkins, J.C.
1400 Camousen Cres.
Victoria, BC V5J 5K9

Social Insurance No.: 978-010-789
Marital Status: Married
Net Claims Code: 4
Pay Rate: $700 per week; overtime $26.25 per hour.
Job Title: Salesperson

Week Ended	Gross Pay					Deductions						Net Pay	
	Hours	Straight time	Overtime	Total	To Date	Federal Income Tax	Province of BC Income Tax	Canada Pension Plan	Employment Insurance	United Way	Total	Amount	Cheque No.
Jan. 4	40	700.00		700.00	700.00	72.00	27.40	31.32	14.70	2.00	147.42		103
Dec. 3	40	700.00		700.00	35,437.50	72.00	27.40	31.32	14.70	2.00	147.42	552.58	1525
Dec. 10	40	700.00		700.00	36,137.50	72.00	27.40	31.32	14.70	2.00	147.42	552.58	1548
Dec. 17	44	700.00	105.00	805.00	36,942.50	118.80	36.65	36.39	16.91	2.00	186.10	618.90	1574
Dec. 24	48	700.00	210.00	910.00	37,852.50	117.00	46.15	41.63	19.11	2.00	227.69	682.31	1598
Dec. 31	46	700.00	157.50	857.50	38,710.00	106.45	41.75	39.36	18.01	2.00	207.57	649.93	1632
Total		36,400.00	2,310.00	38,710.00	38,710.00	4,310.40	1,981.80	1,742.90	812.91	104.00	8,952.01	29,757.99	

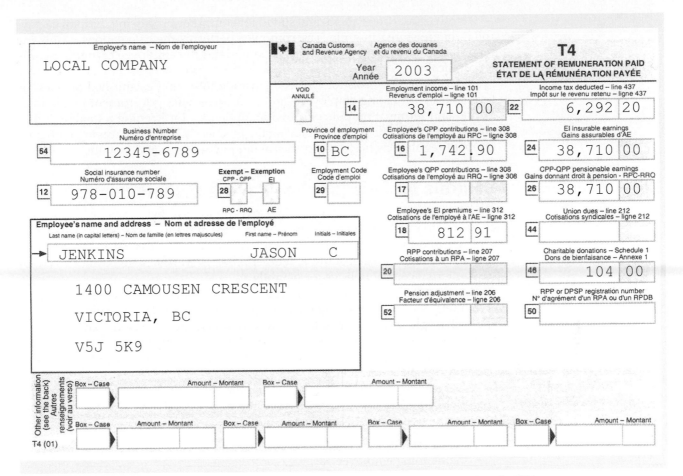

Source: Reproduced with permission of the Minister of Public Works and Government Services Canada, 2004.

EXHIBIT 11-10

Employee Statement of Remuneration Paid (Form T4)

return, while the second copy is for the employee's records. CCRA matches the income on the T4 filed by the employer against the income reported on the employee's income tax return, filed by the employee, to ensure that the employee properly reported his or her income from employment.

Internal Control over Payroll

The internal controls over cash payments discussed in Chapter 8 also apply to payroll. There are two main types of controls for payroll: controls for efficiency and controls for safeguarding payroll disbursements.

Controls for Efficiency

Reconciling the bank account can be time consuming because of the large number of paycheques. There may be a large number of outstanding cheques for the bank reconciliation. To limit the number of outstanding cheques, many companies use two payroll bank accounts. They pay the payroll from one payroll account one month and from the other payroll account the next month. This way they can reconcile each account every other month, and that decreases accounting expense.

REAL WORLD EXAMPLE

Another internal control feature is direct depositing of paycheques into employees' bank accounts (electronic funds transfer, or EFT). This eliminates the possibility of lost or stolen cheques and makes it difficult to distribute cheques to a fictitious employee. It is also useful to compare the current-employee list to a list of former employees to ensure that terminated employees are not still receiving paycheques.

Payroll transactions are ideally suited for computer processing. Employee payroll data are stored in a file. The computer performs the calculations, prints the payroll register and the paycheques, and updates the employee earnings records electronically.

Other payroll controls for efficiency include following established policies for hiring and terminating employees, and complying with government regulations. Hiring and termination policies provide guidelines for keeping a qualified, diligent work force dedicated to achieving the business's goals. Complying with government regulations helps companies avoid paying fines and penalties.

Controls for Safeguarding Payroll Disbursements

Owners and managers of small businesses can monitor their payrolls by personal contact with employees. Large corporations cannot do so. A particular risk is that a paycheque may be written to a fictitious person and cashed by a dishonest employee. To guard against this and other possible crimes, large businesses adopt strict internal control policies for payrolls.

The duties of hiring and terminating employees should be separated from payroll accounting and from distributing paycheques. Issuing paycheques only to employees with a photo ID ensures that only actual employees receive pay. A formal time-keeping system helps ensure that employees actually worked the number of hours claimed. Employees may punch time cards at the start and end of the work day to prove their attendance.

As we saw in Chapter 8, the foundation for good internal control is separation of duties. This is why companies have separate departments for the following payroll functions:

- hiring and terminating employees, and
- maintaining employee earnings records

STOP & THINK

Centurion Homes of Calgary, Alberta, builds houses and has four construction crews. The supervisors hire—and terminate—workers and keep their hourly records. Each Friday morning the supervisors telephone their workers' hours to the home office, where accountants prepare the weekly paycheques. Around noon the supervisors pick up the paycheques. They return to the construction site and pay the workers at day's end. What is the internal control weakness in this situation? Propose a way to improve the internal controls.

Answer: When the supervisors control most of the information used in the payroll system, they can forge the payroll records of fictitious employees and pocket their pay. To improve internal control, Centurion Homes could hire and terminate all workers through the home office. This would prove that all workers actually exist. Another way to improve the internal controls would be to have a home-office employee distribute paycheques on a surprise basis. Any remaining cheques would arouse suspicion. This system would probably prevent supervisors from cheating the company.

OBJECTIVE 6
Report current liabilities on the balance sheet

Reporting Payroll Expense and Liabilities

At the end of each period, a company reports all its current liabilities on the balance sheet. At December 31, 2002, Inco Limited (www.inco.com) had the current liabilities shown in Exhibit 11-11. Inco combines all payroll liabilities under a single heading, Accrued Payroll and Benefits.

Current Liabilities	(U.S. $ in millions)
Long-term debt due within one year........	$ 97
Accounts payable	338
Accrued payrolls and benefits....................	118
Other accrued liabilities	210
Income and mining taxes payable.............	167
Total current liabilities............................	$930

EXHIBIT 11-11

Inco Limited Balance Sheet
at December 31, 2002
(Partial)

The following Decision Guidelines feature summarizes some of the more important payroll decisions that a business must consider.

DECISION GUIDELINES *Accounting for Payroll*

Decision	Guidelines
What are the key elements of a payroll accounting system?	• Personal Tax Credits Return, Form TD1(E) • Payroll register • Payroll bank account and payroll cheques • Employee earnings record • Employee wage and tax statement, Form T4

What are the key terms in the payroll area?	*Gross pay* (Total amount earned by the employee)
	 – *Payroll deductions*
	   a. Withheld income tax
	   b. Withheld Canada (or Quebec) Pension Plan deductions—equal amount paid by employer
	   c. Withheld Employment Insurance deductions—employer pays 1.4 times employee deduction
	   d. Optional deductions (retirement savings plan, charitable contributions, union dues)
	
	 = *Net (take-home) pay*

What is the employer's total payroll expense?	*Gross pay*
	 + *Employer's payroll expenses*
	   a. Canada (or Quebec) Pension Plan expense—equal amount also paid by employee
	   b. Employment Insurance expense—employer pays 1.4 times amount employee pays
	 + *Fringe benefits for employees*
	   a. Insurance (dental, drug plan, and disability)
	   b. Employer's share of retirement savings plan (and other retirement benefits)
	   c. Club memberships and other benefits
	
	 = *Employer's total payroll costs*

Where to report payroll amounts?	• Payroll expenses on the income statement • Payroll liabilities on the balance sheet

Summary Problem
for Your Review

Best Threads, a clothing store in Moose Jaw, Saskatchewan, employs one sales-person, Sheila Kingsley. Her straight-time pay is $420 per week. She earns time and a half for hours worked in excess of 35 per week. For Kingsley's wage rate and "net claim code" on her Personal Tax Credits Return (TD1), the federal income tax withholding rate is approximately 11.5 percent, and the provincial rate is 7.7 percent. Canada Pension is 4.95 percent on income until the maximum total contribution of $1,801.80 is reached, while Employment Insurance premiums are 2.1 percent until the maximum total contribution of $819.00 is reached. In addition, Best Threads pays Kingsley's Blue Cross supplemental health insurance premiums of $31.42 a month and dental insurance premiums of $18.50 a month.

During the week ended February 28, 2003, Kingsley worked 48 hours.

Required

1. Compute Sheila Kingsley's gross pay and net pay for the week.
2. Record the following payroll entries that Best Threads would make:
   a. Expense for Kingsley's wages including overtime pay
   b. Cost of employer's share of Kingsley's withholdings (ignore the basic Canada Pension Plan exemption)
   c. Expense for fringe benefits
   d. Payment of cash to Kingsley
   e. Payment Best Threads must make to Canada Customs and Revenue Agency (CCRA)
   f. Payment of fringe benefits for the month
3. How much total payroll expense did Best Threads incur for the week? How much cash did the business spend on its payroll?

Solution

Requirement 1

Gross pay:

Straight-time pay for 35 hours		$420.00
Overtime pay		
Rate per hour ($420 ÷ 35 × 1.5)	$18.00	
Hours (48 – 35)	× 13	234.00
Total gross pay		$654.00

Net pay:

Gross pay		$654.00
Less: Withheld federal income tax ($654 × 0.115)	$75.21	
Withheld provincial income tax ($654 × 0.077)	50.36	
Withheld Canada Pension Plan ($654 × 0.0495)	32.37	
Withheld Employment Insurance ($654 × 0.021)	13.73	171.67
Net pay		$482.33

Requirement 2

a. Sales Salary Expense... 654.00
    Employee Withheld Federal and Provincial Income Tax
        Payable ($75.21 + $50.36) 125.57
    Employee Canada Pension Plan Payable......................... 32.37
    Employee Employment Insurance Payable 13.73
    Wages payable 482.33
    To record expense for S. Kingsley's wages.

b. Canada Pension Plan Expense...................................... 32.37
   Employment Insurance Expense 19.22
    Employer Canada Pension Plan Payable 32.37
    Employer Employment Insurance Payable...................... 19.22
    To record cost of employer's portion of S. Kingsley's wages.
      CPP is $32.37 ($32.37 × 1).
      EI is $19.22 ($13.73 × 1.4).

c. Medical and Dental Expense.. 49.92
    Employee Benefits Payable.. 49.92
    To record expense of fringe benefits ($31.42 + $18.50).

d. Wages Payable to Employee.. 482.33
    Cash.. 482.33
    To record payment of wages to S. Kingsley.

e. Employee Withheld Federal and Provincial Income Tax
      Payable.. 125.57
   Employee Canada Pension Plan Payable............................. 32.37
   Employee Employment Insurance Payable 13.73
   Employer Canada Pension Plan Payable 32.37
   Employer Employment Insurance Payable 19.22
    Cash.. 223.26
    To record payment to CCRA.

f. Employee Benefits Payable 49.92
    Cash.. 49.92
    To record payment of monthly fringe benefits.

Requirement 3

Best Threads incurred *total payroll expense* of $755.51 (gross salary of $654.00 + employer's cost of Canada Pension Plan of $32.37 + employer's cost of Employment Insurance of $19.22 + fringe benefits of $49.92). See entries a to c.

Best Threads paid cash of $755.51 on payroll (Kingsley's net pay of $482.33 + payment to CCRA of $223.26 + fringe benefits of $49.92). See entries d to f.

Cyber Coach
Visit the Study Guide on the Media Companion CD-ROM and the Student Resources area of the *Accounting* Companion Website for extra practice with the new material in Chapter 11.
www.pearsoned.ca/horngren

Summary

1. **Account for current liabilities of known amount.** *Current liabilities* may be divided into those of *known amount* and those that must be *estimated*. Trade accounts payable, short-term notes payable, interest payable, GST payable, payroll, and unearned revenues are current liabilities of known amount.

2. **Account for current liabilities that must be estimated.** Current liabilities that must be estimated include warranties payable, vacation pay, and corporations' income tax payable.

   Contingent liabilities are not actual liabilities but potential liabilities that may arise in the future. Contingent liabilities, like current liabilities, may be of known amount or an indefinite amount. A business that faces a lawsuit not yet decided in court has a contingent liability of indefinite amount.

3. **Compute payroll amounts.** *Payroll* accounting handles the expenses and liabilities arising from compensating employees. Employers must withhold federal and provincial income taxes, Canada (or Quebec) Pension Plan contributions, and Employment Insurance premiums from employees' pay and send these *withholdings* together with the employer's share of the latter two to the appropriate government. In addition, many employers allow their employees to pay for insurance

and union dues and to make gifts to charities through payroll deductions. An employee's net pay is the gross pay less all withholdings and optional deductions.

4. **Record basic payroll transactions.** An *employer's* payroll expenses include the employer's share of Canada (or Quebec) Pension Plan contributions and Employment Insurance premiums; employers also pay provincial health and post-secondary education taxes in those provinces that levy them and Workers' Compensation. Also, employers may provide their employees with fringe benefits, such as life insurance coverage and retirement pensions.

5. **Use a payroll system.** A basic *payroll system* consists of a payroll register, a payroll bank account, payroll cheques, and an earnings record for each employee. Good *internal controls* over payroll help the business to achieve efficiency and to safeguard the company's cash. The cornerstone of internal control is the separation of duties.

6. **Report current liabilities on the balance sheet.** The company reports on the balance sheet all current liabilities that it owes: current liabilities of known amount, including payroll liabilities; and current liabilities that must be estimated.

Self-Study Questions

Test your understanding of the chapter by marking the correct answer for each of the following questions:

1. A $10,000, 9 percent, one-year note payable was issued on July 31. The balance sheet at December 31 will report interest payable of (*pp. 536–537*)
   a. $0 because the interest is not due yet
   b. $453.70
   c. $377.26
   d. $900

2. Which of the following liabilities creates no expense for the company? (*p. 537*)
   a. Interest
   b. Sales tax
   c. Employment Insurance
   d. Warranty

3. Known liabilities of uncertain amounts should be (*p. 543*)
   a. Estimated and accrued when they occur
   b. Ignored. Record them when they are paid.
   c. Reported on the income statement
   d. Described in the notes to the financial statements

4. Suppose Canadian Tire estimates that warranty costs will equal 1 percent of tire sales. Assume

that November sales totalled $900,000, and the company's outlay in tires and cash to satisfy warranty claims was $7,400. How much warranty expense should the November income statement report? (*p. 543*)
   a. $1,600
   b. $7,400
   c. $9,000
   d. $16,400

5. Nu Systems Company is a defendant in a lawsuit that claims damages of $55,000. On the balance sheet date, it appears unlikely that the court will render a judgment against the company. How should Nu Systems Company report this event in its financial statements? (*p. 545*)
   a. Omit mention because no judgment has been rendered
   b. Disclose the contingent liability in a note
   c. Report the loss on the income statement and the liability on the balance sheet.
   d. Both b and c

6. Emilie Frontenac's weekly pay for 40 hours is $400, plus time and a half for overtime. The federal tax rate, based on her income level and deductions, is 10.5 percent, the provincial rate is 8.8 percent, the Quebec Pension Plan rate is 4.95 percent

on her weekly earnings, and the Employment Insurance rate is 2.1 percent on her weekly earnings. What is Emilie's take-home pay for a week in which she works 50 hours? (*pp. 554–556*)

a. $424.97
b. $460.97
c. $428.42
d. $404.97

7. Which of the following represents a cost to the employer? (*p. 552*)
a. Withheld income tax
b. Canada Pension Plan
c. Employment Insurance
d. Both b and c

8. The main reason for using a separate payroll bank account is to (*p. 556*)
a. Safeguard cash by preventing the writing of payroll cheques to fictitious employees
b. Safeguard cash by limiting paycheques to amounts based on time cards

c. Increase efficiency by isolating payroll disbursements for analysis and control
d. All of the above

9. The key to good internal controls in the payroll area is (*pp. 561–562*)
a. Using a payroll bank account
b. Separating payroll duties
c. Using a payroll register
d. Using time cards

10. Which of the following items is reported as a current liability on the balance sheet? (*pp. 562–563*)
a. Short-term notes payable
b. Estimated warranties
c. Accrued payroll withholdings
d. All of the above

Answers to the Self-Study Questions follow the Similar Accounting Terms.

Accounting Vocabulary

Accrued expense (*p. 541*)
Accrued liability (*p. 541*)
Canada (or Quebec) Pension Plan (*p. 550*)
Current portion of long-term debt (*p. 541*)
Employee compensation (*p. 542*)
Employment Insurance (*p. 551*)

Gross pay (*p. 549*)
Net pay (*p. 549*)
Payroll (*p. 542*)
Short-term note payable (*p. 536*)
Withheld income tax (*p. 550*)
Workers' Compensation (*p. 552*)

Similar Accounting Terms

Current portion of long-term debt   Current maturity
Unearned revenues   Deferred revenues; Revenues collected in advance; Customer prepayments
Payroll register   Payroll journal; Payroll record

Answers to Self-Study Questions

1. c $10,000 \times 0.09 \times ^{153}/_{365} = $377.26
2. b
3. d
4. c $900,000 \times 0.01 = $9,000
5. b
6. a Overtime pay: $400 \div 40 = $10; $10 \times 1.5 = $15 per hour; $15 per hour $\times$ 10 hours = $150
   Gross pay = $400 + $150 = $550
   Deductions = ($550 \times 0.105) + ($550 \times 0.088) + ($550 \times 0.0495) + ($550 \times 0.021)
   $= $57.75 + $48.40 + $27.23 + $11.55 = $144.93
   Take-home pay = $550.00 – $144.93 = $405.07

7. d
8. c
9. b
10. d

Assignment Material

Questions

1. What distinguishes a current liability from a long-term liability? What distinguishes a contingent liability from an actual liability?

2. A company purchases a machine by signing a $50,000, 4-percent, one-year note payable on June 30. Interest is to be paid at maturity. What two current liabilities related to this purchase does the company report on its December 31 balance sheet? What is the amount of each current liability?

3. Explain how GST that is paid by consumers is a liability of the store that sold the merchandise. To whom is it paid?

4. What is meant by the term *current portion of long-term debt*, and how is this item reported in the financial statements?

5. Why is an accrued expense a liability?

6. Describe the similarities and differences between an account payable and a short-term note payable.

7. At the beginning of the school term, what type of account is the tuition that your college or university collects from students? What type of account is the tuition at the end of the school term?

8. Why is a customer deposit a liability? Give an example.

9. Murray Company warrants its products against defects for two years from date of sale. During the current year, the company made sales of $1,000,000. Management estimated warranty costs on those sales would total $30,000 over the two-year warranty period. Ultimately, the company paid $35,000 cash on warranties. What is the company's warranty expense for the year? What accounting principle governs this answer?

10. Identify one contingent liability of a definite amount and one contingent liability of an indefinite amount.

11. What are the two basic categories of current liabilities? Give an example of each.

12. Why is payroll expense relatively more important to a service business such as a public accounting firm than it is to a merchandising company such as Zellers?

13. Two persons are studying Beauregarde Company's manufacturing process. One person is Beauregarde Company's factory supervisor, and the other person is an outside consultant who is an expert in the industry. Which person's salary is the payroll expense of Beauregarde Company? Identify the expense account that Beauregarde Company would debit to record the pay of each person.

14. What are two elements of an employer's payroll expense in addition to salaries, wages, commissions, and overtime pay?

15. What determines the amount of income tax that is withheld from employee paycheques?

16. What is the Canada (or Quebec) Pension Plan? Who pays it? What are the funds used for?

17. Identify three required deductions and two optional deductions from employee paycheques.

18. Identify the employee benefit expenses an employer pays.

19. Who pays Employment Insurance premiums? What are these funds used for?

20. Briefly describe a basic payroll accounting system's components and their functions.

21. How much Employment Insurance has been withheld from the pay of an employee who has earned $52,288 during the current year? What is the employer's Employment Insurance expense for this employee?

22. Briefly describe the two principal types of internal controls over payroll.

23. Why do some companies use two special payroll bank accounts?

24. Identify three internal controls designed to safeguard payroll cash.

Exercises

Exercise 11-1 *Recording note payable transactions* **(Obj. 1)**

Record the following note payable transactions of Taylor Company in the company's general journal. Explanations are not required.

2005
June 1   Purchased delivery truck costing $43,000 by issuing a one-year, 4-percent note payable.

Dec. 31 Accrued interest on the note payable.

2006

June 1 Paid the note payable at maturity.

Exercise 11-2 *Recording sales tax and GST* *(Obj. 1)*

Make general journal entries to record the following transactions of Napanee Products for a two-month period. Explanations are not required.

June 30 Recorded cash sales of $223,400 for the month, plus provincial sales tax of 8 percent collected on behalf of the province of Ontario and goods and services tax of 7 percent. Record the two taxes in separate accounts.

July 6 Sent June provincial and goods and services taxes to appropriate authorities (Minister of Finance for PST and Receiver General for GST). Assume no GST input tax credits.

Exercise 11-3 *Reporting current and long-term liabilities* *(Obj. 1)*

Suppose Mars Technologies borrowed $4,000,000 on December 31, 2003, by issuing 5 percent long-term debt that must be paid in four equal annual instalments plus interest each January 2, commencing in 2005. By inserting appropriate amounts in the following excerpts from the company's partial balance sheet, show how Mars Technologies would report its long-term debt.

	December 31,			
	2004	2005	2006	2007
Current liabilities:				
Current portion of long-term debt............	$ _____	$ _____	$ _____	$ _____
Interest payable...	$ _____	$ _____	$ _____	$ _____
Long-term liabilities:				
Long-term debt..	$ _____	$ _____	$ _____	$ _____

Exercise 11-4 *Reporting current and long-term liabilities* *(Obj. 1)*

Assume Banff Electronics completed these selected transactions during December 2004:

1. Music For You Inc., a chain of music stores, ordered $210,000 worth of CD players. With its order, Music For You Inc. sent a cheque for $210,000. Banff Electronics will ship the goods on January 3, 2005.

2. The December payroll of $1,200,000 is subject to employee withheld income tax of 16 percent, Canada Pension Plan expenses of 4.95 percent for the employee and 4.95 percent for the employer, Employment Insurance deductions of 2.1 percent for the employee and 1.4 times the employee rate of 2.1 percent for the employer. On December 31, Banff Electronics pays employees but accrues all tax amounts.

3. Sales of $300,000,000 are subject to estimated warranty cost of 1.4 percent. This was the first year the company provided a warranty.

4. On December 2, Banff Electronics signed a $500,000 note payable that requires annual payments of $125,000 plus 4 percent interest on the unpaid balance each December 2.

Required

Report these items on Banff Electronics' balance sheet at December 31, 2004.

Exercise 11-5 *Recording current liabilities* *(Obj. 1)*

Link Back to Chapter 4 (Current Ratio). The management of Marquis Marketing Services examines the following company accounting records at August 29, immediately before the end of the year, August 31:

Total current assets	$ 650,000
Capital assets	2,159,000
	$2,809,000
Total current liabilities........................	$ 385,000
Long-term liabilities	495,000
Owner's equity.....................................	1,929,000
	$2,809,000

Marquis's banking agreement with The Royal Bank requires the company to keep a current ratio of 2.25 or better. How much in current liabilities should Marquis pay off within the next two days in order to comply with its borrowing agreements?

Exercise 11-6 *Accounting for unearned revenue* *(Obj. 1)*

The law firm Garner & Brown bills a large corporate client an annual retainer fee of $120,000 on January 1, 2006. The fee is based on anticipated monthly services of $10,000.

Required

1. Using the account title Retainer Fees for unearned revenue, journalize (1) Garner & Brown's receipt of retainer fees, and (2) the provision of services in the month of January 2006.
2. Post the journal entries in Requirement 1 to the unearned revenue account (Retainer Fees) T-account. What is the value of services to be provided to the client in the remaining 11 months?

Exercise 11-7 *Accounting for unearned revenue* *(Obj. 1)*

Assume *The Globe and Mail* completed the following transactions for one subscriber during 2005:

Oct.	1	Sold a six-month subscription, collecting cash of $150 plus sales tax of 8 percent and 7 percent GST.
Nov.	15	Remitted (paid) the sales tax and GST to the Province of Ontario.
Dec.	31	Made the necessary adjustment at year end to record the amount of subscription revenue earned during the year.

Required

1. Using *The Globe and Mail* (assumed) account title Subcriptions Received, journalize the transactions above.
2. Post the entries to the Subscriptions Received T-account. How much does *The Globe and Mail* owe the subscriber at December 31, 2005?

Exercise 11-8 *Accounting for warranty expense and the related liability* *(Obj. 2)*

The accounting records of Sebago Industries included the following balances at the end of the period:

Estimated Warranty Payable	Sales Revenue	Warranty Expense
Beg. bal. 12,400	519,000	

In the past, Sebago Industries' warranty expense has been 4 percent of sales. During the current period, Sebago Industries paid $27,900 to satisfy the warranty claims of customers.

Required

1. Record Sebago Industries' warranty expense for the period and the company's cash payments during the period to satisfy warranty claims. Explanations are not required.
2. What ending balance of Estimated Warranty Payable will Sebago Industries report on its balance sheet?

Exercise 11-9 *Accounting for warranty expense and estimated warranty payable (Obj. 2)*

Honda Canada Inc. warranties its Acura automobiles for five years or 100,000 kilometres, whichever comes first. Suppose Honda's experience indicates that the company can expect warranty costs during the five-year period to add up to 7 percent of sales.

Assume that Open Skies Acura in Regina, Saskatchewan, made sales of $1,200,000 during 2005, its first year of operations. Open Skies Acura received cash for 10 percent of the sales and notes receivable for the remainder. Payments to satisfy customer warranty claims totalled $49,000 during 2005.

Required

1. Record the sales, warranty expense, and warranty payments for Open Skies Acura. Ignore any reimbursement Open Skies Acura may receive from Honda Canada Inc.

2. Post to the Estimated Warranty Payable T-account. At the end of 2005, how much in estimated warranty payable does Open Skies Acura owe its customers? Why must the warranty payable amount be estimated?

Exercise 11-10 *Reporting a contingent liability (Obj. 2)*

Oshawa Security Systems is a defendant in lawsuits brought against the monitoring service of its installed systems. Damages of $500,000 are claimed against Oshawa Security Systems but the company denies the charges and is vigorously defending itself. In a recent newspaper interview, the president of the company stated that he could not predict the outcome of the lawsuits. Nevertheless, he said management does not believe that any actual liabilities resulting from the lawsuits will significantly affect the company's financial position.

Required

Describe what, if any, disclosure Oshawa Security Systems should provide of this contingent liability. Total liabilities are $2.0 million. If you believe note disclosure is required, write the note to describe the contingency.

Exercise 11-11 *Accruing a contingency (Obj. 2)*

Refer to the Oshawa Security Systems situation in the preceding exercise. Suppose that Oshawa Security Systems' lawyers advise that preliminary judgment of $150,000 has been rendered against the company.

Required

Describe how to report this situation in the Oshawa Security Systems financial statements. Journalize any entry required under GAAP. Explanations are not required.

Exercise 11-12 *Interpreting a company's contingent liabilities (Obj. 2)*

Nortel Networks Corporation's 2002 financial statements include the following note:

NOTES TO CONSOLIDATED FINANCIAL STATEMENTS

12. (In Part): Guarantees and Commitments

(c) Lease agreements

Nortel Networks has entered into agreements with its lessors that guarantee the lease payments of certain sub-lessees of its facilities to lessors. Generally, these lease agreements relate to facilities Nortel Networks vacated prior to the end of the term of its lease. These lease agreements require Nortel Networks to make lease payments throughout the lease term if the sub-lessee fails to make scheduled payments. These lease agreements have expiration dates through June 2012. The maximum amount that Nortel Networks may be required to pay under these types of agreements is $40 million.

Required

1. Why are these *contingent* (versus real) liabilities?
2. How could the contingent liability become a real liability for Nortel Networks? What are the limits to the company's guarantees? When will this contingent liability no longer exist?

Exercise 11-13   *Computing net pay   (Obj. 3)*

Marla Johnson is a clerk in the shoe department of The Bay in Winnipeg. She earns a base monthly salary of $1,875 plus a 7 percent commission on her sales. Through payroll deductions, Marla donates $15 per month to a charitable organization and pays dental insurance premiums of $39.15. Compute Marla's gross pay and net pay for December, assuming her sales for the month are $100,000. The income tax rate on her earnings is 30 percent, the Canada Pension Plan contribution is 4.95 percent, and the Employment Insurance Plan premium rate is 2.1 percent. Marla has not yet reached the CPP or EI maximum earning levels

Media Companion CD-ROM

Exercise 11-14   *Computing and recording gross pay and net pay   (Obj. 3, 4)*

Will Wong works for a Quick Burgers takeout for straight-time earnings of $10.50 per hour, with time and a half for hours in excess of 35 per week. Will's payroll deductions include income tax of 14 percent, Canada Pension Plan of 4.95 percent on earnings and Employment Insurance of 2.1 percent on earnings. In addition, he contributes $2.50 per week to the United Way. Assuming Will worked 40 hours during the week, (1) compute his gross pay and net pay for the week, and (2) make a general journal entry to record the restaurant's wage expense for Will's work, including his payroll deductions and the employer payroll costs. Round all amounts to the nearest cent.

Exercise 11-15   *Recording a payroll   (Obj. 3, 4)*

Baie D'Urfé Manufacturing incurred salary expense of $95,000 for September. The company's payroll expense includes Canada Pension of 4.95 percent and Employment Insurance of 1.4 times the employee payment, which is 2.1 percent of earnings. Also, the company provides the following fringe benefits for employees: dental insurance (cost to the company of $5,723.09), life insurance (cost to the company of $461.09), and pension benefits through a private plan (cost to the company of $1,945.60). Record Baie D'Urfé Manufacturing's payroll expenses for Canada Pension Plan and Employment Insurance and employee fringe benefits. Ignore the CPP basic exemption.

Exercise 11-16   *Using a payroll system to compute total payroll expense   (Obj. 5)*

Study the Employee Earnings Record for J.C. Jenkins in Exhibit 11-9, page 560. In addition to the amounts shown in the exhibit, the employer also paid all employee benefits plus (a) an amount equal to 5 percent of gross pay into Jenkins' pension retirement account, and (b) dental insurance for Jenkins at a cost of $35 per month. Compute the employer's total payroll expense for employee J.C. Jenkins during 2003. Carry all amounts to the nearest cent.

Challenge Exercises

Exercise 11-17   *Accounting for and reporting current liabilities*   **(Obj. 1, 6)**

Link Back to Chapter 4 (Current Ratio). Suppose the balance sheets of a corporation for two years reported these figures:

	Billions	
	2004	**2003**
Total current assets	$ 7.25	$ 6.46
Capital assets	22.37	20.48
	$29.62	$26.94
Total current liabilities	5.83	7.56
Long-term liabilities	14.96	11.66
Shareholders' equity	8.83	7.72
	$29.62	$26.94

The notes to the 2004 financial statements report that during 2004, because of some refinancing arrangements, the corporation was able to reclassify $3.5 billion from current liabilities to long-term liabilities.

Required

1. Compute the corporation's current ratio at the end of each year. Describe the trend that you observe.

2. Suppose that the corporation had not refinanced and not been able to reclassify the $3.5 billion of current liabilities as long-term during 2004. Recompute the current ratio for 2004. Why do you think the corporation reclassified the liabilities as long-term?

Exercise 11-18   *Analyzing current liability accounts*   **(Obj. 1, 6)**

Jericho Company recently reported notes payable and accrued payrolls and benefits as follows:

	December 31,	
	2005	**2004**
	(in millions of dollars)	
Current liabilities (partial):		
Notes payable	$ 13	$ 39
Accrued payrolls and benefits	135	149

Assume that during 2005, Jericho Company borrowed $1.5 million on notes payable. Also assume that Jericho paid $125 million for employee compensation and benefits during 2005.

Required

1. Compute Jericho Company's payment of notes payable during 2005.
2. Compute Jericho Company's employee compensation during 2005.

Beyond the Numbers

Beyond the Numbers 11-1

Suppose a large manufacturing company is the defendant in numerous lawsuits claiming unfair trade practices. The company has strong incentives not to disclose these contingent liabilities. However, generally accepted accounting principles require companies to report their contingent liabilities.

Required

1. Why would a company prefer not to disclose its contingent liabilities?

2. Describe how a bank could be harmed if a company seeking a loan did not disclose its contingent liabilities.

3. What is the ethical tightrope that companies must walk when they report their contingent liabilities?

Beyond the Numbers 11-2

The following questions are not related.

a. A warranty is like a contingent liability in that the amount to be paid is not known at year end. Why are warranties payable shown as a current liability, whereas contingent liabilities are reported in the notes to the financial statements?

b. A friend comments that he thought that liabilities represented amounts owed by a company. He asks why unearned revenues are shown as a current liability. How would you respond?

c. Auditors have procedures for determining whether they have discovered all of a company's contingent liabilities. These procedures differ from the procedures used for determining that accounts payable are stated correctly. How would an auditor identify a client's contingent liabilities?

Ethical Issue

Many companies, such as Campeau Corporation, borrowed heavily during the 1970s and 1980s to exploit the advantage of financing operations with debt. At first, the companies were able to earn operating income much higher than their interest expense and were therefore quite profitable. However, when the business cycle turned down, their debt burdens pushed the companies to the brink of bankruptcy. Operating income was less than interest expense.

Required

Is it unethical for managers to commit a company to a high level of debt? Or is it just risky? Who could be hurt by a company's taking on too much debt? Discuss.

Problems (Group A)

Problem 11-1A *Journalizing liability-related transactions* *(Obj. 1, 2)*

The following transactions of Mid West Technology of Regina, Saskatchewan, occurred during 2004 and 2005. The company's year end is December 31.

2004
Mar. 3 Purchased a machine for $66,000, signing a six-month, 4.5 percent note payable.
   31 Recorded the month's sales of $1,345,000, one-quarter for cash, and three-quarters on credit. All sales amounts are subject to the 7 percent goods and services tax, to be calculated on the sales of $1,345,000.
Apr. 7 Sent February's goods and services tax to the Receiver General.
May 31 Borrowed $750,000 with a 5 percent note payable that calls for annual instalment payments of $150,000 principal plus interest.
Sept. 3 Paid the six-month, 4.5 percent note at maturity.
   30 Purchased goods at a cost of $25,000, signing a 4 percent, six-month note payable for that amount.
Dec. 31 Accrued warranty expense, which is estimated at 1.5 percent of annual sales of $14,450,000.
   31 Accrued interest on all outstanding notes payable. Make a separate interest accrual entry for each note payable.
2005
Mar. 31 Paid off the 4 percent inventory note, plus interest, at maturity.
May 31 Paid the first instalment and interest for one year on the long-term note payable.

Required

Record the transactions in the company's general journal. Explanations are not required.

Problem 11-2A *Identifying contingent liabilities* *(Obj. 2)*

Sylvia Lemieux provides skating lessons for children ages 8 through 15. Most students are beginners. Sylvia rents ice time from the local arena. Because this is a new business venture, Sylvia wants to save money and does not want to purchase insurance. She seeks your advice about her business exposure to liabilities.

Required

Write a memorandum to inform Sylvia Lemieux of specific contingent liabilities that could arise from the business. It will be necessary to define a contingent liability because she is a professional skater, not a businessperson. Propose a way for Sylvia to limit her exposure to these possible liabilities.

Problem 11-3A *Computing and reporting payroll amounts* *(Obj. 3, 4)*

The partial monthly records of Johansen Products show the following figures:

Employee Earnings
(a) Regular earnings.................	?
(b) Overtime pay	$6,997
(c) Total employee earnings.....	?

Deductions and Net Pay
(d) Withheld income tax	17,852
(e) Canada Pension Plan	3,584
(f) Employment Insurance.......	2,243

(g) Dental and drug insurance	$ 778
(h) Total deductions....................	?
(i) Net pay	68,924

Accounts Debited
(j) Salary Expense	33,234
(k) Wage Expense........................	?
(l) Sales Commission Expense ..	29,678

Required

1. Determine the missing amounts on lines (a), (c), (h), and (k).

2. Prepare the general journal entry to record Johansen Products' payroll for the month. Credit Payroll Payable for net pay. No explanation is required.

Problem 11-4A *Computing and recording payroll amounts* *(Obj. 3, 4)*

Media Companion CD-ROM

Assume that Marcy St. Laurent is a marketing director in Bell Mobility's head office in Montreal. During 2003, she worked for the company all year at a $6,500.00 monthly salary. She also earned a year-end bonus equal to 15 percent of her salary.

St. Laurent's monthly income tax withholding for 2003 was $1,762.28. Also, she paid a one-time withholding tax of $4,095.11 on her bonus cheque. She paid $307.31 per month towards the Quebec Pension Plan until the maximum ($1,801.80) had been withheld. In addition, St. Laurent's employer deducted $136.50 per month for Employment Insurance until the maximum ($819.00) had been withheld. St. Laurent authorized the following deductions: 1.5 percent per month of her monthly pay to Bell's charitable donation fund and $34.00 per month for life insurance.

Bell Mobility incurred Quebec Pension Plan expense equal to the amount deducted from St. Laurent's pay. Employment Insurance cost the company 1.4 times the amount deducted from St. Laurent's pay. In addition, the company provided St. Laurent with the following fringe benefits: dental and drug insurance at a cost of $65 per month, and pension benefits to be paid to St. Laurent upon retirement. The pension contribution is based on her income and was $5,350.00 in 2003.

Required

1. Compute St. Laurent's gross pay, payroll deductions, and net pay for the full year 2003. Round all amounts to the nearest cent.

2. Compute Bell Mobility's total 2003 payroll cost for St. Laurent.

3. Prepare Bell Mobility's summary general journal entries to record its expense for
   a. St. Laurent's total earnings for the year, her payroll deductions and her net pay. Debit Salary Expense and Executive Bonus Compensation as appropriate for sales and employee benefit expense. Credit liability accounts for the payroll deductions and Cash for net pay.
   b. Employer payroll expenses for St. Laurent. Credit the appropriate liability accounts.
   c. Fringe benefits provided to St. Laurent. Credit Health Insurance Payable and Company Pension Payable.

   Explanations are not required.

Problem 11-5A   *Journalizing, posting, and reporting liabilities*   (Obj. 1, 2, 3, 4, 6)

Collingwood Hardware's general ledger at June 30, 2005, the end of the company's fiscal year, includes the following account balances before adjusting entries. Parentheses indicate a debit balance.

Note payable, short-term...........	$ 37,000	Employee benefits payable	_____
Accounts payable........................	167,840	Estimated vacation pay	
Current portion of long-		liability..................................	$3,948
term debt payable..................	_____	GST payable..............................	2,450
Interest payable...........................	_____	Property tax payable.................	3,642
Salary payable	_____	Unearned maintenance	
Employee payroll with-		revenue	13,500
holding taxes payable............	_____	Long-term debt payable...........	150,000
Payroll costs payable..................	_____		

The additional data needed to develop the adjusting entries at June 30 are as follows:

a. The $37,000 short-term note payable was issued on July 31, 2004, matures one year from date of issuance, and bears interest at 6 percent.

b. The long-term debt is payable in annual instalments of $30,000, with the next instalment due February 28, 2006. On that date, Collingwood Hardware will also pay one year's interest at 5.5 percent. Interest was last paid on February 28, 2005.

c. Gross salaries for the last payroll of the fiscal year were $10,723. Of this amount, employee withholdings were $2,378, and salary payable was $8,345.

d. Employer payroll costs were $1,394, and Collingwood Hardware's liability for employee life insurance was $75.

e. Collingwood Hardware estimates that vacation pay is 4 percent of gross salaries of $120,000 after adjustment for the last payroll of the fiscal year.

f. On March 1, 2005, the company collected one year's service contract revenue of $13,500 in advance.

g. At June 30, 2005, Collingwood Hardware is the defendant in a $50,000 small claims lawsuit, which the store expects to win. However, the outcome is uncertain.

Required

1. Open T-accounts for the listed accounts, inserting their unadjusted June 30, 2005 balances.

2. Post the June 30, 2005 adjusting entries to the accounts opened.

3. Prepare the liability section of Collingwood Hardware's balance sheet at June 30, 2005.

4. Is there a contingent liability? If yes, write the note to describe it and indicate where it should appear.

Problem 11-6A *Using a payroll register; recording a payroll* *(Obj. 5)*

Media Companion CD-ROM

Assume that payroll records of a branch of Indigo Books provided the following information for the weekly pay period ended December 18, 2003:

Employee	Hours Worked	40-Hour Weekly Earnings	Income Tax	Canada Pension	Employ- ment Insurance	United Way	Year-to-date Earnings at the End of the Previous Week
Lucy Quik	45	$440	$ 62.85	$15.22	$12.57	$ 4	$19,130.00
Maura Wells	50	500	73.25	21.37	15.98	4	28,400.00
Carl Keller	49	850	184.10	0	0	10	42,350.00
Maurice Lamont	40	380	42.60	10.25	8.49	1	8,966.00

Lucy Quik and Maurice Lamont work in the office, and Maura Wells and Carl Keller are sales staff. All employees are paid time and a half for hours worked in excess of 40 hours per week. Show computations.

Required

1. Enter the appropriate information in a payroll register similar to Exhibit 11-7.

2. Record the payroll information in the general journal, crediting net pay to Cash.

3. The employer's payroll costs are calculated by matching the employee's Canada Pension Plan contribution (employee rate 4.95 percent; maximum $1,801.80) and paying 1.4 times the employee's Employment Insurance premium (employee rate 2.1 percent; maximum $819.00). Record the employer's payroll costs in the general journal.

4. Why is no Canada Pension Plan or Employment Insurance deducted for Keller?

Problem 11-7A *Reporting current liabilities* *(Obj. 6)*

Following are six pertinent facts about events during the year at Hudson Farm Equipment Manufacturing, an Ontario company:

a. On September 30, Hudson Farm Equipment Manufacturing signed a six-month, 5 percent note payable to purchase a machine costing $120,000. The note requires payment of principal and interest at maturity.

b. Sales of $2,103,000 were covered by Hudson Farm Equipment's product warranty. At January 1, estimated warranty payable was $29,300. During the year, Hudson Farm Equipment recorded warranty expense of 3 percent of sales and paid warranty claims of $55,700.

c. On November 15, Hudson Farm Equipment received $10,000 on deposit for a tractor. The tractor will be delivered in March of next year.

d. December sales totalled $223,000 and Hudson Farm Equipment collected GST of 7 percent on these sales. This amount will be sent to the appropriate authority early in January.

e. Hudson Farm Equipment owes $200,000 on a long-term note payable. At December 31, 4.5 percent interest for the year plus $40,000 of this principal are payable within one year.

Required

For each item, indicate the account and the related amount to be reported as a current liability on Hudson Farm Equipment Manufacturing's December 31 (year-end) balance sheet.

Problem 11-8A *Accounting for current liabilities; making basic payroll entries; reporting current liabilities* **(Obj. 1, 2, 4, 6)**

High Mountain, an Alberta company, is a ski resort with the following information available:

- Goods and Services Tax: 7 percent GST is applicable to all purchases and sales.
- Employer Payroll Costs: the employer's share of Canada Pension and Employment Insurance is 1.0 times and 1.4 times the employees' share respectively. The company pays Workers' Compensation of 3 percent and estimates vacation pay at 4 percent of all earnings.

The company prepares quarterly financial statements and had the following transactions for the first three months of 2003:

Jan.   31   Recorded the month's purchases, $312,000 (not including the GST). All purchases are on credit.

31   Recorded the month's sales of $429,000 (not including the GST), of which 85 percent were on credit.

31   Recorded and paid the payroll for the month. Gross earnings were $95,000, with deductions of:
- Employee income taxes equal to 17 percent of gross earnings
- Canada Pension Plan deductions equal to 4.95 percent* of gross earnings (employees' share)
- Employment Insurance deductions equal to 2.1 percent of gross earnings (employees' share)
- Union dues deduction equal to $1,560.

Feb.   3   Borrowed $50,000 from the bank by signing a 5 percent, 30-day note payable with the principal and interest payable on the maturity date.

7   Paid the GST for the month of January.

17   Sent a cheque for all payroll deductions and contributions, including the employer's share, to the appropriate authorities.

28   Recorded the month's purchases, $349,000 (not including the GST). All purchases are on credit.

28   Recorded the month's sales of $550,000 (not including the GST), of which 75 percent were on credit.

28   Recorded and paid the payroll for the month. Gross earnings were $115,000, with deductions of:
- Employee income taxes equal to 17 percent of gross earnings
- Canada Pension Plan deductions equal to 4.95 percent* of gross earnings (employees' share)
- Employment Insurance deductions equal to 2.1 percent of gross earnings (employees' share)
- Union dues deduction equal to $1,872.

Mar.   4   Paid the note payable from February 3.

7   Paid the GST for the month of February.

17   Sent a cheque for all payroll deductions and contributions, including the employer's share, to the appropriate authorities.

31   Recorded the month's purchases, $365,000 (not including the GST). All purchases are on credit.

31   Recorded the month's sales of $625,000 (not including the GST), of which 80 percent were on credit.

31   Recorded and paid the payroll for the month. Gross earnings were $145,000, with deductions of:
- Employee income taxes equal to 17 percent of gross earnings
- Canada Pension Plan deductions equal to 4.95 percent* of gross earnings (employees' share)
- Employment Insurance deductions equal to 2.1 percent of gross earnings (employees' share)
- Union dues deduction equal to $2,100.

*For purposes of this calculation, ignore the basic exemption of $3,500.

Required

1. Journalize all of the transactions, and any adjustments that would be required on March 30, 2003 (the end of the first quarter). Round all amounts to the nearest whole dollar. Use days, not months, to calculate interest amounts.

2. Show the current liability section of the balance sheet as of March 30, 2003. Assume there are nil balances in all accounts at January 1, 2003.

Problem 11-9A *Accounting for current liabilities; accounting for contingent liabilities; reporting current liabilities* **(Obj. 1, 2, 6)**

McLaughlin Technologies produces and sells customized network systems in Manitoba. The company offers a 60-day, all software and labour—and an extra 90-day, parts-only—warranty on all of its products. The company had the following transactions in 2005:

Jan.	31	Sales for the month totalled $350,000 (not including GST), of which 95 percent were on credit. The company collects 7 percent GST on all sales and estimates its warranty costs at 3 percent of sales.
	31	Based on last year's property tax assessment, estimated that the property taxes for the year would be $19,000 (1 percent of last year's $1,900,000 assessed value). Recorded the estimated property taxes for the month; credit Estimated Property Taxes Payable.
Feb.	4	Completed repair work for a customer. The software ($5,000) and labour ($3,250) were all covered under the warranty.
	7	Remitted the appropriate GST for the month of January (the company had paid $15,610 GST on purchases in January).
	28	Recorded the estimated property taxes for the month of February.
	28	Sales for the month totalled $325,000 (not including GST), of which 90 percent were on credit. The company estimates its warranty costs at 3 percent of sales.
Mar.	7	Remitted the appropriate GST for the month of February (the company had paid $13,648 GST on purchases in February).
	8	McLaughlin Technologies received notice that it was being sued by a customer for an error resulting from the failure of its product. The company's lawyer was reluctant to estimate the likely outcome of the lawsuit, but another customer indicated that a similar case had resulted in a $100,000 settlement.
	15	Completed repair work for a customer. The software ($7,500) and labour ($2,750) were all covered under the warranty.
	21	Completed repair work for a customer. The software ($4,500) was covered by the warranty, but the labour ($1,650) was not. Payment for the labour is due from the customer in 30 days.
	31	Sales for the month totalled $315,000 (not including GST), of which 95 percent was on credit. The company estimates its warranty costs at 3 percent of sales.
	31	Received the property tax assessment for 2005. It showed the assessed value of the property to be $2,300,000 and a tax rate of 1.3 percent of the assessed value. The company made the appropriate adjustment and used the Property Taxes Payable account.

Required

1. Journalize the above transactions.

2. Show the appropriate financial statement presentation for all liabilities.

Problems (Group B)

Problem 11-1B *Journalizing liability-related transactions* **(Obj. 1, 2)**

The following selected transactions of Auto Tooling, a Saskatchewan company, occurred during 2004 and 2005. The company's year end is December 31.

2004

Jan. 3 Purchased a machine at a cost of $175,000 plus 7 percent GST, signing a 4 percent, six-month note payable for that amount.

29 Recorded the month's sales of $785,000 (excludes PST and GST), 80 percent on credit and 20 percent for cash. Sales amounts are subject to 8 percent provincial sales tax plus 7 percent GST.

Feb. 5 Sent January's provincial sales tax and GST to the appropriate authorities.

28 Borrowed $1,500,000 on a 5 percent note payable that calls for annual instalment payments of $150,000 principal plus interest.

July 3 Paid the six-month, 4 percent note at maturity.

Nov. 30 Purchased inventory for $75,000 plus GST, signing a six-month, 4 percent note payable.

Dec. 31 Accrued warranty expense, which is estimated at 1 percent of annual sales of $4,000,000.

31 Accrued interest on all outstanding notes payable. Make a separate interest accrual entry for each note payable.

2005

Feb. 28 Paid the first instalment and interest for one year on the long-term note payable.

May 31 Paid off the 4 percent note plus interest at maturity.

Required

Record the transactions in the company's general journal. Explanations are not required.

Problem 11-2B *Identifying contingent liabilities (Obj. 2)*

Morgan Motors is the Morgan dealer located in Victoria, British Columbia, and the only dealer in Western Canada. The dealership repairs and restores Morgan vintage cars. Hal Irwin, the general manager, is considering changing insurance companies because of a disagreement with Bart LeMesure, agent for the Dominion of Canada Insurance Company. Dominion is doubling Morgan Motors' liability insurance cost for the next year. In discussing insurance coverage with you, a trusted business associate, LeMesure brings up the subject of contingent liabilities.

Required

Write a memorandum to inform Morgan Motors of specific contingent liabilities arising from the business. In your discussion, define a contingent liability.

Problem 11-3B *Computing and recording payroll amounts (Obj. 3, 4)*

The partial monthly records of East Shore Golf Shop show the following figures:

Employee Earnings

(a) Regular employee earnings..............	$19,947
(b) Overtime pay.............	?
(c) Total employee earnings....	?

(f) Employment Insurance...............	$ 536
(g) Medical insurance........................	541
(h) Total deductions...........................	7,147
(i) Net pay	18,395

Deductions and Net Pay

(d) Withheld income tax........	5,109
(e) Canada Pension Plan	?

Accounts Debited

(j) Salary Expense..............................	?
(k) Wage Expense..............................	6,938
(l) Sales Commission Expense	1,681

Required

1. Determine the missing amounts on lines (b), (c), (e), and (j).

2. Prepare the general journal entry to record East Shore Golf Shop's payroll for the month. Credit Payrolls Payable for net pay. No explanation is required.

Problem 11-4B   *Computing and recording payroll amounts*   **(Obj. 3, 4)**

Assume that Shetal Patel is a Vice-President in GE Capital's leasing operations. During 2003 she worked for the company all year at a $7,500 monthly salary. She also earned a year-end bonus equal to 15 percent of her salary.

Shetal's federal income tax withheld during 2003 was $2,398 per month. Also, there was a one-time federal withholding tax of $4,712 on her bonus cheque. She paid $356.85 per month into the Canada Pension Plan until she had paid the maximum of $1,801.80. In addition, Shetal paid $157.50 per month Employment Insurance through her employer until the maximum of $819.00 had been reached. She had authorized GE Capital to make the following payroll deductions: life insurance of $55 per month; United Way of $37.50 per month.

GE Capital incurred Canada Pension Plan expense equal to the amount deducted from Shetal's pay and Employment Insurance expense equal to 1.4 times the amount Shetal paid. In addition, GTE Capital paid dental and drug insurance of $38 per month and pension benefits of 6 percent of her base salary.

Required

1. Compute Shetal Patel's gross pay, payroll deductions, and net pay for the full year 2003. Round all amounts to the nearest cent.

2. Compute GE Capital's total 2003 payroll cost for Shetal.

3. Prepare GE Capital's general journal entries to record its expense for
   a. Shetal's total earnings for the year, her payroll deductions, and her net pay. Debit Salary Expense and Executive Bonus Compensation as appropriate for salary and employee benefit expense. Credit liability accounts for the payroll deductions and Cash for net pay.
   b. Employer payroll expenses for Shetal. Credit the appropriate liability accounts.
   c. Fringe benefits provided to Shetal. Credit Health Insurance Payable and Company Pension Payable. Explanations are not required.

Problem 11-5B   *Journalizing, posting, and reporting liabilities*   **(Obj. 1, 2, 3, 4, 6)**

The general ledger of Super Storage Units at June 30, 2004, the end of the company's fiscal year, includes the following account balances before adjusting entries. Parentheses indicate a debit balance.

Notes payable, short-term........	$ 20,000	Employee benefits	
Accounts payable	235,620	payable	_____
Current portion of long-		Estimated vacation pay	
term debt payable	_____	liability.................................	$ 12,360
Interest payable..........................	_____	Sales tax and GST payable.....	5,972
Salary payable............................	_____	Unearned rent revenue	15,000
Employee payroll		Long-term debt payable.........	250,000
withholdings payable..........	_____		
Payroll expense payable............	_____		

The additional data needed to develop the adjusting entries at June 30 are as follows:

a. The $20,000 short-term note payable was issued on February 28. It matures six months from date of issuance and bears interest at 4.5 percent.

b. The long-term debt is payable in annual instalments of $50,000 with the next instalment due on August 31. On that date, Super Storage Units will also pay one year's interest at 5 percent. Interest was last paid on August 31 of the preceding year.

c. Gross salaries for the last payroll of the fiscal year were $12,655. Of this amount, employee payroll withholdings payable were $2,730, and salary payable was $9,925.

d. Employer payroll expense payable was $1,639, and Super Storage's liability for employee health insurance was $1,982.

e. Super Storage estimates that vacation pay expense is 4 percent of gross salaries of $295,000 after adjustment for the last payroll of the fiscal year.

f. On March 1, the company collected one year's rent of $15,000 in advance.

g. At June 30, Super Storage is the defendant in a $275,000 lawsuit, which the company expects to win. However, the outcome is uncertain.

Required

1. Open T-accounts for the listed accounts, inserting their unadjusted June 30, 2004 balances.

2. Post the June 30, 2004, adjusting entries to the T-accounts opened.

3. Prepare the liability section of Super Storage Units' balance sheet at June 30, 2004.

Media Companion CD-ROM

Problem 11-6B   *Using payroll register; recording a payroll*   *(Obj. 5)*

Assume that the payroll records of a district sales office of Beaver Lumber Products provided the following information for the weekly pay period ended September 21.

Employee	Hours Worked	Hourly Earnings Rate	Income Tax	Canada Pension	Employment Insurance	United Way	Year-to-date Earnings at the End of the Previous Week
Molly Entwistle	43	$30	$374.10	$ 0	$ 0	$25	$47,200
Tally Lafarge	40	13	67.60	22.41	10.92	2	19,760
George White	49	10	63.70	20.92	10.29	2	20,250
Luigi Bos	42	20	252.00	0	0	5	40,050

Tally Lafarge and George White work in the office, and Molly Entwistle and Luigi Bos work in sales. All employees are paid time and a half for hours worked in excess of 40 hours per week. Show computations.

Required

1. Enter the appropriate information in a payroll register similar to Exhibit 11-7.

2. Record the payroll information in the general journal, crediting net pay to Cash.

3. The employer's payroll costs include matching each employee's Canada Pension Plan contribution (employee rate 4.95 percent; maximum $1,801.80) and paying 1.4 times the employee's Employment Insurance premium (employee rate 2.1 percent; maximum $819.00). Record the employer's payroll costs in the general journal.

4. Why was no Canada Pension Plan or Employment Insurance deducted for Entwistle and Bos?

Problem 11-7B   *Reporting current liabilities*   *(Obj. 6)*

Following are six pertinent facts about events during the current year at East Coast Fisheries, a Prince Edward Island fisheries supply company:

a. Sales of $911,000 were covered by East Coast Fisheries' product warranty. At January 1, the estimated warranty payable was $14,600. During the year East Coast recorded warranty expense of 2 percent of sales and paid warranty claims of $25,600.

b. On August 31, East Coast Fisheries signed a six-month, 4.5 percent note payable to purchase supplies costing $45,000. The note requires payment of principal and interest at maturity.

c. On November 30, East Coast Fisheries received rent of $15,000 in advance from a subtenant in their building. This rent will be earned evenly over three months.

d. December sales totalled $80,000 and East Coast Fisheries collected provincial sales tax of 10 percent plus goods and services tax of 7 percent on these sales. These taxes will be sent to the appropriate authorities early in January.*

e. East Coast Fisheries owes $150,000 on a long-term note payable. At December 31, $30,000 of this principal plus 5 percent accrued interest since September 30 are payable within one year.

*Note: Prince Edward Island bases PST on price including GST.

Required

For each item, indicate the account and the related amount to be reported as a current liability on East Coast Fisheries' December 31 (year-end) balance sheet.

Problem 11-8B *Accounting for current liabilities; making basic payroll entries; reporting current liabilities* *(Obj. 1, 2, 4, 6)*

Atlantic Marine of St. John's, Newfoundland, operates a marine supply company with the following information available:

- 15 percent HST is applicable to all purchases and sales.
- Payroll costs—the employer's share of Canada Pension and Employment Insurance are 1.0 times and 1.4 times the employees' share, respectively. The company pays Workers' Compensation of 3 percent and estimates vacation pay at 4 percent of all earnings.

The company prepares quarterly financial statements and had the following transactions for the first three months of 2003:

Apr. 30   Recorded the month's purchases of inventory, $775,000 (not including the HST). All purchases are on credit. The company uses the periodic inventory system.

      30   Recorded the month's sales of $1,415,000 (not including the HST), of which 80 percent were on credit.

      30   Recorded and paid the payroll for the month. Gross earnings were $295,000, with deductions of:
- Employee income taxes equal to 22 percent of gross earnings
- Canada Pension Plan deductions equal to 4.95 percent* of gross earnings (employees' share)
- Employment Insurance deductions equal to 2.1 percent of gross earnings (employees' share)
- Union dues deduction equal to $5,250.

May 2   Borrowed $250,000 from the bank by signing a 4 percent, 30-day note payable with the principal and interest payable on the maturity date.

      7   Paid the HST for the month of April.

      15   Sent a cheque for all payroll deductions and contributions, including the employer's share, to the appropriate authorities.

      31   Recorded the month's purchases of inventory, $600,000 (not including the HST). All purchases are on credit.

      31   Recorded the month's sales of $1,450,000 (not including the HST), of which 75 percent were on credit.

      31   Recorded and paid the payroll for the month. Gross earnings were $315,000, with deductions of:
- Employee income taxes equal to 22 percent of gross earnings
- Canada Pension Plan deductions equal to 4.95 percent* of gross earnings (employees' share)
- Employment Insurance deductions equal to 2.1 percent of gross earnings (employees' share)
- Union dues deduction equal to $5,420.

June 1   Paid the note payable from May 2.

June 7 Paid the HST for the month of May.

16 Sent a cheque for all payroll deductions and contributions, including the employer's share, to the appropriate authorities.

30 Recorded the month's purchases of $850,000 (not including the HST). All purchases are on credit.

30 Recorded the month's sales of $1,500,000 (not including the HST), of which 85 percent were on credit.

30 Recorded and paid the payroll for the month. Gross earnings were $355,000, with deductions of:
- Employee income taxes equal to 22 percent of gross earnings
- Canada Pension Plan deductions equal to 4.95 percent* of gross earnings (employees' share)
- Employment Insurance deductions equal to 2.1 percent of gross earnings (employees' share)
- Union dues deduction equal to $5,697.

*For purposes of this calculation, ignore the basic exemption of $3,500.

Required

1. Journalize all of the transactions, and any adjustments that would be required on June 30, 2003 (the end of the first quarter). Use days, not months, to calculate interest amounts.

2. Show the current liability section of the balance sheet as of June 30, 2003. Assume there are nil balances in all accounts at March 1, 2003.

Problem 11-9B *Accounting for current liabilities, accounting for contingent liabilities, reporting current liabilities* *(Obj. 1, 2, 6)*

Northern Explorations produces and sells customized mining equipment in Labrador. The company offers a 60-day, all parts and labour—and an extra 90-day, parts-only—warranty on all of its products. The company had the following transactions in 2005:

Jan. 31 Sales for the month totalled $80,000 (not including HST), of which 90 percent were on credit. The company collects 15 percent HST on all sales and estimates its warranty costs at 3 percent of sales.

31 Based on last year's property tax assessment, estimated that the property taxes for the year would be $30,000 (1.5 percent of last year's $2,000,000 assessed value). Recorded the estimated property taxes for the month; credit Estimated Property Taxes Payable.

Feb. 4 Completed repair work for a customer. The parts ($500) and labour ($850) were all covered under the warranty.

7 Sent a cheque for the appropriate HST for the month of January (the company had paid $2,700 of HST on purchases in January).

28 Recorded the estimated property taxes for the month of February.

28 Sales for the month totalled $92,000 (not including HST), of which 85 percent were on credit. The company estimates its warranty costs at 3 percent of sales.

Mar. 7 Sent a cheque for the appropriate HST for the month of February (the company had paid $3,750 of HST on purchases in February).

8 Northern Explorations Company received notice that it was being sued by a customer for an accident resulting from the failure of its product. The company's lawyer was reluctant to estimate the likely outcome of the lawsuit, but another customer indicated that a similar case had resulted in a $250,000 settlement.

15 Completed repair work for a customer. The parts ($2,500) and labour ($1,200) were all covered under the warranty.

21 Completed repair work for a customer. The parts ($750) were covered by the warranty, but the labour ($1,100) was not. Payment from the customer is due for the labour in 30 days.

31 Sales for the month totalled $88,000 (not including HST), of which 88 percent was on credit. The company estimates its warranty costs at 3 percent of sales.

Mar. 31 Received the property tax assessment for 2005. It showed the assessed value of the property to be $2,200,000 and a tax rate of 1.8 percent of the assessed value. The company made the appropriate adjustment and used the Property Taxes Payable account.

Required

1. Journalize the above transactions.
2. Show the appropriate financial statement presentation for all liabilities.

Challenge Problems

Problem 11-1C   *Verifying the completeness of liabilities (Obj. 1)*

Public accounting firms acting as auditors of companies are very careful to ensure that all of the company's accounts payable are recorded in the proper period. In other words, they want to ensure that all payables relating to the year under review are recorded as a liability at year end.

Required

Explain why you think auditors are so concerned that all payables owing at year end be properly recorded in the right period.

Problem 11-2C   *Accounting for estimated liabilities (Obj. 1)*

There is no consensus on the proper amount for airlines to record with respect to frequent-flier expense. Two alternative scenarios are presented below:

a. The person claiming a ticket under the frequent-flier program would use a seat that otherwise would be empty.

b. The person claiming a ticket under the frequent-flier program would use a seat that otherwise would be used by a full-fare-paying passenger.

Required

1. Recommend to an airline how much it should record as a liability under each of the scenarios. Which amount would you suggest the airline record since it doesn't know which will occur?

2. Write a response to the person who states that, since it is not known if the frequent-flier miles will be used, the liability is contingent and need not be expensed until the passenger actually uses the frequent-flier miles. This person suggests that because the liability is contingent, not actual, it should be disclosed in the notes.

Extending Your Knowledge

Decision Problem

Identifying internal control weaknesses and their solution   (Obj. 5)

Schneider Construction is a large road-building business in Ontario. The owner is Neil Schneider, who oversees all company operations. He employs 15 work crews, each made up of 6 to 10 members. Construction supervisors, who report directly to Schneider, lead the crews. Most supervisors are long-time employees, so Schneider trusts them to a great degree. The company's office staff consists of an accountant and an office manager.

Because employee turnover is rapid in the construction industry, supervisors hire and terminate their own crew members. Supervisors notify the office of all personnel changes. Also, supervisors forward to the office the employee TD1 forms, which the crew members fill out to claim tax withholding exemptions. Each Thursday the supervisors submit weekly time sheets for their crews, and the accountant prepares the payroll. At noon on Friday the supervisors come to the office to get paycheques for distribution to the workers at 5 p.m.

Schneider Construction's accountant prepares the payroll, including the payroll cheques, which are written on a single payroll bank account. Neil Schneider signs all payroll cheques after matching the employee name to the time sheets submitted by the supervisor. Often the construction workers wait several days to cash their paycheques. To verify that each construction worker is a bona fide employee, the accountant matches the employee's endorsement signature on the back of the cancelled payroll cheque with the signature on that employee's TD1 form.

Required

1. List one *efficiency* weakness in Schneider Construction's payroll accounting system. How can the business correct this weakness?
2. Identify one way that a supervisor can defraud Schneider Construction under the present system.
3. Discuss a control feature Schneider Construction can use to *safeguard* against the fraud you identified in Requirement 2.

Financial Statement Problem

Current and contingent liabilities   *(Obj. 1, 2)*

Details about a company's current and contingent liabilities appear in a number of places in the annual report. Use the Intrawest Corporation financial statements in Appendix A to answer the following questions.

1. Give the breakdown of Intrawest's current liabilities at June 30, 2003. Give the July 2003 entry to record the payment of amounts payable (accounts payable and accrued liabilities) at June 30, 2003.

2. How much was Intrawest's bank and other indebtedness at June 30, 2003? Of this amount, how much was due in one year? Where did you find information about the composition of the bank and other indebtedness? When is the bank and other indebtedness due?

3. Does Intrawest have any commitments coming due in the fiscal year ending in 2004? If so, where did you find information about them? Why are commitments not shown on the balance sheet as a liability?

4. Does Intrawest Corporation have any contingent liabilities at June 30, 2003? How do you know?

Comprehensive Problem
for Part Two

Comparing Two Businesses

Suppose you are ready to invest in a small resort property. Two locations look promising: Sanibel Resort in Victoria, British Columbia, and Hyde Park Resort in Nova Scotia. Each place has its appeal, but Sanibel Resort wins out. The main allure is that the price is better. The property owners provide the following data:

	Sanibel Resort	Hyde Park Resort
Cash	$ 36,500	$ 68,300
Accounts receivable	21,900	19,600
Inventory	79,400	73,200
Land	289,500	716,000
Buildings	1,920,000	2,097,200
Accumulated amortization—buildings	(127,543)	(880,200)
Furniture and fixtures	803,000	998,300
Accumulated amortization— furniture and fixtures	(241,000)	(572,800)
Total assets	$2,781,757	$2,519,600
Total liabilities	$1,203,000	$1,079,100
Owner's equity	1,578,757	1,440,500
Total liabilities and owner's equity	$2,781,757	$2,519,600

Income statements for the last three years report total net income of $568,200 for Sanibel Resort and $302,800 for Hyde Park Resort.

Inventories   Sanibel Resort uses the FIFO inventory method, and Hyde Park Resort uses the LIFO method. If Sanibel Resort had used LIFO, its reported inventory would have been $7,500 lower. If Hyde Park Resort had used FIFO, its reported inventory would have been $6,400 higher. Three years ago there was little difference between LIFO and FIFO amounts for Sanibel, and LIFO and FIFO amounts for Hyde Park.

Capital Assets   Sanibel Resort uses the straight-line amortization method and an estimated useful life of 35 years for buildings and seven years for furniture and fixtures. Estimated residual values are $432,000 for buildings, and $0 for furniture and fixtures. Sanibel Resort's buildings and furniture and fixtures are three years old.

Hyde Park Resort uses the double-declining-balance method and amortizes buildings over 35 years with an estimated residual value of $490,000. The furniture and fixtures, now two years old, are being amortized over seven years with an estimated residual value of $90,900.

Accounts Receivable   Sanibel Resort uses the direct write-off method for uncollectibles. Hyde Park Resort uses the allowance method. The Sanibel Resort owner estimates that $2,150 of the company's receivables are doubtful. Prior to the current year, uncollectibles were insignificant. Hyde Park Resort's receivables are already reported at net realizable value.

Required

1. Puzzled at first by how to compare the two resorts, you decide to convert the Sanibel Resort's balance sheet to the accounting methods and the estimated useful lives used by Hyde Park Resort. Round all amortization amounts to the nearest $100. The necessary revisions will not affect Sanibel Resort's total liabilities.

2. Convert Sanibel Resort's total net income for the last three years to reflect the accounting methods used by Hyde Park Resort. Round all amortization amounts to the nearest $100.
3. Compare the two resorts' finances after you have revised the Sanibel Resort's figures, with the two resorts' finances beforehand. Which resort looked better at the outset? Which resort looks better when they are placed on equal footing?

Krave's Candy Co. and Clodhoppers: The Saga Continues

Two boyhood friends, Chris Emery and Larry Finson, using a recipe developed by Chris's grandmother, went into the candy business in Winnipeg in 1995. The candy, which they called "Clodhoppers," was a Christmas candy, a seasonal purchase in competition with Turtles® and other Christmas candies.

They hoped people would crave their candy and that is how the name, Krave's Candy Co., was developed.

Initially, the company grew quite quickly and demand outpaced the supply. The two partners needed to expand and personally lacked the resources to fund the required expansion. Like many young entrepreneurs, Chris and Larry had invested all their savings plus the money raised from mortgaging their houses in Krave's Candy Co.

At this point many young companies founder because they are unable to raise the needed funds. Chris and Larry had several choices: 1. Sell part of their equity to outsiders such as a venture capital firm; 2. Borrow the money from a financial institution such as a bank; 3. Borrow money from family. The partners chose the third option.

Epilogue

Clodhoppers have gained wide acceptance and can be found in a range of stores across Canada and at more than 2,700 Wal-Mart stores in the United States. *Fortune Small Business* reported that the company's sales in 2002 were $7 million, which represented "1.6 million pounds of candy [and] . . . 3.4 billion calories."

We learn in the video that Dairy Queen has introduced a "Clodhopper Blizzard," a variation on the very popular Dairy Queen Blizzard. You have probably noticed that Rogers Video and Blockbuster tempt customers with 225-gram bags of Clodhoppers.

Chris and Larry have "won" (for $6,500 in a charity auction in support of the Children's Miracle network) a visit from Chuck Moody, President and CEO of Dairy Queen International for a day. Their goal is to persuade Chuck to add the Clodhopper Blizzard to the Dairy Queen menu in the United States with a view to greatly increasing their sales and awareness of Clodhoppers in the United States.

CASE QUESTIONS

1. When Chris and Larry wanted to expand to meet the demand for Clodhoppes, they lacked sufficient resources to grow their business. Discuss why they chose Option 3.

2. When Chris and Larry started Krave's Candy Co. they thought of Clodhoppers as a seasonal, Christmas candy. Subsequently, they began marketing Clodhoppers as a candy that was appropriate year-round. Why do you think they decided to change their marketing strategy?

3. What did Chris and Larry think would be gained by "winning" Chuck Moody for a day?

4. What is Chuck Moody's background? What sort of questions do you think he might have asked Chris and Larry before suggesting they make a presentation to Dairy Queen's Research and Development department at Dairy Queen's head office in Minneapolis?

5. What company is majority shareholder of Dairy Queen and who is that company's president?

Sources: CBC *Venture*, 2002; *Winnipeg Free Press*, March 21, 2003; *Fortune Small Business*, February 2003; *The Dauphin* [Manitoba] *Herald*, February 18, 2003.

Appendix A

fundamentals

Intrawest 2003 Annual Report

YEARS ENDED JUNE 30
(IN MILLIONS OF UNITED STATES DOLLARS,
EXCEPT PER SHARE AMOUNTS)

	2003	2002	2001	2000	1999
CONSOLIDATED OPERATIONS					
REVENUE					
Resort operations	571.5	485.1	492.2	447.4	382.5
Real estate	512.7	495.8	424.3	348.4	221.2
Other	2.4	5.1	6.3	14.7	5.9
Total revenue	1,086.6	986.0	922.8	810.5	609.6
EXPENSES					
Resort operations	454.8	377.8	383.9	353.7	300.9
Real estate costs	437.7	407.7	343.3	285.5	177.4
Interest	47.1	43.1	44.5	35.2	24.8
Depreciation and amortization	67.5	65.4	57.9	51.4	40.2
General, administrative and other	32.4	33.4	29.7	32.6	27.7
Write-down of technology assets	12.3	—	—	—	—
Total expenses	1,051.8	927.4	859.3	758.4	571.0
Income from continuing operations	34.8	58.6	63.5	52.1	38.6
INCOME FROM CONTINUING OPERATIONS PER COMMON SHARE					
Basic	0.73	1.33	1.45	1.20	0.96
Diluted	0.73	1.31	1.43	1.18	0.94
WEIGHTED AVERAGE NUMBER OF SHARES (IN THOUSANDS)					
Basic	47,364	44,206	43,665	43,362	40,237
Diluted	47,590	44,695	44,504	44,252	40,986
Total Company EBITDA*	209.2	211.2	200.3	165.4	128.8
CONSOLIDATED BALANCE SHEETS					
ASSETS					
Resort operations	918.7	841.8	813.7	784.7	699.0
Properties – resort	1,067.3	861.5	700.6	569.3	460.9
– discontinued operations	—	6.3	7.1	9.6	20.6
Other	529.7	457.3	434.9	353.8	311.7
Total assets	2,515.7	2,166.9	1,956.3	1,717.4	1,492.2
LIABILITIES AND SHAREHOLDERS' EQUITY					
Bank and other indebtedness	1,260.9	1,055.9	1,010.0	833.2	727.1
Other liabilities	543.7	433.7	377.9	372.9	226.6
Shareholders' equity	711.1	677.3	568.4	511.3	538.5
Total liabilities and shareholders' equity	2,515.7	2,166.9	1,956.3	1,717.4	1,492.2

*EBITDA = Net income before interest, income taxes, non-controlling interest, depreciation and amortization.

Statements contained in this annual report that are not historical facts are forward-looking statements that involve risks and uncertainties. Intrawest's actual results could differ materially from those expressed or implied by such forward-looking statements. Factors that could cause or contribute to such differences include, but are not limited to, Intrawest's ability to implement its business strategies, seasonality, weather conditions, competition, general economic conditions, currency fluctuations and other risks detailed in the company's filings with the Canadian securities regulatory authorities and the U.S. Securities and Exchange Commission.

Contents

The following discussion and analysis should be read in conjunction with our audited consolidated financial statements for the year ended June 30, 2003 and accompanying notes included in this annual report. The discussion of our business may include forward-looking statements about our future operations, financial results and objectives. These statements are necessarily based on estimates and assumptions that are subject to risks and uncertainties. Our actual results could differ materially from those expressed or implied by such forward-looking information due to a variety of factors including, but not limited to, our ability to implement our business strategies, seasonality, weather conditions, competition, general economic conditions, currency fluctuations, world events and other risks detailed in our filings with Canadian securities regulatory authorities and the U.S. Securities and Exchange Commission.

COMPANY OVERVIEW

Intrawest is the world's leading operator and developer of village-centered resorts. We have a network of 10 mountain resorts, geographically diversified across North America's major ski regions. Our resorts include Whistler Blackcomb (77% interest) and Panorama in British Columbia, Blue Mountain (50% interest) in Ontario, Tremblant in Quebec, Stratton in Vermont, Snowshoe in West Virginia, Copper and Winter Park in Colorado, Mammoth (59.5% interest) in California and Mountain Creek in New Jersey. We assumed control of Winter Park in December 2002 under a long-term capital lease arrangement. Our resorts hosted 8.2 million skier visits in fiscal 2003, 10.7% of the North American market and the most in the mountain resort industry.

We own and operate one warm-weather resort, Sandestin, in Florida. Our resort assets include 18 golf courses and we also manage an additional 11 golf courses for other owners. We have interests in several other leisure-related businesses, including Alpine Helicopters (45% interest) and the Breeze/Max retail store chain.

We are the largest mountain resort real estate developer in North America. We develop real estate at our resorts and at six third-party owned resorts (five in the United States and one in France). We develop real estate for the purpose of sale and to June 30, 2003 we have closed 10,490 residential units at 15 different resorts.

OPERATING SUMMARY

Our operating results in 2003 were below the expectations we set at the outset of the year. The travel and leisure industry continued to feel the impact of the challenges we faced in 2002, i.e., the slow economy and the aftermath of September 11, and it also had to deal with several unforeseen events, including the war in Iraq and the SARS outbreak.

Income from continuing operations was $34.8 million in 2003 compared with $58.6 million in 2002. The decline was caused primarily by reduced profits from our real estate business and a $12.3 million write-down of technology assets. Until the beginning of March our ski and resort operations were performing well, however concerns over the war in Iraq and the SARS outbreak had a dramatic impact on destination visits to our resorts at a time that has historically been the busiest part of our season. Consequently, in the third and fourth quarters, our ski and resort operations lost the ground they had gained earlier in the season.

In Colorado, real estate sales continued to be slow. In Whistler, we had planned to close the second phase of high-end, high-margin single-family lots at Kadenwood but the market for this product type has temporarily stalled. Notwithstanding these situations, demand for real estate has generally been very strong at our resorts, as evidenced by our record backlog of pre-sales. We will realize the benefit of these pre-sales when they close in 2004 and 2005. Our real estate profits were also impacted by delays in the completion of construction of two projects that pushed closings into fiscal 2004.

The write-down of technology assets resulted from our decision to standardize various business systems across our resorts and reflects the write-off of our investment in redundant systems. We expect to realize both efficiencies and cost savings as a consequence of this decision.

Total Company EBITDA was $209.2 million in 2003, down from $211.2 million in 2002. A reconciliation between earnings reported in our statements of operations and Total Company EBITDA is included in "Additional Information" at the end of this discussion and analysis.

REVIEW OF SKI AND RESORT OPERATIONS

Our ski and resort operations are segregated into two reportable segments: mountain resort operations and warm-weather resort operations. The mountain resort operations comprise all the operating activities at our 10 mountain resorts as well as the operations of Resort Reservations (RezRez), Alpine Helicopters and Breeze/Max Retail. The warm-weather resort operations comprise all the operating activities at Sandestin as well as operations at our five stand-alone golf courses.

The key drivers of the mountain resort operations business are skier visits, revenue per visit and margins. Our strategy to increase skier visits has two main elements: improving the quality of the resort experience by upgrading and expanding the on-mountain facilities and building villages at the base to provide accommodation for destination guests. By expanding the amenities on the mountain and in the village, we are able to broaden the customer mix, extend the length of stay and capture a higher percentage of guest spending, all of which increases revenue per visit. Building the accommodation also allows visits to be spread more evenly during the week and during the season, which improves margins since a significant proportion of operating expenses at a resort are fixed. The key drivers of the warm-weather resort operations business are similar; i.e., golf rounds, revenue per round and margins.

The following table highlights the results of our ski and resort operations.

	2003	2002	CHANGE (%)
Skier visits [1]	7,302,000	6,283,000	16.2
Revenue (Millions)	$ 571.5	$ 485.1	17.8
EBITDA (Millions)	$ 116.7	$ 107.3	8.8
Margin (%)	20.4	22.1	

[1] All resorts are at 100% except Mammoth at 59.5% and Blue Mountain at 50%.

Revenue from ski and resort operations was $571.5 million in 2003 compared with $485.1 million in 2002. Revenue from mountain resorts increased from $424.8 million to $506.5 million while revenue from warm-weather resorts increased from $60.3 million to $65.0 million.

MOUNTAIN RESORTS

On December 23, 2002, we closed on a transaction with the City and County of Denver to operate Winter Park on a long-term lease arrangement. Since the lease gives us control over the resort, for financial reporting purposes Winter Park is treated in the same manner as any of our directly owned resorts. This was an important transaction for us, not only because it adds a quality resort in the largest ski market in North America to our portfolio, but also because of the synergies that it will create with Copper and our other Colorado operations. Winter Park, combined with Copper, gives us an operation with over two million skier visits, similar in scale to Whistler Blackcomb, our most profitable resort. By sharing administrative services, collaborating on marketing initiatives, harmonizing operations and developing new product and service offerings, we expect to realize higher margins than either resort could achieve individually.

The results of Winter Park were consolidated from the closing date and accounted for $33.1 million of the increase in mountain resort revenue and 793,000 of the increase in skier visits. In February 2002 we sold our smallest resort, Mont Ste. Marie, which generated $1.6 million of revenue from 62,000 skier visits in fiscal 2002.

On a same-resort basis (i.e., excluding Winter Park and Mont Ste. Marie) mountain resort revenue increased by 11.8% or $50.1 million due to various factors:

(MILLIONS)	
Increase in skier visits	$ 15.9
Increase in revenue per skier visit	15.2
Increase in non-skier visit revenue	10.8
Impact of exchange rate on reported revenue	8.2
	$ 50.1

Same-resort skier visits increased by 4.6% from 6,221,000 in 2002 to 6,509,000 in 2003, despite the difficult conditions in the travel and leisure sector. Skier visits were higher at every resort except for Whistler Blackcomb, Panorama and Tremblant. Skier visits at our eastern resorts, which experienced excellent early-season conditions, were 18.7% ahead of last year through the first week of March but then declined by 7.5% to the end of the season. The changes were somewhat less significant at our western resorts, being 2.3% ahead through the first week of March and 3.9% below for the balance of the season. The decline in visits after the first week of March came entirely from the destination market as evidenced by the fact that during this period season pass visits increased 24.4%. We estimate that the increase in skier visits increased mountain resort revenue by $15.9 million in 2003.

Same-resort revenue per skier visit increased 4.2% from $55.07 in 2002 (after adjusting for the impact of the improvement in the Canadian dollar exchange rate) to $57.40 in 2003. Revenue per skier visit is a function of ticket prices and ticket yields, and revenue from non-ticket sources such as retail and rental stores, lodging, ski school, and food and beverage services. Ticket yields reflect the mix of ticket types (e.g., adult, child, season pass and group), the proportion of day versus destination visitors (destination visitors tend to be less price-sensitive), and the amount of discounting of full-price tickets in regional markets. Revenue per visit from non-ticket sources is also influenced by the mix of day versus destination visitors, the affluence of the visitor base, and the quantity and type of amenities and services offered at the resort.

Revenue per visit from ticket sales increased 1.4% from $27.60 to $27.99. There was a relative shift in the mix of visits from "paid" visits to season pass visits as we sold 16.6% more season passes and frequency cards in 2003 than 2002 and this tended to lower ticket yields. Over the past several seasons we have deliberately sought to increase season pass and frequency card sales in order to increase pre-committed revenue. Revenue per visit from non-ticket sources increased 7.1% from $27.46 to $29.41. This increase is less than we had expected due to softness in the retail business (which was an industry trend) and lower revenues from ski school and rental due to reduced destination visits after February. Approximately half of the increase in non-ticket revenue per visit came from lodging and property management due to a 12.9% increase in the number of occupied room nights, most notably at Blue Mountain, Stratton and Snowshoe. We estimate that the increase in revenue per visit increased mountain resort revenue by $15.2 million in 2003.

For the purposes of this analysis, non-skier visit revenue comprises revenue from golf and other summer activities and revenue from businesses such as RezRez, Alpine Helicopters and Breeze/Max. Revenue from golf and other summer activities increased 8.1% across the mountain resorts from $39.5 million in 2002 to $42.7 million in 2003. Summer lodging and property management revenue increased 20.1%, led by strong room night growth at Tremblant, Blue Mountain and Snowshoe. Our central reservations business, RezRez, expanded its operations into several new warm-weather destinations, leading to a 40.9% growth in revenue to $13.5 million in 2003. We had expected much higher revenues from RezRez, however increased competition in the on-line travel sector and reduced travel by U.S. customers (which account for over 80% of RezRez's business) significantly reduced bookings. Revenue at Alpine and Breeze/Max increased by 4.0% and 1.1%, respectively. Overall, non-skier visit revenue increased by $10.8 million in 2003.

The reported amount of mountain resort revenue was increased by $8.2 million in 2003 because of the increase in the value of the Canadian dollar against the U.S. dollar. In 2003 revenue from the Canadian resorts was translated for financial statement reporting purposes at an average rate of Cdn.$1.51 to U.S.$1.00 compared with an average rate of Cdn.$1.57 to U.S.$1.00 in 2002.

WARM-WEATHER RESORTS

Revenue from warm-weather resorts increased 7.9% from $60.3 million in 2002 to $65.0 million in 2003. Revenue at Sandestin increased by $6.4 million due mainly to a 12.6% increase in occupied room nights. The opening of the new village at Baytowne Wharf in July 2002 increased the accommodation base at Sandestin and added many new amenities to the resort, driving higher lodging, retail, and food and beverage revenue. The sale of the Sabino Springs golf course in Tuscon in June 2002 reduced warm-weather resort revenue by $3.2 million, however this was partially offset by $1.1 million more revenue from Big Island Country Club in Hawaii, which we acquired in January 2002.

REVENUE BREAKDOWN

The breakdown of ski and resorts operations revenue by business was as follows:

(MILLIONS)	2003 REVENUE	2002 REVENUE	INCREASE (DECREASE)	CHANGE (%)
Mountain operations	$ 228.6	$ 193.3	$ 35.3	18.3
Retail and rental shops	95.9	85.0	10.9	12.8
Food and beverage	74.9	63.0	11.9	18.9
Lodging and property management	81.7	61.0	20.7	33.9
Ski school	37.1	30.4	6.7	22.1
Golf	28.0	29.4	(1.4)	(4.9)
Other	25.3	23.0	2.3	10.3
	$ 571.5	$ 485.1	86.4	17.8

Assuming control of Winter Park in December 2002 increased revenue from mountain operations, retail and rental shops, food and beverage, and ski school by $20.7 million, $3.4 million, $4.8 million and $3.5 million, respectively.

The proportion of revenue from mountain operations has fallen from 49.3% of total ski and resort operations revenue in 1997 to 40.0% in 2003. This trend is likely to continue as we build out the villages at our resorts, expanding the inventory of lodging units and changing the customer mix in favor of destination visitors who spend more on retail and rental, ski school, and food and beverage.

SKI AND RESORT OPERATIONS EXPENSES AND EBITDA

Ski and resort operations expenses increased from $377.8 million in 2002 to $454.9 million in 2003. Mountain resort expenses increased by $71.4 million to $397.3 million while warm-weather resort expenses increased by $5.7 million to $57.6 million.

The net impact of assuming control of Winter Park and selling Mont Ste. Marie increased mountain resort expenses by $19.5 million, leaving same-resort expense growth of $51.9 million. The strengthening of the value of the Canadian dollar increased the reported amount of mountain resort expenses by $6.7 million. The strong start in the East in 2003 compared with a very late start in 2002 impacted our expense growth. In 2002 we had a "vertical" ramp-up at Blue Mountain, Stratton, Snowshoe and Mountain Creek with essentially no pre-Christmas season, resulting in abnormally low costs. By comparison, in 2003 these eastern resorts commenced operations much earlier, ramping up more gradually, resulting in higher costs supported by higher revenues. In addition, the impact of the war in Iraq and SARS occurred in our core-operating month of March and happened suddenly, reducing visits significantly. Since we were uncertain how long the decline in visits would last and how great it would be, we had limited ability to ramp down costs. Overall, increased business volumes at these four eastern resorts during the full 2003 season resulted in a 19.3% increase in operating expenses (equivalent to $13.1 million) and a 22.6% increase in revenues.

The expansion of RezRez into new locations added $10.5 million to ski and resort operations expenses. We had set up an organization and infrastructure at RezRez to deal with a significant expected increase in business volumes. With the majority of bookings typically occurring in the period from October to February, the revenue shortfall was evident too late to institute meaningful cost savings before year-end. We have now heavily downsized and reorganized RezRez to focus on the ski and golf destinations where we have inherent advantages and away from warm-weather destinations. We expect these expense reductions, combined with revenue opportunities from the significant interest we are receiving from other travel providers in the RezRez on-line booking engine, to return this business to profitability.

The increase in warm-weather resort expenses of $5.7 million was almost entirely due to Sandestin and the opening of the new village in July 2002. The revenue growth at Sandestin more than offset the growth in expenses.

EBITDA from ski and resort operations increased from $107.3 million in 2002 to $116.7 million in 2003. EBITDA from the mountain resorts increased from $98.9 million to $109.2 million while EBITDA from the warm-weather resorts declined from $8.4 million to $7.5 million.

On a same-resort basis, mountain resorts EBITDA was $96.8 million in 2003 compared with $98.6 million in 2002. EBITDA from the resorts increased by 8.3%, however this was offset by reduced EBITDA from the non-skier visit businesses, i.e., Alpine, RezRez and the Breeze/Max retail chain.

The decrease in warm-weather resort EBITDA was due mainly to reduced profits from our Arizona golf operations due to the sale of the Sabino Springs golf course last year.

REVIEW OF REAL ESTATE OPERATIONS

We have two real estate divisions – the resort development group and the resort club group. The resort development group develops and sells three main products: condo-hotel units (typically, small village-based units that owners occupy sporadically and put into a rental pool at other times), townhome units (typically, larger units outside the main village core that owners retain for their own use) and single-family lots (serviced land on which owners or other developers build homes). In order to broaden market appeal, condo-hotel and townhome units are sold on the basis of both whole ownership and fractional ownership. Currently most of the fractional product has been quarter-share but a high-end tenth-share project is under construction at Whistler and other fractions are under consideration. The resort club group's business is a flexible form of timeshare where owners purchase points that entitle them to use accommodation at different resorts. The resort club group currently generates less than 10% of our total real estate revenue and hence is not reported as a separate business segment in the financial statements.

Our business strategy for real estate has two major elements: the maximization of profits from the sale of real estate and the provision of accommodation for destination visitors, which represents an earnings annuity for the ski and resort operations. Visitors renting the accommodation generate lodging revenue as well as revenue from purchasing lift tickets or golf fees, food and beverage, and retail.

We recognize real estate sales revenue at the time of "closing," which is when title to a completed unit is conveyed to the purchaser and the purchaser becomes entitled to occupancy. Since our standard practice is to pre-sell our real estate, any proceeds received prior to closing are recorded as deferred revenue in our balance sheet.

The following table highlights the results of the real estate business.

	2003	2002	CHANGE (%)
Units closed	1,239	1,290	(4.0)
Revenue (Millions)	$ 512.7	$ 487.8	5.1
Operating profit (Millions)	$ 75.0	$ 85.1	(11.9)
Margin (%)	14.6	17.4	

Revenue from the sale of real estate increased 5.1% from $487.8 million in 2002 to $512.7 million in 2003. Revenue generated by the resort development group increased from $449.8 million to $472.8 million while revenue generated by the resort club group increased from $38.0 million to $39.9 million.

RESORT DEVELOPMENT GROUP REVENUE

We closed a total of 528 units at the Canadian resorts in 2003 compared with 589 units last year. The average price per unit increased from Cdn.$423,000 in 2002 to Cdn.$436,000 in 2003. We also closed the sale of the majority of our commercial properties at Tremblant in 2003, recognizing revenue of $21.5 million. Currently we have approximately 500,000 square feet of remaining commercial properties at nine different resorts. Our plan is to sell all of these properties in the normal course.

We closed 611 units at the U.S. resorts in 2003 compared with 701 units in 2002. The number of units that close in a particular period is dependent on both transacting sales and the timing of construction completion. We had expected to close more units in 2003, however construction delays, due mainly to difficult site conditions, the complicated building design and construction management issues (see below), were experienced on two projects at Lake Las Vegas and Squaw Valley. The average price per unit was $457,000 at the U.S. resorts in 2003 (after adjusting the number of units for the impact of joint ventures at Keystone and Three Peaks), up from $442,000 in 2002. In 2003 we also closed our first 100 units at Les Arcs in France for proceeds of $31.1 million.

The mix of product types (i.e., condo-hotel, townhome and single-family lot) closed was not materially different in 2003 than in 2002.

During 2003 we reorganized the resort development group from a resort-based structure to a regional structure. We have six regional offices providing development and construction services to 17 different resorts. This structure allows us to share resources between resorts and gives us the critical mass in each region to be able to engage specialized development and construction experts that might be uneconomical for an individual resort. The new structure also strengthens our control systems so that, for example, the construction management issues that affected the completion of two projects in 2003 are less likely to impact our business in the future.

RESORT CLUB GROUP REVENUE

The resort club group generated $39.9 million in sales revenue in 2003, up from $38.0 million in 2002. We had expected stronger revenue growth, however sales were impacted by the slow economy and the uncertainty created by recent world events. This product type is more of a consumer purchase than our resort development group product and confidence is an important factor in the purchase consideration. Furthermore, resort club product does not have the same sense of scarcity as other types of real estate so purchasers are under less pressure to buy.

REAL ESTATE OPERATING PROFIT

Operating profit from real estate sales decreased from $85.1 million in 2002 to $75.0 million in 2003. The profit margin was 14.6% in 2003 compared with 17.4% in 2002. The reduction in margin was due to a number of factors, including:

- The write-off of $3.3 million of costs at Copper in connection with various projects that are on hold pending a strengthening of the Colorado market.
- A write-down of $3.0 million in connection with two projects at Mountain Creek. Sales of these projects had slowed because of an environmental lawsuit (that has now been settled), resulting in increased holding costs. In addition we have projected more conservative sales prices for unsold inventory.
- Lower margins in 2003 for the resort club group. Marketing and sales costs increased to 57% of revenue in 2003 from 48% in 2002 as a result of the difficult market conditions.

  Excluding the impact of the factors listed above, the profit margin in 2003 would have been 16.7%.

REAL ESTATE PRE-SALES

At August 31, 2003, we had pre-sold real estate revenue of $460 million that we expect to close in fiscal 2004. This compares with pre-sold revenue this time last year of $370 million for delivery in fiscal 2003. In addition, we have $65 million of pre-sales for delivery in fiscal 2005. This does not include projects that will be undertaken by Leisura (see Liquidity and Capital Resources), which has $260 million of pre-sales for delivery in fiscal 2004 and 2005. Our strategy of pre-selling projects before the start of construction reduces market risk and increases the predictability of real estate earnings.

CAPITALIZATION OF COSTS TO REAL ESTATE

Generally accepted accounting practice for real estate requires that all costs in connection with the development of real estate be capitalized to properties under development and then expensed in the period when the properties are closed and the revenue is recognized. Such costs include land and building costs as well as overhead costs of personnel directly involved in the development, construction and sale of real estate, and interest on debt used to fund real estate costs. The capitalized interest comprises interest on specific real estate debt (i.e., construction financing) and interest on the portion of general corporate debt used to fund real estate development expenditures.

The book value of properties increased from $867.8 million at June 30, 2002 to $1,067.3 million at June 30, 2003. The strengthening of the value of the Canadian dollar from a year-end rate of Cdn$1.52:US$1.00 in 2002 to Cdn$1.35:US$1.00 in 2003 increased the reported book value of properties by $26.3 million. Other factors responsible for the increase include:

- A net increase of $73.3 million in the book value of commercial space resulting from the completion of new properties at Whistler, Mammoth, Sandestin, Squaw Valley, Lake Las Vegas and Blue Mountain and the sale of commercial properties at Tremblant.
- An increase of $26.1 million in the book value of resort club properties mainly due to the new resort club locations under construction at Blue Mountain and Zihuatanejo, Mexico.

The book value of properties to be sold to Leisura was $73.8 million at June 30, 2003. We expect to transfer the majority of these properties in the first two quarters of fiscal 2004.

With the completion and closing of projects currently under construction and with the development of most new projects to take place in Leisura, the book value of our properties is expected to decline significantly in 2004.

Effective July 1, 2002, we changed our plans for commercial properties. Instead of holding them as long-term revenue-producing investments, existing commercial properties would be sold and commercial properties developed in the future would be developed for the purpose of sale. In 2003 we sold the majority of our commercial properties at Tremblant and we plan to sell our remaining portfolio of commercial properties. Rental revenue and rental expenses relating to these properties were capitalized during 2003. In 2002 rental property revenue of $8.0 million and rental property expenses of $5.0 million were included in the statement of operations.

REVIEW OF CORPORATE OPERATIONS

INTEREST AND OTHER INCOME

Interest and other income was $2.4 million in 2003, up from $1.1 million in 2002 due mainly to dividend income from Compagnie des Alpes (CDA) and higher interest income net of losses on asset disposals.

In July 2002 we sold 55% of our investment in CDA and at the same time ceased to exercise significant influence over CDA's affairs. In 2003 we therefore accounted for CDA on a cost basis, whereas in 2002 we used the equity basis and recorded income from equity accounted investment of $3.9 million. Subsequent to June 30, 2003, we sold the balance of our investment in CDA. Both the sale in July 2002 and the sale subsequent to June 30, 2003 were for proceeds approximately equal to the book value of our investment.

INTEREST COSTS

Interest expense increased from $43.1 million in 2002 to $47.1 million in 2003. We incurred total interest costs (including financing fees and amortization of deferred financing costs) of $102.9 million in 2003 compared with $83.4 million in 2002. The increase was due mainly to interest on the $137-million 10.5% senior unsecured notes issued in October 2002, partially offset by interest on the Cdn. $125-million 6.75% unsecured debentures repaid in December 2002. In addition we had higher construction loan interest due to increased construction activity and the Winter Park capital lease added $2.2 million of interest. In total, $55.5 million of this interest was capitalized to properties under development, $14.9 million of which was subsequently expensed in 2003 when the properties were closed.

DEPRECIATION AND AMORTIZATION

Depreciation and amortization expense increased from $65.4 million in 2002 to $67.5 million in 2003. The increase was due mainly to assuming control of Winter Park.

GENERAL AND ADMINISTRATIVE COSTS

All general and administrative (G&A) costs incurred by our resorts in connection with the ski and resort operations business are included in ski and resort operations expenses. Similarly, G&A costs incurred in the development of real estate are initially capitalized to properties, and then expensed to real estate costs in the period when the properties are closed. Corporate G&A costs, which mainly comprise executive employee costs, public company costs, audit and legal fees, corporate information technology costs and head office occupancy costs are disclosed as a separate line in the statement of operations. The breakdown of G&A costs for 2003 and 2002 was as follows:

(MILLIONS)		2003	PROPORTION (%)		2002	PROPORTION (%)
Corporate G&A costs	$	14.9	12.6	$	12.2	11.1
G&A expenses of ski and resort operations business		65.1	55.2		55.9	50.8
Previously capitalized G&A costs expensed in real estate cost of sales		16.5	14.0		15.4	14.0
Total G&A costs expensed during the year		96.5	81.8		83.5	75.9
Net G&A costs of real estate business capitalized to properties		21.5	18.2		26.6	24.1
Total G&A costs incurred during the year	$	118.0	100.0	$	110.1	100.0

Corporate G&A costs increased from $12.2 million in 2002 to $14.9 million in 2003 due mainly to higher compensation and pension costs, and increased insurance, legal and audit expenses. Including the G&A costs of our operations and real estate divisions, we expensed 81.8% of general and administrative expenses in 2003 compared with 75.9% in 2002.

WRITE-DOWN OF TECHNOLOGY ASSETS

When we acquired our network of resorts we inherited many different information technology (IT) systems. This impeded our ability to share information and build synergies across resorts. Where we introduced new IT systems, we used a standardized approach, however we recognized that we needed to move to greater standardization of legacy IT systems. During the fourth quarter of 2003 we therefore wrote off $9.1 million of IT systems that we plan to replace. Furthermore, in 2003 we reorganized and downsized RezRez, our central reservations business. RezRez had expanded into several warm-weather destinations but the expansion was not successful. We therefore decided to abandon these locations to focus on our core ski destinations. In light of this, we reviewed the value of RezRez assets and took a write-down of $3.2 million for various of its IT assets in the fourth quarter.

INCOME TAXES

We provided for income taxes of $6.2 million in 2003 compared with $9.5 million in 2002. This equates to an effective tax rate of 12.0% in both years. Note 13 to the consolidated financial statements provides a reconciliation between income tax at the statutory rate (38.0% and 41.2%, respectively, in 2003 and 2002) and the actual income tax charge.

NON-CONTROLLING INTEREST

We have a 23% limited partner in the two partnerships that own Whistler Blackcomb. The results of the two partnerships are fully consolidated with the outside partner's share of earnings shown as non-controlling interest. Non-controlling interest decreased from $11.7 million in 2002 to $11.3 million in 2003, reflecting reduced ski and resort operations earnings due to the slow start to the season and the impact of the war in Iraq and SARS on business, primarily in March.

DISCONTINUED OPERATIONS

Our consolidated financial statements disclose the results of our non-resort real estate business as discontinued operations. The discontinued operations incurred a loss of $0.6 million in 2003 compared with a loss of $0.1 million in 2002. Losses (or net income) from discontinued operations accrue to the holders of the non-resort preferred ("NRP") shares and any cash flows generated by the discontinued operations are paid to the NRP shareholders to redeem their shares. In December 2002 the discontinued operations were wound up and all the remaining NRP shares were redeemed.

LIQUIDITY AND CAPITAL RESOURCES

Generating free cash flow continues to be a high priority for us. Free cash flow does not have a standardized meaning prescribed by generally accepted accounting principles ("GAAP"). We calculate it as follows:

(MILLIONS)	2003	2002
Cash provided by (used in) continuing operating activities [1]	$ (26.6)	$ 5.7
Investment in ski and resort operations assets ("capex")	(64.5)	(91.5)
Free cash flow	$ (91.1)	$ (85.8)

[1] A reconciliation between net earnings as determined by Canadian GAAP and cash provided by (used in) continuing operating activities is shown in the Consolidated Statements of Cash Flows.

In 2003 our results showed negative free cash flow of $91.1 million compared with negative free cash flow of $85.8 million in 2002. We had expected positive free cash flow in 2003, however the slowdown in the travel and leisure sector, made worse by concerns over the war in Iraq and SARS, reduced operating cash flow from our ski and resort operations businesses. Cash flow from our real estate business was impacted by delayed completions of some projects and slow sales in Colorado, although generally demand for our products has been robust. On the positive side we reduced resort capex to about $65 million, significantly below prior years, and we sold some non-core assets.

Over the past few years, as we started to build out our villages and install infrastructure, our real estate business has been a significant user of cash. In both 2003 and 2002 we were free cash flow positive before making investments to grow our real estate business. During 2003 we implemented a strategy – the Leisura partnerships – that will allow us to both reduce the capital required for real estate and to grow the business.

We are also focused on increasing cash flow from our ski and resort operations businesses. We have a number of initiatives at our resorts to increase revenue (e.g., customer relationship management (CRM) and E-commerce programs, more packaging of services and maximizing sales channels) and to reduce costs (e.g., shared-services model in Colorado and elsewhere, downsizing of RezRez and eliminating discretionary expenses). Given the strong competitive position of our resorts, we do not need to invest as much in capex as we did in 2002 and prior years. We expect future resort capex requirements to remain close to 2003 levels (at approximately the same amount as depreciation and amortization expense). We also plan to grow our fee-based businesses (e.g., golf course and lodging management) and we can do this by investing minimal capital.

We expect to generate free cash flow in fiscal 2004 and to use it to repay debt.

LEISURA PARTNERSHIPS

In 2003 we entered into two partnerships (one in Canada and one in the U.S., collectively referred to as "Leisura") that will have a significant impact on our capital structure and our capital requirements for real estate. Leisura is intended to carry out the ownership and financing of the bulk of our real estate production. By selling the bulk of our production-phase real estate to separate and independent entities we achieve several objectives, including:

■ Significantly reducing the capital requirements needed to support the real estate business.
■ Significantly reducing debt levels.
■ Limiting our exposure to the risks of the production-phase real estate business.
■ Implementing separate and appropriate capital structures for our resort business and our real estate business.

We will continue to undertake some development activity on our own account outside of the Leisura structure. This includes smaller townhome projects and single-family lots, which are not as capital intensive as condo-hotel and larger townhome projects, as well as resort club and fractional projects. In addition, we will carry out all development activity at certain resorts (e.g., Snowmass because it is a joint venture development or Les Arcs because construction is primarily purchaser-financed).

Intrawest is a minority partner in Leisura and we will account for our investment in Leisura on an equity basis. We will continue to identify land parcels for development and complete the master planning, project design and pre-sales process for all future real estate projects. Once a project has reached set pre-sale targets and construction is about to commence, Leisura will acquire the land parcels for the project from us at fair market value. By December 31, 2003, Leisura is expected to acquire land parcels for about 10 projects at seven resorts (none had been transferred at June 30, 2003). In future years, we expect to carry out the bulk of the real estate production at our resorts in a similar fashion. There is no guarantee, however, that Leisura will acquire more land parcels from us in future years. For the projects that are sold to Leisura, we will provide development management services on a fee basis.

The Leisura partnerships have sufficient capital to be strong credit-worthy entities that can comfortably finance and carry out their business on a freestanding basis. Construction financing will be secured by the projects with recourse only to Leisura.

The formation of Leisura will result in a significant reduction in our net debt in 2004. We will recover the bulk of our investment in projects currently under construction as they are completed over the next 12 months and our capital expenditures to support this part of our real estate business in future will be limited to our investment in Leisura. The difference between the large amount of capital recovered from current projects as they complete (approximately 80% of the units in these projects are pre-sold) and the much smaller investment in Leisura will generate significant cash flow that will be used to reduce debt.

CASH FLOWS IN 2003 COMPARED WITH 2002

The major sources and uses of cash in 2003 and 2002 are summarized in the table below. This table should be read in conjunction with the Consolidated Statements of Cash Flows, which are more detailed as prescribed by GAAP.

(MILLIONS)	2003	2002	CHANGE
Funds from continuing operations	$ 122.8	$ 128.6	$ (5.8)
Acquisitions, resort capex and other investments	(39.4)	(107.1)	67.7
Net cash flow from other net assets	14.6	44.3	(29.7)
Funds available before net investment in real estate	98.0	65.8	32.2
Net investment in real estate developed for sale	(163.8)	(163.2)	(0.6)
Net cash flow from operating and investing activities	(65.8)	(97.4)	31.6
Net financing inflows	115.9	87.7	28.2
Increase (decrease) in cash	$ 50.1	$ (9.7)	$ 59.8

Funds from continuing operations generated $122.8 million of cash flow in 2003, down from $128.6 million in 2002 as reduced real estate profits and increased interest and G&A expenses were partially offset by higher EBITDA from ski and resort operations.

Acquisitions, resort capex and other investments used $39.4 million of cash in 2003, down from $107.1 million in 2002. Acquisitions and resort capex used $6.0 million and $26.9 million, respectively, less cash in 2003 than 2002 while proceeds from asset disposals, net of other investments, generated $34.8 million more cash in 2003 than 2002.

Assuming control of Winter Park used $2.8 million cash in 2003 as the majority of the purchase price was financed through a capital lease. In 2002 we had acquired Big Island Country Club in Hawaii for a cash payment of $8.9 million. We do not plan to invest significant capital in acquisitions in the near term. We will continue to seek opportunities to expand our businesses but do so in ways (e.g., engaging in management contracts or entering joint ventures) that limit our capital requirements.

We spent $64.5 million on resort capex in 2003, down from $91.5 million in 2002. Each year we spend $25 million to $30 million on maintenance capex at our resorts. Maintenance capex is considered non-discretionary (since it is required to maintain the existing level of service) and comprises such things as snow grooming machine or golf cart replacement, snowmaking equipment upgrades and building refurbishments. Expansion capex (e.g., new lifts or new restaurants) is considered discretionary and the annual amount spent varies year by year. We expect maintenance and expansion capex to be approximately the same in 2004 as in 2003.

Proceeds from non-core asset sales (mainly 55% of our investment in Compagnie des Alpes and employee housing units at Whistler Blackcomb) net of new investments generated $28.0 million of cash in 2003. Subsequent to year-end we sold the balance of our investment in Compagnie des Alpes for $12.5 million. In 2002 we sold Mont Ste. Marie and Sabino Springs golf course but these sales were offset by new investments, resulting in a net investment in other assets of $6.7 million. We have identified other non-core assets for disposal and we will continue our program of selling these assets in the future.

Other net assets provided cash of $14.6 million in 2003 compared with $44.3 million in 2002. This represents the cash flow from changes in receivables, other assets, payables and deferred revenue.

Our businesses provided cash flow of $98.0 million in 2003 compared with $65.8 million in 2002, before net new investments in real estate. We invested $163.8 million in real estate in 2003, approximately the same as in 2002. We had expected our net investment to be lower in 2003, however the construction delays at Squaw Valley and Lake Las Vegas and slower transfers of properties to Leisura delayed cost recoveries until fiscal 2004. We expect to recover a portion of our investment in real estate in fiscal 2004 as units currently under construction are completed and closed and new real estate production moves to Leisura.

In total, our operating and investing activities used $65.8 million of cash in 2003, down from $97.4 million in 2002. We also paid $12.0 million and $11.3 million, respectively, in 2003 and 2002 for dividends to our shareholders and distributions to the limited partner in Whistler Blackcomb and we expect these payments to be approximately the same in 2004. Amounts paid to redeem and repurchase NRP shares were $6.7 million in 2003 and $0.4 million in 2002. We have now redeemed all the NRP shares. Net borrowings of $129.9 million and $46.3 million in 2003 and 2002, respectively, as well as proceeds of share issuances of $4.8 million and $53.0 million in 2003 and 2002, respectively, funded these cash flows.

DEBT AND LIQUIDITY POSITION

At June 30, 2003, we had net debt (i.e., bank and other indebtedness net of cash) of $1,134.1 million compared with $979.2 million at June 30, 2002. Part of the increase in net debt was due to the strengthening of the Canadian dollar, particularly in the fourth quarter. The change in the exchange rate from Cdn$1.52:US$1.00 at last year end to Cdn$1.35:US$1.00 at this year end increased the reported amount of Canadian dollar-denominated debt by $39.9 million at June 30, 2003.

As discussed above, we expect to generate significant free cash flow in fiscal 2004 and to reduce net debt. We are confident that we can achieve this objective because of the Leisura transaction and the current high level of pre-sales of real estate that is being completed within Intrawest. Not only does the Leisura transaction significantly reduce our capital requirements for real estate but it also reduces the risk that delays in construction completion will result in higher debt balances because these debt balances are obligations of Leisura, not Intrawest.

Over half of our bank and other indebtedness ($658.4 million) at June 30, 2003 is not due for repayment until after 2008. With respect to the balance of our bank and other indebtedness, $287.2 million is due to be repaid in fiscal 2004 of which $229.1 million, or approximately 80%, relates to construction financing that is covered more than 100% by real estate pre-sales. As these projects close, we will repay the construction loans as well as other debt. Our senior credit facility, which had a balance of $240.2 million at year-end, is due in fiscal 2005 and we expect to renew this facility on maturity.

We have a number of revolving credit facilities to meet our short-term capital needs. These include a $365-million facility at the corporate level, of which $240 million was drawn at June 30, 2003. In addition, several of our resorts have lines of credit in the range of $5 million to $10 million each to fund seasonal cash requirements. Since Leisura will be undertaking most of the future real estate development, we have not renewed the three revolving credit facilities that we had last year for real estate construction. Instead we will finance any projects that we develop through one-off project-specific loans. We believe that these credit facilities, combined with cash on hand and internally generated cash flow, are adequate to finance all of our normal operating needs.

BUSINESS RISKS

We are exposed to various risks and uncertainties in the normal course of our business that can cause volatility in our earnings. Our ski and resort operations and real estate businesses are managed to deal with risks that are common to most companies; i.e., the risks of severe economic downturn, competition and currency fluctuations, and the more industry-specific risks of unfavorable weather conditions, seasonality of operations and development issues.

ECONOMIC DOWNTURN

A severe economic downturn could reduce spending on resort vacations and weaken sales of recreational real estate.

Our results in both 2003 and 2002 (years that saw a significant slowdown in the economy) provide evidence of our ability to deal with an economic downturn. Ski and resort operations EBITDA for 2003 and 2002 were only 3.7% and 0.9%, respectively, below our record EBITDA in 2001, on a same-resort basis. There are two main reasons for this:

- The strong competitive position of each of our resorts due to the villages at their base and the quality of their on-mountain facilities. This has also created a loyal customer base that is strongly committed to our resorts.
- The profile of our customer base, who have incomes well above the national average and are therefore less likely to have their vacation plans impacted by a recession.

Real estate developers face two major risks from an economic downturn: land risk and completed inventory risk. Land risk arises when land is purchased with debt and economic conditions deteriorate resulting in higher holding costs and reduced profitability, or worse, loan defaults and foreclosure. We have reduced our land risk by generally acquiring land at low cost with the purchase of a resort or by securing land through options and joint ventures. Completed inventory risk arises when completed units cannot be sold and construction financing cannot be repaid. Often this risk arises because many developers are supplying units to the market and since we control most of the supply at our resorts, this risk is reduced. We have also mitigated this risk by pre-selling a significant portion of units prior to commencement of, and during, construction.

COMPETITION

The mountain resort industry has significant barriers to entry (e.g., very high start-up costs, significant environmental hurdles) that prevent new resorts from being created. Competition therefore is essentially confined to existing resorts. Our resorts compete for destination visitors with other mountain resorts in Canada, the United States, Europe and Japan, and with other leisure industry companies, such as cruise lines. They also compete for day skiers with other ski areas within each resort's local market area. Skier visits in North America have been relatively static over the past 10 years, which has increased competition between resort owners.

Our strategy has been to acquire resorts that have natural competitive advantages (e.g., in terms of location, vertical drop and quality of terrain) and to enhance those advantages by upgrading the facilities on the mountain and building resort villages at the base. Our principal strength compared with industry competitors is our ability to combine expertise in resort operations and real estate development, particularly in building master-planned resort villages. Increasingly the village has become the dominant attraction in generating visits to a resort.

We own substantially all of the supply of developable land at the base of our resorts and hence competition in real estate is somewhat restricted. Expertise in all aspects of the development process, including resort master-planning, project design, construction, sales and marketing, and property management also gives us a distinct competitive advantage.

CURRENCY FLUCTUATIONS

Over the past several years our Canadian resort operations have benefited from the lower Canadian dollar relative to other currencies, and particularly against the U.S. dollar. This has made vacationing in Canada more affordable for foreign visitors and it has encouraged Canadians to vacation at home. A significant shift in the value of the Canadian dollar, particularly against its U.S. counterpart, could impact earnings at Canadian resorts.

We finance our U.S. assets with U.S. dollar debt and our Canadian assets with Canadian dollar debt. Generally we service debt with revenue denominated in the same currency. In addition, cash flow generated by Canadian operations is generally retained in Canada and invested in expanding our Canadian assets. Similarly cash flow generated at our U.S. resorts is generally reinvested in the United States. Cross-border cash transactions and currency exchanges are kept to a minimum.

Since we report earnings in U.S. dollars but our income is derived from both Canadian and U.S. sources, we are exposed to foreign currency exchange risk in our reported earnings. Revenues and expenses of our Canadian operations will be impacted by changes in exchange rates when they are reported in U.S. dollars. We estimate that a 10% increase in the average value for the fiscal year of the Canadian dollar relative to the U.S. dollar would result in a 5% increase in our reported net income, while a 10% decline in the average value of the Canadian dollar would result in a 4% decrease in our reported net income. The impact of Canadian/U.S. dollar exchange rate changes on the balance sheet are reflected in the foreign currency translation amount included in shareholders' equity and does not affect reported earnings.

UNFAVORABLE WEATHER CONDITIONS

Our ability to attract visitors to our resorts is influenced by weather conditions and the amount of snowfall during the ski season.

We manage our exposure to unfavorable weather in three ways: by being geographically diversified, by seeking to spread visits to our resorts as evenly as possible through the season and by investing in snowmaking. Geographically diversified companies like ours can reduce the risk associated with a particular region's weather patterns. Every ski season since 1995, favorable and unfavorable weather conditions at different times across North America have offset one another, allowing us to come within 3% of our budgeted winter season ski and resort operations revenue on a same-resort basis. The more a resort can attract visitors evenly through the season the less vulnerable it is to unfavorable weather at a particular time. We seek to spread visits to our resorts by marketing to destination visitors who book in advance, stay several days and are less likely than day visitors to change their vacation plans, and by attempting to increase visits mid-week and at non-peak times. Investing in snowmaking also mitigates the impact of poor natural snow conditions. Snowmaking is particularly important in the East due to the number of competing resorts and less reliable snowfall. We have an average of 92% snowmaking coverage across our five eastern resorts.

SEASONALITY OF OPERATIONS

Ski and resort operations are highly seasonal. In fiscal 2003, 67% of our ski and resort operations revenue was generated during the period from December to March. Furthermore during this period a significant portion of ski and resort operations revenue is generated on certain holidays, particularly Christmas/New Year, Presidents' Day and school spring breaks, and on weekends. Conversely, Sandestin's peak operating season occurs during the summer months, partially offsetting the seasonality of the mountain resorts. Our real estate operations tend to be somewhat seasonal as well, with construction primarily taking place during the summer and the majority of sales closing in the December to June period. This seasonality of operations impacts reported quarterly earnings. The operating results for any particular quarter are not necessarily indicative of the operating results for a subsequent quarter or for the full fiscal year.

We have taken steps to balance our revenue and earnings throughout the year by investing in four-season amenities (e.g., golf) and growing summer and shoulder-season businesses. As a result of these initiatives, the proportion of ski and resort operations revenue earned outside the historically strong third fiscal quarter has increased to 45.2% in 2003 from 32.7% in 1997.

DEVELOPMENT ISSUES

As a real estate developer we face the following industry-specific risks:

- Zoning approvals or project permits could be withheld.
- Construction and other development costs could exceed budget.
- Project completion could be delayed.
- Purchasers could fail to close.

Our experience in resort master planning equips us to deal with municipal approval agencies. In addition, our approach of consulting with all community stakeholders during the planning process helps to ensure that we run into less resistance at public hearings.

We are not in the construction business – we engage general contractors to construct our real estate projects. Having fixed-price contracts with completion penalties reduces our exposure to cost overruns and construction delays. As our experience showed this year, some construction delays are inevitable in the real estate business, particularly given the location and variable weather conditions at our mountain resorts, however we do not anticipate that they would have a material impact on our earnings in any particular year.

Our pre-sales contracts require purchasers to put down 20% deposits, i.e., generally in the range of $50,000 to $150,000, which they forfeit if they do not close. Historically very few purchasers have failed to close.

Leisura rather than Intrawest is at risk for cost overruns, completion delays and purchaser contract defaults on any project that it purchases. We continue to be at risk for zoning and permit approvals since these approvals must be in hand before projects are sold to Leisura.

There is a risk that Leisura will not purchase land parcels from Intrawest in future years. The Leisura partners have, however, expressed a strong interest in extending their involvement in future years and we expect them to do so. In the event that the current partners decide not to participate in future projects we believe we will be able to identify alternative investors.

WORLD EVENTS

World events such as the terrorist attacks on September 11, 2001, the war in Iraq and the SARS outbreak disrupt domestic and international travel and reduce visits, or change the mix of visits, to our resorts. Often these types of events happen suddenly and cannot be prepared for. As we have shown over the past two years, we have been less impacted by these events than many other leisure and hospitality companies due to the high degree of commitment of our customers (e.g., as season pass holders or property owners), the significant proportion of our visitors who drive to our resorts (approximately 85% of all resort visits) and our ability to communicate with our database of customers and market products to them.

CRITICAL ACCOUNTING POLICIES

This discussion and analysis is based upon our consolidated financial statements, which have been prepared in accordance with GAAP in Canada. The preparation of these financial statements requires us to make estimates and judgments that affect the reported amounts of assets, liabilities, revenues and expenses and disclosure of contingencies. These estimates and judgments are based on factors that are inherently uncertain. On an ongoing basis, we evaluate our estimates based on historical experience and on various other assumptions that we believe are reasonable under the circumstances. Actual amounts could differ from those based on such estimates and assumptions.

We believe the following critical accounting policies call for management to make significant judgments and estimates.

USEFUL LIVES FOR DEPRECIABLE ASSETS Ski and resort operations assets and administrative furniture, computer equipment, software and leasehold improvements are depreciated using both the declining balance and straight-line basis (depending on the asset category) over the estimated useful life of the asset. Assets may become obsolete or require replacement before the end of their estimated useful life in which case any remaining undepreciated costs must be written off.

FUTURE NET CASH FLOWS FROM PROPERTIES **Properties under development and held for sale, which totaled $1,067.3 million at June, 30, 2003, are recorded at the lower of cost and net realizable value. In determining net realizable value it is necessary, on a non-discounted basis, to estimate the future cash flows from each individual project for the period from the start of land servicing to the sell-out of the last unit. This involves making assumptions about project demand and sales prices, construction and other development costs, and project financing. Changes in our assumptions could affect future cash flows from properties leading to reduced real estate profits or potentially property write-downs.**

RECOVERABILITY OF AMOUNTS RECEIVABLE **At June 30, 2003, amounts receivable totaled $203.6 million. We regularly review the recoverability of amounts receivable and record allowances for any amounts that we deem to be uncollectible. Disputes with our customers or changes in their financial condition could alter our expectation of recoverability and additional allowances may be required.**

VALUE OF FUTURE INCOME TAX ASSETS AND LIABILITIES **In determining our income tax provision, we are required to interpret tax legislation in a variety of jurisdictions and to make assumptions about the expected timing of the reversal of future tax assets and liabilities. In the event that our interpretations differed from those of the taxing authorities or that the timing of reversals is not as anticipated, the tax provision could increase or decrease in future periods.**

At June 30, 2003, we had accumulated $117.2 million of non-capital loss carryforwards which expire at various times through 2023. We have determined that it is more likely than not that the benefit of these losses will be realized in the future and we have recorded future tax assets of $35.8 million related to them. If it is determined in the future that it is more likely than not that all or a part of these future tax assets will not be realized, we will make a charge to earnings at that time.

OUTLOOK

As we move into fiscal 2004 we are focused on two primary financial objectives – to improve profitability and returns on capital from our existing businesses and to generate free cash flow.

Our goal is to increase profits in the ski and resort operations business by both growing revenue and containing costs. As we build more accommodation in our villages we will open up revenue-generating opportunities in lodging management and indirectly in our other businesses. We intend to utilize our capability in CRM and direct marketing to increase occupancy levels. Given the shortened booking window, these programs have the advantage that they can be introduced quickly and, since they are targeted to existing customers and good prospects, their rate of success is enhanced. They are also more cost-effective than other marketing programs.

We expect to reduce costs at our resorts by capitalizing on our network to take advantage of economies of scale. Standardized processes and technology will allow us to consolidate operations. The consolidation of our Colorado businesses in fiscal 2004 is the first step. Since new capex for ski and resort operations is expected to remain at about the same level as annual depreciation, these revenue growth and cost containment initiatives are expected to lead to a higher return on capital.

Our new organizational structure for the real estate development group is expected to improve our efficiency and our control, leading to stronger real estate margins in the future. This structure also facilitates growth since resources for multiple resorts are pooled.

As we assembled and improved our network of resorts we were significantly cash flow negative. We are now moving to a less capital-intensive business model with lower capital expenditures for our resorts and reduced infrastructure spending for real estate. We are also focused on growing our fee-based businesses (e.g., lodging, golf course and reservations management), which require minimal capital investment. We expect the Leisura transaction to produce free cash flow from our real estate business in fiscal 2004. This will occur as we recover the book value of current projects, and expenditures for the most capital-intensive projects in the future are restricted to our investment in Leisura. As we generate free cash flow we expect to pay down debt and improve our credit ratios.

The term **EBITDA** does not have a standardized meaning prescribed by GAAP and may not be comparable to similarly titled measures presented by other publicly traded companies. A reconciliation between net earnings as determined in accordance with Canadian GAAP and Total Company EBITDA is presented in the table below.

(MILLIONS)	YEAR ENDED JUNE 30 2003		YEAR ENDED JUNE 30 2002
Income before tax	$	52.3	$ 79.8
Depreciation and amortization		67.5	65.4
Interest expense		47.1	43.1
Interest in real estate costs		32.4	27.9
Write-down of technology assets		12.3	—
Interest and other income		(2.4)	(5.0)
Total Company EBITDA	$	209.2	$ 211.2

QUARTERLY FINANCIAL SUMMARY

(in millions of dollars, except per share amounts)

	2003 QUARTERS 1ST	2 ND	3RD	4TH	2002 QUARTERS 1ST	2ND	3RD	4TH
Total revenue	$ 112.7	$ 208.0	$ 402.6	$ 363.3	$ 93.7	$ 231.4	$ 342.1	$ 318.8
Income (loss) from continuing operations	(11.1)	3.4	56.8	(14.3)	(9.8)	6.0	56.2	6.2
Results of discontinued operations	0.0	(0.6)	0.0	0.0	0.2	(0.1)	0.0	(0.1)
Net income (loss)	(11.1)	2.8	56.8	(14.3)	(9.6)	5.9	56.2	6.0
PER COMMON SHARE:								
Income (loss) from continuing operations								
Basic	(0.23)	0.07	1.20	(0.30)	(0.22)	0.14	1.28	0.14
Diluted	(0.23)	0.07	1.19	(0.30)	(0.22)	0.14	1.25	0.13
Net income (loss)								
Basic	(0.23)	0.07	1.20	(0.30)	(0.22)	0.14	1.28	0.14
Diluted	(0.23)	0.07	1.19	(0.30)	(0.22)	0.14	1.25	0.13

The consolidated financial statements of Intrawest Corporation have been prepared by management and approved by the Board of Directors of the Company. Management is responsible for the preparation and presentation of the information contained in the consolidated financial statements. The Company maintains appropriate systems of internal control, policies and procedures that provide management with reasonable assurance that assets are safeguarded and that financial records are reliable and form a proper basis for preparation of financial statements.

The Company's independent auditors, KPMG LLP, have been appointed by the shareholders to express their professional opinion on the fairness of the consolidated financial statements. Their report is included below.

The Board of Directors ensures that management fulfills its responsibilities for financial reporting and internal control through an Audit Committee which is composed entirely of outside directors. This committee reviews the consolidated financial statements and reports to the Board of Directors. The auditors have full and direct access to the Audit Committee.

Joe S. Houssian
Chairman, President and Chief Executive Officer
SEPTEMBER 2, 2003

Daniel O. Jarvis
Executive Vice President and Chief Financial Officer

Auditors' Report to the Shareholders

We have audited the consolidated balance sheets of Intrawest Corporation as at June 30, 2003 and 2002 and the consolidated statements of operations, retained earnings, and cash flows for the years then ended. These financial statements are the responsibility of the Company's management. Our responsibility is to express an opinion on these financial statements based on our audits.

We conducted our audits in accordance with Canadian generally accepted auditing standards. Those standards require that we plan and perform an audit to obtain reasonable assurance whether the financial statements are free of material misstatement. An audit includes examining, on a test basis, evidence supporting the amounts and disclosures in the financial statements. An audit also includes assessing the accounting principles used and significant estimates made by management, as well as evaluating the overall financial statement presentation.

In our opinion, these consolidated financial statements present fairly, in all material respects, the financial position of the Company as at June 30, 2003 and 2002 and the results of its operations and its cash flows for the years then ended in accordance with Canadian generally accepted accounting principles.

KPMG LLP
Chartered Accountants
Vancouver, Canada
SEPTEMBER 2, 2003

Consolidated Statements of Operations

For the years ended June 30, 2003 and 2002
(In thousands of United States dollars, except per share amounts)

	2003	2002
REVENUE:		
Ski and resort operations	$ 571,527	$ 485,142
Real estate sales	512,695	487,775
Rental properties	—	8,038
Interest and other income	2,417	1,115
Income from equity accounted investment	—	3,901
	1,086,639	985,971
EXPENSES:		
Ski and resort operations	454,861	377,801
Real estate costs	437,690	402,700
Rental properties	—	4,963
Interest (note 16)	47,142	43,072
Depreciation and amortization	67,516	65,434
Corporate general and administrative	14,889	12,175
Write-down of technology assets (note 8(b))	12,270	—
	1,034,368	906,145
Income before undernoted	52,271	79,826
Provision for income taxes (note 13)	6,243	9,549
Income before non-controlling interest and discontinued operations	46,028	70,277
Non-controlling interest	11,274	11,675
Income from continuing operations	34,754	58,602
Results of discontinued operations (note 4)	(578)	(122)
Net income	$ 34,176	$ 58,480
INCOME FROM CONTINUING OPERATIONS PER COMMON SHARE:		
Basic	$ 0.73	$ 1.33
Diluted	0.73	1.31
NET INCOME PER COMMON SHARE:		
Basic	0.73	1.33
Diluted	0.73	1.31

See accompanying notes to consolidated financial statements.

Consolidated Balance Sheets

June 30, 2003 and 2002
(In thousands of United States dollars)

	2003	2002
ASSETS		
CURRENT ASSETS:		
Cash and cash equivalents	$ 126,832	$ 76,689
Amounts receivable (note 7)	126,725	109,948
Other assets (note 8(a))	123,610	88,062
Resort properties (note 6)	662,197	399,572
Future income taxes (note 13)	10,619	7,536
	1,049,983	681,807
Ski and resort operations (note 5)	918,727	841,841
Properties (note 6):		
Resort	405,100	461,893
Discontinued operations	—	6,325
	405,100	468,218
Amounts receivable (note 7)	76,842	64,734
Other assets (note 8(b))	65,070	94,332
Goodwill	—	15,985
	$2,515,722	**$2,166,917**
LIABILITIES AND SHAREHOLDERS' EQUITY		
CURRENT LIABILITIES:		
Amounts payable	$ 218,444	$ 195,254
Deferred revenue (note 10)	134,878	99,484
Bank and other indebtedness (note 9):		
Resort	287,176	279,297
Discontinued operations	—	2,750
	640,498	576,785
Bank and other indebtedness (note 9):		
Resort	973,743	773,790
Discontinued operations	—	82
	973,743	773,872
Due to joint venture partners (note 14)	5,388	3,963
Deferred revenue (note 10)	43,609	23,069
Future income taxes (note 13)	94,986	75,843
Non-controlling interest in subsidiaries	46,359	36,116
	1,804,583	1,489,648
Shareholders' equity:		
Capital stock (note 12)	460,742	466,899
Retained earnings	264,640	241,665
Foreign currency translation adjustment	(14,243)	(31,295)
	711,139	677,269
	$2,515,722	**$2,166,917**

Contingencies and commitments (note 15)
Subsequent event (note 8(b))

Approved on behalf of the Board:

Joe S. Houssian
Director

Paul M. Manheim
Director

See accompanying notes to consolidated financial statements.

Consolidated Statements of Retained Earnings

For the years ended June 30, 2003 and 2002
(In thousands of United States dollars)

	2003	2002
Retained earnings, beginning of year:		
As previously reported	**$ 241,665**	$ 187,922
Adjustment to reflect change in accounting for goodwill and intangibles, net of tax (note 2(t)(i))	**(6,150)**	—
As restated	**235,515**	187,922
Net income	**34,176**	58,480
Dividends	**(5,051)**	(4,737)
Retained earnings, end of year	**$ 264,640**	$ 241,665

See accompanying notes to consolidated financial statements.

Consolidated Statements of Cash Flows

For the years ended June 30, 2003 and 2002
(In thousands of United States dollars)

	2003	2002
CASH PROVIDED BY (USED IN):		
OPERATIONS:		
Income from continuing operations	**$ 34,754**	$ 58,602
Items not affecting cash:		
Depreciation and amortization	**67,516**	65,434
Future income taxes	**(3,914)**	(2,873)
Income from equity accounted investment	**—**	(3,901)
(Gain) loss on asset disposals, net of write-offs	**858**	(323)
Write-down of technology assets	**12,270**	
Non-controlling interest	**11,274**	11,675
Funds from continuing operations	**122,758**	128,614
Recovery of costs through real estate sales	**437,690**	402,700
Acquisition and development of properties held for sale	**(601,524)**	(565,863)
Increase in amounts receivable, net	**(12,109)**	(8,936)
Changes in non-cash operating working capital (note 21)	**26,590**	49,191
Cash provided by (used in) continuing operating activities	**(26,595)**	5,706
Cash provided by discontinued operations	**140**	3,898
	(26,455)	9,604
FINANCING:		
Proceeds from bank and other borrowings	**599,112**	351,259
Repayments on bank and other borrowings	**(469,235)**	(304,933)
Issue of common shares for cash, net of issuance costs	**4,782**	53,037
Redemption and repurchase of non-resort preferred shares (note 12(a))	**(6,697)**	(358)
Dividends paid	**(5,051)**	(4,737)
Distributions to non-controlling interests	**(6,923)**	(6,534)
	115,988	87,734
INVESTMENTS:		
Expenditures on:		
Revenue-producing properties	**—**	(2,353)
Ski and resort operations assets	**(64,546)**	(91,490)
Other assets	**(11,778)**	(8,463)
Business acquisitions (note 3)	**(2,849)**	(8,876)
Proceeds from asset disposals	**39,783**	4,103
	(39,390)	(107,079)
Increase (decrease) in cash and cash equivalents	**50,143**	(9,741)
Cash and cash equivalents, beginning of year	**76,689**	86,430
Cash and cash equivalents, end of year	**$ 126,832**	$ 76,689

Supplementary information (note 21)
See accompanying notes to consolidated financial statements.

Notes to Consolidated Financial Statements

For the years ended June 30, 2003 and 2002
(Tabular amounts in thousands of United States dollars, unless otherwise indicated)

1 OPERATIONS:

Intrawest Corporation was formed by an amalgamation on November 23, 1979 under the Company Act (British Columbia) and was continued under the Canada Business Corporations Act on January 14, 2002. Through its subsidiaries, the Company is engaged in the development and operation of mountain and golf resorts principally throughout North America.

2 SIGNIFICANT ACCOUNTING POLICIES:

(a) BASIS OF PRESENTATION:

The consolidated financial statements are prepared in accordance with generally accepted accounting principles in Canada as prescribed by The Canadian Institute of Chartered Accountants ("CICA"). Information regarding United States generally accepted accounting principles as it affects the Company's consolidated financial statements is presented in note 22.

(b) PRINCIPLES OF CONSOLIDATION:

The consolidated financial statements include:

(i)   the accounts of the Company and its subsidiaries; and

(ii)   the accounts of all incorporated and unincorporated joint ventures, including non-controlled partnerships, to the extent of the Company's interest in their respective assets, liabilities, revenues and expenses.

The Company's principal subsidiaries and joint ventures are as follows:

SUBSIDIARIES	PERCENTAGE INTEREST HELD BY THE COMPANY (%)
Blackcomb Skiing Enterprises Limited Partnership	77
Whistler Mountain Resort Limited Partnership	77
Intrawest/Lodestar Limited Partnership	100
IW Resorts Limited Partnership	100
Mont Tremblant Resorts and Company, Limited Partnership	100
Copper Mountain, Inc.	100
Intrawest California Holdings, Inc.	100
Intrawest Golf Holdings, Inc.	100
Intrawest Resort Ownership Corporation	100
Intrawest Retail Group, Inc.	100
Intrawest Sandestin Company, L.L.C.	100
Intrawest/Winter Park Holdings Corporation (note 3)	100
Mountain Creek Resort, Inc.	100
Mt. Tremblant Reservations Inc.	100
Playground Real Estate Inc.	100
Resort Reservations Network Inc.	100
Snowshoe Mountain, Inc.	100
Intrawest Golf Management (Canada) Ltd.	100
The Stratton Corporation	100

2 SIGNIFICANT ACCOUNTING POLICIES: (CONTINUED)

JOINT VENTURES AND NON-CONTROLLED PARTNERSHIPS (note 14)	PERCENTAGE INTEREST HELD BY THE COMPANY (%)
Alpine Helicopters Ltd.	45
Blue Mountain Resorts Limited	50
Blue River Land Company L.L.C.	50
Chateau M.T. Inc.	50
Intrawest/Brush Creek Development Company L.L.C.	50
Intrawest/Lodestar Golf Limited Partnership	73.7
Keystone/Intrawest L.L.C.	50
Mammoth Mountain Ski Area	59.5
Resort Ventures Limited Partnership	50

All significant intercompany balances and transactions have been eliminated.

(c) ACCOUNTING FOR INVESTMENTS:

The Company accounts for investments in which it is able to exercise significant influence in accordance with the equity method. Under the equity method, the original cost of the shares is adjusted for the Company's share of post-acquisition earnings or losses, less dividends.

(d) USE OF ESTIMATES:

The preparation of financial statements in conformity with generally accepted accounting principles requires management to make estimates and assumptions that affect the reported amounts of assets and liabilities and disclosure of contingent assets and liabilities at the date of the financial statements and the reported amounts of revenues and expenses during the reporting period. Actual results could differ from those estimates.

The significant areas requiring management estimates include the estimates of future net cash flows from properties, useful lives for depreciation, the recoverability of amounts receivable, and the value of future income tax assets and liabilities.

(e) CASH EQUIVALENTS:

The Company considers all highly liquid investments with terms to maturity of three months or less when acquired to be cash equivalents.

(f) PROPERTIES:

(i) Properties under development and held for sale:

Properties under development and held for sale are recorded at the lower of cost and net realizable value. Cost includes all expenditures incurred in connection with the acquisition, development and construction of these properties. These expenditures consist of all direct costs, interest on specific debt, interest on that portion of total costs financed by the Company's pooled debt, and an allocation of indirect overhead. Incidental operations related specifically to properties under development are treated as an increase in or a reduction of costs.

Effective July 1, 2002, the Company determined that it would no longer retain the commercial properties that it developed as long-term revenue-producing properties. Instead existing commercial properties would be sold and commercial properties developed in the future would be developed for the purpose of sale. Consequently from July 1, 2002, commercial properties are classified as properties under development and held for sale and net rental income before depreciation is capitalized to the cost of the property. Properties held for sale are not depreciated.

Costs associated with the development of sales locations of the vacation ownership business, including operating and general and administrative costs incurred until a location is fully operational, are capitalized. The results of incidental operations related specifically to a location are treated as an increase in or a reduction of costs during the start-up period. These net costs are amortized on a straight-line basis over seven years.

The Company defers costs directly relating to the acquisition of new properties and resorts which, in management's judgment, have a high probability of closing. If the acquisition is abandoned, any deferred costs are expensed immediately.

The Company provides for write-downs where the carrying value of a particular property exceeds its net realizable value.

(ii) Classification:

Properties that are currently under development for sale and properties available for sale are classified as current assets. Related bank and other indebtedness is classified as a current liability.

(g) SKI AND RESORT OPERATIONS:

The ski and resort operations assets are stated at cost less accumulated depreciation. Costs of ski lifts, area improvements and buildings are capitalized. Certain buildings, area improvements and equipment are located on leased or licensed land. Depreciation is provided over the estimated useful lives of each asset category using the declining balance method at annual rates as follows:

	(%)
Buildings	3.3 to 5.0
Ski lifts	5.0 to 8.0
Golf courses	2.0 to 3.3
Area improvements	2.0 to 3.3
Automotive, helicopters and other equipment	10.0 to 50.0
Leased vehicles	20.0 to 25.0

Inventories are recorded at the lower of cost and net realizable value, and consist primarily of retail goods, food and beverage products, and mountain operating supplies.

(h) ADMINISTRATIVE FURNITURE, COMPUTER EQUIPMENT, SOFTWARE AND LEASEHOLD IMPROVEMENTS:

Administrative furniture, computer equipment and software are stated at cost less accumulated depreciation. Included in software costs are any direct costs incurred developing internal use software. Depreciation of administrative furniture is provided using the declining balance method at annual rates of between 20% and 30%. Depreciation of computer equipment and software is provided using the straight-line method at annual rates of between 10% and 33 $\frac{1}{3}$%.

Leasehold improvements are stated at cost less accumulated amortization. Amortization is provided using the straight-line method over the lease term.

(i) DEFERRED FINANCING COSTS:

Deferred financing costs consist of legal and other fees directly related to the debt financing of the Company's ski and resort operations. These costs are amortized to interest expense over the term of the related financing.

(j) GOODWILL AND INTANGIBLE ASSETS:

Goodwill represents the excess of purchase price over the fair value of identifiable assets acquired in a purchase business combination. Intangible assets with indefinite useful lives represent costs that have been allocated to brand names and trademarks. Effective July 1, 2002, the Company no longer amortizes goodwill and intangible assets with indefinite useful lives, but they are subject to impairment tests on at least an annual basis (see note 2(t)(i)) and additionally, whenever events and changes in circumstances suggest that the carrying amount may not be recoverable.

Intangible assets with finite useful lives are costs that have been allocated to contracts and customer lists and are amortized on a straight-line basis over their estimated useful lives.

(k) DEFERRED REVENUE:

Deferred revenue mainly comprises real estate deposits, season pass revenue, club initiation deposits, government grants and the exchange gains arising on the translation of long-term monetary items that are denominated in foreign currencies (note 2(o)). Deferred revenue which relates to the sale of season passes is recognized throughout the season based on the number of skier visits. Deferred revenue which relates to club initiation deposits is recognized on a straight-line basis over the estimated membership terms. Deferred revenue which relates to government grants for ski and resort operations assets is recognized on the same basis as the related assets are amortized. Deferred revenue which relates to government grants for properties under development is recognized as the properties are sold.

2 SIGNIFICANT ACCOUNTING POLICIES: (CONTINUED)

(l) GOVERNMENT ASSISTANCE:

The Company periodically applies for financial assistance under available government incentive programs. Non-repayable government assistance relating to capital expenditures is reflected as a reduction of the cost of such assets.

(m) REVENUE RECOGNITION:

(i) Ski and resort operations revenue is recognized as the service is provided. Commission revenues derived from airline ticket, hotel, car and cruise reservations are recognized when the customer first utilizes the service. Commission revenue is recorded at the net of the amount charged to the customer and the amount paid to the supplier.

(ii) Revenue from the sale of properties is recorded when title to the completed unit is conveyed to the purchaser, the purchaser becomes entitled to occupancy and the purchaser has made a payment that is appropriate in the circumstances.

(iii) Points revenue associated with membership in the vacation ownership business of Club Intrawest (which revenue is included in real estate sales) is recognized when the purchaser has paid the amount due on closing, all contract documentation has been executed and all other significant conditions of sale are met.

(n) FUTURE INCOME TAXES:

The Company follows the asset and liability method of accounting for income taxes. Under such method, future tax assets and liabilities are recognized for future tax consequences attributable to differences between the financial statement carrying amounts of existing assets and liabilities and their respective tax bases.

Future tax assets and liabilities are measured using enacted or substantively enacted tax rates expected to apply to taxable income in the years in which those temporary differences are expected to be recovered or settled. The effect on future tax assets and liabilities of a change in tax rates is recognized in income in the period that includes the substantive enactment date. To the extent that it is not considered to be more likely than not that a future income tax asset will be realized, a valuation allowance is provided.

(o) FOREIGN CURRENCY TRANSLATION:

These consolidated financial statements are presented in U.S. dollars. The majority of the Company's operations are located in the United States and are conducted in U.S. dollars. The Company's Canadian operations use the Canadian dollar as their functional currency. The Canadian entities' financial statements have been translated into U.S. dollars using the exchange rate in effect at the balance sheet date for asset and liability amounts and at the average rate for the period for amounts included in the determination of income.

Cumulative unrealized gains or losses arising from the translation of the assets and liabilities of these operations into U.S. dollars are recorded as foreign currency translation adjustment, a separate component of shareholders' equity.

Effective July 1, 2002, exchange gains or losses arising on the translation of long-term monetary items that are denominated in foreign currencies to the applicable currency of measurement are included in the determination of net income (note 2(t)(ii)). Previously these gains and losses were deferred and amortized on a straight-line basis over the remaining terms of the related monetary item except for gains or losses related to foreign currency denominated long-term obligations designated as hedges of investments in self-sustaining foreign operations.

The actual exchange rates used for translation purposes were as follows:

CANADIAN DOLLAR TO U.S. DOLLAR EXCHANGE RATES	2003	2002
At June 30	1.3475	1.5162
Average during year	1.5112	1.5687

(p) PER SHARE CALCULATIONS:

Income per common share has been calculated using the weighted average number of common shares outstanding during the year. The dilutive effect of stock options is determined using the treasury stock method.

The Company has a stock option plan as described in note 12(c). Section 3870 of the CICA Accounting Handbook ("CICA 3870") requires a fair value-based method of accounting that is required for certain, but not all, stock-based transactions. CICA 3870 must be applied to all stock-based payments to non-employees, and to employee awards that are direct awards of shares, that call for settlement in cash or other assets, or are share appreciation rights that call for settlement by the issuance of equity instruments. As permitted by CICA 3870, the Company continues to account for employee stock option grants using the intrinsic value-based method under which no expense is recorded on grant and provides, on a pro forma basis, information as if a fair value methodology had been applied (note 12(h)). Accordingly, no compensation expense has been recognized for the periods presented. Any consideration paid on the exercise of options or purchase of shares is credited to capital stock.

(r) EMPLOYEE FUTURE BENEFITS:

The Company accrues its obligations under employee benefit plans and the related costs as the underlying services are provided.

(s) COMPARATIVE FIGURES:

Certain comparative figures for 2002 have been reclassified to conform with the financial statement presentation adopted in the current year.

(t) CHANGE IN ACCOUNTING POLICIES:

(i)   On July 1, 2002, the Company adopted the new recommendations of section 3062, "Goodwill and Other Intangible Assets," of the CICA Handbook, without restatement of prior periods. Under the new recommendations, goodwill and intangible assets with indefinite lives are no longer amortized but are subject to impairment tests on at least an annual basis by comparing the related reporting unit's carrying value to its fair value. Any write-down resulting from impairment tests made under the new section at adoption effective July 1, 2002 must be recognized as a charge to retained earnings at that date. Any impairment of goodwill or other intangible assets identified subsequent to July 1, 2002 will be expensed as determined. Other intangible assets with finite lives will continue to be amortized over their useful lives and are also tested for impairment by comparing carrying values to net recoverable amounts.

At June 30, 2002, the net carrying value of goodwill was $15,985,000. Upon adoption of these recommendations, it was determined that $179,000 needed to be reclassified from goodwill to ski and resort operations assets, and $3,813,000 needed to be reclassified from goodwill to depreciable intangible assets under CICA recommendations on business combinations. The Company completed its impairment testing on the balance of goodwill and intangible assets with indefinite lives as at July 1, 2002. As a result of this testing, an impairment loss of $6,150,000 (being net of taxes of $5,843,000) was required and has been recognized as an adjustment to opening retained earnings.

A reconciliation of previously reported net income and income per share (basic and diluted) to the amounts adjusted for the exclusion of goodwill amortization is as follows:

	2003	2002
Income as reported	$ 34,176	$ 58,480
Goodwill amortization	—	743
Adjusted income	$ 34,176	$ 59,223
Income per share (basic):		
Income as reported	$ 0.73	$ 1.33
Goodwill amortization	—	0.01
Adjusted income per share	$ 0.73	$ 1.34
Income per share (diluted):		
Income as reported	$ 0.73	$ 1.31
Goodwill amortization	—	0.02
Adjusted income per share	$ 0.73	$ 1.33

(ii)   On July 1, 2002, the Company retroactively adopted the new recommendations of section 1650, "Foreign Currency Translation," of the CICA Handbook which eliminated the requirement to defer and amortize unrealized translation gains and losses on long-term foreign currency denominated monetary items with a fixed or determinable life. Instead the exchange gains and losses on these items are included in the determination of income immediately. The adoption did not impact the financial position and results of operations of prior periods, or the results for the year ended June 30, 2003.

3 ACQUISITIONS:

On December 23, 2002, the Company assumed control of the assets and operations of Winter Park Resort, a major ski and resort operation in Colorado. For accounting purposes the assumption of control has been treated as a purchase of the resort. The fair value of the purchase price of the assets acquired was $47,204,000 of which $38,236,000 was assigned to ski and resort operations assets, $7,817,000 was assigned to real estate development properties and $1,151,000 was assigned to amounts receivable. The purchase was financed primarily through the issuance of a capital lease, the assumption of certain liabilities and the payment of $2,849,000 cash.

During the year ended June 30, 2002, the Company acquired the assets and business of Big Island Country Club Limited Partnership, which operates a golf course on the island of Hawaii, for cash consideration of $8,876,000.

4 DISCONTINUED OPERATIONS:

For reporting purposes, the results of operations and cash flow from operating activities of the non-resort real estate business have been disclosed separately from those of continuing operations for the periods presented.

The results of discontinued operations are as follows:

	2003	2002
Revenue	$ 441	$ 1,128
Loss before current income taxes	$ (578)	$ (104)
Provision for current income taxes	—	18
Loss from discontinued operations	$ (578)	$ (122)

5 SKI AND RESORT OPERATIONS:

	2003		
	COST	ACCUMULATED DEPRECIATION	NET BOOK VALUE
SKI OPERATIONS:			
Land	$ 58,679	$ —	$ 58,679
Buildings	300,351	59,124	241,227
Ski lifts and area improvements	443,889	140,260	303,629
Automotive, helicopters and other equipment	134,654	81,001	53,653
Leased vehicles	4,903	2,814	2,089
	942,476	283,199	659,277
RESORT OPERATIONS:			
Land	23,187	—	23,187
Buildings	68,178	7,486	60,692
Golf courses	124,919	21,173	103,746
Area improvements	95,256	23,431	71,825
	311,540	52,090	259,450
	$1,254,016	$ 335,289	$ 918,727

	2002		
	COST	ACCUMULATED DEPRECIATION	NET BOOK VALUE
SKI OPERATIONS:			
Land	$ 52,490	$ —	$ 52,490
Buildings	248,731	47,556	201,175
Ski lifts and area improvements	411,352	118,993	292,359
Automotive, helicopters and other equipment	120,681	70,499	50,182
Leased vehicles	4,614	2,311	2,303
	837,868	239,359	598,509
RESORT OPERATIONS:			
Land	21,925	—	21,925
Buildings	58,219	8,937	49,282
Golf courses	120,145	16,444	103,701
Area improvements	87,446	19,022	68,424
	287,735	44,403	243,332
	$1,125,603	$ 283,762	$ 841,841

The ski and resort operations have been pledged as security for certain of the Company's bank and other indebtedness (note 9).

6 PROPERTIES:

Summary of properties:

	2003	2002
Properties under development and held for sale	$1,067,297	$ 797,603
Revenue-producing properties	—	70,187
	$1,067,297	$ 867,790

Properties are classified for balance sheet purposes as follows:

	2003	2002
CURRENT ASSETS:		
Resort	$ 662,197	$ 399,572
LONG-TERM ASSETS:		
Resort	405,100	461,893
Discontinued operations	—	6,325
	$1,067,297	$ 867,790

Cumulative costs capitalized to the carrying value of properties under development and held for sale are as follows:

	2003	2002
Land and land development costs	$ 205,709	$ 187,269
Building development costs	704,396	478,175
Interest	103,154	80,082
Administrative	54,038	52,077
	$1,067,297	$ 797,603

During the year ended June 30, 2003, the Company capitalized interest of $55,525,000 (2002 – $38,850,000) (note 16).

Properties have been pledged as security for certain of the Company's bank and other indebtedness (note 9). Breakdown of revenue-producing properties:

		2002	
	COST	ACCUMULATED DEPRECIATION	NET BOOK VALUE
REVENUE-PRODUCING PROPERTIES:			
Land	$ 8,217	$ —	$ 8,217
Buildings	68,298	11,340	56,958
Leasehold improvements and equipment	6,472	1,460	5,012
	$ 82,987	$ 12,800	$ 70,187

7 AMOUNTS RECEIVABLE:

	2003	2002
Receivables from sales of real estate	$ 54,576	$ 59,679
Ski and resort operations trade receivables	34,427	23,053
Loans, mortgages and notes receivable (note 20)	89,189	73,408
Funded senior employee share purchase plans (note 12(f))	4,445	4,475
Other accounts receivable	20,930	14,067
	203,567	174,682
Current portion	126,725	109,948
	$ 76,842	$ 64,734

Amounts receivable from sales of real estate primarily comprise sales proceeds held in trust which are generally paid out to the Company or to construction lenders within 60 days.

Total payments due on amounts receivable are approximately as follows:

YEAR ENDING JUNE 30,	
2004	$ 126,725
2005	19,129
2006	4,037
2007	3,310
2008	1,996
Subsequent to 2008	48,370
	$ 203,567

The loans, mortgages and notes receivable bear interest at both fixed and floating rates which averaged 10.71% per annum as at June 30, 2003 (2002 – 10.91%). Certain of these amounts have been pledged as security for the Company's bank and other indebtedness (note 9).

8 OTHER ASSETS:

(a) CURRENT:

	2003	2002
Ski and resort operations inventories	$ 34,640	$ 30,054
Restricted cash deposits	57,087	34,502
Prepaid expenses and other	31,883	23,506
	$ 123,610	$ 88,062

(b) LONG-TERM:

	2003	2002
Investment in Compagnie des Alpes	$ 12,257	$ 36,142
Deferred financing and other costs	20,053	16,481
Administrative furniture, computer equipment, software and leasehold improvements, net of accumulated depreciation of $19,644,000 (2002 – $15,769,000)	23,856	33,614
Other	8,904	8,095
	$ 65,070	$ 94,332

In July 2002 the Company sold 55% of its investment in Compagnie des Alpes ("CDA") for proceeds which approximated its carrying value. As a result, the Company changed from the equity to the cost method of accounting for its investment at the beginning of the current fiscal year. During July 2003 the Company sold its remaining interest in CDA for proceeds which approximated its carrying value.

During the year ended June 30, 2003, the Company decided to standardize certain information technology systems across its resorts in order to improve efficiencies and eliminate costs. In addition, the Company reorganized its central reservations business and assessed the value of the assets of that business. As a result, the Company wrote down the value of information technology assets by $12,270,000.

9 BANK AND OTHER INDEBTEDNESS:

The Company has obtained financing for its ski and resort operations and properties from various financial institutions by pledging individual assets as security for such financing. Security for general corporate debt is provided by general security which includes a floating charge on the Company's assets and undertakings, fixed charges on real estate properties, and assignment of mortgages and notes receivable. The following table summarizes the primary security provided by the Company, where appropriate, and indicates the applicable type of financing, maturity dates and the weighted average interest rate at June 30, 2003:

	MATURITY DATES	WEIGHTED AVERAGE INTEREST RATE(%)	2003	2002
SKI AND RESORT OPERATIONS:				
Mortgages and bank loans	Demand – 2017	3.68	$ 62,432	$ 124,578
Obligations under capital leases	2004 – 2052	9.09	45,070	3,869
			107,502	128,447
PROPERTIES:				
Interim financing on properties under development and held for sale	2004 – 2017	5.71	264,032	141,337
Resort club notes receivable credit facilities	2006	5.21	28,121	27,436
Mortgages on revenue-producing properties	2004 – 2011	nil	—	12,485
			292,153	181,258
General corporate debt	2004 – 2005	5.63	240,243	184,000
Unsecured debentures	2004 – 2010	10.20	621,021	562,214
		7.91	1,260,919	1,055,919
Current portion			287,176	282,047
			$ 973,743	$ 773,872

Principal repayments and the components related to either floating or fixed interest rate indebtedness are as follows:

| YEAR ENDING JUNE 30, | INTEREST RATES | | TOTAL REPAYMENTS |
	FLOATING	FIXED	
2004	$ 252,630	$ 34,546	$ 287,176
2005	267,620	10,680	278,300
2006	19,257	12,836	32,093
2007	80	2,942	3,022
2008	1,278	653	1,931
Subsequent to 2008	5,231	653,166	658,397
	$ 546,096	$ 714,823	$1,260,919

The Company has entered into a swap agreement to fix the interest rate on a portion of its floating rate debt. The Company had $14,126,000 (2002 – $16,000,000) of bank loans swapped against debt with a fixed interest rate ranging from 4.70% to 5.58% (2002 – 4.70% to 5.58%) per annum.

Bank and other indebtedness includes indebtedness in the amount of $306,458,000 (2002 – $263,691,000) which is repayable in Canadian dollars of $412,952,000 (2002 – $399,808,000).

The Company is subject to certain covenants in respect of some of the bank and other indebtedness which require the Company to maintain certain financial ratios. The Company is in compliance with these covenants at June 30, 2003.

10 DEFERRED REVENUE:

	2003	2002
Deposits on real estate sales	$ 109,075	$ 76,239
Government assistance (note 11)	10,992	7,901
Club initiation deposits	24,845	13,431
Season pass revenue	14,989	13,883
Other deferred amounts	18,586	11,099
	178,487	122,553
Current portion	134,878	99,484
	$ 43,609	$ 23,069

11 GOVERNMENT ASSISTANCE:

The federal government of Canada and the Province of Quebec have granted financial assistance to the Company in the form of interest-free loans and forgivable grants for the construction of specified four-season tourist facilities at Mont Tremblant. Loans totaling $10,464,000 (Cdn.$14,100,000) (2002 – $9,300,000; Cdn.$14,100,000) have been advanced and are repayable over 17 years starting in 2000. The grants, which will total $43,052,000 (Cdn.$58,013,000) (2002 – $38,318,000; Cdn.$58,013,000) when they are fully advanced, amounted to $31,400,000 (Cdn.$42,312,000) at June 30, 2003 (2002 – $24,518,000; Cdn.$37,174,000). During the year ended June 30, 2003, grants received of $3,812,000 (Cdn.$5,138,000) (2002 – $3,513,000; Cdn.$5,326,000) were credited as follows: $1,138,000 (2002 – $1,010,000) to ski and resort operations assets, $573,000 (2002 – $1,461,000) to properties and $2,101,000 (2002 – $1,042,000) to deferred government assistance.

12 CAPITAL STOCK:

(a) SHARE CAPITAL REORGANIZATION:

Effective March 14, 1997, the Company completed a reorganization of its share capital designed to separate the remaining non-resort real estate assets from the rest of the Company's business. Under the reorganization, each existing common share was exchanged for one new common share and one non-resort preferred ("NRP") share. The new common shares have the same attributes as the old common shares.

On December 18, 2002, the Company redeemed all of the remaining NRP shares at a price of Cdn.$2.02 per share for a total of $6,697,000. As a result, the carrying value of the NRP shares was reduced to zero and contributed surplus was increased by $2,661,000 representing the difference between the redemption price and the assigned value of the NRP shares less the foreign currency translation adjustment related to the NRP shares.

(b) CAPITAL STOCK:

The Company's capital stock comprises the following:

	2003	2002
Common shares	$ 458,081	$ 453,299
NRP shares	—	13,600
Contributed surplus (note 12(a))	2,661	—
	$ 460,742	$ 466,899

(i) Common shares:

Authorized: an unlimited number without par value

Issued:

	2003		2002	
	NUMBER OF COMMON SHARES	AMOUNT	NUMBER OF COMMON SHARES	AMOUNT
Balance, beginning of year	47,255,062	$ 453,299	44,026,394	$ 400,262
Issued for cash under stock option plan	305,000	2,685	270,850	1,893
Amortization of benefit plan, net (g)	—	2,097	—	—
Purchased for benefit plan (g)	—	—	(292,182)	(4,807)
Issued for cash, net of issuance costs	—	—	3,250,000	55,951
Balance, end of year	47,560,062	$ 458,081	47,255,062	$ 453,299

(ii) NRP shares:

Authorized: 50,000,000 without par value

Issued:

	2003		2002	
	NUMBER OF NRP SHARES	AMOUNT	NUMBER OF NRP SHARES	AMOUNT
Balance, beginning of year	5,163,436	$ 13,600	5,513,936	$ 13,958
Redemption	(5,163,436)	(6,697)	—	—
Transferred to contributed surplus	—	(2,661)	—	—
Foreign currency adjustment	—	(4,242)	—	—
Purchased for cancellation	—	—	(350,500)	(358)
Balance, end of year	—	$ —	5,163,436	$ 13,600

(iii) Preferred shares:

Authorized: an unlimited number without par value

Issued: nil

(c) STOCK OPTIONS:

The Company has a stock option plan which provides for grants to officers and employees of the Company and its subsidiaries of options to purchase common shares of the Company. Options granted under the stock option plan are exercisable in Canadian dollars and may not be exercised except in accordance with such limitations as the Human Resources Committee of the Board of Directors of the Company may determine.

The following table summarizes the status of options outstanding under the Plan:

	2003		2002	
	SHARE OPTIONS OUTSTANDING	WEIGHTED AVERAGE PRICE	SHARE OPTIONS OUTSTANDING	WEIGHTED AVERAGE PRICE
Outstanding, beginning of year	3,697,900	$ 16.04	3,322,500	$ 15.24
Granted	445,000	15.89	711,800	16.17
Exercised	(305,000)	9.41	(270,850)	6.99
Forfeited	(34,000)	18.03	(65,550)	17.87
Outstanding, end of year	3,803,900	$ 18.68	3,697,900	$ 16.04
Exercisable, end of year	1,867,310	$ 18.20	1,753,950	$ 14.70

The following table provides details of options outstanding at June 30, 2003:

RANGE OF EXERCISE PRICES	NUMBER OUTSTANDING JUNE 30, 2003	WEIGHTED AVERAGE LIFE REMAINING (YEARS)	WEIGHTED AVERAGE PRICE	NUMBER EXERCISABLE JUNE 30, 2003	WEIGHTED AVERAGE PRICE
$ 8.56 – $ 10.74	134,100	1.8	$ 10.17	134,100	$ 10.17
$ 11.67 – $ 17.07	233,500	4.4	14.74	205,500	15.02
$ 17.66 – $ 21.56	3,436,300	6.8	19.28	1,527,710	19.19
	3,803,900	6.4	$ 18.68	1,867,310	$ 18.20

(d) EMPLOYEE SHARE PURCHASE PLAN:

The employee share purchase plan permits certain full-time employees of the Company and its subsidiaries and limited partnerships to purchase common shares through payroll deductions. The Company contributes $1 for every $3 contributed by an employee. To June 30, 2003, a total of 65,809 (2002 – 65,809) common shares have been issued from treasury under this plan. A further 100,000 common shares have been authorized and reserved for issuance under this plan.

(e) DEFERRED SHARE UNIT PLAN:

The company has a key executive Deferred Share Unit Plan (the "DSU Plan") that allows each executive officer to elect to receive all or any portion of his annual incentive award as deferred share units. A DSU is equal in value to one common share of the Company. The units are determined by dividing the dollar amount elected by the average closing price of the common shares on the Toronto Stock Exchange for the five trading days preceding the date that the annual incentive award becomes payable. The units also accrue dividend equivalents payable in additional units in an amount equal to dividends paid on Intrawest common shares. DSUs mature upon the termination of employment, whereupon an executive is entitled to receive the fair market value of the equivalent number of common shares, net of withholdings, in cash.

The Company records the cost of the DSU plan as compensation expense. As at June 30, 2003, 74,381 units were outstanding at a value of $981,000 (2002 – 49,351 units at a value of $827,000).

(f) FUNDED SENIOR EMPLOYEE SHARE PURCHASE PLANS:

The Company has two funded senior employee share purchase plans which provide for loans to be made to designated eligible employees to be used for the purchase of common shares. At June 30, 2003, loans to employees under the funded senior employee share purchase plans amounted to $4,445,000 with respect to 247,239 common shares (2002 – $4,475,000 with respect to 374,387 common shares and 26,939 NRP shares). The loans, which are included in amounts receivable, are non-interest bearing, secured by a promissory note and a pledge of the shares ($3,259,000 market value at June 30, 2003) and mature by 2012. A further 96,400 common shares have been authorized and reserved for issuance under one of the plans.

(g) KEY EXECUTIVE EMPLOYEE BENEFIT PLAN:

The Company has a key executive employee benefit plan which permits the Company to grant awards of common shares purchased in the open market to executive officers. To June 30, 2003, a total of 292,182 (2002 – 292,192) common shares were purchased under this plan. The common shares vest to the employees in part over time and the balance on the attainment of certain future earnings levels. The value of the shares amortized to income during the year ended June 30, 2003 was $2,097,000. None of the shares were vested as at June 30, 2003.

12 CAPITAL STOCK: (CONTINUED)

(h) STOCK COMPENSATION:

Had compensation expense for stock options granted subsequent to June 30, 2001 been determined by a fair value method using the Black-Scholes option pricing model at the date of the grant, the following weighted average assumptions would have been used for options granted in the current period:

	2003	2002
Dividend yield (%)	0.9	0.6
Risk-free interest rate (%)	3.11	4.38
Expected option life (years)	7	7
Expected volatility (%)	36	55

Using the above assumptions, the Company's net income for the year ended June 30, 2003 would have been reduced to the pro forma amount indicated below:

	2003	2002
Net income, as reported	$ 34,176	$ 58,480
Estimated fair value of option grants	(1,909)	(649)
Net income, pro forma	$ 32,267	$ 57,831
PRO FORMA INCOME PER COMMON SHARE FROM CONTINUING OPERATIONS:		
Basic	$ 0.69	$ 1.31
Diluted	0.69	1.29

The estimated fair value of option grants excludes the effect of those granted before July 1, 2001. The fair value of options granted during the year ended June 30, 2003 was $6.35 per option (2002 – $9.15) on the grant date on a weighted average basis.

(i) PER SHARE INFORMATION:

The reconciliation of the net income and weighted average number of common shares used to calculate basic and diluted income per common share is as follows:

	2003		2002	
	NET INCOME	SHARES (000)	NET INCOME	SHARES (000)
BASIC INCOME PER COMMON SHARE:				
Income from continuing operations	$ 34,754	47,364	$ 58,602	44,206
Dilutive effect of stock options	—	226	—	489
Diluted income per common share	$ 34,754	47,590	$ 58,602	44,695

Options aggregating 3,675,300 (2002 – 2,399,800) have not been included in the computation of diluted income per common share as they were anti-dilutive.

13 INCOME TAXES:

(a) The provision for income taxes from continuing operations is as follows:

	2003	2002
Current	$ 10,157	$ 12,422
Future	(3,914)	(2,873)
	$ 6,243	$ 9,549

The reconciliation of income taxes calculated at the statutory rate to the actual income tax provision is as follows:

	2003	2002
Statutory rate (%)	38.0	41.2
Income tax charge at statutory rate	$ 19,683	$ 32,888
Non-deductible expenses and amortization	326	53
Large corporations tax	2,574	1,159
Taxes related to non-controlling interest share of earnings	(4,284)	(4,804)
Reduction for enacted changes in tax laws and rates	—	(2,434)
Taxes related to equity accounted investment	—	(1,605)
Foreign taxes less than statutory rate	(13,182)	(15,589)
Other	1,126	(101)
	6,243	9,567
Current income taxes related to discontinued operations	—	18
Provision for income taxes	$ 6,243	$ 9,549

(b) The tax effects of temporary differences that give rise to significant portions of the future tax assets and future tax liabilities are presented below:

	2003	2002
FUTURE TAX ASSETS:		
Non-capital loss carryforwards	$ 35,823	$ 27,068
Differences in working capital deductions for tax and accounting purposes	5,465	4,004
Other	3,861	727
Total gross future tax assets	45,149	31,799
Valuation allowance	(17,559)	(16,206)
Net future tax assets	27,590	15,593
FUTURE TAX LIABILITIES:		
Differences in net book value and undepreciated capital cost of ski and resort assets and properties	81,824	80,021
Differences in book value and tax basis of bank and other indebtedness	28,844	3,879
Other	1,289	—
Total gross future tax liabilities	111,957	83,900
Net future tax liabilities	$ 84,367	$ 68,307

Net future tax liabilities are classified for balance sheet purposes as follows:

	2003	2002
CURRENT ASSETS:		
Future income taxes	$ 10,619	$ 7,536
LONG-TERM LIABILITIES:		
Future income taxes	94,986	75,843
	$ 84,367	$ 68,307

(c) At June 30, 2003, the Company has non-capital loss carryforwards for income tax purposes of approximately $117,200,000 (2002 – $101,960,000) that are available to offset future taxable income through 2023.

14 JOINT VENTURES:

The following amounts represent the Company's proportionate interest in joint ventures and non-controlled partnerships (note 2(b)):

	2003	2002
Properties, current	$ 53,993	$ 42,178
Other current assets	20,888	21,717
	74,881	63,895
Current liabilities	(59,629)	(49,487)
Working capital	15,252	14,408
Ski and resort operations	161,609	155,964
Properties, non-current	79,032	58,713
Bank and other indebtedness, non-current	(32,213)	(40,376)
Other, net	(14,856)	(14,924)
	$ 208,824	$ 173,785

	2003	2002
Revenue	$ 128,286	$ 131,122
Expenses	122,272	119,960
Income from continuing operations before income taxes	6,014	11,162
Results of discontinued operations	419	385
	$ 6,433	$ 11,547

	2003	2002
CASH PROVIDED BY (USED IN):		
Operations	$ (5,309)	$ 29,206
Financing	30,544	(15,267)
Investments	(25,003)	(20,425)
Increase (decrease) in cash and cash equivalents	$ 232	$ (6,486)

Due to joint venture partners is the amount payable to the Company's joint venture partners on various properties for costs they have incurred on the Company's behalf. Payments to the joint venture partners are governed by the terms of the respective joint venture agreement.

15 CONTINGENCIES AND COMMITMENTS:

(a) The Company holds licenses and land leases with respect to certain of its ski operations. These leases expire at various times between 2032 and 2051 and provide for annual payments generally in the range of 2% of defined gross revenues.

(b) The Company has estimated costs to complete ski and resort operations assets and properties currently under construction and held for sale amounting to $379,019,000 at June 30, 2003 (2002 – $397,642,000). These costs are substantially covered by existing financing commitments.

(c) In addition to the leases described in (a) above, the Company has entered into other operating lease commitments, payable as follows:

YEAR ENDING JUNE 30,	
2004	$ 10,478
2005	9,919
2006	8,987
2007	7,605
2008	7,024
Subsequent to 2008	65,785
	$ 109,798

(d) The Company is contingently liable for the obligations of certain joint ventures and partnerships. The assets of these joint ventures and partnerships, which in all cases exceed the obligations, are available to satisfy such obligations.

(e) The Company and its subsidiaries are involved in several lawsuits arising from the ordinary course of business. Although the outcome of such matters cannot be predicted with certainty, management does not consider the Company's exposure to lawsuits to be material to these consolidated financial statements.

(f) Canada Customs and Revenue Agency ("CCRA") has proposed certain adjustments to reduce the amount of capital cost allowance and non-capital losses claimed by the Company. No notice of reassessment has been issued. The Company has made submissions with respect to these proposals and intends to contest any adjustments, if made. The Company believes that it is unlikely that CCRA would be successful with the proposed challenge. Whether CCRA will ultimately proceed with such proposals, and the outcome of the issues under review if the proposals proceed, cannot be determined at this time. If all of the issues raised by CCRA in the proposals were reassessed as proposed, the Company would be required to pay total cash taxes of approximately $7,500,000 plus interest of approximately $5,000,000. For accounting purposes, the effect of any reassessment would be charged to income in the year the outcome of the proposals is determined.

16 INTEREST EXPENSE:

	2003	2002
Total interest incurred	$ 102,926	$ 83,439
Less:		
Interest capitalized to ski and resort operations assets	192	1,353
Interest capitalized to properties, net of capitalized interest included in real estate cost of sales of $14,872,000 (2002 – $13,314,000)	40,653	25,536
	$ 62,081	$ 56,550

Interest was charged to income as follows:

	2003	2002
Real estate costs	$ 14,872	$ 13,314
Interest expense	47,142	43,072
Discontinued operations	67	164
	$ 62,081	$ 56,550

Real estate cost of sales also include $17,581,000 (2002 – $14,525,000) of interest incurred in prior years.

Interest incurred and interest expense include commitment and other financing fees and amortization of deferred financing costs.

17 FINANCIAL INSTRUMENTS:

(a) FAIR VALUE:

The Company has various financial instruments including cash and cash equivalents, amounts receivable, certain amounts payable and accrued liabilities. Due to their short-term maturity or, in the case of amounts receivable, their market comparable interest rates, the instruments' book value approximates their fair value. Debt and interest swap agreements are also financial instruments. The fair value of the Company's long-term debt including interest swap agreements, calculated using current rates offered to the Company for debt at the same remaining maturities, is not materially different from amounts included in the consolidated balance sheets.

(b) INTEREST RATE RISK:

As described in note 9, $546,096,000 of the Company's debt instruments bear interest at floating rates. Fluctuations in these rates will impact the cost of financing incurred in the future.

(c) CREDIT RISK:

The Company's products and services are purchased by a wide range of customers in different regions of North America and elsewhere. Due to the nature of its operations, the Company has no concentrations of credit risk.

18 PENSION PLANS:

The Company has two non-contributory defined benefit pension plans, one registered and the other non-registered, covering certain of its senior executives. The number of senior executives included in the plan increased from five to 15 in 2002. The Company partially funded the accrued benefit obligation until December 2001. The estimated market value of the plans' assets (i.e., the funded amount) was $3,252,000 at June 30, 2003 (2002 – $2,857,000). A substantial portion of the unfunded benefit obligation, the estimated present value of which was $15,479,000 at June 30, 2003 (2002 – $10,783,000), has been secured by a letter of credit. This obligation is being expensed over a period of 13 years.

In addition to the plans mentioned above, one of the Company's subsidiaries has two defined benefit pension plans covering certain employees. The estimated market value of the plans' assets was $5,989,000 and the estimated present value of the unfunded benefit obligation was $2,229,000 at June 30, 2003. The obligation is being expensed over a period of 10 years.

For the year ended June 30, 2003, the Company charged to operations pension costs of $1,992,000 (2002 – $1,070,000).

19 SEGMENTED INFORMATION:

The Company has four reportable segments: mountain resort operations, warm-weather resort operations, real estate operations, and corporate and all other. The mountain resort segment includes all of the Company's mountain resorts and associated activities. The warm-weather segment includes Sandestin and all of the Company's stand-alone golf courses. The real estate segment includes all of the Company's real estate activities.

The Company evaluates performance based on profit or loss from operations before interest, depreciation and amortization, and income taxes. Intersegment sales and transfers are accounted for as if the sales or transfers were to third parties.

The Company's reportable segments are strategic business units that offer distinct products and services, and that have their own identifiable marketing strategies. Each of the reportable segments has senior executives responsible for the performance of the segment.

The following table presents the Company's results from continuing operations by reportable segment:

	2003	2002
SEGMENT REVENUE:		
Mountain resort	$ 506,483	$ 424,835
Warm-weather resort	65,044	60,307
Real estate	512,695	495,813
Corporate and all other	2,417	5,016
	$1,086,639	$ 985,971

19 SEGMENTED INFORMATION: (CONTINUED)

	2003	2002
SEGMENT OPERATING PROFIT:		
Mountain resort	$ 109,197	$ 98,935
Warm-weather resort	7,469	8,406
Real estate	75,005	88,150
Corporate and all other	2,417	5,016
	194,088	200,507
Less:		
Interest	47,142	43,072
Depreciation and amortization	67,516	65,434
Corporate general and administrative	14,889	12,175
Write-down of technology assets	12,270	—
	141,817	120,681
Income before income taxes, non-controlling interest and discontinued operations	$ 52,271	$ 79,826

	2003	2002
SEGMENT ASSETS:		
Mountain resort	$ 978,719	$ 912,642
Warm-weather resort	145,361	151,924
Real estate	1,311,079	1,032,296
Corporate and all other	80,563	60,720
Discontinued operations	—	9,335
	$2,515,722	$2,166,917

	2003	2002
CAPITAL EXPENDITURES:		
Mountain resort	$ 59,674	$ 81,658
Warm-weather resort	4,872	9,832
Corporate and all other	5,025	10,237
	$ 69,571	$ 101,727

GEOGRAPHIC INFORMATION:

	2003	2002
REVENUE:		
Canada	$ 474,865	$ 424,764
United States	611,774	561,207
	$1,086,639	$ 985,971

	2003	2002
SEGMENT OPERATING PROFIT:		
Canada	$ 102,871	$ 121,707
United States	91,217	78,800
	$ 194,088	$ 200,507

	2003	2002
IDENTIFIABLE ASSETS:		
Canada	$ 886,978	$ 753,885
United States	1,628,744	1,403,697
Discontinued operations	—	9,335
	$2,515,722	$2,166,917

20 RELATED PARTY TRANSACTIONS:

During the year ended June 30, 2002, $3,991,000 was repaid to the Company by a partnership, one of whose partners was a corporation controlled by an officer and a director of the Company.

21 CASH FLOW INFORMATION:

The changes in non-cash operating working capital balance consist of the following:

	2003	2002
CASH PROVIDED BY (USED IN):		
Amounts receivable	$ (17,208)	$ (29,720)
Other assets	(17,557)	20,819
Amounts payable	14,866	48,676
Due to joint venture partners	1,425	(4,788)
Deferred revenue	45,064	14,204
	$ 26,590	$ 49,191
SUPPLEMENTAL INFORMATION:		
Interest paid related to interest charged to income	$ 62,091	$ 56,550
Income, franchise and withholding taxes paid	11,067	11,596
NON-CASH INVESTING ACTIVITIES:		
Notes received on asset disposals	2,226	6,902
Bank and other indebtedness incurred on acquisition	35,172	—

22 DIFFERENCES BETWEEN CANADIAN AND UNITED STATES GENERALLY ACCEPTED ACCOUNTING PRINCIPLES:

The consolidated financial statements have been prepared in accordance with generally accepted accounting principles ("GAAP") in Canada. The principles adopted in these financial statements conform in all material respects to those generally accepted in the United States and the rules and regulations promulgated by the Securities and Exchange Commission ("SEC") except as summarized below:

	2003	2002
Income from continuing operations in accordance with Canadian GAAP	$ 34,754	$ 58,602
EFFECTS OF DIFFERENCES IN ACCOUNTING FOR:		
Depreciation and amortization pursuant to SFAS 109 (d)	(690)	(1,870)
Real estate revenue recognition (i)	(8,931)	4,089
Start-up costs (j)	3,101	(4,772)
Tax effect of differences	2,478	562
Foreign exchange pursuant to SFAS 52 (g)	—	(14)
Results of discontinued operations	(578)	(122)
Income before cumulative effect of change in accounting principle	30,134	56,475
Adjustment to reflect change in accounting for goodwill, net of tax (k)	(6,150)	—
Net income in accordance with United States GAAP	23,984	56,475
Opening retained earnings in accordance with United States GAAP (b)	275,101	223,363
Common share dividends	(5,051)	(4,737)
Closing retained earnings in accordance with United States GAAP	$ 294,034	$ 275,101
INCOME BEFORE CUMULATIVE EFFECT OF CHANGE IN ACCOUNTING PRINCIPLE PER COMMON SHARE (IN DOLLARS):		
Basic	$ 0.65	$ 1.28
Diluted	0.65	1.27
INCOME PER COMMON SHARE (IN DOLLARS):		
Basic	0.52	1.28
Diluted	0.52	1.27
WEIGHTED AVERAGE NUMBER OF SHARES OUTSTANDING (IN THOUSANDS):		
Basic	47,364	44,206
Diluted	47,590	44,695

22 DIFFERENCES BETWEEN CANADIAN AND UNITED STATES GENERALLY ACCEPTED ACCOUNTING PRINCIPLES: (CONTINUED)

	2003	2002
COMPREHENSIVE INCOME:		
Net income in accordance with United States GAAP	$ 23,984	$ 56,475
Other comprehensive income (h)	17,808	2,299
	$ 41,792	$ 58,774

	2003	2002
Total assets in accordance with Canadian GAAP	$2,515,722	$2,166,917
EFFECTS OF DIFFERENCES IN ACCOUNTING FOR:		
Shareholder loans (c)	(4,445)	(4,475)
Ski and resort assets (d)	1,948	2,525
Goodwill (d)	37,471	34,696
Properties (d)	640	650
Sale-leaseback (l)	14,080	—
Start-up costs (j)	(2,551)	(5,682)
Future income taxes on differences	4,222	1,744
Total assets in accordance with United States GAAP	$2,567,087	$2,196,375

	2003	2002
Total liabilities in accordance with Canadian GAAP	$1,804,583	$1,489,648
EFFECTS OF DIFFERENCES IN ACCOUNTING FOR:		
Revenue recognition (i)	24,096	—
Total liabilities in accordance with United States GAAP	$1,828,679	$1,489,648

	2003	2002
Capital stock in accordance with Canadian GAAP	$ 460,742	$ 466,899
EFFECTS OF DIFFERENCES IN ACCOUNTING FOR:		
Extinguishment of options and warrants (a)	1,563	1,563
Shareholder loans (c)	(4,445)	(4,475)
Capital stock in accordance with United States GAAP	457,860	463,987
Closing retained earnings in accordance with United States GAAP	294,034	275,101
Accumulated other comprehensive income (h)	(13,486)	(32,361)
Shareholders' equity in accordance with United States GAAP	$ 738,408	$ 706,727

(a) EXTINGUISHMENT OF OPTIONS AND WARRANTS:

Payments made to extinguish options and warrants can be treated as capital items under Canadian GAAP. These payments would be treated as income items under United States GAAP. As a result, payments made to extinguish options in prior years impact the current year's capital stock and retained earnings. No payments were made during the years ended June 30, 2003 and 2002.

(b) RETAINED EARNINGS:

Opening retained earnings in accordance with United States GAAP for the year ended June 30, 2002 includes the effects of:

(i)　adopting SFAS 109 as described in (d). The net increase in retained earnings was $40,685,000; and

(ii)　treating payments made to extinguish options and warrants as income items as described in (a). The net decrease in retained earnings was $1,563,000.

(c) SHAREHOLDER LOANS:

The Company accounts for loans provided to senior employees for the purchase of shares as amounts receivable. Under United States GAAP, these loans, totaling $4,445,000 and $4,475,000 as at June 30, 2003 and 2002, respectively, would be deducted from share capital.

(d) INCOME TAXES:

As described in note 2(n), the Company follows the asset and liability method of accounting for income taxes. Prior to July 1, 1999, the Company had adopted the Statement of Financial Accounting Standards No. 109, "Accounting for Income Taxes" ("SFAS 109"), for the financial statement amounts presented under United States GAAP. SFAS 109 requires that future tax liabilities or assets be recognized for the difference between assigned values and tax bases of assets and liabilities acquired pursuant to a business combination except for non tax-deductible goodwill and unallocated negative goodwill, effective from the Company's year ended September 30, 1994. The effect of adopting SFAS 109 increases the carrying values of certain balance sheet amounts at June 30, 2003 and 2002 as follows:

	2003	2002
Ski and resort operations assets	$ 1,948	$ 2,525
Goodwill	37,471	34,696
Properties	640	650

(e) JOINT VENTURES:

In accordance with Canadian GAAP, joint ventures are required to be proportionately consolidated regardless of the legal form of the entity. Under United States GAAP, incorporated joint ventures are required to be accounted for by the equity method. However, in accordance with practices prescribed by the SEC, the Company has elected for the purpose of this reconciliation to account for incorporated joint ventures by the proportionate consolidation method (note 14).

(f) STOCK COMPENSATION:

As described in note 2(q), the Company accounts for stock options by the intrinsic value-based method. In addition, in note 12(h) the Company provides pro forma disclosure as if a fair value-based method had been applied for grants made subsequent to June 30, 2001. For United States GAAP purposes, the pro forma disclosures would consider the fair value of all grants made subsequent to December 15, 1995.

Had compensation expense been determined in accordance with the timing of application provisions of United States GAAP using the Black-Scholes option pricing model at the date of the grant, the following weighted average assumptions would be used for option grants in:

	2003	2002
Dividend yield (%)	0.9	0.6
Risk-free interest rate (%)	3.11	4.38
Expected option life (years)	7	7
Expected volatility (%)	36	55

Using the above assumptions, the Company's net income under United States GAAP would have been reduced to the pro forma amounts indicated below:

	2003	2002
NET INCOME IN ACCORDANCE WITH UNITED STATES GAAP:		
As reported	$ 23,984	$ 56,475
Estimated fair value of option grants	(5,228)	(5,215)
Pro forma	$ 18,756	$ 51,260
PRO FORMA INCOME PER COMMON SHARE:		
Basic	$ 0.41	$ 1.16
Diluted	0.41	1.15

22 DIFFERENCES BETWEEN CANADIAN AND UNITED STATES GENERALLY ACCEPTED ACCOUNTING PRINCIPLES: (CONTINUED)

(g) FOREIGN EXCHANGE ON BANK AND OTHER INDEBTEDNESS:

Prior to July 1, 2002 under Canadian GAAP, the Company deferred and amortized foreign exchange gains and losses on bank and other indebtedness denominated in foreign currencies over the remaining term of the debt. Under United States GAAP, foreign exchange gains and losses are included in income in the period in which the exchange rate fluctuates.

(h) OTHER COMPREHENSIVE INCOME:

Statement of Financial Accounting Standards No. 130, "Reporting Comprehensive Income" ("SFAS 130"), requires that a company classify items of other comprehensive income by their nature in a financial statement and display the accumulated balance of other comprehensive income separately from retained earnings and capital stock in the equity section of the balance sheet.

The foreign currency translation adjustment in the amount of $14,243,000 (2002 – $31,295,000) presented in shareholders' equity under Canadian GAAP would be considered accumulated other comprehensive income under United States GAAP. The change in the balance of $17,808,000 would be other comprehensive income for the year (2002 – income of $2,299,000).

(i) REAL ESTATE REVENUE RECOGNITION:

The Company recognizes profit arising on the sale of a property, a portion of which is leased back by the Company, to the extent the gain exceeds the present value of the minimum lease payments. The deferred gain is recognized over the lease term. Under United States GAAP, the Company's continued involvement in the property precludes a sale-leaseback transaction from sale-leaseback accounting. As a result, the profit on the transaction is not recognized but rather the sales proceeds are treated as a liability and the property continues to be shown as an asset of the Company until the conditions for sales recognition are met.

In accordance with Canadian GAAP, the Company recognizes revenue from the sale of serviced lots after receiving a deposit and conveying title to the purchaser. Statement of Financial Accounting Standards No. 66, "Accounting for Sales of Real Estate" ("SFAS 66"), provides that a sale of real estate should not be recognized unless the deposit received from the purchaser is at least a major part of the difference between usual loan limits and the sales value of the property. Accordingly, no revenue and cost of sales would have been recognized under United States GAAP on certain lot sales for the year ended June 30, 2001 where the deposit received was less than 10% of the sales price. During the year ended June 30, 2002, the remainder of the loans receivable was collected.

(j) START-UP COSTS:

As described in note 2(f), the Company capitalizes for Canadian GAAP purposes certain costs incurred in the start-up period of specific operations. For United States GAAP purposes, such costs would be expensed as incurred.

(k) GOODWILL AND OTHER INTANGIBLE ASSETS:

As described in note 2(t)(i), the Company restated opening retained earnings for impairment losses calculated by comparing the carrying values to fair values of goodwill and intangible assets with indefinite lives. For United States GAAP, the Company adopted effective July 1, 2002 the provisions of SFAS 142, "Goodwill and Other Intangible Assets," which are similar to Canadian GAAP except that under this standard the impairment losses are recognized as a cumulative effect of a change in accounting principle and are treated as a charge to net income in the year of adoption.

(l) DERIVATIVES AND HEDGING ACTIVITIES:

For United States GAAP purposes, the Company adopted the provisions of SFAS 133, "Accounting for Derivative Instruments and Hedging Activities," as amended, effective July 1, 2000. Under this standard, derivative instruments are initially recorded at cost with changes in fair value recognized in income except when the derivative is identified, documented and highly effective as a hedge, in which case the changes in fair value are excluded from income to be recognized at the time of the underlying transaction. The only derivative instrument outstanding at June 30, 2003 and 2002 is the interest rate swap described in note 9. As the fair value of this swap is not materially different than its cost at both dates, no reconciliation adjustment is required.

In the U.S., SFAS 143, "Accounting for Asset Retirement Obligations" ("SFAS 143"), addresses financial accounting and reporting for obligations associated with the retirement of long-lived assets and the associated asset retirement costs. SFAS 143 requires the Company to record the fair value of an asset retirement obligation as a liability in the period in which it incurs a legal obligation associated with the retirement of tangible long-lived assets that result from the acquisition, construction, development and/or normal use of the assets. The fair value of the liability is added to the carrying amount of the associated asset and this additional carrying amount is depreciated over the life of the asset. Subsequent to the initial measurement of the asset retirement obligation, the obligation will be adjusted at the end of each period to reflect the passage of time and changes in the estimated future cash flows underlying the obligation. If the obligation is settled for other than the carrying amount of the liability, the Company will recognize a gain or loss on settlement. The Company was required to adopt the provisions of SFAS 143 effective July 1, 2002. Certain of the land lease arrangements related to the Company's ski and resort operations require remediation steps be taken on termination of the lease arrangement. The Company plans to operate its resorts indefinitely and thus is unable to make a reasonable estimate of the fair values of the associated asset retirement obligations.

In the U.S., SFAS 144, "Accounting for the Impairment or Disposal of Long-Lived Assets" ("SFAS 144"), provides guidance for recognizing and measuring impairment losses on long-lived assets held for use and long-lived assets to be disposed of by sale. SFAS 144 also provides guidance on how to present discontinued operations in the income statement and includes a component of an entity (rather than a segment of a business). The provisions of SFAS 144 are required to be applied prospectively after the adoption date to newly initiated disposal activities. The Company was required to adopt SFAS 144 effective July 1, 2002. The adoption of SFAS 144 did not materially impact the Company's consolidated financial position or results of operations.

The FASB has issued SFAS 146, "Accounting for Costs Associated with Exit or Disposal Activities" ("SFAS 146"), which is effective for exit or disposal activities that are initiated after December 31, 2002. SFAS 146 requires that a liability be recognized for exit or disposal costs only when the liability is incurred, as defined in the FASB's conceptual frame-work, rather than when a company commits to an exit plan, and that the liability be initially measured at fair value. The Company expects the adoption of this standard will affect the timing of recognizing liabilities, and the amount recognized, in respect of future exit activities, if any.

The FASB has issued Interpretation No. 45, "Guarantor's Accounting and Disclosure Requirements for Guarantees, Including Indirect Guarantees of Indebtedness of Others" ("FIN 45"). FIN 45 requires additional disclosures as well as the recognition of a liability by a guarantor at the inception of certain guarantees entered into or modified after December 31, 2002. The initial measurement of this liability is the fair value of the guarantee at inception. The requirements of FIN 45 have been considered in the preparation of this reconciliation.

The FASB has issued Interpretation No. 46, "Consolidation of Variable Interest Entities" ("FIN 46"). Its consolidation provisions are applicable for all entities created after January 31, 2003, and for existing variable interest entities as of July 1, 2003. With respect to entities that do not qualify to be assessed for consolidation based on voting interests, FIN 46 generally requires consolidation by the entity that has a variable interest(s) that will absorb a majority of the variable interest entity's expected losses if they occur, receive a majority of the entity's expected residual returns if they occur, or both. The Company is currently evaluating the impact of adopting the requirements of FIN 46.

Appendix B

Summary of Generally Accepted Accounting Principles (GAAP)

Every technical area has professional associations and regulatory bodies that govern the practice of the profession. Accounting is no exception. In Canada, the Canadian Institute of Chartered Accountants (CICA) has the responsibility for issuing accounting standards that form the basis of generally accepted accounting principles (GAAP). The authority for setting GAAP was delegated to the CICA by the federal and provincial governments and the Canadian Securities Administrators in the 1970s.

The CICA's pronouncements, called *Recommendations,* are collected in Volume I of the *CICA Handbook.* The Recommendations specify how to account for particular business transactions and must be followed, except in those rare cases where a particular Recommendation or Recommendations would not lead to fair presentation. In those cases, the accountant should, using professional judgment, select the appropriate accounting principles. An accountant who determines that the *CICA Handbook* is not appropriate and selects some other basis of accounting must be prepared to defend that decision.

Each new Recommendation issued by the CICA becomes part of GAAP, the "accounting law of the land." In the same way that our laws draw authority from their acceptance by the people, GAAP depends on general acceptance by the business community. Throughout this book, we refer to GAAP as the proper way to do financial accounting.

The Objective of Financial Reporting

The basic objective of financial reporting is to provide information that is useful in making investment and lending decisions. Accounting information can be useful in decision making only if it is *understandable, relevant, reliable, comparable,* and *consistent.*

Accounting information must be *understandable* to users if they are to be able to use it. *Relevant* information is useful in making predictions and for evaluating past performance—that is, the information has feedback value. For example, Canadian Tire Corporation, Limited's disclosure of the profitability of each of its lines of business is relevant for investor evaluations of the company. To be relevant, information must be timely. *Reliable* information is free from significant error—that is, it has validity. Also, it is free from the bias of a particular viewpoint—that is, it is verifiable and neutral. *Comparable* and *consistent* information can be compared from period to period to help investors and creditors assess the entity's progress through time. These characteristics combine to shape the concepts and principles that comprise GAAP. Exhibit B-1 on the next page summarizes the concepts and principles that accounting has developed to provide useful information for decision making.

Summary of Important Accounting Concepts, Principles, and Financial Statements

Concepts, Principles, and Financial Statements	Quick Summary	Text Reference
Concepts		
Entity Concept	Accounting draws a boundary around each organization to be accounted for.	Chapter 1
Going-concern concept	Accountants assume the business will continue operating for the foreseeable future.	Chapter 1
Stable-monetary-unit concept	Accounting information is expressed primarily in monetary terms.	Chapter 1
Time-period concept	Ensures that accounting information is reported at regular intervals.	Chapter 3
Conservatism concept	Accountants report items in the financial statements in a way that avoids overstating assets, shareholders' equity, and revenues and avoids understating liabilities and expenses.	Chapter 6
Materiality concept	Accountants consider the materiality of an amount when making disclosure decisions.	Chapter 6
Principles		
Reliability (objectivity) principle	Accounting records and statements are based on the most reliable data available	Chapter 1
Cost principle	Assets and services, revenues and expenses are recorded at their actual historical cost.	Chapter 1
Revenue principle	Tells accountants when to record revenue (only after it has been earned) and the amount of revenue to record (the cash value of what has been received).	Chapter 3
Matching principle	Directs accountants to (1) identify all expenses incurred during the period, (2) measure the expenses, and (3) match the expenses against the revenues earned during the period. The goal is to measure net income.	Chapter 3
Consistency principle	Businesses should use the same accounting methods from period to period.	Chapter 6
Disclosure principle	A company's financial statements should report enough information for outsiders to make informed decisions about the company.	Chapter 6
Financial Statements		
Balance sheet	Assets = Liabilities + Owners' Equity at a point in time (for proprietorships and partnerships). Assets = Liabilities + Shareholders' Equity at a point in time (for corporations).	Chapters 1 and 13
Income statement	Revenues and gains −Expenses and losses =Net income or net loss for the period.	Chapters 1 and 14
Cash flow statement	Cash receipts −Cash disbursements =Increase or decrease in cash during the period, grouped under operating, investing, and financing activities.	Chapters 1 and 17
Statement of retained earnings	Beginning retained earnings +Net income (or − Net loss) −Dividends =Ending retained earnings	Chapter 1
Statement of shareholders' equity	Shows the reason for the change in each shareholders' equity account, including retained earnings.	Chapter 14

Appendix C

Typical Charts of Accounts for Different Types of Businesses
(For Businesses Discussed in Chapters 1–12)

SERVICE PROPRIETORSHIP

ASSETS

Cash
Accounts Receivable
Allowance for Uncollectible
    Accounts
Notes Receivable, Short-
    Term
GST Receivable
Interest Receivable
Supplies
Prepaid Rent
Prepaid Insurance
Notes Receivable, Long-
    Term
Land
Furniture
Accumulated
    Amortization—Furniture
Equipment
Accumulated
    Amortization—
    Equipment
Building
Accumulated
    Amortization—Building

LIABILITIES

Accounts Payable
Notes Payable, Short-Term
Salaries Payable
Wages Payable
Goods and Services Tax
    Payable
Employee Income Tax
    Payable
Employment Insurance
    Payable
Canada Pension Plan
    Payable
Quebec Pension Plan
    Payable
Employee Benefits Payable
Interest Payable
Unearned Service Revenue
Notes Payable, Long-Term

OWNER'S EQUITY

Owner, Capital
Owner, Withdrawals

Revenues and Gains

Service Revenue
Interest Revenue
Gain on Sale of Land (or
    Furniture, Equipment, or
    Building)

Expenses and Losses

Salaries Expense
Wages Expense
Payroll Benefits Expense
Insurance Expense for
    Employees
Rent Expense
Insurance Expense
Supplies Expense
Uncollectible Account
    Expense
Amortization Expense—
    Furniture
Amortization Expense—
    Equipment
Amortization Expense—
    Building
Property Tax Expense
Interest Expense
Miscellaneous Expense
Loss on Sale (or Exchange) of
    Land (Furniture,
    Equipment, or Buildings)

SERVICE PARTNERSHIP

Same as Service Proprietorship, except for Owners' Equity:

OWNER'S EQUITY

Partner 1, Capital
Partner 2, Capital
Partner N, Capital
Partner 1, Withdrawals
Partner 2, Withdrawals
Partner N, Withdrawals

Merchandising Corporation

ASSETS	LIABILITIES	SHAREHOLDERS' EQUITY
Cash	Accounts Payable	Common Shares
Short-Term Investments (Trading Securities)	Notes Payable, Short-Term	Retained Earnings
Accounts Receivable	Current Portion of Bonds Payable	Dividends
Allowance for Uncollectible Accounts	Salaries Payable	
Notes Receivable, Short-Term	Wages Payable	
Goods and Services Tax Receivable	Goods and Services Tax Payable	
Interest Receivable	Employee Income Tax Payable	
Inventory	Employment Insurance Payable	
Supplies	Canada Pension Plan Payable	
Prepaid Rent	Quebec Pension Plan Payable	
Prepaid Insurance	Employee Benefits Payable	
Notes Receivable, Long-Term	Interest Payable	
Investments in Subsidiaries	Income Tax Payable	
Investments in Stock	Unearned Service Revenue	
Investments in Bonds	Notes Payable, Long-Term	
Other Receivables, Long-Term	Bonds Payable	
Land	Lease Liability	

ASSETS (continued)

Land Improvements
Accumulated Amortization—Land Improvements
Furniture and Fixtures
Accumulated Amortization—Furniture and Fixtures
Equipment
Accumulated Amortization—Equipment
Buildings
Accumulated Amortization—Buildings
Organization Cost
Franchises
Patents
Leaseholds
Goodwill

Revenues and Gains

Sales Revenue
Interest Revenue
Dividend Revenue
Equity-Method Investment Revenue
Gain on Sale of Investments
Gain on Sale of Land (Furniture and Fixtures, Equipment, or Building)
Discontinued Operations—Gain
Extraordinary Gains

Expenses and Losses

Cost of Goods Sold
Salaries Expense
Wages Expense
Commission Expense
Payroll Benefits Expense
Insurance Expense for Employees
Rent Expense
Insurance Expense
Supplies Expense
Uncollectible Accounts Expense
Amortization Expense—Land Improvements
Amortization Expense—Furniture and Fixtures
Amortization Expense—Equipment
Amortization Expense—Buildings
Incorporation Expense
Amortization Expense—Franchises
Amortization Expense—Leaseholds
Amortization Expense—Goodwill
Income Tax Expense
Loss on Sale of Investments
Loss on Sale (or Exchange) of Land (or Furniture and Fixtures, Equipment, or Buildings)
Discontinued Operations—Loss
Extraordinary Losses

Manufacturing Corporation

Same as Merchandising Corporation, except for Assets and Certain Expenses:

ASSETS	EXPENSES (CONTRA EXPENSES IF CREDIT BALANCE)
Inventories:	Direct Materials Price Variance
Materials Inventory	Direct Materials Efficiency Variance
Work in Progress Inventory	Direct Labour Price Variance
Finished Goods Inventory	Direct Labour Efficiency Variance
Factory Wages	Overhead Flexible Budget Variance
Factory Overhead	Overhead Production Volume Variance

Glossary

Account The detailed record of the changes that have occurred in a particular asset, liability, or owner's equity during a period (p. 52).

Account payable A liability that is backed by the general reputation and credit standing of the debtor (p. 12).

Account receivable An asset, a promise to receive cash from customers to whom the business has sold goods or services (p. 12).

Accounting The system that measures business activities, processes that information into reports and financial statements, and communicates the findings to decision makers (p. 2).

Accounting cycle Process by which accountants produce an entity's financial statements for a specific period (p. 163).

Accounting equation The most basic tool of accounting: Assets = Liabilities + Owner's Equity (proprietorship) or Assets = Liabilities + Shareholders' Equity (corporation) (p. 11).

Accounting information system The combination of personnel, records, and procedures that a business uses to meet its need for financial data (p. 333).

Accrual-basis accounting Accounting that recognizes (records) the impact of a business event as it occurs, regardless of whether the transaction affected cash (p. 109).

Accrued expense An expense that has been incurred but not yet paid in cash (pp. 119, 541).

Accrued liability Another name for an accrued expense (p. 541).

Accrued revenue A revenue that has been earned but not yet received in cash (p. 120).

Accumulated amortization The cumulative sum of all amortization expense from the date of acquiring a capital asset (p. 117).

Acid-test ratio Ratio of the sum of cash plus short-term investments plus net current receivables to current liabilities. Tells whether the entity could pay all its current liabilities if they came due immediately. Also called the quick ratio (p. 455).

Adjusted trial balance A list of all the ledger accounts with their adjusted balances (p. 125).

Adjusting entry Entry made at the end of the period to assign revenues to the period in which they are earned and expenses to the period in which they are incurred. Adjusting entries help measure the period's income

and bring the related asset and liability accounts to correct balances for the financial statements (p. 113).

Aging-of-accounts method A way to estimate bad debts by analyzing individual accounts receivable according to the length of time they have been due (p. 442).

Allowance for Doubtful Accounts A contra account, related to accounts receivable, that holds the estimated amount of collection losses. Also called allowance for uncollectible accounts (p. 441).

Allowance for Uncollectible Accounts Another name for allowance for doubtful accounts (p. 441).

Allowance method A method of recording collection losses based on estimates made prior to determining that the business will not collect from specific customers (p. 441).

Amortizable cost The asset's cost minus its estimated residual value (p. 491).

Amortization The term the CICA Handbook uses to describe the systematic changing of the cost of a capital asset; it is often called depletion when applied to wasting assets. The term is also used to describe the writing off to expense of capital assets (pp. 116, 489).

Amortization expense That portion of the cost of capital assets or natural resources used up in a particular period (p. 504).

Asset An economic resource a business owns that is expected to be of benefit in the future (p. 12).

Audit The examination of financial statements by outside accountants, the most significant service that public accountants perform. The conclusion of an audit is the accountant's professional opinion about the financial statements (p. 391).

Average-cost method Another name for the weighted-average cost method (p. 302).

Bad-debt expense Another name for uncollectible-account expense (p. 440).

Balance sheet List of an entity's assets, liabilities and owner equity (proprietorship) or shareholder equity (corporation) as of a specific date. Also called the statement of financial position (p. 20).

Balance-sheet approach Another name for the aging-of-accounts method of estimating uncollectibles (p. 442).

Bank collection Collection of money by the bank on behalf of a depositor (p. 399).

Bank reconciliation Process of explain-

ing the reasons for the difference between a depositor's records and the bank's records about the depositor's bank account (p. 398).

Bank statement Document for a particular bank account showing its beginning and ending balances and listing the month's transactions that affected the account (p. 395).

Batch processing Computerized accounting for similar transactions in a group or batch (p. 338).

Betterment Expenditure that increases the capacity or efficiency of an asset or extends its useful life. Capital expenditures are debited to an asset account (p. 488).

Brand name Distinctive identification of a product or service (p. 506).

Canada (or Quebec) Pension Plan All employees and self-employed persons in Canada (except in Quebec where the pension plan is the Quebec Pension Plan) between 18 and 70 years of age are required to contribute to the Canada Pension Plan administered by the Government of Canada (p. 550).

Capital Another name for the owner's equity of a business (p. 12).

Capital asset Long-lived asset, like property, plant and equipment, wasting asset, and intangible asset used in the operation of a business. Its value is in use (pp. 116, 175, 484).

Capital cost allowance Amortization allowed for income tax purposes by Canada Customs and Revenue Agency; the rates allowed are called capital cost allowance rates (p. 497).

Capitalize a cost To record a cost as part of an asset's cost, rather than as an expense (p. 487).

Carrying value of a capital asset The asset's cost less accumulated amortization (p. 118).

Cash-basis accounting Accounting that records only transactions in which cash is received or paid (p. 109).

Cash flow statement Reports cash receipts and cash disbursements classified according to the entity's major activities: operating, investing, and financing (p. 20).

Cash payments journal Special journal used to record cash payments by cheque (p. 350).

Cash receipts journal Special journal used to record cash receipts (p. 346).

Chart of accounts List of all the accounts and their account numbers in the ledger (p. 69).

Cheque Document that instructs the bank to pay the designated person or business the specified amount of money (p. 394).

Closing entries Entries that transfer the revenue, expense, and owner withdrawal balances from these respective accounts to the capital account (p. 170).

Closing the accounts Step in the accounting cycle at the end of the period that prepares the accounts for recording the transactions of the next period. Closing the accounts consists of journalizing and posting the closing entries to set the balances of the revenue, expense, and owner withdrawal accounts to zero (p. 168).

Collection period Another name for the days' sales in receivables (p. 456).

Computer virus A malicious computer program that reproduces itself, gets included in program code without consent, and destroys program code (p. 393).

Conservatism Concept by which the least favourable figures are presented in the financial statements (p. 303).

Consistency principle A business must use the same accounting methods and procedures from period to period or disclose a change in method (p. 303).

Contra account An account that always has a companion account and whose normal balance is opposite that of the companion account (p. 117).

Control account An account whose balance equals the sum of the balances in a group of related accounts in a subsidiary ledger (p. 345).

Controller The chief accounting officer of a company (p. 390).

Copyright Exclusive right to reproduce and sell a book, musical composition, film, or other work of art. Issued by the federal government, copyrights extend 50 years beyond the author's life (p. 506).

Corporation A business owned by shareholders that begins when the federal government or provincial government approves its articles of incorporation. A corporation is a legal entity, an "artificial person," in the eyes of the law (p. 6).

Cost of goods sold The cost of the inventory that the business has sold to customers, the largest single expense of most merchandising businesses. Also called cost of sales (pp. 218, 274).

Cost of sales Another name for cost of goods sold (pp. 218, 274).

Cost principle States that assets and services are recorded at their purchase cost and that the accounting record of the asset continues to be based on cost rather than current market value (p. 10).

Credit The right side of an account (p. 55).

Credit memorandum (credit memo) The document issued by a seller for a credit to a customer's Account Receivable (p. 353).

Creditor The party to a credit transaction who sells a service or merchandise and obtains a receivable (pp. 437, 450).

Current asset An asset that is expected to be converted to cash, sold, or consumed during the next 12 months, or within the business's normal operating cycle if longer than a year (p. 175).

Current liability A debt due to be paid within one year or one of the entity's operating cycles if the cycle is longer than a year (p. 175).

Current portion of long-term debt Amount of the principal that is payable within one year (p. 541).

Current ratio Current assets divided by current liabilities. Measures the ability to pay current liabilities from current assets (p. 179).

Database Computerized storehouse of information that can be systematically assessed in a variety of report forms (p. 334).

Days' sales in receivables Ratio of average net accounts receivable to one day's sales. Indicates how many days' sales remain in Accounts Receivable awaiting collection (p. 456).

Debit The left side of an account (p. 55).

Debit memorandum (debit memo) The document issued by a buyer to reduce the buyer's Account Payable to a seller (p. 354).

Debt ratio Ratio of total liabilities to total assets. Gives the proportion of a company's assets that it has financed with debt (p. 179).

Debtor The party to a credit transaction who makes a purchase and creates a payable (pp. 437, 450).

Default on a note Failure of the maker of a note to pay at maturity. Also called dishonour of a note (p. 453).

Deferred revenue Another name for unearned revenue (p. 121).

Depletion Another word to describe the amortization of wasting assets (p. 504).

Deposit in transit A deposit recorded by the company but not yet by its bank (p. 398).

Direct write-off method A method of accounting for bad debts by which the company waits until the credit department decides that a customer's account receivable is uncollectible and then debits Uncollectible-Account Expense and credits the customer's Account Receivable (p. 445).

Disclosure principle A business's financial statements must report enough information for outsiders to make knowledgeable decisions about the business (p. 303).

Dishonour of a note Failure of the maker of a note to pay a note receivable at maturity. Also called default on a note (p. 453).

Double-declining-balance method A type of amortization method that expenses a relatively larger amount of an asset's cost nearer the start of its useful life than does the straight-line method (p. 492).

Doubtful-account expense Another name for the uncollectible-account expense (p. 440).

Due date The date on which the final payment of a note is due. Also called the maturity date (p. 450).

Electronic funds transfer (EFT) System that transfers cash by digital communication rather than paper documents (p. 395).

Employee compensation Payroll, a major expense of many businesses (p. 542).

Employment Insurance Act All employees and employers in Canada must contribute to the Employment Insurance Fund, which provides assistance to unemployed workers (p. 551).

Encrypting The process of rearranging plain-text messages by some mathematical formula to achieve confidentiality (p. 394).

Enterprise resource planning (ERP) system Integrates all company data into a single data warehouse (p. 399).

Entity An organization or a section of an organization that, for accounting purposes, stands apart from other organizations and individuals as a separate economic unit. This is the most basic concept in accounting (p. 9).

Estimated residual value Expected cash value of an asset at the end of its useful life. Also called residual value, scrap value, and salvage value (p. 490).

Estimated useful life Length of the service that a business expects to get from an asset; may be expressed in years, units of output, kilometres, or other measures (p. 490).

Expense Decrease in owner's equity (proprietorship) or shareholders' equity (corporation) that occurs in the course of delivering goods or services to customers or clients (p. 12).

Financial accounting The branch of accounting that provides information to people outside the business (p. 4).

Financial statements Business documents that report financial information about an entity to persons and organizations outside the business (p. 2).

Firewall Barriers used to prevent entry into a computer network or a part of a network. Examples include passwords, personal identification numbers (PINs), and fingerprints (p. 394).

First-in, first-out (FIFO) inventory cost method Inventory costing method by which the first costs into inventory are the first costs out to cost of goods sold. Ending inventory is based on the costs of the most recent purchases (p. 295).

Franchise Privileges granted by a private business or a government to sell a product or service in accordance with specified conditions (p. 506).

General journal Journal used to record all transactions that do not fit one of the special journals (p. 341).

General ledger Ledger of accounts that are reported in the financial statements (p. 344).

Generally accepted accounting principles (GAAP) Accounting guidelines, formulated by the CICA's Accounting Standards Committee, that govern how businesses report their results in financial statements to the public (pp. 7, 47).

Going-concern or continuity concept Accountants' assumption that the business will continue operating in the foreseeable future (p. 11).

Goodwill Excess of the cost of an acquired company over the sum of the market values of its net assets (assets minus liabilities) (p. 506).

Gross margin Excess of sales revenue over cost of goods sold. Also called gross profit (p. 218).

Gross margin method A way to estimate inventory based on a rearrangement of the cost of goods sold model: Beginning inventory + Net purchases = Cost of goods available for sale. Cost of goods available for sale − Cost of goods sold = Ending inventory. Also called the gross profit method (p. 306).

Gross margin percentage Gross margin divided by net sales revenue. A measure of profitability (p. 239).

Gross pay Total amount of salary, wages, commissions, or any other employee compensation before taxes and other deductions are taken out (p. 549).

Gross profit Another name for gross margin (p. 218).

Gross profit method Another name for the gross margin method (p. 306).

Hardware Electronic equipment that includes computers, disk drives, monitors, printers, and the network that connects them (p. 334).

Imprest system A way to account for petty cash by maintaining a constant balance in the petty cash account, supported by the fund (cash plus disbursement tickets) totalling the same amount (p. 409).

Income from operations Another name for operating income (pp. 235, 280).

Income statement List of an entity's revenues, expenses, and net income or net loss for a specific period. Also called the statement of operations (p. 20).

Income-statement approach Another name for the percent of sales method of estimating uncollectibles (p. 441).

Income summary A temporary "holding tank" account into which the revenues and expenses are transferred prior to their final transfer to the Capital account (p. 171).

Intangible asset An asset with no physical form, a special right to current and expected future benefits (pp. 484, 505).

Interest The revenue to the payee for loaning out the principal, and the expense to the maker for borrowing the principal (p. 450).

Interest period The period of time during which interest is to be computed, extending from the original date of the note to the maturity date (p. 450).

Interest rate The percentage rate that is multiplied by the principal amount to compute the amount of interest on a note (p. 450).

Internal control Organizational plan and all the related measures adopted by an entity to meet management's objectives of discharging statutory responsibilities, profitability, prevention and detection of fraud and error, safeguarding of assets, reliability of accounting records, and timely preparation of reliable financial information (p. 388).

Inventory All goods that a company owns and expects to sell in the normal course of operation (p. 217).

Inventory turnover Ratio of cost of goods sold to average inventory. Measures the number of times a company sells its average level of inventory during a year (p. 240).

Invoice A seller's request for cash from the purchaser (p. 221).

Journal The chronological accounting record of an entity's transactions (p. 58).

Last-in, first-out (LIFO) inventory cost method Inventory costing method by which the last costs into inventory are the first costs out to cost of goods sold. This method leaves the oldest costs—those of beginning inventory and the earliest purchases of the period—in ending inventory (p. 297).

Leasehold Prepayment that a lessee (renter) makes to secure the use of an asset from a lessor (landlord) (p. 506).

Ledger The book of accounts (p. 52).

Liability An economic obligation (a debt) payable to an individual or an organization outside the business (p. 12).

Licence Privileges granted by a private business or a government to sell a product or service in accordance with special conditions (p. 506).

Liquidity Measure of how quickly an item may be converted to cash (p. 175).

Long-term asset An asset other than a current asset (p. 175).

Long-term liability A liability other than a current liability (p. 176).

Lower-of-cost-or-market (LCM) rule Requires that an asset be reported in the financial statements at the lower of its historical cost or its market value (current replacement cost for inventory) (p. 304).

Maker of a note The person or business that signs the note and promises to pay the amount required by the note agreement. The maker is the debtor (p. 450).

Management accounting The branch of accounting that generates information for internal decision makers of a business, such as top executives (p. 4).

Matching principle The basis for recording expenses. Directs accountants to identify all expenses incurred during the period, measure the expenses, and match them against the revenues earned during that same span of time (p. 111).

Materiality concept A company must perform strictly proper accounting only for items and transactions that are significant to the business's financial statements (p. 303).

Maturity date The date on which the final payment of a note is due. Also called the due date (p. 450).

Maturity value The sum of the principal and interest due at the maturity date of a note (p. 450).

Menu A list of options for choosing computer functions (p. 337).

Module Separate compatible units of an accounting package that are integrated to function together (p. 339).

Moving-weighted-average cost method A weighted-average cost method where unit cost is changed to reflect each new purchase of inventory (p. 298).

Multi-step income statement Format that contains subtotals to highlight significant relationships. In addition to net income, it also presents gross margin and income from operations (p. 238).

Net earnings Another name for net income or net profit (p. 16).

Net income Excess of total revenues over total expenses. Also called net earnings or net profit (p. 16).

Net loss Excess of total expenses over total revenues (p. 16).

Net pay Gross pay minus all deductions; the amount of employee compensation that the employee actually takes home (p. 549).

Net profit Another name for net income or net earnings (p. 16).

Net purchases Purchases less purchase discounts and purchase returns and allowances (pp. 242, 273).

Net sales Sales revenue less sales discounts and sales returns and allowances (p. 218).

Network The system of electronic linkages that allow different computers to share the same information (p. 334).

Nominal account Another name for a temporary account (p. 169).

Nonsufficient funds (NSF) cheque A "bounced" cheque, one for which the maker's bank account has insufficient money to pay the cheque (p. 399).

Note payable A liability evidenced by a written promise to make a future payment (p. 12).

Note receivable An asset evidenced by another party's written promise that entitles you to receive cash in the future (p. 12).

Note term Another name for the interest period of a note (p. 450).

Objectivity principle Another name for the reliability principle (p. 10).

Online processing Computerized processing of related functions, such as the recording and posting of transactions, on a continuous basis (p. 337).

Operating cycle The time span during which cash is paid for goods and services that are sold to customers who then pay the business in cash (p. 175).

Operating expense Expense, other than cost of goods sold, that is incurred in the entity's major line of business: rent, amortization, salaries, wages, utilities, property tax, and supplies expense (pp. 235, 278).

Operating income Gross margin minus operating expenses plus any other operating revenues. Also called income from operations (pp. 235, 280).

Other expense Expense that is outside the main operations of a business, such as a loss on the sale of capital assets (pp. 235, 280).

Other revenue Revenue that is outside the main operations of a business, such as a gain on the sale of capital assets (pp. 235, 280).

Outstanding cheque A cheque issued by the company and recorded on its books but not yet paid by its bank (p. 398).

Owner's equity In a proprietorship, the claim of an owner of a business to the assets of the business. Also called capital (p. 12).

Owner withdrawals Amounts removed from the business by an owner (p. 12).

Partnership An unincorporated business with two or more owners (p. 6).

Patent A federal government grant giving the holder the exclusive right for 20 years to produce and sell an invention (p. 505).

Payee of a note The person or business to whom the maker of a note promises future payment. The payee is the creditor (p. 450).

Payroll Employee compensation, a major expense of many businesses (p. 542).

Percent-of-sales method A method of estimating uncollectible receivables as a percent of the net credit sales (or net sales) (p. 441).

Periodic inventory system Type of inventory accounting system in which the business does not keep a continuous record of the inventory on hand. Instead, at the end of the period the business makes a physical count of the on-hand inventory and applies the appropriate unit costs to determine the cost of the ending inventory (p. 220).

Permanent account Another name for a real account—asset, liability, or owner's equity—that is not closed at the end of the period (p. 169).

Perpetual inventory system Type of accounting inventory system in which the business keeps a continuous record for each inventory item to show the inventory on hand at all times (p. 220).

Petty cash Fund containing a small amount of cash that is used to pay minor expenditures (p. 409).

Postclosing trial balance List of the ledger accounts and their balances at the end of the period after the journalizing and posting of the closing entries. The last step of the accounting cycle, the postclosing trial balance ensures that the ledger is in balance for the start of the next accounting period (p. 174).

Posting Transferring of amounts from the journal to the ledger (p. 60).

Prepaid expense A category of miscellaneous assets that typically expire or get used up in the near future. Examples include prepaid rent, prepaid insurance, and supplies (p. 114).

Principal The amount loaned out by the payee and borrowed by the maker of a note (p. 450).

Principal amount Another name for the principal (p. 450).

Promissory note A written promise to pay a specified amount of money at a particular future date (p. 450).

Proprietorship An unincorporated business with a single owner (p. 6).

Purchases journal Special journal used to record all purchases of inventory, supplies and other assets on account (p. 348).

Quick ratio Another name for the acid-test ratio (p. 455).

Real account Another name for a permanent account (p. 169).

Real-time processing Computerized processing of related functions, such as the recording and posting of transactions, on a continuous basis. Also called online processing (p. 338).

Receivable A monetary claim against a business or an individual, acquired mainly by selling goods and services and by lending money (p. 437).

Reliability principle Requires that accounting information be dependable (free from error and bias). Also called the Objectivity principle (p. 10).

Repair Expenditure that merely maintains an asset in its existing condition or restores the asset to good working order. Repairs are expensed (matched against revenue) (p. 488).

Retail method A method of estimating ending inventory based on the total cost and total selling price of opening inventory and net purchases (p. 307).

Revenue Increase in owner's equity (proprietorship) or shareholders' equity (corporation) that is earned by delivering goods or services to customers or clients (p. 12).

Revenue principle The basis for recording revenues; tells accountants when to record revenue and the amount of revenue to record (p. 110).

Reversing entry An entry that switches the debit and the credit of a previous adjusting entry. The reversing entry is dated the first day of the period following the adjusting entry (p. 213).

Sales Another name for sales revenue (p. 218).

Sales discount Reduction in the amount receivable from a customer, offered by the seller as an incentive for the customer to pay promptly. A contra account to sales revenue (p. 227).

Sales journal Special journal used to record credit sales (p. 343).

Sales returns and allowances Decrease in the seller's receivable from a customer's return of merchandise or from granting the customer an allowance from the amount the customer owes the seller. A contra account to sales revenue (p. 227).

Sales revenue Amount that a merchandiser earns from selling inventory before subtracting expenses. Also called sales (p. 218).

Salvage value Another name for estimated residual value (p. 490).

Scrap value Another name for estimated residual value (p. 490).

Server The main computer in a network, where the program and data are stored (p. 334).

Shareholder A person who owns stock in a corporation (p. 6).

Short-term note payable Note payable due within one year, a common form of financing (p. 536).

Single-step income statement Format that groups all revenues together and then lists and deducts all expenses together without drawing any subtotals (p. 238).

Software Set of programs or instructions that cause the computer to perform the work desired (p. 334).

Special journal An accounting journal designed to record one specific type of transaction (p. 341).

Specific identification method Another

name for the specific-unit-cost method (p. 295).

Specific-unit-cost method Inventory cost method based on the specific cost of particular units of inventory (p. 295).

Spreadsheet A computer program that links data by means of formulas and functions; an electronic work sheet (p. 339).

Stable-monetary-unit concept Accountants' basis for ignoring the effect of inflation and making no adjustments for the changing value of the dollar (p. 11).

Statement of earnings Another name for the income statement (p. 20).

Statement of financial position Another name for the balance sheet (p. 20).

Statement of operations Another name for the income statement. Also called the statement of earnings (p. 20).

Statement of owner's equity Summary of the changes in an entity's owner's equity during a specific period (p. 20).

Straight-line method Amortization method in which an equal amount of amortization expense is assigned to each year (or period) of asset use (p. 491).

Subsidiary ledger Book of accounts that provides supporting details on individual balances, the total of which appears in a general ledger account (p. 344).

Temporary account Another name for a nominal account. The revenue and expense accounts that relate to a particular accounting period and are closed at the end of the period are temporary accounts. For a proprietorship, the owner withdrawal account is also temporary (p. 169).

Time-period concept Ensures that accounting information is reported at regular intervals (p. 112).

Time Another name for the interest period (p. 450).

Trademarks and trade names Distinctive identifications of a product or service (p. 506).

Transaction An event that affects the financial position of a particular entity and may be reliably recorded (p. 13).

Trial balance A list of all the ledger accounts with their balances (p. 64).

Trojan horse A computer virus that does not reproduce but gets included into program code without consent and performs actions that can be destructive (p. 393).

Uncollectible-account expense Cost to the seller of extending credit. Arises from the failure to collect from credit customers. Also called doubtful-account expense or bad-debt expense (p. 440).

Unearned revenue A liability created when a business collects cash from cus-

tomers in advance of doing work for the customer. The obligation is to provide a product or a service in the future. Also called deferred revenue (p. 121).

Units-of-production (UOP) method Amortization method by which a fixed amount of amortization is assigned to each unit of output produced by the capital asset (p. 492).

Wasting assets Capital assets that are natural resources (p. 504).

Weighted-average cost method Inventory costing method based on the weighted-average cost of inventory during the period. Weighted average cost is determined by dividing the cost of goods available for sale by the number of units available. Also called the average cost method (p. 302).

Withheld income tax Income tax deducted from employees' gross pay (p. 550).

Work sheet A columnar document designed to help move data from the trial balance to the financial statements (p. 164a).

Workers' Compensation A provincially administered plan that is funded by contributions by employers and that provides financial support for workers injured on the job (p. 552).

Index

Check Figures

P1-1A	Total assets, $219,200
P1-2A	Total assets, $23,600
P1-3A	Total assets, $165,000
P1-4A	No check figure
P1-5A	Net income, $20,000; total assets, $63,000
P1-6A	Net income, $10,480; total assets, $82,440
P1-7A	No check figure
P1-8A	Total assets, $187,700; net income, $14,700
P1-1B	Total assets, $121,200
P1-2B	Total assets, $160,000
P1-3B	Total assets, $480,000
P1-4B	No check figure
P1-5B	Net income, $35,000; total assets, $167,500
P1-6B	Net income, $31,600; total assets, $142,600
P1-7B	No check figure
P1-8B	Total assets, $244,000; net income, $100,000
P1-1C	No check figure
P1-2C	No check figure
DP 1	No check figure
DP 2	No check figure
FSP 1	No check figure
P2-1A	Net loss, $14,000
P2-2A	No check figure
P2-3A	Trial balance total, $68,250
P2-4A	Trial balance total, $107,400
P2-5A	Trial balance total, $692,850; net income, $11,460
P2-6A	Trial balance total, $121,000
P2-7A	Net income, $2,800; total assets, $111,200
P2-8A	No check figure
P2-9A	No check figure
P2-1B	Net income, $105,000
P2-2B	No check figure
P2-3B	Trial balance total, $76,125
P2-4B	Trial balance total, $79,400
P2-5B	Trial balance total, $35,000; net income, $2,935
P2-6B	Trial balance total, $246,400
P2-7B	Net income, $10,800; total assets, $230,800
P2-8B	No check figure
P2-9B	No check figure
P2-1C	No check figure
P2-2C	No check figure
DP 1	Trial balance total, $43,600; net income, $10,400
DP 2	No check figure
FSP 1	No check figure
P3-1A	Cash net loss, $8,100; accrual net income, $2,400
P3-2A	No check figure
P3-3A	No check figure
P3-4A	No check figure
P3-5A	Adjusted trial balance total, $152,190
P3-6A	Net income, $138,090; total assets, $188,430
P3-7A	Net income, $22,800; total assets, $137,700
P3-8A	Trial balance total, $346,500; net income, $96,900
P3-1B	Cash net loss, $5,350; accrual net income, $2,300
P3-2B	No check figure
P3-3B	No check figure
P3-4B	No check figure
P3-5B	Adjusted trial balance total, $49,875
P3-6B	Net income, $277,880; total assets, $480,120

P3-7B	Net income, $16,762; total assets, $96,862
P3-8B	Trial balance total, $712,800; net income, $136,800
P3-1C	No check figure
P3-2C	No check figure
DP 1	Ending adjusted owner's equity, $166,200
DP 2	No check figure
FSP 1	Ending balance (thousands): Prepaid expenses and other, $31,883,000
P3A-1	Ending balances: Unearned service revenue, $4,800; Service revenue, $1,600
P3A-2	Total liabilities and owner's equity, $1,800
P4-1A	Net income, $14,820
P4-2A	Net income, $118,960; total assets, $650,640
P4-3A	Net income, $216,000; total assets, $357,000
P4-4A	Postclosing trial balance total, $408,000
P4-5A	Net income, $35,955; total assets, $535,860
P4-6A	Total assets, $70,560
P4-7A	Net income overstated by $2,940
P4-8A	Net income, $207,000
P4-9A	Net income, $43,350; total assets, $189,150
P4-1B	Net income, $50,880
P4-2B	Net income, $101,556; total assets, $297,216
P4-3B	Net income, $171,000; total assets, $294,000
P4-4B	Postclosing trial balance total, $429,000
P4-5B	Net income, $77,250; total assets, $312,960
P4-6B	Total assets, $772,800
P4-7B	Net income understated by $1,380
P4-8B	Net income, $61,200
P4-9B	Net income, $112,800; total assets, $395,400
P4-1C	No check figure
P4-2C	No check figure
DP 1	Net income, $160,620; total assets, $175,170; total owner's equity, $105,360
DP 2	No check figure
FSP 1	Current ratio, 2003, 1.64; debt ratio, 2003, 0.72
P4A-1	Ending balances: Salary payable, $0; Salary expense, $360
P5-1A	No check figure
P5-2A	No check figure
P5-3A	Receivable amount, $2,400; no discount
P5-4A	Net income, $108,820
P5-5A	Ending capital balance, $189,280
P5-6A	Net loss, $25,200; total assets, $517,050
P5-7A	Net loss, 25,200; total assets, $517,050
P5-8A	Net income, $27,150
P5-9A	Gross margin, $48,020
P5-10A	Gross margin, $21,936
P5-11A	Net loss, $15,048; total assets, $147,672
P5-1B	No check figure
P5-2B	No check figure
P5-3B	No check figure
P5-4B	Net income, $181,404
P5-5B	Ending capital balance, $240,336
P5-6B	Net income, $179,180; total assets, $401,880
P5-7B	Net income, $179,180; total assets, $401,880
P5-8B	Net income, $97,875
P5-9B	Gross margin, $37,050
P5-10B	Gross margin, $29,720

P5-11B	Net loss, $21,150; total assets, $54,900
P5-1C	No check figure
P5-2C	No check figure
DP 1	Net income, $120,340; total assets, $211,260
DP 2	No check figure
DP 3	No check figure
FSP 1	Closed to Retained earnings, $52,271,000
P5S-1	No check figure
P5S-2	No check figure
P5S-3	Receivable balance, $4,800; no cash discount
P5S-4	Gross margin, $392,320; net income, $176,100; total assets, $436,220

P6-1A	Cost of ending inventory, $800
P6-2A	Operating income, $2,484
P6-3A	Gross margin, $1,465
P6-4A	Net income, $1,540
P6-5A	Gross margin: Weighted-average $34,293; FIFO $35,484; LIFO $33,092
P6-6A	Gross margin, $115,000
P6-7A	Gross margin, $4,000
P6-8A	Cost of goods sold, $38,350,000
P6-9A	Net income: 2005 $114,000; 2004 $106,000; 2003 $22,000
P6-10A	Gross margin $5,144,000
P6-11A	Estimated ending inventory at cost, $45,000
P6-12A	LIFO ending inventory $16,000; FIFO ending inventory $18,750
P6-1B	Cost of ending inventory, $300
P6-2B	Operating income, $945
P6-3B	Gross margin, $3,270
P6-4B	Net income, $8,040
P9-5B	Gross margin: Weighted-average $7,555; FIFO $7,833; LIFO $7,242
P6-6B	Gross margin, $232,000
P6-7B	Gross margin, $2,856
P6-8B	Cost of goods sold, $34,845,000
P6-9B	Net income: 2005 $29,000; 2004 $16,000; 2003 $27,000
P6-10B	Gross margin $1,403,700
P6-11B	Estimated ending inventory at cost, $60,800
P6-12B	LIFO ending inventory $42,900; FIFO ending inventory $59,400
P6-1C	No check figure
P6-2C	No check figure
DP-1	Net income before tax with purchase: FIFO $66,750; LIFO $51,938
FSP 1	Other inventory, $1,067,297,000

P7-1A	No check figure
P7-2A	Total cash, $144,014
P7-3A	Total cash, $13,190
P7-4A	Total accounts payable, $6,800; total cash, $12,652
P7-5A	Total cash, $40,755
P7-6A	Total cash, $54,348
P7-1B	No check figure
P7-2B	Total cash, $139,812
P7-3B	Total cash, $8,300
P7-4B	Total accounts payable, $10,750; total cash, $14,186
P7-5B	Total cash, $43,740
P7-6B	Total cash, $38,160
P7-1C	No check figure
P7-2C	No check figure
DP 1	Total cash receipts on account, $15,816
DP 2	No check figure
CP 1	Net income, $58,800; total assets, $567,220
CP 2	Net income, $513; total assets, $58,363

| P8-1A | No check figure |

P8-2A	No check figure
P8-3A	Adjusted balance, $12,147
P8-4A	Adjusted balance, $6,424.42
P8-5A	No check figure
P8-6A	No check figure
P8-7A	Cash short $29.90
P8-8A	Adjusted balance, $2,059
P8-9A	No check figure
P8-1B	No check figure
P8-2B	No check figure
P8-3B	Adjusted balance, $15,329
P8-4B	Adjusted balance, $19,931.75
P8-5B	No check figure
P8-6B	No check figure
P8-7B	Cash over $8.17
P8-8B	Adjusted balance, $3,328
P8-9B	No check figure
P8-1C	No check figure
P8-2C	No check figure
DP 1	Adjusted bank balance, $21,228; adjusted book balance, $22,228
DP 2	No check figure
FSP 1	Increase in cash, $50,143,000

P9-1A	No check figure
P9-2A	Uncollectible-account expense, direct write-off method, $21,650; allowance method, $12,870
P9-3A	Allowance for uncollectible accounts, $14,474
P9-4A	Req. 3. Accounts receivable, net, $426,950
P9-5A	Req. 2. $365.04
P9-6A	Dec. 1, 2006, Dr. Cash, $15,525
P9-7A	Feb 1, 2005, Cr. Interest revenue, $4,166.67
P9-8A	2006 current ratio, 1.83
P9-9A	Uncollectible account expense, allowance method, $12,517
P9-10A	Uncollectible account expense, $12,825
P9-1B	No check figure
P9-2B	Uncollectible-account expense, direct write-off method, $3,500; allowance method, $8,600
P9-3B	Allowance for uncollectible accounts, $19,514
P9-4B	Req. 3. Accounts receivable, net, $250,520
P9-5B	Req. 2. $246.40
P9-6B	Sept. 14, 2003, Dr. Cash, $4,100.00
P9-7B	June 1, 2006, Cr. Interest revenue, $520.83
P9-8B	2005 current ratio, 1.59
P9-9B	Uncollectible account expense, allowance method, $4,755
P9-10B	Uncollectible account expense, $17,300
P9-1C	No check figure
P9-2C	No check figure
DP 2	Net income, 2006, $195,060; 2005, $170,880
DP 1	Net income $3,800 less under allowance method
FSP 1	Acid-test ratio, 2003, 0.396

P10-1A	Total for Land, $299,775
P10-2A	Amortization Expense—Buildings, $99,450
P10-3A	No check figure
P10-4A	Dec. 31, 2005 amortization amount: Straight-line, $56,943; Units-of-production, $71,178; Double-declining balance, $121,385
P10-5A	Dec. 31, 2006 Amortization Expense—Limousines, $19,350
P10-6A	Capital assets at cost, ending balance, $5,593,400,000
P10-7A	Amortization Expense—Bauxite Mine, $434,750; Amortization Expense—Franchise, $43,250
P10-8A	Total capital assets, $396,769
P10-9A	Total capital assets, $4,079,584
P10-1B	Total for Land, $523,737

P10-2B	Amortization Expense—Buildings, $255,000
P10-3B	No check figure
P10-4B	Dec. 31, 2004 amortization amount: Straight-line, $59,750; Units-of-production, $61,021; Double-declining balance, $137,000
P10-5B	Dec. 31, 2005 Amortization Expense—Forklift, $3,972
P10-6B	Req. 1. Book value, $81,322,000
P10-7B	Amortization Expense—Oil Properties, $1,327,889; Amortization Expense—Patent, $225,000
P10-8B	Total capital assets, $338,083
P10-9B	Total capital assets, $6,877,834
P10-1C	No check figure
P10-2C	No check figure
DP-1	Net income: Krug Associates, $152,000; Tsui Co., $72,000
FSP 1	Req. 5. Interest expense, $55,525,000
P11-1A	No check figure
P11-2A	No check figure
P11-3A	Wage Expense, $30,469
P11-4A	Total annual cost of employee, $98,778.40

P11-5A	Total current liabilities, $275,657
P11-6A	Total net pay, $2,261.20
P11-7A	Estimated warranty payable, $36,690
P11-8A	Req. 2. Total current liabilities, $1,182,984
P11-9A	Req. 2. Total current liabilities, $36,226
P11-1B	No check figure
P11-2B	No check figure
P11-3B	Salary Expense, $16,923
P11-4B	Total annual cost of employee, $112,304.40
P11-5B	Total current liabilities, $372,745
P11-6B	Total net pay, $2,394.06
P11-7B	Estimated warranty payable, $7,220
P11-8B	Req. 2. Total current liabilities, $2,842,334
P11-9B	Req. 2. Total current liabilities, $25,100
P11-1C	No check figure
P11-2C	No check figure
DP-1	No check figure
FSP 1	Req. 2. Current portion of bank and other indebtedness, $287,176,000
CP1	Req. 2. Sanibel Resort net income for last three years, revised, $106,039